W9-BWD-447

MESSAGES, ADDRESSES, AND
PUBLIC PAPERS
OF
TERRY SANFORD

Governor Terry Sanford

MESSAGES, ADDRESSES, AND PUBLIC PAPERS

OF

TERRY SANFORD

GOVERNOR OF NORTH CAROLINA

1961-1965

Edited by

MEMORY F. MITCHELL
Editor, Division of Publications
STATE DEPARTMENT OF ARCHIVES AND HISTORY

Raleigh
Council of State
State of North Carolina
1966

PREFACE

Before he left office, Governor Terry Sanford expressed the opinion that the public addresses and papers of his administration should be held to one volume. The overwhelming number of addresses, dedication ceremonies, informal talks, statements for the press, news conferences, articles, and reports made the job of elimination of material the most difficult phase of preparing this volume for the press. Even a hasty review of the complete file of material would impress anyone with the tremendous energy of, work done by, and contributions made by Governor Sanford.

Several criteria were used in determining which addresses to include in full, which to summarize, and which only to list. Appearances at significant meetings and events, speeches in which new policies or ideas were brought to light, and typical addresses on various subjects were considered; an effort was made to publish in full meaningful materials fitting one or more of these standards. Where summaries in a page or less were substituted for full addresses, the central theme and main points were given without the inclusion of much detail.

Relatively few of the many proclamations, executive orders, and statements could be used; here again, an effort was made to select those of particular significance and those which were illustrative of the activities and programs of the Governor and of his administration.

Funds for this volume were provided by the Council of State, as has been the custom for volumes of papers of other governors. The editor wishes to thank Governor Sanford himself for his suggestions and advice; his press secretary, Mr. Graham Jones, for checking many points, answering innumerable questions, helping with the selection of illustrations, and giving valuable advice throughout the months the volume was in preparation; and Dr. Christopher Crittenden, director of the North Carolina State Department of Archives and History, for his encouragement, support, and guidance. Mrs. Nancy S. Bartlett and Miss Marie D. Moore, editorial assistants with the State Department of Archives and History, deserve and are hereby given recognition and thanks for their many hours of tedious and painstaking work. Mrs. Bartlett prepared the list of appointments, and she and Miss Moore did research for headnotes and footnotes, helped prepare copy for the printer, and rendered assistance in ways far too numerous to mention. Appreciation is also expressed to Miss

34924

Brenda M. Smith, Mrs. Elizabeth C. Swindell, and Mrs. Ann W. Little, who assisted with the proofreading and the indexing. All illustrations used in the book were furnished by Mr. Graham Jones.

Memory F. Mitchell

November 1, 1966

TABLE OF CONTENTS

---

* Summarized

* Summarized

_____

* Summarized

* Summarized

* Summarized

---

* Summarized

* Summarized

---

* Summarized

LIST OF ILLUSTRATIONS

TERRY SANFORD

By

GRAHAM JONES

"The hopes of North Carolina, the hopes of America and the hopes of our world will rise higher from the desks of the classrooms than from the launching pads at Cape Canaveral."

Thus did Terry Sanford evaluate education in the early 1960's during the race for space.

Terry Sanford made quality education the overriding issue of three arduous campaigns for office in 1960 and he made quality education the number-one goal of his four years as Governor.

Two weeks after his election, Sanford addressed an audience of educators from across North Carolina at Memorial Auditorium on the campus of the University of North Carolina at Chapel Hill.

During the preceding year, he had outlined the broad general framework of the Quality Education Program. On the campus of the oldest state university in the nation, that November night, he delivered one of the longest addresses of his career. In that address, he spelled out the specifics of the Quality Education Program.

Dr. James Bryant Conant, President Emeritus of Harvard University called the program "a landmark in American education."

An elderly professor, sitting on a back row of the large auditorium, said: "Good Lord! He meant what he said during the campaign."

It was perfectly natural that the young Governor-elect of North Carolina should have chosen Chapel Hill for his "Statement of Faith and Purpose in Education."

For it was at the University of North Carolina that he had worked his way through to an undergraduate degree. It was at Chapel Hill where he had met, courted, and won for his wife a vivacious and charming young coed from Hopkinsville, Kentucky, Margaret Rose Knight.

It was at Chapel Hill that he and Margaret Rose had set up housekeeping following his years of service in Europe during World War II. And it was at Chapel Hill where, following World War II, he earned his law degree and served as Assistant Director of the Institute of Government.

But more important than his many personal attachments to Chapel Hill, was the influence of the university on the state of North Carolina for more than a century and a half.

Often when newsmen from other states interviewed the Governor, they would raise the question: "What makes North Carolina different?" Invariably, Governor Sanford ranked the University of North Carolina as one of the major reasons.

Terry Sanford came to the university from the farm trading town of Laurinburg where he was born August 20, 1917. His father was the soft-spoken Cecil L. Sanford, an independent merchant and realtor. His mother, Elizabeth Martin Sanford, a native of Salem, Virginia, taught in the public schools for forty years.

When, in 1966, Sanford published his first book *But What About the People?* he dedicated it to his mother "who heightened my interest in education" and to his father "who heightened my interest in politics."

Terry Sanford's entry into politics came in 1928, when, as an eleven-year-old, he marched in a torchlight parade in Laurinburg for Al Smith. He carried a sign proclaiming, "Me and Ma Is For Al."

After graduating from Laurinburg High School, Sanford studied for a semester at Presbyterian Junior College at Maxton before transferring to the university at Chapel Hill. Like many of his classmates during the depression of the 1930's, Sanford worked. He delivered newspapers. He washed dishes in a cafe. He was a bus boy at Swain Hall. He was an assistant manager of a dormitory and he was a laundry agent.

During his student days, Sanford found time to win the presidency of his dormitory and a seat in the Student Legislature. In student politics, he met many of the men who twenty years later would help elect him Governor.

As for his courtship with the coed majoring in English, he says with a grin that he knew Margaret Rose Knight a year before he got up nerve enough to ask her for a date.

However the shyness did not stop him from marrying Margaret Rose on July 4, 1942, while Sanford was serving as a special agent for the Federal Bureau of Investigation.

Shortly after their marriage, Sanford left his draft-exempt post with the FBI to enlist in the paratroops. He won his jump boots and the bars of a second lieutenant before being shipped to Europe.

During the war, he fought in five campaigns in Italy, France, Belgium, and Germany. Included in those campaigns was a jump with the 517th Parachute Combat Team into the invasion of Southern France and action in the Battle of the Bulge, the last German attack of the war.

After returning to the States, Sanford returned to Chapel Hill to complete work on his law degree which he earned in 1946. For the next two years, he served as an assistant director of the Institute of Government.

In 1948 he moved to Fayetteville where he set up his law practice. In Fayetteville, he was active in church, veterans, and civic affairs.

In the Methodist church, he was a district lay leader and chairman of the Board of Trustees of Methodist College.

He served as a charter member of the Fayetteville Area Industrial Development Commission, as president of the Fayetteville Junior Chamber of Commerce, as director of the Chamber of Commerce, as chairman of the Fayetteville Red Cross, as president of the United Services Fund, and as a director of the Children's Home Society of North Carolina. He was active in the Masons, the Shrine, and the Rotary Club.

Fellow veterans elected him Judge Advocate of the North Carolina Department of the American Legion.

It was from Fayetteville that he launched his first state-wide campaign for political office. In 1949 Sanford successfully sought the presidency of the Young Democratic Clubs of North Carolina. In a vigorously contested race at New Bern, Sanford won over two opponents.

In that YDC campaign, Sanford had the strong support of O. Max Gardner, Jr., of Shelby. In 1960, from the bed that multiple sclerosis confined him to, Gardner wrote the check for Sanford's filing fee for Governor.

In 1950 North Carolina's "Go Forward" Governor W. Kerr Scott appointed Sanford as a member of the State Ports Authority which he served during a period of major expansion of North Carolina's deep-water ports at Morehead City and Wilmington.

By 1952 Sanford was running for and winning the State Senate seat from Cumberland County.

When Scott began to get ready to run for the United States Senate in 1954, he chose Terry Sanford as his state campaign manager. The Scott family and the "Branchhead" leadership rallied behind Sanford's campaign of 1960.

So did Charles M. Johnson, the man Kerr Scott had defeated for Governor in 1948.

Sanford's campaign organization was diverse and so was his support across the state. That support included men of as widely varying views as Charles A. Cannon, head of the historically nonunion Cannon Mills, and W. Millard Barbee, president of the State AFL-CIO. It included strong advocates of civil rights and strong advocates of state rights. It included distinguished professors on college campuses and men and women who could barely write enough to vote.

In short, the Sanford team included the kind of coalition that elected Franklin Roosevelt, and it was a fair composite of the populace of North Carolina.

Sanford left no doubt as to where he stood on the major issues of the day.

He detailed those positions in an address to the Young Democratic Club at Chapel Hill early in 1960 in a 32-point "Positive Program for Progress." And he spelled them out as he traveled into every one of the state's 100 counties.

Running against Sanford in the campaign were three strong candidates: Malcolm E. Seawell, Attorney General of North Carolina under Governor Hodges; John D. Larkins, Democratic National Committeeman and former Chairman of the State Democratic Executive Committee; and Dr. I. Beverly Lake, former Assistant Attorney General and former Professor of Law at Wake Forest College.

During the first primary, the attacks centered on Sanford, who was generally acknowledged as the front-runner.

Because of his strong support for the Quality Education Program and his frank pledge to raise new taxes if necessary to pay the cost, Sanford was labeled "High Tax Terry" and accused of playing Santa Claus.

One opponent charged that Sanford was promising "pie in the sky."

To that charge, Sanford answered with a quick grin: "If it's pie in the sky, let's put it in the oven and start cooking."

Seawell and Larkins were eliminated in the first primary and Sanford led Dr. Lake by an 88,000-vote plurality.

In the runoff, the race issue was a major question.

Sanford's position was short and clear: "What we need," he said, "is massive intelligence, not massive resistence."

Sanford and his supporters took a lesson from the 1950 Democratic primary runoff for the United States Senate when the race question became the decisive factor.

Rather than lose the initiative, they took the offensive. Sanford workers, who had been up until dawn counting votes of the first primary, were back at work in Room 4-B of Raleigh's Carolina Hotel by noon of Sunday, May 29, 1960. At 8 A.M. on Monday, Sanford was holding his customary Monday morning press conference at the Carolina.

There followed four weeks of campaigning from the Atlantic to the Appalachians and from the dawn shifts at mill gates to midnight handshaking at factory doors.

Sanford's theme during the second primary was: "Let's not

close our schools, let's improve them."

For a week or two of those hot June days, the electorate of North Carolina seemed precariously balanced between moderation and massive resistance, between a New Day and a return to Rip Van Winkle, between moving out into the mainstream of American life and a trip up a dead-end tributary.

But when North Carolinians voted on Saturday, June 25, they cast a 76,000-vote majority for Sanford and for his New Day programs.

Within a couple of weeks of his nomination, Sanford was in Los Angeles for the National Democratic Convention. The morning after arriving, he held a press conference and strongly endorsed Senator John F. Kennedy.

Some of Sanford's strongest supporters had warned him before he left North Carolina for the convention that if he backed Kennedy, he would never be Governor. Sanford not only endorsed the Massachusetts Catholic, he made one of the seconding addresses.

Sanford and eleven other Tar Heel delegates voted for Kennedy and promptly were dubbed "the Dirty Dozen."

A deluge of angry telegrams and irate letters descended on Sanford headquarters at the Carolina Hotel and the Sanford quarters in Los Angeles.

Anti-Catholic newspaper ads and literature began to pop out across North Carolina. The man who had just won a tremendous victory over racial prejudices, with the passions still running hot, returned to North Carolina to face a fight against religious prejudices.

Sanford did not hesitate for a moment. He told the voters in town after town that he believed Jack Kennedy would make North Carolina and America a great President, "another young Roosevelt." And, he said in effect, if you don't want to vote for Kennedy, don't vote for me!

Historical precedent seemed against Kennedy and Sanford. The only time that North Carolinians had voted for a Republican for President since the Civil War was in 1928 when Catholic Al Smith headed the Democratic ticket. Moreover, North Carolina's Democratic majorities for President had been dwindling ever since 1936—to the point that Adlai Stevenson squeaked out a majority of only 15,000 in 1956.

When the votes were counted on November 8, North Carolina was still Democratic, with a 57,000-vote majority for Kennedy and a 122,000-vote majority for Sanford.

In his inaugural address, Sanford repeated his campaign promises for the Quality Education Program, for an accelerating drive for new industry, for a reinvigorated farm economy, and for new roads.

In general, he pledged his administration to a New Day in the Old North State.

"I call," he said, "on all citizens to join with me in the audacious adventure of making North Carolina all it can and ought to be."

The youngest Governor of North Carolina since Charles Aycock was not long is displaying his own audacity.

Sanford had been in the Capitol but sixty days when he went upstairs on Monday night, March 6, 1961, to deliver his Special Budget Message on Education before a joint session of the General Assembly.

It is a story as old as parliamentary government that legislators and constituents like to vote for appropriations but dislike the taxes that make the appropriations possible.

In his address that winter night, Governor Sanford asked for both: a Quality Education Program that would add $100 million of enrichment funds to North Carolina's public schools, and removal of hundreds of exemptions in North Carolina's sales tax and called for additional levies on alcoholic beverages to pay the cost.

One of the sales tax exemptions that was to be removed was that on food.

In concluding his address, Governor Sanford told the legislators in whose hands the Quality Education Program rested:

The hour is at hand when North Carolina can begin its bold march forward. We begin this march in these halls by reaching out and grasping the hands of our greatest possession, our children and our grandchildren.

The hand we grasp today is the strong handclasp to the future, the hand of a leader in the world's struggles.

I thank you for your attention to the future of North Carolina.

As he had anticipated, the tax was unpopular.

Why, shouted critics, didn't he recommend a tax on luxuries? Wasn't he taking bread out of the mouths of children with the food tax?

He answered promptly, on March 9 in an address at Smithfield:

If we tax bread, we also will be taxing cake. If we tax fatback, we also will tax caviar. If we tax corn meal, we also will tax filet mignon.

No one is going to go hungry because of this tax. But the children of North Carolina will go thirsty for quality education if we do not enact this program for better schools.

The Governor took the same kind of message across the state during the following ninety days. It made no difference whether he was speaking to bankers or barbers, businessmen or farmers, at country clubs or county fairs. His speeches invariably turned out to be pleas for the Quality Education Program and the tax to support it.

The Governor also passed along the message to members of the General Assembly morning after morning over red-eye gravy at the Mansion, day after day over coffee at the Capitol, and night after night over cigars back at the Mansion.

On the key votes, Governor Sanford and the Quality Education Program won by a three-to-one majority in the House and a four-to-one majority in the Senate.

The North Carolina Education Association, whose members had been among Governor Sanford's strongest supporters, provided this checklist of what the Quality Education Program entailed:

1. Pay increases for teachers and all other school personnel. (The pay raises for the teachers averaged 22 per cent.)

2. Addition of 2,826 teachers for North Carolina's rapidly multiplying student enrollment, and the addition of 44 assistant superintendents, 25 supervisors and more home economics and vocational teachers.

3. Clerical assistants for schools with $1.50 per pupil allocated to provide the clerks.

4. Library allotment doubled—from 50 cents per pupil to $1.00, and instructional supplies raised from $1.12 to $1.50 per pupil.

5. In-service courses for professional improvement of teachers provided at a cost of $300,000, and 300 additional teacher-training scholarships offered.

6. Increased salaries for college personnel and an additional $70,100 for expansion of television teaching.

7. Increased funds for industrial education centers and a strengthened Department of Public Instruction.

8. Establishment of the Department of Curriculum and Research to keep curriculums of the public schools abreast of the latest developments and techniques.

The National Education Association ranked North Carolina as the pace setter in the nation in the advancement of education.

Sanford went on the stump again. This time he told superintendents, principals, and teachers that the burden now rested upon their shoulders.

He carried his quality education message directly to school children across the state. He told the students—whites, Negroes, and Indians, first graders through seniors: "You can't get quality education out of a 'Ready Mix Box.' You have to work for it."

He warned them that "brainpower has replaced backpower."

Altogether, Sanford spoke to an estimated 279,000 students in their schools.

The influence of the Quality Education Program extended far beyond the borders of North Carolina. When the Governor and a team of other North Carolinians visited Cincinnati on a travel mission in May, 1961, they were shown an Ohio education journal urging action in the Buckeye state comparable to that which Sanford had begun in North Carolina.

Several successful candidates for high public office in other states asked for, and received, copies of Governor Sanford's Quality Education Program.

During his four years as Governor, Sanford was invited to speak on quality education from Columbia, South Carolina, to Los Angeles and Seattle; and from Biloxi, Mississippi, and Dallas, Texas, to Harvard and Yale universities.

In all, he spoke in thirty other states during his administration, almost always on quality education.

When he attended his first Southern Governors Conference at Nashville, Tennessee, in the summer of 1961, Sanford was elected chairman of the Southern Regional Education Board and was re-elected the following year.

Throughout his campaigns for Governor and throughout his administration, Sanford spoke for education as a whole, "from the first grade through the graduate school."

After the 1961 legislative victory for public education, the Governor appointed a blue-ribbon Commission on Education Beyond the High School. Headed by noted Winston-Salem attorney Irving E. Carlyle and including strong educational and lay leaders from across North Carolina, the commission submitted to the Governor a thorough study of the state's needs for education beyond the high school and recommendations on how to meet those needs.

Governor Sanford strongly endorsed the program and threw the weight of his administration behind its adoption by the 1963 General Assembly.

The highlights of the Governor's Higher Education Act were:

1. Establishment of a network of comprehensive community colleges across the state so that higher education would be within the geographic and economic reach of tens of thousands of North Carolina boys and girls who could not afford to go away to school. The comprehensive community colleges were to be financed jointly by state and local governments. They were to provide courses ranging from teaching illiterate adults how to read and write to vocational training and college parallel work.

2. Establishment of three new senior colleges—one in the East at Wilmington, one in the Piedmont at Charlotte, and one in the West at Asheville.

3. Stipulation that North Carolina should have one university with its campuses at Chapel Hill, Raleigh, and Greensboro, and such other campuses in the future as the trustees and the General Assembly should deem advisable.

The section on the Consolidated University paved the way for full university status at Raleigh and Greensboro and made possible the subsequent addition of Charlotte College as the University of North Carolina at Charlotte.

The consensus of educators was that Governor Sanford's Higher Education Act of 1963 ranked in importance with the Revolutionary Constitutional provision for a university and with the consolidation of the university in 1931.

In education, as in other fields, Governor Sanford constantly searched for new ideas on how to do the job better.

Among the new ideas in education that he translated into being were the following:

The Governor's School at Winston-Salem where gifted children could study each summer in an eight-week course of instruction from talented teachers.

The North Carolina School of the Arts, a resident school providing training in the arts by outstanding instructors.

The Advancement School to afford under-achieving students the chance to catch up and to provide the state a laboratory for teaching teachers how to reach students who were not performing up to their abilities.

The Learning Institute of North Carolina at Durham to provide research programs for the improvement of education.

Operation Second Chance, a retraining program for dropouts in three sections of the state.

A privately financed loan program to help high school graduates get the money to go on to college. "If you have the will and the skill," Sanford told high school seniors, "we will help you find the way." He did so with the aid of the North Carolina Bankers Association.

One group that weighed heavily on the Sanford conscience was the mentally retarded, whom he called "the forgotten children."

The first trip he made after returning to North Carolina following the Los Angeles convention in 1960 was to the mental hospitals of the state. Escorting Sanford from hospitals at Morganton to Goldsboro was John W. Umstead, Jr., Chairman of the State Hospitals Board of Control and a champion of the mentally retarded and the mentally ill.

The young gubernatorial nominee and the veteran legislator spent a week visiting with boys and girls who, at the time, seemed to have no chance in life other than to be treated as well as some pet animal.

Later, Governor Sanford was to remember the wards he saw on that trip. He summed up his feelings this way:

> Of all the inventions down through the centuries, of all the discoveries since the time of Eden, of all the miracles of nature, there is none that approaches the magnificence, the intricacies or the potentials of the human mind.
>
> It is an indictment of our society and the society of other nations that while learning to open canned foods electrically, to broadcast voices and pictures electronically; to manufacture cars with automatic gears and power steering and power brakes and without cranks, to dam the greatest of our rivers; to irrigate the most arid of our lands; to travel safely under the polar cap; to fire missiles across oceans and continents; and to reach toward the stars themselves—that while doing all of these things, we have failed to find the solution to the problems of mental retardation.

To speed the search toward the solution, Governor Sanford asked the 1963 General Assembly for funds to establish a Center for Mental Retardation at Chapel Hill for the training of special teachers, for expansion of vocational training, and for an allotment to the State Board of Health for the identification and evaluation of retarded children.

The members of the 1963 General Assembly strongly approved the program.

Although education was the overriding issue of his campaigns for office and the overriding goal of his administration, Sanford was keenly aware of the need for new industry with new and better-paying jobs in North Carolina.

The children who were studying under the Quality Education Program would need good jobs when they finished their education.

The rural people coming off the farms because of mechanization needed jobs.

Industrial employees being automated out of work needed jobs.

Governor Sanford sought to secure those jobs in a number of ways. He took a tour of industrial centers in the Ohio Valley (Pittsburgh, Columbus, Dayton, Indianapolis, and Cincinnati) in May, 1961, with leaders from across the state. He provided strong leadership for two International Trade Fairs at Charlotte to bring buyers from other states and foreign countries to North Carolina to see Tar Heel products. He invited industrialists with prospective new plants to the Mansion on Blount Street. And he told the North Carolina story to audiences of businessmen in New York, Chicago, and other major cities.

At the end of his administration, the State Department of Conservation and Development reported the score for new industry during the Sanford years:

The greatest investment in new and expanded plants in any four-year period in North Carolina's history was made from 1961 to 1965, more than $1.2 billion worth. This investment created 120,489 new jobs and increased annual payrolls in the state by more than $400 million.

The United States Department of Labor later reported that during the period in which Terry Sanford was Governor, North Carolina outstripped all other states in the rate of increase for nonfarm jobs.

In agriculture, Governor Sanford placed his greatest emphasis on food processing.

Symbolic of that emphasis were scores of new food plants and a new Food Science Building at North Carolina State University.

Speaking on the Raleigh campus, Sanford summarized his thoughts on food processing: "Today, the most important thing is not how many pecks of pickled peppers Peter Piper picks. What's important is how many pecks of pickled peppers Peter Piper processes, packages and make profits on."

Despite advances on education, industrial, and agricultural fronts, Governor Sanford worried about the low living standards of many North Carolinians.

Among the things that worried him was the fact that North Carolina suffered from one of the highest rates of illiteracy, one of the lowest rates of per capita income and some of the poorest housing in the nation.

As a strong advocate of the free enterprise system, he believed the economy was only so strong as its weakest links.

As a devout church member, he felt he was his brother's keeper. He was concerned for the underfed and underclothed child, for the physically and fiscally disabled and for the indigent old.

The Governor moved in several ways to lift the hopes and the lives of the underprivileged. Included in those moves was action to improve the lot of migrant farm workers and support for extending and increasing the state's minimum wage act.

Governor Sanford expressed his concern for the underprivileged in a letter to state agency heads after Christmas of 1962.

He wrote: "I saw a raggedly-clothed boy who had worn his shoes through to the cold December ground. I wondered whose job it is to help him. . . . I talked with a little girl who had not had a decent meal since school was out."

The Governor concluded his letter this way: "Those in need

of help are not just 'cases.' These are people. Our people. They need our help. We cannot do our job by sitting down and waiting for them to come to us. Reach out. Find them. Seek them out. Don't miss one."

In 1963 Governor Sanford led in the establishment of the North Carolina Fund which was designed to seek out the poor and to help them become self-respecting and self-supporting.

The fund was incorporated after months of preliminary work with the Ford Foundation and the Z. Smith Reynolds and the Mary Reynolds Babcock foundations. The Ford Foundation contributed $7 million to the fund, the Z. Smith Reynolds Foundation gave $1,625,000, and the Mary Reynolds Babcock Foundation allocated $875,000.

Sanford summarized the need and the goal of the North Carolina Fund:

In North Carolina there remain tens of thousands whose family income is so low that daily subsistence is always in doubt. There are tens of thousands who go to bed hungry, get up hungry and go to school hungry. There are tens of thousands of young people who have no skills and no present likelihood to get a skill. There are tens of thousands who live in houses that are a blight on the landscape.

There are tens of thousands whose dreams will die. Some of this poverty is self-imposed and some is undeserved. All of it withers the spirit of children who neither imposed it nor deserve it. These are the children of poverty who tomorrow will become the parents of poverty.

We hope to break this cycle of poverty. That is what the North Carolina Fund is all about.

Governor Sanford and the North Carolina Fund invited Tar Heel communities to submit proposals for comprehensive attacks on poverty that would serve as pilot projects. The Community Action Programs were designed to tie together the efforts of educational, welfare, health, employment, and other public and private agencies.

The call brought in 51 proposals covering 66 counties.

Another major effort of the fund was designed especially for the children of poverty. Under the Comprehensive School Improvement Program, often called the "3-R's Project," the fund allocated $2 million to the State Board of Education with matching funds from the state. Under that project, hundreds of schools throughout the state worked to improve the foundation courses for children in the first three grades.

When the United States Congress was holding hearings on the federal anti-poverty program, Governor Sanford was invited to Washington to testify on the progress of North Carolina's program which already was underway. After adoption of the federal legislation. President Lyndon B. Johnson invited the Governor to Washington to witness the signing of the act.

During the four years of the Sanford administration a constant question was a problem that is as old as pigmentation— the problem of people of different races living together peacefully.

After the Revolutionary War, North Carolinians had refused to ratify the constitution until the first American civil rights act had been approved—the Bill of Rights.

North Carolinians took pride in that heritage. They also took pride in the fact that during the Civil War Tar Heels were "first at Bethel, farthest at Gettysburg . . . and last at Appomattox."

To this old state the young Governor brought a new message for a New Day. In his inaugural address, he said: "As we move into the challenging and demanding years ahead, no group of our citizens can be denied the right to participate in the opportunities of first-class citizenship."

In an address to a convocation of South Carolina educators in Columbia, on July 18, 1961, the Governor declared: "The South is rising again! It is not rising through secession from the Union, nor through insurrection, nor through nullification. It is rising through education, through commerce and through agriculture."

He concluded that address by noting that "the South can rise and march again. We will make this march not with bayonets but with textbooks. We will not be firing on Fort Sumter. We will be firing on the dungeons of ignorance."

Throughout his administration, Terry Sanford worked to translate his words of good will into concrete action.

When Freedom Riders traveled through North Carolina there was precious little news filed. The rides didn't make news because there were no incidents.

Sanford recalled afterward with a happy chuckle that the closest thing to a riot during the travels occurred at the bus station in Raleigh. A mob of people—whites and Negroes—converged there one night. The soft drink machine had stripped a gear and was dispensing free drinks. Everyone wanted a free drink.

Another incident that permitted a bit of laughter in the usually grim and potentially explosive confrontation occurred when the American Nazi Party sent self-styled "Hate Riders" through the state. As he did so often to prevent racial conflict and possible bloodshed, Governor Sanford called quietly on the State Highway Patrol for assistance. A patrol car was assigned to follow the car from the time it entered North Carolina from Virginia until the time it made its exit. As he was nearing the South Carolina border, the driver of the "hate" car took a wrong turn and got lost. The patrolman, following the best tradition of courtesy and helpfulness of the Highway Patrol, gave the driver directions to the road out of North Carolina and bade him goodbye.

There were militants in both races who seemed determined to break North Carolina's record of moderation and restraint.

One was Robert Williams of Monroe, whom the National Association for the Advancement of Colored People had expelled. Williams collected a small arsenal of weapons and grew a Fidel Castro beard. Williams' activities in North Carolina came to an end when he and several others were charged with kidnapping a white couple. Williams fled the state and made his way to Cuba where for several years he made propaganda broadcasts for the Cuban Communists. From Cuba, he reportedly went on to Communist China.

In an address to the Southern Association of Colleges and Secondary Schools in Dallas, Texas, on November 28, 1962, Governor Sanford again tied his belief in the human dignity of all men to education:

"We need our own and a new kind of Emancipation Proclamation which will set us free to grow and build, set us free from the drag of poor people, poor schools, from hate, from demagoguery. . . . This kind of proclamation can be written in one word: Education."

Early in his term, Governor Sanford began laying the groundwork for major and positive action on the race question.

He led up that action deliberately. Key steps along the way were a statement on North Carolina's economy and an address to fellow Methodists at Polkville.

In the statement, Governor Sanford noted that North Carolina's per capita income would jump ten places on the national scale of states if Negro income were as high as the income of white citizens.

In the address at Polkville, he argued that the religious beliefs of North Carolina could not be reconciled with second-class citizenship.

Then, on January 18, 1963, Governor Sanford went again to Chapel Hill to address the North Carolina Press Association. In less than five minutes Sanford delivered probably the shortest address a Governor had ever made to the newsmen. And, most of the editors agreed, the most important.

Noting that 1963 was the one-hundredth anniversary of the emancipation of Negroes from slavery in America, Governor Sanford said:

"Now is a time not merely to look back to freedom but forward to the fulfillment of its meaning. Despite great progress, the Negro's opportunity to obtain a good job has not been achieved in most places across the country.

Reluctance to accept the Negro in employment is the greatest single block
to his continued progress and the full use of the human potential of the
nation and its states.

"The time has come for American citizens to give up this reluctance, to
quit unfair discriminations, and to give the Negro a full chance to earn
a decent living for his family and to contribute to higher standards for himself and all men. . . ."

The Governor then announced establishment of the Good
Neighbor Council whose duties would be to encourage employment across North Carolina without regard to race and to urge
all young people to become better educated and, thereby, qualified for employment opportunities as they opened.

To head the Good Neighbor Council, Sanford appointed
veteran state official David S. Coltrane. Dr. James T. Taylor of
North Carolina was named vice-chairman and the places on the
council were filled by leaders of both races, including representatives of some of the most important companies in the state.

The editors and reporters who heard the Good Neighbor address gave the Governor a standing ovation. More important, the
news media of the state carried support of the council across the
state.

That pleased the Governor, but it did not surprise him. He
knew as personal friends the editors and reporters of Tar
Heel newspapers, radio and television stations from Manteo to
Murphy. During his four years in office, a large majority of
North Carolina's "Fourth Estate" supported the Governor on
his major programs, while never abdicating the right to take
shots at him whenever the mood arose.

Newsmen were frequent visitors at the Governor's Mansion
during the Sanford years. They came for breakfasts and for
briefings. Included were editors of the smallest weeklies in North
Carolina and such nationally syndicated columnists as Scotty
Reston of the *New York Times*, Drew Pearson, and author
Theodore White.

Under the guidance of the Governor and Margaret Rose Sanford, an open door policy was maintained at the old Victorian
house on Blount Street. Tens of thousands of Tar Heels and
visitors from other states and other nations were welcomed there.

During the Sanford tenancy, the Mansion was the site for
such white tie occasions as the symphony balls, initiated by the
Governor to raise funds for the North Carolina Symphony, and
such blue jean parties as an old-fashioned peach ice cream churn-
ing the Governor arranged for several hundred orphans.

Adding enthusiasm and laughter to the stately rooms of the
Mansion were the Sanford children, Betsy and Terry, Jr. From

time to time, Governor Sanford would momentarily suspend conferences with top state officials to listen to a report on young Terry's football game and to hear about a new dress Betsy wanted.

Toward the end of his administration, Governor Sanford sat down in the Mansion Library with one of his long legal pads and began to jot down a list of programs he had underway.

He compiled a list of 88 projects, a number that members of his staff thought was conservative. "He has more irons in the fire than a blacksmith," noted one friend.

Among the highlights of the achievements made by North Carolina under the Sanford administration were:

The Quality Education Program, which Dr. Frank Porter Graham called the greatest advance in education throughout North Carolina's history.

The accelerating drive for new industry, which produced 120,000 new jobs and which, according to United States government figures, made North Carolina the pace setter in the nation.

A reinvigoration of the agricultural economy with a new emphasis on food processing.

The establishment of an anti-poverty program that served as a model for states across the nation.

The encouragement of peaceful and progressive race relations based on decency and democracy during a time of upheaval in America.

The first court reform in North Carolina in the twentieth century.

The establishment of the State Board of Science and Technology to assure that North Carolina, which was a century late in the Industrial Revolution, would be at the launching of the Space Age.

The first reapportionment of the State House of Representatives and the State Senate in twenty years.

Prison policies that led to a decreasing prison population in North Carolina while most states were suffering increases.

The construction of thousands of miles of new secondary, primary, and interstate roads.

A budget policy that was "fiscally sound and forward bound" and under which some of the largest surpluses in Tar Heel history were compiled.

During Terry Sanford's administration, a lot of roads were built. A lot of buildings were raised. And a lot of crops were planted.

But the roads will wear out and the buildings someday will be razed and the crops will be rotated.

The lasting monument to Terry Sanford will rise in the minds of the boys and girls who went to school during the Sanford years and in the minds of their children and their grandchildren.

He said that education was the rock on which he would build the house of his administration.

Education also was the rock on which his stature rose.

INAUGURAL ADDRESS

INAUGURAL ADDRESS

MEMORIAL AUDITORIUM, RALEIGH

January 5, 1961

[As one newspaperman described the inauguration ceremonies of Governor Terry Sanford, "Pomp and politics dominated the day." The formalities marking the beginning of a new administration were brought to a colorful climax at noon on Thursday, January 5, 1961, when, in Raleigh's Memorial Auditorium, official acceptance of the office of chief executive occurred. In ceremonies lasting less than an hour, Governor Sanford, Lieutenant Governor Cloyd Philpott, and numerous other state officials took their respective oaths of office administered by members of the North Carolina Supreme Court. Immediately after the ceremonies, an inaugural parade was staged on Fayetteville Street, witnessed by Governor Sanford and other dignitaries.]

There is a new day in North Carolina!

I am here not to proclaim it, but rather to acknowledge its arrival.

It is here because our people are seeing, with new vision, the richness and vastness of the resources of North Carolina. It is here because they have seized upon the ideas which will turn these resources into limitless achievement.

There is an eagerness, an alertness, a confidence, a will to move ahead, that has now caught up our people and fired them with the reality of a new day.

It is here because of the past achievements of the people who have dreamed and worked and sacrificed for North Carolina throughout this century.

It is here because Charles Brantley Aycock[1] had a great heart and dauntless vision, and because he made North Carolina believe in universal education in an uncertain, uneasy and difficult day.

The new day is at hand because Glenn,[2] Kitchin,[3] Craig,[4] and

---

[1] Charles Brantley Aycock (1859-1912), lawyer, Governor of North Carolina, 1901-1905. During his administration improvements in state educational standards were realized, including the establishment of three colleges, expansion of public schools, and increase of teachers' salaries. Beth G. Crabtree, *North Carolina Governors, 1585-1958: Brief Sketches* (Raleigh: State Department of Archives and History, 1958), 113-114, hereinafter cited as Crabtree, *North Carolina Governors*.

[2] Robert Broadnax Glenn (1854-1920), lawyer, state legislator, state solicitor, United States district attorney, and Governor, 1905-1909. Crabtree, *North Carolina Governors*, 114-115.

[3] William Walter Kitchin (1866-1924), editor, lawyer, Governor, 1909-1913. Crabtree, *North Carolina Governors*, 116-117.

[4] Locke Craig (1860-1925), farmer, lawyer from Asheville, Governor, 1913-1917. Crabtree, *North Carolina Governors*, 117-118.

Bickett[5] were willing to step out in bold leadership when the day was still dark.

The arrival of the new day acknowledges the imagination of Morrison[6] in anticipating the transportation requirement of a growing state in a growing region.

It acknowledges the fiscal soundness and responsibility contributed by McLean[7] and Gardner,[8] and the advance of higher education under Morrison, McLean, and Gardner, culminating in the consolidation of the Greater University.

It acknowledges the courage of Ehringhaus,[9] who led the way to unpopular decisions in order that our public schools could be financed during the depression.

It acknowledges the stability and public conscience of the Hoey[10] and Broughton[11] administrations, the medical care and the human concern of a great and good state.

It acknowledges the sturdy courage of Cherry[12] and Umstead,[13] the still-broadening public conscience in the goal of total care for the mentally ill and retarded.

It acknowledges the tough-minded, warm-hearted, unbeatable

---

[5] Thomas Walter Bickett (1869-1921), teacher, lawyer from Franklin County, legislator in 1907, Governor, 1917-1921. Crabtree, *North Carolina Governors*, 119-120.

[6] Cameron Morrison (1869-1953), lawyer and political leader widely credited with the final overthrow of Republicanism in North Carolina. While Governor, 1921-1925, he helped unify the state through the expansion of the primary road system, and he championed improvement in educational facilities. Crabtree, *North Carolina Governors*, 120-121.

[7] Angus Wilton McLean (1870-1935), Democratic party leader, Governor, 1925-1929. He re-established the sound credit rating of the state, expanded executive power, and consolidated state departments. Crabtree, *North Carolina Governors*, 122-123.

[8] Oliver Max Gardner (1882-1947), Governor, 1929-1933, state legislator, Lieutenant Governor, delegate to Democratic conventions. Among his accomplishments as chief executive was the consolidation of the University at Chapel Hill, State College in Raleigh, and Woman's College in Greensboro. Crabtree, *North Carolina Governors*, 123-124.

[9] John Christoph Blucher Ehringhaus (1882-1949), lawyer, Governor, 1933-1937. Advances made under his leadership in social welfare included the rural electrification program, workmen's compensation legislation, and crop control. Crabtree, *North Carolina Governors*, 125-126.

[10] Clyde Roark Hoey (1877-1954), printer and newspaper publisher, lawyer, legislator, Governor, 1937-1941. He advocated progressive educational ideas and the modern parole system. Crabtree, *North Carolina Governors*, 126-127.

[11] Joseph Melville Broughton (1888-1949), lawyer, principal, community leader, state legislator, Governor, 1941-1945. He supported teacher pay increase, a retirement plan for all state employees, and an improved health program. Crabtree, *North Carolina Governors*, 125-126.

[12] Robert Gregg Cherry (1891-1957), lawyer, World War I veteran, state legislator, Governor, 1945-1949. He championed expansion of the state's health program. Crabtree, *North Carolina Governors*, 129-130.

[13] William Bradley Umstead (1895-1954), teacher, civic and religious leader from Durham, Governor, 1953 until his death in November, 1954. Crabtree, *North Carolina Governors*, 132-133.

drive of the "Great Agrarian," Kerr Scott,[14] bodily lifting up the rural segment of our economy, putting a new pulse-beat into the progressive heart of North Carolina.

It acknowledges the life of Luther Hodges,[15] whose energy paved the road of industrial development, and whose calm skill steered us through the threatened storms of racial strife to the shores of wisdom.

It acknowledges these and many other things, and it acknowledges in the names of these governors the tens of thousands of loyal and selfless members of the General Assembly, the teachers, the state employees, the institutions, the agencies, and the countless citizens who have shared each other's love of North Carolina.

It acknowledges the spirit of North Carolina—that we are doing well but we must do better—that we can do whatever we set out to do.

For many years our progress was impeded by the shackles of inadequate capital, the limitations of an economy in which agriculture was not sufficiently matched with high-wage industry, and the overwhelming obstacles of inadequate transportation facilities. That was yesterday.

Gone are the shackles.

Gone are the limitations.

Gone are the overwhelming obstacles.

North Carolina is on the move and we intend to stay on the move.

We are on the move because the leaders have drawn their strength from the people in a state which requires her leaders to stay close to her people.

We are on the move because we have put our fundamental faith in universal education.

We are on the move because we are making the most of the natural resources God has given us, and because we are driving hard to lift our agricultural and industrial income.

We are going to continue to put our faith in these funda-

---

[14] W. Kerr Scott (1896-1958), Governor, 1949-1953, farmer, champion of agrarian causes as farm agent, Grange leader, State Commissioner of Agriculture, 1936-1948. As Governor, he expanded state services in such areas as health, education facilities, transportation and communication, especially in rural areas. Crabtree, *North Carolina Governors*, 131-132.

[15] Luther Hartwell Hodges (1898-   ), industrialist from Leaksville, civic leader and public servant, Lieutenant Governor, 1952-1954. Following Governor Umstead's death, he succeeded to the governorship, and was elected in his own right to the next term, 1956-1960. Appointed Secretary of Commerce by President Kennedy, 1961. Crabtree, *North Carolina Governors*, 134-135; William S. Powell (ed.), *North Carolina Lives: The Tar Heel Who's Who* (Hopkinsville, Kentucky: Historical Record Association, 1962), 606-607, hereinafter cited as Powell, *North Carolina Lives.*

mentals: universal education, supporting, and supported by, a stronger economy.

I am not going to rely on dire statistics to prove my determination to lift the quality of education and to broaden the opportunities of earning a better living. Instead I am going to rely on faith. We have come a long way from a beginning which rose out of the ashes of disaster and despair.

We all are proud of our universal education. But now, in the closing decades of the twentieth century, we must do more than merely make education universal. We must give our children the *quality* of education which they need to keep up in this rapidly advancing, scientific, complex world. They must be prepared to compete with the best in the nation, and I dedicate my public life to the proposition that their education must be of a quality which is second to none. A second-rate education for our children can only mean a second-rate future for North Carolina.

Quality education is the foundation of economic development, of democracy, of the needs and hopes of the nation. Quality education put in its bleakest terms is survival. In its brightest terms, it is life, and growth, and happiness.

I have already detailed my program for quality education in North Carolina. It is a model program which represents the best thinking in the education field. Already it has received national attention and comment. We are confident that this is the program that the children of North Carolina need.

If it takes more taxes to give our children this quality education, we must face that fact and provide the money. We must never lose sight of the fact that our children are our best investment. This is no age for the faint of heart.

I believe that the people of this state will rise in boldness and will go forward in determination that we have chosen wisely when we base our future hopes on quality education. I need your help, your understanding, your firmness of purpose, and your hard work if we are to achieve this goal.

While quality education is the rock upon which I will build the house of my administration, we are not going to fall into the error of thinking that this, or any other single emphasis, will alone build a better North Carolina.

Education supports the economy but education must be supported by the economy. As we work for quality in education we must at the same time work just as boldly for broader opportunities to lift the income of our people.

Our goal is not only full development of the talents of our children, but also the creation of an expanding economy which will give everyone a better chance to make a better living.

Governor and Mrs. Sanford and Governor and Mrs. Luther H. Hodges are pictured leaving Raleigh's Memorial Auditorium on Sanford's inauguration day, January 5, 1961.

The Governor and his family were photographed in the Mansion in 1961. Terry, Jr., the Governor and his wife, Margaret Rose, and their daughter, Betsy, are shown in this family picture.

I see for us three points of greatest economic emphasis: lifting farm income; expanding industry and developing new industry; and properly using, conserving, and developing our water resources, which we have been given in such abundance, and which in turn will contribute to the industrial and agricultural pursuits.

I promise these next four years will demonstrate that I believe in the future of farming and that I have carried on with the Kerr Scott fervor.

I promise these next four years will demonstrate that I believe in the potential of industrial development and that I have carried on with the Luther Hodges energy.

And with this fervor and energy I pray that I will always carry on with the faith of Aycock and Gardner and all the other governors of North Carolina whose leadership and love have brought North Carolina to its new day.

As we work here to build a better state, we will also do our part to build a better nation.

Today we stand at the head of the South, but that is not enough. I want North Carolina to move into the mainstream of America and to strive to become the leading state of the nation. We can do it.

As the dynamic leadership of President John F. Kennedy moves us into the New Frontiers of a changing world, we will accept for North Carolina our responsibilities as citizens of the most powerful nation in the world, the last, best hope of the free world. We pledge to march with President Kennedy.

When the story is written it will be said that North Carolina did its part, that North Carolina contributed to the peoples of the world in the unending struggle for world peace and world understanding.

We can do this by appreciating that we are a leading part of the leading free nation of the free world, and that everything we do reflects good or bad upon that leadership. We can do this by appreciating that if America is to be strong for its job of leadership, then it is up to us to make North Carolina strong for its important part of that leadership. Quality education and a stronger economy thereby take on added significance of a most sobering nature.

In our segment of the free world, North Carolina will conquer, settle, and civilize the New Frontiers. While we are observing the big responsibilities, we will not forget the total responsibilities. If we achieve prosperity, prosperity will not harden our hearts.

We are not going to forget the progress we have made in the treatment and care of the mentally ill and the mentally deficient. We will improve our program and facilities which already stand with the most enlightened and advanced in America.

We are not going to forget the ill, the old, the dependent, the helpless, the handicapped.

We are not going to forget the modernization of our programs for penal institutions and juvenile correctional institutions.

We are going to find more effective ways to reduce the slaughter on our highways.

We are not going to forget the working man, the laborer, the small businessman, who often find the cards being stacked against them.

We are not going to forget the importance of our libraries, our symphony, our dramas, our art museums.

We are not going to forget, as we move into the challenging and demanding years ahead, that no group of our citizens can be denied the right to participate in the opportunities of first-class citizenship. Let us extend North Carolina's well-known spirit of moderation and goodwill, of mutual respect and understanding, in order that our energies and our resources, our abilities and our wills, may be directed toward building a better and more fruitful life for all the people of our state.

I stand firmly in the footprints of Aycock when he chose the creed for North Carolina:

I would have the strong to bear the burdens of the weak and to lift them up and make them strong, teaching men everywhere that real strength consists not in serving ourselves, but in doing for others.

All these things can be done, but they cannot be done in bitterness of factional strife. We need the help of all people of goodwill. I promise not to look back to past partisan differences, but to keep my eyes forward on the hopes and goals of North Carolina. If we work together for the common good, then all things are possible.

The General Assembly, the Council of State, the school people, the administrative officers, the state employees across the state can help move North Carolina forward, but they are powerless without the support and goodwill of the entire citizenry.

I call on all of us to put aside partisan differences, to turn our backs on those things which divide us and join hands on those things which can help us grow great. I promise to do this.

North Carolina is on the march. We are going forward. We will continue to march forward.

I pledge to North Carolina my devotion, my time and my energies, the full measure of all that there is within me to move in the faith of our fathers for a future bright with promise.

I call on all citizens to join with me in the audacious adventure of making North Carolina all it can and ought to be.

MESSAGES TO JOINT SESSIONS
OF THE GENERAL ASSEMBLY

MESSAGES TO JOINT SESSIONS OF
THE GENERAL ASSEMBLY

[Governor Sanford delivered two addresses to the joint sessions of the House of Representatives and the Senate during 1961 and four during 1963. When an extra session of the General Assembly convened in October, 1963, the Governor again addressed the legislators in joint session. All these messages were delivered by the Governor in person. They are printed in the *Journal of the Senate of the General Assembly of the State of North Carolina, Session 1961*, pp. 11-22, 73-79; the *Journal of the House of Representatives of the General Assembly of the State of North Carolina, Session 1961*, pp. 19-31, 123-129; the *Journal of the Senate . . . , 1963*, pp. 16-38, 39-44, 191-195, 386-389; the *Journal of the House of Representatives . . . , 1963*, pp. 20-46, 49-54, 307-311, 625-628. The journals of proceedings of the 1963 special session are included in the 1963 volumes. Governor Sanford's message to the special session is found on pages 799-800 of the *Senate Journal* and on pages 13-15 of the Extra Session section at the back of the *House Journal*.

In addition, routine messages concerning appointments were sent to the Senate and the House by the Governor (pp. 535-536, *Senate Journal, 1961*, and 241-242, *Senate Journal, 1963*; pp. 458-459, *House Journal, 1961*, and 565-567, *House Journal, 1963*). A special message was sent to the Senate concerning the resignation of Representative John W. Umstead (*Senate Journal, 1963*, p. 112). Messages on tax reduction (*Senate Journal, 1963*, p. 46, and *House Journal, 1963*, p. 72) and the Trade Fair (*Senate Journal, 1963*, p. 87, and *House Journal, 1963*, pp. 143-144) were sent by Governor Sanford to the legislators.]

BUDGET MESSAGE TO THE GENERAL ASSEMBLY
February 9, 1961

[In his first message to the General Assembly, Governor Sanford outlined needs of the state and stressed the need for adequate financial support to assure a new day for North Carolina. He dissected the budget prepared by the Advisory Budget Commission, concluding that additional funds were needed. He told the legislators that he would discuss the matter of additional revenue at a later time. Reaction was mixed, but the representatives and senators on the whole reacted favorably. At least three members of the Advisory Budget Commission were themselves convinced of the need and soon joined in efforts to provide funds beyond their own initial recommendations.]

INTRODUCTION

Under the Executive Budget Act, it is the responsibility and privilege of the Governor to come before you at this time and set forth the financial policy and program of the state for the next biennium in the form of a recommended budget.

"Budgets," said the great British Prime Minister Gladstone three-quarters of a century ago, "are not merely matters of arithmetic, but in a thousand ways go to the root of the prosperity of individuals, interrelations of classes, and the strength of kingdoms." This statement belongs among the truths that are eternal.

The consideration and adoption of the State Budget is the heaviest single responsibility that rests upon you as the representatives of the people of North Carolina. All that our state is, and all that we hope her to become, is closely tied to the budgets which have been and will be adopted by the legislature over the years. It is in this light that I urge you to consider all budget proposals—not merely as dollars to be collected and spent, but as a plan for providing the public services which the citizens of this enlightened state need, can afford, and should have. The budget is the most powerful tool available to you with which to fashion and carry out sound state governmental policy, and thereby to promote the well-being of our citizens.

Look about us, where North Carolina is strong today, our budgets have been strong in the past. Where North Carolina lags today, our budgets have needed and today need strengthening. We have not always been able to do all that we needed to do to strengthen our state in major respects; but our past progress is a firm foundation upon which, with our increasing ability to afford improved public services, we can build for the future.

In dealing with such a broad and complicated subject as our state budget, I will have to speak at this time in somewhat summary form. I am, however, attaching to your copies of this message the Budget Report of my predecessor, Governor Luther H. Hodges, and the Advisory Budget Commission. The Budget Report explains very fully the budget recommendations, and I urge that you read it carefully before you go into the details of budget requests and recommendations. From that report you can quickly obtain a view of the budget as a whole that will make the details much more meaningful to you.

I am also submitting herewith copies of all of the budget documents. These are in four volumes: the "A" Budget, the "B" Budget, the Capital Improvement Budget, and the Budget Digest. These documents contain the specific requests and recommended appropriations for every agency and institution.

The Budget Report was signed by the Director of the Budget, all six members of the Advisory Budget Commission, the Director of Administration, and the Acting State Budget Officer. I am sure that they gave careful consideration to the requests and needs of all of the state's institutions and agencies and apportioned the estimated available funds in accordance with their best judgment. I commend them for a job well done. I know that more time and effort have been expended on this recommended budget than on any previous budget in our history. I thank all state employees who assisted in its preparation for their faithful service to the state of North Carolina.

I especially express the gratitude of the state of North Carolina to J. K. Doughton,[16] distinguished public servant, splendid gentleman, who with thoroughness and with vision led the deliberations of his able associates, O. Arthur Kirkman,[17] J. William Copeland,[18] H. Clifton Blue,[19] Clyde H. Harriss,[20] and Joe C. Eagles, Jr.,[21] all of whom labored long in the public interest.

It was my privilege to attend nearly all of the hearings before the Governor and Advisory Budget Commission. Under the Constitution and the Executive Budget Act, however, responsibility for the preparation of this budget rested entirely with the previous administration.

Given the decision of those responsible for preparing this budget to limit their recommendations to the income which existing revenue sources will yield, this is a good budget. Generally, I approve it. It is a forward-looking budget, and provides a sound base upon which to build toward a new day in North Carolina.

There are, however, a few important areas in which I am convinced that this budget must be increased. In a relatively short time I shall come before you with additional recommendations for strengthening the budget at certain points, particularly in its provisions for education. At that time I shall also recommend to you specific measures for obtaining the additional revenue which my appropriation recommendations will require.

In the meantime, I commend the proposed budget to you. It is worthy of the most careful analysis and the soundest judgment you can give it. Ultimate responsibility for the adoption of the budget rests solely with the General Assembly. In the exercise of your independent judgment, you may see fit to increase appropri-

[16] James Kemp Doughton (1884-   ), farmer, banker from Sparta, representative in General Assembly, 1949-1955, Speaker of the State House of Representatives, 1957. *North Carolina Manual, 1957* (Raleigh: Office of the Secretary of State, 1957), 479, hereinafter cited as *North Carolina Manual*.

[17] O. Arthur Kirkman (1900-   ), railroad executive, bank official from High Point, representative in House of Representatives, 1949-1951, state senator, 1953-1959. *North Carolina Manual, 1959*, 483-484.

[18] James William Copeland (1914-   ), lawyer, judge, legislator from Woodland, state senator, 1951-1953, 1957-1959, Legislative Counsel to Governor Sanford, 1961, and special judge of Superior Court since 1961. Powell, *North Carolina Lives*, 285.

[19] Herbert Clifton Blue (1910-   ), publisher and public servant from Aberdeen, representative in the General Assembly since 1947, Speaker of the State House of Representatives, 1963. *North Carolina Manual, 1963*, 554.

[20] Clyde Hampton Harriss, Sr. (1902-   ), businessman, insurance agent, farmer from Salisbury, representative in the General Assembly, 1955-1963. *North Carolina Manual, 1963*, 579.

[21] Joseph Colin Eagles, Jr. (1910-   ), tobacconist and farmer from Wilson, state senator in General Assembly, 1949, 1951, 1957, and 1961. *North Carolina Manual, 1961*, 478.

ations beyond those recommended; or you may see fit to reduce recommended appropriations. Throughout your deliberations, bear in mind that the Executive Budget Act, and responsible management of the state's finances, require a balanced budget at all times.

Throughout the remainder of this message, I shall have occasion to mention many figures. In the interest of simplicity, I shall round off dollar figures and percentage figures and shall talk in terms of biennial, rather than annual, revenue and appropriations.

FISCAL CONDITION

I find the state of North Carolina today to be in sound fiscal condition.

We shall begin the next biennium with a very substantial General Fund credit balance of $53 million. Improved economic conditions and resulting General Fund revenue increases account for $42 million of this credit balance, while the remaining $11 million will come from savings effected by keeping expenditures below appropriations. And, let me make it clear now that the budget recommendations already provide for the expenditure of this $53 million General Fund credit balance.

The Highway Fund will on July 1, 1961, have an estimated balance of $26 million in state funds and $32 million in federal funds. This total Highway Fund balance of $58 million is fully committed and is not available for appropriation in addition to budget recommendations.

The gross debt of the state is $253.5 million, with an additional $11.5 million in bonds authorized but not yet issued. Of this total, $37 million is fully provided for by sinking funds and $106 million of secondary-road bonds are serviced by a 1-cent-per-gallon gasoline tax. Thus, for all practical purposes the net debt of the state is the $120 million in outstanding General Fund bonds issued since 1949.

THE TOTAL STATE BUDGET

The resources estimated to be available for expenditure by the state during the 1961-1963 biennium total $1,496 million. Recommended appropriations of $1,455 million will leave an estimated credit balance on June 30, 1963, of $42 million, nearly all of which is committed to specific purposes, such as highway construction and debt service.

The figures just mentioned include all receipts—state tax and other revenues, bond proceeds, federal funds, and agency receipts. They include, also, all proposed appropriations for current operations and for capital improvements.

Our budget is organized into three major operating funds—the General Fund, Highway Fund, and Agriculture Fund—and several smaller special funds earmarked to finance specific programs. Because their size dwarfs all others, I shall concentrate on the General Fund and Highway Fund in the remainder of what I shall have to say today.

THE GENERAL FUND

General Fund resources for the coming biennium, after excluding federal funds and agency receipts, are estimated at $747 million. This sum consists of an estimated $53 million in beginning credit balance, recommended capital improvement bond issue proceeds of $54 million, and current revenues of $640 million.

Recommended General Fund appropriations total $747 million, of which $689 million is for current operations and $58 million is for capital improvements. The estimated credit balance on June 30, 1963, will be only $15,000.

I take note of the fact that this budget proposes that the state spend on current General Fund operations during the 1961-1963 biennium $49 million more than the state is expected to receive in General Fund revenue during that period. The budget is kept in balance by spending all of the $53 million credit balance accumulated during the 1959-1961 biennium.

If the expectations of the makers of this budget hold true, there will be no comparable credit balance with which to begin the 1963-1965 biennium. This means that we will leave difficult problems for the 1963 General Assembly in maintaining the level of services under the "A" Budget.

REVENUE

General Fund revenue for the current biennium is estimated at $620 million. For the next biennium, General Fund revenue is estimated at $640 million, an apparent increase of only $20 million, or 3 per cent. Budgets, however, must be built upon revenue which is expected to come in year after year. As you know, revenue for the current biennium includes $28 million in "windfall" receipts resulting from the adoption of the income tax withholding system two years ago. This $28 million can be spent but once and will not come again. Deducting those "windfall" receipts gives 1959-1961 General Fund revenue collections of a recurring type in the sum of $592 million. By comparison with that figure, the $640 million in revenue projected for the 1961-1963 biennium represents an increase of $59 million, or 8 per cent.

In view of the exceptionally good General Fund revenue collections of this biennium in comparison with 1957-1959, there
may be a strong temptation in some quarters to argue that an
8 per cent General Fund revenue increase is too conservative,
and that additional appropriations can be provided for by the
painless expedient of raising the revenue estimates. The Advisory
Budget Commission does not, and I do not, and dare not, share
that hope. On the basis of all the evidence now available, including general economic conditions and trends and the relatively
conservative revenue growth estimates now being made by the
federal government and by our sister states—averaging less than
4 per cent—I see no present justification for raising the Advisory
Budget Commission's 8 per cent revenue increase estimate. To
take any other position would be dangerous and would border
upon fiscal irresponsibility. Should new information cause a
change in this view while you are in session, I shall so advise you.

APPROPRIATIONS

Requests for General Fund appropriations for current operations during the coming biennium totaled $783 million, and
88 per cent of that amount is recommended for appropriation.
Recommended General Fund appropriations of $689 million
constitute an increase in current operation appropriations of
$103 million, or nearly 18 per cent above comparable expendi-
tures for the current biennium.

"A" Budget recommendations for maintaining present services
at existing levels, with suitable allowance for the increased
number of people to be served, are $626 million, virtually the full
sum requested. This is an increase of more than $40 million
above current expenditures. "B" Budget recommendations, providing for improved services, new programs, and salary increases,
total $61 million in comparison with the $156 million requested.

General Fund capital improvements requests added up to $105
million. The budget recommends the appropriation of $58 mil-
lion for capital improvements, of which $4 million will be pro-
vided from current revenue, $6 million from bonds to be issued
on legislative authorization, and $48 million from bonds to be
issued on approval of the voters of the state.

The budget is arranged into about a dozen major functional
groupings: education, public welfare, corrections, debt service,
and the like. The budget of each agency and institution will be
found under the appropriate functional heading. This enables
you, in apportioning state funds, to think primarily in terms of
the programs of public service to be performed and secondarily in

terms of the specific agencies and institutions which will perform them.

In discussing the provisions which this budget makes for the various functions of state government, I shall talk more about programs and activities than about figures, and refer you to the appropriate budget documents for the details.

GENERAL GOVERNMENT

The general government function includes the General Assembly, the Governor's Office, the courts, the fiscal control and revenue agencies, the personnel agencies, and a few others. Recommended General Fund appropriations for general government total $24 million, up 34 per cent from current expenditures. A large part of the increase is a $2.5 million appropriation for administrative distribution to state agencies to continue in force the new salary schedules adopted July 1, 1960. These salary schedules were adopted too late for the necessary funds to be included in the "A" Budget requests of the agencies. Other increases in the sum of $864,000 raise the salaries of Supreme Court justices and Superior Court judges and solicitors, and provide for expanded activities of the Department of Revenue, Department of Administration, and State Bureau of Investigation.

Another large item is the Contingency and Emergency Fund, which is distributed almost entirely to agencies and institutions outside of general government.

EDUCATION

The most important and the most expensive function of our state government is education: support of the public schools, maintenance of our institutions of higher education, aid to five community colleges, operation of schools for handicapped children, and support of the State Library, Department of Archives and History, and several other educational and cultural undertakings.

Recommended General Fund appropriations for the entire education function, including a proper share of retirement contributions and debt service, total $520 million. This is 75.4 per cent of total recommended General Fund appropriations for all purposes. While that percentage figure is down slightly from prior years, the budget nevertheless carries an absolute increase of $70 million, or 16 per cent, over current expenditures for education.

For the public schools, on which the major share of state education funds are spent, recommended appropriations total $442 million. This is $51 million, or 13 per cent, above comparable expenditures for 1959-1961, which include the contingent supplemental salaries voted by the General Assembly two years ago.

The "A" Budget contains a public school appropriation increase of $25 million to take care of an enrollment growth of 19,000 pupils a year and otherwise to continue current levels of instruction and supporting services. The "B" Budget recommendations provide for salary increases and other improvements in the public schools to the extent of $40 million, which includes $14 million to convert the contingent supplemental salaries now being paid into a part of the continuing salary base for public school employees.

I know that improving the salaries of public school teachers and other school employees is of major concern to all of you. Appropriations of $35 million, which is the greater part of the public school budget increase, will make possible a new salary range for public school academic teachers of $3,300 to $5,000 a year, compared with the present range of $2,946 to $4,557 a year. Salary increases in the same proportion are recommended for principals, superintendents, and supervisors. Vocational teachers' salary schedules, already higher than those of academic teachers, are also to be increased proportionately.

In addition to salary increases, the new funds recommended will strengthen state-level supervisory and administrative activities in the public school system, and, in many other respects, implement the requests of the State Board of Education.

The annual rate of state support for public school libraries is increased from $1.50 to $3.00 per pupil, and the annual state allotment for instructional supplies is raised from $1.12 to $1.50 per pupil. Adequate provision is made for a new program for the professional improvement of teachers, for a permanent curriculum study and research program under the State Board of Education, for the administration of the National Defense Education Program, and for the development of vocational education instructional materials.

Local school supervision will be improved by the addition of twenty-five local unit supervisors to the present 256. The program for mentally retarded children received the full financial support requested.

In vocational education, the budget recommendations allow expansion of vocational instruction and vocational rehabilitation programs. A new agricultural technology program is recommended. The nineteen industrial education centers which are contributing so much to the industrial growth of our state will receive $763,000 for additional equipment.

You can readily see that public schools have not been exactly neglected, but it has been deliberately left to us to initiate the fulfillment of the bright promise of quality education which holds so much for the future of our people.

The over-all increase in General Fund appropriations from the last budget to this one is 18 per cent.

The total increase for public schools is 13 per cent.

The percentage of the total General Fund budget is 67.7 per cent. With all that was done by this Budget Commission, and it is considerable, we have shown little progress. In 1959-1961 the percentage of our total General Fund resources going to public schools was 70.4 per cent. This budget, I repeat, allots only 67.7 per cent.

So you can see that in spite of all we have done, we are losing ground.

The programs of enrichment cannot be implemented under this budget. At least, forgetting the small percentage differences which can be explained away in several creditable ways, this is pretty good evidence that we are not making the progress we must make.

It can be argued that we can get along on this level of appropriations, and we can, but at this rate we will never achieve opportunities of education second to none.

I have talked with Governor Hodges and with the members of the Advisory Budget Commission. They realize this budget will not achieve the goals in education we must now reach. But they have done the best possible within the framework of the tax structure with which they worked, and they have properly left to us the challenge of achieving high quality in our system of public schools.

I am sure, I am positive, that there is contained in this budget no implied admonition to "hold the line" at the proposed figures.

Rather, I am satisfied, I know, that it was and is expected that this budget will serve as a "line of departure" from which we will move to the objective of quality education to meet the demand of a rapidly advancing, changing, scientific, complex world.

Because of the importance of public schools, I have chosen to talk about expanding our educational opportunities at a later time when we can devote our attention exclusively to that subject, and therefore I request your indulgence in allowing me to deliver another and special message on the budget for public education.

Turning now to higher education: Appropriations recommended for the Consolidated University of North Carolina and the nine other institutions of higher education total $58 million, an increase of $12 million, or 26 per cent, beyond current appropriation expenditures.

Our university and colleges now enroll 36,500 students, or 53 per cent of those attending college in this state. A further rise of 4,000, or 11 per cent, is expected in the next two years.

The Advisory Budget Commission recommends as a policy matter that college tuition rates be increased, on the ground that the per-student cost to the state for higher education has risen more in proportion than has the cost to the student in tuition and fees. It is recommended that the proceeds from these additional tuition receipts, totaling $2.2 million, be distributed 50 per cent to scholarships, 40 per cent to faculty salaries, and 10 per cent to libraries. The scholarships would offset the impact of tuition increases on needy students.

Competition for qualified college faculty members is keen through the nation, because college enrollment pressures are felt nationwide. Faculty salary funds will be increased under the terms of this budget by $3.4 million from General Fund appropriations and an additional $900,000 from tuition increases. Distribution of these salary funds will be left to the discretion of the administrators of the various institutions, as has been the recent practice.

The increase in higher education appropriations will, in addition to salary raises, provide for teaching larger numbers of students and for the purchase of additional library books and instructional and scientific equipment.

Appropriations in aid of summer school programs at the state institutions will be regularized by the appropriation of $960,000, to be distributed among the institutions in proportion to hours of summer school instruction given. Grants to community colleges will be increased from $3.25 to $4.00 per student quarter hour of instruction in approved courses.

HEALTH AND HOSPITALS

Appropriations recommended for health and hospitals total $65 million, an increase of 17 per cent over current expenditures. Most of this increase represents the cost of continuing and expanding operations of the mental institutions and the training schools for mentally retarded children and the extension and enrichment of programs of the State Board of Health.

Funds are recommended to continue operations at the present levels of service in Memorial Hospital at Chapel Hill, the sanatorium system, and other state hospitals and health agencies.

PUBLIC WELFARE

General Fund appropriation recommendations for all public welfare activities total $25 million, an increase of 17 per cent over current expenditures. These state appropriations together with federal and county contributions, will provide $168 million for public welfare. This is $18 million more than will be received during the current biennium.

The funds recommended for public welfare will support the caseloads and average grants projected by the state welfare agencies in the Old Age Assistance, Aid to Dependent Children, Aid to the Permanently and Totally Disabled, and Aid to the Blind programs. These projections of average caseloads and average grants are based on the continuation of recent trends, all of which are upward except for the Old Age Assistance caseload.

I suggest that you carefully evaluate the welfare proposals and assure yourselves that the recommended funds are sufficient to support reasonable increases in the public assistance programs.

CORRECTIONS

The budget recommends appropriations of $4.5 million for the state juvenile correction program, an increase of 29 per cent over 1959-1961 expenditures.

Included are funds for the establishment of a new Juvenile Evaluation and Treatment Center on the Moore General Hospital property near Asheville, recently given to the state by the federal government. This center will be used for processing and classifying all students assigned by the courts to the correctional schools, as well as for the psychiatric care and rehabilitation of difficult cases.

The Probation Commission and Board of Paroles have heretofore been supported by the Highway Fund. The Budget Report recommends their transfer to the General Fund. Moderate appropriation increases are proposed for each of these agencies.

PUBLIC SAFETY AND REGULATIONS

For public safety and regulation, which includes the military and civil defense departments as well as several regulatory agencies, appropriations of $7 million—an increase of 9 per cent —are recommended. The increase will go chiefly to the financial responsibility program of the Department of Motor Vehicles, the civil defense program, and expanded activities of other regulatory agencies.

NATURAL RESOURCES AND RECREATION

Appropriations recommended for natural resources and recreation are $8 million, which is 15 per cent more than current expenditures. This increase will strengthen the programs in forest management, industrial development, commercial fisheries resources, and water resources.

AGRICULTURE

The agricultural agencies will, under the recommended budget, receive General Fund appropriations totaling $12 million. The increase over current expenditures is $800,000, or 7 per cent.

Included is a General Fund appropriation to the Department of Agriculture of $2.9 million, an 18 per cent increase over comparable current expenditures. This sum, together with a $2.8 million appropriation from the Agriculture Fund, will furnish appropriations of $5.7 million to the Department of Agriculture. The increases will permit improved inspectional activities and better tax collection by the department.

Salary increases for academic personnel in the Agricultural Experiment Station and the Cooperative Agricultural Extension Service, both of which are administratively controlled by State College, are included in the appropriations to the Consolidated University of North Carolina. Modest increases are proposed in other phases of the budgets of those agencies.

Several farms now being operated at state institutions no longer serve their original purposes, take too much of the time of administrative personnel, and their orderly discontinuation is recommended.

RETIREMENT AND PENSIONS

Teachers and other state employees belong to the Teachers' and State Employees' Retirement System. The state's contribution to the Retirement System covers the employer's contribution for both Social Security and the state retirement plan.

General Fund appropriations to the Retirement System will total $46 million. The increase of 40 per cent over current expenditures for this purpose is attributable to the normal growth in the number of people on the state payroll, the state's contribution required to match increased salaries, higher Social Security contribution rates, and larger contributions required to keep the Retirement System in actuarially sound condition.

DEBT SERVICE

General Fund debt service appropriation recommendations of $25 million are 50 per cent higher than expenditures for the current biennium. Of the increase, $3.4 million will be required to service the debt outstanding on July 1, 1961, and another $4.9 million will be necessary to service the capital improvement bonds which the budget recommends be authorized and issued.

SALARY INCREASES

Budget recommendations for salary increases in education have already been discussed. For full-time, permanent employees subject to the State Personnel Act, the budget provides salary increases of $3 million from the General Fund and $2.85 million from the Highway Fund. If this amount were distributed on a percentage basis, it would provide an across-the-board pay raise of 3 per cent. Recommended salary increases and additional merit salary increments combined add 7 per cent to the total cost of salaries for this group of state employees.

CAPITAL IMPROVEMENTS

Recommended General Fund appropriations for capital improvements total $58 million. These appropriations will be financed by a direct appropriation of $4 million from current revenues, $6 million in bonds to be issued on legislative authorization, and $48 million in bonds to be issued upon approval by the legislature and a favorable vote of the people.

Nearly half of the capital improvement recommendations— $26.5 million—is for the institutions of higher education. This sum represents about half of the capital improvement requests submitted by those institutions.

The voted bond issue will finance $13.5 million for expanded state port facilities.

To relieve overcrowding of our state offices in Raleigh, the budget provides that the State Highway Building, which was financed from the Highway Fund, and the Highway Commission's testing laboratory building be purchased by the General Fund from the Highway Fund at a price of $2.365 million. The building will furnish office space for General Fund agencies. The Highway Commission will apply the sale proceeds to the construction of a new highway building in the Raleigh area.

The state has long needed an appropriate building for its very fine archives collection and historical museum, and for its State Library. To erect such a building, an appropriation of $2.692 million is recommended.

The Raleigh Farmers Market is currently operated by the State Department of Agriculture on an experimental basis under a lease contract with the owner of the facility. The lease expires this spring. It is recommended that the state purchase the Farmers

Market facility at a price of $500,000, in order to continue and improve the services which the market is rendering to the farmers of the state.

THE HIGHWAY FUND

Highway Fund revenues are currently earmarked for the support of the State Highway Commission, the Department of Motor Vehicles, and the State Prison Department.

All of the balance of $58 million with which the Highway Fund will begin the next biennium is already committed. Current revenues, state and federal, are estimated at $331 million for 1961-1963. Recommended Highway Fund appropriations total $358 million, leaving a balance at the end of the next biennium of $31 million, practically all of which is already reserved for debt service and aid to municipalities.

REVENUE

Estimated Highway Fund state revenue for 1961-1963 is $295 million—or 7 per cent above current revenue. This increase rate would have been higher, but for the depressing effect of growing numbers of compact and small foreign cars upon gasoline consumption. It is estimated that gasoline consumption during this year will be about 1 per cent less than it would have been if no compacts had been sold.

APPROPRIATIONS

In spite of the anticipated gain in Highway Fund state revenue, recommended appropriations from state and federal funds combined total $358 million, down $63 million—or 15 per cent—from current expenditures. This decrease is almost wholly due to a drop of $62 million in federal funds to be spent in 1961-1963. Appropriations from state funds are almost identical with those of the current biennium.

STATE HIGHWAY COMMISSION

Recommended appropriations of state and federal funds to the State Highway Commission are $317 million, which is 19 per cent down from current expenditures. Again, this reduction is due to a falling-off in federal construction funds.

The decrease in federal funds for highway construction comes from the fact that in prior years North Carolina, because it was in a position to take immediate advantage of federal interstate system grants, received higher annual allocations for the interstate system than are now being allocated to us. During 1961-1963, interstate allocations and expenditures, as well as other federal aid funds, are likely to remain constant unless some change is made in the present federal highway program.

DEPARTMENT OF MOTOR VEHICLES

Highway Fund appropriations recommended for the Department of Motor Vehicles are $19 million, an increase of 6 per cent over 1959-1961 expenditures. Included in the recommendations are fifty Highway Patrol clerks who will relieve fifty patrolmen for road patrol service.

STATE PRISON DEPARTMENT

Recommended Highway Fund appropriations for the State Prison Department are $32 million, an increase of 22 per cent over current expenditures.

This increase of $5.6 million will provide primarily for reduction of working hours of custodial employees from more than sixty to forty-eight hours a week, for salary adjustments already authorized for certain classifications of prison employees, for expansion of rehabilitation and training activities, for improved security measures, and for new programs of adult education and vocational education for youthful offenders. A major reorganization of the prison system, especially as to the number and size of field units and facilities, is also contemplated by the budget.

CAPITAL IMPROVEMENTS

Capital improvements recommendations for Highway Fund agencies total $5.7 million, of which $2.6 million will come from the Highway Fund and the remainder from other sources. No bonds are proposed for these capital improvements.

The recommended appropriations will finance construction of a new State Highway building; necessary new prison facilities; and Highway Patrol facilities, offices, radio towers, and equipment.

CONCLUSION

In conclusion, let me say again that the recommended budget which I have just outlined to you, and which is about to be placed in your hands, constitutes a sound basic plan of state expenditures for the upcoming biennium. With the additions, which I shall shortly recommend to you, I firmly believe that it will enable us to make a long stride toward the new day which all of us covet for our beloved North Carolina.

Thank you.

SPECIAL MESSAGE TO THE GENERAL ASSEMBLY

March 6, 1961

[After outlining in broad terms the needs of the state, particularly in the field of education, when he addressed the General Assembly in February, the Governor felt it necessary to go into more detail in a later speech. In March he appeared before another joint session to present in detail a plan for raising needed revenues to meet what he considered pressing needs. To carry out his program in the field of education, Governor Sanford recommended the elimination of the sales tax exemption on food and other items, effective July, 1961. He also suggested that a state-wide vote on the proposal be held in November to determine whether the tax should be continued after July 1, 1963. The "food tax" became the subject of debate throughout the state before it was finally enacted into law. A day or so after the address to the General Assembly, the Governor began receiving letters on the subject of a food tax for education. A supporter wrote that he had resided in North Carolina for two years and had three daughters in the public schools and wanted "to express my wholehearted support of your recommendations for aid to Education. I know that every ounce of your aggressiveness and determination will be required before your proposals are adopted by the legislators." He concluded by saying that "The results from your program will be better citizens for North Carolina and better Americans." Another wrote, "I am so proud that you are Governor of my State and I want to take this opportunity to tell you so." Despite the fact that the writer stated that she and her husband did not have a child in school, she knew that increased taxes would be needed and thanked the Governor "for the foresight you have for children and the future of our state." Still another wrote, "I have two sons, aged three and four. My wife and I want the best educational opportunities for them that we and our state can afford. We *can* afford what you have asked. If we cannot afford this minimum, we cannot afford anything." This citizen promised the Governor "support . . . to the very best of our abilities and resources." Not all, however, expressed appreciation for the Sanford proposal. About seventy mimeographed letters, individually signed, were sent with the statement: "I am *HIGHLY* opposed to *ANY* tax on the most essential item (food). I thoroughly believe in higher education and will support it 100%, but in my opinion, revenue can be obtained from other sources. . . . If this proposal becomes law, believe me—YOU WILL BE THE MOST UNPOPULAR GOVERNOR NORTH CAROLINA EVER HAD." One writer asked, "How do you have the nerve, and inconsideration for the people of N. C. to put tax on food?" Still another told the Governor, "Terry Sanford's 'NEW DAY' is certainly dawning in North Carolina, but instead of bringing relief to the already over-taxed inhabitants, *it is realy* [sic] *adding insult to injury.*" In a letter addressed to the Governor, the Lieutenant Governor, members of the General Assembly, and the Speaker of the House, an irate citizen, after criticizing the food tax, continued by saying, "But if your [sic] will stop the hole where our tax money is being wasted, you now have enough. The Welfare Department is one that is so large that an elephant could fall through, and the Board of Health is in the same class. The Highway Department is still worse. There is more tax money wasted than spent for the good of the children. There are a good many more places that I could name." The Governor's Office received hundreds of letters on the subject of a food tax to support quality education after the presentation of this address, which was televised on a state-wide network.]

Tonight—on this sixth day of March, 1961—we must take a deliberate, penetrating look at the future.

Tonight we must begin to swing wide the doors to the future for our children, for beyond the threshold lie the hopes and aspirations of not only our children but all the world's children.

The last great hope of the world is democracy as we know it; and North Carolina must once again rally to the cause just as it has from Kings Mountain to the Yalu River.

Today we do not take up the sword. Instead, we take up the pen, the educational pen. We put the pen into the uncertain, eager hands of our youth, for we know they must—and they will— write the future history of North Carolina, and indeed of the nation and the free world.

Any achievement by man requires sacrifice—and tonight we must look together at a small measure of sacrifice.

I do not come to you expecting popular acclaim for what I have to say. I do come to do my duty in full confidence that you in turn will do your duty.

When I presented the budget to the General Assembly, I asked that you allow me to return to recommend additional funds to meet the basic needs for school improvement.

I have explained time and again that I believe the economic, social, and moral development of our state depends largely on an expanding program of quality education second to none.

I have explained time and again that I believe it is time that North Carolina provide the opportunities that will put this state in the front ranks of our community of states.

I have explained to you my reasons for believing that the budget is inadequate to achieve the public education goals we must set for our state. I am sure that it is generally acknowledged that we have not done all we can do.

I come to you now with the most difficult decision that I have had to make since assuming the office of Governor, and, perhaps, the most difficult of my term of office.

I come to you now with the most difficult decision of your service in this session.

It has not been difficult, however, to decide that something must be done about our schools. This is obvious to all.

It has not been difficult to concede that if we want to do the job we will have to pay for it. This is admitted by all.

Having concluded we must take decisive steps for school improvement, and having concluded we must have more money, the difficult decision is what sources will best distribute equitably the costs among all the citizens of the state.

I have examined many sources and I have come to decisions

which I recommend to you now in the firm belief that this is the way to move North Carolina forward—the way to swing open the doors to our children.

I have considered every possible source of taxation, and I will mention some of these sources which have been widely discussed.

I looked carefully at the tax on whisky, beer, and wine. Beer and wine are already taxed at a rate which appears to me to be as high as reasonably consistent with our regulatory responsibilities. I have studied the effect of a recent tax increase on whisky in Virginia, which drove the sale "to the woods" and diminished the total receipts from this source. Therefore, I concluded that to make the tax on whisky too high would be self-defeating and therefore ought to be avoided. I am convinced, however, that to increase this tax by an amount of 20 per cent of the present tax would not reach the point of diminishing returns. Such an increase from 10 per cent to 12 per cent would bring in an additional amount of $3 million for the biennium, and therefore I recommend this as one of our sources.

I have looked carefully at the so-called crown tax on soft drinks. It is argued with considerable merit that there is no more justification for a special tax on soft drinks than on an ice cream cone, a chocolate soda, a Baby Ruth or a package of potato chips. It is a fact that one cent on a bottle would result in taxing soft drinks at almost double the rate we tax whisky. The states which have adopted this source have discovered that sales diminish and a large percentage of bottlers go out of business. Thus the tax defeats itself. Only two states now have such a tax, and I am advised that one of these will probably repeal the tax this year. It seems fairer to me to tax soft drinks at the rate of 3 per cent as a part of the regular sales tax, and this is already being done.

A great many people have said to me that we should tax tobacco products, and a great many people have said we should not. The principal reason given for putting a tax on cigarettes is that people who smoke, whether rich or poor, can afford to pay the tax. Representatives from over half of the counties have advised me that they do not believe it wise to put a special tax on tobacco. Many of them report that they pledged against such a special tax during their campaigns for election. Many people will be surprised to find such a widespread sentiment against this special tax, and frankly I do not fully understand the sentiment. The most logical explanation I have heard is that North Carolina is the leading tobacco producer and the leading manufacturer, and our leaders of the industry have the burden of fighting such taxes in other states, where, in many instances, they have been levied in unfair amounts. Consequently, I do not now recommend a special tax, but recommend that tobacco products be taxed at the rate of 3 per cent along with other similar commodities, as is now the case.

I have considered a state tax on real estate and other property. Most states put the greatest burden of school support on real estate taxes. We departed from that concept some years ago, deciding to leave this source to the limited use of county and city governments. Real estate is more static, and in time of economic depression has little or no earning capacity, so taxation of this source has in times past resulted in hardships and loss of farms and other property by foreclosure. More than a quarter of a century ago we made the basic decision to tax money, rather than property, and I oppose any change in this long-accepted approach.

We decided then to obtain our chief support for schools and state functions from money earned and money spent. Thus, the sales tax, the income tax, and the gasoline tax have been the basic support of state operations.

The income tax has been a steady, expanding source of revenue for the state and has distributed the burden to those best able to pay as measured by income. This is a fair and equitable tax, but already the state is receiving substantial revenue from the income tax, and the federal government is taxing this source almost to the breaking point. There is no real hope of relief from federal taxation until the cold war is won, and an increase by the state would, it must be admitted by all, be too burdensome. I believe those best able to pay should carry the heaviest burden of taxation, but even a casual glance at income tax rates will convince you that this is already the case. Therefore, I recommend that we do not change our rate of income tax.

I have considered two possibilities with the sales tax: an increase in the rate to 3½ per cent or 4 per cent, or a removal of exemptions.

The sales tax is fair in distributing the costs of the state services to all who share in these benefits. When balanced with the present income tax schedules, it is about as fair a method as possible for distributing the costs because the more a man spends, the more he pays in sales tax.

The chief difficulty with the present sales tax is that because of so many assorted exemptions, it is extremely difficult to administer. It is difficult for the small merchant to know what he has collected, what he should collect, and what he should pay in to the state. It is impossible for the ordinary consumer to know what is taxed and what is not.

Our statistics and study show that: (1) increasing the tax to 4 per cent on shoes and clothing and other items would reach approximately the same people, in the same amounts, as a tax across the board, on all items, without exemption; and (2) we now collect the lowest sales tax per capita of all the thirty-four states having a sales tax, probably because of our many exemptions which make administration and collection difficult.

Therefore, it is my recommendation that you remove all exemptions from the sales tax.

I will submit a proposed bill which will place the tax at 3 per cent across the board, except it will place only 1 per cent on the farm and industrial group of items and equipment used in production, and only 2 per cent on motor vehicles with the present top limitations. It will not tax those items such as products of the farm sold for further processing and subsequent taxation, and gasoline already taxed by another method.

I am well aware of the hardships of paying tax on necessary items by those whose income is so low that every penny counts. But I am also aware of the greater hardship placed upon the children of these same people by inadequate school opportunities, and I have been able to devise no way that the poorest can be exempt from a general sales tax. Welfare payments and the distribution of free food answer this complaint raised in behalf of the poorest among us, and the poor who do not receive these payments, I predict, will be willing to do their share in order that we might have a strong tax structure which will support the schools which will give their children a better chance in life. A patchwork tax structure, with special taxes on special items, will not give us the kind of tax structure we must have if our schools are to grow as our population grows.

I know that this will place extra burdens on many merchants. However, I have no doubt about their general response. They are responsible and civic-minded. I think that the merchants of this state have never been given adequate praise for their participation in the support of the needs of the people of North Carolina. Through their efforts to make the sales tax effective beginning in 1933, they literally saved the public schools. Now again, they are called on to do their part in making our school system better. I express my thanks for what they have already done for the state and deep appreciation for what they are yet to do.

If you will authorize these taxes we will be able to take a giant stride forward in lifting up the chances of our boys and girls.

We will be able to adopt the "B" Budget requests of the State Board of Education, a group of conscientious, dedicated and prudent business, professional, and civic leaders who are devoted to the cause of education and the state of North Carolina.

There is no better informed group than your State Board of Education. I have studied all their requests. They have carefully balanced all of the most urgent needs, and we must have the program they have laid before us. I recommend it to you without reservation. It will be explained in detail at hearings before the Joint Appropriations Committee, by the Board of Education and Department of Public Instruction representatives.

The recommended changes in the tax structure will bring in an estimated $83 million during the next biennium.

Meeting the budget requests of the Board of Education will require $70 million. This will leave a balance of $13 million.

All of us have been able to take great pride in our university and colleges. We can demonstrate that they have contributed much beyond their cost to the life and growth and happiness of our state.

I would not have us slow their progress as the price of accelerating our efforts for secondary education. Rather, I know we must continue to improve our colleges if we are to continue to prosper and grow. The budget I presented earlier provides for substantial improvements.

Each president is presenting to you requests above the Advisory Budget Commission recommendations, but less than the original "B" Budget requests. I believe that we can adjust these figures to about $3 million and continue to have a vital, moving program of higher education.

There will be some other urgent needs, and I recommend that you consider adding to the proposed appropriations as already submitted the following increases: mental hospitals, $500,000; welfare, including a wider distribution of surplus food, $2 million; other agencies and institutions, plus a reasonable margin for a reserve, $3.5 million.

Through the Budget Bureau, I will consider carefully with you the line items involved in these increases.

This will leave a balance of $4 million. I will later have a detailed report for you on the status of the finances of the State Highway Department, but I can tell you now that because of matching federal funds there is virtually nothing left for secondary road construction. This ties in with the proper consideration of school needs, because an urgent requirement is road improvement if we are to be able to move the school buses. One superintendent in an adjoining county reported more than forty school buses stuck in one week. I recommend that this sum of $4 million be applied in partial support of the prison budget, that an equal amount be released to the Highway Fund for use in urgently needed secondary road construction.

I want to remind the professional school people what I have said in many ways and on many occasions. I am asking the General Assembly to ask the people to provide more adequate financial support for the schools, but I am going to be even more demanding of the school people for improved performance up and down the line. If the General Assembly and the people provide increased appropriations, then it is up to us to do our part in improving our performance in every other respect. I propose to work in every field of school activity to improve the level and standard of performance. We will continue our curriculum study and improvement, our search for methods of rewarding merit and superior performance, our efforts to achieve all of those things we can do without additional money. In other words, I am saying that we realize that money is only a part of what we need to achieve the quality we seek, and we are pledging to the people to complete the job in every respect.

I realize the task of the public servant is never easy and frequently extremely difficult. I know, however, that you are here because of an abiding desire to serve the cause of democracy, and I know that your presence here involves a personal financial sacrifice in every instance.

You will receive some good advice, some bad advice, some fair and some unfair pressure. I know that you realize this is part of the price of public service, and that you will take it all, good and bad, without complaint.

Over two years ago at Durham I outlined my hope that the people would become so interested in education that they would demand better schools and would be willing to support this effort. I said then that I wanted some way to get the people involved, concerned, excited, and ready to go to work to achieve quality education.

The quality we seek cannot be delivered by the General Assembly, although only you can start the march. Quality is complex, difficult, constant in required attention; and it will demand the best in effort by school boards, the state agencies, the superintendents, the principals, the teachers, the parents, the students, and indeed all of the citizens of the state. And this is no single-shot affair. It will require attention year after year after year. It is, as Admiral Rickover points out, "an essential civic duty for every intelligent and educated person, for every person with deep love of his country and her children, to participate in the public debate on education. . . . there is no valid reason why the United States cannot have the best school system in the world."

I would like to see every citizen understand the need and the problem, caught up and taking part, willing not only to supply the money but anxious to supply the continuing interest without which our expenditures will have been in vain.

I think I know how we can obtain this interest and continuing support.

I recommend that you enact the tax revision I have suggested, that the new schedule become effective July 1, 1961, for the coming biennium, and that the proposition be submitted to a vote of the people next fall to determine whether this tax and level of support will be continued after July 1, 1963.

As we start this mighty crusade, the first and fundamental decision should be supported by all of the people. We should give notice that every person is involved. We should demonstrate that we are united, and that we will continue our dedication until we lead the nation in school opportunities for our children.

In this way you are not "passing the buck." We are simply asking all the people to join with us.

I have faith in the vision of our people. If you will do this, I will join with you this fall in carrying our crusade to every county in this state.

In this way the people will understand what we are doing, will participate in our decisions, and we in North Carolina will be ready to move.

In reaching the decisions I have outlined today, I have been guided in my deliberations by my trust in people and my faith in the Divine Power without whose help no human endeavor can succeed. As I turn these decisions over to you, I leave with you the refrain that has in these past weeks occupied my mind. It comes from a well-known hymn:

> Grant us wisdom,
> Grant us courage,
> For the facing of this hour.

The hour is at hand when North Carolina can begin its bold march forward. We begin this march in these halls by reaching out and grasping the hands of our priceless possession, our children and our grandchildren.

The hand we grasp today is the strong handclasp to the future, the hand of a leader in the world's struggles.

I thank you for your attention to the future of North Carolina.

BIENNIAL MESSAGE

February 7, 1963

[Governor Sanford was the first governor to address the General Assembly in the new Legislative Building. Rather than read his message, he distributed copies to the legislators for their reference as he "talked" with them for thirty minutes about the comprehensive and creative programs for the new biennium. This "State of the State" message was carried on state-wide television and radio.]

Mr. President, Mr. Speaker, and Members of the General Assembly of North Carolina:

This occasion is a historic one for the reason that this is the first session to meet in the beautiful new Legislative Building. This building will long be the pride of North Carolina, a symbol recalling our sturdy history and our important future.

Further, this is an important occasion for me because I come to meet you as a group for the first time.

I look forward to our joint venture in the cause of North Carolina progress. You follow the most constructive General Assembly in the history of our state; and I am glad to see that so many of the men and women of vision and courage who set this high mark last time are back here today to begin another session.

The accomplishments of the 1961 General Assembly were marked by an optimistic awareness that North Carolina had reached the point in history when we could do many more things toward providing better chances in life for all of our people.

On their record you have the opportunity to build an even greater record of service and dedication.

You will hear some whisperings abroad saying that we have done enough, have moved well and far and rapidly, and so it is time now to slow down, rest, and catch our breath.

These whispers come from the fearful and timid who have always opposed the accomplishments from which they now would rest. This cannot be and is not the spirit of North Carolina. We are moving wisely and firmly. Much remains to be done, to provide better educational opportunities for the competition our children will surely face, to encourage broader economic development so everybody will have a better chance to make a better living. Now is the time to move forward. Now is no time to loaf along.

I do not intend to present the "Governor's Program." I intend to say to you that there is much to be done, that the opportunities are here as never before, and that I pledge to work with you to achieve the good things in life which are ours for the reaching.

You know, as well as I, that the last two years have seen many gains, much progress. The next two can see even more.

You know, as well as I, that the last decade has brought more advances than any in our history. The next decade can double these advances.

In almost all fields, in almost all sections, in almost all programs, the heartbeat of North Carolina is healthy, and is getting stronger all the time.

SCIENCE

We are not neglecting any of the other broad concerns of our people when we conclude that science will have more influence than ever before in the future of our state.

Science in its broadest meaning of interrelated disciplines is the secret of future development as it unfolds the secrets of space and man and earth.

Our responsibility cannot be fulfilled by a legislative act or a simple appropriation, or the best of intentions.

It starts with the first grade. It involves all business. It radiates from graduate schools. It finds strength in faculties, in the Research Triangle, in the attitudes of people, in industry, in agriculture, in government.

We already have the Governor's Scientific Advisory Committee, made up of leading scholars. With their guidance, adding to them groups of leaders in every field, plotting the course, we are attempting to enter the age of science with wisdom and understanding.

AGRICULTURE

In agriculture, Commissioner L. Y. Ballentine[22] continues to furnish the drive needed for consumer protection and the vision required for agricultural development.

Technology in producing, processing, and packaging products has considerably increased the variety and volume and the need for vigilance in carrying out the department's responsibilities for protecting the health and pocketbook of consumers.

There is not a man, woman, or child in North Carolina who does not derive benefit from the service and regulatory programs

---

[22] Lynton Yates Ballentine (1899-1964), dairy farmer from Varina and Raleigh, active in agrarian and civic groups such as the Agriculture Foundation of North Carolina State College, Raleigh Kiwanis Club, and the Grange; politically active as state senator, 1937-1943, Lieutenant Governor and Chairman of Board of Education, 1945-1949, State Commissioner of Agriculture from 1948 until his death in 1964. Powell, *North Carolina Lives,* 59; Governor Sanford's statement issued July 19, 1964.

of one or more of the department's sixteen divisions.

Of the new programs authorized by the last session of the General Assembly and initiated by the department during this biennium, none has been of more vital importance to every citizen of the state than the compulsory meat and poultry inspection, assuring wholesome and healthful food.

Another important new addition to the Department of Agriculture during the past biennium was state purchase of the Farmers Market at Raleigh. Purchased under a self-liquidating agreement and operated on its own revenues at no cost to the taxpayer, this facility is making a major contribution not only to North Carolina agriculture, but also to North Carolina consumers through the increased quantity and enhanced quality of fresh produce made available to them the year round.

Working in partnership with the Department of Agriculture is the School of Agriculture, which Dean H. Brooks James[23] has made even more effective in public service.

The Agricultural Opportunities Program provides a blueprint for all agencies, organizations, and groups to assist in increasing farm income; providing adequate markets and facilities, including processing; and improving family and community living through education.

A Department of Food Science and Processing has been created at State College; and the development of the food processing industry is an important part of the Conservation and Development program and is a major part of all related state agencies as we embark on a planned goal to make North Carolina the food supplier for the nation. Food processing is now one of our major projects.

The Agricultural Extension Service's "1.6 in '66" Program was developed from 100 county programs. We called on the Extension Advisory Boards in each county to work with the extension staff, and thus more than 1,500 farmers directly developed this approach to new income, and thousands more contributed to it indirectly.

Extension home economics agents, the 4-H Club program, the FFA, the community and area development activities indicate that farm life and economy are on the move.

Research in the departments of the School of Agriculture and the North Carolina Agricultural Experiment Station will reduce

---

[23] Herman Brooks James (1912-   ), educator, author; Dean of the School of Agriculture at North Carolina State University since 1960. Albert Nelson Marquis and Others (eds.), *Who's Who in America: A Dictionary of Notable Living Men and Women* (Chicago: A. N. Marquis Company, 1898–[annually]), XXXIII, 1012. hereinafter cited as *Who's Who in America*.

the cost of production and improve the product through the elimination of the many hazards of plant and animal diseases, insects, weeds, and weather.

The levels of living will be limited only by the imagination of the researchers. Much is going on to make farming more valuable to everybody in the state.

COMMERCIAL FISHERIES

Still another food resource of great importance is our commercial fishing industry. We are seeking greater use through food processing.

Our Conservation and Development Department director recently toured the coastal area to discuss the problems of commercial fishermen. Rigid and frozen conservation practices would impose hardships, and inadequate conservation measures would be disastrous for the future. We are continually striving for that program that will insure wise use of this resource; and our Commercial Fisheries Division considers itself the advocate and protector of the person who draws his living from the commercial waters.

TOURISTS

Any time we speak of our resources in North Carolina, we cannot overlook the fact that North Carolina is a natural vacation state. The variety of our attractions, from mountains to coast, are unequaled. Last year more than 25 million travelers visited our state. In 1961 some 75,450 people were employed in 18,600 travel-serving industries which had a gross income of $888 million. As our third largest dollar-producing industry, we must continue to give our increased support to this enterprise.

ROADS AND HIGHWAYS

Good roads help the tourist business, and also business, agriculture, and industry profit from roads.

The most significant road-building achievement in the past two years has been in the over-all improvement of secondary roads in North Carolina. A total of $15 million was spent in 1961, most of it after July of that year; and in 1962, $36 million was expended, representing the largest expenditure since the Scott bond issue. In 1962 over 1,100 miles of secondary roads were stabilized and 900 miles paved.

I would point out to you that these funds for secondary roads were squeezed out by a better budget arrangement and careful management. Adequate appropriations are not available to build as rapidly as we should. We will continue to do all that we can to improve as much secondary mileage as possible with existing revenues.

The primary and the interstate systems were not neglected.

North Carolina is one of the leaders in the nation in terms of the amount of interstate system open to traffic.

In 1962 a total of 2,569 miles of highway work was let to contract at a total value of over $66 million dollars, representing the largest single year's work in the highway history of North Carolina.

There are many other reasons for being proud of your Highway Commission and Highway Department under the direction of Chairman Merrill Evans[24] and Director W. F. Babcock.[25] Traffic engineering for safety is being expanded to save lives. New research has been set up to save us money and make our operations more effective. Plans are being made for advance right-of-way acquisition which will prevent blockage of future highway projects. Our Advance Planning Unit is considered one of the finest in the nation.

Finally the basic problem is money. Ten per cent of all state highway mileage in America is in the North Carolina system, and we support it on 3 per cent of the highway taxes collected. With all of the money directed toward highways and no longer supporting the prisons and other such agencies, the best possible analysis of our highway system indicates that we are still falling approximately $25 million a year behind in our construction program; and this means primary, urban, and secondary roads.

I am convinced that an improved highway system promotes the economy in such a way that it pays for itself, and that the investments we make in better roads will be returned.

You will also receive legislation dealing with roadside billboards, and these certainly need proper control.

INDUSTRIAL DEVELOPMENT

The past two years have been eventful ones for the continued economic growth of North Carolina. This growth has been highlighted especially by our industrial expansion.

Growth of our industrial labor force and gains to the payrolls of our wage earners have also been significant for 1961-1962.

---

[24] Merrill Evans (1904-   ), farm supply and life insurance dealer from Ahoskie, former county commissioner and member of the General Assembly, Chairman of State Highway Commission, 1961. *North Carolina Manual, 1963,* 464.

[25] Willard Farrington Babcock (1917-   ), engineering professor and consultant from Raleigh, author of professional publications, Director of Highways since 1959. *North Carolina Manual, 1963,* 480.

Gross gains to our working force in industry have been over 60,000 persons and wage gains have been some $200 million.

Secretary of State Thad Eure[26] has authorized more new corporations during the past two years than at any other similar period in the history of the state. During 1961 and 1962, 6,133 new domestic corporations were organized. Seven hundred ninety-six corporations from other states were domesticated to do business in North Carolina.

In 1961 our per capita income scored a 5 per cent gain over the average for 1960. Comparable figures for 1962 are not yet available, but it is believed there will be some gain over 1961. Hargrove Bowles[27] and Robert Stallings[28] have provided vivid and vigorous leadership.

The full weight of our industrial education program is now beginning to be felt in our promotion efforts. Our Department of Conservation and Development states, without reservation, that the industrial education program, and in fact the state's total new efforts toward improving education, represent one of the most effective promotional tools ever provided.

The developers over the state are anxious to learn what new and effective things this legislature will do to assist the program. They and we know that some of our closest competitors are girding themselves to do serious battle with us on every worthwhile project contemplated for the Southeast.

We must not follow in the steps of some states in the nation that make unrealistic concessions to industry. We cannot, however, because we are leading, afford to become staid and self-satisfied. We strive constantly to improve our attractiveness to reputable business. Those factors which hinder our economic growth in competition with other areas must be corrected or we will miss some of the progress which would naturally come our way.

I especially solicit your thinking and advice on how we might keep this progress moving for the benefit of all of our people.

SCHOOLS

Since the General Assembly was last here much progress has

---

[26] Thad Eure (1899-   ), lawyer from Winton, former mayor of Winton and representative from Hertford County, Secretary of State of North Carolina since 1936. *North Carolina Manual, 1963*, 448-449.

[27] Hargrove Bowles, Jr. (1919-   ), insurance executive and industrial developer from Greensboro; appointed Director of Conservation and Development by Governor Sanford in January, 1961. *North Carolina Manual, 1961*, 413.

[28] Robert L. Stallings (1912-   ), businessman, former mayor of New Bern; appointed Director of Conservation and Development, August, 1962, by Governor Sanford. *North Carolina Manual, 1963*, 462-463.

been made in our schools. State Superintendent Charles F. Carroll[29] and State Board Chairman Dallas Herring[30] are leading the way.

The most dramatic change has been the beginning of a new life in education across the state, in large counties and little ones. Teachers are working harder, stretching for new ideas, doing a better job day by day, exhibiting a high morale and a higher sense of duty and dedication.

More smart and dedicated young people than ever before are choosing teaching as a career. More new teachers, graduating from our colleges, are staying in North Carolina to teach.

More consolidation, more improvement in courses of study, fewer dropouts, more dedication from principals, greater interest by parents, are positive signs of progress. Along with the emphasis by our state, there has been great new help from the counties and districts, where ultimate responsibility lies. I am pleased to see so much local interest and work, for without this we cannot make much progress. We must urge even greater local support.

Students, the key and the purpose of all your efforts, are showing that they realize studying is important, that learning is going to mean so much in their lives. They are serious but, with the full enthusiasm of youth, are giving a new dimension to our schools. Student leadership is meaning more than ever. Your efforts and faith are being well rewarded by students who have come to full understanding that there is no place tomorrow for the uneducated brain or the untrained skill.

School administrators are seeking new ways, better methods, fresh ideas, to make the most of the human resources of the state.

When we first decided to accelerate our school efforts, I pointed out that there is no magic button, there is no easy way, that our sustained efforts for about ten years would be required to reach the top, and then full steam would be necessary to keep us there.

All over this nation, North Carolina is recognized as a foremost leader in new effort for better schools. Other states are looking, asking, following, and maybe getting ahead of us.

This is no time to get smug. When I asked the last General Assembly for new money, I said I would be just as demanding

---

[29] Charles Fisher Carroll (1900-   ), educator and civic leader from Williamston; member of Southern Regional Education Board, North Carolina Recreation Commission, and North Carolina Symphony Society; Superintendent of Public Instruction of North Carolina since 1952. *North Carolina Manual, 1963,* 452-453.

[30] William Dallas Herring (1916-   ), manufacturer; educational, religious and political leader; former mayor of Rose Hill; Chairman of North Carolina Board of Education since 1957. Powell, *North Carolina Lives,* 593-594.

of teachers and school people. I have tried to do this and will continue. There is plenty of room for improvement in teachers, school principals, school systems, superintendents, board members, and governors. We know it, and we will try to find that improvement.

There is also need for continued legislative support, and the budget requests of the State Board of Education are realistic and reasonable.

We are moving, moving in the right direction. If we keep up this rate of effort and improvement and support through this session, and the next two, the General Assembly arriving at this statehouse in February of 1969 should find that North Carolina has a school system equal to the best in the nation.

TALENTED CHILDREN

In the age when excellence is in demand, we have a rapidly expanding public school program to seek out and challenge unusual talent. Last year, 2,065 students were involved, and this year 5,206 are taking part, and next year, it will reach far more.

In addition, we have established a summer school for talented high school juniors and seniors to be held at Salem College, to give incentive and recognition to excellence throughout the state. This project, the first of its kind, has national significance. It will be supported for three years by a grant from the Carnegie Foundation and Winston-Salem individuals, companies, and foundations.

RETARDED CHILDREN

We have never given proper attention to children with limited ability. I appointed a special commission last year to outline a state program in this field. I will later ask you to make this a permanent commission, and will present to you the very thoughtful suggestions the program presented.

EDUCATIONAL TELEVISION

We expect to utilize television in education to the best possible extent. Last year I set up a special study committee and already we are actively seeking complete coverage for all parts of the state. This approach holds great promise for the improvement of quality in instruction.

EMPLOYMENT

As a state, we are concerned with employment, and the Employment Security Commission's role is almost wholly concerned with activities designed to promote fuller use of the state's manpower resources.

North Carolina's rate of insured unemployment during the biennium remained consistently below the national average.

A low average industrial wage has disturbed us until we analyze it, and we find the reasons are more good than bad. We now have 40,000 people in needlework averaging $1.32 per hour, which pulls down our total average. A few years ago, however, we did not have these jobs now held largely by displaced farm people, and it must be admitted that $1.32 is far better than unemployment. We will, however, continue to do everything possible to improve the chances our people have to earn a better living.

The total wage payments to insured workers rose between the first half of 1960 and first half of 1962 by more than 13 per cent, meaning that the 1962 payroll for these workers will be $3.8 billion as compared with 1960 earnings of less than $3.3 billion.

We paid out $82 million in insurance to unemployed, which did much to relieve the distress of those experiencing unemployment and served as a cushion to bolster the North Carolina program.

Our employment security trust fund increased by $7 million, and all indications are that North Carolina's program remains one of the most solvent in the nation.

There are certain minor amendments and adjustments to be made, including increasing the benefits in certain cases.

As a state, we have a responsibility of helping find jobs. The Chairman of the Employment Security Commission, Colonel Henry E. Kendall,[31] has taken the lead in this. We take it as our mission to reduce substantially unemployment, and we are working in that direction.

LABOR

Frank Crane,[32] Commissioner of Labor, has brought exceptional skill to his assignment.

Labor-management relations continued on their traditional even keel, with relatively few strikes and low totals of lost man-hours. North Carolina's record of industrial peace and productivity is one of the best in the nation.

---

[31] Henry E. Kendall (1905-   ), engineer, civic leader, World War II veteran from Raleigh; appointed Chairman of Employment Security Commission, July, 1946, and since reappointed by Governors Scott, Umstead, Hodges, and Sanford. *North Carolina Manual, 1963,* 463-464.

[32] Frank Crane (1907-   ), public servant from Raleigh; former safety director of the North Carolina Industrial Commission and administrative assistant of the North Carolina Employment Service; State Commissioner of Labor since 1954. *North Carolina Manual, 1963,* 455.

We have just come through a year of record growth.

The state has received national publicity and recognition for its achievement in industrial safety.

The North Carolina Minimum Wage Law is well accepted now, and it appears appropriate to increase the 75-cent minimum set by the 1959 statute to a figure more in keeping with present-day economic realities. I hope you will consider this favorably, and I hope it might be raised to $1.00.

This would substantially help the earnings of many thousands of our fellow citizens and would boost the entire economy.

WORKMEN'S COMPENSATION

Chairman J. W. Bean[33] of the Industrial Commission and his associates are administering the Workmen's Compensation Law with great efficiency and with fairness to all.

The percentage of injuries has been decreasing, but the employment in industrial plants has been increasing and thus the caseload is growing.

It is likely that the coverage and maximum amounts provided in the statutes are no longer adequate, and I would hope you would give some consideration to adjusting these provisions.

SENATE REDISTRICTING

There are some other specific things we need to do during this session.

The Constitution requires that the Senate be redistricted. It is just that simple, and we need to get on with the job.

I hope also you will consider a constitutional amendment which will make this automatic in the future, as we provided in the case of House reapportionment in the last session and elections.

INSURANCE LAWS

North Carolina is known nationally as a state of honest and fair insurance law administration, with the chief passion being the complete protection of the public. We need some tightening up here and there and we can count on Commissioner Edwin S. Lanier[34] to present sound proposals to us.

---

[33] J. W. Bean (1893-   ), educator; railroad official from Raleigh; public official in various capacities under Governors Hodges, Scott, Cherry, Broughton, and Hoey; Chairman of North Carolina Industrial Commission since 1954. *North Carolina Manual, 1963*, 465.

[34] Edwin Sidney Lanier (1901-   ), public official from Raleigh; former mayor of Chapel Hill, county commissioner, state senator, and North Carolina Personnel Director; appointed Commissioner of Insurance, 1962. *North Carolina Manual, 1963*, 456.

ELECTION LAWS

Our elections are honest but in some cases the absentee ballot provisions have been abused. Chairman William Joslin[35] has proposed sound changes for your consideration.

SCHOOL BOARDS

School boards and school committees are a key to success of our hopes in achieving a new quality in our schools. We must attempt to devise several methods of selection which will diminish partisan attitudes, and I am thinking about nonpartisan rather than bipartisan attitudes. We need to attract the best possible citizens to these jobs.

MIGRANT LABOR

The Governor's Committee on Agricultural Migrants approved and sponsored a bill in the 1961 General Assembly which authorized minimum sanitation standards in labor camps. This bill failed to pass. It was decided to prepare such minimum standards, which would be followed on a co-operative basis with the Employment Security Commission, the local health departments, and local growers. These standards were approved by the Governor's committee and released to the press December, 1961. We are doing many other things on a voluntary basis.

Many growers co-operated in 1962, and 202 permits were issued by the local health departments in contrast to 147 issued during 1961.

A number of new camps were constructed and physical improvements were made but many continued to operate without adequate sanitation protection.

We should consider legislation for minimum protection of migrant workers.

PUBLIC HEALTH

Most public health programs are necessarily of an ongoing nature to undergird continually the total health of the citizens of North Carolina, and Dr. J. W. R. Norton,[36] State Health

---

[35] William Joslin (1920-   ), attorney from Raleigh; former law clerk to United States Supreme Court Justice Hugo Black, member of General Statutes Commission, associate city attorney; Chairman of State Board of Elections since 1962. Governor Sanford's news release of July 31, 1962.

[36] John William Roy Norton (1898-   ), physician from Raleigh, State Health Director since 1948, member of North Carolina Conference of Social Service, consultant to Surgeon General's Committee on Mental Health; author of professional articles. *North Carolina Manual, 1963,* 476-479.

Officer, and many associates are to be commended for their diligence.

Our state has maintained its outstanding record in the control of communicable disease. This is especially true in poliomyelitis in which the 1959 total of 277 paralytic cases with twenty deaths was cut down to nine cases in 1961 with one death and to eleven cases in 1962 with no deaths.

Remarkable progress can be seen in the control of diphtheria and typhoid fever.

Progress in the control of whooping cough is also encouraging.

Influenza, however, is still largely uncontrolled with epidemics occurring every two to three years.

The board constantly monitors for radiation fallout and is prepared for wide-scale operation in an emergency.

Aid to counties is a pressing need at the present time in order to enable local health departments to add sufficient staff to cope with immediate public health problems.

We will have presented for our consideration legislation authorizing the State Board of Health to intensify its study of the air pollution problem in the state and to encourage adoption of measures to abate these hazards.

THE SANATORIUM SYSTEM

Tuberculosis is treated in four sanatoriums: McCain, Black Mountain, Wilson, and the Gravely Sanatorium at Chapel Hill.

The system is extremely well administered under Dr. Henry Stuart Willis, Superintendent and Medical Director,[37] and Ben H. Clark, Administrator.[38] Costs of operation compare most favorably.

Treatment has improved remarkably. The average stay in 1950 was sixteen months; now it is less than seven months.

There is a slight increase in admissions with a drug-resistant bacilli which could create serious future problems. There is also a shift in the age of the patients with the largest group now being elderly people, and this also could create some future problems. Both of these situations could cause increased costs in the next biennium which we cannot now anticipate.

To determine just where we stand, I appointed an Advisory

---

[37] Henry Stuart Willis (1891-   ), physician from Chapel Hill; Superintendent and Medical Director of North Carolina Sanatorium System since 1947; Clinical Professor of Medicine at the University of North Carolina since 1959. Powell, *North Carolina Lives*, 1318.

[38] Ben H. Clark, Administrator of North Carolina Sanatorium System from Chapel Hill; member of Governor's Committee on Tuberculosis. Governor Sanford's news release of November 10, 1961.

Committee on Tuberculosis and the members have just made a report. This indicates there is still much work to be done in public health and other areas and we are taking the recommended steps.

ATOMIC ENERGY

The use of atomic energy will have growing meaning for the people of this state, and its regulation, development, and control are supervised and co-ordinated by a group of businessmen, educators, and public employees constituting the North Carolina Atomic Energy Advisory Committee.

We have six subcommittees—Agriculture, Medicine and Public Health, Education and Research, Power, Industry and Labor, and Radiation Standards—all concerning themselves with vital problems.

A number of state institutions and agencies are involved with the problems and opportunities of atomic energy, and industrial development will be assisted by our clear understanding of the possibilities.

The committee has recommended for our consideration certain legislative action, which I believe would be of benefit to us, especially relating to regulation, licensing, and supervision.

SPACE TECHNOLOGY

Space projects have not naturally sought North Carolina because we were not located to provide a launching site and did not have the basic aircraft industry, but there will be many things we can contribute to the exploration of space secrets, and many benefits we can derive from this contribution. Right now we are working on a program which will do just this.

The development of stronger departments in engineering and the physical sciences is a major effort, and these and related fields must receive our complete support as we chart our course into a century of technology and change.

We are going to continue to drive to develop the educational contributions to the atomic and space age, drawing together the brains and resources of industry, business, education, and government to plan our place in this fantastic future.

UTILITIES

The regulation of utilities is under the chairmanship of Harry T. Westcott,[39] who is doing a conscientious and able job, along

---

[39] Harry Tracy Westcott (1906-   ), marketing specialist, North Carolina Department of Agriculture; appointed by Governor Scott as member of Utilities Commission, 1950; accepted chairmanship, 1958. *North Carolina Manual, 1963,* 470-471.

with his colleagues.

At his suggestion, I recommended that a thorough study be made to bring our utilities laws up to date and this has now been done.

I hasten to point out to you and for the record the facts we point out almost daily to industrial prospects. Statistics disclose that our electric rates, with the exception of several relatively small areas, are well below the national average; residential rates are 10 per cent lower, and commercial and industrial rates are 25 per cent to 30 per cent lower. North Carolina rates are lower than those in our neighboring states. In the past two years the generating capacity has been increased from 3,624,983 kilowatts to 4,435,833 kilowatts, and this is dramatic proof of economic growth.

The number of telephones in service in North Carolina is increasing at the rate of approximately 65,000 per year. Held orders have decreased from 37,000 in 1954 to less than 3,000 at present.

The present commission operating under the present laws has done an outstanding job, and this fact is so recognized at the national level.

Give them clearer laws and they will do an even better job.

We need a full-time legal advocate for the public.

We need a full-time expert representing the public.

There is a need to define the lines between the private companies and the co-operatives. We need to change the method of increasing rates under bond prior to any hearing.

There is need to have a workable and understandable rate-making law, protecting the public and fair to the companies.

The General Statutes Commission will present a report and recommendations to you, and in addition you will have available the study made by Mr. Edward Hipp[40] and the recommendations of our own Utilities Commission.

RURAL ELECTRIFICATION

The North Carolina Rural Electrification Authority, under the chairmanship of Gwyn B. Price,[41] has successfully promoted an expansion program which now has 98 per cent coverage in

---

[40] Edward B. Hipp, lawyer, public official from Raleigh; served as attorney to Utilities Commission since 1963. Information supplied by Utilities Commission personnel.

[41] Gwyn B. Price (1900-   ), farmer from Warrensville; member of Farmers Cooperative Council of North Carolina; Director, Farmers Cooperative Exchange; leader in State Grange; Chairman, North Carolina Rural Electrification Authority since 1941. *North Carolina Manual, 1963,* 496.

dependable electric service and dependable telephone service for 50 per cent of our rural people, reaching 212,000 consumer members.

The growing problem of duplication of service must be solved with fairness to all, especially the rate payer, and this will be one of our jobs during this session.

MENTAL HOSPITALS

The North Carolina mental care system is not only in the mainstream of America; John Umstead [42] has put it in the first flotilla, and the professional leadership of Dr. Eugene Hargrove [43] will keep us setting an example for the rest of the nation.

To a great extent our potential rests with the mental health of our people. We have risen above the old concept of custodial care. Our philosophy now, rising from the public attitude and spirit and promoted by professional knowledge, is treatment and rehabilitation.

While yearly admissions have risen extraordinarily, the average daily population of the hospital has almost leveled off. For the first time, this halts a rise in resident population which has been going on since the establishment of the hospitals. This has been accomplished, of course, only by the discharge rate keeping pace with admissions which means a much more active treatment program within our hospitals.

We are requesting support for additional research.

The guideline for the future in North Carolina is the development of an integrated, comprehensive patient-family-community oriented system of care for major and minor mental disturbances, including mental retardation.

You will also be asked to consider the establishment of a mental health department which will expand the scope of services.

North Carolina is in a position to play a leading role in a national trend toward the maximum realization of human resources through research, training, and service in the mental health field.

MUSIC

The North Carolina Symphony, under the leadership of our

---

[42] John Wesley Umstead, Jr. (1889-   ), Democratic leader from Orange County; insurance agent active in various affairs of the state: University Board of Trustees, Hospitals Board of Control, Grange, Masonic Order, legislator, 1931, 1939, 1941-1961. *North Carolina Manual, 1961,* 562-563.

[43] Eugene Alexander Hargrove (1918-   ), physician, specializing in psychiatry, from Raleigh; member of American Medical Association; Clinical Professor of Psychiatry at the University of North Carolina; author of many professional articles. *North Carolina Manual, 1963,* 492-493.

imaginative pioneer, Dr. Benjamin Swalin,[44] adds to the enrichment of the education of our children across the state, as it presently begins its eighteenth annual tour. We must assure the permanent establishment of the symphony.

DRAMA

The outdoor dramas, a North Carolina creation, give us a first ranking position and add to the appeal to tourists and the enjoyment of our citizens.

ART

The North Carolina Museum of Art continues to amaze visitors, influence industrial prospects, enrich the lives of our young people, and reflect credit on our state.

Dr. Justus Bier, Director,[45] internationally recognized, has carried on his work with great skill and imagination. The exhibition on Tilmann Riemenschneider last fall, supported by the governments of France, the Netherlands, and West Germany, was a tremendous success with our people, and widely reported in popular as well as in art periodicals. *Life* magazine, for example, devoted eight full-color pages to the North Carolina exhibition and carried one of the exhibition sculptures on the cover of its Latin American edition.

During the year the Kress Foundation turned over to the state the title to the seventy-two works of art valued at $2.5 million. The total value of our collection is about $7.5 million.

TRAFFIC SAFETY

We continue to be disturbed by the national increase in traffic accidents. One of our positive accomplishments has been the establishment of the privately-endowed North Carolina Traffic Safety Council, which is digging hard for solutions.

I have already outlined publicly a program which I think will save some lives. All of our experience in this and other states indicates drastic action is necessary if you really want to reduce injuries and fatalities. I will send you a special message relating to this problem.

---

[44] Benjamin Franklin Swalin (1901-   ), violinist, Associate Professor of Music at the University of North Carolina, 1935-1949; Director of North Carolina Symphony Orchestra since 1949. Powell, *North Carolina Lives*, 1195.

[45] Justus Bier (1899-   ), art professional from Germany; member of International Art Critics Association; Fulbright Fellow, University of Wurzburg; art editor and critic; Director, North Carolina Museum of Art since 1961. *North Carolina Manual, 1963*, 489-490.

COURT IMPROVEMENT

The people voted for the amendments to improve the administration of justice.

Appropriate research material for legislation is being prepared by a committee of representatives of the General Assembly, the Bar Association, the Judicial Council, and the public. This will be presented to your proper committees for guidance in determining what actions might be taken this year. I think the public expects us to start implementation.

In addition, the Judicial Council will make meritorious recommendations for the general improvement of the courts and court procedure.

STATE PERSONNEL

Personnel Administration has made continuing progress in the past two years, and is now under the direction of Walter E. Fuller,[46] an able civil servant. In this area, continued progress and accomplishments are of utmost importance, not only to recognize fairly the many capable and conscientious employees of the state, but also to meet the future needs for competent management and leadership. The dynamic nature of state government makes it imperative that we maintain an employment atmosphere attractive to the highest caliber of well-trained and qualified career employees; more emphasis will be needed on the development and training of our personnel.

A longevity pay plan, as provided by the Enabling Act passed by the last legislature, has been adopted by the State Personnel Council, and I have recommended that the State Personnel Council study the feasibility of increasing these payments.

Contrary to the belief of many, there are a good number of state employees who do not enjoy the commonly referred to standard work week of forty hours. Significant improvements have been made; for example, in our mental institutions some 900 employees have had their working hours reduced since July 7, 1961. On January 1, 1962, the hours of custodial employees of the Prison Department were reduced from sixty to forty-eight hours. Five years ago these employees worked seventy-two hours per week. The objective is to get and keep better guards, and you can see the quality of the work reflected in the reduction in hours.

---

[46] Walter Erwin Fuller (1912-   ), agriculturist, farm and civic leader from Louisburg; former Assistant Director, Department of Conservation and Development; State Personnel Director, 1962-1963; Director of Department of Water Resources, 1964. Governor Sanford's news release of December 10, 1963.

The 1961 Appropriation Act included a salary adjustment fund for each of the two years. During the past two years, the State Personnel Council has authorized salary range revisions for some 200 classes of positions which included approximately 8,000 employees.

Although this is not in the budget, we need a continuation of a salary adjustment fund to be provided in the 1963-1965 budget. You will receive requests for across-the-board salary increases which are not set forth in the budget. You will receive requests for higher salaries for professional personnel. I recommend that the joint appropriations committee study these three problems so that we might reach fair and equitable decisions.

COUNTY GOVERNMENT

I am pleased to report much success in the co-operation between state government and the 100 counties.

The state and the counties are partners in the financing of public schools, in the financing of community colleges, in the support of industrial education centers, in the administration and financing of public welfare and public health, in library operation, hospital construction, and agriculture extension. We work with them in the development of plans for roads and water resources and many other programs.

Last year I was privileged to attend their national meeting and observed that most other states look to North Carolina as a model of co-operation which they hope to achieve.

We have sought the advice and suggestions of county officials in all things relating to joint responsibilities, and they have been most co-operative and helpful.

We shall continue to seek their assistance, and shall continue to furnish advice available to us and to assist them in every possible way in the discharge of their responsibilities.

We cannot hope to make progress unless county officials are willing to do their share, to accept their responsibilities, and to lead out in education and other programs vital to the future of our people.

CITIES AND TOWNS

Thirty years ago only 25 per cent of our citizens lived in town. Now it is 40 per cent. In the perspective of history, it will be but an instant before a majority of North Carolinians are city residents.

As people crowd together, their problems multiply geometrically, and they need help.

There are three ways in which the state can assist: (1) with money; (2) with enabling legislation; and (3) with planning and advisory services. I propose action in all three categories.

There is a way in which the state can give financial aid and save itself money. I have instructed the Highway Department to set up a revolving fund for the advance acquisition of highway rights-of-way. Where future thoroughfares are engineered, the state can use its money to purchase and hold rights-of-way, protection of open spaces, tightening of Powell Bill procedures, and other changes which should help the towns and cities.

Finally, we can give all the cities a point of contact in state government where they can receive planning advice, economic development assistance, and find an advocate with federal agencies.

COMMUNITY PLANNING

In striving for the economic and educational growth of our people, I know that we must always be aware that rapid growth brings not only benefits but also problems.

To cope with these problems of development in a sound and orderly manner, sound planning principles must be employed. Our larger cities are meeting the problem by employing professional planning staffs. Our smaller communities, however, often lack the financial resources to do this even though the problems confronting them are not less acute than those of the larger cities.

In recognition of this problem, the General Assembly of 1957 authorized the creation of a Division of Community Planning within the structure of the Department of Conservation and Development. Since its activation, the division has concentrated its efforts in the smaller municipalities and counties having populations of less than 50,000 persons. After the first full year's operation, in late 1958, the division was serving only four municipalities. Now, some four years later, sixty-seven municipalities and eleven counties are being served, and additional communities are being added to the list as rapidly as assistance can be provided.

We can avoid the crowded cities, the slums, the breeders of crime and disorder, by making planning a part of our growth.

RECREATION

The North Carolina Recreation Commission under the leadership of Ralph J. Andrews,[47] its imaginative director, primarily

---

[47] Ralph James Andrews (1906-   ), park executive from Raleigh; leader in various professional activities, including the American Recreation Society, American Red Cross, and North Carolina Travel Council; since 1950, State Director of Recreation. *North Carolina Manual, 1963,* 485.

is in the business of furnishing advice and stimulus to public, private, and commercial recreation interests throughout the whole state.

North Carolina of the future will need vast recreational facilities. People will be living in more crowded conditions—predictions have been made that we will have one vast city ranging from the Research Triangle to Charlotte—leisure time is a certainty, and more millions will be traveling to "Variety Vacationland" for recreation.

Only a few years ago, we were giving little or no attention to the development of recreation; now it is suddenly important. We have asked the North Carolina Recreation Commission to draw together all agencies directly or indirectly concerned with recreation, and to plan now for the 1980's.

FORESTS

We are doing much with our natural resources and, of equal importance, are practicing conservation measures that will enhance their value for future generations.

Management practices and fire-control programs of our forest land make us a leader in these programs in the Southeast. The assistance being rendered to woodland owners by our State Forest Service continues to be of considerable value to local economy and our forest tree seedling program is helping to insure an abundant growth of trees for the future. Some 43 million seedlings will be sold this year, and increased interest in the program indicates even greater distribution for the coming years.

The serious loss of woodlands from forest fires has been reduced through modern fire-fighting techniques and equipment. During the past two years the average size of our forest fires has been reduced drastically and the percentage of protected acreage actually burned has been brought to a new low figure.

PARKS

We must not ignore the preservation and protection for the benefit of our people those things of our natural and native surroundings that are so much a part of the beauty and history of our state. Over the past two years state parks were visited by more than 3.25 million people, an all-time high attendance figure. As our state continues to grow economically and industrially, the demand for park facilities will increase rapidly. During the past two years two new areas have been added to bring to thirteen our total of state parks.

We also have been expanding greatly the facilities at Kerr

Reservoir under the Kerr Reservoir Development Commission.

The North Carolina National Park, Parkway and Forest Development Commission concerns itself with the development of the Great Smoky Mountains National Park, the Blue Ridge Parkway, and the North Carolina National Forests. This spring we have called a conference on outdoor recreation in the Appalachians which should be of great help in the development of western North Carolina.

The Hatteras National Seashore Park Commission is concerned with the development and promotion of the greatest seashore park in the country.

We need to plan today for adequate parks for the future.

WILDLIFE

The Wildlife Resources Commission is supported from hunting and fishing license fees and certain federal funds.

Headed by Clyde P. Patton, Executive Director,[48] we have a program of intensive fish and game management building for the present use and protecting for the future use.

WATER RESOURCES

Water resources development in North Carolina has gained momentum rapidly during the current biennium under the direction of Harry E. Brown.[49]

Steps aimed at full development of major river basins for purposes of water supply, water quality improvement, flood control, navigation, irrigation, and recreation are moving steadily ahead.

The completion of the W. Kerr Scott Reservoir on the Yadkin River will provide for future industrial development, for flood control, and many advantages including the growing demand for recreation facilities.

Similar possibilities are included in the 100-year plan for the comprehensive development of the Cape Fear Basin which is now under consideration by Congress.

Similar studies for the Neuse will be ready in 1963, and for the Upper French Broad in 1965. Surveys for the Catawba, New, and French Broad river basins are in progress. Similar studies

---

[48] Clyde Pharr Patton (1913-   ), biologist, author, civic leader from Raleigh; Director, North Carolina Wildlife Resources Commission since 1948. *North Carolina Manual, 1963*, 498.

[49] Harry Emerson Brown (1898-   ), industrial engineer and World Wars I and II veteran from Raleigh; former administrator of Department of Conservation and Development; Director of Department of Water Resources, 1961-1964. *North Carolina Manual, 1963*, 486-487; Governor Sanford's news release of December 10, 1963.

for the Yadkin, Broad, and Tar river basins have been authorized.

Waterway development is moving forward at the fastest rate in the state's history.

Studies of the coastline are in progress. Hurricane protection plans for Carolina Beach, Fort Fisher, Wrightsville, and Fort Macon are authorized by Congress. Plans for protection against storm flooding for areas of Craven and Pamlico counties are near completion.

The state is a partner with New Hanover County, the town of Wrightsville Beach, and the federal government in the Saline Water Conversion Research and Development Test Station.

North Carolina's state-wide antipollution program has made great progress; all basins studies have been completed; thirteen basins have been classified (90 per cent of the state's area), leaving only three which will be completed by the end of this session. Chairman Vivian Whitfield [50] deserves commendation.

The eroding shoreline is particularly acute. The Water Resources Department and a special committee headed by Woodrow Price[51] are making extensive studies, and will have recommendations to make to you.

There will be other modest requests, but I hope you will see the importance, the new momentum, and will work to keep us moving rapidly to conserve and develop this great and valuable natural resource.

STATE PORTS

The State Ports Authority is adding new life to the economy of North Carolina in a way that will bring benefits for many years. No longer are we required to look to the north and the south for exports and imports, having some of our profits rub off as we of necessity relied on the ports of Norfolk and Charleston.

During the last biennium, we have completed a new warehouse and equipment garage at Morehead City and have acquired the former shipyard at Wilmington under a lease-purchase option.

We have also built at Wilmington a new T-head pier for the purpose of handling bulk liquid cargos, and have seen new companies come in to use this and other port facilities.

---

[50] James Vivian Whitfield (1894-   ), farm leader from Burgaw; former member of United States Foreign Service; legislator, 1945-1953; Chairman, State Stream Sanitation Committee and member of Advisory Committee on Forestry. *North Carolina Manual, 1953*, 445; Governor Sanford's news release of February 21, 1962.

[51] Woodrow Price, managing editor of the *News and Observer* from Raleigh; Chairman of North Carolina Outer Banks Seashore Commission. Governor Sanford's news release of August 31, 1962.

Ports business has increased.

We need additional berths and warehouses if we are to stay in the competition.

Our sister states are moving rapidly. Port development is an important segment of our total economic development, as important as roads and airports. Our ports are fast approaching self-support, but we need now to make the wise investments which will keep our economy moving.

HISTORY

This is the three hundred seventy-sixth year since the birth of Virginia Dare and the three hundredth anniversary of the Carolina Charter by King Charles II, and we are going to have many things remind us of a full and proud heritage.

We should not let this tercentenary pass without building a hall of history. We are the only state between Pennsylvania and the Gulf Coast without a proper place to display and preserve our history, and our documents are in constant jeopardy in their present temporary storage.

LIBRARY

A strong State Library, supporting local libraries, is a part of a wise program of education, and indeed the extent of libraries is a measure of the civilization of a people.

One example of the work is the State Library Processing Center which orders, catalogs, processes, and delivers ready for use books selected by participating libraries in sixty-four counties. Consultant services, extension services, and the State Aid to Public Libraries Fund are examples of other assistance to local communities and the very fine services directed by Mrs. Elizabeth H. Hughey.[52]

We do not really have a library in the physical sense. We need this badly if we are to develop our facility properly, and it is believed that it should be built in conjunction with our hall of history.

PRISONS, PAROLES, PROBATION

You are the first General Assembly in at least two decades to be free from the responsibility of providing funds for a growing prison population. Your Prison Department is the only one in the nation with a decreasing population, and we expect a reduc-

---

[52] Elizabeth House Hughey (1916-   ), State Librarian from Raleigh; member of American Library Association, Adult Education Association of America, and North Carolina Family Life Council. *North Carolina Manual, 1963,* 494-495.

tion of more than 1,200 inmates from what the figure would have been if the average inmate population had continued to grow as it did from 1945 through 1961.

I am sure we are pleased when the cost of crime is reduced and the tax-dollar is saved. The savings in human resources, gainful employment, and the reduction in heartbreak and mental anguish are the most significant gains from stopping the growth of the prison population.

Close co-operation between the Prison Department and free community agencies and citizens in aiding alcoholics has helped to remove many from the list of repeated offenders.

The rapid growth and remarkable success of the Work Release Program has attracted national and international attention. This program has not only helped to reduce the prison population by its effectiveness as a rehabilitation measure, but has also shifted the cost of supporting more than 1,250 work release prisoners and their dependents from the state to the prisoners themselves.

Another especially noteworthy aspect of the Work Release Program is the fact that court, probation, prison, parole, welfare, and employment officials and personnel all have important functions in its development and operation. Credit for and pride in the success of this program is, therefore, widely shared.

We need to have the Work Release Law modified so that its proven value as a pre-parole program can be extended to prisoners serving sentences longer than five years.

We need to expand and extend the programs and measures conducted co-operatively by the Prison Department and the Hospitals Board of Control to determine what can and should be done for prisoners who are mentally ill or inebriates.

We need to make a comprehensive study of possible alternatives for treating the alcoholic offender.

We need to encourage and facilitate co-ordination of the programs of all agencies concerned with crime prevention and control, and in this regard I commend to you the recommendations of the Commission on Reorganization of State Government.

With rare exceptions it is far better to place a person on parole than to give an outright discharge from prison. Parole procedure provides some supervision and some help in readjustment and makes return to prison less likely. Of the 7,000 paroled, only 1.4 per cent committed while on parole what would be termed really serious offenses.

We need additional parole officers to do the job in the proper manner, giving personal attention which will lessen the chances of return to prison. Reformation of the prisoner is the most important work of the Board of Paroles, and it is obvious that Chairman Johnson Matthews[53] has made the policy work.

The financial side is no small matter. In the last two years alone over $6 million has been saved by placing men on parole who otherwise would have been an expense to the prison system, and over $700,000 has been saved in welfare payments to the families of these men. In addition, in the same period the men on parole have earned almost $8 million on which they paid taxes to help support the men they left in prison, to say nothing of adding to the support of schools for their children.

Probation also has been of significant value because it gives careful supervision to the person in trouble before he suffers the many bad effects of being in the prison system, associating with people who may cause additional trouble. The probation system, under the able leadership of Charles Cohoon,[54] is being used more and more by the judges; if we are to make this work, to redeem lives, to save money for the state, we need additional probation supervisors.

We can supervise a man on probation or parole for a year at the cost of keeping him in prison for one month, and records show this person will earn his own money, pay taxes, and is less likely to get into trouble again.

These agencies—Probation, Prison, Parole—will continue to move forward in the twofold task of protecting the public and rehabilitating offenders. We expect to reduce further the cost of crime by closer guidance, expanding rehabilitation programs for youthful offenders, alcoholics, and inmates needing medical and psychiatric treatment, by group counseling, pre-release preparation, academic and vocational education, and the expansion of the Work Release Program.

PUBLIC WELFARE

North Carolina is known across the nation for its progressive public welfare program, a program which has placed great emphasis on a wide variety of services that help people to help themselves.

Despite this range of services, public welfare in North Carolina has been marked by economy of administration.

---

[53] Johnson Matthews (1899-   ), lawyer, World War I veteran from Durham; state legislator, 1927; Chairman, North Carolina Board of Paroles under Governors Hodges and Sanford; helped set up state's Work Release Act; retired September, 1963. *North Carolina Manual, 1963,* 467; *News and Observer* (Raleigh), March 16, 1960, hereinafter cited as *News and Observer.*

[54] William Charles Cohoon (1917-   ), from Columbia; jobber of petroleum products; former county commissioner; legislator, 1959 and 1961; Director of State Probation Commission. *North Carolina Manual, 1963,* 482.

The 1961 General Assembly strengthened the public welfare program in a number of ways through both legislation and appropriations. These measures have all been implemented during the biennium to the end that grants are slightly higher for needy people and services are on a sounder basis.

Good as the record is, we are not doing enough in the public welfare area. We must see to it that every child deprived of the support and care of his parents has his basic needs for food, clothing, and shelter met at such a level that he can in turn take full advantage of educational opportunity and become a well-adjusted, self-supporting adult.

We will have some good recommendations coming from the special commission set up by the last General Assembly and under the chairmanship of former Senator Dallas Alford.[55]

We also need to turn our attention to the necessarily high cost of medical care for the medically indigent and also for older people no longer able to work, not medically indigent, but with limited funds, who have worked hard all of their lives, who have not been able to save much from limited earnings, and who face having all of their life's savings wiped out by extended illness. I do not believe this is socialized medicine, and I do not believe it leads toward socialized medicine, and I do not think we can continue to ignore the needs of these people in the face of increasing medical care costs. We have a special committee working on the implementation of Kerr-Mills legislation and will have this available for your consideration.

SCHOOLS FOR BLIND AND DEAF

We have the State School for the Blind and Deaf at Raleigh with Egbert N. Peeler[56] as superintendent; and in Morganton the largest school for the deaf in the nation, under the direction of Ben Hoffmeyer.[57]

We also are in the process of building an additional school for the deaf at Wilson under authorization of the last session of the General Assembly. You are being asked to implement this new school, which is much needed to provide training for children who live in the eastern half of the state.

---

[55] Dallas L. Alford, Jr., realtor, former county commissioner and state senator from Rocky Mount; member, Governor's Commission to Study Public Welfare. *North Carolina Manual, 1961*, 469; Goveror Sanford's news release of December 15, 1961.

[56] Egbert Noll Peeler, educator, school superintendent from Raleigh; Superintendent of State School for the Blind and Deaf. Powell, *North Carolina Lives*, 960.

[57] Ben Earl Hoffmeyer (1914-   ), religious and educational leader from Morganton; Superintendent of State School for the Deaf at Morganton since 1955. Powell, *North Carolina Lives*, 608.

Also, we need to remember as we improve the public schools that this specialized training is also a part of public education, and should not be overlooked. These children need too the advantages of the increased appropriations which attract and hold the best possible teachers.

COMMISSION FOR THE BLIND

The North Carolina State Commission for the Blind, with H. A. Wood[58] as its able secretary, charged with all services for the blind except the schools, has the support of volunteers to a degree unequaled in any other state in the nation.

In rehabilitation North Carolina has led the nation for the past fifteen years in the number of blind persons rehabilitated into employment.

Home industries, medical services, prevention of blindness, restoration of vision are a part of this remarkable state service.

We will ask you to strengthen these services.

VETERANS

North Carolina has always made a heavy contribution in manpower to our nation's armed forces. As evidence of this, we have a veteran population of some 436,000 persons. There are over 96,000 veterans and dependents in North Carolina now receiving some form of disability or death benefits, and it is significant to note that we have about 2,000 Tar Heels who were disabled in the so-called "peacetime" actions around the globe since Korea. These men, together with their dependents—widows, orphans, and aging parents who lost sons—comprise about 45 per cent of our population. Last year alone, federal expenditures for veterans in North Carolina exceeded $143 million.

For the most part, assistance in obtaining and continuing to receive these benefits must come from outside the federal government. These benefits are not automatic; entitlement must be proved. Such assistance is provided all over North Carolina through the work of the North Carolina Veterans Commission, headed by Collin McKinne.[59]

CIVIL DEFENSE AGENCY

Recurrent international crises and the grave dangers that face our nation in this nuclear age leave little room for doubt that

---

[58] Henry Alton Wood (1904-   ), leader in service to the blind; member of American Association for the Blind; United States delegate, World Council for Welfare of the Blind in Rome; North Carolina Executive Secretary of Commission for the Blind. *North Carolina Manual, 1963,* 490.

[59] Collin McKinne (1921-   ), industrial engineer and civic leader from Louisburg; former civil defense leader; World War II veteran; appointed Director, North Carolina Veterans Commission, 1957. *North Carolina Manual, 1963,* 486.

realistic civil defense is essential to our continued well-being and security as a free people. It is considered vital to our national diplomacy and generally accepted as part of our American defense. As such, it is vital to us as a state and as individual citizens.

North Carolina civil defense, established with a small coordinating agency operating under the Governor, directed by General Edward F. Griffin,[60] has made outstanding progress during the biennium.

Emergency services are established with responsibilities assigned to twenty-seven state agencies and organizations. Training has been conducted by many of the services at state, area, and local levels.

Every county and 275 cities and towns in North Carolina have named local civil defense directors. Eighty-three counties have emergency plans written and approved, and 159 cities and towns are covered by published plans. These plans, prepared under supervision of the state agency, meet Department of Defense criteria and enable the local agency to qualify for matching federal funds and government surplus property.

Nobody knows whether all these defense measures will ever have to be used, but as long as there is any possibility that they will be required to preserve our state and its people, the effort to establish and maintain a state of operational readiness is fully justified.

NATIONAL GUARD

The North Carolina National Guard is a volunteer organization composed of citizen-soldiers who devote part of their time to training to be ready for any state or national emergency requiring the services of disciplined and armed forces.

In the event of enemy attack. the National Guard has standing orders to mobilize immediately as a part of our civil defense plan and will serve in the state pending its call to federal duty.

The organization consists of units of the Army and Air National Guard located in 102 cities and towns across the state. The Adjutant General, Claude T. Bowers,[61] is an able and experienced veteran and administrator.

Financial support is provided jointly by the state and federal

---

[60] Edward Foster Griffin (1900-   ), lawyer from Louisburg, former state senator; Director of North Carolina Civil Defense since 1954; former president of National Association of State Civil Defense Directors; civil defense consultant to NATO Council Meeting, 1960. *North Carolina Manual, 1963,* 461-462.

[61] Claude Thomas Bowers (1899-   ), civic leader from Warrenton; distributor of petroleum products; veteran of World Wars I and II; Adjutant General of the State National Guard since 1960. *North Carolina Manual, 1963,* 458-459.

governments, with the bulk coming from national defense funds.

The field training periods conducted during 1961 and 1962 indicate that all units were in the best state of training and readiness ever achieved.

Notable in the achievements of the Army National Guard is the development and implementation of a Physical Fitness Program for all members of the Guard, developed with the assistance of the North Carolina Recreation Commission and physical education personnel of North Carolina State College. The chief of the National Guard Bureau was so impressed that he requested us to demonstrate the program to National Guard personnel of all the states. This was done at conferences held in Raleigh and Salt Lake City. As a result, the program has been adopted by the majority of the states and North Carolina has received much favorable comment and praise across the nation.

The National Guard is now in the process of reorganization under the "ROAD" concept, along with regular army divisions. This is being done in a manner which will best serve the national defense interests, which is our primary goal in the North Carolina National Guard.

We should consider legislation authorizing the establishment of a North Carolina State Guard on a cadre basis. A cadre thus established, with a few volunteers in each community where National Guard units are now located, would provide for a rapid organization of a State Guard as a replacement for the National Guard in the event of mobilization for national service.

MEDICAL CARE COMMISSION

We can all be proud of the accomplishments of the North Carolina Medical Care Commission and William F. Henderson,[62] the Executive Secretary.

During the past two years the commission has approved twenty-nine community health facility projects involving a total cost of $34 million.

Under this program, North Carolina is leading the nation in the number of medical projects constructed.

With the state loan program, we have attracted sixty new students to medical careers in the mental hospitals and in the state's rural communities.

Our programs for the future concentrate on providing adequate personnel to staff our medical programs, and we are giving

---

[62] William Freeman Henderson (1913-   ), former teacher, social service and hospital administrator from Raleigh; professional leader currently serving as Director of the Medical Care Commission. *North Carolina Manual, 1963*, 481.

attention to attracting more people to health careers.

We are giving more attention to the development of long-term care programs to lessen the strain on acute general hospital beds, and to provide less costly services for the chronically infirm.

During this session, we will need to consider budget requests to encourage local facilities for the chronically ill, to aid in building mental health clinics, and to continue the student loan programs.

JUVENILE CORRECTION

The guidance, training, and correction of juveniles who violate the law are responsibilities of the state.

North Carolina now enjoys the reputation of having one of the best correction and training programs in the nation. This is carried out by the Board of Correction and Training under the dedicated direction of Blaine M. Madison.[63]

Six schools across the state plus the new Juvenile Evaluation Center authorized by the last session of the General Assembly constitute our institutions, and their success and competence are measured by the fact that 90 per cent of the children trained never again become involved with violations of the law.

The Juvenile Evaluation Center, providing services for the children from the six schools with acute emotional and behavior problems, treats those psychologically disabled, emotionally disturbed, and physically handicapped.

This center is a significant forward movement toward our goal of providing therapy for children so they can solve their problems and return to their own communities as compatible and productive citizens.

It is not enough to rely on the correctional institution. Juvenile delinquency springs from many causes, and to the extent we can work on these causes we can reduce institutional treatment.

We have established the Governor's Committee on Juvenile Delinquency and Youth Crime, bringing together all of the various public and private agencies that can have an influence for the good of young people. This has met with enthusiastic response, and only last week this program was pointed out as a model for the other forty-nine states.

HIGHER EDUCATION

Recently I had a chance to outline the position of education

---

[63] Blaine Mark Madison, educational and welfare leader from Raleigh; author of many professional articles; appointed Commissioner of State Board of Correction and Training, 1956. *North Carolina Manual, 1963,* 491.

beyond the high school when I spoke at the Methodist College in Fayetteville. This report, position, and projection was based on the study of Irving Carlyle's[64] Commission on Education Beyond the High School, which in itself is a landmark in higher education in the state and nation.

The Board of Higher Education is doing an excellent job and we are fortunate to have Dr. William C. Archie[65] as Director. The report of the board will soon be available and distributed to each of you, so I will not attempt to review its accomplishments in this message.

North Carolina has been able to attract able men and women to lead our institutions of higher education. President William C. Friday,[66] the chancellors, the college presidents all are giving outstanding leadership.

I hope you would consider four main objectives in higher education, and if you do, I think historians will look back to your session as the year North Carolina started getting ready for the space age. Certainly, countless generations of boys and girls will have their lives and opportunities made better by your actions.

The first objective is a better definition of the university, drawing closer together the three campuses, strengthening the position of each, providing for the expansion to Charlotte and other communities as they can justify professional and graduate training, giving us one, great, strong university.

The second objective is to provide for greater co-operation with the private colleges, assuring that the influence of this great resource is not diminished. I have asked a special committee to work on this and I will keep you informed.

The third objective is to enrich the program at all of our state colleges, to prepare for the expansion which is sure to come, and to authorize four-year colleges at Wilmington, Charlotte, and Asheville.

The fourth objective is to establish under the Board of Edu-

---

[64] Irving Edward Carlyle (1896-   ), lawyer, civic and political leader from Winston-Salem; former president of North Carolina Bar Association; member, North Carolina Board of Public Welfare; World War I veteran; former state legislator. Powell, *North Carolina Lives,* 215.

[65] William Council Archie (1908-   ), college professor and administrator; author of language and literature articles; Director of North Carolina Board of Higher Education, 1961-1965. *North Carolina Manual, 1963,* 479; Governor Sanford's news release of February 22, 1961.

[66] William Clyde Friday (1920-   ), lawyer, civic leader from Chapel Hill; President of the University of North Carolina since 1956; elected Chairman of American Council on Education, 1964. Powell, *North Carolina Lives,* 463-464; Governor Sanford's statement of October 2, 1964.

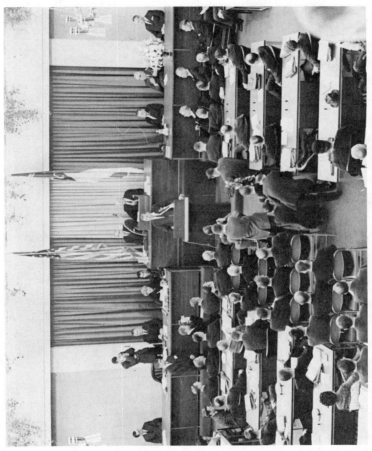

Governor Sanford addressed a joint session of the General Assembly on February 7, 1963. The session was held in the Hall of the House in the new Legislative Building.

Governor Sanford and the Council of State were photographed on September 3, 1964. With the Governor are James Allen Graham, Commissioner of Agriculture; Edwin Sidney Lanier, Commissioner of Insurance; Charles Fisher Carroll, Superintendent of Public Instruction; Edwin Maurice Gill, State Treasurer; Frank Crane, Commissioner of Labor; Thomas Wade Bruton, Attorney General; Henry Lee Bridges, State Auditor; and Thad Eure, Secretary of State.

cation, in conjunction with our industrial education centers, a system of comprehensive community colleges.

In your deliberations, you have a chance to set the philosophy which will turn our history, as your action gives to every boy and girl a finer chance to get ready for the competition of the space age.

FISCAL AFFAIRS

Edwin Gill,[67] State Treasurer, an outstanding public servant, shows why North Carolina is recognized as the state "where good government is a habit."

He reports, "Sound fiscal policy has characterized North Carolina over a period of more than sixty years. Credit, of course, for this splendid record belongs to all of the fiscal agencies of the State, as well as to the General Assembly itself. The fact that our bonds are rated AAA, the highest rating given any State bonds, reflects the fact that North Carolina has managed her debt well, preserved a balanced budget, and carried on the general affairs of State in a businesslike manner."

The State Auditor, Henry Bridges,[68] able guardian of public funds, reports sound fiscal management in state government.

CONCLUSION

I have surveyed the various activities of our state government. Each time I do this I come to see again that our government is the people's massive, orderly effort to achieve together what no one of us can so well achieve alone.

During these two years we have been guided by the concept that the purpose of government is to serve the people, to assist in progress, to lead in education and economic development, to do it economically, efficiently, honestly, and always guided by the best interests of our progressive people.

Progress has been made—enough to show us that much more progress is possible.

The progress has been made with the lowest number of public employees and the lowest per capita tax rate consistent with the hopes and expectations of our citizens—fourth from the bottom in employees, next to the bottom in per capita tax expenditures.

---

[67] Edwin Maurice Gill (1899-   ), lawyer and public official from Raleigh; veteran in state government, having held such positions as representative in the General Assembly, gubernatorial private secretary, Commissioner of Paroles, and Commissioner of Revenue; State Treasurer since 1953. *North Carolina Manual, 1963,* 450-451.

[68] Henry Lee Bridges (1907-   ), lawyer and civic leader from Raleigh; World War II veteran; deputy clerk in Guilford County Superior Court; State Auditor since 1947. *North Carolina Manual, 1963,* 449-450.

The greatest thing in North Carolina is the faith and spirit of our people. It is that faith and spirit represented in this legislature, which you exemplify as leaders of our people.

Now is the time to move forward. You and I have this joint responsibility.

BUDGET MESSAGE

FEBRUARY 8, 1963

[In a televised message on the budget, Governor Sanford incorporated fewer figures and statistics than had been included in most budget addresses and chose to concentrate on the "whys" and "wherefores." He analyzed the proposed budgets for operating expenses, expanded services, and capital improvements in the perspective of future North Carolina growth; he also suggested the possibility of tax relief.]

I am happy to have the responsibility, imposed upon me by the Executive Budget Act, to come before the General Assembly to recommend the budget for the 1963-1965 biennium.

About this same time one year ago, the first memorandum was sent out asking all state agencies to submit their budget requests for study by the staff of the Budget Division, the Advisory Budget Commission, and the Governor. This was the beginning of a process that has consumed the time and thought of many people over the twelve-month period which followed.

I would like to thank, on behalf of the state, the men of the Advisory Budget Commission. As you know, four of the six members serve in their capacity as chairmen of the House and Senate Finance and Appropriations Committees. These members are Representative Thomas H. Woodard,[69] who also served as chairman; Senator James G. Stikeleather, Jr.;[70] Senator Thomas J. White;[71] and Representative J. Shelton Wicker.[72] In addition to these members, Senator Ralph H. Scott [73] and Mr. David S. Coltrane[74] and later Mr. E. D. Gaskins[75] served in the two ap-

[69] Thomas Hadley Woodard (1901-1966), president of insurance company, bank vice-president and civic leader from Wilson; representative in the General Assembly, 1957-1963. *North Carolina Manual, 1963,* 620.
[70] James Gudger Stikeleather, Jr. (1911-   ), general insurance and real estate dealer from Asheville; served in legislature, 1955-1963. *North Carolina Manual, 1963,* 546-547.
[71] Thomas Jackson White (1903-   ), lawyer, public servant from Kinston; served in legislature, 1953-1957 as representative, and 1961-1963 as state senator. *North Carolina Manual, 1963,* 549-550.
[72] J. Shelton Wicker (1917-   ), wholesale gas and oil jobber, civic leader from Sanford; representative in the General Assembly, 1953-1963. *North Carolina Manual, 1963,* 617-618.
[73] Ralph H. Scott (1903-   ), president of Melville Dairy, civic leader from Haw River; state senator in General Assembly, 1951-1955, 1961-1963. *North Carolina Manual, 1963,* 543-544.
[74] David Stanton Coltrane (1893-   ), farmer, public official from Raleigh; former Assistant Commissioner of Agriculture and Commissioner of Agriculture; Director of North Carolina Department of Administration; Chairman of the North Carolina Good Neighbor Council. Powell, *North Carolina Lives,* 273; Capus M. Waynick, John C. Brooks, and Elsie W. Pitts (eds.), *North Carolina and the Negro* (Raleigh: North Carolina Mayors' Cooperating Committee, 1964), 257.
[75] E. D. Gaskins (1912-   ), President of American Bank and Trust Company

pointed positions. I commend these men for their devotion and their service to North Carolina.

The first major objective in constructing the budget was to determine what would be required in order to continue all necessary state services and programs at the existing level. This, as you know, we have come to call the "A" Budget. While the decisions are limited to determining exactly how much will be required to continue these services at the existing level, still much negotiation and study are necessary.

The "B" Budget provides for new programs, or for improvements or additions to existing programs. Of course, the "B" Budget is limited by the amount of money available, and I can assure you that there are many more needs than there is money to meet those needs. Public hearings were held, and the Advisory Budget Commission deliberated over a period of more than three months before the final decisions were made.

The Capital Improvements Budget is the third category of recommendations making up the total budget. These are the requests for additional dormitories, additional hospital space, and other capital construction. The Advisory Budget Commission went out across the state for three and one-half weeks, traveling more than 1,800 miles, in order to have firsthand knowledge of our various institutions.

The Capital Improvements Budget, like the "B" Budget, is limited by the resources available, and the pressures of both these areas of need had to be judged in making the final recommendations.

I am now submitting to you four documents: Volume I of the Budget, which contains the "A" Budget; Volume II, which contains the "B" Budget and certain summary statements; Volume III, which contains the Capital Improvements Budget; and Volume IV, a digest of all three of these budgets with a number of graphs and other illustrations.

At the front of Volume I you will find the Budget Report, which is a very concise and yet thorough summary of the total budget. I am not going to use the Budget Message as a mere restatement of the Budget Report. Rather than make that duplication, I am sure you would benefit more by studying that report at your convenience and at length.

---

in Monroe; former member of State Banking Commission; member of Board of Conservation and Development before becoming member of the Advisory Budget Commission in 1962. Governor Sanford's statements of July 23, 1962, and July 16, 1963.

I will use this occasion to discuss and emphasize the major decisions contained in the budget.

THE GENERAL FUND

Of the three major operating funds, the General Fund is the largest (74 per cent of tax-supported funds). It finances almost all programs other than Highway (including Motor Vehicles) and part of Agriculture.

The General Fund derives its revenue mainly from the income tax (40 per cent), sales tax (36 per cent), and certain franchise and excise taxes. There are also various agency receipts and some federal matching funds.

I am most happy to report to you that North Carolina is in an excellent financial condition. In 1961 our per capita income rose by 5 per cent, while the average percentage increase for the nation was only 2 per cent. We have had rapid growth both on the farms and in industry. Never has there been greater confidence in the economy of North Carolina.

I am happy to report we can continue to make sound progress without thinking about new taxes, and in fact I intend to recommend some tax relief.

This economic growth has produced additional revenue for the state, mainly in the personal income tax area. Other revenues have increased significantly, though not so dramatically as personal income. While our 1961 revenue estimates were optimistic, they did not attempt to foresee this unusual prosperity. As a result, additional collections of revenue are now estimated to total $77 million at the end of this biennium.

When savings from appropriated funds are added, we will have an opening balance (also called surplus) for the coming biennium of $104 million. This balance is healthy, a sign of economic progress and economy in government, but it doesn't mean we will have all the money we need. This compares with $74 million surplus which we had when the last session of the General Assembly made up the last budget. In other words, we needed a surplus of at least $74 million this time just to be even with the board.

The official General Fund revenue estimates for the coming biennium total $840.825 million. When you add the $104 million to these estimates, we will have total General Fund resources of $944.825 million with which to finance General Fund programs.

Against these resources we had first to determine the amount required for the General Fund "A" Budget. This is $814 million, to keep programs going at the existing levels of service.

The 1961 General Assembly appropriated $779 million for these same programs in the present biennium. Thus you see we expect and estimate normal growth of our existing programs to be about 4½ per cent. Normal growth means that for about every twenty-seven new students we need one more teacher and additional supplies. It means that as the population increases we must anticipate that more people will need hospital and other such services.

Therefore, to keep programs operating as they now operate we need "A" Budget expenditures from the General Fund of $814 million, a 4½ per cent increase. Subtract this from the money available and we have left $131 million.

We turn now to Capital Improvements. We found that we need to finance many construction projects. In effect, we were faced with the needs of four years. The Advisory Budget Commission decided that critical needs for improvement projects will require $117 million and that certainly we should do no less than this.

In facing these critical needs we followed a very sound and conservative approach in the financing of this program by recommending $47 million in direct appropriations to capital construction.

This means that we shall not have to ask the people for additional bonded indebtedness in the next two years.

The other funds needed for this construction program can be secured from self-liquidating funds, other receipts, and a legislative bond issue. Such a legislative bond issue would be only two-thirds of the amount by which the state debt was reduced this biennium.

In considering the "B" Budget requests, major decisions were made in several areas. I will discuss, first of all, education.

The last General Assembly moved our public school program forward swiftly, and our state led the country in the rate of improvement. That took real political courage because they backed up their beliefs with the necessary money. The advance was a major one. The school tax has turned out to be one of the best investments we have ever made for our boys and girls. It cannot be repealed unless we want to repeal school improvements. We don't.

I firmly believe, and there are thousands across this state who believe with me, that the surest way in which we can give our people a better life is to prepare our children to compete effectively in the age in which they live. We will make every effort to give our adults a better opportunity through better training and more job opportunities, but the fact remains that our soundest investment is in our boys and girls. They still have the time to learn; their lives are not yet shaped to the patterns which restrict so many of us who are older. In them lies the hope of North Carolina.

We are recommending, therefore, that this state invest during the coming year an additional $51 million in our children. This program will provide a teacher allotment formula which will provide the student more attention in the classroom; five days sick leave for teachers, the first and only sick leave teachers have had; aid for purchase of high school textbooks, $4.00 per pupil; salary increases for teachers of 3 per cent in the first year, and 2 per cent in the second year of the biennium, which is not much, but priorities were given to other things by education leaders, including teachers themselves; additional equipment for our industrial education centers; other improvements in our school bus program, clerical help, and other functions.

In higher education we have many needs. One of the most pressing is the strengthening of our faculties to a point at which they can effectively match other institutions of similar status and character throughout the United States. We recommend that this can be done at a cost of $7 million.

As was pointed out by the Governor's Commission on Education Beyond the High School, we need to convert three of our community colleges into four-year institutions. To convert institutions at Charlotte, Wilmington, and Asheville will cost $2 million.

Also, as the commission's report said, we need a system of two-year comprehensive community colleges to offer both college and technical-vocational training. These community colleges are to be developed as part of a large program, and should have local support and interest. To begin the development of this important system, the Board of Education needs $1 million.

We turn now to the area of correction. A significant change is being recommended by sizable increases in probation and paroles programs, and a corresponding leveling off of prison expenditures. Substantial savings to the state should be realized in that it costs approximately twelve times as much to keep a man in prison as it does to supervise him on probation. There are also the indirect savings to the Welfare Department by keeping the man on the job as a wage earner.

Further, the educational and rehabilitation services of the Prison Department have recommended increases. With these improved services, and the improvements recommended in the paroles and probations programs, we hope to continue North Carolina's enviable record of a decreasing prison population while the nation's prison population as a whole is increasing.

For mental institutions, we are recommending appropriations of $52 million, an increase of $9 million. This provides for the increase in the number of mentally retarded children coming under the care of our institutions under the "A" Budget concept, and for a significant improvement in the "B" Budget in the level of medical care and treatment service in all of our mental institutions.

Following approval by the voters for the constitutional amendment authorizing salary increases for the members of the Council of State, we have recommended that the salaries of these elected officials be set at $18,000. These loyal public servants have long been neglected, and I am happy to endorse wholeheartedly remuneration for their services which will be in keeping with the responsibilities they bear.

The "A" Budget also provides $9 million for our long-established automatic and merit increment programs for state employees.

AGRICULTURE FUND

We are recommending an increase of about $3 million for continued growth and for a number of programs essential to help improve our farm economy. I will mention four: first, our meat and poultry inspection program; second, the Cooperative Agriculture Extension Service; third, the food and drug control program; and fourth, the programs of marketing fruit and vegetables.

HIGHWAY FUND

The third major fund is the Highway Fund.

While it is still very strong, this fund has not experienced the exceptional growth of our General Fund revenue.

Highway Fund revenues are derived almost entirely from the gasoline tax and motor vehicles license fees, supplemented by federal aid construction funds.

Since much the greater part of the Highway Fund budget is dedicated to highway construction and maintenance, this fund cannot be considered in the same way as the General Fund. As soon as a project is begun, the funds for completing that project are encumbered, and there are balances, of both state and federal money, which are carried forward each year for completion of these projects. These factors prohibit a one-sentence analysis.

Let me generalize, however, by saying that there are sufficient revenues in the Highway Fund to continue both the Highway and the Motor Vehicles departments at generally the same level at which they now operate.

This is no mean accomplishment, in view of the fact that during this biennium we have had the largest secondary road building program since the Scott farm-to-market roads.

Sufficient money is recommended to match all federal aid construction funds apportioned for North Carolina. As you know, our interstate and primary highway system is being developed as rapidly as possible, and this program will be continued.

It would be misleading, however, for me to indicate that we are building all the roads we should. There simply isn't enough money and we have limited our recommendations to money which is now available in existing funds.

The major change in this area is the recommendation to eliminate Highway Fund diversions in the form of gasoline inspection fees not related to the administration of that program, and the cost of prison labor not actually used by the Highway Department. By ending these diversions, $12 million is made available for secondary road construction, or an increase of 29 per cent over that which would have otherwise been available.

Also of special significance is the addition of twenty-five highway patrolmen for the strengthening of our traffic safety program. We may need more. This support, added to our increased attention to traffic safety engineering in highway construction and improvements, should help save lives and property of our people on the highways.

This, then, is our recommended budget for 1963-1965. It is a substantial budget, in that it totals $1.8 billion when federal and all other funds are added. However, it should be viewed in a proper perspective.

It must be remembered that in North Carolina there are no county roads, no county prisons, and that basic school support is provided by the state. This state-wide philosophy has made it possible for us to get more from our tax dollar than any other state in the union. We move forward with our 7-cent gasoline tax while other states demand the same 7 cents, or even 8 cents, in state taxes, and then depend on the counties to provide substantial road building and maintenance with revenues from local property taxes.

We must remember that when we compare North Carolina to all the other states, with all of these factors in mind, we rank forty-ninth in the nation in the amount which is spent per person for governmental services.

When we compare the number of government employees in the same light, we rank forty-sixth in the nation.

When we compare the amount of debt each citizen must bear because of these same services, North Carolina ranks forty-sixth.

Even with these comparisons in mind, however, we know that our state has moved to the forefront in many areas. Today, as in years past, we are sensitive to the needs of our people in schools, roads, hospitals, industry, agriculture, and all the facets of this modern world. Yet these services, at a very high standard, are within our means.

The growing needs of a growing people demand a forward-looking budget, a budget that matches the spirit of aggressive progress of North Carolina.

Progress with fiscal integrity is the tradition of North Carolina, and this tradition has been our guiding light in preparing and presenting the budget for 1963-1965.

SPECIAL MESSAGE ON TRAFFIC SAFETY

April 2, 1963

[Because traffic safety was the subject of much talk and little action, Governor Sanford made a third personal appearance before the 1963 General Assembly to urge strong legislation in the field. The delivery of this message dramatized the need and the legislators backed the Governor by enacting many of the provisions he recommended. Despite the new legislation, traffic accidents and deaths continued to increase, resulting in what Sanford called his "greatest disappointment as Governor."]

Mr. President, Mr. Speaker, Members of the North Carolina General Assembly:

I thank you for the advantage of appearing before you, rather than dispatching a written message, because this subject requires all the prominence we can gain for it. You and I need the attention and concern of the public, because in the normal course of things you are not going to win any popularity contests working with the problems of highway safety.

The ones who are pinched by traffic laws often complain, and often bitterly, and the ones whose lives are saved never know it.

Project Impact, an experiment in six counties, saved at least nineteen lives. Those nineteen people should be up here lobbying for an extension of that experiment to all of the state, but they are not, for it is obvious that they cannot be identified because no one knows where misfortune might have struck had it not been for this official safety action.

But they are alive, and many others avoided painful or disabling injuries, and many hundreds of others can be saved in the future if the public will understand and support our efforts.

The problem is that in 1962, in just one calendar year, 1,320 people lost their lives, 37,000 persons were injured, and $200 million were lost on the highways of North Carolina, just one of fifty states. Think of that: 1,320 dead; 37,000 injured; $200 million lost. Just one year, just one state.

Automobile wrecks are the sixth leading cause of death in the United States.

Automobile wrecks are the number-one cause of death among young people from five to twenty-five.

This is an epidemic. You are the doctors.

Your immediate reaction to this staggering description of destruction might be one of hopelessness. We are tempted to wring our hands in despair, or to reach out for one simple, single cure-all.

We cannot afford to do either. We know from our own North Carolina experiences that we can whittle away at the destruction by the systematic action exerted by public officials.

In 1935 we had 1,095 people killed, and in 1962 we had jumped up 225 beyond this figure. This is much better than it seems. In 1935 we had only a half million vehicles traveling only 4 billion miles. The death rate was twenty-six for every 100 million miles of travel. In 1962, with 2 million cars, the rate of death was 6.2 per 100 million miles. So you can see that we have been making progress, for if the 1935 rate had not been reduced, we would have lost more than 5,000 North Carolinians in 1962.

Last year, for the first time since 1941, the number of Americans killed in automobile accidents climbed back up to more than 41,000. This shows that for a period of twenty years we were successful in holding the line. But 1962 showed us that we are unable to hold the line any longer with the present resources.

Many areas in the country have been able to achieve dramatic reductions in traffic accidents through the use of what is known as "the managed approach." This is the approach which has been re-emphasized in North Carolina in the last several months. First, to define a total program and to mobilize public participation, we organized the North Carolina Traffic Safety Council, consisting of leading citizens, employing a professional staff, paid for from private nontax funds. Then we called together all state officials with traffic saftey responsibilities, and constituted them the Governor's Coordinating Committee for Traffic Safety (representatives of the General Assembly, Health, Education, Justice, Motor Vehicles, Insurance, Highways, Institute of Government, and Safety Council).

I want to assure you that no one feels that the traffic accident problem will be solved by the simple passing of laws. This is a job for everybody, and the most important responsibility falls to the understanding citizen who is willing to support the necessary official action. These two organizations concern themselves with a number of avenues through which official and unofficial action must be exerted, including accident records, laws and ordinances, engineering, education, police traffic supervision, motor vehicle administration, traffic courts, public information, and organized citizen support. We are working on all of these. Today we look to our legislative part in the total effort. I am suggesting nine points for your consideration. The Coordinating Committee, using studies of accident records as a foundation, has agreed on two things: (1) the most important causes of accidents and (2) the means to control or eliminate these causes.

Therefore, the suggestions I am about to make are neither the result of one man's investigation nor are they any so-called pet projects of individual state agencies. Rather they are the result of agreement by public officials in every place of accident preventive work, and are related directly to the accidents now occurring on highways in our own state of North Carolina.

COORDINATING COMMITTEE

We need to provide for the continuing co-ordination of official traffic safety effort, and North Carolina's official agencies with traffic safety responsibilities should be bound together by statutory authority. This has worked well, but the united effort should not be dependent on the mere invitation of the Chief Executive, but should be given the status of being a creation of the General Assembly. This would require no money. The role of such a Coordinating Committee on Traffic Safety, similar to the one already existing by invitation of the Governor, would be to examine continually the accident problems of North Carolina, to determine the needs of the represented agencies in dealing with these problems, to determine the priorities to be given these needs, and to provide for continuing co-ordination of the state's accident preventive efforts. In this way we would have a single group charged with the leadership in reducing highway wrecks. This committee should include in its membership representatives of the General Assembly, perhaps the chairman of each committee on highway safety, thus obtaining spokesmen for the legislative bodies.

COURTS

Implementation of the court improvement amendments will contribute much to traffic accident prevention, and I hope you will do all that you can to assure the orderly adoption of a uniform court system in the state. I realize that we cannot move too hastily in arranging these complex provisions which must be designed to serve for perhaps a hundred years, but I do hope you will at least adopt the recommendations of the North Carolina Bar Association.

INTERSTATE COMPACTS

In accordance with legislation recommended by your Commission on Interstate Cooperation, I urge the adoption of interstate compacts dealing with drivers licenses and motor vehicle safety equipment. These two compacts will help protect our citizens from unsafe drivers who accumulate records of accidents and violations in a number of states and will help assure the prompt adoption of uniform standards for new motor vehicle safety equipment.

THE POINT SYSTEM

The point system has worked well, but there are certain loopholes which should be closed. The systems should reflect the factual realities of a driver's conduct as decided by a court, and not courtroom technicalities which allow evasion of the point system.

ADDITIONAL PATROLMEN

We know additional patrolmen will reduce accidents. Elimination of paper work with insurance reports, if you see fit to enact this, will free many, but we probably could make out a case for needing several hundred more patrolmen. We cannot afford this many, but we should add as many as possible during the next biennium.

SEAT BELTS

Experts call the seat belt the most important safety device that can be added to a motor vehicle. One thing we know positively is that seat belts save lives, and that their use reduces greatly the chance of getting killed if you are involved in an accident. We are not suggesting that we require them on all cars but we do recommend them for all cars. We are asking simply that they be required on new cars in the future, just as safety glass is required. I hope you will pass the bill now pending.

BEGINNING DRIVERS

I don't believe in blaming teen-agers for all of our problems. There is too much of that. Neither do I believe in putting them in any dangerous situation without adequate training and advice, and that is exactly what we have been doing.

Our accident records show that drivers under the age of twenty have more than twice their share of accidents occurring in the driving population. This is pretty good evidence we have been placing them in a dangerous and deadly situation without proper care.

I believe most parents and most young people believe we can attack this problem without penalizing young people.

Perhaps our best approach would be to require driver education in the school system or in the Motor Vehicles Department driver-training program, for all new drivers under the age of eighteen. We could waive or relax their requirement in the few places where such training is not available. We would be saving young lives if we also added a requirement for the issuance of a provisional license for all drivers under the age of twenty. We should also make training available before the sixteenth birthday.

We are not meeting our duty as parents unless we do provide some safeguards, and ultimately our best hope for a lasting solution of the traffic-accident problem is driver education.

TESTS FOR ALCOHOL

This always runs into opposition, but how can we turn away from the clear proof that one-third of all of North Carolina's fatal accidents involve a drinking driver? The nondrinking driver is entitled to what protection we can give him, and we are not giving him very much.

We need a chemical test law requiring persons accused of driving under the influence to take a scientific test to determine how much they have been drinking. We should make it simple—perhaps the breath test. I believe this would be a strong deterrent.

First, we could take one of two approaches. We could require this as additional proof under the existing laws and drivers' license penalties.

As an alternative, we could make it simply against the law to be a drinking driver by specifying that driving with a specified percentage content of alcohol is against the law, coupled with a provision that the commissioner could revoke the license for not more than one year in place of the present mandatory revocation for one full year as the penalty for driving under the influence of alcohol. This latter course would be preferable because it would eliminate the doubtful situation of attempting to define "under the influence" and would give the commissioner discretion in individual cases.

CHECK OF SAFETY EQUIPMENT

I am opposed to the mechanical inspection we found so burdensome, but I am far more opposed to neglecting to check the safety equipment which we require on automobiles for the purpose of saving lives. I think a periodic check of the five or six items on a motor vehicle relating to our safety—brakes, horn, tires, steering, lights, windshield wipers—at any garage or service station which cares to qualify for approval, would reduce substantially our deaths. Not only would a safety-check program require safe equipment, but it would create an increased awareness of safety on the part of every individual driver. Records in other states, as well as our own records, demonstrate a safety check would reduce materially highway accidents.

Those are the items. I leave the details to you. These are simple things, and yet they are substantial things. These do not increase the encroachment upon individual liberties. Rather they enhance individual liberty, and improve the chance we all seek to lead a healthy and productive life.

We look to you for the leadership which will call to a halt the increasing epidemic of traffic deaths and injuries.

MESSAGE TO GENERAL ASSEMBLY
AT ITS CULLOWHEE SESSION

May 14, 1963

[The General Assembly made several junkets throughout the state during the Sanford administration. Proponents of these trips maintained that the legislators were able to see and hear firsthand various local problems; opponents insisted that the trips were so tightly scheduled that such a purpose could not be fully realized. After an overnight railroad trip from Raleigh, the legislators went to Western Carolina College where they, about 2,000 college students, and citizens of the area heard the Governor urge co-operation between the sections of North Carolina rather than a continuation of a feeling of sectionalism.]

Mr. President, Mr. Speaker, members of the General Assembly, citizens of western North Carolina, and students from all across North Carolina and, indeed, the nation:

This is a day when Americans were scheduled to reach upward toward the stars and I think it was very appropriate that our legislative branch and officials of North Carolina should today come up to this "Land of the Sky."

There was, as a great many of you will remember, a time when it took all day and most of the night to get from Raleigh here. In those days you had to point your T-Model somewhere in the general direction of the West and go through South Carolina and Georgia in order to get to Cullowhee.

There was a time, and I put emphasis on there *was* a time, when this area was closer to the capitals of South Carolina, Georgia, and Tennessee than to Raleigh. But today you can fly from here to Raleigh in an hour, or you can drive it in six hours and not violate the safety program. Or, as our legislators can tell you, you can take a nice leisurely overnight train trip, doing your work and getting a good night's rest on the way up here.

And thanks to the rapid advances in communications, you can, in a matter of seconds, communicate from here to Raleigh—as the people in the Budget Bureau and the Highway Building know.

Today as you know, Cooper [Astronaut Gordon Cooper] and the officials of NASA are still reaching for the stars. And the General Assembly too is still reaching for the accomplishments which will help develop North Carolina's great potential. As we reach, I think it is well to remind ourselves that the problems and the opportunities which face one part of North Carolina are the problems and the opportunities of all of North Carolina.

I hold a strong conviction that the problems and the opportunities which face the tourist industry in these western counties should be the concern of eastern and Piedmont counties.

The harvests and the failures of the cabbage and corn crops are of considerable importance to you here, of course, and also to the textile workers of Kannapolis and Concord, Greensboro and Burlington.

The number of tourists who drive the Blue Ridge Parkway, across the roof of North Carolina, has a strong correlation to the number who drive down the new History Highway on the Atlantic coast.

The food processing plants up here have given farmers and businessmen of eastern North Carolina some good pointers.

On the other side of the coin, you who live and work in this area are adversely affected when the waves of the ocean erode the Outer Banks. It takes a little longer for you to feel those waves, and that loss, but you will feel them.

When the looms are stopped in the Piedmont because of improper foreign competition, when cancer scares threaten the tobacco plants of the farms of Pitt and Lenoir and the factories of Forsyth and Durham and Rockingham, the economy of these western counties suffers. And, indeed, as we look now to your problems and your opportunities, I am convinced absolutely that the problems of the Appalachian are the problems of the state of North Carolina and we take them seriously.

In short, the town of Jackson down east and the county of Jackson up here rise or fall together; Nags Head and Nantahala are in the tourist business together; the distance between Manteo and Murphy is an ever narrowing one.

I would say to the citizens of this section that your representatives and your senators are well aware of this unity of purpose and unity of opportunity. I could call their names one by one, and say that they understand and that they are representing all of North Carolina and that their work and their contributions indicate that they understand that all of North Carolina will stand or fall as we stand together.

There is no longer any place for sectionalism. There is no longer one part playing the state off against the other. Indeed, if we are going to reach our opportunities as we can, we need to do it working together.

These members of the General Assembly—I say to you who live here and to you students—are people who are dedicated and who are working diligently every day and almost every night to develop North Carolina's future, to give everybody a better opportunity to earn a better living and to have a better life, to give young people a chance to have the kind of education which will enable them to compete with young people from any part of the nation and any part of the world. These are the people who have laid those plans, these are the people who are fulfilling those programs.

These are the men who are accelerating the drive for new and diversified industry to improve the economy of our state.

These are the men who are considering ways to improve and enhance the third largest income-producing industry in our state: the tourist industry.

These are the men who made possible more secondary road funds during the last two years than in any two years since Governor Scott's road bond program. In the counties that compose the group we usually consider western North Carolina, you may be interested in knowing that more than $8 million was spent in the last two years on secondary roads alone. Translated into mileage, that means 245 miles of paving and 535 miles of improvement, and we are just beginning to demonstrate by stopping diversion, and by more careful economy that we can continue to speed up road-building progress. We are going to do all we can to help you through road construction to open up this country and improve the economy.

Most important, these are the people helping in education, the ultimate denominator of all of North Carolina. These are the men who lifted high in 1961, and who are lifting still higher in 1963, the educational opportunities of all the boys and all the girls in all the counties of North Carolina.

It is right that today's joint session of the General Assembly should be held on a college campus. It is just about ninety-six hours since the lawmakers of North Carolina endowed every student in North Carolina.

The members of the 1963 General Assembly made that permanent endowment through adoption of the broadest based and the most far-reaching legislative act in all of the United States.

Benefits of this measure, which was adopted with overwhelming approval on Friday, will be appreciated by many generations of North Carolinians, and I believe the historians of this state will place the accomplishments of this General Assembly along with the provision of the Revolutionary Constitution of North Carolina providing for the University of North Carolina and later the establishment of colleges like Western Carolina and Appalachian.

This act is but part of North Carolina's twentieth century

commitment to give its children the best possible opportunity to get ready for the competition of life.

Other measures reaffirming that commitment are now under careful consideration by the members of the General Assembly.

The representatives and senators are now considering a substantial increase in the public schools and our continuing drive to make our schools second to none.

For the first time in the history of our state, the entire budget requested by the State Board of Education, which carefully screened all of the needs, has been approved by the administration and the Advisory Budget Commission. The chairman of the Board of Education was able to come to the Committee on Appropriations and say: "We have nothing new to request because for the first time in all of the history of this state, education has been put absolutely in the first place."

There are increased funds in the budget for Western Carolina and for the other senior colleges.

And we know of the influence of this college, Appalachian, and Asheville-Biltmore on western North Carolina; and we look to these institutions to provide the leadership to continue the progress to make North Carolina what it must be.

There is continued support in the budget for industrial education centers, which are meaning so much to so many, many students who for various reasons are not going on to college. You also will find appropriations to establish a strong basis for industrial education at the high school level. This is something about which we have concerned ourselves. Perhaps in paying attention to many other problems in the past we have not given adequate attention. I am satisfied that this General Assembly will write a new record and a new start for broader industrial and vocational opportunities for high school students.

There are funds for the mentally gifted children challenging them to do their utmost to make all the contributions that they can make to this state, because of their unusual abilities. And, incidentally, this program got its start right here on the campus of Western Carolina College.

There are steps under way to broaden the chances in life for the mentally retarded children. This legislature is going to show that we have come to the place where we are going to remember these long forgotten children.

These are but a few items of North Carolina's number-one purpose of education.

There are many other challenges and many other opportunities and many other things which the General Assembly will do to speed the progress of our state.

There is the proposed space center.

There is the important matter of democratic redistricting.

There is the vital question of traffic safety legislation.

There is the need for improving our mental health and hospital system.

There are the questions of parks, community planning, forests, recreation, wildlife, and water resources—altogether 1,500 to 2,000 questions contained in bills introduced in this session to which attention is given every day by these distinguished legislative bodies.

This General Assembly is working for you. This General Assembly is working for all of the people of North Carolina. And I am satisfied that when the record is written, that this General Assembly will stand at the very top in contributions made to all of the people of North Carolina.

And I am very happy to have been associated with it.

Thank you very much.

ADDRESS TO THE SPECIAL SESSION
OF THE GENERAL ASSEMBLY

October 14, 1963

[The North Carolina Senate had not been redistricted since 1941 despite the constitutional requirement that such be done after every federal ten-year census. By 1963 changing regional patterns and political and judicial pressures joined to accentuate the need for redistricting legislation; the result was a General Assembly which struggled with the problem but failed to find a solution. On June 26 Governor Sanford said that a special session would be necessary and that he would appoint a special committee to study the problem and recommend legislation. In speaking to the legislators meeting in October, Governor Sanford urged the passage of the law "with dispatch," and the members of the two houses took him literally, passing the redistricting bill four days after their arrival in Raleigh.]

As you return to a special session, I have the opportunity to express to you as a group my gratitude for your help to me and for your contributions to the forward progress of North Carolina during the regular 1963 session. There has seldom been a session of the General Assembly which provided so well for education, and never a session which provided so well for higher education, with new funds for faculties, with support for new and improved programs in an age of increasing complexities, and with a blueprint for the future of our university and colleges which forever will mark an upward turning point in the history of North Carolina.

There were many other accomplishments, for those in need of mental health treatment, and especially a comprehensive program of hope for our long forgotten children, the retarded. Because of your work and devotion there is a new vitality about our state, and many generations will profit from your good works.

We did not do everything that we might have done, but it is a mighty record of solid achievement. I am proud of your record. I hope all North Carolinians will understand these accomplishments.

We did leave undone the little matter of redistricting the Senate.

Things became so harried and hurried and confused in the closing weeks, with so many important programs and policies being developed, that we just could not adequately wrap up this one responsibility.

I well understand, and I believe those who have been close to the scene well understand, that the majority has always intended to meet this responsibility. That you did is best expressed by your resolution, passed in the waning hours of the regular

session, requesting the Governor to call a special session because
the General Assembly, in your phrase, had "been unable to agree
on the provisions of an Act to redistrict the State Senate, as required by the Constitution of North Carolina."

I have complied with that request, and I have welcomed the
chance over the summer, with calmness and care, to work with
most of you in preparing for the final action we have come to
take.

The constitutional duty of the governor is to state the purpose
of this special session and to recommend the action which he
believes should be taken.

That is a very easy duty. I will report to you what you already
know, and recommend an action which I am sure you already
are prepared to take. My report and recommendation are best
wrapped up in the words of your resolution which I have already
quoted, "to redistrict the State Senate, as required by the Constitution of North Carolina."

You and I, in preparing for this session, have indeed been
guided by the constitutional mandate that "each Senate District
shall contain, as near as may be, an equal number of inhabitants."
During these several months I have met both formally and in-
formally with many of you. We have discussed, considered, adjusted, and agreed in order to get the job done.

Our plan, the consensus bill I call it because so many had a
hand in its formulation, cannot be completely pleasing to everyone. It is the result of conscientious resolve to follow the Constitution regardless of all other considerations, political, personal,
regional. Some of you doubtless cannot return because of the
new plan, but this has not caused you to shirk your duty.

The districts have not been redrawn for more than twenty
years, and this same period has seen the greatest changes in our
population. These facts have forced us to present a bill which
makes substantial changes in our senatorial district boundaries.
The result has been that almost every district has been redrawn.
In spite of this degree of adjustment required, our legislators
have co-operated in the true spirit of North Carolina, and we
are able to present a bill which has the majority support in both
houses of the General Assembly.

I do not know whether there can be a constitutional amendment which will satisfy the necessary three-fifths majority. A
number of proposals were discussed during the regular session.
In the course of working out the redistricting bill submitted today, a questionnaire was sent to each legislator. From this it
became apparent that there was much sentiment for constitu-

tional change, but wide variation as to what the change should be.

I think some constitutional amendment is justified. We could use some guidelines for setting up districts better than the present terse, "as near as may be" equal in population. Also, I think it would be to our benefit to have some provision for "automatic" redistricting in the future. This could mean a commission authorized to draw the lines, to present it to the General Assembly, to become final after ninety days, for example, if not amended by the General Assembly. Or we could provide that a commission would take over if the first session after the official census failed to redistrict. Both of these proposals would leave the duty with the legislature but would eliminate many headaches for future legislators and governors.

As to other forms, I have no recommendations at this time.

Whatever you do about amending the Constitution, we cannot let our desire to improve it prevent us from following our clear and present duty under the present Constitution.

A bill to do this, "to redistrict the State Senate, as required by the Constitution of North Carolina," has been signed by a majority in each of the houses.

I trust you will pass it into law with dispatch.

PUBLIC ADDRESSES AND
SUMMARIES OF
PUBLIC ADDRESSES

PUBLIC ADDRESSES AND SUMMARIES OF PUBLIC ADDRESSES

[During his term of office, Governor Sanford made 369 speeches, of which more or less complete copies were preserved. In addition, he made approximately 425 others from rough notes or extemporaneously. Addresses selected to be included in full in this volume were chosen because of their importance, their relevance to the over-all Sanford program, and the diversity of their subject matter. Summaries of 165 other addresses are printed in this section; the remainder are listed by date, title, and place of delivery and may be found on pages 491-521.]

A STATEMENT OF FAITH AND PURPOSE IN EDUCATION

University of North Carolina at Chapel Hill

November 21, 1960

[Prior to assuming the office of Governor, Terry Sanford outlined in clear and unmistakable terms his belief in the necessity of quality education for North Carolina. In "A Statement of Faith and Purpose in Education," Sanford called education "the foundation of economic improvement," "the foundation of democracy," "the foundation of the needs and hopes of the nation," "survival," and "life and growth and happiness." In this address he made clear his intentions of putting education first during the four-year term of his administration and of embarking on a ten-year plan for making the dream of quality education become a reality in his state. Because of its significance, the address is included here despite the fact that it was delivered before Sanford's term of office began.]

On many occasions and in many ways I have tried to emphasize during the past weeks and months my conviction that North Carolina is facing a new day. All around us I see the evidence of a brightening dawn of opportunity, unmatched in its potential by anything in our past.

A new day brings new opportunities. It also brings new responsibilities. The dawn cries to a people to awake. Now is the time to get up and go to work. North Carolina faces an exciting future, and we must be up and doing.

North Carolinians have always understood that education is the means by which our state must reach its full potential growth in both economic and human values. At the turn of the century, Walter Hines Page made the following statement of faith and it's good today:

I believe in the free public training of both the hands and the mind of every child born of woman.

I believe that by the right training of men we add to the wealth of the world. All wealth is the creation of man, and he creates it only in proportion to the trained uses of the community; and, the more men we train, the more wealth everyone may create.

I believe in the perpetual regeneration of society, in the immortality of democracy, and in growth everlasting.[76]

This brave and penetrating grasp of the importance of education in the life of the state was supported in the political arena by Page's able contemporary, Charles Brantley Aycock, who has come to be known as "educational governor." In terms of political action, he issued this clarion call that we know still today: "Equal! That is the word! On that word I plant myself and my party—the equal right of every child born on earth to burgeon out all that there is within him."

The people of North Carolina were not deaf and they did not turn away. Many other leaders arose. The people responded. North Carolina was poor, extremely poor, just struggling up out of the period of Reconstruction; but gradually schools were built, the school term was lengthened, and people in other states began to be aware that this "valley of humiliation between two mountains of conceit" was taking the lead among all the other states who started at the bottom of the ladder along with us after the period of Reconstruction collapse.

But what was good enough for yesterday will be totally inadequate tomorrow. Whatever our success, it is not enough for the rapidly advancing scientific, changing world we now enter.

We are justly proud of North Carolina's position. We came up the hard way. We have come a long route. We have no apologies, but too many of us have become somewhat self-satisfied and complacent about our reputation as "first in the South," and too many have thought the job was finished.

The job is not finished. What we have really done is to create new and unlimited opportunities.

Dr. Howard Odum[77] of the University of North Carolina showed clearly that North Carolina did not need to stay in the group of states called the "nation's economic problem number one." While we do not have everything, he pointed out, we do have in abundance those resources that really matter—soil, water, climate, rainfall, and people—most of all we have a stock of sturdy

---

[76] Walter Hines Page, *The Rebuilding of Old Commonwealths* (New York: Doubleday, Page and Company, 1905), 102, hereinafter cited as Page, *Rebuilding of Old Commonwealths*.

[77] Howard Washington Odum (1884-1954), author, teacher, sociologist; Kenan Professor of Sociology at the University of North Carolina at Chapel Hill, 1920-1954; recipient of O. Max Gardner award, 1953; contributor to improved race relations in the South. Stanley J. Kunitz, *Twentieth Century Authors: A Biographical Dictionary of Modern Literature* (New York: H. W. Wilson Company [First Supplement], 1955), 733.

and able people. We only need to develop fully this human resource.

I am not satisfied with being first in the South. I want the title "first in the country." Why shouldn't North Carolina strive to lead the nation?

To that goal I dedicate the full measure of my devotion. I believe that a fearful, hesitant approach to the future will, indeed, cause us to "lose our ventures." I believe, like Page, in universal education, in the eternal values of democracy, and in growth everlasting. I pledge myself and my party, like Aycock, to achieving for each child the opportunity "to burgeon out all that there is within him," regardless of where he lives or who his parents are.

Quality education is no mean goal! For all other goals we seek for North Carolina can be measured by the quality, the scope, the reach of our educational efforts.

Education is the foundation of economic improvement. I am concerned, vitally, and will be throughout this administration, with industrial development, farm income, the economic growth, and the chance of all to make a better living. Because I am concerned I have chosen quality education as the rock on which to build the house of my administration.

Education is the foundation of democracy. I am concerned with defending the principles of freedom, of individual liberties, of free enterprise, of equality and dignity of man, and therefore I seek the fulfillment of these principles through quality education we offer our boys and girls.

Education is the foundation of the needs and hopes of the nation. I am concerned with our part in the world, and I am concerned with the peace of the world, and therefore I propose that we adequately educate the scientists, the statesmen, and the citizenry who will fully understand and are equipped to defend and promote the ideals of our dynamic democracy of the twentieth century.

Education, put in the bleakest terms, is survival. Here in our own small part of the free world, we can do no less than seek the best as we prepare to do our part to defend America and the free world.

And education, put in its brightest terms, is life and growth, and happiness. We are not here merely to make a living. We are talking about the fundamental when we talk about education, and our goal is worthy of the best we have in mind, and heart, and spirit.

As Governor of North Carolina, I will work for a program

which provides educational opportunity, appropriate and available, second to none in quality, for all the children of our state, and I will work to obtain adequate support for that program.

The *program* is up to the State Board of Education, the Department of Public Instruction, the local school boards, the superintendents, the principals, the teachers, and the parents.

The *support* is up to the General Assembly, the county and city officials, or, in other words, put in its broadest sense, to the entire citizenry of North Carolina.

I know we have an excellent blueprint for the program, and I know we have the people who have the ability to put it into effect. I am also confident that the people of North Carolina, believing that we can build a better state through quality education, will provide the support for this program.

We cannot know for several months exactly how much money we will have available in the budget to be adopted next spring, although I do know that happily the revenue picture is extremely bright. I do know that the members of the Advisory Budget Commission are conscientious, dedicated, and share with me a faith in public education.

But I go back to my original statement, made February 23 in Greensboro, in the middle of a political campaign, when I outlined our school needs and our state's potential, and called on the women of the state to lead a "crusade for education." I said then, and on numerous occasions since then, that I value children more than money, and my position remains as I stated then:

> I believe the people are eager to pay for quality education. They know this is the only basis for improvement. They know good men and women leave the teaching profession every month because they have to support families. They know that a disproportionately high percentage of college graduates, educated to a large degree by public expense, leave this state to teach elsewhere because of our inadequate salaries. They know that ultimate salaries are extremely inadequate for career people. They know that to attract enough of the right quality teachers we cannot rely upon love of teaching, alone, but must offer salaries commensurate with their training and education.

I said then and I repeat now, *I would not be honest if I did not promise that, if revenues are inadequate, I will have the courage to recommend to the General Assembly and the people the proper sources.*

I will also recommend to the General Assembly where we can get the money. That was my campaign promise, and it is my pledge to North Carolina tonight. The plan is worth the money. We must do no less. This is the way everyone can share in building a better state through quality education.

The North Carolina plan might be called a "four-star program," and I will outline the basic elements of these four guiding stars, by pointing out that we seek for our state public education which is (1) appropriate, (2) available, (3) excellent, and (4) supported.

First, the educational opportunities must be appropriate.

1. This means we seek education which meets state and national needs, along with and as a part of the needs of the individual.

It recognizes that individual talents vary, that a total school program must fit the needs of each child, and that individuality must not be crushed in a common mold. To achieve this, we need an adequate counseling and guidance service for our students.

It recognizes that all students need a basic education in English, mathematics, the humanities, elementary sciences, the social sciences, if we are to develop fully for intelligent citizenship.

It recognizes that education in depth in these basic subjects, plus other disciplines such as foreign languages, should be provided for those students with greater academic abilities.

It recognizes that the school has some responsibility for a program of physical education and health.

It recognizes that vocational courses should be provided, in addition to the basic academic courses, for those who will seek employment or technical training after graduation. It should provide opportunities for education in the practical arts.

It recognizes that we must provide special challenges for the gifted child.

It recognizes that training must be provided for the handicapped child.

It means our human resources, whatever they are, must be developed fully up and down the line.

2. Having outlined the objectives for educational opportunities which will be appropriate, how can we go about achieving such a program? Aware that much has been done, we can do more in the following ways:

The courses of study to make and keep education appropriate, in line with the principles outlined, will be left to local school administrators and teachers with encouragement and assistance from local school boards, with advice and leadership from the State Board of Education and State Department of Public Instruction, and guidance from the Curriculum Study. The Curriculum Study is the most important single effort now being made to improve the quality of the schools, and we will urge the

General Assembly to increase financial support of the study for the next two years.

We will present a specific program to the General Assembly to achieve an advance in providing teachers and training for retarded children.

We will present a specific recommendation to the General Assembly to begin a program of special school opportunities for gifted children.

Second, while making education appropriate for individual development and for the state and national need, we must be certain that this kind of education is available to all boys and girls of North Carolina, no matter where they might live.

1. This means that we must continue to recognize that, largely because of widely diverse circumstances in county wealth, North Carolina, unlike many states, has assumed primary financial responsibility for the operation of its schools.

I reaffirm that we will not shift this primary responsibility back to the counties, and we will not sit idly by awaiting federal assumption of this responsibility.

2. The state (Board of Education, Department of Public Instruction, General Assembly, Governor) should encourage consolidation wherever and however possible. Better transportation and Kerr Scott's roads have expanded the reach of every school building and have altered our thinking of the proper size of a school community. I accept Dr. James Bryant Conant's standard that a high school with a graduating class of less than 100 is too small to be either appropriate in scope or adequate in quality. Community pride is an admirable trait, but it should not get in the way of quality education for the children of the community. We are moving in the right direction across North Carolina, and local school boards should give careful attention to consolidation, where possible, to achieve quality and an adequate range of courses of instruction.

3. This means we must make educational opportunity available for those students who are so handicapped mentally or physically that they cannot profitably attend a regular school. Much is now being done in institutional care and in special day classes, and continued expansion of this training will be made so that the "forgotten children" will be reached with special training.

4. Transportation of students must be safe and adequate. Local school boards need pay special attention to the situation where school buses serve separate elementary and high schools, necessitating long delays in the return home of the smaller chil-

dren. Part of the answer to this is adequate consolidation, and part of the answer may be in state aid for the financially-strapped counties.

5. Availability includes the question of adequate school buildings. I believe that this should remain essentially a county responsibility, that we should be certain that we get the most for our building dollar (the buildings should be standardized to a reasonable degree and a limit should be placed on the amount which can be spent per square foot), and that the state will have to provide some matching funds for the next immediate period which will see an unusual influx of students. So I will propose to the General Assembly a state school bond issue for this purpose.

6. If appropriate education is to be available to a degree that our full potential of human resource is developed, then we need to expand community colleges and industrial education centers, and I shall have more to say about these items at a later date. We must also be concerned with the quality of higher education, and I shall discuss this in detail at a later date. I want it understood clearly that I am in no way discounting the responsibility for doing more—and doing more now—for higher education.

Third, the educational opportunities must be *excellent,* must be of the highest quality, must be second to none.

To achieve quality, to achieve excellence, will require the best efforts of all who are concerned with public education.

There is no easy road; there is no clearly-marked road; there is no sure road; but I do have some landmarks which will lead us onward.

1. We need to attract able people to the teaching profession and keep them there once they have become good teachers. We need to make salaries for teachers competitive. Over the next ten years we must increase salaries until we can draw and keep an adequate number of quality teachers. I will recommend to the General Assembly in 1961 substantial salary increases, but this is only the first step. We will need to go on and on until we are not losing teachers, or failing to attract young people to the teaching profession, because of inadequate salaries. It is that simple. If we are going to get and keep an adequate number of the kind of teachers we must have, we must compete for them in salary scales. We can do no less. This is fundamental.

2. Excellent teachers must have excellent education for their profession. This education and the institutions in which it is provided must be strengthened. Scholarships for prospective

teachers have been proved worthwhile. The number must be increased and extended to teachers and administrators in service.

3. The professional help the teacher needs must be provided. This applies to supervision, special teachers, and to in-service education opportunities. I will recommend to the General Assembly an appropriation to start a program of in-service training. This is the best way to improve the quality of classroom teaching.

4. The classroom teaching-learning situation must be improved. This is essential if excellence is to be achieved. The teacher must be given time to teach. This means that interruptions and nonteaching duties must be reduced to a minimum. The pupil must be given time to learn. This means that conflicting demands on student time and effort must be eliminated.

Class size must be adjusted. In the primary grades, no teacher should have more than twenty-five students. In the upper grades, some classes might include a larger number of students, but all students should also meet sometime during the day in very small groups. Some individual attention is essential. A minimum of fifty professional people for each 1,000 students should be our goal. I will recommend to the General Assembly a first step in this direction.

The special services and teaching tools such as textbooks, laboratories, shops, television, and electronic aids must be adequate. Libraries, the center of the school's instructional program, have been neglected in too many schools, and this requires our immediate action. I will make recommendations for additional appropriations to the General Assembly concerning these needs.

Supporting services by noninstructional personnel are part of the total school effort, and these employees are entitled to fair treatment and proper consideration and are not going to be neglected.

5. The student must be given the help he needs to choose and to follow successfully the right courses. Our goal is that all of the necessary guidance services needed must be provided. I will recommend to the General Assembly that we strengthen guidance services for students.

6. Educational opportunity that is excellent must have excellent leadership. This is true on the state level and on the local level. Salaries and standards of State Department professional positions must be established comparable to those of college professors. Salaries and standards of local educational leadership positions must be made competitive with leadership positions in other professions.

7. Constant study of school performance is some assurance of achieving quality and excellence. We need continuing study and research into methods, courses, techniques, and teacher education, if we are to achieve constant improvement. Every business knows the value of research. Witness the Research Triangle. The State Board of Education has already started this job of research and study in education, and I will recommend making it a permanent part of the public school structure. In other words, we will keep on asking ourselves, "How good a job are we doing? How can we improve what we are doing?"

Fourth, and the last guiding star, we need to *support* our schools, and this means everybody must support them. We need to support them with money, understanding, encouragement, with determination that we are entitled to the best, and that we have the capacity and the resources to obtain the best.

This is not so nebulous. Let me point out a few of many ways we can give such far-ranging support.

1. The taxpayers have been getting their money's worth in North Carolina. The trouble is that we haven't been buying enough. I am certain that North Carolina gets more for its school dollar than, for example, New York or California, where much more per student is spent. But we are not doing the job because we are not spending enough. While it is almost meaningless to compare figures with national averages, this nevertheless furnishes some guide to our thinking. The national average spent on a student is $369. It is the average of wealthy states and poor states; it is not the top amount. North Carolina, state and local, spends $230. That doesn't look right, and it isn't. We can't spend what we ought to next year, no matter how much we might try, but we can start out now on a determined goal to increase this amount from year to year. If we had unlimited funds, we would not want to spend them next year. The job cannot be done in a year or two, but we can, during the next ten years, increase our appropriations year after year until we reach, not necessarily the national average, but the point where we are achieving the excellence we seek.

2. We must make the teaching profession a truly attractive one. "Attractive" is probably a poor word because it may suggest relaxed ease and comfortable security and no more. But I mean "attractive" in the sense that it is of critical importance to the scholarly mind. This includes an atmosphere of respect as well as circumstances of comfortable security.

We must provide an atmosphere which will show always its respect and concern for the teaching profession. It is not enough for this respect to be shown in the isolated act of belated public recognition for a long career of devoted teaching service come to an end. It must be a continued concern throughout that career that the teacher have not only a salary commensurate with the public service performed, but those added essentials to a feeling of dignity which all of us, even teachers, must have in order to give sustained performance.

For example, should a public school teacher, on the theory that she has three summer months in which to have all her illnesses, not be allowed a single day of sick leave without paying her own substitute? I think this is unrealistic, as well as unfair, and not in keeping with the spirit of a state which seeks the best possible teachers.

3. Recognition of teacher quality is essential. To quote a resolution of the National Education Association, "It is a major responsibility of the teaching profession, as of other professions, to evaluate the quality of its services. To enable educators to meet this responsibility more effectively, the association calls for continued research to discover means of objective evaluation of the performance of all professional personnel and their interrelationships for the purpose of improving instruction."

I agree with this statement and think this should be the approach in North Carolina, where, as a matter of fact, such study and research is presently being carried on.

This is not the so-called subjective merit rating which has been found unworkable in other states.

I would hope that this study could point the way for a lively program of encouraging private endowments to reward exceptional teaching, similar to the plan of Kenan Professors at Chapel Hill.

4. It means that parents must understand and support and believe in the kind of school system we hope will be developed in North Carolina. It means they must stand behind the school board in difficult decisions of consolidation and school locations. It means they must support the school administrators who have the courage to curtail midweek extracurricular activities. It means they must insist on homework being assigned and insist on homework being done.

5. It means that students in school must accept the responsibility of learning. I have difficulty in getting this point across to two at home, and I have no illusions about getting it across to the more than a million in the school system; but it is a challenging job for teachers properly to challenge all children to do their best. Schooling is not a mother-bird activity. The

students must feed themselves.

There is no magic ten-year plan. The Governor cannot force educational standards upward. There is no push button marked "quality education."

This will be everybody's job. This is a call to arms. It is time for North Carolinians to march—to start our march from the forefront of the South to the forefront of the nation.

The route-of-approach is outlined in our plans and programs, but the marching must be done by the people of North Carolina—all of the people of North Carolina.

The objective is quality education for our boys and girls, second to none. The objective is quality education which will lift North Carolina in its every endeavor.

I have not covered everything. Education, like life in North Carolina, is expanding, dynamic, and difficult to define in an exactly outlined framework. Our plans can never be put in a neat package in a showcase. They will be altered as we learn, as we move forward.

It will take the best thinking of local school boards. I am thankful for the dedicated citizens who make up these school boards. I am thankful that tradition in North Carolina has caused these school boards, with few exceptions, to be guided by nonpartisan and nonpolitical motives.

It will take the best in leadership of the school administrators. It will take the devotion and determination of the teachers.

Above all, it will take the understanding and support of all the citizens, a willingness to go forward in the conviction that all progress stems from education.

Shakespeare put it this way:

> There is a tide in the affairs of men,
> Which, taken at the flood, leads on the fortune,
> Omitted, all the voyage of their life
> Is bound in shallows and in miseries.
> On such a full sea are we now afloat;
> And we must take the current when it serves,
> Or lose our ventures.

The "full sea" of which Brutus spoke is around us. The rising tide is lapping at our feet. We cannot fail to see it unless we are blind and cannot see or are fearful and will not open our eyes.

Education is the barque on which we must launch our hopes. Through education of our people, the promise of the New Day will be achieved. If we cling to it strongly enough it will lift us on the floodtide of opportunity.

My faith always has been that the people of North Carolina

are ready to go—ready to make this New Day of opportunity a New Day of achievement.

ASSOCIATION OF U. S. ARMY
BRAXTON BRAGG CHAPTER

FORT BRAGG

January 24, 1961

[Within a month after assuming the governorship, Sanford presented an address which he entitled "President Kennedy and the Quest for Peace." He endorsed Kennedy's foreign policy and spoke of its meaning to persons in uniform and to civilians who were concerned with the struggles for peace and the future of the United Nations.]

President Kennedy at his inauguration aptly expressed the determined spirit of this generation of Americans: "Born in this century, tempered by war, disciplined by a hard and bitter peace, proud of our ancient heritage—and unwilling to witness or permit the slow undoing of those human rights to which this nation has always been committed."

No group could better understand this determination and no group could be more ready to fight to preserve these national commitments than soldiers and ex-soldiers like yourselves. There is no question about this readiness and willingness to fight and die; the question is will we take the leadership in defending "our ancient heritage" *without fighting*. Will we, again in the words of John F. Kennedy, "begin anew the quest for peace, before the dark powers of destruction unleashed by science engulf all humanity in planned or accidental self-destruction"?

It is a paradox that fighting is less difficult for the democratic mind to grasp than is the "quest for peace." Fighting unleashes the native spirit, while the quest for peace requires all the restraints, and all the patience, and all the understanding with which man, unhappily, is not naturally endowed at birth.

That has been the story of most wars. Patience, understanding, restraint, not fully developed in man, failed.

You know better than many that talking is better than shooting, that negotiating is easier than digging foxholes, and that debating—however vitriolic—burns a man less than white phosphorous or radiation.

The United States and the other nations of the world have found in the last fifteen years around the tables of the United Nations that restraint and patience are not natural attributes of man, but they know bombast is better than bombs, and the insult of words is less disrespectful than the insult of death.

When we are tempted to despair of the fruitless argument around West 92nd Street, we might well remember the lethal arguments around Bastogne, around Guadalcanal, and around Pusan.

We all know that American military might is capable of destroying Soviet cities, and Khrushchev's missiles could destroy ours. This is the cold fact that has helped to keep the cold war from growing too hot. This is why we continue to fight our fights around the conference tables at the UN. I firmly believe that the United Nations, supported by the strength of the United States and other free nations, has kept us out of World War III.

Let's look at the United Nations. It has its shortcomings. It has its frustrations, and it has had its failures. But the shadows of its failures are not as wide as the brightness of its potential and are not as dark as the threat of war. I believe any student of the history of man would agree with me that the very existence of the United Nations is remarkable. It is a remarkable, even if a somewhat faltering, step toward the universal peace for which men have strived and for which women have yearned since Cain killed Abel.

Here are sovereign nations sitting down together in the spotlight of international attention and arguing their cases. Here are the smallest nations of the earth occupying, on the platform of the world, space equal to the largest countries. Here the poorest government is afforded the same rights as the richest government. Here in the United Nations are represented every race, color, and creed.

The United Nations logically resulted from the devastation of war and the aspirations of all men to be free, to be fed, and to be able to face the future without fear.

If the United Nations has failed to do all that a war-weary world in 1945 hoped it would do, we should remember that it was a long and painful time in being formed. When early men came down from the trees and out of the caves, it was natural they should establish governments: first the family, then the tribe, then the city-states and the kingdoms and empires.

Now the kingdoms and the nations and the empires long have entered into alliances for mutual protection. There were confederations, the ententes, the axes.

Woodrow Wilson came along with his proposal for a new kind of international combination, the League of Nations.

The United States, following the poor advice of that little group of willful men, declined to join in Wilson's great experiment. We refused to sit at the tables in Geneva.

I do not believe it an exaggeration to say the wounds we suffered at Pearl Harbor, on the Anzio Beach, at the Battle of the Bulge, and all the other battlefields of World War II were a direct and tragic sequel to that refusal to enter the League.

In World War II we learned as we suffered. In 1945 America, first under Franklin Delano Roosevelt and then under Harry S. Truman, took the lead in establishing the United Nations.

I think I should point out here that North Carolinians individually and North Carolina as a state helped pour the concrete for the foundation of the United Nations. In 1941, before Pearl Harbor, the North Carolina General Assembly, by an act known as the Humber Resolution, called on the nation to move toward the establishment of a world order with powers limited to matters of armament for the purpose of stopping war.

That action on March 3, 1941, by the General Assembly of North Carolina will, I believe, rank in importance in our history along with the Halifax Resolves and the Mecklenburg Declaration, which were forerunners of the Declaration of Independence. This was the first time in history that a state had taken such a stand. More than thirty states followed suit.

I concur completely with the President of the United States, who stated last week the official policy of this nation, that the United Nations is "our last best hope in an age where the instruments of war have far outpaced the instruments of peace."

North Carolina will move in the front lines with the President in the march to the New Frontiers of freedom and peace. We will honor and support his pledge "to prevent the United Nations from becoming merely a forum for invective—to strengthen its shield of the new and the weak—and to enlarge the area to which its writ may run."

There are many here who wear the United Nations ribbon for service in Korea. By many standards that war—or "police action" if you prefer—was not a satisfactory war.

Of course, I have never heard of a war that really was satisfactory. But before the partisan critics of the Korean War dismiss that conflict as "Mr. Truman's War," let them be reminded of some places where the League of Nations did not fight. Let them be reminded of the Rhineland, Austria, and Czechoslovakia.

The United Nations, in Korea, fought and halted communism. The United Nations served notice that aggression would not be tolerated. It is hard to estimate how many other small nations have been able to preserve their integrity through this timely warning of Korea. I am one who believes that those who died in Korea did NOT die in vain.

The failures and the shortcomings of the UN have been well publicized. But let's look at some of the other accomplishments besides Korea.

Soviet troops were withdrawn from Iran after World War II after the United Nations adopted a resolution calling for withdrawal.

Fighting between India and Pakistan over Kashmir was halted after the United Nations Good Offices Committee intervened. Dr. Frank Porter Graham[78] of North Carolina was a key conciliator in that cessation of hostilities.

Of course, the UN played a vital role in the Suez crisis, in the Berlin blockade and right now is playing a vital role in the Congo. Any one of these situations could have pushed us into World War III.

But the United Nations has said to aggressors: "Halt!"

Aggression may succeed momentarily, but we will not let them use Hungary as a stepping stone to further aggression like Hitler used Czechoslovakia.

We will not let Korea or Laos go undefended like Manchuria in 1931.

We will not permit imperialism, no matter under what name it parades, use the Congo as a proving ground like Mussolini used Ethiopia.

The United Nations has said to all: Trespassers will be prosecuted!

When aggressors and would-be aggressors recognize this fact, then we can devote our efforts toward the abolition of disease and hunger and make the United Nations the organization to promote the welfare of all nations and of all men, women, and children.

You as soldiers have been the protectors in war and the policemen of peace. The cause for which you fought in Korea was not only the defense of America but also defense of free men

---

[78] Frank Porter Graham (1886-   ), teacher, public official, World War I veteran; President of the University of North Carolina at Chapel Hill, 1930-1949; member of various boards of importance, including the Carnegie Foundation, Woodrow Wilson Foundation, National Council of Churches, Hampton Institute; United States senator, administrator of United States Department of Labor, United Nations representative for India and Pakistan. Powell, *North Carolina Lives*, 504.

everywhere. The Second, Third, Seventh, Twenty-fourth, Twenty-fifth, Fortieth, and Forty-fifth Infantry Divisions and the First Cavalry and the Marines and the Navy and the Air Force were fighting under the United Nations flag as well as under the Stars and Stripes.

Now the cynics throw up their hands in horror when the United Nations fails as it failed at the time of the Hungarian Revolution. The United Nations is impotent, they charge.

The United Nations has had its setbacks—Hungary was the biggest.

But we don't abolish our Congress when it enacts a law which doesn't work. And we do not disband our police force when someone gets away with murder. We strengthen them!

To abandon or weaken the United Nations now would lead to international anarchy.

Rather than abandoning the United Nations, rather than diluting our support of it, let us work from the blueprint drawn by President Kennedy: "To invoke the wonders of science instead of its terrors . . . to explore the stars, conquer the deserts, eradicate disease, tap the ocean depths and encourage the arts and commerce."

NORTH CAROLINA PRESS ASSOCIATION

Chapel Hill

February 2, 1961

As he was to do on several occasions, Governor Sanford addressed members of the North Carolina Press Association. At the 1961 meeting, he compared the power of the press to the courtroom prosecutor, judge, and grand jury. This power carried with it tremendous responsibility, and the Governor commended the group for accepting its role. He congratulated the press for the goodwill and good sense exhibited by North Carolina newspapers in backing the sensible approach to the integration-segregation question, giving credit to them for helping keep the schools open during the crisis. The Governor then charged them to help with the "equally difficult task of helping to improve these schools."

Throughout the years of his tenure, Sanford's primary concern was education. He addressed groups throughout North Carolina and the nation on the subject, and his speech to the

North Carolina Press Association was no exception. He praised the newspapermen for supporting the report of a fact-finding group which had shown the critical needs of the public schools. After discussing plans for the financial support of the schools, the Governor remarked that money was not the sole answer but that the job could not be done without money. He concluded that the story of education was important to all segments of the public, was vital to those working on newspapers, and would be the top story for the year 1961.

WILSON INDUSTRIAL COUNCIL
INDUSTRY AND EDUCATION DINNER

WILSON

February 6, 1961

As Governor Sanford traveled, he became more and more convinced that North Carolinians were determined "to move forward economically by taking full advantage of the considerable potential we possess in the fields of agriculture, industry, and education." With human and natural resources being marshaled into one big effort for higher standards and opportunities for all, he said that citizens were building for the future and should not concentrate selfishly on the present. He commended the Wilson Industrial Council for accepting such responsibility. The Governor observed that economic diversity, a problem in the eastern counties, had to become a reality. In that area, "Agriculture is the backbone of the economy and tobacco is the backbone of agriculture." Change was imperative; diversification of agriculture and the establishment of an industrial balance would reveal new economic activity in the east, provide challenge and opportunity. To keep young people at home, they would have to be supplied with knowledge, technical training, and desire. The burden of responsibility of meeting the goals would have to be met by each individual who would "dedicate himself to the task."

GRIFTON JUNIOR CHAMBER OF COMMERCE

GRIFTON

February 10, 1961

Early in his administration, Governor Sanford undertook the task of carrying his message of quality education to the people of North Carolina. His talk to the Grifton Junior Chamber of Commerce was one of those occasions in which the Governor explained his program. He believed that the primary work of the governor, the legislature, parents, and citizens was the education of children. He explained the need for new classrooms, more books, more teachers, attention to the mentally retarded and the exceptionally talented. Programs for the groups at both ends of the scale as well as for the average children would mean provision "whereby the weak could grow strong and the strong could grow great." The Governor concluded his talk with an appeal to the Jaycees of Grifton and throughout North Carolina to help in the effort to improve the educational opportunities in the state.

FARMERS COOPERATIVE COUNCIL OF NORTH CAROLINA

RALEIGH

February 21, 1961

[In its February 20 issue, the *News and Observer's Farm and Home Magazine* carried a message from the Governor in which he stated that "Kerr Scott got the farmer out of the mud; it is our job to get the farmer out of the hole." The next day he spoke to farm leaders and reiterated his stand to give emphasis to agriculture as the previous administration had concentrated on industry. He encouraged a realistic understanding of the situation and called for ideas which would result in a stronger farm economy. Appearing in September before the Farmers Cooperative Exchange, Sanford again urged that steps be taken to move the farm economy upward.]

This conference here tonight is proof that farming is not dead in North Carolina. This meeting of the leaders of all major farm organizations in our state is an excellent example that farmers are working together like never before to assure a healthy growth in North Carolina's most fundamental industry —agriculture.

For the past several years, as I have traveled over our state, I have pointed out something that all of you know but something that the skeptical seem to doubt: Far from being dead, North Carolina's farms contain the seed for a great new harvest of rural prosperity.

This conference shows that that was one campaign statement which is irrefutable.

If anyone needs further evidence of the vitality and the potential growth of our farms and of our farmers, let him read the calendar of farm meetings in this state this week. To cite only a few:

Monday through Saturday, cotton growers from the northeast to the southwestern corners of our state are observing the Agricultural Stabilization and Conservation "Highlight Week." Monday through Wednesday, the first North Carolina barrow show is being held in Johnston County. Monday, two-bale cotton growers were honored at State College. Yesterday, a program on cattle feeding was held at the Nash County courthouse. Yesterday, a meeting on corn production was held in Martin County. Tomorrow, a meeting on egg production will be held in the same county. Tuesday through Thursday, a regional conference on marketing is being held at the YMCA here in Raleigh. Tomorrow, Ayshire breeders meet in Greensboro. Day after tomorrow, Guernsey breeders meet in Durham. Thursday, Landrace hog breeders will hold a sale in Rocky Mount Friday, Poland hog breeders will hold a sale at Greenville. Thursday, a peanut product meeting will be held in the Halifax County courthouse. Thursday, a sweet potato show and a Negro 4-H Club sale will be held in Rocky Mount. Friday, a beef cattle tour will be held in Northampton County. Saturday, the Raleigh Production Credit Association holds its annual meeting down the street from here. Monday through Saturday is Future Farmers of America Week.

May I say here that it's easy to see from a schedule like this why farm families find it easy to obey the Fourth Commandment and observe Sunday as a day of rest.

These meetings indicate the increasing diversity of North Carolina's farming business. They show that farming is important not only to the rural areas of our state but also to our largest cities.

They suggest that what happens on the farm is significant to what happens in the factory and the mill and the business office.

But, then, you here tonight don't need a lawyer to tell you this. You know it.

You also are aware of the great irony of the rural economy in our state: North Carolina, with some of the richest farmland in the nation, has some of the poorest farms, and some of the most underpaid farmers.

Why is this?

It can't be because North Carolina farmers don't work as hard as farmers elsewhere. The acres of this state have been well irrigated with the sweat of farmers.

It can't be because we've lacked rural leadership. We've grown in this state some of the great farm leaders of the nation. To mention just a few, our state produced Hugh Bennett,[79] who fathered the soil conservation program. We've had men like Flake Shaw[80] and M. G. Mann[81] and Kerr Scott and Clarence Poe.[82] And as of tonight three of the most important agricultural posts in President Kennedy's administration are filled by Harry Caldwell,[83] Charles Murphy,[84] and Horace Godfrey.[85] Congressman Harold Cooley[86] from this district is chairman of the House Agriculture Committee. L. Y. "Stag" Ballentine has worked long and well as Commissioner of Agriculture.

I could go on, but those are enough to show that any poverty of our farms cannot be blamed on poor leadership.

Nor can our farm problems be blamed on poor climate. We have one of the best in the world. We have a long growing season.

---

[79] Hugh Hammond Bennett (1881-1960), soil scientist, public official in state, national, and international capacities; first chief of United States Soil Conservation Service; named "father of soil conservation." Jaques Cattell (ed.), *American Men of Science: A Biographical Directory* (Tempe, Arizona: Jaques Cattell Press, Incorporated [Tenth Edition, revised, 1960]) , Vol. A-E, 274.

[80] R. Flake Shaw, farm leader from Greensboro; Executive Secretary of North Carolina Farm Bureau Federation, 1940-1957; member of Board of Directors and the Executive Committee of the American Farm Bureau; member of Federal Reserve Bank of Richmond. Information supplied by Irby Shaw Walker, daughter of Flake Shaw and employee of State Farm Bureau Federation.

[81] Manly G. Mann (1889-1958) , farm leader, railroad employee, bank official; Director of North Carolina Cotton Growers' Association and of Farmers Cooperative Exchange. *News and Observer*, November 16, 1952.

[82] Clarence Hamilton Poe (1881-1964) , editor-publisher from Raleigh; holder of honorary degrees from Wake Forest, University of North Carolina at Chapel Hill, Washington College in Maryland, Clemson, and North Carolina State University; editor of the *Progressive Farmer*, 1899-1953; member of the State College Board of Trustees, State Board of Agriculture, Agriculture Committee of the United States Chamber of Commerce, Committee on Rural Electrification; master of the State Grange; elector for the Hall of Fame of Great Americans, 1925-1964. Powell, *North Carolina Lives*, 981.

[83] Harry B. Caldwell, farmer, co-operative executive from Greensboro; active in North Carolina agrarian causes; Chairman of the Agricultural Advisory Committee in Washington; holder of other federal posts in the Hoover and Eisenhower administrations. Powell, *North Carolina Lives*, 203.

[84] Charles S. Murphy (1909-   ) , lawyer, government official from Wallace; educated Duke University; legislative counsel, United States Senate, 1934-1946; administrative assistant to Harry S. Truman; lawyer engaged in active practice, 1953-1961; Under Secretary of Agriculture under John F. Kennedy. Powell, *North Carolina Lives*, 896.

[85] Horace David Godfrey (1915-   ) , government executive; former Wake County farmer; holder of long record of government service, beginning with work in the U. S. Department of Agriculture, 1934-1943; Mason and Grange leader; administrator of Agricultural Stabilization and Conservation Service. Powell, *North Carolina Lives*, 491.

[86] Harold D. Cooley (1897-   ), lawyer and member of Congress from Nashville; studied at Duke University and Law School of Yale University; member of Congress from the Fourth District, 1934-19—; chairman of House Committee on Agriculture. Powell, *North Carolina Lives*, 282; *North Carolina Manual, 1961*, 504.

The farm problem of this state certainly cannot be explained by a lack of water. We are heaven-blessed in this respect. Of course, we have tended to squander this great resource. We have let it flow down to the Atlantic without using it, and we have, for entirely too long, let it carry away some of our best topsoil.

One of the outstanding extension programs is the one carried on in this state.

So, we see that we have the people, we have the soil, we have the climate and the water. We have everything necessary for rural prosperity. In spite of all of these ingredients, we have not discovered the proper recipe for putting them together. For last year hundreds of North Carolina's family farms went out of business. Many others operated in the red or barely broke even. And our farm children moved away in droves as they reached maturity.

The census of 1960 showed that the counties which lost heaviest in population were the agrarian counties. Real farm income continued to go down.

The low income of the majority of North Carolina's farms is in large measure responsible for the low per capita income standing of North Carolina.

I have heard it happily explained that new industry, a new plant, would solve the needs of people making inadequate incomes on the farms now. This is misleading.

We cannot convert them all to industrial workers. The answer is not to send them all to town. You know what there is in town tonight. There are large numbers of unemployed and underemployed workers already. Industrialization is one of the most urgent needs of this state, but industrialization is not the answer to our farm problems. We need new industry and will work toward this goal, but we also need new income from the soil, and we must work even harder for this goal, because the path is more obscure.

I have no magic answer to the farm needs. I would hope that you here tonight might from time to time suggest programs that would help. From talking with you and farmers across the state, it seems obvious that you have solved many of the problems of production.

Now you face the problems of distribution. We need to grow what will sell, and we need to sell it at a profit. The enormity of the distribution problem can be grasped when we consider the wheat and eggs and other commodities overflowing the storage bins in this nation and the millions upon millions of hungry men, women, and children in other nations.

As a matter of fact, we don't have to go to India or the Congo or Latin America to find hungry people. When we acted last week to bring North Carolina into the federal surplus food program on a full-time basis, we found that upward of 500,000 North Carolinians are underfed. Incidentally, I believe this surplus food program is going to help two ways: First, it's going to help feed the hungry; and secondly, it's going to help reduce farm surpluses which have a habit of depressing the prices of the current harvests.

One of the programs on which Kerr Scott was working when he died was a World Food Bank. I am happy to see others are continuing that work. I am happy to see that President Kennedy has carried this idea to the point of creating programs to carry out this goal.

Our farm surpluses are greater weapons in this cold war with communism than our atomic stockpile. Unhappily, they are weapons we have barely used. These food surpluses are especially potent weapons in a year when the Soviet and Chinese collective farms have suffered one of their periodic failures.

If communism breeds on hunger, democracy can grow on nourishment. It may well be that the minds of those uncommitted millions around the globe will be won through their stomachs.

Now let's come back closer to home in our look at government and the farmer. Here in Raleigh for the last six years we saw what a determined policy by state government could do in expanding industry.

This administration means to give the same emphasis to farming in the next four years as was given to industrialization in the last administration. First of all, let me say the door to the Governor's Office is going to be open as wide and as quickly to a farmer as it is to an industrial prospect. And, I might add, it's going to be open at all times to both.

I want your ideas and will help you put them to work.

I am happy to see the electric and telephone co-ops represented here.

These co-ops lighted farm houses and brought phones to them when they were needed. I am not picking any fight with the commercial utility companies when I say that the co-ops will be protected. There is room and there is need aplenty for both the commercial and the co-operative utilities. You have done much to lay the foundation for better rural life.

So long as people need food to eat, so long as they want tobacco to smoke, so long as they require clothes to wear, and so long as they need wood to build, then farming will be the major industry of our state.

Let us use our imagination to develop our resources, to improve our income, to widen our opportunities.

The answer to most of our problems—schools, roads, income—lies in a stronger farm economy.

NORTH CAROLINA
PRISON DEPARTMENT PERSONNEL

RALEIGH

February 22, 1961

Addressing personnel of the Prison Department, Governor Sanford talked about prison administration. He discussed the challenge facing these people, a challenge created by the growing knowledge of human behavior and the science of government. The Governor commended the state's prison officials for their courage and competence, saying that the policies followed by them reflected the thinking of foremost penologists and prison administrators in the world. He explained that policy-making was subject to change, but the basic guides, such as those outlined in the *Prison Department Guidebook,* had to be followed. The co-operation betwen the prison system and the Institute of Government in Chapel Hill in planning courses for personnel was cited as a good example of the dynamic progress being made. More and more use of probation and parole meant a higher percentage of serious offenders remaining under the care of the prison officials. Rehabilitation had taken on new meaning as programs such as Alcoholics Anonymous, work release, education while in prison, recreation, and job placement had been put into effect. Governor Sanford made it clear that the prison personnel had his support in the job they had to do.

CITY-WIDE PTA RALLY

FAYETTEVILLE

February 28, 1961

Governor Sanford stated that North Carolina had the resources, the will, the opportunity to move; the result would be a new day through education. He spoke of the PTA as a powerful force, and he urged three lines of action: (1) increased attention to the development of closer relationships between parents and teachers with mutual trust, exchange of information, and extension of the schools' guidance programs so that each child would have two advocates—one at home and one at school; (2) promotion of united efforts to secure for every child an educational opportunity of high quality, though the achievement of this goal would require agreement as to the kind of job the school should do so that its primary objective of education would not be forgotten; and (3) aggressiveness in political action to assure laws and appropriations which would promote better public education for all children. "Money will not do the job but we cannot do the job without money." The Governor concluded by saying that the support of quality education had to be "the first order of our public business."

EDUCATION RALLY

SMITHFIELD

March 9, 1961

[To emphasize Sanford's program of quality education for North Carolina, a series of education rallies were held throughout the state; the gubernatorial address was a feature of nearly all of these meetings. The Governor often visited several schools in more than one county in a single day, making as many as ten or twelve speeches. His ideas in the field of education were repeated on numerous occasions, not only at rallies such as the one at Smithfield but to the state's citizens by means of television and radio. His first televised "Report to the People" incorporated many of the thoughts presented to this smaller group; the "Report" is summarized on page 21.]

I come to you here tonight to continue the campaign seeking the support of the adults of this state for the children of this state. I have traveled many more miles across North Carolina during the last thirteen months, asking for this support for the schools, than I traveled all through World War II. I believe this campaign we are waging for better schools is of equal—if, indeed, not greater—importance than those campaigns of World War II. For the first prerequisite to democracy is an educated citizenry.

The decision on whether our schools shall be improved and whether the education of our children shall be the first order of business is now in the hands of the people of this state and their elected representatives.

I have promised to work for the improvement of educational opportunities. I have always said that I would do my duty in recommending new taxes, if needed, to pay for those opportunities.

I have proposed a far-reaching program.

I have now proposed to your elected representatives in the General Assembly the means of financing the part of the program which requires expenditures.

The question of our schools and the question of our children's education is now in your hands and the hands of your fellow citizens across the state. Are you willing to pay the price for the education of your children?

I think that all of us, no matter what our views on a particular tax may be, can agree that there is no greater need in North Carolina today than the improvement of the public schools. There are too many unhappy statistics which cry out that need.

Let's look at the record and see how our state compares with our sister states in education.

North Carolina ranks forty-fifth among the fifty states in the amount of money we spend on each child going to school. We spend an average of $240 a year for the education of each of our school children in North Carolina. The average American child has $369 a year spent on him.

North Carolina ranks fortieth in the per capita expenditure of state and local governments for local schools.

North Carolina ranks forty-first in per capita expenditure of state and local governments for all public education.

North Carolina in the last decade raised the rate of teachers' salaries less than *any* other state in the union. Our teachers' salaries were low in 1950 and far below the national average. After ten years, those salaries were appreciably farther below the national average.

North Carolina ranks forty-first in pupil-teacher ratio. That means that forty states give teachers smaller class loads than we require teachers of this state to teach.

Now let's look at some figures with a close correlation to those I have just listed. Let's look at the result of our poor support of our children's education.

North Carolina ranks forty-first among the states in the per cent of adults with college diplomas.

North Carolina ranks forty-first among the states in the per cent of our population fourteen years old and older who are illiterate.

North Carolina ranks forty-fourth among the fifty states in the percentage of adults with less than five years of schooling.

North Carolina ranks forty-fifth in the percentage of men rejected by the armed forces because they were illiterate.

North Carolina ranks forty-seventh among the fifty states in the median school years completed by adults—that is, persons twenty-five years old or older.

North Carolina ranks forty-eighth among the fifty states in the percentage of our adult population who are high school graduates.

Now, let's look at one more brief set of statistics. I rather suspect there is a strong cause-and-effect relationship between the figures I have already listed and these I am about to list.

North Carolina ranks thirty-seventh among the states in migration.

North Carolina ranks forty-third in per capita disposable income.

North Carolina ranks forty-fifth in per capita income.

Lest someone accuse me of looking only on the dark side, let me point out that North Carolina ranks eighth among the states in the number of school children. That is our greatest asset.

But we have cultivated our children's minds less well than we have cultivated our tobacco and cotton and peanut acres.

We have given proportionately less attention to the maintenance of schools than we have to the maintenance of wardrobes, our automobiles, and our kitchen stoves.

North Carolina is rightly concerned when anyone attempts to lower our tobacco parity of 90 per cent.

Yet we have let our children's educational parity fall to less than 66 per cent.

I could go on reciting statistics until midnight, but I believe the ones you have just heard will convince any sensible person of the need.

These are the facts, these are the figures that we must weigh when we consider the admittedly unhappy prospect of new taxes. These are the facts that I had to consider before I went before the General Assembly of North Carolina Monday night with the special budget message on education. These are the facts your elected representatives of the General Assembly must weigh in the coming months.

These unhappy facts are the facts that every citizen must weigh.

The decision on the future of North Carolina schools is the decision that will determine in large measure the future of our children. And, it is true, that the future of North Carolina will be determined by the children.

That decision is in the hands of you, the adult citizens of North Carolina.

Now in the last three days, there has been some talk that runs about like this: "Yes, I favor the Governor's program for better schools and better educational opportunities for my children, but I don't like his tax idea."

Now we all agree that taxes are unpleasant.

But I know of few things in this world, though, that don't require a price of some sort.

The Battle of the Bulge was not something that GI's went into because they wanted to. They went in it and they fought and they stuck because it was absolutely necessary to do so. The alternative was worse than the fighting, the freezing, the bleeding, and even the dying.

There was never a church built in North Carolina that didn't require someone's sacrifice. There was never a foreign mission established for which someone didn't have to pay in discomfort or even suffering.

I am confident of the answer the General Assembly of North Carolina will give to this program. I have faith in the people's decision on this program.

Our state's record is too clear to doubt that decision. Our grandfathers who supported Aycock at the turn of the century and our fathers who supported the sales tax during the depression have left a strong heritage to guide us.

Now let us look at the cost of better schools and better educational opportunities for our children.

I have proposed an across-the-board sales tax to pay for the program.

I did so only after the most careful and conscientious consideration. I eliminated getting the money for improving the schools from the income tax because the federal government has just about exhaused that source.

I eliminated the property tax because that is the chief and one of the few taxes for local and county governments in paying for the necessary services they provide.

I did not propose the crown tax on soft drinks for the same reason that I did not propose a tax on candy bars, peanuts, or ice cream cones. We already have a 3 per cent tax on these items.

I did not propose additional taxes on cigarettes. Cigarettes are heavily taxed by the federal government, we tax them at 3 per cent, and it would not bring in enough money to begin to do the job.

I did propose as large an increase in whisky taxes as I believe we could collect without driving trade to the woods.

This talk that tax should be put on whisky and cigarettes and luxuries before we tax food and the other items that we will tax by eliminating the exemptions is misleading and ignores the fact that whisky, beer, wine, cigarettes, and the "luxuries" are already taxed.

So, we must turn inevitably to the sales tax. There we have two choices: Raise the rate on the items now taxed from 3 to 4 per cent or eliminate the exemptions.

I fail to see that you treat the poor man any better by raising the tax he must pay when buying his children blue jeans and shoes and socks and underclothes than by eliminating the exemptions.

For that matter, an additional tax on cigarettes or on soft drinks will hit the poor man just as hard as it does the wealthy. The poor man drinks as much "pop" and smokes just as much as the rich man. I'm not saying a poor man should smoke or drink soda. But you and I know he does.

Now what about this tax on food. And when we talk of eliminating the sales tax exemptions to raise the funds for better schools we are talking about a tax on food. There is no beating around the bush about it, for $50 million in the program for education will be derived from the tax on food. This brings us to a very simple decision. Do we want to pay 30 cents on every $10 worth of food in order better to prepare our children for life? I honestly know of no other way.

I am well aware of the hardships of paying tax on necessary items by those whose income is so low that every penny counts. But I am also aware of the greater hardship placed upon the children of these same people by inadequate school opportunities, and I have been able to devise no way that the poorest can be exempt from a general sales tax.

Welfare payments and the distribution of free food answer the complaint raised in behalf of the poorest among us. I have worked with other state officials to secure for the poor of this state full advantage of the federal food surplus program. This program already is underway.

I hope that those who may be tempted to speak out against the food tax will suggest some painless way we can get the money.

I hope they will explain why it is fair to tax the food which persons, including the poor, who must "eat out" pay on food at cafes and restaurants. As you know, we have been taxing that food since 1933. I hope they will remember that twenty-six of the thirty-five states with sales tax, do NOT exempt food.

I hope also they will remember that if we tax bread we also will be taxing cake; if we tax fatback, we also will tax caviar; if we tax cornmeal, we also will tax filet mignon.

No one is going to go hungry because of this tax.

But the children of North Carolina will go thirsty for quality education if we do not enact this program for better schools.

Sanford carried out his campaign promises despite the "Pie in the Sky" label given by his opponents during the campaign. The event pictured here occurred on May 11, 1960, in front of the Wake County Courthouse.

The Governor and his wife are shown participating in the Civil War Centennial observance.

The decision is just as simple as that. I am not trying to thrust anything upon the people. I am trying to do my duty to serve the future of our children, and I hope you will decide to help pay the cost in order to have the quality of schools the future demands.

CONFEDERATE CENTENNIAL DAY

LOUISBURG

March 18, 1961

Speaking early in the observance of the Confederate Centennial, Governor Sanford observed that the past was being commemorated and the future surveyed. Commemorating the first raising of the Confederate flag in North Carolina, which occurred in Franklin County when Major Orren Randolph Smith and his neighbors flew their homemade one on March 18, 1861, the Governor said that North Carolina rose to the need when volunteers were called. Though citizens of the present might not agree with all the issues of the South of 1861, the courage and devotion with which North Carolina served was cause for admiration. Those who survived deserved recognition for their part in creating one prosperous nation. The observance in 1961 of what archivist and historian R. D. W. Connor called a "victory of the vanquished" was a commemoration of the end of the struggle which brought about a better union. Governor Sanford voiced the opinion that if North Carolina of 1961 exercised the courage and devotion of North Carolina of 1861, the fight for better schools would be won. The state, because of its preparation for the future, had never wasted time moaning. It would continue to fight for educational opportunities, would continue to rise, and would continue to grow and move.

[In the absence of Governor Sanford, this speech was read by Thomas N. Lambeth, Administrative Assistant.]

EDUCATION RALLY

GOLDSBORO

March 20, 1961

Speaking on the topic, "A Sense of Values," Governor Sanford pointed out the fact that Governor Charles B. Aycock, whose home was near Goldsboro, heralded a message similar to that of his administration. He referred to the magic of radio, on which this speech was carried, as illustrative of the different degrees of education demanded of present-day students. He emphasized the added significance of education, which could no longer be considered a luxury for the well-bred but was a matter of survival. Leading authorities who had visited North Carolina had considered the long-range plan for quality education significant and outstanding in America. Needs and costs had to be measured, but the Governor expressed the belief that quality education was worth almost any temporary sacrifice. The tax on food was less objectionable than the neglect of full and adequate education for all children. Expressing hope that the people of North Carolina would support the program, the Governor urged consideration by the General Assembly of ways of paying for the program. Though the food tax seemed the only way to support quality education, Sanford promised to consider any suggestions submitted to him. In 1949, 1953, and 1959, the people voted clearly for education when they approved multimillion-dollar bond issues; a vote in the affirmative in this case would mean a vote for the future of North Carolina.

FUTURE FARMERS OF AMERICA

Coats

March 23, 1961

The Governor congratulated the Future Farmers group for honors it had received, saying the teachers and the families deserved credit for their contributions. He reviewed briefly the history of the organization, pointing out that it had promoted instructional programs and rendered valuable service to students and to the entire agricultural industry since its beginning in 1928. He observed that action of the group was indicative of the fact that North Carolina did not intend to get out of the farming business.

Because students were concerned with subjects other than agriculture, Governor Sanford discussed education in general, talking about the program for a new day in North Carolina. He said the state had to provide financial support, had to make teaching a profession with the highest quality of training and performance, had to insist on a better balance in the curriculum, and had to guard time so as not to waste it on nonessential activities.

Governor Sanford elaborated on these points. He commented that any youth failing to get the best education of which he was capable had failed in his responsibility to himself, his state, his nation. In the field of agriculture awards and competition had been carried to the extreme; a balance in the curriculum had to be maintained.

In conclusion, the Governor urged the fathers to support education with taxes, the students to support education by hard work and study. He said students should not consider their education completed when they finished high school; opportunities for further training were available. He expressed confidence that the youth of North Carolina would respond to the promise of a new day and to the challenge before them.

REPORT TO THE PEOPLE
STATE-WIDE TELEVISION NETWORK

RALEIGH

March 23, 1961

In a speech originating in the Raleigh studio of WUNC-TV, Governor Sanford gave the first of many televised reports dealing with the issue of North Carolina education. He urged citizens to consider facts. The Governor cited many of the figures given in his education rally speech in Smithfield on March 9 (see pages 114-119). Confronted by "these unhappy facts," Governor Sanford urged each citizen to weigh his own set of values and decide for or against a program of better education. Many people, he said, favored lifting the educational standards but opposed new taxes with which to implement the program. He reminded them that few things required no price. Though the final decision would be left to the General Assembly and the people of North Carolina, the Governor's view was that the food tax was the only feasible way of obtaining the needed solid financial foundation. This conclusion was based on a study of the tax structure and precedents set by other states and was drawn only after all alternate proposals were deemed inadequate. Harder work from teachers, more homework from students, more encouragement from parents would make taxation seem the least of the sacrifices. "Upon no other basis—at no less cost—can we fulfill the possibilities of North Carolina."

NORTHEASTERN NORTH CAROLINA
INDUSTRIAL DEVELOPMENT CONFERENCE

TARBORO

April 5, 1961

[The Department of Conservation and Development sponsored six conferences to stimulate industrial development in various sections of North Carolina. The Governor spoke at each of these gatherings, adapting his message to fit local conditions. This address to the northeastern group is given in full as it presents the over-all philosophy of the Governor in the field of industrial development. The addresses presented in other areas on May 3, June 6, September 7, November 2, and November 29 are summarized; the summaries may be found on pages 129, 136-137, 174, 190-191, and 211-212.]

I am happy to meet with you today in this important conference of business, civic, and government leaders of northeastern North Carolina. Your very presence here indicates to me that you recognize the need for close co-operation in the development of this area.

You have the guarantee of assistance from the Board and the Department of Conservation and Development and all other agencies of state government in building the economy of northeastern North Carolina. I want to extend to you my personal pledge that the Governor's Office will be working with you and for you as you move ahead.

By the same token, I challenge you to work with state government and its agencies and, above all, to work with each other in developing this area.

The time for petty rivalries is past. Neither northeastern North Carolina nor any area of North Carolina can afford them. The time for complacency also is gone. All we have to do to know that we can and should do better is to read the population figures for the last decade for the counties represented here today.

Of the twenty-one counties comprising this conference, eleven lost population during the last decade. Most of the rest of your counties barely held their own.

When we consider the high birth rate in northeastern North Carolina, we begin to get the picture of how great the out-migration from this area really was.

In these twenty-one counties of northeastern North Carolina, there was a bare 1.48 per cent gain in population in the 1950's. In the state as a whole, there was a gain of 12.2 per cent in population.

Some of the greatest losses North Carolina suffered in World War I, World War II, and the Korean War did not occur on the battlefields. Perhaps the greatest losses were the men and women who went away to the service and to the war industries and never came back because they found greater opportunities in other states.

There's not a person here today who doesn't know of some talented young persons who have moved away from this area and this state to make a better living elsewhere.

You and I can understand the reason. North Carolina suffers from one of the lowest per capita incomes in the nation. Yet the per capita income of northeastern North Carolina is almost a third less than the state's per capita. And, I repeat, the state's per capita of $1,485 is nothing to brag about. The per capita for this twenty-one-county area is only $1,052. Five of these twenty-one counties did not build a single new industry in the fifties. I know there are many reasons for this low figure. But there are equally strong reasons why we can raise it substantially.

A good illustration of what we can do in northeastern North Carolina, and in all of North Carolina, can be seen right here in Tarboro. In recent years this town has added the payrolls of Glenroit Mills, Carolina Plastics, and other companies.

These companies have pumped new opportunities not only into Tarboro but also into all of Edgecombe County and northeastern North Carolina. They didn't just happen. These companies came to Tarboro because the leaders here worked to bring them to this town.

Now I'm not down here to tell you that industry is the answer to all of our problems. It certainly is not. We are not going to try to build here in this area—or in any other section of the state—a Jersey City, or a Detroit, or a Pittsburgh.

I'm not sure we could if we wanted to and I don't think we want to. One of the strengths of North Carolina has long been its small towns and its medium-sized cities, drawing their manpower and their raw materials from the nearby countryside.

What we need in northeastern North Carolina, and what we need throughout North Carolina, is a balance between agriculture, industry, and commerce. In this area, industry and commerce haven't achieved the proper balance with agriculture. If we have two bad crops running, the courthouse yard is filled with people.

The industry that we need in this area doesn't have to be of the great proportions of DuPont at Kinston. We are very proud to have the DuPont plant, but you know and I know that that type of plant isn't built very often.

We are equally proud to have the home-grown and home-manned plants like Monk Harrington's at Lewiston and Long

Manufacturing Company.

The biggest employer in North Carolina, Burlington Industries, started as a small home-grown company. Cannon Mills and Reynolds Tobacco Company are other examples which prove that North Carolina can build great industries—as well as import them.

So when we put the welcome mat out for the out-of-state plants—and it is out and it's going to stay out as long as I am Governor—we must not forget to leave the door open for our neighbors down the street.

Whether we are seeking the plants of an out-of-state corporation or the expansion of established firms or the construction of new home-grown companies, there are certain foundation stones we must place. I believe the chief of these foundation stones is attitude. The attitude we need in northeastern North Carolina and the attitude we need all across this state is one that discards with equal vigor defeatism on the one hand and complacency on the other hand. There really is no excuse for a defeatist attitude anywhere in this state, least of all in northeastern North Carolina. The people are here and the land and water and climate are here. The heritage of greatness also is here.

In this area are located some of the great historic shrines of America: the first English colony in the New World, the first airplane flight, the first declaration for American Independence; all of these took place in the area you represent. They are natural tourist attractions, as are the excellent hunting and fishing that abound in this area.

As these great new interstate Highways 95 and 85 open up, this area is going to become more and more a route of the tourists moving south for the winter and north for the summer. I hope you will help us in our efforts to persuade these travelers to spend some time—and some money—in North Carolina. The State Highway Commission, under the leadership of two men from northeastern North Carolina, Merrill Evans and Ben Roney,[87] is working on plans to see that northeastern North Carolina benefits fully from the new Cheasapeake Bay Tunnel.

Now while we're talking about transportation, I would like to discuss an area airport with you. I know you have discussed it many times in the past and some of you are still working for it. I would hope that out of this conference would come the spirit

---

[87] Benjamin E. Roney, from Rocky Mount; Administrative Assistant to W. Kerr Scott during his terms as Governor and Senator; appointed Director of Secondary Roads by Governor Sanford, July, 1961. See Governor Sanford's news release of June 29, 1961.

of co-operation and determination that would at long last make such an airport possible.

Last week, I had the opportunity of helping to celebrate the first flight on Piedmont Air Lines route from Norfolk to Tennessee. That route will include stops at Elizabeth City and Rocky Mount. This was a step—or a flight—in the right direction.

But we know that in order to gain adequate airline service, this area of Rocky Mount, Wilson, Greenville, Goldsboro, and Kinston needs a consolidated airport. If cities the size of Raleigh and Durham or Greensboro and High Point find it beneficial to consolidate their efforts in joint airport operations, wouldn't it be likely that your cities could also benefit from a joint effort?

This takes us back to attitude. No one of the counties or cities of this area can achieve its full potential working by itself. Working together, with an attitude of enlightened self-interest, you can change the face of this area.

A good illustration of what can be accomplished by joint effort is East Carolina College, Atlantic Christian College, the College of the Albemarle, and Elizabeth City Teachers College. These institutions were not the result of the efforts of a single community. They resulted from the devotion and work of people all across this area.

The attitude that we need to build this area and this state starts at the individual level. There is not a single person here today, and I doubt if there is a person living in northeastern North Carolina, who would not readily agree that we need improvement. We're all for progress. But whether we achieve progress or not will require something more than a vague desire.

Here are some of the hard questions we must answer if we truly want a better economy for ourselves and a better opportunity for our sons and daughters in this area: Are you willing to sell land that has been in your families for generations, and sell it at reasonable prices, to give new companies a place to locate? Are you willing to face some competition from new firms for workers? Are you willing to extend some honest-to-goodness southern hospitality to new people with different accents? Are you willing to restore and maintain the cleanliness of our streams for the man and the town downstream? Is your civic pride strong enough to make you clean up the eyesores of your town and county and build the facilities we need to attract industries and tourists—and to hold your own sons and daughters who have been leaving this area in great number? Is your civic pride enlightened enough to thrust off petty jealousies in order to work in a co-operative campaign for the good of this whole area? Are you willing to invest your time, your effort, and your money to make your town, your county, your area, and your state a better place?

If I were not confident of your answers, I would not be here today.

Northeastern North Carolina is rich in history.

It's richer still in its potential.

I look forward to working with you to achieve that potential.

NORTH CAROLINA MOTHER'S DAY PROGRAM

RALEIGH

April 10, 1961

In this tribute to the mother of the year, Governor Sanford spoke both personally and as a representative of the state. Charles B. Aycock's mother, he pointed out, could neither read nor write; this factor inspired her son toward a successful career and helped give birth to the reality of universal education in North Carolina. Sanford paid tribute to the debt he owed his mother for instilling in him a keen interest in education. The Governor praised mothers and their many roles, challenging them to help build the quality of North Carolina education by co-operating with teachers and by encouraging children to take advantage of their opportunities.

FOURTH ANNUAL AUTHORS LUNCHEON

GOLDSBORO

April 18, 1961

This annual literary tribute at which Governor Sanford spoke was sponsored by the Goldsboro Rotary Club and the libraries of Wayne County. He praised the interest of the group in good literature, adding that too often leaders failed to appreciate and promote cultural activities. Turning his remarks to the particular author and book being honored, Oliver Orr, *Charles Brantley Aycock,* he said this was an appropriate time "to take cognizance of the high ideals and dedication to the common good" expressed by Governor Charles B. Aycock. The Governor described Oliver Orr's biography of Aycock as a real contribution to literature, a book in which Aycock was divested of abstractions and vague

Pictured above are the Governor's parents, Mr. and Mrs. Cecil Sanford of Laurinburg.

The Honorable Terry Sanford
Dear Governor Sanford:
    Described in your speech I do believe
Is an education, I hope to receive.
    Of this I want to be a part,
And I think I've had a right good start.
    I want to go to college- so
I really hope that I can go.
    I think it's good to be a writer
Or maybe a teacher, but not a fighter.
    After the speech you gave last night
It makes me really want to fight
    To pull up my grades, and make my mind grow,
So the United States will have reason to glow.
    Every child needs to be educated,
But you need to be congratulated.
                    Sincerely yours,
                    Judy Pleasant

Over 40,000 letters were received and answered after the Governor asked school children to write to him on the subject of quality education. He is shown here with Judy Pleasant, of Sherwood Bates School in Raleigh, and her letter on March 3, 1962.

references and a book which revealed an image in which the man stood tall. The book contributed to an understanding of present-day objectives, and in closing, Governor Sanford quoted Aycock's words:

"I would have all our people to believe in the possibilities of North Carolina; in the strength of her men; the purity of her women, and their power to accomplish as much as can be done anywhere on earth by any people. I would have them to become dissatisfied with small things; to be anxious for higher and better things; to yearn for real greatness; to seek after knowledge; to do the right thing in order that they may be what they ought. I would have the strong to bear the burdens of the weak and to lift up the weak and make them strong—teaching men everywhere that real strength consists not in serving ourselves but in doing for others."

1961 CONVENTION OF NORTH CAROLINA CONGRESS OF PARENTS AND TEACHERS

WINSTON-SALEM

April 19, 1961

When he addressed the 1961 meeting of the Congress of Parents and Teachers, Governor Sanford was careful to direct his remarks on education so that they were appropriate for his audience. He spoke of the broad interests of the group and of the purposes of the PTA organization. Sanford challenged the group "to move out into a fuller realization of this broad area of responsibility that you have set for yourselves." Welfare of children was a primary concern of the PTA, and the Governor reminded those in attendance that they, as parents and teachers, were in a strategic position to accomplish this aim. Citing education as the only means of achieving a new day, the Governor called for the support of the PTA in the endeavor to raise the educational level of North Carolina. He specifically called for co-operation in three areas: the formation of a closer relationship between parents and teachers; aggressive promotion to secure for every child educational opportunity of high quality, including, of necessity, selectivity with regard to extracurricular activities and use of school time; and active political action to win approval by the legislators of laws and appropriations which would promote education. Governor Sanford elaborated on each point and again concluded with a call for co-operation and a pledge of his help.

SALUTE TO EAST CAROLINA COLLEGE

GREENVILLE

April 26, 1961

The Governor expressed pleasure at the opportunity of joining Pitt County and the state in this salute to East Carolina College. From an opening in 1909 to 106 students, the enrollment had grown to 4,599. The institution was approved by ten major accrediting associations, had a faculty of which half had doctoral degrees, and trained more teachers than any other college in North Carolina and was fifth in the nation in this regard. The Governor called the school "the artery of the educational bloodstream of eastern North Carolina." He recognized the indebtedness of the state to the administration, the trustees, and the faculty of former and present years. In urging students to pay the greatest salute possible to East Carolina College by remaining in North Carolina to live and work, he referred to the state as one "on the go!" He said the state had expressed faith in the students by supporting the college, and he had confidence that the students would prove their faith in the state by remaining in North Carolina.

BATH HIGH SCHOOL CHAPTER OF FUTURE FARMERS OF AMERICA

BATH

April 28, 1961

The occasion for this address was a father-son banquet, which Governor Sanford noted as particularly appropriate because of the close relationship between farm and home. He praised the Future Farmers program, saying that an enviable record of group activity and individual accomplishment had been set at Bath. He then discussed vocational agriculture and its role in North Carolina's new day. Pointing out the obvious need for production and prosperous agriculture in the state led to the comment that all FFA members studied subjects other than agriculture and all should be interested in education in general. The Governor proceeded to discuss the over-all program for quality education. As he had done on other occasions, the Governor stressed the need for fathers to support public education with taxes, for students to support it by hard work and study, and for students to remember that their education would not be completed with high school graduation. In concluding his address, Sanford told the audience that a bright future, through hard work, was ahead for North Carolinians in the new day.

SOUTHEASTERN NORTH CAROLINA INDUSTRIAL DEVELOPMENT CONFERENCE

CLINTON

May 3, 1961

The Governor, in his second industrial development conference address, again urged the people of the area to seek to realize the full potential which was awaiting them. He outlined resources of a good water supply, the deep-water ports, forests, rich soil, and excellent climate of the southeastern region, adding that these were the advantages to be used in attracting industry rather than tax gimmicks and tax rebates. Sanford also reminded his audience of the man-made resources, such as good roads. He urged the southeastern citizens to provide needed facilities so that big conventions could be held in the area; he also encouraged the establishment of additional food processing plants. North Carolina, once called the "Rip Van Winkle State" had been more recently called the "State on the Go"; this change was attributed to the attitude and hard work of citizens like those attending the Clinton conference.

DEDICATION ADDRESS AT WASHINGTON COUNTY UNION SCHOOL

ROPER

May 4, 1961

Speaking at the dedication of Washington County Union School, the Governor again sounded his keynote of education. After referring to the importance of this school to the economic future of Washington County and North Carolina, he referred to quality education as a prerequisite, as the foundation of the needs and hopes of the nation. He called education "life and growth and happiness." The Governor continued by explaining the program for education, its cost, and its need. He said that

North Carolina's rank of eighth in the number of school children was the state's greatest asset. "But we have cultivated our children's minds less well than we have cultivated our tobacco and cotton and peanut acres." This school was called proof that the state would pay for quality education, and the Governor concluded by calling on educators, teachers, and students to meet their respective responsibilities.

SIXTY-FIFTH ANNUAL CONVENTION
NORTH CAROLINA BANKERS ASSOCIATION

PINEHURST

May 9, 1961

The Governor began by praising bankers for their willingness to accept community responsibility. The promotion of economic growth in the state was advantageous to bankers and to all North Carolinians, and the Governor stressed the importance of the fact that a large number of people looked to those in the banking profession for "guidance and leadership, for advice and encouragement in many activities affecting, not just themselves, but their communities as well." He expressed the opinion that those living today would have to dedicate themselves to the obligations and opportunities of the day so that future generations would look back to this generation with pride and gratitude. While many parts of the nation were standing still or losing ground, North Carolina was moving ahead. With the future looking brighter for the nation as a whole, North Carolina stood in an excellent position to accelerate its economic development. Bankers as individual citizens and as leaders were faced with a big responsibility; Governor Sanford assured them that he knew they would measure up to this challenge as they had done to those of the past.

OHIO VALLEY INDUSTRIALISTS AND BUSINESSMEN

PITTSBURGH, COLUMBUS, DAYTON, INDIANAPOLIS, CINCINNATI

May 22-26, 1961

[Though Governor Sanford stressed quality education as his number-one interest, industrial growth was not neglected. Accompanied by thirty-five of the state's leading businessmen, who traveled at their own expense, the

Governor launched a five-day "good will" industrial promotional tour. He spoke at several major cities, advertising North Carolina's assets and denying allegations of piracy and gimmicks to attract industries to the state. Leaving Raleigh during the meeting of the General Assembly for a tour such as this was considered by some to be unorthodox, but the timing proved perfect. By June 6 Press Secretary Graham Jones issued a preliminary report showing that eighty-eight companies had expressed interest in the possibility of locating plants in North Carolina, with three firm commitments to locate in the state immediately. Excerpts from the Ohio Valley speeches are given here.]

North Carolina once was called, by one of its own historians, the "Rip Van Winkle State."

We're here to tell you that this Rip Van Winkle woke up.

Today North Carolina truly is the "State on the Go."

It is the "State on the Go" in industry, in commerce, in agriculture, and in education.

In the last decade, more than $1.5 billion was invested in new and expanded industrial plants in North Carolina.

In the first quarter of this year, our state broke all records in erecting new industry—more than $42 million worth.

During the recession of 1960, North Carolina's economy expanded. A recent United States Department of Commerce report pointed out: "Business in North Carolina generally held firm during 1960 despite reported recessive downtrends in the nation."

The truth of the matter is that during the recession year of 1960, North Carolina was compiling a new record of industrial growth. In 1960 we added more than $235 million in new and expanded manufacturing plants.

Now my administration and the citizens of North Carolina don't mean to slow down in our industrialization campaign. We mean to accelerate that industrial drive!

That's why we're here.

There is profit in North Carolina for new industry. North Carolina is the leading industrial state of the fastest growing new market in America, the Southeast.

We have not come here to beg handouts. We've come to talk business with the leaders of this great industrial area who have plans for expanding into new markets.

We have not come here to try to uproot or transplant established factories. We have come to get the seeds for industrial plantings for our fertile fields of North Carolina.

This North Carolina industrial mission is not an invasion. It is an invitation to businessmen interested in expanding their industries and increasing their profits.

This is not a raid. It is a good will mission.

We are not here to engage in plant piracy. We are here to

encourage industrial expansion. We haven't come to steal, we've come to sell—to sell North Carolina as a profitable site for expanding industries.

We're not offering gimmicks. We're offering reciprocal and mutually profitable interstate trade.

For more than a century, North Carolina has exported young people to this area. And for more than a century, we have imported your manufactured products. Now we're ready to trade our production and market opportunities for your branch plants.

I would like to list briefly some of the assets of North Carolina which have attracted new industry, both native and out-of-state, and some of the assets which have made these new industries profitable to their management and to their stockholders.

First, North Carolina has an abundance of rich land from the Coastal Plain of eastern North Carolina to the red clay of the Piedmont and the Blue Ridge and Smoky Mountains of western North Carolina.

North Carolina has a heaven-blessed water supply. Our precipitation is almost double the national average. We have an annual average rainfall of fifty inches and a practically untapped volume of ground water.

North Carolina has an excellent temperate climate which gives the farmer a long growing season and the industrialists a year-round manufacturing season.

North Carolina has one of the best moving transportation systems in the nation.

We have long been known as the "good roads state." This was true when George Washington and General Lafayette traveled over our roads in the eighteenth century. It also is true today when 99 per cent of North Carolina's population live either along paved roads or within a mile of a paved road. Recently, the United States Bureau of Roads issued a report showing that North Carolina ranks ninth among the states in the number of miles of the new interstate highway system open to traffic.

Complementing our highway system—which, incidentally is the largest in mileage maintained by any state government—are the tracks of twenty-eight railroads.

We have excellent passenger and freight service by airlines, and we're improving that service almost daily.

As far as port facilities for import and export trade are concerned we are this year approving a multimillion dollar expansion program at our deep-water ports. That expansion program is going to increase the shipping capacity of the state ports at Morehead City and Wilmington by 65 to 70 per cent.

All of these transportation facilities combine to give North Carolina manufacturers easy accessibility to national and international markets.

Now let's turn to government.

North Carolina's state government always has reflected the will of the people that it serves. Like the citizens of North Carolina, our state government has been not the last to cast the old aside, nor yet the first the new to accept. We have been in North Carolina neither radical nor reactionary. We have built steadily and we have built solidly.

Since the year of 1900, there has not been so much as a breath of scandal in North Carolina's state government. Without any self-praise, I can honestly report: "Good Government is a Habit in North Carolina."

Because of this stable and business-like operation of our state government, North Carolina's credit rating ranks at the very top—triple A—on Wall Street. Moody's lists our state bonds as among the safest buys in the nation.

Of course, North Carolina's government—state, county, and municipal—is simply a reflection of our state's greatest asset: the citizens of North Carolina.

We have enjoyed excellent labor relations in North Carolina. In 1960, North Carolina lost less than .005 per cent of total working time to strikes. In fact, strike-caused production and working time losses dropped to an all-time low in North Carolina in 1960.

We also have enjoyed in North Carolina harmonious race relations. Not a single school has been closed a single day in North Carolina since the Brown decision on school desegregation. I might add that when a Negro student earns the editorship of the *North Carolina Law Review*,[88] as he did recently, it makes more news in other states than it does in North Carolina. There is a mutual respect between the races—white, Negro, and Indian—in our state.

Another blue chip stock that North Carolina has to offer is our educational system, from the first grade through the graduate school. This year I have proposed, and the General Assembly is now considering, a major advance for our public schools. I proposed this program, and the General Assembly is considering it with favor, because we believe good educational opportunities are the first prerequisite to industrial, agricultural, and personal growth.

We believe you will be interested in this education program

---

[88] J. Le Vonne Chambers, editor of the *North Carolina Law Review,* 1961-1962 (Vol. 40).

of progress because it is that program that will train the executives and the employees for the plants you locate in North Carolina. Incidentally, to raise the revenue for that program, I have proposed elimination of sales tax exemptions. The one tax source that both the administration and the legislature ruled out from the beginning was any increase in income taxes—either corporate or personal.

A good example of the interdependence of industry and education in North Carolina is our new Research Triangle. That triangle, composed of Duke University at Durham, the University of North Carolina at Chapel Hill and North Carolina State College at Raleigh, is designed to utilize to the fullest possible extent for industry, commerce, and government the brain power of those three great institutions of higher learning.

The businessmen of North Carolina have contributed millions of dollars for the establishment of the Research Triangle Park on which are being built great new laboratories for science and technology.

These, then, are some of the assets of North Carolina.

These are the assets that attracted to North Carolina in recent years new plants of companies like DuPont, General Electric, Westinghouse, Western Electric, Douglas Aircraft, Ford Motors, Alcoa, Pittsburgh Plate Glass, Sperry Rand, Dayton Rubber, Firestone, and U. S. Rubber—to mention just a few.

These are some of the assets that have helped such companies grow in North Carolina and grow profitably.

North Carolina has not gone in for tax rebate gimmicks in the past and we have no intention whatsoever to dangle them in the future. We don't offer such gimmicks because they would be unfair to established industries and because we have learned by observation that the industry looking for such gimmicks makes a poor corporate citizen.

We are not seeking new industry just to add smokestacks to the skyline of North Carolina. We are seeking new industries to provide better opportunities for North Carolinians to make better livings.

North Carolina is advertising efficient and hard-working employees—not cheap labor.

North Carolina is selling its good climate—both industrial and weather—not a sweatshop atmosphere.

North Carolina is promoting an equitable corporate and individual tax rate—not tax gimmicks and rebates.

North Carolina is a good site on which to manufacture and a good market in which to sell.

Most important of all, North Carolina, with its historical,

cultural, and vacation varieties that extend from the Atlantic to the Smokies, is a good place to live.

There is profit in North Carolina. We invite you to come and share it with us.

GRADUATION EXERCISES, HIGH POINT COLLEGE

HIGH POINT

May 28, 1961

Speaking on the topic, "The Private College in the Pattern of Educational Opportunity," Governor Sanford told students that they were graduating from a time-honored institution. With 47 per cent of North Carolina students in institutions of higher learning attending church-related colleges, the role of these schools was of concern and interest to the state. The church schools served the dual purpose of promoting Christian education and filling a need as part of the total higher education effort. The Governor remarked that a partnership existed between private and public colleges, but the theory of separation of church and state was jealously guarded.

The magnitude of the operation of educational institutions of higher learning meant the necessity of examining the total picture, including curriculums, quality of instruction, and the role of liberal education. The Governor elaborated on each of these points, concluding that co-operative effort on the part of both public and private institutions was required. He explained to the graduates that they owed a debt to their schools and to the state, a debt which could be paid only by serving in positions of leadership and by helping find answers to the problems of the day.

WOMAN'S COLLEGE ALUMNAE OF WAKE COUNTY

RALEIGH

May 29, 1961

In addressing the alumnae of Woman's College, the Governor spoke on the total co-ordination of public education. With student population increasing, the best possible education would have to be made available at the lowest cost. He discussed three alternative decisions facing those in positions of planning for the state's education: to do nothing; to continue in the pattern the state was then following; to develop a planned pattern of educational opportunity from elementary school through the graduate school. The latter course, involving further development of community colleges and industrial education centers, was imperative to the state's future. Sanford spoke of the need for leadership which was not "saddled to the *status quo*." The consolidation of the University of North Carolina in the 1930's required vision and planning; results of that move had been applauded. The Governor said he wanted to urge groups such as this to contribute to the solution of problems facing education in North Carolina by study, criticism, and support.

PRESBYTERIAN JUNIOR COLLEGE COMMENCEMENT

MAXTON

June 5, 1961

More than 4,000 students, including the Governor himself, studied at Presbyterian Junior College between the time of its opening on September 4, 1929, and the time of the 1961 commencement exercises. Governor Sanford expressed the hope that the 1961 graduates would be stimulated to assume roles of leadership by the contributions of former students and the ideals of higher education learned at the school. He noted plans for the opening of St. Andrews College, observing that the new college showed the strong faith of the Presbyterians in higher education. He praised expansion being made by many denominations, pointing out the need of support for church-related colleges. Stressing the importance of education, Sanford said, "Quality education is the vitamin for personal growth and economic growth." In his closing remarks, the Governor said he "did not come to preach a eulogy for Presbyterian Junior College," but "to take part in the baptism of a larger education endeavor." He expressed belief that the spirit of the old would thrive as an integral part of the new St. Andrews College.

WESTERN NORTH CAROLINA INDUSTRIAL DEVELOPMENT CONFERENCE
(Delivered by Hargrove Bowles, Jr.)

WAYNESVILLE

June 6, 1961

The recreational potential of western North Carolina would

have to be complemented with industry, the Governor told the Western North Carolina Industrial Development Conference, and he pledged the co-operation of state agencies. Industry would have to be offered technical services, repair services, and stability in community and area growth. Sanford said that businessmen investigating the suitability and potentials of a city would consider whether or not the community had measured its future needs and had realistically planned and budgeted for those needs. A city needed to know which sites were available for industry and should require appropriate zoning. Development of resources, however, included development of human resources. In this area lay the importance of industrial education centers. The Governor spoke of the importance of the Western North Carolina Regional Planning Commission, established in 1957, in helping answer questions about sound growth for the future. A plan of action for the full development of the area would demand local initiative and hard work, co-ordinated with local and regional programs.

NORTH CAROLINA ASSOCIATION OF BROADCASTERS

DURHAM

June 8, 1961

[In his address to the broadcasters of North Carolina, the Governor reviewed the action of the 1961 General Assembly. He dubbed this legislature one "with a conscience," and he gave a sympathetic appraisal on most points. He singled out for praise the educational program adopted by the session. The address was carried "live" to the citizens of North Carolina.]

I appreciate the opportunity of meeting with the radio and television leaders of North Carolina.

I especially appreciate the "live" coverage of these remarks on the state-wide networks you have set up.

As those of you here in this room know, I was one of your frequent customers last year. The only difference is that last year you made me pay every time I went on the air.

Now to demonstrate my appreciation for this free time you've given me today, let me assure all the stations on this network that I will quit in plenty of time for the commercial.

I am grateful for the opportunity not only to speak to the radio and television broadcasters but also to address the citizens all across North Carolina. I have said on several occasions that as Governor of a state with four and a half million citizens, who live from the Atlantic to the Smokies, there is only one way I know to speak directly to the entire citizenry at one time, and that is through the radio and television networks of the state.

Since my inauguration six months ago this week, I have had several occasions to request the radio and television stations to clear time so that I might report directly to the people on matters of importance to the state.

I am happy to say, the radio and television stations have never let us down.

This co-operation is typical, I believe, of the strong public service spirit that prevails in the broadcasting industry of North Carolina. Recently, my desk has been flooded with letters from stations agreeing to carry—without any charge to the taxpayers— "spots" advertising North Carolina as a "Variety Vacationland" and as a good place for new industry to earn profits.

But broadcasting is more than just a "fair weather" friend.

I would like to remind the listeners of this broadcast that every time they hear the buzz of a Conelrad test on their radios, they are hearing another example of the support the broadcasting industry of North Carolina is rendering our national preparedness program.

The television and radio stations have given generously of their time and their money in alerting the citizens of our state of impending natural disasters. The hurricanes we have suffered in recent years in North Carolina cost the state many millions of dollars in property damage. But imagine, if you can, the lives that were NOT lost because the population had the advance warning from the "hurricane watch" broadcast by TV and radio stations.

I want to express particular praise for the television stations that have participated in the "in-school" teaching programs and those which have helped teach adults how to read and write. This is a vital program in a state where the adult illiteracy rate is almost the worst in the nation.

On behalf of the people of North Carolina, I thank the radio and television stations of North Carolina for their public service programs.

It has been suggested that I use this occasion to give the people of North Carolina a report on their 1961 General Assembly, which, at this very moment, is working in Raleigh to build a stronger North Carolina with greater opportunities for all the citizens. I welcome the opportunity.

I understand, from a radio news report I heard en route to Durham, that the General Assembly is expected to begin voting within the hour on the most important single piece of legislation that has come before a North Carolina General Assembly since the days of Governor Charles Brantley Aycock.

That legislation, of course, is the educational program.

I would not be so presumptuous as to predict the exact vote on either the appropriations bill or the revenue bill. But I will tell you this: If I were not absolutely confident that majorities in both the Senate and the House share with me a strong determination that our sons and daughters shall receive educational opportunities equal to the best and second to none, I would not be addressing you today.

Last year I broadcast from Wilmington to Asheville the fact that if the citizens of North Carolina elected me their governor, quality education would be the overriding goal of my administration. I have tried not to backtrack a single step and not to deviate a single degree from that goal.

On occasion in the past six months, some have suggested that I might twist some legislative arms on the many issues before the General Assembly.

I have chosen not to twist any arms. I made that choice because I have complete confidence in the vision, judgment, and integrity of the General Assembly.

North Carolina has moved into the mainstream of America.

I am happy to acknowledge that this move has been made possible by the strong oarsmanship of the members of the 1961 General Assembly.

The education program is en route to passage. Its adoption is going to mean a stronger state—a state stronger in industry, stronger in commerce, stronger in agriculture. For the children of our state, this quality education program is going to mean richer minds—as well as richer pocketbooks.

There are those who have agreed with us that we needed to appropriate substantially greater sums to teach the children. But they kick up their heels in horror over the taxes needed to pay for quality education if we had not adopted this program.

Let me very briefly summarize my feelings on the new school taxes. It would have been nice to get the money for better educational opportunities from taxes on luxuries like mink coats.

But there just aren't enough mink coats sold in North Carolina to raise the revenue the state must have if it is to adopt the quality education program.

No one is going to go hungry because of the tax on food items not presently taxed.

But the children of North Carolina would have gone thirsty for quality education if we had not adopted this program.

I am happy to report to the citizens of North Carolina that a majority of their legislators have the courage to stand up and be

counted—not only for appropriating the funds for quality education but also to pay the cost of that program by voting for the
revenue—a revenue vote without which the appropriation vote
would be meaningless.

Now some honest and conscientious persons have objected to
the tax on food on the grounds that there are undernourished
people in North Carolina.

There are undernourished people in North Carolina—entirely
too many.

It would be a pittance, and a fraud to claim we would be
alleviating their poverty by allowing them to retain the few
pennies involved in the new school taxes. To do this would not
help them, but it would damage seriously the opportunities of
their children, and all children, for a better education and a
better living.

We have a better solution to help the poor. The administration,
working closely with the General Assembly, has moved quickly
and definitely to do something about empty stomachs. We have
brought North Carolina for the first time into active participation
in the surplus food program. A number of counties already have
joined in this program. And, I am reliably informed, many more
counties will join soon after the start of their new fiscal year next
month.

The General Assembly has tentatively approved substantial
increases in the appropriations for welfare funds.

The record of the 1961 General Assembly on the entire matter
of helping the needy of our state has been the best of any legislature in a long time. This General Assembly has tentatively adopted
appropriations that will provide for increased benefits for the
hungry, the indigent old, the crippled, and the dependent children of North Carolina.

On another highly important measure, the 1961 General
Assembly overwhelmingly adopted an amendment to the State
Minimum Wage Act that raised the wages of 19,000 North
Carolina workers.

The General Assembly is still working on measures to improve
the unhappy lot of migratory farm workers—to assure safe transportation and decent sanitary conditions for those workers.

We are beginning to open up the dead-end roads. The lot and
future of these people are major concerns of mine.

The General Assembly is still working on bills to abolish the
abuses of loan sharks who have given the lending business a bad
name. I expect a good bill will be passed.

Yes, the 1961 General Assembly has been a legislature with a
conscience.

Now let me speak for a minute on that most difficult of legislative problems: reapportionment and redistricting.

On this perennial problem I would point out that the 1961 General Assembly has made more progress than has been made since 1941.

The General Assembly did reapportion the House of Representatives.

The General Assembly did adopt an automatic reapportionment act that I hope may set the pattern for speedy and equitable reapportionment in future sessions.

It is true that the General Assembly has not found an agreeable way to redistrict the seats of the State Senate. On the matter of congressional redistricting, the General Assembly is now moving toward enactment of a bill.

Some people are unhappy with that bill. Of course, there is no way the General Assembly could possibly eliminate one congressional district—as it must under the 1960 census—and make everyone happy.

I will say this with all the force at my command: Anyone who says the Senate-approved bill is unfair to the minority party must have overlooked the fact that the county in which the minority party has its greatest membership and the home county of the minority party congressman would be included in the new district. Gerrymandering is done by the Republican-controlled legislatures in other states, and the proposed map has less of the gerrymander than the present districts in North Carolina.

I can tell you the Democratic legislature of North Carolina is a lot more considerate of the minority party than the Republican legislatures are of Democratic congressional districts north of here.

The 1961 General Assembly adopted, and sent to the people for approval in a state-wide constitutional vote, one of the best court improvement programs of any state at any time.

The bill that was adopted was not all that its sponsors hoped for. On the other hand, it went further than some of its opponents would have liked. But this General Assembly worked in the best tradition of democratic government and both sides deserve great credit for the resulting bill which is a good bill and a vast improvement.

If the people of the state approve the proposed amendment to the Constitution, and I believe they will, our administration of justice in North Carolina would be more expeditious, more nearly exact, and more equitable.

On highway safety legislation, the 1961 General Assembly made some marked advancements.

The Assembly extended the compulsory automobile liability

insurance act to protect the citizens of the state against un-
insured drivers.

The Assembly improved substantially the point system to slow
down habitual traffic violators.

The Assembly also increased the penalties for prearranged
racing. Other safety measures are awaiting action.

On reorganization of state government, the General Assembly
has adopted major administration proposals including enlarging
the membership of the State Highway Commission and bringing
it closer to the people. The Assembly also reorganized the Board
of Conservation and Development to assure that proper attention
will be given to all aspects of the conservation and development
program.

Road building is always a question of prime importance to the
citizens of North Carolina. It is especially important to those who
still live on muddy roads.

On the recommendation of the administration, this General
Assembly has established a major policy that will mean more
roads in both the secondary and primary systems.

That is the policy of halting the diversion of highway tax
money to non-highway uses.

The General Assembly is in the process of relieving the Highway Fund of the cost of the Prison System and the cost of the
boards of Paroles and Probation. The Assembly also has tentatively approved the bill to let the Highway Commission use
interest on Highway Fund money to build roads.

Under these three important and excellent measures, funds
have been made available to build roads that would not have
been available under the old system of diverting highway funds.

This is especially important when we consider that highway
revenues have not been keeping pace with General Fund increases.

In brief, under the three measures to halt diversion of Highway
Fund money, more rural roads will be built during the next two
years than could have been built under the old system.

Now I could talk for hours about other significant achievements
of the 1961 General Assembly.

But I'm not sure you would give me that much free time on
the radio and television stations.

Let me simply sum up my personal appraisal of the 1961
General Assembly this way:

I have neither seen in my lifetime nor read in my histories of
any General Assembly of the twentieth century that has rendered
greater service to the people of North Carolina.

I will always be proud to have served as the Governor who
worked with the General Assembly of North Carolina of 1961.

YOUTH FITNESS COMMISSION

RALEIGH

June 10, 1961

[About 200 people attended this conference, including more than 180 teen-agers representing 91 counties of North Carolina. After the address, in which he called for a rededication of youth fitness in mental and spiritual realms, as well as in the physical sense, Governor Sanford presented awards to a boy and girl selected for their outstanding fitness.]

I appreciate the honor of meeting with you and of discussing with you briefly our plans and our efforts to make North Carolina physically, as well as fiscally, mentally, and spiritually stronger.

On behalf of all the citizens of our state, I want to thank each of you for your unselfish and unpaid service to the state in this vital field of physical fitness.

It has become a trite, but true, commentary on our times that we parents of today hurry to drive our children to school so that they won't be late for their physical education classes.

Youth fitness plays an important role in the current cold war just as it did in the world wars and the Korean conflict. We all pray that this cold war will never boil over into a hot war. But we must be prepared collectively as a nation and individually as citizens if it should.

The physical and mental fitness of the young people of the nation is as great a deterrent to communism as the launching pads at Canaveral.

Those Americans who enjoy amateur sports have been dismayed in recent Olympic games to have the regimented Soviet teams outscore us repeatedly. Year after year in the last decade, the Australian tennis teams defeated the American teams in the Davis Cup play-offs.

Now, I am not so concerned by the Soviets outscoring us in the Olympics or the Australians winning the Davis Cup as I am of the fact that these losses may well reflect a general softening of the traditional American physical vigor.

Today, as never before, our way of life is being besieged from every corner. There is not only the communist threat, but also the many domestic obstacles that seem to multiply daily.

These challenges must be met, grappled with, and conquered. They are like hurdles in a race which must be vaulted to reach the finish line.

I have spent the greater part of the last two years talking about and working for quality education for all the sons and daughters of North Carolina. I have been speaking of quality education in the broadest sense of those words: from the first grade through the graduate school, and from physical education to physics.

I think it appropriate that a conference such as this one should consider this quality education program. Because, I know, when you speak of youth fitness you are not restricting yourselves to a kind of vegetable care and growth for our children. If you were interested in the physical side of fitness only, you probably would be forced to the conclusion that the children of our state should spend all their time on the gym floors or at the beaches.

What you're interested in and what I am interested in is the fullest possible development of every boy and girl of this state. That includes proper attention to physical education, and that includes proper attention to the mental, social, and spiritual education of every child.

In balancing the time allotments for each of these aspects of growth, I want it clearly understood that I am not advocating taking more time from the textbooks for interscholastic or intercollegiate sports. On the contrary! I believe we have cheated too many students by permitting too many midweek out-of-town games in the public schools.

It is just possible that the recent basketball scandals were blessings in disguise, for they made us re-examine our whole intercollegiate and interscholastic programs.

There has been too much "spectating" and not enough participating by the vast majority of our high school and college students in this field of sports.

On many occasions, I have pointed out that we must not rob the classroom time for extracurricular activities. If we are to build quality education programs that will develop the whole personality of the child, we must give the teacher time to teach.

I believe the time has come to re-examine out-of-town games in the middle of the school week. Studies must take first priority if our state is to develop youth fitness in the true sense.

There is a strong interdependence between the intellect, the morality, and the physique of the child.

We must not permit intellectual and mental stagnation. We must not tolerate moral decay. And we must not condone physical dissipation.

These three elements are inseparable. They are like the mathematical equation: A equals B; B equals C; therefore, A equals C. They represent the three corners of the equilateral triangle which is the same regardless of which side is used as the base.

Intellectual brilliance can only be utilized when it is bound together by fibers of moral strength and propelled by physical vigor.

Moral depth comes only from knowledge that gives us appreciation of the rights of others and an intellectual and physical stamina that allows us to stand up in the face of adversity,

None of these component parts of the total personality is achieved easily. We cannot attain intellectual brilliance, moral depth, or physical stamina just by wishing. It takes diligence and practice—every day and every month and every year.

As I have said, physical fitness is an integral part of the development of the child—and of the program for letting every boy and every girl of North Carolina burgeon out the best that is within him.

Recently, I had occcasion to speak to automobile liability insurance company executives in New York City. We were discussing highway safety for North Carolina. I told those insurance executives that one way to help solve the traffic problem would be for all of us to walk to work. I have tried to practice, whenever my schedule permits, that preaching by walking to the Capitol.

Besides cutting down on wrecks and frayed nerves of rush-hour driving at the start of every day, such a practice would also cut down the bulging waistlines of North Carolina.

North Carolina's rate of rejections by Selective Service has been entirely too great. Many of those rejected were turned down because of illiteracy. With our quality education program, North Carolina is going to solve that problem.

I am counting on groups like this to help us solve the problem of persons rejected for physical reasons. Because as well as the large number rejected for illiteracy, there also was an unusually large number of persons in our state rejected for physical reasons.

Now I realize no physical fitness program can make the blind see or the deaf hear. But we can certainly trim down the incidence of heart disease due to overweight, and we can certainly curtail other preventable physical deficiencies.

If North Carolina is to swim in the mainstream of American life, every man, woman, and child must recognize the need for individual strength—mental strength, moral strength, and physical strength.

I shall look forward to working with you to build a stronger North Carolina by building stronger North Carolinians.

ANNUAL CONFERENCE
TEACHERS OF VOCATIONAL AGRICULTURE
Greensboro
July 13, 1961

Governor Sanford told the vocational agriculture teachers that they occupied key positions, but they would have to realize the importance of inevitable change. He said it was man's nature to go forward, though change might create hardship and problems. He proceeded to discuss his program for improvements in the educational system of the state, including a review of legislation adopted by the 1961 General Assembly. He explained that intelligent action and a real spirit of enthusiasm would be needed on the part of farming interests. Sanford expressed the opinion that the teachers at this meeting had accepted the responsibility facing them, that the attitude of the group was one of confidence, and that confidence was a force which would overcome any obstacle, achieve any goal.

DEDICATION OF
FEDERAL HOUSING ADMINISTRATION OFFICE
Greensboro
July 13, 1961

The dedication of the Federal Housing Administration's new office marked the twenty-sixth year of business headquarters in Greensboro and afforded Governor Sanford another opportunity to praise the co-operative partnership between government and free enterprise. An organization synonymous with sound fiscal policies, intelligent planning, efficient management, and constructive policies, the FHA had helped house America since 1934, with no cost to taxpayers. Governor Sanford attributed the enactment of the Housing Act of 1961 partially to the success of the FHA program. The new act would help government and private citizens "to get on with the job of *razing* the slums and of *raising* new homes. . . ." The Governor pointed out the benefits to be derived by North Carolina citizens—the poorer group, the elderly, and the students—from the legislation. He pledged the support of his administration to work with the FHA and private enterprise in taking full advantage of the provisions of the new act. He concluded with the statement that good housing helped "make a stronger neighborhood, a stronger community, a stronger state and a stronger nation."

DEDICATION OF BENSON NATIONAL GUARD ARMORY

BENSON

July 16, 1961

[Governor Sanford, participating in the dedication of a new National Guard Armory at Benson, spoke meaningfully of America's desire for peace but willingness to fight to preserve freedom. He reiterated his belief in the desires and goals of Americans to foster both peace and freedom throughout the world in this talk and in a number of other speeches delivered during his administration.]

I appreciate the honor you have extended to me in inviting me to participate in the dedication of this new National Guard Armory. This armory will serve as an integral part in the Table of Organization and Equipment of our national defense effort. And the men who train in this armory will march as part of the American army of freedom. The men who will train here will be primarily citizen-soldiers. They will be the kind of citizen-soldiers who answered that first call to rally around the flag of freedom at Bunker Hill. They will march in the footsteps of the citizen-soldiers who fought and won under Andy Jackson at New Orleans a century and a half ago. They will also march in the footsteps of the citizen-soldiers who answered Woodrow Wilson's call and fought under "Black Jack" Pershing "to make the world safe for democracy."

I know the men who train here will be faithful to our heritage of freedom just as their older brothers were faithful to that heritage in Bataan, at Bastogne, at Guadalcanal and Iwo Jima.

Our nation has never had a Junker military caste like Bismarck and the Kaiser and Hitler had to call on. And as long as Americans are willing to leave their civilian jobs to defend freedom, we never will! Americans do not march just to hear hobnail boots striking the ground. We are a nation that would rather hear the beat of rock'n'roll than the beat of Wagner's militaristic music.

The order of the day in America is peace—not war. The uniform of the day is the overall of the farmer or the Ivy League suit of the salesman or the dungarees of the factory worker—not battle dress of militarists. Our chow lines are at a civilian hot dog stand or a Dairy Queen—not at military messes. But let no dictator misinterpret this traditional love of peaceful pursuit. Civilian-soldiers have proved since 1776 that they will fight if fight they must!

The dictators in the Kremlin and the dictators in Peiping should take a long hard look at the history of America before they start anything. The American eating peanuts at the ball park will sacrifice that bag of peanuts for a can of C-rations if he must. And the American civilian will exchange his golfing putter for an M-1 if it is necessary to do so to safeguard freedom here and elsewhere.

This armory that we are dedicating here today is symbolic of the fact that while Americans prefer peaceful pursuit, they are willing to take up arms to protect their right, and the right of their families, to freedom. In short, we are willing to work for peace, but we are also willing to fight for freedom.

President Kennedy has demonstrated to the Soviets and to the world that America does not fear to negotiate. But he also has said, and he has shown, that we will never negotiate out of fear.

President Kennedy is willing to go to Vienna—to negotiate.

But Jack Kennedy will never go to Munich—to appease.

If Nikita Khrushchev is as smart a man as he is supposed to be, he must know that a man like Jack Kennedy who fought to defend this nation against Tito and Hitler will also fight to defend the free world against imperialistic communism.

All Americans who sweated in the jungles of the Pacific and shivered in the mud of Italy and froze in the snows around Bastogne pray in their hearts that we will never again have to sweat and freeze and bleed and die just to prove to a dictator that we are willing to do so to preserve democracy.

We pray that the Communists, who profess to base their beliefs on historical dialectics, will read in their histories the unmistakable lesson that has been written in blood: the lesson that Americans will fight though they prefer peace; the lesson that Americans will negotiate, but will never surrender; the lesson that the assembly lines which turn out the consumer goods which we enjoy also can turn out tanks and planes and rockets.

It is because dictators sometimes misinterpret the American mood that we need armories like this one. It is because dictators sometimes overlook the hard lesson of history that it is necessary for civilian-soldiers to learn to handle weapons in this armory.

I was happy to see the report issued recently by North Carolina's Adjutant General, Claude Bowers. General Bowers appraised the state of readiness of the North Carolina National Guard as the best in his memory. And as you old soldiers and you veterans know, General Bowers' memory of the Guard goes back to World War I. It is reassuring to have a man like General

Bowers leading the civilian-soldiers of North Carolina. It is reassuring to have men like Colonel Ivan Hardesty[89] and their fellow officers here at Benson and across the state in command of our civilian-army corps in North Carolina. It also is reassuring to have the excellent cadre of noncommissioned officers that the North Carolina National Guard has.

And as a man who served his time as a private, I will say to the beginners in the Guard: An army couldn't exist without you —for as you know, the buck stops with you, and you do most of the work.

The civilian-soldiers of North Carolina and the civilian-soldiers of the other forty-nine states are ready to mobilize—if mobilization is ordered by the President.

General Bowers has noted that the civilian-soldier "has always fought well" and that the strength of the civilian-soldier is in being able to make do with what he has.

Marching alongside of the RA's in a half dozen wars, the civilian-soldiers of North Carolina have never failed in their mission, their mission to defend freedom.

We have, in recent days, reached one of those crises in history when the fate of the free world hangs in the balance. At this very hour, the fate of Berlin hangs precariously. And the fate of Berlin is just as important to all the free world in the summer of 1961 as was the fate of the Polish Corridor in the summer of 1939.

I wish Nikita Khrushchev could have been here today and seen the demonstration of America's willingness to fight if he forces us into a fight. I would hope that *Pravda* and *Isvestia* and *Red Star*, the main newspapers of the Soviet Union, might mention this dedication somewhere in their news columns tomorrow morning. For this dedication is a striking example that America is ready to answer the call of President Kennedy if that call to arms is forthcoming.

We are prepared and we will fight to save Berlin and to safeguard the free world.

I, therefore, am happy to dedicate this building as a citadel to the defense of the liberties of America—and to the defense of liberty throughout the world.

---

[89] Ivan Hardesty, Assistant Chief Engineer of Highway Department from Raleigh, career National Guardsman since 1926; promoted from colonel to brigadier general, May, 1962. Governor Sanford's news release of May 29, 1962.

SOUTH CAROLINA EDUCATION WEEK CONFERENCE

COLUMBIA, SOUTH CAROLINA

July 18, 1961

[An early morning flight enabled Governor Sanford to leave Raleigh and arrive in Columbia in time to address the South Carolina Education Week Conference. The conference was made up of representatives of the School of Education of the University of South Carolina, the South Carolina Association of School Administrators, the South Carolina Association of School Boards, and the Congress of Parents and Teachers. He urged the South to move forward in the field of education and was critical of areas in which the region was backward. His address was not, however, without the characteristic Sanford optimism.]

The South is rising again! It is not rising again through secession from the union, nor through insurrection, nor through nullification. It is rising again through education, through industry, through commerce, and through agriculture.

It is rising through the exercise of its long-neglected literary talents, through its research in the scholarly fields and in the applied sciences. It is rising to heights that will make the great accomplishments of the "Old South" pale by comparison.

The South is moving again into the mainstream of American life.

Now that it is moving, the South deserves a chance to work out its future without free advice from people who neglect their own problems in order to give ill-informed attention to ours. It is doubtful that we will have it. The issues are too alive, too complex, too pressing, and too emotional.

The South has been on the defensive too long. The defensive position is not conducive to positive thought and action. But positive thought and action are what we must have today in the South and in the nation. We must and we intend to move out of the defensive. If there is to be a New South, it must have a new policy—a policy consistent with the national conscience, to be sure, but a policy which also will preserve that which is best of the South's distinctive culture and enable it to realize its highest potential for good. We can move from the defensive to national leadership, and this we must do because the very future of the nation depends on what we are able to accomplish.

What should the new southern policy be? To the extent that education is basic to the achievement of our national goals, and nothing is more basic to it, education must be the foundation of progress in the South. The issue must not be whether there will be education. The issue must be whether the education that is available is appropriate, of excellent quality, and adequately supported.

North Carolina has settled the question. It does not intend to turn back. We have faced the bleak alternatives to better schools, and we have chosen to expand and improve our schools.

The clarion call for better schools has replaced the rebel yell as the voice of the South, and it deserves the attention of a national audience which usually is only too willing to hear the opposite. Education across the nation is crying for direction and leadership. Well, let's lead.

North Carolina is on the move as is South Carolina and, indeed, the entire South. It is backing up its promises with money in unprecedented amounts.

The General Assembly of North Carolina recently appropriated over $100 million in enrichment funds for public education.

The General Assembly of North Carolina has met the challenge of the times by that action. The South Carolina legislature, I am told, also has moved to meet that challenge. We cannot do the job that needs doing in education without money provided by those legislatures.

But money, whether it is provided by the city council, the legislature, or the Congress, cannot do the job alone.

As James Bryant Conant put it: "The road to better schools will be paved by the collective action of the local citizenry. The responsibility for the sorely needed upgrading of our schools cannot be passed to the state legislatures or to Congress. The responsibility rests on every citizen in the land."

But though the support must come from the people and their elected representatives, the educating must come from the teachers. You educators must not fail, for all else depends on you as we seek our regional and national goals.

I would hope that those in education, self-assured in their own competency, would leave their minds wide open for all criticism and new ideas. Those who are motivated to sharp criticism of existing institutions from their own sincere concern make a valuable contribution to the advancement of our society.

Now is the time for fresh approaches, bold action, tearing away from any tinge of self-satisfaction, an appreciative willingness to give all thoughts and suggestions a fair audience.

I have noted in some of my friends and associates in the field of education, a group in which I count myself to be a member, a tendency to be oversensitive. Criticism of the school system too often evokes criticism of the person making the criticism.

I welcome all ideas, thoughts, suggestions, criticism—even harsh and blunt criticism. I do not pretend to take all advice, but I do try to listen and weigh and profit by all advice which comes my way.

A case in point is Admiral Hyman C. Rickover. Here a distinguished scientist, a patriot of the highest order, a man moved by an overriding concern for the future of democracy is suspected of being against the school system because he is harsh in his criticism. I will admit that I suspect he occasionally deliberately overstates his case, takes an unusually blunt stance, slaps harder than is needed, in order to shock us to attention. This is his method, but not his purpose, and we might in candor concede that his method is justified by our laxness in many areas.

I say those of us charged with the future of education in a democracy can take criticism and that we will expect and welcome it. In this way we will profit, and democracy will profit and survive.

I would not follow all the suggestions of Admiral Rickover, and perhaps not any of them exactly, but I use him as an example because the reaction to his prodding has been extreme.

For example, consider these statements of Rickover:

We are now confronted with clear-cut evidence that in the all-important field of education our true competitive position against other certain advanced nations is unsatisfactory. The wall behind which we have been nursing the illusion that "our schools are the best in the world" is being rudely pulled down and we must face up to the truth, remedy our educational errors and do a great deal better by our children.

There is no answer in this statement, but there is much truth, and we will do well to look back over our shoulders to see indeed that our adversaries are gaining on us.

Continuing to quote:

The enormous wealth [of America has been] a mighty prop to self-esteem. . . . Thus protected against the harsh facts of life, it is easy to imagine oneself superior, not just in wealth but in other things as well. This is a pleasant illusion, but it may have consequences not even the richest can afford.

Here, perhaps, is a key to the reason the youth is in a better position to move into national leadership. We have had less reason to become haughty and vain, and we know we have a job to do in building our opportunities.

And again:

. . . not even so rich a people as we can *afford* underpaid and undereducated teachers, absence of academic standards, and a philosophy of fun and games at school. . . .

Now don't jump at conclusions by saying to yourself we can't have inflexible national standards. Maybe we can't, but put your mind to working on how we can have academic standards which afford goals and measure achievement. That is the way to put blunt criticism to work running in your favor.

And don't get miffed when I quote "fun and games" by thinking, "well, we certainly don't have that in our schools." Maybe you don't, but too many do, and we are all too lax in too many ways.

I am saying to educators let's be our own harshest critics. Let's seek out our shortcomings, look for ways of improvement, and get on with the job.

Take the four things I have just mentioned: underpaid teachers, undereducated teachers, absence of academic standards, "fun and games."

Teachers are underpaid. I am responsible for that, and all citizens are responsible. I said across my state that this was problem number one. The people agreed, the General Assembly agreed, and we are moving to higher pay.

Many people have asked: "How will paying a teacher more convert her into a better teacher than she was last year?" The answer is twofold. We have to start paying more before we start attracting an adequate number of qualified people. This is no chicken or egg dilemma. Higher pay must come first.

The other answer is immediate. Higher pay demonstrates that we have confidence in our teachers, that we understand the priority of education, and that we believe in upgrading its importance. This leads to improved morale and a terrific challenge, and every teacher worth his salt immediately starts trying to do a better job.

When I speak of undereducated teachers, I am not restricting myself to the teachers in the classrooms who hold something less than "A" certificates. I am speaking also of those teachers who have taken an overdose of courses of *how* to teach and who have had far too few courses of *what* to teach.

It is time that our schools of education bring the courses on subject matter into balance with the courses on teaching methods.

I think there would be no argument from this audience if I observe that in the field of academic standards an "A" on arithmetic in one school, or in one county, does not equal an "A" on the same subject in another school or in another county. The results of entrance examinations for college freshmen prove the inequality of academic standards of various schools and various counties and various states.

We might sum up the problem of the overemphasis on "fun and games" this way: It is true that all work and no play makes Johnnie a dull boy. But all play and no work at school will make

Johnnie an ignorant boy. And it will make him a poor boy when
he goes out into the world to compete for a job.

Carolinians have always understood that education is the means
by which our states must reach their full potential growth in both
economic and human values. At the turn of the century, Walter
Hines Page made the following statement of faith:

> I believe in the free public training of both the hands and the mind of
> every child born of woman.
> I believe that by the right training of men we add to the wealth of the
> world. All wealth is the creation of man, and he creates it only in proportion
> to the trained uses of the community; and, the more men we train, the more
> wealth everyone may create.
> I believe in the perpetual regeneration of society, in the immortality of
> democracy, and in growth everlasting.[90]

We have had our successes and we have made progress and
we have a remarkable record considering that we suffered many
years of struggle against the oppressive tactics of vindictive victors
as an aftermath of the Civil War. But whatever our successes, it
is not enough for the rapidly advancing scientific, changing world
we now enter.

The job is not finished. What we have really done is to
create new and unlimited opportunities.

The late Dr. Howard Odum of the University of North Carolina, and a native of Georgia, showed clearly that the South need
not continue to be known as the "nation's economic problem
number one." While we do not have everything, he pointed out,
we do have in abundance those resources that really matter—
soil, water, climate, rainfall, and people—most of all we have a
stock of sturdy and able people. We only need to develop fully
this human resource. That again justifies our reliance on education as the path to all other objectives.

Quality education is no mean goal! For all other goals we
seek for the South can be measured by the quality, the scope, the
reach of our educational efforts.

Education is the foundation of economic improvement. We in
the South are concerned, vitally, with industrial development,
farm income, the economic growth, the chance of all to make a
better living; and because of this we must give top priority to
education.

Education is the foundation of democracy. We are concerned
with defending the principles of freedom, of individual liberties,
of free enterprise, of equality and dignity of man; and therefore,
we seek the fulfillment of these principles through quality education we offer our boys and girls.

---

[90] Page, *Rebuilding of Old Commonwealths*, 102.

Education is the foundation of the needs and hopes of the nation. We are concerned with our part in the world, and we are concerned with the peace of the world, and therefore, we must adequately educate the scientists, the statesmen, and the citizenry who will fully understand and are equipped to defend and promote the ideals of our dynamic democracy of the twentieth century.

Education, put in the bleakest terms, is survival. Here in our own small part of the free world, we can do no less than seek the best as we prepare to do our part to defend America and the free world.

And education, put in its brightest terms, is life and growth, and happiness. We are not here merely to make a living. We are talking about the fundamental when we are talking about education, and our goal is worthy of the best we have in mind, and heart, and spirit.

The training the teachers are giving in the classrooms is ultimately going to be more important than the training being given on the parade fields of Fort Jackson and Fort Bragg—and I am not minimizing the importance of the army posts.

How well the students perform is going to have a greater effect on history than how well a missile performs at Cape Canaveral.

The South must improve its schools if it expects to improve its economy.

Yet despite this, we have for too long in the South expected our teachers to work for apples and yearbook dedications.

North and South Carolina are properly concerned when anyone attempts to cut our tobacco parity below 90 per cent. Yet we have been giving our sons and daughters something less than 66 per cent of the national educational parity.

The South, like the rest of the nation, needs to take a long, hard look at itself to see where it stands now, and to see where it hopes to stand and where it will stand twenty years from now.

.   .   .   .

Our public school system is southern, and we have no desire to make it northern or anything other than southern. But that does not require us to be provincial in our efforts to prepare our children to take part in life. We have been forced, by the sheer impact of the change taking place in this modern day America, to place our children in competition with children from every section of the country.

The present day businessman cannot rely on competition solely from his own county or even his own state. Products from all over America, and indeed all over the world, flow in daily to compete against the products he is selling here in this state. If he is a manufacturer, he can rest assured that a new industry from outside the South will soon come in, and he will have to meet the new demands for labor and other resources.

If the child is setting out to become a lawyer, he can no longer plan to make a living on criminal cases and a few civil actions in the JP courts. He may be practicing in what we think of as a one-horse town, but he still must match wits with bonding attorneys from Wall Street, tax attorneys trained by the federal government, and corporation lawyers sent out by General Motors and Standard Oil. The attorney today competes with these experts, and beats them from time to time, or he must give up any hope of a successful career.

Even to get into a medical school today, a student must match his wits against those who come from all over the country to get the relatively few openings in our crowded medical schools. In practice, the doctor must make use of the most complex medicines and methods of modern science.

In all of these areas, the child from the South can no longer think in terms of how good he is in his own community; he must be competent to equal those all across the nation. We may still revel in the stories of the Old South, but when it comes down to the hard, everyday problem of making a living, there just aren't many of us picking cotton anymore. And the public school system which is geared to those times will do our children the greatest disservice in preparing them for a race they can never win, a life they can never live to its fullest.

The South, like the rest of the nation, needs to ask itself again the questions which Edwin Markham angrily asked:

> Is this the thing the Lord God made and gave
> To have dominion over sea and land. . . ?
> How will you ever straighten up this shape;
> Touch it again with immortality:
> Give back the upward looking and the light;
> Rebuild in it the music and the dream? [91]

Through education! That is how. Education will straighten up this shape, touch it again with immortality, give it back the upward looking and the light. But education that is designed for the few, the rich and the privileged will not do it. Education that does not take him into account, or rejects him if it notices him at all, will never straighten up this shape or heal his immedicable woes.

Great southerners have long recognized this truth. Thomas Jefferson knew that an educated citizenry is a necessary pre-

---

[91] Edwin Markham, *The Man With the Hoe and Other Poems* (New York: Doubleday, Page and Company, 1922), 16-17.

requisite to free government. Woodrow Wilson, another souther-ner, knew that universal education is a necessary prerequisite to making the world safe for democracy.

But this is not the only area of educational need. The South, like the rest of the nation, needs also to look at the other end of the educational system—the colleges and the universities.

Only three of the thirteen southern states rank above the national average in the percentage of their adult population with four or more years of college education. North Carolina is not among them. It is thirty-ninth among the fifty states. South Carolina ranks higher, but not high enough to boast. Your state is thirty-second among the fifty states.

I do not minimize the need for more money in higher educa-tion, either public or private. More money must be provided—substantially more money. But the South will not keep faith with the future if we do not take into account the tremendous backlog of educational demand that exists on the part of honest, hard-working people who simply do not have the price. It is a reality we must face. It is a reality the South must take into account as it shapes a new college policy for the future.

Universal quality education will provide the cornerstone for a prosperous New South—a South that can again lead the nation.

The place to begin is with the beginning: in the public schools. Here we must reappraise our curriculum. North Carolina is seeking a new curriculum, a curriculum with power—"power in itself to challenge the latent germ of genius, great or small, classical or modern, academic or technical, that every educable human being has within him in some degree." It is only in the light of this curriculum study that we are investing another $100 million toward the achievement of this goal. We await results with hope and with confidence, but meanwhile we work.

This, however, is not enough for the foundation. The key to quality education is quality teaching. And one of the keys to quality teaching is quality teacher education, both pre-service and in-service teacher education. It must be said to the credit of professional education in North Carolina and South Carolina that it, too, is taking a positive stand for progress. There can be no doubt that the leadership now being exerted by the profession will bring new quality, of rich meaning, to the instruction in tens of thousands of classrooms in the state.

The junior colleges and the church-supported colleges must play important roles in the higher education of our states. How else shall we face the doubling of college enrollments certainly within the next decade? How else will we be able to reach the young men and women who simply do not have the price of a residential college education?

The need for industrial, or the so-called terminal-technical education is increasing. At the present time a survey of every job opportunity in North Carolina is being made, and this survey will lead to complete, accurate descriptions of the requirements of each of these thousands of jobs. On the basis of this survey, curricular standards will be set up and state-wide courses of instruction leading to certification of technicians will be established. These will form the curriculum of North Carolina's new system of industrial education centers, which, although begun only in 1958, are now reaching over 15,000 adults.

I am informed that South Carolina is moving quickly in this field of industrial education.

At the head of our educational system, and carrying the heaviest responsibility for its leadership are our senior colleges and universities with their graduate schools and various professional programs. These institutions serve as the brain centers, as sources of ideas and plans for much of our life. The specialized leaders who come from these institutions become the trusted leaders in many fields, and the standard they set is determined in a large part by the standard to which they have been challenged by those institutions. As we support these institutions to the best possible performance, we insure that our leadership will have the opportunity to develop to its fullest.

Quality education which we seek cannot be delivered by a city council, or a legislature, or the Congress, although their help is essential in starting the march. Quality education is complex, difficult, constant in required attention, and it will demand the best in effort by school boards, the state agencies, the superintendents, the principals, the teachers, the parents, the students, and indeed all the citizens of this university, this city, this state, and this nation.

The hour is at hand when South Carolina, North Carolina, and all the South can rise again and march again. We will make this march not with bayonets but with textbooks. We will not be firing on Fort Sumter. We will be firing on the dungeons of ignorance.

We will make this march by reaching out and grasping the hands of our most priceless possession, our children and our grandchildren.

Thank you.

STATE 4-H CLUB WEEK MEETING

RALEIGH

July 26, 1961

[Some 1,400 members of the 4-H Clubs of North Carolina met in Raleigh for their annual convention. Discussions, dress revues, contests, and elections filled the days, but the highlight of the week was the address by Governor Sanford. Speaking at William Neal Reynolds Coliseum, the Governor discussed the influence of farming on the international scene and then launched into an analysis of the farm situation and opportunities in North Carolina.]

Each of you sitting here today is living testimony to something that I have been saying across our state for years: Farming is NOT dead in North Carolina. In fact, this remarkable audience and this remarkable demonstration of the work of 1,400 young farm leaders is proof positive that there is new hope, new vigor, and new promise for profitable harvests on North Carolina's farms.

There is, indeed, a new day in North Carolina agriculture!

I grew up in the farm trading town of Laurinburg, although it has grown to three times the size and the designation of "All American City" since I left and I know something of the work involved in your activities. I know the toil and sweat that go into suckering tobacco. And I also know the rich sense of personal satisfaction, as well as the enrichment of the pocketbook, that comes at the end of a good season.

Then I know too what the work that you and your parents are doing this summer means to the economy of a town like Laurinburg, and cities like Durham and Winston-Salem and Raleigh, and even that metropolis of Charlotte.

If you have a bad year on the farm, the urban people have a bad year in town. The merchant's sales drop. The banker's deposits fall off. The manufacturer's orders go down.

When the farmer prospers, we know there are going to be good profits in town. But when the farmer suffers, we all are going to suffer.

This is especially true in North Carolina, a state that has more family-sized farms than any state in the union except Texas.

We know of the close correlation between the prosperity on the farm and the prosperity of the town. We learned that lesson before any one of you 4-H Club members here today was born. We learned it the hard way. There was a farm depression in the early 1920's. Those were the Roaring Twenties in the big cities so very few people in town worried very much about the plight of the farmer out in the country.

But we found out in 1929 that the farm economy plays an integral role in the over-all national economy.

The farm depression of the early twenties caught up with the cities in the fall of 1929. If you've studied your history of that period, you know that mighty Wall Street did something then that generally has been left to the inhabitants of the barnyard.

It laid an egg.

We had to relearn this lesson the hard way again in the 1950's. These were the years you here today will remember. You know that we had some officials in Washington who thought the solution to the farm problem was to shut down the small farms.

You know what happened. We first had a farm recession. Then we had a national recession. In fact we had a couple of them.

Now, we are in the happy position of having an administration in Washington under the capable leadership of President Jack Kennedy, who fully appreciates the importance of keeping our farm programs strong.

As you know, President Kennedy and Secretary of Agriculture Orville Freeman have relied heavily on North Carolina and North Carolinians in maintaining and developing the agricultural resources on our New Frontier.

Three of the major policy makers in Secretary Freeman's department are North Carolinians: Charles Murphy from Wallace is Under Secretary of Agriculture; Harry B. Caldwell of Greensboro is chairman of the President's Farm Advisory Committee; and Horace Godfrey is administrator of the Commodity Credit Corporation. They are working, as are the President and Secretary Freeman, with Congressman Harold Cooley, the veteran chairman of the House Agriculture Committee, and with Senator B. Everett Jordan,[92] a member of the Senate Agriculture Committee. (Parenthetically, I would like to say that Senator Jordan's committee's recent vote on the farm bill was not fully understood. In the complicated legislative process, which is hard to understand, he was working for the kind of farm bill which would best serve North Carolina. If you will watch with patience you will see my prediction come true that Senator Jordan will play an important role in helping the farm situation in our state and nation.)

This position in national leadership is important to a state like ours that still is primarily an agricultural state. And this effort to reinvigorate the farm economy is vital to the nation.

It is vital because, as we have seen, the nation's domestic

---

[92] B. Everett Jordan (1896-   ), businessman from Saxapahaw; political and civic leader; successor in United States Senate to W. Kerr Scott, who died in 1958. *North Carolina Manual, 1963*, 501-502.

economy is as strongly tied to the agricultural economy as it is to the steel or the automotive industries.

It is vital to the United States in our foreign policy.

One of America's secret weapons in this cold war with communism is our agriculture.

True, you don't kill a man with an ear of corn or a bag of peanuts. You use rifles and hand grenades and bombs and missiles for killing. But it is equally true that with the food we raise here in North Carolina you can keep a man from dying.

In this crisis over Berlin, our surplus food is as important to the defense of the free world as our stockpile of atom bombs.

I'm sure you've read the Biblical story of the seven years of feast that were followed by the seven years of famine. Young Joseph may well have been a 4-H Club member had he lived today. For he had the good sense to conserve—to store the surpluses of ancient Egypt against the time of drought and hunger.

There is a more modern example of this object lesson.

I wonder how many of you noticed the story in the Sunday newspapers by Ovid Martin, the Associated Press farm editor. Martin pointed out that "The Berlin crisis and the possibility that it might develop into a shooting war has put this nation's farm surpluses and its excessive agricultural productive capacity in a new light."

He went on to point out that when World War II broke out, the United States was struggling with overproduction and excess supplies.

It didn't take long to exhaust our surpluses in that war.

And, should we have to fight over Berlin, or any of the other danger spots around the globe, it would not take long to exhaust all our farm surpluses.

In fact, the only farm surplus that we now have which is large enough to make our defense leaders feel easy is the wheat stockpile. And that wouldn't last but twenty-five months. It wouldn't last that long if we helped to supply our allies—as we did in the last war and as we certainly would be expected to do in any future war.

Our surpluses of corn would last only six months under wartime conditions. Our surpluses of tobacco, cotton, butter, dry milk, dry beans, rice, peanuts, oats, barley, cheese, rye, flaxseed, and soybeans would hardly last until the next year's crops were in.

You young members of the 4-H Clubs here today may not remember the food rationing of World War II. But all of you adult leaders do.

I hope and I pray that we will never have to use our farm surpluses for wartime purposes. As a former GI, I can tell you that those canned K and C rations never tasted half as good as fresh vegetables and fresh milk and fresh fruits and fresh meats from the farms of North Carolina.

But it is important for all Americans, including those who moan about full storage bins, to bear in mind the vital role farm surpluses play in winning wars.

The Soviet Union may be running neck and neck in the missile race. But they're not even within hog-calling distance of the United States in farm production.

The Communists of Russia and the Communists of China have tried to catch up. But their collective farms have been a miserable failure in comparison with our privately owned farms operated by free farmers.

Incidentally, I would again refer you to your history books and the great role farmers around the globe have played in the defense of freedom against communism. Whenever communism has encroached or attempted to encroach on free men, the farmers have been frontline fighters against it. The Kulaks in Russia fought it and Stalin had to exterminate them before he could get on with his communization and his collective farms. Many thousands, and probably millions, of Chinese farmers have resisted the nationalization of their lands, their homes, their lives.

The farmers in Poland were among the first to help slow down communism of that once free land.

Farmers the world over will fight communism, when they know what it really is, as hard as they fought serfdom.

So we can see that farmers as well as farm surpluses are mighty weapons in the arsenal of democracy.

This state, as one of America's great agricultural states, and America as the greatest agricultural nation in the world, must go on the offensive.

You young ladies already know that the way to a man's heart is through his stomach.

Both you young ladies and you young men should also know that the way to a man's mind also is often routed through his stomach. You don't find many of the people in the emerging new nations who are turning to communism on a full stomach.

But, by the same token, you don't find many starving people worrying about political theories of democracy or communism on empty bellies.

Here is where free America can and must go on the offensive.

We can use our farm surpluses to feed a hungry world. And we should do so not merely to win over the uncommitted nations—which is, of course, reason enough itself. But we should divide our farm surpluses with a hungry world because it is morally the right thing to do.

It has been truthfully said that our farm surpluses are America's blessing, not a national burden. We should share this blessing with the underfed around the world.

Now I've been discussing with you the importance of farmers and farming in the international situation. But what about down home on the farm in North Carolina?

You young farm leaders of North Carolina know better than most what is right—as well as what is wrong—with the farms of North Carolina.

You know that it's time to be planting and growing in North Carolina, not for plowing-under our farms.

To this end, the agricultural leaders of North Carolina, including your own 4-H Club adult leaders, met with me recently and put forward North Carolina's new agricultural opportunities program.

Objectives of the program are to lift the farm income, to develop marketing and processing facilities and services, and to promote education for family and community development.

A blueprint for accomplishing these objectives was prepared by the North Carolina Board of Farm Organizations and Agricultural Agencies. The program calls for tackling farm income and marketing problems on the basis of "economic areas" rather than on the basis of county or community enterprises alone.

True, the farm economy of North Carolina, like the farm economy of the nation, has suffered its ills. But we have made significant gains in farm income in the past few years despite the downward trend over the nation at large.

We are neither going to plow under our family farms nor our farmers. We are not going to run them off the farms and into cities where there already is too much unemployment.

Instead, we are going to work for new agricultural opportunities through every available resource at our disposal.

The time has come to do some pruning of outdated farming and marketing practices and ideas. We have been doing a fairly good job in the past, but we are not reaping anything like our potential. We need to revitalize our farm programs with greater emphasis on agriculture as one of the cornerstones of our economy.

North Carolina is not getting out of the farming business. We can't afford to. Six out of every ten persons in North Carolina live in rural areas. The total agricultural business is worth $3.5 billion a year to North Carolina. What's more, North Carolina has over 190,000 farms.

I believe there are certain areas where more emphasis needs

to be placed and where the Governor's Office can work effectively with the Commissioner of Agriculture, State College, and other farm agencies and organizations.

1. The Governor and the Highway Commission can see that proper consideration be given to rural roads. I recommended and the General Assembly adopted a far-reaching program to stop highway fund diversion so that millions of dollars can be freed to work on rural roads.

2. The Governor's Office and the Department of Conservation and Development are already working day and night to encourage the establishment of more farm-related plants in North Carolina. We have made good progress in this field already.

Since January, I have had the pleasure of helping to announce a new strawberry packing plant in southeastern North Carolina, a new sweet potato drying and packaging plant in northeastern North Carolina.

Next month, I will help dedicate an important new feed mill at Wilson.

You and I know that such plants serve the double purpose of providing new markets for farm commodities and new job opportunities for farm families.

3. The state can and is promoting to the fullest the great export market possibilities. To this end I have recommended and the General Assembly has approved and sent to the people a program to expand the deep water ports of North Carolina. Through these ports we are developing ways to ship our crops to the four corners of the world.

4. The Governor can and will give top priority to promote "agricultural opportunities" at banking conventions, county fairs, industrial meetings, farm conventions, and other meetings from Tryon to Chinquapin. This is a program which has meaning for every family living in rural North Carolina. And because of that, it has a meaning for every citizen of the state.

For example, North Carolina grows only a quarter of a million dollars worth of aromatic tobacco a year. Yet the tobacco manufacturers of North Carolina buy $90 million worth every year. North Carolina farmers are furnishing less than half the hogs that the new meat processing plant at Wilson needs and is ready to buy. That plant imports the rest from the Midwest, but we can grow hogs as profitably within North Carolina as any state in the union.

We can grow economically and profitably more fruits and vegetables, more cattle, and can grow the feed to support an expanded livestock industry.

5. The Governor's Office, working with the farm agencies and

organizations and with other economic development groups and agencies, can serve as the focal point for all the programs and unify them into one great effort to move North Carolina's agriculture forward.

We have the resources to get the job done, but we need better to utilize them.

Finally, the door to the Governor's Office is always open to the leaders of the farm agencies and the farm organizations and, in fact, to every farmer of North Carolina who is working to revitalize the agricultural economy of our state. The Governor's Office has enjoyed an excellent working relationship with the Commissioner of Agriculture and his department, with the North Carolina State Grange, the Farm Bureau, North Carolina State College and all the other agencies working to lift the level of living of the rural families of our state.

So long as man must eat, so long as man must clothe himself against the weather, so long as man enjoys a smoke, there will be a place of leadership for agriculture in North Carolina.

We intend to give farming the rightful place in building a greater North Carolina.

PRESENTATION OF FREEDOM ASSOCIATION WORLD PEACE AWARD TO DR. FRANK PORTER GRAHAM, EIGHTH ANNUAL SOUTHEASTERN WORLD AFFAIRS INSTITUTE

BLUE RIDGE

July 29, 1961

After praising President Kennedy's quest for peace, Governor Sanford added that the honoree of this occasion, Dr. Frank Porter Graham, was also a champion of peace and freedom. He briefly reviewed Dr. Graham's military career, his service to the cause of education in North Carolina, and his political career. He described Graham as a radical in that he believed and practiced the radical belief of the golden rule; as a liberal in that he worked for progress; as a conservative in that he believed in preserving the customs, traditions, and history of the past; and as a reactionary in that he believed in the power of the individual as did Jefferson, Jackson, Lincoln, and Wilson. Sanford, commenting on the fitness of honoring Frank Porter Graham again, said that the tallest monument to him was to be found in the minds of men all over North Carolina, the United States, and the world.

SUMMER LEADERSHIP CONFERENCE
NORTH CAROLINA CLASSROOM TEACHERS
ASSOCIATION

MARS HILL

August 2, 1961

The Governor, in this address on education, stressed the role of the teacher in the formative years of a child's growth. He compared the teacher to an actor on the stage, saying many were full-time professionals though some, while paid to work full time, actually put other interests first and devoted only part of their time to teaching. He urged teachers to analyze their own attitudes and make constant efforts to improve the quality of their work. For those behind the scenes, for all the citizens, the burden was heavy, but it remained the full-time professional teacher who had the direct responsibility of molding the nation's future. Governor Sanford said he had insisted on salary increases of 22 per cent because he felt teachers earned the increase. As Governor, he was going to require more than a 22 per cent increase in teaching proficiency. He told the teachers that the spotlight was on them and suggested that they "raise the curtain and get on with this high drama of educating the boys and girls of our state."

ANNUAL SUPERINTENDENTS CONFERENCE

MARS HILL

August 9, 1961

As he had done when he addressed the classroom teachers a week earlier, Governor Sanford again emphasized the role of the group to which he was speaking as he discussed quality education. "I Am Climbing Jacob's Ladder," the theme song of the conference, was taken by the Governor as a means of comparing the job of the superintendents with the challenges presented by the spiritual. He said that when financial support granted by the General Assembly became a reality, school people were faced with the decision of how to get the job done and that there was no time for self-congratulation. Again Sanford compared the educational program with a drama, this time calling the superintendents the directors of the production. He called for them to value the needed sense of timing, the making of decisions, and the sensitiveness to social change with the constant effort toward improvement. So as to bring in all interested people, lines of communication had to be kept open, but the single most important segment of the superintendents' job was to help the teachers do a better job. He urged the group to keep up with events as they happened and evaluate the school program regularly; he recommended accreditation of the schools by the Southern Association of Colleges and Secondary Schools as a *"stimulation for improvement...."* The desire to fill new jobs would be great, even where qualified persons could not be found, and the temptation to lower standards would have to be resisted. As the last rung in the ladder, Sanford asked that the superintendents build "a public image of the school that will reflect its true worth." In conclusion he called for co-operation, saying, "As we all work together in response to this challenge, I am proud to be numbered among your company!"

AGRIBUSINESS CARAVAN LUNCHEON

RALEIGH

August 10, 1961

On numerous occasions during his administration, Governor Sanford emphasized the fact that farming was not dead in North Carolina. To the group at this luncheon he said leaders of agriculture and business were working together. While North Carolina had some of the richest farm land in the nation, it also had some of the poorest farms and the most underpaid farmers. The state needed new industry; it also neded income from the soil. The Governor reminded the group that many problems of production had been solved but that the problem of distribution was still to be faced. In this connection he mentioned hungry people in North Carolina and abroad, recalling the leadership of Kerr Scott in the World Food Bank program, a program which had been carried further during the Kennedy administration. Sanford said that his administration intended to place emphasis on farming. North Carolina's new Agricultural Opportunities Program, with its objectives of lifting farm income, developing marketing and processing facilities and services, promoting education for family and community development, was cited as proof of North Carolina's stand. With six out of every ten persons in the state living in rural areas, there were over 190,000 farms; the total agriculture business was worth $3.5 billion a year. The Governor promised that his administration would see that proper consideration was given to rural roads, would work to establish farm-related plants, would promote export marketing possibilities, would give priority to "agricultural opportunities" at conventions and similar gatherings, and would see that the Governor's Office served as the focal point for all programs. Farming would be given a rightful place in building a greater North Carolina.

DANIELS FAMILY REUNION

WANCHESE

August 19, 1961

[Governor Sanford addressed members of the Daniels family at their reunion at Wanchese. He talked about the contributions made by this particular family and then broadened his outlook to the "good family of man on the new frontiers. . . ." The latter he called "the one hope of our world."]

It is good for a Governor of North Carolina to meet with one of the strong families which have been so long among the keepers of this shore of brave American beginnings. Probably there never was a time when we needed more than now the recollection of men who dared in the effort to establish a brave new world. For after the centuries that remains our task still, and one as hedged about with hazard as in the days when men crossed wide sea to an unknown wilderness.

The seas are narrower now. And the wilderness we face all over this globe is one of man's own making. Yet the vision which prompted the voyage to this shore must be the same today in terms of the hopes and hungers of people. I believe that the courage of four centuries has never lapsed.

Like other North Carolinians, I have been aware of the uninterrupted courage of men bearing the Daniels name who manned the Coast Guard.

I like to remember, too, that when the very idea of flight in the air seemed a great foolishness to many, there was a Daniels in the group which helped the Wright brothers break the ignorance which kept man earthbound.

Sometimes in this day of missiles, it is easy to wish that men had never left the ground. Still we know that when men could cease to soar, the qualities which made them dare the seas would be gone, too.

Our task greater than mere courage is to understand that we must face every wilderness, and to know that there is no shore anywhere which is not our concern. A Daniels gave us example of that, too, and in days as threatening almost as those in which we live today. Like most North Carolinians, I am proud of Josephus Daniels who in the years when World War II was inevitably approaching exemplified the Good Neighbor policy of Franklin Roosevelt in Latin America. I like to think that it was the good neighbor policy, which has always been our pattern in eastern North Carolina, that was the basis of the quality which helped Josephus Daniels keep Mexico our great friend next door when we were endangered in the whole world. And being here today helps in understanding that only such similar good neighborliness, as President Kennedy now means to put into creative action, will keep us secure in time of threat of even greater war.

I like to attend such family reunions as this one. They give us not only a time of pleasure meeting of families and friends but an opportunity, too, to recall the good, strong men who built America in neighborliness and can now only build a strong, free world in neighborliness, too.

I know that sometimes such things as the foreign aid program President Kennedy proposes, and which is jeopardized this very week end by men failing in full vision and understanding, seem complicated, costly, and distant from our daily concerns. Actually, the Kennedy program is an extension of the vision and courage which dared to broach the beaches here in daring for a new and better world.

Here on the oldest American frontier, men like your families and your fellows should understand the new frontiers best. And in the reunion of an honored North Carolina family, we can understand the need and meaning of the effort to build the family of free men despite savagery at our doors and dangers in the distance which are really as close as the waves on our own shores.

The good family of man on the new frontiers is the one hope of our world.

NATIONAL SECURITY SEMINAR

FORT BRAGG

August 25, 1961

[A diverse group of some 300 civilians, soldiers, businessmen, and top military experts participated in this two-day seminar meeting in Fort Bragg. Discussions on the nature of the Soviet threat and methods for fighting the cold war were led by such proficient men as Dr. Frank Barnett, Director of the Institute for American Strategy; Dr. Stefan Possony, Georgetown University professor; and Arbor Gray, official of the Federal Bureau of Investigation. In this opening night address, Governor Sanford expressed the determined spirit of this generation, "willing to work for peace, but . . . also willing to fight for freedom."]

We have, in recent days, reached one of those crises in history when the fate of the free world hangs precariously in the balance. At this very hour, the fate of Berlin rides on a dictator's whim and a democracy's determination. And the fate of Berlin is just as important to all of the free world in the summer of 1961 as was the fate of the Polish Corridor in the summer of 1939.

The safety of the free world is endangered in the jungles of not-so-far-away Laos. And the outcome of the Chinese Communist aggression in Laos is as important to the free world in 1961 as was the outcome of the Japanese aggression in Manchuria in 1931.

The threat to the independence of the newly free nations of Africa is as grave to the free world in August of 1961 as was the threat against Ethiopia by the strutting Mussolini in 1937.

. . . .

[In the deleted portions, the Governor discussed the preference Americans had for peace rather than for war, but he emphasized the fact that Americans would fight if necessary. The portions omitted were similar to parts of the Governor's address on the occasion of the dedication of the Benson National Guard Armory. See pages 148-149.]

This seminar—composed as it is of civilians and soldiers, representatives of management and representatives of labor, big businessmen and small businessmen—shows the broad base of American strength.

As vitally necessary as are military posts like Fort Bragg, I believe that the ultimate strength of America will be found in the schoolyards of our nation, rather than on the parade grounds. I believe that what is going on in the classrooms is of equal, if not greater, importance than what is going on in the briefing rooms. I believe that the future of America will rise higher from the laboratories of the schools than from the launching pads at Cape Canaveral.

America's greatest fortress is not a Maginot Line, nor a Siegfried Line. America's greatest fortress is the schoolhouse.

This nation's future will not be found at the end of the tunnel to a fall-out shelter, even though those shelters are a necessary safeguard in a time of crisis. The nation's future will be found rather at the end of an academic procession at commencement time. Therefore, I believe, it is as imperative to strengthen our educational system as it is to strengthen our defense system.

I would like to add that free minds at work in free schools are a far greater bastion of strength than the semisecret cells of superpatriots. It seems to me that the neofascistic rantings of the

superpatriot organization in vogue at the moment are as dangerous to our freedoms as any foreign enemy.

As Mr. Sam Rayburn pointed out in Raleigh a few months ago,
America has had to suffer through these superpatriot groups
before. Some of Mr. Thomas Jefferson's friends were imprisoned
in the eighteenth century—for trying to exercise their rights as
free men. Then we had outfits like the Know-Nothing Party in
the nineteenth cenutry. We had the "American Firsters" around
the time of World War II. As a veteran of World War II, I am
as suspect of superpatriots of today as I was of the American-
Firsters.

President Kennedy at his inauguration aptly expressed the
determined spirit of this generation of Americans: "Born in this
century, tempered by war, disciplined by a hard and bitter peace,
proud of our ancient heritage—and unwilling to witness or
permit the slow undoing of those human rights to which this
nation has always been committed."

No group could better understand this determination and no
group could be more ready to fight to preserve these national
commitments than one like this. There is no question about this
readiness and willingness to fight and die; the question is will we
also take the leadership in defending "our ancient heritage"
without fighting. Will we, again in the words of John F. Kennedy,
"begin anew the quest for peace, before the dark powers of destruction unleashed by science engulf all humanity in planned or
accidental self-destruction?"

It is a paradox that fighting is less difficult for the democratic
mind to grasp than is the "quest for peace." Fighting unleashes
the native spirit, while the quest for peace requires all the restraints, and all the patience, and all the understanding with
which man, unhappily, is not naturally endowed at birth. That
has been the story of most wars. Patience, understanding, restraint, not fully developed in man, failed.

You know better than many that talking is better than shooting,
that negotiating is easier than digging foxholes, and that debating—however vitriolic—burns a man less than white phosphorous
or radiation.

The United States and the other nations of the world have
found in the last fifteen years around the tables of the United
Nations that restraint and patience are not natural attributes of
man, but they know bombast is better than bombs and the insult
of words is less disrespectful than the insult of death.

When we are tempted to despair of the fruitless argument
around West Ninety-second Street, we might well remember the

lethal arguments aroung Bastogne, around Guadalcanal, and around Pusan.

We all know that American military might is capable of destroying Soviet cities—and Khrushchev's missiles could destroy ours. This is the cold fact that has helped keep the cold war from growing too hot. This is why we continue to fight our fights around the conference tables at the United Nations. I firmly believe that the United Nations, supported by the strength of the United States and other free nations, has kept us out of World War III.

The battle of the free world is being fought today around the corridors of the United Nations and around the lobbies of Capitol Hill in Washington, as well as around the Brandenburg Gate in Berlin. The battle in Washington may not be as dramatic. But in the long run, it may well be more important than that show of force in Berlin.

I refer, of course, to the battle on the President's foreign aid program. Men of little vision have threatened to cripple the President's foreign aid program. If they crippled his military preparedness program, they could hardly do more damage.

We must in this hour of peril keep our military guard up. But we must go further. We must also keep our educational system moving forward. We must keep our industrial might on the march. We must revitalize that great secret weapon in our arsenal—our agricultural resources.

Finally, I believe, we must extend the hand of help to the underdeveloped nations. Foreign aid is costly. But when you measure the cost of it against the cost of war and against the cost of suffering and against the cost of limb and life, foreign aid is the least expensive investment with the greatest promise of return that America could make.

CHARLOTTE-MECKLENBURG SCHOOL CONVOCATION

Charlotte

August 30, 1961

Governor Sanford, at the opening of a new school year, referred to education as the foundation of all other North Carolina programs. With supplemental funds appropriated by the 1961 General Assembly, the time had come to implement the quality education program. The Governor reminded the group that professional educators could not do the job alone, that much

President John F. Kennedy, appearing in Chapel Hill for University Day on October 12, 1961, is shown with Governor Sanford, President of the University of North Carolina William C. Friday, Dean J. Carlyle Sitterson, and Chancellor William B. Aycock.

The U.S.S. "North Carolina" was towed to its permanent berth in the Cape Fear River on October 2, 1961.

reliance would be placed on top school units such as those of the Charlotte-Mecklenburg area. He suggested that wasted time could not be afforded, that inefficient teachers and lazy students and selfish parents could not be tolerated. Students would have to desire to learn if quality education were achieved. Parents would have to take an interest in the work of their children, see that homework was assigned and done, and encourage extra reading; they would also need to seek to know teachers and understand guidance programs. Teachers, the key personnel, would have to devote full time to teaching and periodic reappraisals of their individual attitudes and work. Superintendents, principals, board members would have to know what needed to be done; they were asked to inform members of the community about the school program and to help teachers do a better job. The Governor commented that individual responsibility and co-operative endeavor would succeed in improving the schools.

CEREMONY OF TRANSFER OF
U.S.S. "NORTH CAROLINA" FROM NAVY TO STATE

BAYONNE, NEW JERSEY

September 6, 1961

The U.S.S. "North Carolina" was heading home to North Carolina, thanks to the contributions of the many who made the project possible. Governor Sanford expressed appreciation to those people and said that the ship would serve as a constant reminder of the determination of free men to fight despotism and oppression. The ship, scheduled to begin its final voyage near the Statue of Liberty, was to sail past the origins of the nation: Philadelphia, Washington, Yorktown, Jamestown, Roanoke Island. The order of the day was peace; Americans were willing to work for peace but were determined to fight for freedom. Governor Sanford called the ship, headed for its final port of call, a "memorial to the men who dared the deep for freedom's sake."

SEMIANNUAL MEETING
TIDEWATER ALUMNI CHAPTER
UNIVERSITY OF NORTH CAROLINA

NORFOLK, VIRGINIA

September 6, 1961

Governor Sanford's address to the Norfolk area group of alumni of the University of North Carolina dealt with the problems and potentials surrounding the rapid growth of the institution. The Governor remarked that North Carolina was rapidly moving into the mainstream of American life, and part of the credit for this progress had to be attributed to the university. Under the leadership of President Harry Woodburn Chase, the school became a member of the Association of American Universities. To recruit and retain good faculty members had long been a goal, but the salary scale had to be high enough to hold competent people. Sanford commented on criticisms made to growth, but he added that it was both undesirable and impossible for the school to stand still. The advantages of a large library, cultural and intellectual events, student self-government, extracurricular activities, and student publications would be obvious, but students needed also the advantages of small classes and individual attention. To achieve this happy combination, the Governor suggested a system of small classes and laboratories with large lectures by outstanding professors. Governor Sanford referred to the proposed visit of President Kennedy to Chapel Hill, saying the President would see a beautiful campus, an institution of heritage and distinction, and would be introduced to students of high caliber. Achievements at the university had been made because of men with vision and faith; the Governor pleaded for continued courage, vision, and sacrifices on behalf of the Chapel Hill school.

<hr />

NORTHWESTERN AREA
INDUSTRIAL DEVELOPMENT CONFERENCE

WILKESBORO

September 7, 1961

In speaking to the Area Industrial Development Conference in Wilkesboro, Governor Sanford discussed opportunities available in the area. He referred to the fact that part of northwestern North Carolina had been considered a distressed area, but he spoke of the potential which was there. Opportunities and resources made planning imperative. Again he stressed the importance of local citizens taking the initiative, with the help of the state, to build a sounder economy than ever before.

WEEKS LAW GOLDEN ANNIVERSARY CELEBRATION

BILTMORE FOREST, ASHEVILLE

September 26, 1961

In introducing Secretary of Agriculture Orville Freeman on the occasion of the observance of the enactment of the Weeks Law fifty years earlier, Governor Sanford recalled that the first tract of land purchased under the act was in North Carolina at Pisgah National Forest. Since that time more than 20 million acres across the nation had been acquired under this legislation. North Carolina's interest in forestry was briefly reviewed. The Governor said that of the 31,267,000 acres in the state, more than 64 per cent was occupied by forests. The value of the manufacture of forestry products annually exceeded $1 billion. North Carolina furniture factories used lumber, 45 per cent of which was produced in the state. A wider variety of trees was found in North Carolina than on the entire European continent. In 1960, 17.4 per cent of the state's manufacturing labor force derived its livelihood from forestry-related occupations. Problems existed, but faith in the land and in the people would be shown and forests would become more productive in the years ahead than they had been in the past.

DEDICATION OF
BUSINESS AND PROFESSIONAL WOMEN'S
CLUB HEADQUARTERS

CHAPEL HILL

October 1, 1961

At the dedication of a new headquarters building for the Business and Professional Women's Clubs, the Governor had an opportunity to express his philosophy concerning the vital role played by women in North Carolina. Under the leadership of women such as those in this organization, Sanford said that North Carolina women "have moved from the skillet and the spinning wheel to the drafting board and the Univac." Though women still retained their rightful place in the kitchen and in the home, they also had a place "in the classroom, the salesroom, the business office, the laboratory, and the operating room." The leadership of women throughout history was cited by references to Isabella of Spain, Joan of Arc, and Elizabeth of England; in North

Carolina history Cornelia Phillips Spencer, who played a major role in the reopening of the University of North Carolina at Chapel Hill following the Civil War, was mentioned as another example of leadership. As time passed, more and more women occupied positions of trust, including Justice Susie Sharp, Representatives Grace Rodenbough and Rachel Davis, and Welfare Commissioner Ellen Winston. Sanford said he had appointed more than 100 women to boards, commissions, and agencies. The need for women's idealism along with their clear thinking and their practical ideas was keenly felt, and the chief executive urged those in his audience to lend support to the bond issues to be voted on November 7. He told the women that they were "not clothed in old lace of a time gone by," and that he knew they would join "in moving out to build a better North Carolina. . . ."

SOUTH PIEDMONT DISTRICT NCEA

KANNAPOLIS

October 3, 1961

[With the passage of the quality education program by the General Assembly, a major victory had been won, but the implementation of the program was the responsibility of the school people and the citizens of North Carolina. Governor Sanford undertook to travel to all 100 counties to convince the people of their part in making quality education a reality. In this address he called for unified action from teachers, parents, students, and professional administrators; he outlined briefly the responsibility which he expected each group to assume.]

It is appropriate that the educational leaders of this great industrial area convene here today to map battle plans in the war against ignorance and to prepare blueprints for the erection of better schools in a state where the weak truly can grow strong and the strong will grow great.

In a world where the freedom, and, indeed, the very existence of man is threatened, it is in keeping with the finest tradition of North Carolina and of America that our rallying point should be the schoolhouse and not a military parade field.

Human liberties, gained over a period of thousands of years, are at this moment being threatened in the divided streets of Berlin and in the jungles of Laos and Africa. Human life itself, evolved over the span of tens of thousands of years, is imperiled.

A week ago, President Kennedy acutely appraised the world crises we face today: "The events and decisions of the next ten months," he noted, "may well decide the fate of man for the next 10,000 years. . . ." And, the President continued, "Unless man can match his strides in weaponry and technology with equal strides in social and political development, our great strength, like that of the dinosaur, will become incapable of proper control —and man, like the dinosaur, will decline and disappear."

You probably noticed that the period of time forecast by the President to be the months in which civilization, as we know it, will move forward or go the way of the dinosaur coincides with this school year.

President Kennedy's forthright challenge to the Soviets to replace the arms race with a peace race makes your jobs as educators all the more vital.

Whether the Soviet and Chinese Communists will accept that challenge will be determined by Moscow and Peiping. But whatever their answer, your job and mine this school year is the same.

For, put in its bleakest terms, education is survival. If the Communists insist on continuing the arms race and should they cross that narrow line between this cold war and a hot war, education will constitute one of the greatest weapons in our arsenal of defense.

I strongly believe that what is happening in the classrooms in North Carolina today will ultimately be more important to mankind than what is happening in the briefing rooms at Seymour-Johnson Air Base. And what is happening in the laboratories of the schools of this district and this state eventually will have a greater bearing on our future than what is happening on the launching pads at Cape Canaveral. The schoolyard is as vital to our defense as the military parade fields at Fort Bragg and Camp Lejeune.

If, in a moment of sanity at the Kremlin, the Communists should accept the President's challenge and offer for a peace race, then our schools will set the pace for a better world.

This decision of a peace race or an arms race is not one that we can resolve here in Kannapolis. But you and I can play our part. Here in our own small part of the free world, we can do no less than seek the best as we prepare to do our part in defending America and the free world.

Education is the foundation rock on which North Carolina, America, and free nations everywhere must build.

Here in the South Piedmont and here in North Carolina, we must adequately educate the scientists, the statesmen, and the citizenry who will fully understand and who are equipped to defend and promote the ideals of our dynamic democracy of the twentieth century.

If you call the roll of individual goals, or district goals, or state, national, or international goals, you will return to one ringing conclusion: The way to all these objectives is education!

What is the best device for increasing economic skills so the students of today can make better livings tomorrow? Education!

What is the best method for picking up the per capita income of this district and this state? Education!

What is the fundamental for military defense in an age of space and rocket races? Education!

What is the hope for developing statesmen and leaders and a comprehending citizenry? Education.

And so it goes. Indeed, education of our boys and girls is the most compelling single ambition and the most promising hope in the lives of the people of this district, state, and nation.

Because of the vital role education plays in national defense, because of the integral part education exerts in economic development for both individual citizens and the state and nation, because all our goals and all of our hopes for North Carolina rest on the rock of education, this school year may well be the most important in our lifetime.

Another compelling reason why this school year is so important is that we have now reached in North Carolina the time for action in implementing the quality education program for which so many have struggled so long against so many obstacles.

The people have voiced approval of bold and giant strides. The elected representatives of the people in the General Assembly have provided the money requested by the State Board of Education.

Now it is your job as educators to carry out this mandate and to prove that the investment in quality education is an investment that will net our citizens excellent returns.

We have reached in North Carolina a time for action. We cannot afford the luxury of wasted time or ineffective teachers or lazy students or selfish parents. Nor can we afford to use our schools to provide a winter resort for students, a baby-sitting nursery for parents, a Roman holiday entertainment spectacle for the public, and for teachers a part-time way to make a full-time salary.

I recognize that achieving quality education cannot be accomplished solely by educators. It is going to require the united efforts of us all. The state administration will do its part. This rally here today is one of at least 100 that are being scheduled in each of the counties of North Carolina. Moreover, the Governor's Office is working closely with committees that are seeking solutions to the problems facing you, the educators.

Just last Friday, I had the privilege of discussing three of the major school problems with three separate committees: the Stay

In School Committee, the Committee on Education Beyond the High School, and the leaders of the Curriculum Study.

We must look to students, parents, other citizens, school boards, teachers, principals, superintendents, and all people connected with the schools. Where does each of them fit into the pattern of a program to make our schools second to none?

What has the student to do with achieving quality education?

I say to students that quality education is not something that you get out of a box, ready-mixed. It is not something that is going to be given to you. It cannot be said to students: "Here it is. Now come and pick it up." Quality education stems from the fact that you have earnest students who want to learn. Unless there is a desire on the part of the student to learn and to take advantage of the opportunities and the teaching that we hope to continue to move up in quality, then we are not going to have any quality education.

Unless students work at it, unless they want to learn, there'll be no quality education for them. If they do want to learn, if they are sincerely trying to prepare for their opportunities in life, then we hope to improve the chances of their being properly prepared. I am sure that any student now going back can make a great contribution to his own future, realizing that this is not something to be handed to him, but something that he must want and for which he must work.

What have the parents to do with quality education?

First, they should take a direct and daily interest in the school-work of their children. Unless the parents are willing to insist that homework be assigned and that homework be done, unless the parents encourage extra reading and study from time to time, unless the parents concern themselves with the student and the school, we will not make much progress.

I would like to see every local school and every local PTA make a major effort to get parents and teachers to know each other better. Somehow, we tend to distrust people we do not know. It is tragic when parents and teachers distrust each other. I would like to see the major portion of each PTA meeting given over to getting parents and teachers better acquainted with each other and better acquainted with the program in the public school designed to provide quality education for the children in the schools. This would mean that routine business would be handled by giving out mimeographed bulletins. Things like the minutes of the last meeting, committee reports, budget information, and announcements could be handled in a monthly PTA newsletter.

This getting acquainted and better understanding would be an extension of the school's guidance program. Each child needs two advocates, one in the home and one in the school. Certainly, any intelligent effort at counseling can be much more effective if the home and the school pool their knowledge about and concern for the welfare of the child.

There is another thing it would do. It would make parents understand better and appreciate more the educational opportunities the school offers and it will help teachers understand better and be more sympathetic toward the needs of individual children.

If we are going to promote united efforts to improve education, we must first agree on what the job of the school should be. The school's job is an educational job and its primary responsibility is to provide for intellectual development. It shares with other agencies like the home and the church responsibility for health and citizenship and home membership. We cannot, however, give the school such a large part of these responsibilities that it cannot accomplish its major job, the promotion of intellectual development. Sometimes we parents are at fault. There are so many good things we want for our children and the school is such a convenient place to dump these responsibilities. We must redouble our efforts to educate the public to expect a quality educational effort from the school but not to expect the school to accomplish everything for our children. We are going to have to be willing to let the school give up some of the outside jobs we now expect it to assume.

What can the teachers do?

The classroom teacher is the key, the on-stage actor in the drama of quality education. I want you to know that I fully recognize this fact. All that has been done in the General Assembly, by the State Board of Education, by school officials and local boards, and by the Governor's Office has merely served to set the stage. The play is yet to be given. And on the teachers' performance in the classrooms of North Carolina will depend the success of our venture.

Success is the product of a united effort by many people. Without this united effort, all else may fail. But the success of the teacher depends heavily on his own ability and effort. It is toward following this united effort with personal effort that I want to urge all teachers with all the earnestness at my command.

The new day is dawning in North Carolina. The stage is set. The props that we asked for have been provided. The audience is waiting, expectantly, for this new day in education, this program of quality education for which they have bought their tickets. They have been sold on the advertising. Now they want to see the play!

There are many teachers who have parts in this play, nearly 40,000 of them. Most are full-time professional people who give to teaching their full measure of devotion. They even give of their own time in the summer and at other times to becoming better prepared, professionally.

There are others who are part-time teachers with two jobs or divided loyalties. While paid for full-time teaching, they do not give their full measure of devotion to teaching.

I am convinced that quality education will not be achieved by depending on part-time teachers.

The success of our venture will depend on devoted, full-time teachers, and enough of them to play all the key roles. It will depend on an effective curriculum, on good books and enough of them, on strong leadership and direction, on all the props that help the teacher do a good job in the classroom.

But I emphasize again that there will be no quality education across North Carolina unless individual teachers clearly understand that they must deliver quality education in the classrooms.

I recommend, first, that every individual teacher at the beginning of school engage in careful self-examination. I would suggest these eight questions:

How can I do a better job?

What are my shortcomings and how can I overcome them?

How can I reach every child and bring out the best within him?

Have I been lazy at times, or indifferent, or unconcerned?

And don't just ask these questions. Answer them!

Am I taking every opportunity to improve my professional competence?

Do I realize that this child's future is in my hands, and my failure now will mar him in some degree for life?

Have I set high standards for myself which I am willing to follow?

Am I living up to the severe challenge of my noble calling?

I recommend to teachers that they write these questions down, add others of their own, and paste them on their mirrors for review each morning. There is no end to improvement.

No professional person advances or succeeds without daily self-examination and constant effort at improvement. I know this is true of the legal profession, and I am sure it is true of the teaching profession.

What can principals, superintendents, and boards of education do?

Principals, superintendents, members of boards of education, and school committees must move together if we are going to have quality education.

In terms of leadership, superintendents are the key people, and principals are their field lieutenants. These are the executive officers of the most important business in North Carolina.

To give effective leadership, superintendents and principals must either know themselves what needs to be done or they must be able to use the knowledge of experts in an effective way. They must lead out with ideas and provide guidance in giving constructive direction to change—or at least not stand in the way of improvement. There is no set pattern. It takes daily decisions, constant intelligence, positive determination to find ways every day to make their schools better. They must involve in school improvement all of the people concerned. This means students and parents as well as teachers. It means citizens who have no children in school, as well as school board and school committee members. This means leadership, and it will not be achieved by the dictator who doesn't want any opinion expressed but his own. It will not be reached by the principal or superintendent who is afraid to let the lay public in the school for fear they will find out what is going on.

It will require that lines of communication be kept open. The school board, the PTA, and the public in general must be kept informed and must have an open channel to make suggestions.

The school executive must be able to inform members of the community in such a way as to raise high the level of the kind of education they expect. He must not be afraid to tell the truth about the schools, even the unpleasant truth. Citizens cannot be left behind while the professional school man runs the schools. He must be able and willing to present a point clearly and forcibly through contacts with his board and with leaders in the community.

It must be remembered that superintendents, principals, and their staffs exist solely to make more effective the instructional program. They must remember that their job is to help the teacher do a better job, and not to think up more ways to dissipate the teacher's time and energy attending more meetings and making out more reports. I sincerely hope that the new assistant superintendents and supervisors across the state assigned to instruction and curriculum will provide for teachers the help they do not have time to provide for themselves rather than to demand more of the teachers' time and energy and thus take time away from the students.

School boards and committees have the job of knowing what is going on and working for improvement. They make and support sound policy. They make and support the essential decisions which will lead to improvement.

Still another important characteristic is the election to school boards and school committee membership of well-qualified people who are dedicated and informed in the services that they render. I cannot overemphasize the importance of this. Real unity in any school community cannot be achieved without united, dedicated board and committee members who put child welfare first, last, and always!

I am encouraged to know that the State Department of Public Instruction is actively engaged in strengthening the state accreditation policies and procedures. As soon as possible, every school should be re-evaluated. Much of the value of accreditation will lie in the stimulation for improvement that will come to the local school. This is the basic purpose and the most important outcome of evaluation.

North Carolina is seeking a new curriculum, a curriculum with power—"power in itself to challenge the latent germ of genius, great or small, classical or modern, academic or technical, that every educable human being has within him in some degree." It is only in the light of this curriculum study that we are investing another $100 million toward the achievement of this goal. We await results with hope and with confidence, aware that this is a never-ending task.

The duty of improving the schools and thereby the future of North Carolina is laid upon the shoulders of every citizen of the state.

The state administration is doing all it can; the school leaders and the teachers will exceed all that is expected of them. I call on students and parents to take seriously their part. In fact, we need the help of everybody if we are to make our schools and our opportunities second to none.

As James Bryant Conant put it: "The road to better schools will be paved by the collective action of the local citizenry. The responsibility for the sorely needed upgrading of our schools cannot be passed to the state legislatures or to Congress. The responsibility rests on every citizen in the land."

STATE CONVENTION OF
DEMOCRATIC WOMEN OF NORTH CAROLINA

Winston-Salem

October 5, 1961

[This convention was the first state-wide meeting of its kind to be staged by Democratic women of North Carolina. Governor Sanford, who in his first year of office had filled some 100 state positions of responsibility with women, was well qualified to speak on women's role in government. He called for support from the women in the November 7 bond election.]

It is a happy privilege to participate with you in this convention of Democratic women of North Carolina.

I see here tonight the leaders who left your flower gardens to do the spade work for the victory the Democratic party achieved in North Carolina last November 8. You are the ones who left your cookstoves to stoke the fires that produced the steam that made possible the majorities for president and governor and the other offices. You took the needle from your sewing basket and stuck it into the over-inflated balloon of our opposition.

In short, you blazed the trail in a new day to the New Frontier.

Your work of 1960 surpassed that of any women's group in any campaign since the days of the suffragettes.

Since that day when women reached out and grasped the ballot, North Carolina and American politics have improved. The domination of special interest groups and the control of machine bosses have diminished in direct proportion to the activity of women Democrats.

In forty short years, you have moved from the disenfranchised who was supposed to stay in her place in the kitchen to positions of trust and leadership in practically every department and agency of local, state, national, and international government. All the citizens—men, women, boys and girls—have been the beneficiaries.

In an age that tends to be cynical, women Democrats have brought idealism to government. You also have brought integrity and ability. When some of the male leaders have been tempted to close their minds on various projects, you have been there to ask your sharp question of "Why not?" When some of the local, state, and national agencies threatened to get into ruts, you have manned the bulldozers of political action and filled in those ruts.

It has been my happy privilege to fill some 100 of the most important positions of trust in state government with women. I will appoint many more before this administration is over.

I am here to admit, to acknowledge, and to testify to the fact that this administration could not have been inaugurated without your great help, and it could not have achieved the goals of quality education that we have thus far achieved for the children of North Carolina without you, and it will of necessity rely heavily on you for the next three years and three months.

[At this point in the address, Governor Sanford cited thirty or forty women appointed to various boards, commissions, and committees during his administration. See the list of appointments in the Appendix to this volume.]

. . . .

It is easy to see from this list, and I could go on reading it until midnight, that women are occupying more positions of trust in North Carolina's governmental life than ever before.

Susie Sharp of Reidsville[93] is one of North Carolina's outstanding jurists. Grace Rodenbough of Stokes County[94] and Rachel Davis of Lenoir County[95] are leading legislators. Dr. Ellen Winston[96] is one of the most capable administrators in state government.

That precedent goes back through the history of our state, nation, and world. In North Carolina, striking examples of the leadership of women through the ages are pointed up in our history books by the ringing of the bell at Chapel Hill by Cornelia Phillips Spencer to reopen our university after the Civil War had closed it. And you know of the way Dorothea Dix came into North Carolina and turned the bright spotlight of public attention on the "snakepits" in which persons suffering mental illnesses had been cast.

But what we are concerned with primarily tonight is not the past but the future.

The future of this state is bound up with organizations like the Democratic Women of North Carolina. I don't have to tell this organization the progress that North Carolina has achieved

[93] Susie Marshall Sharp (1907-   ), lawyer, 1929-1949, from Reidsville; Judge of Superior Court, 1949-1962; first woman to be appointed Associate Justice of State Supreme Court, March, 1962; re-elected in own right on November 6, 1962. *North Carolina Manual,* 1963, 517.

[94] Grace Taylor Rodenbough (1896-   ), educator, homemaker, civic and cultural leader from Walnut Cove; member of legislature since 1953. Powell, *North Carolina Lives,* 1058-1059.

[95] Rachel Darden Davis III (1905-   ), physician and farmer from Lenoir County; member of state legislature, 1959-1963. *North Carolina Manual, 1963,* 566.

[96] Ellen Black Winston (1903-   ), author, professor, and public servant from Raleigh; Commissioner of State Board of Public Welfare, 1944-1961; appointed 1961 as United States Welfare Commissioner. *North Carolina Manual, 1961,* 434-436; *News and Observer,* December 20, 1962.

under the Democratic party—the progress in education, in good roads, in mental hospitals, in the arts and cultural activities, and in all the many other activities of state government.

And I don't have to reiterate the part women of North Carolina have played in the Democratic party.

I trust that as citizens first, women second, and Democrats third, you will assume as one of your major projects in these next thirty-three days the adoption of the bond issues.

Every one of the issues has been carefully scrutinized, first by college administrators and trustees and the agency heads, then by the Advisory Budget Commission of 1960, then by the appropriations subcommittees and full committees in both the State House of Representatives and the State Senate.

Now these ten bond issues are up to the voters. Every cent of the $61,665,000 proposed in these issues is needed: it is needed so your children and mine will have classroom space when they go to college; it is needed for the treatment and rehabilitation of the mentally ill; it is needed to develop our ports so they can boost the economy of North Carolina; it is needed for the training schools so that we can help delinquent children become self-respecting and self-supporting adults; it is needed for agricultural research stations so that we may reinvigorate our farm economy; it is needed for protecting and preserving our historical assets; it is needed to conserve and develop our rich forest potential and our park system; it is needed for working space for state employees at the state capital.

In short, these ten bond issues are needed for the future of North Carolina.

North Carolina has never trembled at the future. North Carolina has never fainted at a challenge. North Carolina has never shirked her duty to her posterity.

I don't believe North Carolina's women, and men, intend to tremble or faint or shirk now.

I believe you and all the citizens of the state will vote "yes" on November 7.

I am counting on your help.

FIFTY-FIFTH ANNUAL MEETING OF THE NORTH CAROLINA TEXTILE MANUFACTURERS ASSOCIATION

PINEHURST

October 6, 1961

The Governor began by commenting that approximately 44 per cent of all manufacturing employees in North Carolina were in the textile industry, a fact which proved that the hopes and dreams of a large segment of the population lay with the business. Sanford said that state government had assured its support to textile leaders when he urged adoption of a resolution at the Southern Governors' Conference calling for federal action to strengthen the position of the American textile industry. The resolution called for help in preventing textile imports from weakening the industry's economic strength. The pessimism of those who prophesied doom for the industry was largely unjustifiable, for new population would create new demand, but research was also a key factor. The Research Triangle was cited as a symbol of the state's dedication to research; the textile enterprise would have to follow suit. The Governor urged an interest in insuring the development of quality cotton within North Carolina, saying this was a joint responsibility of the textile industry and such groups as the North Carolina Cotton Growers Cooperative Association and the Farmers Cooperative Exchange. Governor Sanford encouraged the group to face the challenges and take advantage of the opportunities in North Carolina.

ANNUAL MEETING
FIFTH DISTRICT MEDICAL SOCIETY

PINEHURST

October 11, 1961

The future of North Carolina and the part the medical profession would play in that future demanded great responsibility of each member of the medical society. Calling on the membership to assume positions of leadership in civic affairs, the Governor particularly urged support of the bond election to be held on November 7, 1961. He explained ways in which the money would be spent. Under essential capital improvements, a variety of programs across the state would progress, including expansion of the North Carolina Health Center in Chapel Hill. The needs of mental health programs would also be covered, and mental institutions would reap benefits by a favorable vote on the bonds. Funds would be made available for participation, by the Medical Care Commission, in local hospital construction. Other issues, while of less direct concern to the medical profession, would benefit North Carolina; these, too, deserved and needed the support of each member of the medical society.

DEDICATION CEREMONIES
JUVENILE EVALUATION CENTER

SWANNANOA

October 14, 1961

Governor Sanford turned his attention westward to Swannanoa and to the newest facility for combating juvenile delinquency. Speaking of the new center, he said the state would "be richly rewarded for . . . [its] investment each time a child finds love and understanding and real purpose in a life once clouded with confusion, antagonism, fear, and, in many instances, hopelessness." He spoke of the rapid progress made in the field of youth rehabilitation. That responsibility had been accepted and supported by the majority of citizens was evidenced by the seven correction and training facilities maintained by the state. The Governor called attention to a national study which showed the programs of North Carolina and Florida to be the best in the Southeast and among the best in the nation. He thanked the dedicated persons who actually administered the programs, adding that the increase in juvenile delinquency and violence of juvenile crimes meant a greater challenge of working with these young people. The Governor said that the dedication of this facility was only the beginning; he expressed hope that this ceremony would be used as a "source of inspiration for the battles yet to be fought."

KENTUCKY DEMOCRATIC DINNER

LEXINGTON, KENTUCKY

October 14, 1961

In an address in Kentucky, Sanford spoke of the strong ties between Kentucky and North Carolina. He referred to the 1949

Jefferson-Jackson Day Dinner in Raleigh, while he was serving
as president of the Young Democratic Clubs of North Carolina,
at which Kentucky's Alben W. Barkley spoke. Barkley attracted
an overflow crowd to hear him trace the history of the Democratic party, a history which Sanford told the group was as vital
as ever, with the addition of a chapter on the New Frontier. The
principles of the Democratic party were unchanged. Sanford
described the party as one willing to "use a round wheel when
it is proved that a round wheel will carry the needs of the people
better than a square wheel," one that believed in free enterprise, that believed in the responsibility of a prosperous nation
to help the indigent, that believed in reinvigorating the farms
and in educating the people. The Governor observed that the
Democratic party was the one that "votes YES to the future."
To further his support of the party and its principles, he cited
goals and achievements made in Kentucky and in North Carolina under Democratic administrations, mentioning specifically
education, highways, and agriculture. He praised Governor Bert
T. Combs for his leadership in Kentucky. Calling the Democratic party's program in North Carolina and Kentucky and in
all America "adventurous and . . . more governed by hopes than
fears," Sanford remembered that the party had led the country
through nearly every difficult period in its history, and that
history had made "clear the wisdom of most of the startling reforms proposed by the Democrats over the years." He said that
"history almost forces one to be a Democrat. . . ." Sanford ended
his address by remarking that the Democratic party was willing
to help people and willing "to take the courageous steps that
today's changing world requires."

OPENING CEREMONIES OF THE
NINETY-FOURTH NORTH CAROLINA STATE FAIR

RALEIGH

October 16, 1961

This gubernatorial speech was a ringing invitation to North
Carolinians and to out-of-state visitors to attend the State Fair.
The Governor commented that anyone who went to the fair
would see North Carolina on display, that agriculture would be
emphasized because North Carolina was an agricultural state
with a future closely associated with farming. The fair provided
abundant evidence to support faith in the future of North

Carolina agriculture. He added that agriculture and industry complemented each other and that evidence of this was shown by the Trade Fair in Charlotte. The State Fair stood as a symbol of what North Carolina had become and what it could do. Governor Sanford closed with a commendation to Commissioner L. Y. Ballentine of the State Department of Agriculture, the fair staff, and the exhibitors.

GOVERNOR'S CONFERENCE ON
ECONOMIC DEVELOPMENT

CHAPEL HILL

November 1, 1961

North Carolina, in seeking to provide more jobs at higher wages, had made great strides in economic development, but since Governor Sanford chose to talk about "hard facts and hard work," he emphasized the goals yet to be won rather than past accomplishments. He discussed the problem of the migration of Tar Heel workers to other regions for greater opportunities, for example, saying that statistics showed that the state would have to work hard to overcome obstacles. He suggested that the citizenry was intelligent and productive, and that conferences such as the one held in Chapel Hill could help work out solutions to problems in the economy. Because of the economic differences in various sections of the state, programs for area development were needed. The Governor said that local governments could do a great deal independently, but that some projects required cooperation between localities. He concluded with a commendation for this conference, which he called "a forum for North Carolina's future."

SOUTH CENTRAL PIEDMONT NORTH CAROLINA
INDUSTRIAL DEVELOPMENT CONFERENCE

CONCORD

November 2, 1961

Governor Sanford again called for self-evaluation by communities seeking new industry. He reminded the group that a community as a potential industrial site would have planned for its future needs, shaped a budget to finance those needs, and exhibited a progressive attitude. Industries expected to pay their share, but they wanted high-quality services in return. The Governor discussed various factors which had to be considered by communities. After he talked about labor, and the asset of industrial education centers; natural assets, such as water and agrarian resources; and a good highway system, Governor Sanford stressed the need for long-term planning. He cited the Western North Carolina Regional Planning Commission as a good example of a group serving seventeen counties and their municipalities. To bring to fruition the benefits of the multifaceted economy of North Carolina would require hard work, co-operation, money, time, and adequate community services. Sanford summed up his idea by saying that "more goes into economic development than industrial development and . . . more goes into industrial development than merely seeking an industry." He expressed confidence in this group and in the citizens of the state in their ability to do the job.

LUNCHEON MEETING OF NEW YORK CITY BANKERS

New York, New York

November 6, 1961

First Citizens, Wachovia, North Carolina National, First Union National, and Branch banks sponsored a meeting in New York at which Governor Sanford spoke. He discussed the significance of banks in the continuing progress of North Carolina, commenting on their role in such programs as traffic safety, industrial development, and improved schools. Citizens were soon to vote on a $61.5 million bond issue, and North Carolina was aware of its AAA bonds, expecting a ready market for them, but the Governor asked the bankers to consider the state on its own merits rather than merely on its financial standing. He reminded the audience of North Carolina's good race relations, of its improved public school system, of its cultural programs and institutions, of its road system, of its agricultural achievements, and of its desire for new industries and promotion of established businesses. Sanford asked the bankers to judge North Carolina "on the basis of its sound sense of responsibility, on its dynamic, aggressive spirit and growth, and on its integrity and character." He expressed the opinion that the bankers would find a state "which has in fact made its way to the mainstream of America."

COLLEGE OF THE ALBEMARLE
DEDICATION AND INAUGURATION CEREMONIES

ELIZABETH CITY

November 7, 1961

Governor Sanford, at the dedication of the College of the Albemarle, called education "vital . . . to the national defense as well as to the promotion of a better life for our people." He urged North Carolina to provide educational opportunities appropriate for each individual throughout his life. Reminding the audience that the southern region had to catch up, Sanford said that North Carolina had embarked on an exciting crusade to improve educational opportunities. He prophesied that the College of the Albemarle would become increasingly important and that the new college would carry people on the eastern seaboard "to a future bright with promise."

NORTH CAROLINA STATE
SCHOOL BOARDS DELEGATE ASSEMBLY

CHAPEL HILL

November 8, 1961

Addressing the Delegate Assembly of the North Carolina School Boards Association, Governor Sanford stressed the responsibility of the group which had broad legal powers and which represented "a powerful moral force." The fact that the people had the ultimate responsibility for government in the United States, including the responsibility for education, resulted in the American system of lay boards of education. The boards worked as a partnership with the State Board of Education and also with local citizens to carry out the job of educating children. Not being fiscally independent in this state, the boards had to co-operate with the boards of county commissioners who had the taxing authority. It was the duty of the school boards to present the needs of the schools to the commissioners and to the legislators to assure adequate support for the public schools. Keeping those groups and the citizens as a whole informed was one of the chief functions of the school board members. The Governor stressed the importance of teamwork, which involved teachers, students, parents, and members of the boards. The members were responsible for setting the tone for the educational program and for establishing local policies. Each school board was called on to "survey all school needs and chart a long-range plan for school improvement." Governor Sanford called education the chief concern of the people of North Carolina; he told the board members that they were leaders and he expressed his trust in their ability and willingness to meet their responsibilities.

TENTH ANNIVERSARY CEREMONIES UNIVERSITY OF NORTH CAROLINA SCHOOL OF NURSING

CHAPEL HILL

November 8, 1961

Governor Sanford commended those who had a role in developing the growth of the School of Nursing, a school which had brought credit to the University of North Carolina and to the state. He pointed out the need for sound preparation in social, psychological, and public health fields as well as the need of nurses for qualities of leadership, citizenship, and social development along with professional training. The increase in population would mean an expansion of health services. The fact that the South's ratio of nurses to the population was the lowest in the country was a matter of grave concern. Sanford reminded the group of the facilities for training available in North Carolina. He then discussed the School of Nursing in particular and described attainments of this school. He congratulated the school on the fine record of its first ten years and suggested that this record "serve as an inspiration . . . [for] the tasks of the years ahead."

NORTH CAROLINA RESOURCE-USE EDUCATION CONFERENCE

DURHAM

November 16, 1961

Sanford reminded persons attending the Resource-Use Education Conference that as resources were being depleted rapidly and demands on those resources increasing, man's relationship to his natural environment was jeopardized. Indecision, irresponsibility, and a lack of vision meant that people were denying themselves a wonderful bounty and imposing on future generations the prospect of a struggle for survival. A new, positive approach to the matter of resource-use would have to be developed. He urged people to educate themselves in the complex field of resource-use and conservation, defined as "an effort to maintain and replenish the supply of resources we now need and use." People being the most important resource, the Governor urged that no effort be spared to develop the physical, mental, and moral capabilities of rising generations. He called this a great challenge, saying that success in meeting the challenge would mean that future generations would enjoy the greatest prosperity in the history of man. He credited this group with working to meet that challenge.

NORTHEASTERN SOIL AND WATER CONSERVATION DISTRICTS

EDENTON

November 16, 1961

Governor Sanford began by reminding North Carolinians of their "long and honorable record in the field of soil and water conservation." The oldest conservation district in America, the Brown Creek Soil and Water Conservation District in Anson County, was organized in 1937. The northeastern districts were founded in 1942. The Governor reviewed accomplishments and explained the significance of the program. He reminded the group that the state realized its responsibility in the field though soil and water conservation district programs were in local hands. In closing, Sanford emphasized North Carolina's responsibility of using natural resources, not abusing them.

TWENTY-SIXTH ANNUAL MEETING OF THE NORTH CAROLINA FARM BUREAU FEDERATION

RALEIGH

November 21, 1961

[Two weeks after the defeat of the state-wide bond proposals, Governor Sanford took the opportunity to discuss needs of the state and to interpret the political situation. He had received innumerable letters from North Carolinians who expressed their feelings on the bond situation after the election had been held. One woman wrote, "Don't blame yourself for the outcome of the bond issue. You worked hard and sincerely for what you believed to be for the best interest of North Carolina. You gave the issue your best effort. If you want my autopsy report, the timing was bad, and too many issues for one swallow—one spoonful of castor oil could be swallowed before you know it (tax in this case) but you would know it before you had downed ten. . . . Well, I pulled all ten of the 'for' levers—I lost—so did you, and the State, but at least we live in a State that we can say what we want to, without fear of reprisal—your popularity is probably at its lowest ebb right now, but in six months it will be up again, and eventually you will have been one of N. Carolina's great governors." On the other side of the ledger, one person attached a newspaper clipping in which the Governor expressed concern because of lack of facilities which would have been provided had the bond issue passed. Commenting on the news item, the citizen wrote, "But he evidently *does not* worry about the thousands of children who go to bed hungry every night as a result of HIS Food Tax, while HE gads around six days out of every week in a $200,000.00 airplane. 'SIC SEMPER TYRANNIS.' "The Governor received a cash-register tape showing a tax of 64 cents; on the back were the words, "This is one good reason I am going to do all I can to help defeat any bond or taxes you try to get passed." On November 10, 1961, the Governor received the following communication which also brought in the matter of the state's plane, the "Kitty Hawk," which was used by the Governor and by other state officials:

OUR

NEW NEW

READER

SEE

SEE TERRY GO

GO GO GO!

RIDE

RIDE, TERRY, RIDE

RIDE, RIDE, RIDE!

BLAH

BLAH, TERRY, BLAH

BLAH, BLAH, BLAH!!!

HEAR

HEAR, TERRY, HEAR

HEAR, HEAR, HEAR!

FLY

FLY, TERRY, FLY

FLY, FLY, FLY

GIVE

GIVE TERRY PLANE

GIVE, GIVE, GIVE

While this writer failed to mention the bond issue specifically, the person obviously wrote to express his personal opinion of the Governor and his program in the wake of the bond defeat. In his address to the Farm Bureau Federation, Governor Sanford went into considerable detail as he elaborated on his feelings of concern for the future of North Carolina.]

I want to talk to you a little this morning from the heart because I want to touch on this theme that you have for this program, "Moving Ahead Together in '62." True, you furnished a great part of the agricultural leadership in the past. But more important than that, you must continue your leadership in all segments of the forward march of North Carolina.

We are at a time of peril in America. We are at a time of opportunity in the South. And that combination of moving into our opportunities in the South can help furnish the kind of leadership which will enable America to remove the peril.

I know of no time, looking back over the broad sweep of the history of America, when this nation faced greater difficulty, including the time of the Revolutionary War. Never before has the very existence of mankind been threatened as it is threatened today. Never before has such a severe challenge been faced by free people to live up to the demands and the responsibilities of making democratic government strong and making it work.

President Kennedy has asked the question and sounded the call to duty in asking the American people: Do we have the skill, the nerve, and the will as a free people to make democracy strong enough, to improve our leadership to the degree where we can indeed save mankind, save the free world, and save American democracy?

In our own part of the free world, are we going to do our part to develop the scientists, to develop the statesmen, and to develop the informed citizenry which America needs?

It cannot be done on any other level. We cannot look to Washington for it and should not look to Washington for it. We cannot look to the United Nations for it, as important as is the UN to world peace.

What is done to develop the kind of citizens who can make democracy carry through under the greatest strains must be done right here in North Carolina, by us, by you. You can furnish the kind of leadership that we need. You can furnish the kind of leadership that the free world must have. You already have furnished that leadership, and I come before you today to express my thanks and the thanks of a grateful state for the part that you played as an organization, in setting the tone, in sounding the call to arms, for the people of North Carolina to mobilize their forces and their resources to do something about education. We stand now in a position of leadership across the nation in terms of what we are attempting to do to prepare free men and women for leadership.

I think that you may take great pride in the fact that during the days when there were many doubtful people, and during the days when many people wondered whether we were attempting to do too much, and during the days when people of little faith did not quite have the courage to do the things that must be done if we are to meet this test of leadership, this organization responded. And this organization cast its vote and its lot with the education of the young people of the state.

Now out of that vote, out of that determination have come many things, some negative and most positive. All across North Carolina right now, in every local community, almost without exception, people are moving toward the improvement of educational opportunities with a new morale and with a new vigor, I believe, the like of which has never been seen in North Carolina before.

People are determined that we can do the job. People are proud of the fact that North Carolina sees this as a great mission and that we are going to do something to prepare the young people in this state who will make the state even greater than it has been.

I thank you for what you have done because North Carolina, indeed, is on the move and will, with your leadership, continue to be on the move going forward together in 1962 and in all the years to come.

Some bad things came out of the decision, as inevitably they must. First of all, we knew that if we were going to do something about schools and public education we had to start with the fundamental problem. The fundamental problem is this: Just this morning I was reading an advanced report that will be made the last of this month to the Southern Governors concerning the problems of education in our region. One set of statistics caught my attention. We have known it, but here it is. This whole region of sixteen states needs around 55,000 to 60,000 new teachers each year. We in the region are producing now around 40,000 teachers. That is, we are graduating 40,000 and all of them do not go into teaching.

The fundamental need was to attract the attention of outstanding students in high school and in college and direct their interests toward the teaching profession. In other words, our fundamental need was to get better people in adequate numbers to come into the teaching profession and keep them there once they became good teachers.

That was the fundamental need. The fundamental way to go about it, we thought, and you agreed, was to make the teaching profession more attractive, to give it a high level of dignity on the local level, to make it the kind of thing that a young person would seek with pride and seek with the satisfaction of knowing that he not only would fulfill the desire to have a vital role in his generation, in his time, in his state and country, but also where he could be adequately compensated and could adequately provide for his family.

So the first need, among many, many needs all of which are not yet met, was to increase the attractiveness of the teaching profession. Now that can be done by you locally in many ways. It can be done by more adequate facilities. It can be done by just an attitude toward the teaching profession which cast it, cast the teaching profession in the important role that it does occupy in the future of the country.

It could also be done on the state level by increased financial support. So as we analyzed and studied and thought about the needs of education, one of the many things that had to be done was an increased level of financial support for the teaching profession to reverse this downward trend where less and less teachers were coming and start it moving upward so that we would have tomorrow and in 1962, 1965, and 1970 an adequate number of teachers—well-qualified, confident teachers to do the job that must be done.

In order to reverse that trend, the General Assembly of North Carolina took the greatest forward step that has ever been taken by a General Assembly in the history of North Carolina. They voted the appropriations. They provided the foundation on which you locally can build a better school system. They did their job. And in doing their job, it was necessary to find additional money.

Now, that ought not to surprise anybody. It ought to be perfectly obvious that if you are going to expand a business operation, you must pay for it. If you are going to increase your standard of living at home, you must pay for it. If you are going to extend your farming operations, you must make additional investments. So this General Assembly, knowing that it must make an additional investment, faced up to the job and made that additional investment in face of much opposition and much criticism and a degree of unpopularity. It was a painful decision because I knew it would evoke bitter criticism from many places across the state. It was a painful decision because I was disturbed at one time that we could not muster enough support to get it across, and if we didn't, of course, the whole concept of the future greatness of North Carolina's educational system and the future of North Carolina as based on education would fall backward.

But I made that decision knowing that there would be many months of unpopularity. I made that decision knowing that it could not be a popular decision. I made that decision knowing that there would be many people who would insist that we had done wrong by the people of the state. But I made it, and the General Assembly made the decision on the firm understanding that we did not come to office merely to seek popularity. If that had been the only mission in seeking office, then it wouldn't have been worth the effort. If that had been our only guiding light, then we would not have been worthy of the high office.

And, therefore, we decided that we would face the lack of popularity and take it in our stride, confident in the long run that the people of North Carolina would realize that this indeed was the only step and this indeed had to be done if North Carolina was to build to its future greatness. So we did take it.

The General Assembly, with great courage, did pass it, and to your eternal credit this organization endorsed and supported it from the very beginning; I admire your courage and appreciate it.

The General Assembly also submitted a bond issue. I am humble enough to recognize that my own position and my lack of popularity growing out of some difficult decisions might very well have had something to do with the failure of those bond issues. I think, also, that there were many other things that entered.

But let's conclude for a moment that some people decided that this would be a good opportunity to get even with the Governor for things that he has done that they didn't like.

Now I have said before, and I reiterate here, that I do not believe many North Carolinians would vote on the bond issue and the future needs of the state for such a shallow reason. I do not believe that they did.

But right now those people who would make political advantage out of North Carolina's failure to provide these things are making political sport in saying that this was because the people of North Carolina did not like what had been done in this administration in the past, particularly as far as the sales tax is concerned.

They have come up with all kinds of letters to the editors and all kinds of gossip back and forth in order to take political advantage against the future needs of North Carolina.

Now what happens to me and what happens to any popularity that in this office I might have is unimportant. But what happens to the future of North Carolina, a decision for you to make and leaders like you across the state, is extremely important. And I would hope that we could clear aside, with your leadership and with your talking to other people, any partisan look, any narrow look at the future needs of North Carolina, and that we could measure those needs and those requirements now against the future greatness of North Carolina and not against some petty dislike of the moment.

I have seen letters to the editor here in recent weeks that have complained bitterly about the food and medicine tax and cited that as the chief cause without bothering to look at the fact that the legislature did not put any tax on medicine. But hardly a day passes that a letter to the editor doesn't complain about the tax that was not put on. Hardly a day passes that they do not complain about some other part of the state government. Hardly a day passes, and I might as well mention this to you, that they do not complain about the airplane the state owns, which is primarily used for the economic development of North Carolina.

While the insidious Republican leadership—and I speak of the Republican leadership, not of the many Republican members who did work and work enthusiastically for the passage of these bonds—the insidious Republican leadership walked down Front Street publicly announcing that they favored the building of educational and institutional buildings, that they favored the mental hospitals and meeting this humane need of the state, and at the same time they circulated on the back street literature which was misleading, which was false, and which gave an entirely different picture in opposition to the very things that this same leadership was proclaiming on Front Street.

I think that is carrying politics too far. I think that is taking advantage of a partisan position attempting to damage your opposition in a way that doesn't really damage the opposition, but indeed, damages the opportunities of every child and every person in North Carolina.

North Carolina has had too bright a history. North Carolina has too great an opportunity to let that opportunity go down in a mass of personal petty politics. And I hope that we can rise above it. I hope that we can see beyond it, and where I am at fault I earnestly promise to do my best to correct the bad situation.

We are attempting to meet the needs. We are attempting to meet the responsibility, and I need your help if we are going to be able to be successful. In North Carolina right now if we do not do something immediately to provide opportunities in the colleges and universities across the state, if we do not do something right now to provide dormitory space, the cafeteria space, and classroom space, then your sons and daughters and your grandsons and granddaughters are not going to be admitted to college opportunities because in this state we simply will not have enough facilities to provide for them.

And right now, in this state, we have young boys and girls who have strayed from the proper paths, who are in the jurisdiction of the juvenile authorities, and who cannot be admitted to our correctional homes because we simply do not have enough space.

If you are going to do something about that, we are going to need your help and your understanding and your leadership.

And we have in this state crippled children with defective minds, with mental illnesses who are still on waiting lists, and next year the waiting lists will be even greater, the following year even greater because somebody measured the immediate situation against the future needs and because we did not live up to the responsibility to understand something about these needs.

Now, I don't mean to be critical of the people who voted against the bond issue. I am critical of myself, and I am critical of other people in this state charged with the responsibility of explaining these things because we did not do an adequate job.

But North Carolina cannot wait to build its colleges. North Carolina cannot wait to build its mental institutions. North Carolina must move now in this respect if it is to live up to its great tradition and if it is to provide for its bright tomorrow.

In North Carolina over the years, in the darkest times, the people have risen up and the people have always exhibited a spirit of moving forward.

North Carolina stands in the forefront of the South right now. It stands in the forefront of the South for many reasons, going back to the same spirit of North Carolinians who had faith in the future, who had vision to build and courage to do those things now which might seem unpopular but which are essential to the future of the state.

After the Civil War, when everything was torn all apart and the pieces were strewed around, North Carolina was the first in the South to pick up the call, to challenge greatness, to do something about it.

Governor Aycock put our faith in education. Our faith has been in education ever since that day. Our faith has been well rewarded because North Carolina has marched to the forefront of the South. The time has come when the South can move to the forefront of the nation. The time has come.

Now we are celebrating the one hundredth anniversary of the Civil War. To my way of thinking that centennial marks the end of our being here in a little segment behind in so many ways, economically, socially, and educationally, to other parts of the country. That marks the time for moving forward. The war is over. It has been over one hundred years. We have built back. We have built back to a position of leadership in the South.

The time has come for North Carolina to move and to seek a position of leadership in the nation. It is not good enough for our boys and girls to have the best education in the South. We should see that that opportunity is the best in the nation.

We can do it! We've got the people. We've got the spirit. We've got the resources. I am sure that we've got the courage and the vision, and I know that we can do it with people like you and if particularly you will assume this leadership.

We need your help. We must have it. And with it there indeed will be no holding us back as we go forward together in 1962.

Thank you.

REPORT TO THE PEOPLE OVER STATE-WIDE TELEVISION AND RADIO NETWORK

RALEIGH

November 27, 1961

[Near the end of his first year in office, the Governor reviewed the accomplishments and the disappointments of his administration in a thirty-minute report to the people. In his concluding minutes he elaborated on his decision not to call a special session of the General Assembly to consider a new bond issue.]

I welcome the occasion at the beginning of the Christmas season, and at the end of a year's work, to talk about the forward steps taken by the state of North Carolina. This is not, and should not be, a time for false pride and boasting, but rather a point in the course of the administration when we can measure what has been accomplished against the opportunities of what can be done.

After the Civil War, when life was bleak, the future dim, and all things in the South were torn apart, North Carolina was the first to sound the bugle to start the march to greatness and leadership.

Governor Aycock put our faith in education. Our faith has been in education ever since. Our faith has been well rewarded, for it enabled North Carolina to build back from the ashes of war to new and greater opportunities. Never before have our opportunities been as promising as they are today.

I want to call the roll of some of the progress made in North Carolina in the past year pointing to some continuing opportunities.

In industrial development and expansion, North Carolina is continuing to make dramatic headway. This year, North Carolina led the South, and the South led the nation, in the percentage of industrial expansion. We are going full-speed to continue to seek the right kind of new industry to provide the right kind of jobs.

What does this mean? It means that 23,000 of you watching or listening tonight will go to work again tomorrow morning in a job which wasn't even in existence January 1. It means that the 23,000 of you will earn $80 million this year in those jobs. This has been done with work and seeing many people and going many places. The work continues. We have a working team in Raleigh which is working with people across the state.

A further way to illustrate it is is to note that each week since this administration has been in office 515 new jobs have been created for the jobless from new and expanded industry.

Let me say this to textile workers across North Carolina. I know personally many of you who are now listening to this program. I know how important your jobs are to you, and let me tell you that they are extremely important to the whole state.

I couldn't report this to you before, but I have made several trips to help protect your jobs. You can't expect increased wages if you are dragged down by low-wage countries, and this unfair competition has already cost us too many jobs. Just last week the White House took the first real action to protect your jobs that has been taken in ten years, and I am sure they are going to follow through in other ways.

In the Budget Division, this administration has taken determined steps for economy. One of the reasons is that in this time when so much of the national resource must go to national defense, I am determined that we are going to do everything possible to demonstrate that new ways of economy can be found in all levels of government. We have tightened our budget control. We have smashed the racket of price-fixing in bidding for state business. We are carefully examining every phase of the operation of government with a view to saving money.

In the Prison Department, we are doing some new things in new ways. The first purpose of a prison is a place of punishment, but there is a secondary purpose. You who have friends or relatives or loved ones in prison can readily understand that these people are in need of rehabilitation. We are attempting to help every prisoner help himself through training and study and a change in attitude. It saves money for the state; it helps the prisoner to find his way to a proper and rewarding life.

I have been particularly interested in the alcoholic rehabilitation program. We have provided the means for those who feel the desire to stop drinking, and in most of the prison camps, and ultimately we hope in all the camps, we will have a group of Alcoholics Anonymous. In the brief time we have been carrying on this program, we can already measure great success in lives redeemed. Incidentally, 75 per cent of the people in prison are there because of some connection with whisky.

We have concentrated the greatest single effort this year on the public schools because this was the greatest single need. If we are to build properly for the future of North Carolina, if we are to have industrial, agricultural, economic, social, individual growth and advancement, then our schools must be second to none.

Our challenge is to give our children the best opportunities. This does not mean that we expect every one of our children to be a college scholar. It means that our projected program anticipates the needs of the retarded child, gives the average child a wider choice, and provides the very talented child some extra challenges.

The General Assembly had the vision to vote for a program of school improvement for your children. The General Assembly had the courage to vote the taxes from the only adequate source.

Let me say this to the mothers of children: I share with you a desire to give your child the best opportunities in life. But we cannot improve our schools by just talking about it. You and I are doing something about it, and when you pay 15 cents on a $5.00 basket of groceries, you may do so with confidence that you are broadening the horizons for your child and all children.

What has been done in agriculture? There are so many opportunities in agriculture, which is the backbone of the economy of North Carolina, that I could take the entire period talking about what can be done and what is being done to improve farm income across the state. Let me say to the farmers, improvement of farm income has more far-reaching effect on the economy of this state than any other single segment of income. All of our ideas for the improvement of farm income have been tied up now in one program known as "Agricultural Opportunities." In this way each county has been challenged to define the ways in which it might add to its income, joining with other counties across the state in a massive effort to lift the farm economy. In co-operation with Mr. L. Y. Ballentine of the Department of Agriculture and Dean Brooks James, the School of Agriculture, and the Extension Service at State College, and with other related agencies and organizations, I am satisfied that the state has a vigorous program and will continue to do its share to promote those things which will bring more money to the farmers and through the farmers to the entire state.

In meeting our responsibility for helping children who have managed to get in trouble, the state is broadening the scope of its responsibility in the correction of the wayward child, having just opened a new evaluation center at Swannanoa for determining the cause of delinquency and helping set straight those children who come into the state system for correctional training.

In highway construction, we have stepped up farm-to-market road program construction, without cutting down our primary program. This was done by stopping diversion from the highway fund.

You who live on a muddy and dusty road, or have children riding in school buses on narrow roads and treacherous bridges are not forgotten. We promised to put the Highway Commission closer to the people, and you probably have already seen a highway commissioner for the first time in many years. They have been out riding the roads and talking to delegations. This couldn't be started until July so we are just getting cranked up. But we still have more than three years to go and you will witness a lot of improvement during that time.

When I came to office, I was determined to do something about the terrible slaughter on our highways. The loss of life, the injuries to thousands of people, and the extensive property damage are inexcusable. We are going to apply the best energy and determination we possess to reducing this awful loss. In addition to carrying on our official responsibilities, we have organized with voluntary contributions the finest Safety Council in America. I hope that we are going to be able to see progress in saving lives, in reducing injuries, and with your help we can make the most intensive effort of any state in the union.

Along with other accomplishments of a voluntary nature, such as the Highway Safety Council, the Trade Fair should be listed. This was a great success. It brought new business to the industry of North Carolina. This required the energy and efforts of many people on a voluntary basis, but their work paid off in the display of the diversified industrial might of North Carolina for all the world to see. This not only indicated what is being done, but more important, it indicates what can be done in North Carolina.

Another voluntary effort I must mention is the stay-in-school program, which is being conducted by the state with the help of the Optimist Clubs of North Carolina. This attempts to get at the reason for dropouts, to meet the human and economic needs, and to give the added encouragement, where necessary, to have the student return to school.

These are some of the more than 100 such projects, programs, and activities directly under the supervision of the Governor's Office. In addition to these, there are as many more in which the Governor participates. There are more than fifty heads of boards, agencies, or institutions who report directly to the Governor. During the past year, I have appointed and enlisted in the service of the state more than 500 people who have volunteered their services as members of the various boards and commissions. In the many things required of the state administration, government could not well function were it not for the voluntary service of these people who contribute of their time and talent to the progress of North Carolina. I am most grateful that these people make their abilities available for the welfare of the entire state and all its people.

Democracy is the best method known to man for providing everybody a fair opportunity to express themselves. In a democracy, there are always disappointments for some people. When two candidates run for office, only one can win. When a proposition is put to the people, it either passes or fails. This is the way democratic government operates. I not only have never quarreled with this process, but I have fought to defend it.

It so happened that from the opinion I have of the urgent needs, I thought that the recent bond issues should be approved. I knew that failure of the bonds would mean your children and grandchildren, even if qualified, might be denied a college education. I knew failure meant your neighbor's crippled or deaf child might have no place to go for training. I keenly feel these needs, but even so, as I said on the night of the election, it is not for me to quarrel with the decision of the majority of the voters.

It is my duty, however, again to call to the attention of the people that we do have needs. These needs, if unfulfilled, could damage the future of your children.

If we are to do our job in the correction of juveniles who have strayed from the proper paths, then we need to expand our institutions so that juvenile judges desiring to send children to training schools will not be faced with long waiting lists and delays. The longer the delay, the more serious the problem of correcting the child becomes. We do not now have adequate facilities, and to me personally, I believe this was the most disappointing aspect of the bond election.

We need very badly improvements in some of the older buildings of our mental institutions if we are to provide the kind of care which can return patients to normal life as rapidly as possible. This is not only the humane objective, but it has an economic value because the sooner we can cure them, the less expense we will have in their maintenance. This need remains to be faced and fulfilled, and along with it the need for more adequate and extensive treatment for children who need the care of these institutions.

I would go so far as to say that the air conditioning proposed for the hospital ward where live the children with bodies so crippled that they cannot move about, is one of the urgent needs of these institutions. A visit to this ward during the months of summer would convince anyone that this is in no way a luxury.

North Carolinians have always put their faith in education. Historically, our ancestors provided for the necessities of life, organized government, and then built colleges. In 1776, North Carolina made provision in the Constitution that "schools [should] be established . . . and all useful learning [should] be duly encouraged and promoted in one or more universities." Thirteen years later it provided for the first state university.

Since these Revolutionary days, North Carolina has seldom faltered. The schools, colleges, and university have always stood high among the objects of public confidence, public appreciation, and public support. The forward march of our society always brings new problems. Our educational institutions face increasing enrollment demands. They face demands for increased research to improve agriculture, business, industry, health programs, and many other meaningful areas of society. It is clear that our very survival in the world today demands that we redouble our efforts in education. Indeed, the responsibility to educate is an inseparable part of our responsibility to guard and advance the ideals of democracy. Further, if we neglect education, we block our growth economically and industrially; through education we open ways to agricultural, economic, and industrial advancement that will improve our standard of living.

We have been benefited by the fact that the state-supported institutions of higher learning and the Board of Higher Education, in the late fifties, developed a long-range building program for our institutions, including the community colleges, for the decade 1959-1969. This long-range plan demonstrated a need for $89 million in construction over a ten-year period. It was reviewed by Governor Hodges and the Advisory Budget Commission prior to the 1959 session of the General Assembly and again by them prior to the 1961 General Assembly. The 1959 session authorized the first step in this long-range program of capital improvements. Over $22 million, $17 million by a bond vote, in new construction and renovation projects was authorized. The second phase of this long-range plan was approved by the 1961 General Assembly and submitted to the people in the bond election on November 7.

This failure of bond approval means that the well-planned program of expansion in higher education, to take care of anticipated growth, was interrupted on November 7. The requirements remain, and indeed have increased.

Three items show the increase:

1. This report estimated that we would have at least 72,000 students in North Carolina colleges, state and private, by 1969. Right now, eight years ahead of schedule, we have reached this number. And the most conservative estimate now for 1969 is 100,000 students. The state-supported institutions must take their share of this increase.

2. High school enrollments increased by 18,000 students this fall. A large percentage of these students will be seeking admission to college in several years.

3. Enrollments in state-supported institutions increased by 4,162 this fall, an increase of 11.3 per cent over 1960, and private colleges experienced an almost equal increase.

It is necessary to understand that to plan for the future over two years is required to construct a facility once it is authorized. Building cannot be done overnight, so we must think and act ahead of time in order to be ready for students when they are ready for college.

Here, then, is a broad sketch of the immediate needs. I have not mentioned them all, so to these add the parks, the forests, and the ports; the test farms; the housing of archives, library, and other functions; and the medical care program of local hospital construction.

All of these things are important to you, and there is a degree of urgency involved in each.

What can we do to meet these needs?

We could call a special session of the General Assembly and submit the bonds, or at least the most urgent ones, to the people again. Many leaders have recommended this course of action, and I understand and value their reasoning and their desires. I have given this decision my most sincere and careful attention and thought. There is a good argument for calling a special session right now, but there are also some reasons for not calling a special session. The most compelling reason is this: It is not in keeping with the soundest principles of popular government. To call another election now would be to say that when a democratic election is lost, call another if you can. This would be a bad precedent, it is haphazard, and this is not conducive to the orderly processes of democratic government.

The people made the decision, and I will abide the decision. The people made the decision, and the urgent needs must abide the decision. Therefore, I will not call a special session of the General Assembly.

This doesn't mean that there is nothing we can do to lessen the ill effects of these pressing needs. There is much we can do. I have already pledged to do the best possible in working with what we have.

During the summer of 1962 the new Advisory Budget Commission will travel to all of the state institutions, looking into building requirements, and making decisions on a program to be presented in the 1963 General Assembly.

Thus, through the orderly procedure established by our excellent budget control act, we will again have a chance to present to the General Assembly a program to be presented to the people. In the meantime, we will stretch what we have as the demand grows.

I have conferred with Mr. John Umstead and others on ways we can do the best job possible with the mental hospital facilities we have. We cannot expect to do the full job, but we will do the best we can as applications increase beyond our present capacity.

I have conferred with the correctional training school people, and we are trying to find temporary means of accepting some of the juveniles; but we cannot expect to accept all who should have this training.

I have conferred with college presidents. Meeting the needs of students of college age will take extraordinary effort, because this need is growing so much faster than anyone dreamed.

I suggest seven ways we can do something about higher education requirements now:

1. The Advisory Budget Commission and the institution heads will review the capital improvement projects to determine those deemed absolutely essential for the biennium 1963-1965.

2. In order to speed up the program of construction, I have asked the Department of Administration to seek ways now to prepare plans and specifications of these needed facilities. This will save valuable time if dormitories are ultimately approved, and could enable us to make up as much as a year.

3. I now ask citizens living in the communities where our private and public colleges are located to let college officials know if they have any available rooming spaces in their residences that students might use.

4. I shall work with the presidents of our state-supported institutions in every possible way to see if more can be done to accommodate this situation, and I particularly note and commend their attitude expressed last week to "endeavor to utilize our present resources wisely and efficiently."

5. I now ask our private institutions to review their situations, looking to the possibility of accepting more students.

I promise to work closely with the leaders of private colleges in making certain that adequate student loan funds are available and in any way they might call on me for assistance. I would remind many of you that if you have been contemplating a gift to your favorite private college, now is the best possible time you could make it.

6. I am requesting Mr. Irving Carlyle, the able chairman of the Commission to Study Education Beyond the High School, to accelerate the study of the program of higher education, since these recommendations will be of great value in determining what facilities we must have now.

7. I shall ask the presidents, faculty members, trustees, alumni, friends, and students to join me in interpreting the facts concerning higher education to the people of the state. It is important for the people to know the truth about enrollments; research demands to improve our farms, businesses, industries; research in the health fields; the services rendered by our institutions to the people.

This, then, is to say to you that all of those working in this administration will do our best, and we will meet most of the most pressing needs on a temporary basis. But to do so we will need the help of every citizen who loves North Carolina and has faith in her future.

There are many forward moving programs not affected by this bond vote.

In these, which fortunately include the public schools, we will continue to move with full force and vigor. We need your help with these activities.

All of our problems come from growth and expansion and progress. These are problems, but also expansion and progress and growth are new opportunities. These are all around us. We have many things to attract the energy, the devotion, and the zeal of North Carolinians. We need your help in reaching for all of these objectives.

In these areas directly affected by the bond program, we will not falter in the face of a temporary setback.

It may indeed be difficult for the moment, but in the long run we will in this way comprehend better our obligations to the future. In the long run we will recover and we will eventually fulfill these obligations. Indeed, in the long run, democracy is always right. I trust implicitly the democratic process. The people have spoken on this issue at this time.

But now on the broader issues let's speak louder than ever in our spirit of progressiveness, in our determination to provide the opportunities for every child born on earth to develop fully all his talents for the benefit of himself and for mankind, in our determination to provide a better chance for every citizen to make a better living, in our determination to provide for the weak and the ill, in our determination to take our proper place of leadership as strong men and women in a frightened world.

North Carolina is on the move. The people of North Carolina can do anything they want to do.

We need your help, each of you, in reaching out for the chance that today belongs to North Carolina.

NORTH CENTRAL NORTH CAROLINA INDUSTRIAL DEVELOPMENT CONFERENCE

ELON COLLEGE

November 29, 1961

In the sixth and last of the industrial development conferences held in various sections of the state, Governor Sanford reviewed the problems and the opportunities of the area. An area which represented "about the best potential in the South for industrial development" was failing to utilize its resources of people, water, good location within overnight distance of great population centers, capital, and good local governments and local organizations working for development. The Governor cited facts to support his thesis that the area had not measured up. The per capita income was low; people, particularly younger citizens, had moved out of the area to seek employment. Though national and state help was available, the local people were the ones primarily responsible and the ones who had to work to see that there was over-all improvement. Sanford advised the group that "You must make industry want you." He reminded those attending the conference that not only industry but also agriculture had not been developed as fully as possible and that co-operative endeavor would result in mutual benefits. In his concluding statements he stressed the role of education in the picture, reminding his audience that education was a vital development resource which should never be overlooked.

FIRST CONGRESSIONAL DISTRICT
YOUNG DEMOCRATIC CLUBS RALLY

NAGS HEAD

December 8, 1961

Governor Sanford recalled his election as president of the North Carolina YDC in 1949. He said that the Young Democratic Clubs of the nation were founded in North Carolina in 1928; since that time, they had been "the trail blazer" for the party. The Democratic party had "placed great accent on young people and young ideas." Examples of young leadership since the Democrats began "uninterrupted service to North Carolina" in 1901 and accomplishments under this leadership were remembered. The Governor said that Democrats did not always agree, but that the ties which bound them were far greater than the divisive factors. He spoke of the Democratic party as a party of principles and progress, re-enforcing his evaluation with a review of the basic tenets and philosophy of the party. Sanford commented that young Democrats like those at the rally would assure North Carolina's progress with the Democratic party.

NORTH CAROLINA ANNUAL MEETING OF TRAFFIC SAFETY COUNCIL

RALEIGH

December 18, 1961

Sanford spoke of the magnitude of the traffic safety problem in North Carolina. In 1960, 1,226 persons were killed, 26,947 were injured, and economic loss was estimated at around $200 million. He said the state realized its responsibility in this area, but in spite of efforts in many directions, statistics of death and destruction continued to rise. The over-all responsibility rested with the Governor's Coordinating Committee on Traffic Safety, made up of state officials most directly concerned with traffic and highways. The Safety Engineering Committee was studying traffic accident localities and was seeking to improve highway engineering. Legislation to require motor vehicle inspection was needed, and the courts would have to shoulder the burden of traffic law enforcement. Governor Sanford commented that everyone agreed on the goal of greater traffic safety, but the means to this end were often disputed. He emphasized the need "to shoot at specific objectives with careful aim, rather than just pulling the trigger on a big blast and sitting back to hope it does some good." The state should try to eradicate prejudice and listen to the advice of professionals. He cited the use of seat belts as an illustration of this point. Sanford concluded that traffic safety was not receiving the public support it needed, making the need for the Traffic Safety Council greater than ever.

NORTH CAROLINA YOUNG DEMOCRATIC CLUBS MEETING

STATESVILLE

January 6, 1962

Sanford again addressed the Young Democratic Clubs in 1962. In this speech he illustrated the contribution of the Democratic party by discussing several areas: Tobacco farmers were assured an honest 90 per cent of parity and the over-all farm picture was brighter; the textile industry had prospered with increased allowance for depreciation provided by the Kennedy administration; loosening of tight Republican money policies meant more new homes under FHA; slums were cleared under the 1961 Housing

Act; Social Security covered more people than ever before; conservation practices were being carried out in the Appalachian and Cape Fear areas. He said that the Democrats had proved that progress could be made by going forward in school improvement, mental hospitals, correctional institutions, and road systems. Sanford reminded the YDC members that the biggest straw man of the Republicans was socialism, followed by inflation, but that the Republican answer to inflation was recession and depression. Though Republicans had said, throughout the years, that the Democrats were going to bankrupt the state, North Carolina's credit rating was AAA. He promised that Democrats would continue to work to achieve full potential for North Carolina.

NORTH CAROLINA
INDUSTRIAL DEVELOPMENT FOUNDATION

GREENSBORO

January 11, 1962

At the second annual meeting of the North Carolina Industrial Development Foundation, Governor Sanford said the state had just completed the largest year in history for industrial investments. The state's profits from industry were impressive. In 1961 businesses invested more than $279 million in new plants in North Carolina, meaning new payrolls of over $117 million and new jobs for 35,154 persons. Nationally, investments in new plants were down about 3 per cent; North Carolina had an increase of 18.5 per cent. Sanford said North Carolina sought new industries to provide better opportunities for North Carolinians to make better livings. The Governor asked for continued united effort, pledging his administration to see that tax money was well spent. He reminded the group that North Carolina was noted for good, progressive government, and he cited examples to prove the point. Despite the high grade of service, the state rated among the lowest three of all the states in the amount of taxes paid per person for state and local governments. In his final remarks, Sanford observed that North Carolina's problems were those of progress and growth and new opportunity.

MID-YEAR CONFERENCE
MARATHON CHAPTER NUMBER TWO
ORDER OF AHEPA

Charlotte

January 14, 1962

Governor Sanford described the organization to which he spoke on this occasion as one dedicated to fellowship, progress, perpetuation of human dignity and individual freedom and as one which drew on the ideals of Greek traditions, such as free thought and action. After expressing appreciation for the honor of being selected the outstanding Ahepan of 1961, he discussed the roots of democracy in the Greek heritage. He showed how Western civilization was indebted to Greek civilization in democratic theory, in Greek names, in architecture, and in other traditions. He said that North Carolina was proud of its Greek citizens, and the Governor emphasized the need of carrying on the Greek tradition of democracy and citizenship.

MOORESVILLE CHAMBER OF COMMERCE

Mooresville

January 16, 1962

In speaking to this group of Mooresville citizens, Governor Sanford observed that the expansion of industry in the local area, through fuller use of natural resources, was typical of growth throughout the state. He said that the North Carolina Trade Fair of 1961 was designed to promote sales of Tar Heel products; its success was evident when plans were made for a 1962 fair. The Governor then specifically discussed textiles, the number-one industry in Mooresville and the state. The state's textile mills produced approximately half of the nation's entire hosiery output, and nearly half of the American public used towels and linens produced in North Carolina. Textile companies paid approximately 17 per cent of all corporate taxes in the state; about one of every two manufacturing employees was employed by a textile company. The Governor then discussed federal administration programs to help rejuvenate the textile industry; he urged the citizens to rally behind the foreign trade program in return. He ended with a reminder that challenges produced opportunties, and that this part of "the free world has the talent, the courage, and the determination to meet those problems and achieve those potentials."

NORTH CAROLINA PRESS ASSOCIATION

CHAPEL HILL

January 18, 1962

After opening his address with a bit of sarcasm directed at the press and a few jibes at his own public image, Governor Sanford turned to a thoughtful reflection on the role of the press in contemporary society. Constructive criticism from the press helped raise schools and raze slums, helped the poor, helped bring in industry, and helped build new schools. The newspaper, "a daily diary and a daily forecast for all of man's activities and all of his world," naturally emphasized the dramatic and the controversial. There were many stories, however, of equal significance though perhaps less dramatic, on such matters as the results of the school tax, on new industry, and on other aspects of state governmental activities. The Governor expressed hope that many of these would be written during 1962. He predicted that the state would have problems but they would be problems of progress and growth and opportunity; these, too, would be stories of sufficient interest to be covered by the press.

FOURTH ANNUAL HIGHWAY CONFERENCE

RALEIGH

January 30, 1962

[In a three-day meeting, persons concerned with highway building met to exchange ideas, hear prominent speakers, and attend technical discussions. Among other speakers were D. Grant Mickle, Deputy Highway Administrator for the United States Bureau of Public Roads, and J. M. Sprouse, Director of Associated General Contractors of the Highway Construction Division. In his address, Governor Sanford traced progress in the field of transportation and then took the opportunity to support his faith in the integrity of state government despite the basketball scandals and the irregular dealings in the Highway Department, troubles which had occurred during the previous months. See statement on Burch-Brewer Case, January 7, 1962, pages 560-563.]

It is a pleasure to join personnel of the State Highway Department, faculty members and students of North Carolina State

College's School of Engineering, and road builders in this Fourth Annual Highway Conference.

On behalf of the state, I am happy to welcome all of the out-of-town guests to this conference.

As I interpret the purpose of this conference, you are here to develop and exchange ideas on how to give the citizens of this state good roads at the most economically feasible price.

North Carolina has a long history of road building. Many of you here today will recall that North Carolina bore the nickname of "good roads state" some time before many of our sister states thought it was necessary to pave roads.

As a matter of fact, our good roads policy goes back to the time of Revolutionary War. When President George Washington made his tour of the southern states, shortly after his first election, he rode in North Carolina on good roads.

One of the earliest long-range road planners of whom we have any record in this country was a North Carolinian named Daniel Boone. As you engineers know, there are superhighways today along parts of the route he took west.

My only argument with Boone's long-range planning was that he didn't stake off rights-of-way when he made his journey and save us all of those costs today.

In the 1920's, when the use of automobiles was just getting into high gear, Governor Cameron Morrison had the vision to see that if North Carolina was going to grow and prosper she would need good roads. So he, and later Governor Angus McLean, proposed bond issues to link the county seats of our state. That was an awesome task and it involved many millions of dollars. Some critics thought those road bonds were paving the way straight to the poorhouse. But you and I know that those bonds were paving the route to a more prosperous citizenry.

In the forties, Governor W. Kerr Scott had the foresight to recognize that if we wanted to build the economy of all the state, we couldn't leave over half the state bogged down on muddy roads.

Kerr Scott knew that if you provided all-weather roads to the country, the farmer could get his produce to town to sell it. And Kerr Scott knew that if the farmer got his produce sold, he would buy the manufactured goods in the stores in town to haul back to the farm.

Scott had the courage to propose a $200 million road bond program to get the farmer out of the mud. And the citizens of North Carolina had the courage to adopt that program.

Many of you will remember criticism of the Scott bond issue. It was supposed to pave the way to bankruptcy. But it didn't. It helped pave the route to the greatest era of industrialization we have ever enjoyed in North Carolina.

Today those farm-to-market roads are among the strongest selling points our state has. For the industrial employees can travel those "Scott-tops" to their jobs in town every working day in the year. And plants can be located away from congested areas.

North Carolina was ready in the fifties to get a running start on the interstate highway system. Because we were ready, we were able to translate the drawings of the drafting board into highways in an expeditious manner. The motorists of North Carolina today are driving on superhighways that were only pencil lines on a map at the Highway Department a few years ago.

Now before any of you folks at the Highway Department start asking for a raise and before any of you contractors start taking bows, let me say that the taxpayers of this state are not going to be satisfied until every mile and every foot of this interstate system allocated to North Carolina is paved, and every shoulder is built, and every detour sign is removed.

The job I have requires a lot of travel. And despite some suggestions to the contrary, a lot more of my trips are made by car than by plane. I believe I am speaking for all the traveling citizens of North Carolina when I tell you that there is nothing quite as frustrating as riding down a crowded two-lane highway month after month and look across an island and see another two lanes blocked off because they're not quite finished. I realize you sometimes run into rock. And I know the weather washes you out from time to time. And I know there are 100 good reasons for delay in building a highway the way it ought to be built. But there are 1,907,988 good reasons to keep those delays to a minimum and to get those roads open as quickly as good engineering permits. Those 1,907,988 reasons are the number of vehicles registered in our state. And I'm not even counting the backseat drivers of those vehicles.

In 1961 this administration took a long, hard look at the money available for roads in our state, especially money available for secondary roads. We found that after we deducted all the money we had to deduct to match federal road funds, and after we deducted all the money necessary to maintain the roads we already have, and after we made all the other deductions that are necessary, we hardly had enough money left to pave a secondary road from here to Hillsboro Street.

So the administration proposed, and the 1961 General Assembly approved, measures to stop the diversion of highway funds. And we shook loose some bookkeeping funds that hadn't been working for us. As a result, the State Highway Commission intends to pave more secondary roads this year than in any year since Kerr Scott's road bond program.

This does not mean we are going to neglect our interstate and primary system. On the contrary, we are going to spend approximately 10 per cent more on the interstate and primary system than the average for the last two years. We intend to spend this money where it is most needed and where it will do the most good in developing the state of North Carolina. And let me say with all the force of my command, that we intend for this money to be spent without favoritism.

The state of North Carolina and the State Highway Department have a deservedly high reputation for honesty and efficiency. This reputation goes back over many, many years. And it goes out to all the corners of this country.

The honest and hard-working employees of the State Highway Department have built that reputation over the years—ever since we started building roads in North Carolina. I am proud of them, and I know the citizens of North Carolina, who are the employers, are proud of them.

In recent years, a malignant idea has grown in our nation that greasing a palm here and there is good business. This notion has nothing to do with a particular political party. It's a disease that threatens the great majority of honest and law-abiding citizens who foot the bill. Sometimes it comes in the form of vicuna rugs at the White House. Sometimes it comes in the form of a deep freeze.

In recent years, this corrupt concept that everything can be fixed has stretched its slimy paws up into the offices of some of the largest companies in our country and resulted in price-fixing. And it has stretched down onto the basketball courts of colleges and resulted in point-fixing.

Last spring, North Carolina let it be known to everyone doing business with the state of North Carolina that we were not going to let the citizens of this state be cheated through price-fixing. Last summer, we let it be known that we were not going to tolerate the corruption of our sports. This month, we have said in as clear a language that I know that this administration and this state will tolerate irregular dealings neither on the roads of North Carolina nor in any other departments for that matter.

That's not the way we do business in North Carolina.

State employees are honest and we are not going to jeopardize their reputations or the reputation of the state.

The citizens of North Carolina pay into public funds for public roads. And there are not going to be any under-the-table, or back-street deals going on as long as this administration is in office.

The state of North Carolina and the State Highway Commission have a policy of spending public money honestly and carefully. Nowhere in our system of purchase and contracts or in our low bid system or in our allocation of the taxpayers' money is there a clause which mentions or implies that somebody's hand should be greased.

Let me make it as clear as I possibly can: Companies doing business with the state of North Carolina do not have to go through influence peddlers. If a company goes through influence peddlers, it will lose its business with the state of North Carolina the day we catch them. The state of North Carolina does not do business with fixers.

Any company that thinks it has found an "in" for getting the state's business through a back door is going to find a little later that it is barred from doing business with this state.

The state of North Carolina is going to protect its reputation against any isolated case of irregularities.

And the state of North Carolina is going jealously to guard every penny, nickle, dime, and dollar of the taxpayers' money.

Thank you.

SALEM CHAMBER OF COMMERCE ANNUAL DINNER

SALEM, VIRGINIA

February 1, 1962

In speaking to the Salem, Virginia, Chamber of Commerce, Governor Sanford took again the theme of education. He stressed the responsibility of the state in the field of education, adding that the state was well repaid for carrying out its responsibilities. The economy was raised when the citizens were educated; the ranks of unemployed were primarily from the group lacking education. Sanford reminded the audience of Roosevelt's commentary on the South as the number-one economic problem of the nation. He said the South had worked to move forward, and North Carolina was cited as an example of a state which had succeeded in attracting new industry. Chambers of commerce, governmental agencies, and others worked toward this goal, but provision for training made by the state was a chief factor. Industrial education centers provided technical skills, but the state was also concerned for a broad education for its citizens. Sanford said that education was fundamental for long-range economic development and was also vital for short-range goals. Education was essential if the income of the South was to rise. He concluded with a definition of education as "the golden door to liberty and opportunity."

TEMPLE EMANUEL BROTHERHOOD MEETING

GREENSBORO

February 2, 1962

As part of the observance of Brotherhood Week, Governor Sanford commented that nearly all religions subscribed to a belief in the ultimate aim of universal brotherhood. He added that men had compromised their beliefs by relying on themselves rather than God, that the ideal of brotherhood still existed though its application was hard. Governor Sanford called on the people to draw on their heritage for courage and inspiration, saying that the United States was founded on brotherhood and the belief of responsibility to one's fellowmen. Brotherhood Week, 1962, offered a challenge to meet the goal of universal brotherhood.

GRANVILLE INDUSTRIAL DEDICATION DAY

OXFORD

February 6, 1962

The Governor spoke in Granville County on the occasion of the etablishment of two new plants: JFD Electronics-Southern and Outdoor Supply Company, Inc. He commended the local citizens for their initiative, adding that promotion and work undertaken by state government in Raleigh existed because of local needs and wishes. He pointed out the inability of state government to educate a million children, to grow agricultural products, and to perform other tasks needed by the people. What the government could do was provide texts and teachers, supply the results of research from laboratories and offices, and give assistance in many fields. Attracting new industry had been a joint local-state project; new plants, new payrolls, and a better economy resulted. Sanford commented that North Carolina had extended advantages to all businesses: an excellent climate; a tax structure of equality; a labor market made up of efficient and hardworking employees rather than cheap workers; a good place to live, with its educational program, mental health hospital system, credit rating, and transportation facilities. North Carolina, a good place to work and a good place to live, welcomed the two new industries locating in Granville County.

NORTH CAROLINA CITIZENS COMMITTEE FOR BETTER SCHOOLS

RALEIGH

February 22, 1962

As he had done many times before and would do repeatedly in the future, Governor Sanford spoke on the subject of education, which he called "the chief weapon in the arsenal of democracy. . . ." He observed that ignorance and freedom did not go together, that improvement in public education was, therefore, the primary goal of his administration. He applauded members of the General Assembly who had carried out the wishes of the people for improved educational opportunities and had voted funds to support the program. With additional financial support, improvements had been made and were being made. The Governor advocated a conference on education in every county during 1962, with as many people as possible in attendance. He told the North Carolina Citizens Committee for Better Schools that certain areas belonged to the professionals and others to the laymen. In closing, he stated, "What our schools are today will determine, in large measure, what our people will be tomorrow."

TO STUDENTS OF NORTH CAROLINA OVER STATE-WIDE TELEVISION

RALEIGH

March 1, 1962

[Governor Sanford many times observed that the ultimate success of the quality education program lay in student hands. In this television address to the students of North Carolina, he spoke to more than a million young people, explaining to them their opportunities and obligations under the quality education program enacted by the 1961 General Assembly. The "folksy" language used in this talk was typical of the many short speeches Sanford made to school children; this speech easily shows how he was able to establish rapport with his young audiences.]

For some time I've wanted to get all of you together, all of the students of the state. I want to talk to you. And I hope you'll remember as I talk that you form a complex audience. Some of you are in high school and think like adults; others of you are little tots just starting out. You are varied company, not only in ages, either. You come from fishing families down on the coast; maybe a few of you spent last Saturday on a trawl boat. Others of you are from the cities, where your fathers might work in factories or in offices or might keep the streets safe and clean. Many of you are from the country. Your parents grow tobacco or livestock or maybe goats, as does Mr. Carl Sandburg up in the mountains.

You are of different religious faiths. You are of different races. Some of you live in rich houses, some of you don't. Some of you are Indians—did you think of that? So you see what sort of audience you are. Indians and non-Indians, you're all members in good standing of the student population of our state.

And you're just about the most important part of all because the future belongs to you, and the future—the future of you, our children—is our most valuable possession.

My purpose in talking to you tonight is to tell you about the things you can do to help in North Carolina's program of education, because that is our future.

Why, all of a sudden, are we talking so much about education? What is this "quality education" you've been hearing about? Is this something new? Is this something we haven't had before?

As a matter of fact we have had a comparatively good school system across the state since the days of Charles Brantley Aycock and an excellent school system in some counties.

But now as never before, education is becoming more and more esssential. Because it is more important than ever before, everybody is working to make it more effective.

I'd like to think with you about your future. I want you to try to get a picture of it in your mind. It won't be easy to see the future. It wasn't at all possible for me, when I was a boy in Laurinburg, to see the future well. For example, when I started school we didn't have television. Not only did we not have it, we didn't even believe it. If you had told me about television, I would have thought you were trying to be funny. When I started school there were very few electric refrigerators. We bought our ice from an ice wagon which was drawn by a horse. In hot weather your mother would buy 10 cents worth of ice, unless you had company and iced tea and then you bought an extra nickle's worth. I thought this was the way it would always be, that the future would always have ice wagons in it.

Back then there wasn't so much danger of being run over by a car, either. There weren't many cars. To get from Laurinburg to Winston-Salem was quite a trip, and to go as far as Asheville was a journey, and going as far as Memphis, Tennessee, wasn't even talked about. I remember writing a theme about the great progress of mankind after completing an automobile trip to Maxton and back—twelve miles.

But there has been at least one miracle performed every year since I started the first grade. And just the other day our country sent a man around the world. He went around the world three times in less than half a workday. It's impossible, but it's so. Before long somebody will be going to the moon. Some of you will go and see what the man in the moon looks like from close up. Maybe you can explore Mars and see what Venus has on it, or go on into the distant universes. It's true. Yet I never could have foreseen it as a boy. I remember when the comic strip Buck Rogers first came out. It showed a rocket ship circling the earth, and nobody that I knew believed it.

We know now that your future will be full of miracles. How do you prepare for a future like that? How can you get ready for 1980, or for 2010? The only reasonable answer is to advise you to stock up now on education.

That means readin', writin', and 'rithmetic, among other things. An elderly man told me years ago that those three were all a person needed. This was possibly true when he was a boy. He had a nice big farm and a happy family. The family had most of what it needed there at home. The cloth was made from cotton, or linsey-woolsey, made from wool and linen. They had droves of hogs. They had big mules to pull the plow. They had a buggy to drive to worship in or to go to town to fetch salt or sugar or coffee. Their life was well ordered. They did what others had done before them, and about the most change that ever happened from day to day was the change that came in the weather.

But now our times have changed, haven't they? And you'll need to know readin', writin', and 'rithmetic, but you'll also need to know more. Unlike that old gentleman, and unlike the time when I started to school, you happen to be living in the most rapidly moving, fastest changing, complex age the world has ever known. That makes education—in many fields, and about many things—more necessary than ever before.

Maybe you're interested in sciences and engineering. They've become a big part of our world, and they'll be important in yours. Many of you little children know how to turn a television set on. It seems to me that there's not a child in the state too young to learn that. But how do you suppose the set works? How does my picture get on your screen? How does my voice get into your set? The answers are in the sciences.

How does your father's car or truck work? You can sit in the front seat and see that the pedals are pushed and the steering wheel is turned, but you know as well as I do that foot pedals and a steering wheel don't make much of a car. You have to know engineering to make a car.

Or how is a book printed?

Or why is it that the doctor can put a spot of liquid on your arm and keep you from getting smallpox?

How is it that an X-ray machine can see through your clothes, and right through your skin, and take a picture of your lungs, so that a man trained to do so can tell you if you have TB?

How is it that a building can be made forty stories high and stay put? Try sometimes to set forty blocks on top of one another and see if they stay.

Think about your house. Most of you have electricity in it. What is that? How did it get there? How does it make machinery work?

Farming is another profession you might be interested in, scientifically tending to the cattle and the crops, raising chickens and pigs. In that case, you surely need a sound education. Farming has become a complicated procedure. Farmers tell me that they feel like chemists part of the time. They have to buy their chickens special tablets and drops. They have to get their soil tested and buy the fertilizer prescribed for it. There are sprays for insects and poisons for rodents.

There are many other types of jobs, of course. You might want to go into business. Well, you'd better get an education, hadn't you? You might want to operate a grocery store; better get an education. Do you see how far the supermarket has changed from the little country stores? Do you think they've stopped changing? No, chances are that stores will change more in the next twenty years than they have in the last twenty years. How will they be different? I don't know. They'll be different in the ways educated men and women make them different. And if you want to run a store, you'll need to be an educated man or woman.

Some of you will want to be teachers. Some of you will want to be religious leaders. Some of you might want to work on the railroad. Well, you'll need to know as much as you can grasp and contain. And let me say this to you, that I hope you will settle on a high ambition for yourself, on a good one. You have a right to dream of playing a special part in our country.

Our schools will train you to go to college if that is what you want to do. I hope you will. Not enough of our boys and girls with great ability go on for advanced training. Why not? If you have the ability and the ambition you can go to college. Don't let anyone discourage you. In North Carolina our schools will help you find a way. We don't want you to waste your talents.

But our schools aren't limited by any means to training people for college. We are trying to develop the kind of program which will train you for life. There is no reason in the world why you should finish school and face life without having a skill that will enable you to earn a better living. If you've got the ambition, we've got the school. If you can't get it in your local school, you can go on to our industrial training centers, a part of our school system.

Our purpose is to say to every boy and girl, "What is your ambition? What do you want to do?"

And our answer to your response is, "We can help you do it."

Do you want to be an automobile mechanic, a practical nurse, a welder, a dental assistant, a machinist, a space scientist, a lab technician, a better farmer, a chemist, a bookkeeper, an electrical engineer, a surveyor, a teacher, a veterinarian?

We can provide the training for these and a thousand other occupations. But you have got to provide the ambition. You have got to provide the "get-up and go."

Make up your mind that you are not going to drift through life, that you are going to develop your skills and your mind. If you do, we can help you. Talk to your teacher, or principal, or counselor. Pick a career.

If you are out of high school, or didn't quite finish, it is not too late to make a new start. Perhaps you have an older brother or sister who dropped out. Talk to him or her and say that we have the means of providing training if he or she will provide the ambition.

If you can't find out locally what you need to know, write to me.

I am personally interested in every young person in this state, and I say to you that there is no reason for anyone not to be trained in a skill. This is our program. This is our goal. There is no place for unskilled labor tomorrow, and today is the time to learn.

Thomas Wolfe once said that we should give every man his chance, his shining, golden opportunity to work, to be himself, and to become whatever thing his manhood and his vision could combine to make him. He said this was the promise of America. And so it is for all of you, rich and poor, girl and boy, white and colored of this state. Maybe you haven't been taking seriously your school up to now. It's time you did. I don't mean school should be a burden. It shouldn't, but don't sell yourself at a bargain counter. Get a goal in mind and work toward it, prepare yourself. Sharpen your ax keen. One thing we can all say about the future. The only ax that's going to cut a thing is going to have to be keen.

I'd like to go a step further with you, not to talk about other jobs, but to say another word about education. Schooling isn't a matter of jobs only. Schooling joins with your parents and your community and religious leaders to help you become a productive person in your own right. And you as a person, and you and the family you will have someday, are of major consequence. And so is your relationship with the community as a whole.

The communities we live in today have widened and enlarged themselves. We travel faster now. In a sense, science has brought all of us closer together and into a community. Thirty years ago Asia wasn't much more than a romantic word; today products made by Asiatic workers are trying to compete with products made in North Carolina, competing not only in Asia, but in this country, and even in this state. Time was when a plague might strike a country, and we wouldn't even hear about it until it was over. Today we hear about it a few minutes after it's detected, and we can fly medicine to the place, if we choose to, if we want to save lives.

The Bible teaches us to love our neighbors. It teaches us to love even enemies, too, which is asking more than some of us seem to be able to deliver. We live in a time when almost all of the world's people are neighbors, in a sense, and when many of them are enemies. This is so today, and in the future it is likely to become even more important, as we are brought even closer together in a community.

Some people are afraid of this association. They don't want to get involved in other people's affairs, or to have others telling us what they think we ought to do. They suggest we withdraw, pull back. What they haven't told us is where we are going to withdraw. In effect, they are saying that they prefer the olden days to the atomic age, that they had rather have the ice wagon than rocket power. I can understand their view, and so, I'm sure, can you. But you probably can understand, too, their faulty thinking. We cannot abandon the rocket world, even if we wanted to, and there are no ice wagons.

Well, we're going into this new age. We have no choice about that, and how do we get ready for it?

I know many of you are studying a foreign language. Please learn it well, and if you have the courage and mind for it, learn two.

Some of you are studying the literature of other peoples. Absorb as much meaning from it as you can. Literature helps us understand a people.

Many of you are studying world history. Please come to grips with it intelligently. You are going to need to know it long after you have finished the course, if you are to participate intelligently in the affairs which are ahead for us all.

I know you are studying American history. Study it carefully. Consider its spirit and its power. Our Declaration of Independence was the first clear call to freedom sounded by a nation's leaders; it began a revolution which has spread throughout the world, and the echoes of it still reverberate in this country, in this state, and they are coming back to us from other places.

I know many of you are studying North Carolina history. I recommend that, too. Let me tell you about a few men in that story. There's William Davie,[97] who founded our state university. Before that, he was a cavalryman in our Revolution. With a handful of men he stood at the crossroads of the little town of Charlotte and held at bay for more than a day the entire army of the British General Cornwallis.

Another man is Archibald Murphey,[98] who came later. We were a poor state in a new struggling country, and in the early part of the nineteenth century, Murphey begged us to make better roads, to build canals, to begin educating our children. But he was rejected, and the state languished in deeper and deeper poverty. We become known as the "Rip Van Winkle State."

But once we reached the twentieth century, we found such men as Charles Aycock, and for the four years he was governor a school was built every day. Other men made our roads, opened our harbors. So in our century North Carolina has moved into the forefront of the South and has attracted the admiration of the country.

Yes, study the history of North Carolina. It has some sad stories in it, but there's good spirit and plenty of hope in it, too.

And seek to grasp the feelings of poetry, of music, of paintings,

[97] William Richardson Davie (1756-1820), Revolutionary soldier, early statesman; Governor of North Carolina, 1798-1799; called "father of the University of North Carolina" for his many efforts on behalf of that institution. Crabtree, *North Carolina Governors,* 56-57.
[98] Archibald Debow Murphey (1777-1832), statesman and lawyer from Hillsborough, teacher at the University of North Carolina; state senator, 1812-1818; champion of internal improvements, universal education, and constitutional reform. Samuel A. Ashe and Others (eds.), *Biographical History of North Carolina: From Colonial Times to the Present* (Greensboro: Charles L. Van Noppen, 8 volumes, 1905-1917), IV, 340, 348, hereinafter cited as Ashe, *Biographical History.*

of the best plays and writing. Through such achievements we come face to face with the best, most sympathetic understanding of ourselves. And it's through such achievements that we are able to present ourselves to others.

So I recommend to you that all of us learn to communicate better what we are and believe, and that we learn to listen intelligently to others, so that the community of mankind will have in your time its greatest flourishing.

You see there is quite a bit to do and to learn. I'm urging you to become educated men and women. I'm counting on you. So were the 170 men and women who met here in Raleigh last summer. About the time the weather was getting sticky hot, when you were out playing baseball or drinking sodas at the drugstore, they were here working for you. They were your state legislators, and they were involved with certain problems in arithmetic. For example, they were asking why our state was forty-fifth in the amount of money spent for each student.

Also, they were asking why it is that we were forty-first in the size of our classes. The more students a teacher has, the harder it usually is to teach and learn. Our classes in North Carolina have been too big. They asked why North Carolina almost leads the nation in the number of men turned down by the armed forces because they can't read or write, even well enough to be buck privates.

The 170 men and women in Raleigh decided the state could afford to sacrifice enough money to solve these problems. They did their part. They put a great deal of money into a new program of education for you. And our state now hopes to rise toward national leadership.

Many people have worked and are working to improve our schools.

This work by the legislators, the teachers, the parents, the county commissioners, the State Department of Public Instruction, the principals, the superintendents, the school boards, the Curriculum Study, the taxpayers, the State Board of Education, is done for you. It is all going to be wasted work if you don't take advantage of it. The whole key to all this effort is you.

What have you, the student, to do with achieving quality education? I say to students that quality education is not something that you get out of a box, ready mixed. It is not something that is going to be given to you. It cannot be said to students, "Here it is. Now come and pick it up." Quality education stems from the fact that we have earnest students who want to learn. Unless there is a desire on the part of the student to learn and to take advantage of the opportunities and the teaching that we hope to continue to move up in quality, then we are not going to have any quality education.

Unless students work at it, unless you want to learn, there'll be no quality education for you. If you do want to learn, if you are sincerely trying to prepare for the opportunities in life, then all the rest of us are working to improve the chances of your being properly prepared.

But it doesn't make any difference how well the superintendents and principals plan, it doesn't make any difference how much harder the teacher works, there will be no quality education for you unless you want it and unless you are willing to work hard to get it.

Your fathers and mothers and the other adults of North Carolina are paying more taxes so you can have better educational opportunities. We have set as our goal giving you educational opportunities as good as any enjoyed by any children anywhere in the nation. We have done this because there is no reason that North Carolina boys and girls should not have the best.

We cannot move North Carolina to the forefront of the nation unless we have everybody working together.

You know in the western part of our nation there is a large desert. As you approach the desert in your car, you drive by signs which warn you: "Last chance. Last chance for gas and water." If you fail to heed these, you may find yourself in trouble in the middle of the desert. Well, that's the way it is with what you are doing now in school. This is your last chance to get the education you will need in the world that lies ahead—not just to make money, but to be a good citizen in this complicated world.

There will not be another chance. Now is the time. The school is the place.

We need teachers who will work harder to do a better job, and we have these. We need to continue planning and working in the Board of Education and the Department of Public Instruction, and we are. We need legislators and county commissioners who are willing to pay the price, and we have them. We need citizens who are willing to support the future through education, and we have them. We need parents who will take an active interest in the education of their children. Most of all, we need you. In the final analysis, it is your reaction that tells us how well we succeed.

Talk it over in your home room tomorrow. I'd like to have a letter from your class telling me that you understand what we are doing, that you believe in it, and that you want to be a part of our efforts, that you want to join our crusade to make North Carolina's school system the best in the world.

If you are willing to take part, you will be starting right now doing your part to defend the nation, to carry the banner of freedom and human liberty, to promote world peace, and to move North Carolina to its greatest days.

BOARD OF DIRECTORS MEETING OF THE NORTH CAROLINA TRAFFIC SAFETY COUNCIL, INC.

GREENSBORO

March 15, 1962

This meeting, Governor Sanford reminded the audience, represented the first anniversary of the Traffic Safety Council and was, therefore, a good time to take stock. A comparison of figures released by the Department of Motor Vehicles for 1961 and 1960 was shocking in that it showed an increase of twenty-eight deaths and an increase of 7,485 injuries. The Governor said the public was concerned, and for the first time the state had a co-ordinated attack planned. Though on the right track, the program could take years to mature. Sanford placed the courts "on the front line of this struggle" as he launched into a discussion of traffic problems and the court amendment under consideration. Despite the existence of hundreds of conscientious judges and solicitors, the court system was called the weak link in the traffic safety chain. The trouble stemmed from the inability of the courts "to cope with both the volume and the intricacies of automobile litigation." The tendency of some thinkers to feel that the courts should deal sternly only with problem drivers overlooked the fact that everyone was a "problem driver" at one time or another. Attitudes should be developed but the right attitude would not substitute for the administration of justice. Governor Sanford urged the Traffic Safety Council members to expend as much of their resources as possible on the passage of the court reform amendment.

EIGHTY-FIRST ANNUAL MEETING OF THE NORTH CAROLINA TEACHERS ASSOCIATION

RALEIGH

April 12, 1862

Speaking to many of the state's Negro educational leaders at their meeting in Raleigh's Memorial Auditorium, Governor Sanford presented a vivid and perceptive study on the qualifications of a good teacher and the meaning of good teaching. He reminded the group that money could not do the entire job and that good teaching was the prime requisite to the achievement of quality education. He gave several definitions of good teachers and quoted a number of outstanding men from John Locke to Henry Steele Commager on the subject of education and teaching. The Governor ended with an expression of confidence in the members of the teaching profession in North Carolina.

NORTH CAROLINA CREDIT UNION LEAGUE

RALEIGH

April 14, 1962

Since the enactment of the North Carolina Credit Union Act in 1915, credit unions contributed toward a higher standard of living for thousands, the Governor told those who attended the Credit Union League. He reviewed briefly the history of credit unions and then discussed financial stability of the state, stressing the importance of fiscal soundness for a government and for an individual. He gave statistics to show the strong financial position of North Carolina and concluded by urging citizens to move ahead with confidence in themselves and in the future of the state.

INAUGURATION EXERCISES LUNCHEON
GARDNER-WEBB JUNIOR COLLEGE

BOILING SPRINGS

April 16, 1962

The occasion for this speech by Governor Sanford was the inauguration of Dr. Ernest Eugene Poston as the new president of Gardner-Webb Junior College. His address dealt with the challenge of higher education in society. As he frequently did, the Governor emphasized the importance of education. Where citizens had the right to vote, a literate people was vital. He said that elementary and high school were, at one time, sufficient, but increased knowledge of mankind meant the need to teach more and more subjects. It was impossible for all of them to be taught in high schools. With opportunities limited, the Governor urged a partnership between private and public institutions. The progressive heritage of Gardner-Webb was indicative of the important role the school would play, and the Governor concluded by expressing appreciation for the contributions made by this college and its leaders.

CONFERENCE ON FOOD PROCESSING AND MARKETING

RALEIGH

April 17, 1962

Sanford reviewed progress made in North Carolina in the area of food processing and marketing, commenting on such endeavors as the establishment of the Department of Food Science and Processing at State College. He said that North Carolinians were realizing the importance of every phase of the food industry: production, processing, packaging, marketing, management, and research. The state offered practically limitless agricultural potential which, matched with business vision, intelligent leadership, hard work, and close co-operation, could result in a successful food processing operation. He offered suggestions as to ways in which the processing dollar could be kept in North Carolina, but he stressed the requirement of high quality as being essential in the endeavor. To meet the challenge, the state needed experts in packaging and processing. With the native products produced in the state, Governor Sanford said there was no reason why North Carolina could not become a leader in the new field.

DINNER HONORING JOHN W. UMSTEAD, JR.

CHAPEL HILL

April 18, 1962

Speaking at a dinner in honor of John W. Umstead, Jr., Governor Sanford expressed appreciation for Umstead's many outstanding contributions in the roles of businessman, trustee, politician, legislator, and chairman of the Hospitals Board of Control. This leader gave priority to mental hospitals; as a result of his efforts, North Carolina's mental hospitals and training schools were highly esteemed throughout the nation. Umstead finally proved that investment in mental hospitals paid rich dividends to the state. He also worked tirelessly for the cause of education and academic freedom. Governor Sanford commented that Umstead represented in his many programs people all over the state in all walks of life.

SAVINGS BOND MEETING

RALEIGH

April 19, 1962

Governor Sanford, speaking in the Senate chambers in the State Capitol, favored the purchase of United States savings bonds. He said that the bonds helped finance John Glenn's flight into space, the "Nautilus" trip under the North Pole, the winning of World War II. He added that bonds were then helping provide for this country's obligations in trouble spots of the world, and he encouraged the purchase of bonds as a way of fulfilling the duties of citizenship and investing in the future at the same time. State government encouraged the purchase of bonds through the Payroll Savings Plan; the press, radio, and television personnel had co-operated by giving free advertising to the program which had a goal of 17,000 savers in 1962 in North Carolina.

DEDICATION OF
U.S.S. "NORTH CAROLINA" MEMORIAL

WILMINGTON

April 29, 1962

The Governor thanked those who made this occasion possible. To show appreciation, the state and the Battleship Commission pledged their best to make this the greatest World War II memorial in the United States. The drive to bring the ship to North Carolina was successful, and the "North Carolina" was conditioned for public display. The Governor told of plans for landscaping, parking lots, and other facilities which would be made possible by donations and by garden clubs. He said the Battleship Memorial Museum would catch the imagination of the state and of the nation, that exhibits would tell the ship's history which would also be the history of the offer.sive war in the Pacific. Sanford called this the chance to preserve North Carolina's most historical link with World War II, concluding that the prospect awaiting Tar Heels was an exciting one.

NORTH CAROLINA CONFERENCE
FOR SOCIAL SERVICE

RALEIGH

April 30, 1962

[The North Carolina Conference for Social Service, an organization of both laymen and professionals in the field of social welfare, heard Governor Sanford urge North Carolinians to acquire a keen social awareness through historical understanding and to accept the philosophy that government was necessarily involved in the lives and happiness of its citizens. Two years later, Sanford was awarded the North Carolina Conference for Social Service Award for the many programs undertaken during his administration on behalf of human welfare.]

As we spend millions of man-hours and tens of millions of dollars in the race to the other side of space, it is incumbent on us to remember fellow citizens on the other side of the tracks. This golden anniversary of the North Carolina Conference for Social Service makes it apparent that North Carolinians are remembering these human beings on the "wrong" side of the tracks and are working to remedy the social ills of our time.

North Carolina has traveled a long way in many areas of human need since this organization was founded under the leadership of people like Clarence Poe and J. Y. Joyner[99] in 1912.

When this organization was formed, chain gangs were considered an essential part of our penal system. Child labor was defended as necessary in industry. Mental patients were locked away in filth and misery. Compulsory vaccination for smallpox and other communicable diseases was unknown. There was no program to care for the dependent child, the lame, and the aged. Workers hurt on the job received sympathy and very little else, for there was no workmen's compensation laws in those days.

I believe those who now cry "socialism" when any legislation is proposed to meet human needs might find it very informative to review histories of the early part of this century.

For that matter, those who see government as a necessary evil, at best, might well improve their perspective by reviewing the newspapers and the histories of the thirties.

As North Carolina moved slowly forward in the twentieth century to remove the abuses and to relieve the suffering of our society, there was rarely a forward step taken that wasn't attacked. Moves to protect the weak and to defend the poor and to heal

---

[99] James Yadkin Joyner (1862-1954), lawyer, educator, alumnus of the University of North Carolina at Chapel Hill; teacher, principal, professor; State Superintendent of Public Instruction under Governor Charles B. Aycock; leader in shaping educational policy and legislation. Ashe, *Biographical History*, VI, 335-341.

the ill and to give all of our citizens better opportunities have almost invariably been challenged on the grounds that their sponsors were "Reds" or spendthrifts, or at least "visionary, impractical, do-gooders." This opposition continues today. Happily, the good sense and the good conscience of the large majority of the citizens of North Carolina and of America have not been scared away from social progress by the bogy men erected by the shortsighted.

In free elections, the people of this state and of this nation voted twice for the social reforms embodied in Woodrow Wilson's New Freedom, and they voted four times for Franklin Roosevelt's New Deal. They voted for John Kennedy's New Frontier.

The people of North Carolina do not believe it is unduly radical to use a round wheel when it is proved that a round wheel will carry the needs of the people better than a square wheel. The people of North Carolina do not believe that our free enterprise system is going communistic when you take the children out of the mills, women out of sweatshops, and men off the sixty-hour week. The people of North Carolina believe that a prosperous state and nation must, in good conscience, give a helping hand to the indigent old, to the physically and fiscally disabled, and to the underprivileged child.

The state of North Carolina, working with county and municipal governments, has adopted many programs for the benefit of the less fortunate. Our religious training teaches us that we are our brother's keeper. And we would be obligated to provide these programs on that basis alone. But these programs go far beyond helping the persons who are the direct recipients of the benefits.

We learned long ago that an epidemic is no respecter of boundary lines between poor and well-to-do neighborhoods. We learned that a criminal bred by slums has no particular scruples against carrying out crime on the other side of town. We learned that a community or a state or a nation is just so strong as its weakest link.

That's why North Carolina moved to correct the weak links in the social structure of our state. That's why North Carolina abolished chain gangs and turned its attention to rehabilitation of prisoners. That's why this state and this nation set up minimum standards and maximum hours for industrial workers. That's why North Carolina in 1959 became the first state in the Southeast to enact a State Minimum Wage Act, and that's why the 1961 General Assembly strengthened that act. That's why North Carolina enacted the mandatory smallpox vaccination bill some years ago, and that's why North Carolina became the first state to enact the polio vaccination program. That's why we replaced our "snakepits" with decent mental hospitals where the mentally ill are cared for and cured rather than imprisoned.

We have come a long way since 1912, but we still have a long way to go. And that's why we are moving ahead with important programs in the area of social legislation.

First and foremost is the quality education program which was designed to give North Carolina's sons and daughters the same opportunities as those offered to children in other states. The 1961 General Assembly had the vision to appropriate the funds needed to improve the educational opportunities of our children. And the legislators had the courage to raise the funds needed to pay for those improvements. That program already is paying the state dividends in many ways.

In 1961, North Carolina ranked first among all the fifty states in the rate of advancement in public education.

Much remains to be done in the schools. In fact, it is a never-ending job that we must continue to face so long as there are children to educate. But the important thing is that North Carolina is moving in the right direction.

In the field of education, we have a serious problem of drop-outs—the students who leave school before they have completed their high school work. We are working to solve this problem through the Stay-In-School Committee. One of the major civic clubs of North Carolina has taken this problem as a state-wide project and is doing excellent work in this field. I am happy to know that this conference is planning a follow-up meeting on this problem of dropouts later this year.

An accompanying problem to that of dropouts is juvenile delinquency. Now North Carolina does not suffer as critically from juvenile delinquency as do the more highly populated states. But we would be deluding ourselves if we thought it did not exist in our state. Because juvenile delinquency is much more easily prevented than cured, I have asked some 300 experts and leading laymen to discuss this matter at a conference in Chapel Hill on May 14.

Commissioner Blaine Madison and the State Board of Correction and Training have, over the years, developed a highly effective program at the state training schools. The purpose of these schools is to take young people who have gotten off on the wrong track and to help them become self-respecting and self-supporting citizens. The center for youthful offenders at Camp Butner is an important project in this effort to set young people who have strayed on the right paths. These correctional institutions have one of the best rates of rehabilitation in the nation.

An expanding prison population increases the importance of the work being done by our Prison and our Probation departments. Our prison program is considered one of the soundest and most enlightened, by just about everyone, except two escaped prisoners and one lawyer in Rhode Island. [Reference was to a case in which extradition was recommended following a tour of North Carolina prisons by the defense attorney and Rhode Island officials.]

Plans are now underway to provide psychiatric treatment within the prison system so that the antisocial attitudes which send people to prison in the first place may be corrected. Efforts are being expanded rapidly for the cure and rehabilitation of alcoholics in prison.

Our probation system is designed to give men and women the supervised opportunity to prove that, given another chance, they can conduct themselves as law-abiding citizens. This probation program is not set up to forgive crime. It is operated to correct crime. The results show that it is succeeding.

Another important facet of the state's efforts to replace incarceration with rehabilitation is the work release law under which certain first offenders may continue to work during the daytime. This program means simply that the offender, who shows good promise of going straight, continues to support his family and himself during his sentence.

A serious problem facing this state and most farm states is that of migrant farm workers. The citizens of North Carolina were shocked into an awareness of this problem several years ago when a truck overloaded with migrants was involved in a wreck near Fayetteville. The General Assembly has enacted legislation to prevent recurrences of that particular aspect of the problem and to establish requirements for sanitation at the camps. The Committee on Agricultural Migrants and other state agencies concerned are now at work to see that this legislation is enforced.

There are other programs being conducted by the state and other problems facing our citizenry: the surplus food program, special classes and special schools for the mentally retarded, programs for alcoholics, the blind, the deaf, the handicapped. All of these human needs, and others, demand our attention and our best efforts.

I invite your advice and your assistance on the meeting of these problems.

Only by facing up to these problems and solving them can we truly say that North Carolina is a state where the weak grow strong and the strong grow great.

ATLANTA ALUMNI CHAPTER OF THE UNIVERSITY OF NORTH CAROLINA

Atlanta, Georgia

May 2, 1962

In this speech to fellow alumni, Governor Sanford reminisced about the University of North Carolina. After describing a recent visit to the Chapel Hill campus, the Governor compared the institution with the University of Georgia; he concluded that the distinctions were small as compared to the close co-operation between the two schools. Sanford then turned his attention to problems of out-of-state enrollments and faculty recruitment. At the time of the address, there were 800 U.N.C. alumni living in Atlanta and 194 Georgia students attending the Chapel Hill university. The value of having out-of-state students attend North Carolina schools, when many North Carolinians needed an education, was unquestioned in his mind; the Governor commented on the advantages of having new people and new ideas coming into North Carolina schools. With the increase in student population would come additional problems related to recruitment. The Governor indicated that some faculty members for North Carolina colleges would come from the University of North Carolina; many would come from elsewhere. He stressed the need for a faculty of high quality, saying that North Carolina wanted to be compared with the nation rather than the region. The University of North Carolina, as one of only forty-one institutions belonging to the Association of American Universities, ranked as a top university. Sanford predicted that its future would be one of continued achievement and that with the support of the alumni its growth could mean positive gains for the state and the nation.

MEDICAL SOCIETY OF NORTH CAROLINA

Raleigh

May 8, 1862

Governor Sanford discussed with the Medical Society a grave illness: traffic accident deaths and injuries. In addition to the human tragedy involved, he commented on the tremendous property and economic loss. Prevention of such waste was imperative, but the trouble in efforts to educate the public came when many felt the campaign was directed at the other fellow and others felt that accidents could not be prevented. The Governor's Coordinating Committee on Traffic Safety was working to determine the cause of accidents and to answer obvious questions before an official action program could be implemented. The role of the physician was stressed, and Sanford urged the doctors to assume positions of leadership to win citizen support for the program. He called preventive medicine a thankless task but added that it was often the best medicine. After winning citizen support, the second major step was legislation to combat the epidemic. The court improvement amendments would permit the General Assembly to establish traffic courts under a unified judicial system. Questions of drunken driving, teen-age drivers, safety equipment, and others were being studied and solutions sought. The Governor concluded with a plea to doctors to help in the "crash program to stop the crashes."

NORTH CAROLINA STATE DEMOCRATIC CONVENTION

RALEIGH

May 17, 1962

North Carolina, called a "Dixie Dynamo" by a national magazine, might have been called a "Democratic Dynamo" had the magazine been partisan, according to Governor Sanford. In addressing the state Democratic convention, he reviewed twentieth-century progress in North Carolina under Democratic leadership. The party, realizing the value of education, continued to move forward; and the Democratic majority in the 1961 General Assembly, with the help of only one Republican vote, met the challenge and chose the unpopular way in providing for quality education. The party knew that the path to a brighter future lay in education. Sanford observed that the people of North Carolina recognized courage as being the primary requisite of a legislator, and he prophesied that the legislators who voted for quality education would be returned to the 1963 General Assembly. "Courage, and vision, and a willingness to move forward will keep the party strong," Sanford said, predicting that the Democratic party would continue to fulfill its role of leadership.

GRADUATION EXERCISES
APPALACHIAN STATE TEACHERS COLLEGE

BOONE

May 26, 1962

Appalachian State Teachers College, primarily concerned with the education of teachers, was reminded to look to its founder and first president, B. B. Dougherty, for setting the tone for the high professional training for teachers. The Governor discussed education and the excellence required in teaching, saying that this was an appropriate topic for a school which trained teachers. "Civilization has made progress and is continuing to make progress in many ways, but progress makes problems, and problems are always with any people." The Governor said that problems had been solved through the pursuit of excellence, but that modern standards had been lowered in too many ways, resulting in a weakening of the individual soul and a weakening of the national character and strength. He challenged everyone to pursue excellence, saying that "Excellence in one pursuit spills over into other activities." This was given as the reason teaching was important, and the Governor urged those who were going to teach to "define it and live by it and teach by it." He urged the graduates to set excellence as their example and to remember the influence they would have on hundreds of lives. "There isn't any more constructive way to spend your life," the Governor said in conclusion.

JUNE DAIRY MONTH "KICK-OFF" BREAKFAST

RALEIGH

June 1, 1962

The Governor took this opportunity to discuss the growth of the dairy industry as part of the over-all program to develop and co-ordinate food production, processing, and marketing across the state. Enthusiasm for such a program was not new to dairymen, who blazed the trail in many ways. The North Carolina food industry, the Governor said, stood in 1962 where the dairy industry had been two decades earlier. In 1945 a group of people who recognized the dairy industry potential organized and raised money for the establishment of a dairy teaching and research program at North Carolina State College. As a result North

Carolina produced milk for its own requirements and exported a quantity. The Governor gave statistics, citing the dairy industry as an example of what could be achieved.

COMMENCEMENT EXERCISES
NORTH CAROLINA SCHOOL FOR THE DEAF

MORGANTON

June 6, 1962

Governor Sanford praised the graduates of the North Carolina School for the Deaf on their demonstrated ability to overcome handicaps. He then turned to the subject of their future, which he described as "bright with promise." True education, he reminded them, was lifelong in scope; this commencement, which marked the end of one phase of education, was the beginning of another. Graduation meant an opportunity to "move into the full stream of responsibility as a citizen of North Carolina." It also carried an obligation to serve those who would come later. The Governor reminded his audience that schools were owned by the people, and the people had the ultimate responsibility of providing for education.

REPORT TO THE PEOPLE OVER
STATE-WIDE TELEVISION AND RADIO NETWORK

RALEIGH

June 6, 1962

[The tragedy of highway traffic deaths continued to haunt the Governor. Early in his administration he initiated programs whereby an emphasis would be placed on traffic safety. In this direct report to the people of North Carolina, by means of television and radio, the Governor previewed a five-point highway program being planned by the state to curb senseless killing and injury and property damage. Following the address, the Governor received a number of letters on the subject of traffic safety. A man who had lived in North Carolina twenty-four years wrote that he had never agreed more than 50 per cent with any statement made by leading political figures, but he could "honestly say that I agreed one hundred per cent with the message which you brought to the public. . . . I firmly believe that the five points presented in your message will, and should, concur with the feelings of the majority of North Carolinians." He told Sanford that the Governor had "shown your intestinal fortitude in presenting five issues which you know will be a 'hot potatoe' [sic] in political circles and in the next legislature. I feel that you have done your part, but it is now time for the citizens of

North Carolina to match your intestinal fortitude and let their representatives know their desires in this matter." In his closing sentences, the writer said that reform could not begin at the state level, that there had to be "desire for reform . . . in the brain and heart of every individual. Law and reform are not for the 'other fellow' alone; they are for me." A few days later, Governor Sanford received a letter outlining a number of personal experiences and ending with the question of blame. The writer answered her own question by saying parents, who would not say "no" to their children, and "*you,* and our *law-makers,* who are cognizant of these facts, yet continue to *talk* and *talk* and *talk,* while our children (too many) never attain their best capacities, become delinquents, or die *so needlessly."* The Governor's concern continued, and in the spring of 1963, Sanford went to the General Assembly to deliver in person another address on this subject. For this speech to the legislators, see pages 75-80.]

About three or four weeks ago a letter arrived at the Mansion. Usually my mail goes to the office, which is in the Capitol, but this letter turned up at the house, and my wife, Margaret Rose, gave it to me.

The letter was from a woman down east who took me to task. She told me that her son had been killed a few days before. He had been driving up from Wilmington and another car had appeared, coming extremely fast and slipping suddenly across the center line. Her son evidently tried to avoid a collision, but he couldn't make it. The woman asked me what kind of roads we have in this state, when death is a constant traveler.

I have the letter here that this mother wrote, and I'll read this paragraph from it:

If there was a man shooting at people on US 421, you would try to have him arrested. Why don't you have the speeders and reckless people arrested? Somebody is being killed nearly every day. What's the matter with you in Raleigh?

I sympathize with this woman. It's a tragic thing to lose a member of one's family. I know that. And I agree with her that more must be done if our highways are to be safe. Actually, they are even more dangerous than she thinks. She says traffic accidents take a life every day in North Carolina. They take one life every seven hours. Not only that, but somebody is injured every fifteen minutes. That totals about 100 people a day, killed or injured.

We have grown accustomed to viewing statistics coldly. After all, they are merely numbers. But I remind you that we are talking about families, and about individuals who bleed if cut.

I want this lady down east who lost her son to know, and I want you to know, that I am in sympathy with those who suffer on the roads and highways of this state.

There's a big problem here, and it won't be solved by good intentions alone. It will not go down before a renewed siege of determination, either. We must take action if we are to solve it, and I intend to talk about action tonight. I would like to review with you a program for our highways which I'm considering, and I would welcome your views about it.

In fact, you might even want to get a pencil and piece of paper to jot down notes as I talk, for there are several ideas in all. I will tell you what has been suggested to me, and what I think about it. We will go down the line point by point, idea by idea.

The first one is this: that we put out more literature and safety announcements on the radio and television, to keep the people aware of the problem.

My impression is that the existing publicity programs are adequate. We don't need to spend money adding to them. By now all of us know that safety is a serious problem, and surely nobody in the state is in favor of accidents. I think too that the people who really need educational programs on highway safety don't listen to them. And the rest of us don't either. We seem to feel the programs are for the other people. Therefore, it's my impression that we don't need to press for more publicity about highway safety.

There you have one idea which has been suggested to me, which I feel will not yield additional results. What we need is action.

Two types of drivers cause a high proportion of our accidents, and we can use special legislation to deal more adequately with them. One type is composed of young people between the ages of sixteen and twenty-one. There's no doubt about it, these drivers are far more likely to have accidents than are other age groups—two or three times as likely, as the record shows. Some young drivers seem to be reckless by nature, to enjoy moving at high speeds, to seek out danger. Not only are our young people involved in a great many accidents, but they are involved in some of the most violent, tragic ones. Right on the threshold of a good life, they get broken up or cut down. Some of you listening are in this age group. I'm not criticizing all of you, but your group needs criticism. There was an accident recently in which a car driven by a young man struck a tree. The car's motor was ripped out and went sailing into a field. The car was demolished. The speed of the car was reckoned at 100 miles an hour. The young man driving that car thought he would never be involved in an accident. He doubtless liked to speed. Maybe he would object to my suggesting tonight that special legislation is needed to deal with his age group and its driving problems. Maybe his youthful companions in the car would object, too. But they won't, for he and they are dead, except for one, and she is in the hospital badly crippled. It might be that special regulations would have saved their lives.

Of course, a young man who will drive 100 miles an hour will break any other rule. We have to take the drivers' licenses of such people, that's the point of it. My feeling as of tonight is this: that the drivers' licenses of our young people (and this is particularly true of our young men), should be issued with stricter requirements. Any serious infringement of the driving privilege should bring about immediate cancellation of the license. We cannot continue to have daredevil driving on the public roads. I believe we need stricter rules for young drivers than for the older ones.

A second type of driver causes far more than his share of accidents, too. That's the drunken driver. Nobody believes a drunken driver should be permitted to operate a car, not on the roads as they are today. I've asked the highway people for a count on how many of our accidents involve drivers who are drinking, and the report is significant. Of the fatal accidents in our state, drinking drivers are involved in at least one out of every three of them.

It's time to press for better ways to get these people off the roads. Our present ways are not the best. If a drinking driver is brought in by a patrolman today, the question often arises as to whether or not the driver is drunk. The driver often says he isn't, while the patrolman says he is. This is a matter of opinion. What's needed is a legal definition of what constitutes drunkenness—a definition that can be measured exactly. Also, we need equipment so that tests can be given drinking drivers to find out if they are drunk. That is, when the scientific tests show that a driver has a certain percentage of alcohol in his system, then he is marked down as being a drunken driver, drunk as defined by law, not drunk as a mere matter of opinion.

Therefore, we need a new law defining what constitutes drunkenness on our roads, and we need equipment to make the test. With that out of the problem, we can get the problem under better control, and our roads will be that much safer.

The third suggestion which I recommend is that we hire additional traffic engineers in order to get more of the dangerous places out of our present roads. It was a surprise to me to find out recently that the state has only three traffic engineers in the Highway Department. When we think of all the miles of roads, and the new roads being planned and built, we suspect that more men would be useful. If the Highway Department had more traffic engineers, it would be able to put our roads in safer shape, to correct dangerous places.

I have traveled a great deal in North Carolina. This is a big state. Anybody who travels it knows that. We need more traffic engineers than we have. We need five times as many. They in turn can help us fix up our existing roads and make new highways safer.

The fourth suggestion is that we add patrolmen to the Highway Patrol. I've looked into this matter and have asked the patrol to tell me how many patrolmen they have on duty at any one time for every thousand miles of road in the state. The patrolmen we have must be spread around the clock, so I guessed that they would say five or six, at any one time day or night, for every thousand miles of road.

They don't say anything like that. They have only two. They have one patrolman on duty for every 500 miles of road. A patrolman can't even travel that far in an eight-hour shift. That's the distance from Murphy to Morehead City. All the patrolman can hope to do is patrol a section of this. Usually he has to stay on the heavily traveled and most dangerous sections of the primary roads. But accidents occur on all the roads.

You will perhaps agree that the Highway Patrol we have is excellent. It's competent, it's dedicated, it's well-run. It repeatedly wins national awards. An enlarged patrol, however, can do an even better job, can make the roads safer.

It will take some money to hire additional patrolmen, and to keep these cars going, but the patrol makes the roads safer; each one saves many times his cost in property damage alone, and whenever there is an accident, the first helping hand is likely to be the hand of a patrolman.

There is one more suggestion that I can recommend to you. It pertains to the courts. Many of you will agree that something needs to be done to revise our court system. There is too much red tape and delay and inconsistency. I'm a lawyer and I respect the courts, but from my experience it's clear that the system is cumbersome, has loopholes, and lacks uniformity. Certainly this is so in terms of our highway cases.

In November you will have a chance to vote on a new system of courts. A constitutional amendment will be put on the ballot. At that time you can tell the General Assembly to set up a uniform court system. I hope you will do so. Please set it firmly in your memory to vote for court improvement at the election in November.

So there you have five suggestions, which have been made to me, which I am convinced we need. The first will help us get the youthful driver problem under better control. We need to do that.

The second will help us get the drunken driver off the roads. Certainly he has no place there.

The third suggestion is that we hire more highway traffic engineers, in order to improve existing roads, to get rid of hazards, and to help with the planning of new highways.

Then the last two suggestions deal with law enforcement. We should increase the size of the Highway Patrol, and we should insist on a uniform system of courts.

These five measures will bring results. They are firm and reasonable. They go straight to the core of five major problems. They are needed in our state now.

However, they will not come about without support from you. Most of them have opposition of one sort or another. For example, whenever the state takes away a man's driver's license, the man and his family strongly object. Occasionally the man can't continue on his job, and this causes the entire family to suffer. At the same time, we know some people shouldn't drive; we need to get these unsafe drivers out from behind the wheel. This is a life and death matter. And *their* lives, as well as ours, are involved, even though they don't realize it.

Traffic judges need your support. They need for you to give your approval when they convict according to the law. The judge's job is a thankless job if there ever was one. Here's an illustration of what I mean. If you build a hospital, people can see it and appreciate it because they and their loved ones receive the benefits of it. If you reduced accidents by 25 per cent, you would save 300 lives in one year and avoid 10,000 injuries, but the 300 people and their families would never thank the judges because it is incomprehensible to them that they might have been killed. Instead of thanking the judges, the solicitors, the patrolmen, the mayors who save the lives, they are more likely to complain and condemn these very people. But on the brighter side, I believe these complainers are in the minority. I believe the vast majority of the people are ready for a strong, firm solution for these problems.

The five suggestions for action which I have made in this talk are necessary, and I trust those of you listening will let your own views be known.

I have here a few notes, other ideas which have been given to me, which I am not ready to say should be a part of our program. There might be value in some of them. One is the old question of safety inspection of automobiles. This can become a heated debate, as you might remember from past experience. Fifteen years ago we had an inspection system for cars, and some people raised the dickens. They complained that the system got

jammed up—and it did—and that the cars which needed most of
the repair work done were old cars, which they said caused few
of the accidents on the roads. The poor people said that they
would have to spend a large amount of money to fix up *their*
cars, while the rich man got by free. His brakes were good, his
windshield wipers worked well, his lights were most often in
adjustment, and so forth.

But surely we can agree that a car should have proper safety
equipment, no matter how old it is. I'm inclined to believe now
we might need a safety inspection program. If we do, I hope one
can be devised which can be easily administered and which will
be fair to everybody covering only the safety equipment, such
as brakes, tires, lights, steering, without a lot of petty rules and
restrictions in it. Your views on this matter will be helpful to me
in making up my own mind.

Here's a card with another idea on it. It suggests that we require
safety belts. Well, it is true it is almost impossible to get killed
if you are buckled in with a safety belt. It is now required that
brackets be installed in new cars, so you can put belts in if you
want to. I don't know about requiring them. What do you think?

Here's another card which reads as follows: "Would it be
possible to get the billboards off our highways? They cause
accidents." I don't know that they cause accidents. Of course, I
don't like billboards when they get to be lined up down a highway, or clustered, as they sometimes are. I noticed that Luther
Hodges complained recently to the people in the Maggie Valley,
near Waynesville, about the number of billboards there. It's
true that highway billboards add little to the roads, but I'm
not convinced that they cause accidents.

However, I admit that our attitudes toward our highways do
influence our use of them. Improvements such as roadside picnic
parks, things of that sort, help a great deal. It might be that the
state could work more than it does with citizen groups in order
to beautify stretches of our highways. I am thinking here that a
club in your town might be willing to undertake the planting
of flowering trees along a highway. They might use dogwood
trees, or redbud trees, which I call the Judas tree. Why not use
them more than we do? Up in the mountains, a laurel highway
is now planted, and that's a good thing, an asset to the state.
Rose bushes could be used everywhere more than they are. We
can plant them in patches, or we can plant a long stretch with
them. In other words, we can make our highways sources of pride,
and this will certainly have a bearing on their usefulness and
safety.

There are doubtless other ideas. You have some of your own,

I suspect. We will be pleased to consider them. We need good thinking. But I am pretty well sold already on the need to seek the five things I outlined earlier: special legislation for young drivers, special legislation for drinking drivers, more traffic engineers, more highway patrolmen, and needed court improvements. If you will join me on those five, we can make a dent in this problem. We will begin to turn the tide, which now works so painfully against us.

And please give some thought to inspection of safety equipment and safety belts, and any other ideas you might have.

We asked the Institute of Government to analyze all of the causes of accidents. We have already distributed the report to all students sixteen to eighteen years old. The staff there has also prepared this short, concise, concrete, and specific analysis.

Beginning in the morning we will distribute these to every civic club member in the state, and to a half-million other drivers. This is *not* the outline of a program. This is a study of the problem. We are not trying to "sell" a program. We are trying to find solutions.

I want to call on the civic clubs for a special project. All of them have safety chairmen. Sometime this summer, I hope you will distribute this analysis, consider it, have a program concerning safety actions, discuss the problem, make recommendations, or pass resolutions, giving me your advice on what we should do to stop this killing on the highways. This problem will not be solved by drivers, as such, but by citizens.

Last year we managed to get the North Carolina Traffic Safety Council started. It's an organization of citizens; it doesn't cost the taxpayers anything. We also have the Governor's Coordinating Committee on Traffic Safety, and it consists of top state officials. They are preparing their recommendations for us, and I believe they will recommend some of the actions we have discussed tonight. When their report is ready, it will be released to all the news media, and I hope you will give it your best thinking. You, and they, and those of us in government need to work closer together. We can't solve complex problems any other way. We can help with the roads—and we're doing that in Raleigh and Washington. We need new laws, and I can recommend them to the General Assembly and you can recommend them to your representatives. Beyond that we need to seek good ideas and to create a more healthy attitude toward this predicament, which involves us and our families. In olden times travel was dangerous because of robbers; today it's dangerous because of ourselves and our powerful machines.

I have chosen this special time to discuss this with you because we're going into the summer season. That means more traffic and perhaps more accidents. At this time I need to know what legislation on this matter I should present to the General Assembly. I have reviewed the entire matter with you; I will be happy to receive your cards and letters. They will be read and entered into the total consideration of this problem. Send them to the Governor's Office here in Raleigh.

A while ago I read you one paragraph from the letter written by a woman in the eastern part of the state. I will read you the remainder of the letter.

> What are you going to do about the problems we have in this state? What do you do for us when a son is killed on the roads that you people in Raleigh have made? I have lost a son, and I don't know what to do. Such accidents go on and on. I read about them in the paper. What are you going to do about them? I wonder if you care about us, sitting in your big office in Raleigh.
>
> It is very lonely in my house now. I think it is all over for me. I feel as if my life has come to an end. My boy is gone, and he was the best part of my life. What can you do now that he is gone?

We will do all we can.

OPENING SESSION OF SUMMER WORKSHOP AT SOUTHERN REGIONAL EDUCATION BOARD MEETING

WILLIAMSBURG, VIRGINIA

June 15, 1962

Governor Sanford, as chairman of the Southern Regional Education Board, explained that the formal meeting of the board, held at the time and place of the Southern Governors' Conference, was usually limited by time. For a full study and evaluation of the board's activities, a summer meeting was devised in 1957. The Governor turned to a consideration of the report of the Commission on Goals for Higher Education in the South; the report contained a master plan for improving higher education and had received widespread recognition. Sanford said the report revealed the poor position of the South, socially, economically, and educationally. The reality of the situation was confronted with four objectives: to provide full opportunity for all citizens through a variety of institutions and through co-ordinated programs of adult education and extension work; to achieve the highest degree of excellence in teaching, scholarship, and research; to operate at maximum efficiency by making better use of physical facilities and technological aids; to serve as an invigorating force in the economic and social improvement of each state. The report met with positive response, but Sanford called for a sustained effort to see that the report's recommendations were enacted into law by southern legislators. He felt that the Southern Regional Education Board could exert powerful leadership to insure a meaningful follow-up to the commission's report.

NORTH CAROLINA ASSOCIATION OF COUNTY COMMISSIONERS

MOREHEAD CITY

June 18, 1962

Governor Sanford recognized the responsibility of county officials in moving North Carolina forward. He pointed out that "The quality of state government reflects, to a large degree, the quality of local government." North Carolina's position existed because " (1) the potential for unprecedented progress has long existed in North Carolina, (2) because our people have become united in both their desire to develop fully this potential and their confidence in their ability to do so, and (3) because the state's leadership, at all levels of government, has recognized the value of close co-operation in the formulation and execution of intelligent, realistic, carefully co-ordinated plans of action." Sanford called aggressive leadership the key to the future of the state. He urged public officials to do more than was expected and never be satisfied. He concluded by assuring county officials of his confidence in their willingness to help in working co-operatively for "a more prosperous state and a better life for the people we serve."

NORTH CAROLINA METHODIST CONFERENCE

KINSTON

June 19, 1962

Beginning with a story illustrative of a period of transition, Governor Sanford continued with the observation that mankind had always been faced with transition and change. He gave examples of changes in farm life in the twentieth century and changes in community life of rural people. These changes required readjustments; mechanization, for example, meant a smaller rural population; the income of many farm families was not on a par with other citizens. Despite problems, Sanford expressed the opinion that farms on a family-size scale should not be foreclosed but should be reinvigorated. As an example of positive steps taken to improve the farm situation, the Governor discussed the Agricultural Opportunities Program, with its goal of farm income of $1.6 billion by 1966—"1.6 in '66." Food processing as an expanded industry would provide farmers with new markets and new employment and would make for opportunities near farms. Paved rural roads, a quality education program, and conservation of water resources were only a few of the assets which would prove to be a boost to farms. The Governor then discussed agriculture as a weapon against communism, with surplus food being important to the defense of the free world. Wartime conditions would require more than the surpluses on hand, though the Governor expressed the hope that it would never be necessary to use the surpluses for war. He said that farmers in communist areas had resisted nationalization of their land, homes, lives, and that free America had to take the offensive in using the farm surpluses to feed a hungry world. This step had to be taken, not only to win friends, but because it was morally right. Sanford called the surpluses a blessing, not a burden, and asked that this blessing be shared with underfed people around the world.

SOUTHERN ASSOCIATION OF BAPTIST COLLEGES AND SCHOOLS AND EDUCATION COMMITTEE OF THE SOUTHERN BAPTIST CONVENTION

Winston-Salem

June 27, 1962

Governor Sanford chose the sometimes controversial topic of church-state relationships on which to speak to this Baptist group. He called religion the foundation of culture in America; he explained that, though separation of church and state had been a basic principle of the country, that did not mean that government should be godless. The Governor questioned the Supreme Court decision banning prayer in the public schools. He said no school should require prayer but citizens should "continue to use, encourage, and promote prayer in the schools, out of schools, in government, and out of government." He spoke of the partnership between church and state, citing the establishment of educational institutions as an example. Educational institutions had to be provided by both government and churches and the cost to the individual had to be kept within reach. He commended the Baptists for their stand in favor of the separation of church and state, saying that decisions regarding educational needs and facilities would have to be made without violating this principle or the basic belief in the right of private groups to establish and maintain schools. At the same time, plans could and would have to be made together. He urged citizens to "demonstrate . . . qualities of citizenship as well as . . . qualities of loyalty to . . . religious beliefs. . . ." He added that they needed to "merge these two and wear . . . [the] two hats of citizenship and religion with dignity and with commitment to basic human welfare."

NATIONAL GOVERNORS CONFERENCE

HERSHEY, PENNSYLVANIA

July 2, 1962

Governor Sanford took advantage of another opportunity to sell North Carolina when he addressed the National Governors Conference. He discussed industrial development as one of many efforts to raise income, but he explained that the North Carolina program did not include tax concessions. The state had not stolen industry, though it welcomed industries which chose to come to North Carolina. Programs to train individuals in twenty industrial education centers, appropriations at the state level, hard work at the local level, and constructive programs in the Department of Conservation and Development were all factors which had resulted in success. Sanford explained that the state paid particular attention to existing industries. Trade fairs and "Made in North Carolina Week" were cited as examples of two ways of showing appreciation to industries established in the state. In turn, industries became good-will ambassadors for North Carolina. The whole purpose of the program of **industrial development** was "to help people, men and women, have a better chance to make a better living."

NATIONAL ASSOCIATION OF COUNTY OFFICIALS

New York, New York

July 11, 1962

[The responsibilities of local governments, as opposed to those of state and national governments, were often argued by laymen, legislators, and administrators. In his address at the National Association of County Officials in New York, Governor Sanford discussed this subject and emphasized the advantages of local leadership in specified areas.]

There is a lot of talk about home rule. Our theme this morning is what we can do about it.

Not many years ago the roads were designed, built, and maintained by decisions made by county governing bodies. The welfare responsibilities were met by the operation of a county home, or the "poor house" as it was called in Scotland County when I was a boy. The schools, although they might have received a little "encouragement" money from the state government, were built and the teachers paid by local governments which thereby established educational standards. Law enforcement was a county or town undertaking. How far to go, or not to go, was a matter of home rule.

But that was yesterday. When Adam and Eve were being banished from the Garden of Eden, Adam turned to Eve and said, "My dear, we are living in a period of transition." And so it is.

Changes not in government but in conditions brought a transition in home rule. The mule and "drag pan" and the man with the pick passed on. The need for more roads, the necessity for multicounty planning, and the coming of heavy construction equipment combined to shift many road decisions from courthouses to state capital, or at least to state divisional offices.

The depression, demonstrating that the counties where people most needed welfare financial assistance were least able to provide it, moved other decisions to the statehouse and the nation's capitol.

So change brought change and will continue to bring more change.

There were valid reasons for some shifts toward more centralization away from local decisions. Faster transportation and communication made crossing county lines by state authority and state lines by federal authority imperative.

In too many places, however, it was a matter of abdication. Local leaders got tired of leading. They failed to respond to demand for needed governmental services, and citizens turned away to higher governments for solutions to their problems.

This has been true not only of the shift from local to state, but from state to national, and the basic reason is that it is far easier to let someone else solve our problems.

I get disheartened almost every time a conference of state or local officials is conducted about any specific problem because, more likely than not, their labors bring forth the decision in profound words that what we need is more federal aid. This is a "national problem," they declare.

For example, I don't think we need to look to the federal government for a juvenile delinquency program. If there is one thing that can be cared for better the closer to home we can keep it, it is juvenile correction. Maybe our interest can be promoted by national groups, but the solution is not national action.

I see no reason to call for federal help because urban transportation is a knotty problem. Sure it is, but all of the leadership for solving knotty problems is not in Washington. Sure it is easier to get money from the federal government, but that is exactly what we are talking about, or rather talking against, when we seek more local authority.

I know how hard it is to get tax money locally, but it will cost all of us less if we get it locally to spend locally rather than letting the federal government get it locally to spend locally.

This is like pouring buttermilk from one glass to another. By the time it gets to the third glass there is about 20 per cent less to drink.

I am sure that the President, and most cabinet members, and substantial leadership in the Congress would like to stop the trend to centralization, but they can't do it unless the public will tolerate it; and the public will not accept it until we as state and local officials demonstrate our competence and our willingness to handle the legitimate needs of the people.

So this puts the burden of home rule on us. Nobody else is going to take up this cause because nobody else is in the position of responsibility for home rule.

Home rule and local decisions are particularly important today. In these days of rising state and local taxes, and very high federal taxes, all governmental activity is subject to the closest scrutiny and people everywhere heed the call for economy.

There is a strong cry against centralization, because of the inflexibility, the duplication, the remoteness, the waste, the delays which result when government is too far away from the people it is designed to serve.

If we do not put our governmental house in order in a way that brings greater economy and greater service, we will play into the hands of the right-wing extremists who believe that government is not designed to serve and who, in the false name of economy, would eliminate or curtail the services of education, roads, health, welfare, and the other essential and common purposes of democratic government.

This is why home rule is so important today. If we fail to check centralization, government may very well sustain a loss in public confidence.

Your program impresses me. This is your third day of examining home rule in its many aspects. You began with Bill Mac-Dougall's[100] description of home rule in the democratic process. You have considered various approaches and have heard specific examples.

There is much to know about home rule, and a complexity of variations, but one thing is certain: We are in favor of it!

What action will strengthen it is a different story.

We are talking about a fundamental ideal of democratic government when we promote home rule and local decision, for this means keeping government as close as possible to the people. That is an easy and proper position to take.

The difficulty lies in applying this ideal to individual functions, structures, and situations of government. What political action should we take to extend home rule?

What should be a local decision, and how is it to be made and paid for, and who decides what is local and what is not, are matters of application.

County governing boards, whether called commissioners or supervisors, or juries, or courts, or one of twenty-three other titles, and with membership ranging from one to more than fifty, charged with duties ranging from all schools to no schools, all roads to no roads, all prisoners to no prisoners, make impossible one single and simple suggestion of political action necessary to protect the right of home rule.

For example, do you want anything to do with rural roads? Do you want to plan, build, or maintain them? Do you want to pay for them or share in the price? Do you want to play a part in planning or paving or setting priorities? In some states 90 per cent of the rural roads belong to the counties, along with the

---

[100] William R. MacDougall, general counsel, County Supervisors Association of California; keynote speaker at 1962 national conference of county officials. *1962 County Yearbook* (Chapel Hill: North Carolina Association of County Commissioners, 1962), 123.

problems and the payments. In other states, North Carolina included, 100 per cent belongs to the state.

Is this good or bad, and can greater efficiency, and therefore, more roads be a justifiable price to pay for this diminished bit of home rule?

Do you want to control totally the purse strings of education, as you do in some counties, or do you want to share this as is done in some counties, or do you want to give this over to other agencies as is done in some counties?

There is one certain pattern to the government of American counties and that is a total lack of uniformity.

This has given us flexibility and provided examples of progress and is a tradition well worth maintaining. We do not seek uniformity and conformity to the master plan, not even in our definition and goal of home rule.

There is a reason for centralization and a reason for maintaining local decision. We need to test each issue and each function individually.

Some things can be done more efficiently and effectively from the courthouse, some from the statehouse, and some from Washington.

It seems to me that there are three parts to the action we should take.

First, we should define for ourselves, within the context of our counties and our states, what is desirable and what is possible. Obviously a Delaware county would not set out the details in the same matter defined by an Oklahoma county. Surely each state association could propound its home rule goals in definite fashion. In this way we can know what we seek and the people can know why we seek it.

Second, we need, as always in democratic government, to consider the appropriate political action. It would be very easy to say that in order to obtain more home rule, or more authority to decide questions locally, all you have to do is put the pressure on the state legislature to increase your statutory authority, or to insist that state agencies impose fewer state restrictions and authorize more local decisions. But this would be as misleading as it is inaccurate, for this is not all that there is to it.

Legislatures act in response to citizen demand, or at least with the tacit approval of the voters. So a case must be made to the legislature to get it to act, and this must have general public support. Also, state agencies have their own responsibilities and their own ideas as to the best way of discharging these responsibilities. Like the counties, they depend on a grant of authority from the legislature. But unlike the counties, they look at things

on a state-wide basis which often conflicts with the way particular
areas look at the same things. Some areas may want more, and
some less, activity. And the state agency's responsibility is to arrive
at a workable happy medium—which, like compromises, generally
tend to satisfy nobody.

I emphasize this particular aspect of state-county relations—
for after all home rule and local decisions in the major concerns
of county activity exist in the context of state-county relations.
This is true of public schools, public welfare, and public health.
These three activities involve 90 per cent of the expenditures of
our North Carolina counties, and more than 75 per cent of our
state budget, excluding roads and highways. In most states,
it is also true in roads and highways.

My point is that necessarily there is a state-wide interest and
a local interest in most of our responsibilities. The state-wide
interest is often phrased in terms of a minimum, or basic program. The state, acting in response to citizens' demands, provides
that each child shall be given a certain minimum education; that
each needy person shall receive a grant based on a minimum
standard of decency and health; that certain conditions detrimental to public health shall be eliminated. Home rule, then,
cannot mean a reduction of the state-wide minimum level, no
matter what the wishes of a particular area. A majority of people
of the entire state have decided the matter, and they will not
have their will frustrated by local inaction.

The proper responsibility for local decision is how to provide
each child with the minimum education that child needs, plus
additional education to make the child as productive an adult
as possible; how to distinguish the needy from the lazy, and how
to rehabilitate the physically and mentally disabled; how to
identify and deal with public health problems that truly are
harmful.

This is the position for home rule and local decision in the
state-county relationship context. The states will not and cannot allow local decision to override state-wide policy. And as
you approach state agencies to obtain more local authority, you
must understand and appreciate their position just as they must
understand and appreciate yours. While local decision cannot
override state-wide policy, state agencies should not attempt to
use the cloak of state-wide policy to interfere in local decisions.
This makes continuous negotiation and compromise necessary.
This negotiation and compromise must be conducted in the spirit
of good will, in an attempt to harmonize state-wide interest with
local administration to achieve efficiency and economy.

I can speak for myself on this point, and I have made myself clear to the county officials of my own state. I have worked and will continue to work with our North Carolina counties to provide maximum local authority and autonomy. I believe local government, carried out close to the people served, should be and can be responsive government. I believe it should be and can be efficient and economical government. I believe it can be productive. For these reasons I believe as much as possible should be decided locally. But the Governor of the entire state cannot and will not allow the decision of a particular locality to frustrate or override a state-wide interest.

You county officials can and must help to achieve home rule and local decision. If political action is the key to home rule, the political atmosphere is the key to political action. If county officials and state officials are to work together to increase home rule and local decision, they must have the approval of citizens and voters. And if state and local officials disagree, the victor on a particular issue will be the side having the greater popular support.

My point is this: To create the political atmosphere necessary to increase home rule and local decisions, you must act responsibly in areas where you now have authority. It is often said that responsibility and authority go together. If you are to have more authority, you must be responsible.

Look at it this way. If counties do not respond to citizens' desires for services, these citizens will not be willing to see more authority granted to counties. If counties do not provide existing services economically and efficiently, citizens will not be willing to provide more opportunity for waste. If counties do not merit confidence in the existing operations, they will not have opportunity for additional operations. This is no easy task. Like a stone wall, built by adding stone on stone, public confidence is earned and won by a steady succession of satisfactory actions. Some counties have further to go than others, just as some states have further to go than others.

The third suggestion sums up the first two in a word. The word is leadership. You occupy the positions of leaders. You were elected to lead, not just to preside. Home rule and local decisions flourish when local leaders are willing to fight for better educational opportunities for local children. Overcentralization in government is retarded when local leaders get out on a limb to stand for planning, and development, and slum avoidance, and proper endeavors which promote a stronger economy and a more wholesome community.

Home rule follows leadership. If your mission is vigorously the mission of the people, then you are promoting, developing, and achieving home rule.

DEDICATION OF THE CHARLOTTE INDUSTRIAL EDUCATION CENTER

CHARLOTTE

July 18, 1962

[Industrial education centers, established during the administration of Governor Hodges, were made components of the comprehensive system of community colleges and were greatly expanded during the Sanford administration. With part-time instruction in various trade and specialty courses for high school juniors and seniors and adult education courses, the centers featured an "open door" policy of admission and stressed individualized learning. These dedicatory exercises at Charlotte gave the Governor another opportunity to discuss education and its relation to the total economy. Sanford suggested the inclusion of a liberal arts program to complement the practical instruction given at the centers.]

I am happy to have a part in the exercises dedicating the Charlotte Industrial Education Center. This is part of our state-wide declaration of war on poverty.

Such a complete and effective job has been done in remodeling this building that it is hard to recognize it as the old Central High School which was erected in the early twenties and in which Dr. Garinger[101] served as the first principal.

While this building has been extensively remodeled and while the industrial education center, now housed here, is a different type of institution, in no small degree it inherits the mantle of Central High School. Many successful men and women in Charlotte and Mecklenburg County, but also in many other areas of our state and nation, have moved out from this building to successful careers and to lives of valuable service to their state and their nation. All of these have carried with them the very fine reputation that Central High School built for providing excellent educational opportunity. This reputation for excellence was due in no small measure to the leadership of Dr. Garinger, as well as to the leadership of many other people here in Charlotte.

I am certain that this industrial education center will uphold

---

[101] Elmer Henry Garinger (1891-   ), educator from Charlotte; Superintendent of Charlotte-Mecklenburg Schools, consultant in education, Visiting Professor of Education at Appalachian State Teachers College, University of North Carolina at Chapel Hill, University of Missouri, and Peabody College; civic and government worker; representative in the General Assembly, 1963. *North Carolina Manual, 1963,* 573-574.

this record of excellence in providing education. There is no more important task that we face than the task of extending educational opportunity beyond the high school. In doing this, your industrial education center here in Charlotte fills a place in a pattern of such institutions throughout our state.

In all areas of life, the welfare of our state will move forward on the feet of educated people. This is as true in economic welfare as it is true in the area of citizenship in general.

The economic pattern of life in North Carolina has changed radically since the day that this building was first erected. In fact, even during the twenty years from 1940 to 1960, there have been great changes in the way that people make a living in North Carolina. For example, in 1940 agricultural employment accounted for 33.8 per cent of our labor force. By 1950 this had fallen to 24.6 per cent, and in 1960 it has declined sharply to 12.8 per cent. The twenty-year period from 1940 to 1960 showed a 49.6 per cent decline in the proportion of the labor force engaged in agriculture.

At the same time, the percentage of the population engaged in manufacturing has increased sharply. In fact, manufacturing employment in North Carolina has advanced consistently since the mid-fifties in contrast with a near stable level in manufacturing employment for the nation as a whole. We now find in 1960, 1,200,500 people in nonagricultural employment; and manufacturing industries account for 42.4 per cent of this nonfarm employment. This ratio is considerably above the national ratio which is 30.6 per cent. Expansion of industries that we have had in our state for a number of years has accounted for a great deal of this increase. At the same time, we are making significant progress in attracting new industries.

Last year over a quarter of a billion dollars was invested in North Carolina in new industrial plants in our state. Last year some 35,000 new jobs, with an annual payroll of more than $117 million, were established for the people of North Carolina. The Department of Conservation and Development reports to me that for the first six months of this year, we ran ahead of the same period in the record-setting year of 1961.

While we are proud of our record in industrial expansion, we plan to continue working hard to create a balance in the types of manufacturing in North Carolina. Our manufacturing is largely devoted to nondurable goods. These producers provide approximately 72 per cent of the state's manufacturing employment. At the same time, employment in durable goods manufacturing in this state accounts for only 28 per cent of the total.

We can compare four industries in durable goods and four in nondurable goods in order to see just what this picture is. In the United States, furniture, lumber and wood products, metal products, and electrical goods account for 36.1 per cent of the manufacturing industries. In North Carolina, these same four account for 24.4 per cent of the total manufacturing output. Four industries in nondurable goods—textiles, tobacco, apparel, and food—account for 23.7 per cent in the United States and 63.1 per cent in North Carolina.

Not only are we somewhat out of balance as we compare durable goods manufacturing with nondurable goods manufacturing, but in specific areas we are out of balance. For example, in the durable goods, North Carolina is far ahead of the nation in furniture manufacturing and in lumber and wood products manufacturing, but we are far behind the nation in metal products and some behind the nation in electrical goods manufacturing. We are working to attract more of the metal products manufacturing and electrical goods manufacturing businesses to North Carolina, while we work to hold our lead in the other areas.

If we look at the nondurable goods industries, we find that North Carolina is heavily engaged in textile manufacturing which accounts for 43.8 per cent of our manufacturing operations; whereas, this per cent is 5.3 per cent for the nation. We are also far ahead in tobacco, but we are behind in apparel and in food. Certainly, we should not be behind in processing of food through manufacturing enterprises. Our percentage in North Carolina in food manufacturing is 6.5 per cent compared with 10.6 per cent for the nation as a whole.

This concentration of manufacturing in a few relatively major industry groupings indicates that we do not have the kind of balance in our manufacturing structure that we should have. We have made excellent progress, but we need to make much more. We are going to give every assistance possible to the growth of the great established industries of our state, including textiles, tobacco, and furniture. But at the same time, we are also going to be seeking more diversified industry.

I have already mentioned the sharp drop in agricultural employment. There are, however, many activities that are closely related to agriculture, such as food processing, that we need to develop.

Dr. Rupert Vance[102] of the University of North Carolina says that a fully industrialized society will have a large proportion of the labor force engaged in service, distribution, and clerical activities. There are many types of jobs in all of these areas that we have not developed fully in North Carolina.

In the final analysis, industrial welfare means human welfare. While we must be concerned that the manpower needs of industry, agriculture, and business are met, we must also be concerned that the needs of the people of the state shall be met; and among these needs is the need for education, including vocational education.

This industrial education center and others like it are being established to provide the manpower needs of the state. But first of all, they are to provide for human needs. The Employment Security Commission of North Carolina has just completed a very able study of the manpower needs of our state. These findings are to be used in many different ways. Among these ways, they will be used to determine the types of training programs needed in the industrial education centers in North Carolina. In addition to the information we secure from this study of manpower needs, we have also secured information about the flood of high school graduates who will be moving into the labor force or institutions for education beyond the high school. Information of this nature being developed by the Carlyle Commission on Education Beyond the High School ties closely in with the information from the Employment Security Commission study in order to give us the kind of data that we must have if we are going to meet the needs of our people in terms of economics and in terms of education.

I have been pointing out to you that we in North Carolina can be proud of the improvement we have been making in the economic posture of our state and in the job opportunities made available for our people. We cannot be as proud of our record in providing educational opportunities. For example, North Carolina has the poorest record of any state save only Mississippi in the percentage of our young people who attend college. We can hardly hide behind a feeling of pride in economic advancement, while, at the same time, we follow policies that keep half of our college-capable youngsters out of college. We may also extend this by saying that there are many more of our people who should

---

[102] Rupert B. Vance, Arkansas native; Professor of Sociology at the University of North Carolina at Chapel Hill since 1929; research professor at the Institute for Research in Social Science at Chapel Hill. *The University of North Carolina at Chapel Hill Record: The General Catalogue Issue, 1962-1963* (Chapel Hill: University of North Carolina Press, 1962), hereinafter cited as *University Record, 1962-1963*.

not go to college to train for the professions but are fully capable of being educated as technicians and skilled craftsmen in all phases of work.

The state must educate; the state must be educated. The alternative is slavery—economic, cultural, social, and political slavery. The choice is between ignorance and enlightenment on a vast scale. We must double our enrollments in institutions giving education beyond the high school or we will certainly double our problems and our poverty.

The people of this state are hungry for the type of education that will be provided and is now being provided in this institution. How else can we explain that in the space of three years we are reaching 35,000 young people in the industrial education centers, many of whom would not have gone to any type of training institution beyond the high school if these centers had not been available. They have enrolled because they need education for economic survival in an economy that is changing more rapidly than our ideas about education are changing. Now the questions must be: Is terminal education, alone, adequate for them? Is vocational education all that they need? Do they not also need an opportunity for certain liberal studies in the program of education in this institution and in other institutions that may be developed in North Carolina?

At the same time that we see clearly the need for improvement in our economic posture in North Carolina, we also must have an equal concern, if not a greater concern that the human values shall be recognized and provided for. We must be concerned that every child have an excellent, appropriate educational opportunity available for him, and we must also see that in a changing world this educational opportunity can no longer be ended with the public school program.

Walter Hines Page pointed out very clearly the need for recognizing the importance of education for all. This is the way he expressed it:

Society forever needs reinforcement from the rear. It is a shining day in any educated man's growth when he comes to see and to know and to feel and freely to admit that it is just as important to the world that the raga-muffin child of his worthless neighbor should be trained as it is that his own child should be. Until a man sees this he cannot become a worthy democrat nor get a patriotic conception of education; for no man has known the deep meaning of democracy or felt either its obligation or its lift till he has seen this truth clearly.[103]

I am sure that you believe as strongly in the potential future of North Carolina as I believe. I am sure that you are as dedicated

---

[103] Page, *Rebuilding of Old Commonwealths*, 89-90.

as I am to raising the economic level and the general cultural level of our people. The existence of this institution demonstrates concretely that you understand that the way to achieving our goals is through improved educational opportunity. I am certain that you are concerned that all people shall have appropriate, excellent educational opportunity and that we cannot, if we love our state and if we have any hope at all for the future, neglect providing educational opportunity beyond the high school for all who need this opportunity.

AVERY COUNTY CHAMBER OF COMMERCE

Crossnore

August 1, 1962

Governor Sanford, speaking in Avery County, reminded his audience that other counties were engaged in programs to create employment and raise incomes, but he cited Avery as a county which had taken action. The county's average income per person was less than a quarter of the national average and the communities faced loss of population. It was assumed that the county had to have industry, but the people came to realize that industry was only one solution. The decision was made to develop tourist facilities, engage in agricultural enterprises such as the raising of fruits and Christmas trees, and establish small industries. Lack of capital was a problem until funds became available through the Federal Area Redevelopment Act. The County Planning Board, building on the groundwork laid by the Chamber of Commerce, was formed. The board did not displace any existing group, but in its advisory and co-ordinating capacity it represented all major economic interests. Reminding the group that neighboring counties had also made outstanding progress, the Governor advised the Avery County people not to become complacent but to concentrate on continued improvement. He solicited the help of every citizen in selling the area.

ANNUAL MEETING, NORTH CAROLINA POLICE EXECUTIVES ASSOCIATION

Raleigh

August 3, 1962

Governor Sanford told this group of police executives that law, the backbone of society, was worthless unless it was respected and enforced. He said that the policeman personified law for the majority of the people. The Governor then launched into a discussion of the proposed court reform amendment, saying that an efficient court system was imperative to modern law enforcement, that times changed and old machinery needed replacement, and that North Carolina was being asked to support a revision of an outdated system. The purpose of the amendment was to establish a uniform system of lower courts. Though there were many excellent courts, the state had 1,400 of them operating independently. The amendment provided for the division of the state into local court districts. The plan would be worked out by the General Assembly in conjunction with an administrative office which would be established to free judges of details. Sanford remarked that justice was everybody's business and that court improvement should be important to every citizen. He closed with a word of confidence that law enforcement in North Carolina would face up to the challenge of progress.

CEREMONIES COMMEMORATING THE ESTABLISHMENT OF THE FIRST SOIL CONSERVATION DISTRICT IN AMERICA

Wadesboro

August 7, 1962

Governor Sanford, speaking on the spot on which the first soil conservation program was initiated twenty-five years earlier, briefly reviewed accomplishments of the program. The original district of 120,000 acres in Anson and Union counties grew to 3,000 districts covering more than 92 per cent of the nation's farm and range land. The Governor stressed the need to continue the program to assure proper use of natural resources. He said the responsibility was one which would produce rewards if properly assumed; future generations would enjoy prosperity if the present generation assumed its rightful responsibility.

STATE-WIDE TELEVISION ADDRESS ON THE FOOD PROCESSING INDUSTRY

Durham

August 7, 1962

[One of the top-priority programs of the Sanford administration was the expansion of the food processing industry. A thirty-minute documentary (produced by WTVD, Durham, in its "Dixie Dynamo" series), showing food crops and processing plants filmed from the coast to the mountains, was shown while the Governor discussed efforts being made to capitalize on the multibillion dollar market. For another address in which Sanford presented the need for expansion in the area of food processing, see the summary of the April 17, 1962, speech on page 233.]

During the coming months I hope to discuss with you the vital issues that are important to every citizen of the state. Among these issues are such things as court improvement, the state's prison system, North Carolina's water resources, the welfare program, and other subjects of equal importance.

On this program I want to talk with you about food processing in North Carolina—its accomplishments and its opportunities.

Since the Colonial days we have been known as an agricultural state, primarily for our cotton and tobacco. For more than two centuries our entire economy was geared to the production of these commodities. It has only been during this century that food crops have supplemented farm income to any degree, and only in the past few years has food processing started to move into its own in the state.

Feeding 180 million persons three meals a day not only is a great responsibility but is also a great challenge. The farms of North Carolina and the nation are providing the foodstuffs to make this the best fed nation in history.

At this season of the year when fresh produce reaches the market in quantity we are all impressed with nature's abundance in North Carolina: the fields of corn, apples ripening in the mountains, tomatoes on the vine, green fields all over the state, and those taste-tempting strawberries and Sandhills peaches.

If we limited ourselves entirely to the fresh produce market, we'd find ourselves in the position of providing fewer and fewer job opportunities for our people while at the same time paying a premium for food processed out of state. We have made a start and now we have the opportunity of greatly expanding what we are dong toward providing those 540 million American meals a day.

It hasn't been too long ago that a good sized grocery store carried no more than a thousand different food items on its shelves. When you go into a modern supermarket today you find up to 7,000 articles, and the number is increasing constantly. Some of these are presently being processed in North Carolina, some for purely local distribution, others for regional or even national markets.

Just a few years ago the state had to import many products that weren't grown in sufficient quantity to make processing

worthwhile. Now that picture is rapidly changing and many of
the items we were getting from as far away as the Pacific North-
west or even Japan are being profitably produced and processed
in this state.

Some of North Carolina's food plants have been around for
many years. Others are almost brand new. Pickles have long been
a favorite; consequently it was no great surprise when a new
plant began operation in Henderson three years ago. An aggressive local industrial group convinced some hardheaded in-
vestors that what had been done successfully in Mount Olive and
Faison could be done in Vance County. The only surprising thing
has been the rapid growth and expansion of this organization.
This company employs from 200 to 600 persons, depending on
the season, and puts more than $2 million into the economy of
the surrounding counties. Along with its counterparts it has
helped raise North Carolina into the second largest cucumber
producing state in the nation. Management of the firm gives much
credit to North Carolina State College for one of its developments
that has been a boom to the industry. Researchers at the college
were able to isolate a bacteria that caused cucumbers to soften
during fermentation. This research saved the industry thousands
of dollars.

Ten years ago sweet red and green peppers were a negligible
crop in North Carolina when a company began operations in
Dunn. Now several hundred acres of the vegetable are being
harvested every year. The first two seasons were bad crop years,
but persistence and faith in the future paid off. Next time you
eat a stuffed green pepper or have a pizza with pepper strips,
more than likely it will have been grown and processed in North
Carolina.

Men of vision have been responsible for the growth of North
Carolina's three great industries: tobacco, textiles, and furniture.
Men like Reynolds and Duke had the inspiration and determi-
nation to take North Carolina's tobacco and process it into the
finished product. They know that what we can grow in North
Carolina, we can process in North Carolina. The Loves and the
Cannons used this principle in the development of textiles. The
same is true of the furniture industry.

The Department of Food Science and Processing has been
established at State College under the leadership of Dr. William
Roberts.[104] This department is equipped to provide technical

---

[104] William Milner Roberts, head of department and Professor of Food Science
at North Carolina State University at Raleigh. *North Carolina State College General Catalog, 1962-1964* (Raleigh: Office of Information Services of North Carolina
State College of Agriculture and Engineering, 1962), 410, hereinafter cited as
North Carolina State College Catalog.

assistance to farmers and processors alike. A development of this department is responsible for a totally new food industry being started. Through the research of Dr. M. W. Hoover[105] a method of drying sweet potatoes and pumpkins and transforming them into flakes was developed. This laboratory project was translated into full plant operation down in Windsor by produce processors. A combination of local initiative and outside financial help and know-how resulted in a successful operation. They also have plans for developing a white potato flour which could revolutionize the food industry. Their pumpkin operation is in full swing at the present time. You can see that plants such as this can't depend on leftover produce from the fresh market. Rather they need the highest quality raw product available.

With a state as large and diverse as North Carolina no one can keep up with all the things that are happening. Each of us is generally aware of developments in the area in which we live, but occasionally very important happenings somewhere else can pass almost unnoticed. Here's a case in point. In 1958 the Gerber Company started construction on its huge baby food plant near Asheville. I was amazed to discover recently that many people didn't know this plant existed. When this plant was built it took into account the much publicized population explosion. It had expansion plans due for completion in 1970. Their North Carolina operation has been so successful they have already reached the projected 1970 size. As far as it's available, produce for this plant is purchased in North Carolina. Farmers grow beets, carrots, peaches, apples, green beans, and other produce for this plant. This operation is another excellent example of an industry making use of the resources of the community. In addition to making use of the land, it is employing several hundred persons. It is purchasing related products, such as glass jars and other supplies, locally. In addition, it is distributing Gerber products produced in other plants to a ten-state area. One production line of this operation produces 650 jars of baby food a minute.

In nearby Henderson County a state research farm is exploring avenues of food production that promise to provide opportunities for farmers and food processors. One crop on which they are working is cauliflower, now mostly grown on Long Island. If the experimental planting is successful—and it appears it will be—another food crop opportunity will open up for North Carolina farmers.

Another crop on which considerable work is being done is

---

[105] Maurice W. Hoover, Professor of Food Science at North Carolina State University at Raleigh. *North Carolina State College Catalog,* 401.

beets. These are just some of the tools the state food team is providing farmers and industry to make food processing more practical and profitable in North Carolina.

Making use of the assets we have is a very necessary step in our industrial growth. We aren't going to interest steel mills and automobile manufacturers in moving their multibillion dollar operations to North Carolina, at least not overnight. But by judicious use of the assets we have we can upgrade the economy of the state tremendously. We have vast areas of land that can be developed to produce needed agricultural products on the volume basis necessary for processing. We have good supplies of labor for food factories; we have good water supply; we have good plant site availability. Another necessary asset we have is assurance of the needed capital for establishment of worthwhile industries.

Recently the peanut industry in the state was given a boost. Traditionally, peanuts have been thought of on the national market as a Virginia product because the first large plants were built in the tidewater section of that state—this in spite of the fact that North Carolina grows more peanuts than Virginia. Two years ago a blanching plant was established in Edenton that has become something of a model for the industry. Millions of pounds go through this plant a year in wet and dry blanching processes. There has been a considerable growth of packaging of North Carolina peanuts in recent months but not as much as we would like to see. The latest use of this multimillion dollar crop is being developed by a company down in Duplin. It is manufacturing and marketing peanut mixes for pies, cakes, and cookies. This is an example of individual initiative and research being put to work.

All the effort being expanded is not in big plant operation. Here is a case of a small operator struggling to make a product saleable. For nearly four years this man has been smoking marlin, amberjack, dolphin, blues, and other fish so abundant in our coastal waters. His results have been a prized food, but he just couldn't make the smoked fish keep long enough to be commercially successful. Now State College has come along with a chemical answer to that problem. We have more than enough fish available to supply thousands of such smokehouses in eastern North Carolina. Good merchandising could make this the multimillion dollar industry it is in Florida.

One of the seafood products generally associated in the public mind with New England has a strong foothold in this state. Down at Williston, Mr. Elmer Willis is processing clams. Other seafoods being processed that are important to the economy of the state include a new pasteurized crab meat, shrimp, oysters, and of course, a large variety of fish. North Carolina has the potential for becoming the national leader in this most important food source.

Recognizing opportunity when it comes their way is an accepted condition for the Hartsfield family in Holly Ridge. You can put their product on fruit cakes. They took advantage of a native crop—here when Sir Walter Raleigh's colonists arrived—to establish the only winery in the state. Their principal product is the scuppernong. In addition to some fourteen acres of vineyards of their own they buy all the scuppernong grapes they can find and they still need more. In fact, they set out 30,000 cuttings this summer which they plan to offer to farmers at cost in an effort to get them to grow scuppernongs. These are the highest priced grapes on the American market, and it offers an excellent extra cash crop. In a normal year a vineyard will gross a thousand dollars an acre or more. California growers have been in North Carolina this summer exploring the possibilities for scuppernongs in that state. The potential for jellies and preserves has never been fully explored.

A company that has done a splendid job of exploring preserving possibilities is the Garner Company in Winston-Salem. This is one of the oldest forms of food processing and one of the most competitive. The competition is not only from other companies, but from millions of housewives. First known for its Texas Pete Hot Sauce, the company now produces thirty kinds of preserves, jellies, and sauces. It buys most of its raw materials in bulk from North Carolina frozen food plants. A high degree of automation, quality control, and technical know-how have made it possible for this company to produce a superior product that has distribution over a five-state area. This is a success story that can be duplicated by those willing to devote time and energy and imagination.

In this land of plenty not many of us give a great deal of thought to our food—where it comes from, how it gets to us. We take for granted the things that millions of people across the world think about constantly. The bottle of milk, the loaf of bread, the soft drink, the dried beans, the canned vegetables are all things most of us can't remember being without—at least not since the depression. Our children can't remember being without TV dinners and frozen pies. Another generation will demand further refinements in food processing.

Twenty years ago North Carolina had to import much of the fresh milk sold in the state. With the help of the State Department of Agriculture and State College, dairy herds are much enlarged and improved. In spite of greatly increased domestic consumption we are now net exporters of milk. All sections of the state have benefited from this expansion.

A factor in milk production that hasn't received much notice was a twofold development by the Agriculture Department and State College. First a new type grass suited to the needs of dairy cows was developed and found to grow well in North Carolina. The only difficulty was that milk from cows eating this grass had an undesirable flavor. The Food Science Division then developed a machine to remove the objectionable characteristics, but which retained all the desirable qualities of processed milk. Here again an industry has taken advantage of changing tastes and demands to provide a better product.

Another food industry that has grown by leaps and bounds has been the producing and processing of poultry. The broiler demand has caused the entire poultry and egg business to expand many times over with still more room to grow. A plant such as this Farmers Exchange in Durham processes several thousand chickens an hour. In addition to those sold on the fresh market, many more are frozen and shipped to national and even foreign markets. In fact, one of the greatest opportunities for this burgeoning industry is the shipment to overseas points through the ports of Wilmington and Morehead City.

Livestock raising and meat processing are other phases of the food industry that have become vital parts of our economy and offer a great opportunity for the state. The large Swift and Company plant in Wilson is an excellent example of outside capital seeing an opportunity in North Carolina and taking advantage of it. Other big packers such as Newbern Provision are expanding already large operations so they can take care of the ever increasing food demands.

Swine markets are increasing with the advent of pig parlors and the more modern methods of hog production. More and more farmers are feeding out hogs and furnishing packers and curers with a better product. In fact, the country ham business is becoming big business in the state. Tomahawk Farms in Dunn has a capacity of 10,000 dry-cured hams a week.

Impressive as our progress has been in the last few years we need to do much more to raise North Carolina from its position of forty-second in per capita income to a point nearer to the national average.

Raw food products being shipped out of the state and being returned as processed food can be reversed in flow so that we become a net exporter of manufactured food items. We can be to the food industry what Detroit is to the automobile industry, and there is more money spent on food than on new cars. The farmer receives less than 40 per cent of the food dollar with the largest share going to the middleman—the processor. We need more middlemen in North Carolina to keep this huge source of income at home.

Let's not kid ourselves. Mama's not going back to the kitchen to spend five or six hours a day in food preparation when she can get better, tastier products cheaper than grandma knew. One of America's improvements in living standards has been brought about by the emancipation of women from the drudgery of day-long food preparation. The time has come for us to give mama what she wants: better food, more easily prepared, and processed in North Carolina.

Many agencies of the state are co-operating in helping the farmer and businessman in the co-operative venture of preparing food items for the shelves of today's pantry. The Extension Division at State College and the School of Agriculture, under Dean James, with its new Department of Food Science, are bringing scientific research and enthusiastic promotion to food processing. The Agriculture Department, under the direction of my close associate L. Y. "Stag" Ballentine, is taking the lead in finding ways to keep the family-size farm profitable. Just recently the Department of Conservation and Development added a three-man food processing section to its Department of Commerce and Industry.

This might be a good time to remind businessmen of North Carolina that the opportunities in food processing in this state are not closed. On the contrary, the period of greatest growth is just beginning. If you need help or advice in starting or enlarging a food processing plant let us know about it. If you need assistance in merchandising or if you need to know what to grow and where to sell, we'll help you find the answers. Just write to me at the State Capitol in Raleigh and I'll see that your letter is sent to the department that has the answers.

During this program we have mentioned the names of just a few firms and individuals who are doing great work in this field. We could list ten times the number and still only scratch the surface. We'd like to pay tribute to all those fine people and the job they are doing. With all of us working together we can accomplish all we have the courage to set out to do.

ELEVENTH ANNUAL
LEGISLATIVE WORK CONFERENCE
SOUTHERN REGIONAL EDUCATION BOARD

Biloxi, Mississippi

August 16, 1962

This Legislative Work Conference was planned by the Legislative Advisory Council, the permanent advisory body of the Southern Regional Education Board. The need for courageous legislative action was apparent if educational opportunity for all and quality education at every level was to be provided. The objectives of the Commission on Goals for Higher Education in the South were cited; to reach those goals would demand courage and money. Governor Sanford expressed the opinion that money was available though it might have to come from new taxes. He explained that the task of each state was different, but the report of the board and the goals listed there would serve as an excellent guide. He then told the group about the establishment in North Carolina of the Commission on Education Beyond the High School. He urged all states of the South to move forward without delay.

INTRODUCTION OF SIR EDWARD BOYLE AT THE
THREE HUNDRED AND SEVENTY-FIFTH ANNIVERSARY
CELEBRATION OF THE BIRTH OF VIRGINIA DARE

Manteo

August 18, 1962

Gathered at the Waterside Theater in Manteo to commemorate the birth of the first child born of English parentage in America, the audience heard Governor Sanford speak of the courage and daring of the first people to come to the shores of America. He compared their vision with the vision of man today as he seeks passage to the stars. The Governor remarked that the course to the moon could be charted with more certainty than the course to the New World could have been charted by Sir Walter Raleigh's ship. The settlement, the birthday, the first airplane flight were all called "highly important," and this ceremony recognized the "re-establishment of the common heritage and common cause of two free nations," England and the United States. The occasion called attention to the hopes and aims of the free people, and the Governor reminded his audience that "Those aims were enunciated in a not-too-distant past by Winston Churchill and Franklin D. Roosevelt." The common bonds of the two countries were being renewed on this occasion, and Sanford welcomed the representative of Queen Elizabeth's government, Sir Edward Boyle, Minister of Education of Britain. He spoke of education as a "historically vital force in North Carolina and . . . the chief goal of the administration. . . ." After giving a brief sketch of the career of Sir Edward, the Governor presented him as the speaker of the evening.

DEDICATION OF INTERSTATE 85 LINK IN GASTON COUNTY

McAdenville

August 25, 1962

The opening of a new segment of highway would initiate new economic opportunities for Gaston County, the South Piedmont, and all of North Carolina, according to remarks made by Governor Sanford on this occasion. A good system of roads was part of state policy, with the result that there had been development of streets in the largest cities and farm-to-market paved roads in rural areas. Roads meant commerce and trade and economic growth; industrial development came because of good schools and roads which paved the way. In 1961 over a quarter billion dollars in new plants, with new payrolls of over $117 million and jobs for 35,000 North Carolinians made for a new-plant growth of 18.5 per cent, while the national plant investments fell 3 per cent. In the 1920's, Governors Cameron Morrison and Angus McLean proposed bond issues to link county seats; in the 1940's, Governor Kerr Scott realized the necessity of paving rural roads; these projects led to expansion and prosperity. North Carolina was, therefore, ready to start building the interstate system under Governors William B. Umstead and Luther H. Hodges. Governor Sanford observed that much remained to be done, and that North Carolina's programs in the fields of industry and agriculture were dependent on good transportation. America was "pushing toward new frontiers of economic and human opportunities"; North Carolina intended "to pave the road to those opportunities."

DEDICATION OF ROYSTER BUILDING
AT CHERRY HOSPITAL

GOLDSBORO

September 12, 1962

In his address at the dedication of a new building at Cherry Hospital, the Governor reminded his audience of the contribution of Dorothea Dix, who helped convince North Carolina citizens that they should care for those suffering from mental illness. As a result of her efforts, the state substituted care for incarceration. Later, John W. Umstead sold the citizens on the idea of cure as well as care, proving that an investment in mental health would pay rich dividends to the state. Sanford said that crusaders were often called free spenders, but the state had learned that it was cheaper to cure a man and return him to normal life than to incarcerate him. The new building at Goldsboro would pay for itself by making restored lives available to many, by alleviating anguish, and by offering other tangible benefits. He called attention to the obligation of citizens to participate in a mental health program which provided an opportunity to invest in the greatest resource of all—human life.

ANNUAL REUNION OF AIRBORNE ASSOCIATION

WASHINGTON, D. C.

September 13, 1962

Governor Sanford, addressing the annual reunion of Airborne Association, referred to the military reserve of the United States as an effective force. He told of steps taken by President Kennedy to improve the nation's military posture, but he added that there was still need for adequate and efficient reserve forces. Discussing the National Guard, Sanford urged the Pentagon to have a better understanding of the citizen-soldier, who could not be expected to give but so much time to military obligations but who should seek to live up to his responsibilities. After outlining needs and proposals with regard to the National Guard, Sanford observed that more was needed than a priority reserve. The governors of the fifty states, concerned with problems of civil defense, saw the National Guard playing a vital role in this area. Though it was primarily an organization to augment the active army and air force in time of national emergency, the Guard was a state organization, available to governors in times of peace. Sanford ended with a plea for stability in the National Guard so that it would not have to fight for its existence with each change of administration.

METHODIST MEN OF GASTONIA DISTRICT

POLKVILLE

September 13, 1962

[At various times the Governor took the opportunity to express his philosophy concerning race relations and civil rights. Speaking to the Methodist Men of Gastonia District, Sanford brought up the idea of the Good Neighbor Council, an idea which was to develop into reality the next year. See Governor Sanford's press statement of January 18, 1963.]

It is most appropriate that I announce some important plans at a meeting of church laymen because our most difficult problems of race differences must be worked out in the spirit of Christian fellowship.

The situation at highway restaurants has inadvertently delayed long-range plans on which people of good will have been working for some months. We must continue to work on these broader plans because they can have so much real meaning for the people of the state. In the meantime, you will remember that I have asked some people to work with both sides of the restaurant situation. The two matters should not be confused.

The long-range plans center on economic opportunities. There are three factors involved in my planning:

First, people all over North Carolina, in and out of government, are working to improve the economy of North Carolina, to lift us from the forty-second position in per capita income. A major reason, as Census Bureau figures show, for North Carolina's low per capita standing is that Negroes do not have adequate economic opportunities. If we counted the income of white citizens only, North Carolina would rank thirty-second in per capita income instead of forty-second.

Second, Negro youths are not taking full advantage of the technical training available to them. Admittedly, this may be due to the lack of motivation as a consequence of poor economic opportunities for qualified Negro workers.

Third, we need always to understand the hopes of all people. North Carolina has a tradition of good human relations, and nothing must be permitted to detract from that record.

For a long time I have been working on an idea to set up what I think should be called the North Carolina Good Neighbor Council. It will take several more weeks to complete the membership of the council but the purposes are too important to be rushed. It would consist of representatives from all segments of our economy and all sections of our state. This council would have as its mission: (1) helping to provide greater economic opportunities for all North Carolinians; (2) encouraging all young people to become better educated and better trained; (3) dealing with problems which require human understanding and co-operation. It also would work with state agencies and local groups, which already have been established in some North Carolina towns, and would encourage the establishment in others.

In these days in America, we need to show living proof that people of different backgrounds and races can work together. If we are true to our religious heritage in North Carolina and if we believe the lesson of the parable of the Good Samaritan, we should help those in need of help. It is as simple as that. But it is powerful in its capacity to achieve broader opportunities for everyone, the helped and the helpers alike.

COURT IMPROVEMENTS AMENDMENT TALK
WTVD, DURHAM
September 28, 1962

In 1868 the General Assembly set up a court system for 1868. Amendments in 1875 and later provided for various courts, but the Governor insisted that courts had to be uniform to assure equal justice. He said the 1961 General Assembly proposed an amendment on which the people would be asked to vote on November 6. Sanford referred to North Carolina as a state on the go, with progress evident in many areas. The Governor invited people with questions about the court improvement amendment to write to him and promised that the questions would be answered. He closed with a plea for a favorable vote for the constitutional change.

SOUTHERN REGIONAL EDUCATION BOARD
HOLLYWOOD, FLORIDA
October 1, 1962

Governor Sanford told the Southern Regional Education Board that the South was emerging from a long economic struggle, that the new era was in evidence, that abundant resources were available but the question of developing them to their full potential remained. He stressed the idea that the answer was in quality education. Each citizen should have the opportunity to learn to the limit of his ability. New institutions, opportunities for adult education, and financial support for higher education were requirements for the South to reach its full potential. Sanford referred to the great impact of the report of the Commission on Goals for Higher Education in the South. He urged the governors to accept their responsibility and use their influence to see that the recommendations of the report were implemented. He advised the group to "Tell the people where we stand and what we must do, and they will provide the support and the means."

"PROBLEMS OF A GOVERNOR" PANEL
SOUTHERN GOVERNORS CONFERENCE

HOLLYWOOD, FLORIDA

October 4, 1962

All governors faced a multitude of problems, according to Governor Terry Sanford, but all knew that they had volunteered for their jobs. He said that North Carolina had problems of mutual concern to all states: education, low income, the paving of highways and secondary roads, the revitalization of agriculture, prisons and rehabilitation, welfare and hospitals. On this occasion, however, the Governor talked on the problems of modernizing the system of justice in North Carolina. In 1955 the North Carolina Bar Association and lay leaders took a look at the courts and found that the system of justice had not kept up with the times—that the system, not the judges or juries or lawyers or court officials, was at fault. One system, for example, provided for fees to jaypees for convictions. Over a thousand lower courts operated with variations in procedures, costs, and organization. Dockets were crowded. Recommendations made to the 1959 General Assembly for a constitutional amendment were defeated, but another proposal was made in 1961 and a compromise system was accepted by the legislators. The plan was to be voted on by the people on November 6. The Governor commented that up-to-date law enforcement required a modern system, and that the new organization would provide a uniform system of courts below the level of the superior courts, and would establish an administrative office to free judges of mechanical details. Because some lower courts had been making big profits, and because there had been no uniform fee system, the amendment contained provisions to correct these faults. Details regarding the new system were spelled out by Governor Sanford, who concluded with a reminder that "In a democracy, justice is everybody's business."

FIRST CONGRESSIONAL DISTRICT DEMOCRATIC RALLY

EDENTON

October 9, 1962

The Governor began with an expression of appreciation for the privilege of participating in the First Democratic District Rally and with praise for the congressman from the district, Herbert C. Bonner. He said that Democratic records from the courthouse to the White House spoke for themselves, and he reviewed Democratic accomplishments in North Carolina, mentioning the program for quality education, industrial expansion, and revitalization of agriculture. Such a record would force the opposition to smear tactics and would cause them to talk about "spending," about a "two-party" system, and about the Democratic President. Sanford said the First District supported Kennedy in 1960 and the state gave him one of the largest majorities in the nation. Governor Sanford observed that when they talked about a "two-party" system, the Republicans wanted their own party's system; and that when they discussed "deficit spending," they should remember North Carolina's Triple-A credit rating. Though North Carolina's Democrats had their differences, the ties that bound them were stronger than their differences, and the principles of the Democratic party were "unchanged and unchangeable." Sanford called the Democratic party the one that believed in the people, believed in free enterprise, and believed in helping the weak.

STATE-WIDE SCHOOL DROPOUT MEETING

RALEIGH

October 11, 1962

Discussing one of the major problems facing those in the field of education, the Governor made several comments concerning dropouts. He indicated that the responsibility for keeping children in school rested with many individuals, but it was primarily that of the young person himself. Many factors—difficulties with reading, failure, monetary problems—entered into the decision of a child to continue or discontinue his schooling. Nearly half of those who entered the first grade failed to graduate from high school. Sanford urged parents, school officials, and all citizens to help provide the incentive needed to keep young people in school. He felt that they had to be convinced of the value of an education and had to realize that by dropping out they robbed themselves and the state. The Governor referred to this meeting as a step in the right direction; he suggested that the task, of taking the program into every North Carolina home and seeing that every child understand what was at stake, be carried out.

HAYWOOD COUNTY DEMOCRATIC RALLY

WAYNESVILLE

October 22, 1962

[The need for court reform in North Carolina was urgent long before the Sanford administration. The North Carolina Bar Association, in 1955, began a study of the judicial system of the state and recommended a constitutional amendment to the 1959 General Assembly. Because of differences of opinion, the proposal was defeated; two years later, after compromises had been effected, the legislators approved the amendment enthusiastically. In this address the Governor urged all North Carolinians to ratify the amendment in the November 6 election; his request was granted by an overwhelming vote in favor of the issue.]

The improvement of our courts is one of the most vital issues to face the people of North Carolina since 1868. We now have the opportunity to establish a uniform state-wide court system. You can join in making this possible.

The time is here for those who like the idea of equal justice for all—whether they live in the mountains of western North Carolina or the Piedmont or on the Coastal Plains of eastern North Carolina, the big city or the small community—to get interested.

As you know, action of the 1961 session of the General Assembly permits us to vote on this proposed amendment. If we approve it, every family in North Carolina will benefit. If we do not, the cause of court improvement in our state will have suffered such a tremendous blow that it could well be another generation before North Carolinians would have such an opportunity again.

What would this amendment do? We often hear that it is difficult for laymen to understand the courts, that everything said or written on judicial matters is so complicated that only lawyers know what it is all about. This certainly is not true in this case, for the plan for court improvement which will be submitted to the people in November is simple and clear.

I am a lawyer by profession and I respect the profession. But let me say right here, the courts of the state don't belong exclusively to lawyers and they don't belong to judges. Courts belong to all the people.

This amendment is strongly supported by most lawyers and most judges.

But the amendment was approved in a General Assembly by lawmakers, most of whom are not lawyers.

And the "jury" which will determine its fate are all of the citizens of North Carolina.

The court improvement amendment goes straight to the place where changes are needed most and where the majority of our citizens have their only court experience—to the lower courts, those beneath the Superior Court level—and groups them into a uniform system. It also establishes an administrative office to free judges of vexing mechanical details and assist in the business management of the courts.

The proposed amendment is not something which was developed overnight. It resulted from the co-operation of many of North Carolina's public spirited citizens who studied our courts, prepared recommendations for making the administration of justice what it should be in this progressive state, and worked together as private citizens and as members of the legislature to devise a program which would give our citizens the kind of administration of justice they have a right to expect.

The court study which formed the foundation from which the proposed amendment evolved was made by a group of leading lawyers and laymen who undertook this job seven years ago. Many thousands of man-hours were spent in getting the facts and preparing recommendations. This committee found that we had approximately 1,400 so-called lower courts, including the recorder-type and special courts and justices of the peace. Operating as separate units, these courts had different costs, practices, and procedures. A man tried for an offense in one county might, for instance, be charged $36.00 in costs, while someone in an adjoining county might have costs of $8.00 for an identical offense.

The committee found also that some local courts were making big profits. In the case of justices of the peace, we were reminded that they were paid for their services only upon conviction and that these officers often were chosen in a way which did not necessarily require that they be suited to their jobs. Without supervision and in many cases not qualified to dispense justice, they quite frequently proved to be unfit for their responsibilities. There definitely is, however, a place for honest, capable justices of the peace in the administration of justice. We have many of these. The amendment would establish this proper place for them by bringing them into the district courts as officers of the court and giving them and those who have business with them the advantages which will result from having their work supervised.

The amendment would abolish the method of basing their pay on convictions, for they would be paid for their services on a fair plan.

Just how essential it is that the present system for selecting magistrates be changed is indicated in the fact that under the present law, each township is entitled to three magistrates, with one additional for every 1,000 people living in an incorporated city or town.

A large city such as Charlotte would be entitled to elect 204 justices of the peace under this plan. Think of how easy it might be for some completely unfit candidate to be elected by the simple act of voting for himself. And what is true in Charlotte is true in towns and cities across North Carolina.

The amendment provides that the state be divided into a convenient number of local court districts by the General Assembly. The General Assembly also will prescribe where the district courts shall sit, but one must sit in at least one place in each county. Judges of these courts will be elected for each district for terms of four years. It is provided that every district judge shall live in the district for which he is elected. Thus, each county will have at least one seat of a district court, and there will be more if needed. The number of judges serving a district will be determined by the General Assembly on the basis of the need.

This, then, is the court improvement program we will vote on in November. It does away with the glaring evils that have existed and paves the way for a modern, efficient system of courts in which the administration of justice is uniform in practice, procedures, and costs, is not delayed by inefficiencies resulting from lack of proper administration, and is of a high standard because it is administered by well-qualified persons.

I wonder how many of you have thought seriously about our courts. Although many citizens may never have to go to court, the well-being of all citizens depends to a large extent on the quality of the administration of justice in our state.

For example, one of the most serious problems in our state today is the deadly toll we suffer through automobile accidents. Experts in traffic safety tell us that the right kind of traffic courts is the only basic answer to this problem. We can do more by handling violators of highway safety regulations in a modern, scientific way in the courts than through any other program or plan. Judges who are able to become expert in traffic matters would protect you and your family from the dangerous driver and convince those who are good, careful, safe drivers 99 per cent of the time of the importance of extending this performance through that extra 1 per cent.

Think of the lives that would be saved and the losses in money and usefulness that could be avoided by reducing the number and severity of traffic accidents! It can be done better than any other way through the proper handling of traffic offenders in court, and this proper handling can come to North Carolina if we approve the amendment as the first step.

We read and hear every day of new tragedies on our highways. Last year there were 1,254 deaths in the 100 counties in our state. This year the slaughter continues. No matter what else we try to do, we are not going to make our roads as safe as we can make them until we have an efficient, state-wide system of courts presided over by able, safety-minded judges. Just recently I read an editorial deploring the high accident record in a North Carolina county. The editor said:

> There is no doubt but what the public can do but so much about traffic accidents. There must be respect for the laws, and this can only be created by the courts. . . . One weak link here is the lack of a uniform court system. This can be remedied by voting in the Constitutional Amendment in November. There is little hope for justice as long as the fee system for the justices of the peace is continued. The courts should not be set up to make a profit, but to administer justice. Only when traffic cases get quick action, tried when the witnesses are there, and under uniform system can the public hope to correct abuses.

This statement is repeated in substance many times a day by thoughtful, informed people across North Carolina.

All of us know the problem and the answer. You are in a position to understand especially well the operation and structure of the courts and your leadership from now to November can help assure for North Carolina the uniform system of courts that is so essential to the protection of your family and the members of every family in the state.

The question facing all North Carolinians on November 6 is this:

Do we want to give the judges, the solicitors, the attorneys, the plaintiffs, the defendants, the juries, and the law enforcement officers the tools to provide equal and exact justice in the second half of the twentieth century?

Do we, the citizens of North Carolina, want to try to maintain justice in a T-model system, or are we going to do it in a system that recognizes more modern times?

In a democracy, justice is everybody's business. That's why this court improvement is important to every citizen.

NORTH CAROLINA STATE GRANGE CONVENTION

KINSTON

October 26, 1962

Governor Sanford told an appreciative audience that the State Grange had contributed substantially to the progress of North Carolina. Qualified agricultural leaders had been placed in key policy positions so that farm people would have a strong voice in state government. Such men as Kerr Scott and his son, Bob Scott, both of whom had served as masters of the State Grange, were cited as notable leaders of both the state and this particular organization. As he outlined some of the goals of the organization, the Governor called its program an ambitious one. He said state government was also trying to promote opportunities through education, observing that the rural population stood to gain most from increased educational opportunities. Good roads needed to be built, water resources to be guarded, flood control to be studied, and new industry to be attracted; these programs would complement those in the field of agriculture and would benefit the rural people. Because a balanced program of education, agriculture, and industry would pay rich dividends to all, Sanford called on members of the State Grange to help keep North Carolina going forward.

REPORT TO THE PEOPLE OVER
STATE-WIDE TELEVISION AND RADIO NETWORKS

RALEIGH

October 31, 1962

[Civil defense was a matter of grave concern in October, 1962. Though President Kennedy's firm action in seeking to eliminate Russian missiles

from Cuba did not trigger militant repercussions, national tension had
mounted and the realities of defense were uppermost in the minds of citizens throughout the United States. The Cuban crisis soon diminished, but
the need for adequate civil defense preparations continued; and the Governor encouraged North Carolinians to prepare for a lifetime of crises. The
state's concern for civil defense preparations had been shown in a dramatic
way some months earlier. In April, 1961, Mr. and Mrs. Thomas C. McAden
were chosen from many applicants to test a fall-out shelter at the Governor's Mansion. Living in simulated wartime conditions for three days, the
Charlotte couple reported regularly to the public on the problems of survival
in event of nuclear attack.]

President Kennedy has taken bold steps to eliminate Russian
missiles from Cuba. His success could very well be the turning
point in the cold war. The Cuban crisis may be over but the cold
war continues, and we are "destined . . . to live out most, if not
all, of our lives in uncertainty and challenge and peril. . . ." The
intense danger during the Cuban crisis could arise again at any
time. To use this experience to urge greater preparedness, I
want to talk with you about what we are doing in North Carolina and what you can do to protect your family and yourself.

If our civil defense is good enough to save the lives of most of
you, then the chances of any enemy attack are reduced. So, good
civil defense is vital to us personally, to our nation's diplomacy,
and to the American defense.

There has been and will be no reason for panic and no need
for hysteria in North Carolina. We are prepared, and we are
strong, and we know what to do.

In North Carolina we can have 8,000 National Guardsmen
on duty within thirty minutes. Within sixty minutes we could
have 11,400 Guardsmen ready for action. Standing orders for
this purpose already have been issued by the Governor's Office
and company alert and mobilization plans have been polished to
perfection. Your National Guardsmen are trained and disciplined
and prepared to act immediately on orders demanded by any
situation. This is only a part of our readiness. We have other
groups and agencies poised to move into action.

Civil defense rests with the civilians, and we have thousands
who have prepared themselves to be ready, and the entire state
is grateful for their devotion.

We have a state civil defense director, five area directors, and
local directors in ninety-eight counties. The job of these people
should not be misunderstood. They are not in possession of
magic devices to take over our protection in time of emergency.
In time of preparation, which is *now*, they serve as advisers to
government leaders. They also serve as "promoters of civil
defense," and for a number of years they have been trying to

get more of you interested in civil defense. In time of emergency they serve as the staff for the elected heads of cities, counties, and the state, supervising communications, gathering information, and assisting as a staff assists a wartime commander.

It is important to remember that the responsibilty to get ready for emergency action and to direct activities during an emergency rests with the elected officials. All county and city officials have a civil defense mission and responsibility, and you can help them. Civil defense is not for the purpose of planning ways of hiding, but rather for ways of protecting and strengthening and continuing the productive capacity of our people.

The question is how to withstand the initial assault, then get up and keep going.

Thousands of people in almost every county have worked to formulate state and local emergency plans. We have tested the readiness of our Emergency Operational Plans.

At the state level for state-wide emergency communications we have nine radio systems. These are RACES, the Radio Amateur Organization with over 1,500 volunteer operators, the splendid radio system of the Civil Air Patrol, the State Highway Patrol Radio System functioning as our Civil Defense Radio Warning Network on a twenty-four hour per day basis, the Highway Commission Radio Network, the State Forestry Radio Network, Wildlife Commission Radio System, the National Guard Radio Network and the Radio Units of the Prisons System and SBI.

Reporting normal enemy or emergency activity will follow traditional patterns, but reporting fall-out is more complicated. We are prepared to do a complete job here. The Board of Health has been given the radiological monitoring and testing equipment. It has trained people and will keep a state situation map from information constantly supplied by several thousand trained monitors. This information will be passed on to the public by radio.

The State Board of Health also is assigned the responsibility for all health measures, and many hospitals have formulated emergency plans. In addition, we have thirty-five complete 200-bed emergency hospitals stored across the state which, if needed, we can move on short notice.

The Highway Patrol is a strong arm in any emergency; this has been demonstrated during hurricanes. They work with local police and sheriffs.

Rescue squads and rural fire departments are a part of local civil defense, and frequently the center of it. Fire, police, and public works departments are a part of every mayor's emergency plans.

Every other state agency has a mission for the emergency. Every basic industry, such as fuels, building materials, food, has a plan for making its resources available.

I haven't time in a limited broadcast to tell you everything, but here is the state plan, 4½ inches thick, and 8½ feet of county and city plans, showing that all of the many details have been worked out.

There are plans worked out at most schools. This is a responsibility of the local school board, with advice from civil defense. You parents may check in advance on the plans at the school your children attend. Your principal, superintendent, or school board members can talk with you about this.

Many of you have asked about evacuation plans. Evacuation is not as likely as it was several years ago because of changed concept of warfare, and it is not as important in North Carolina as it is in New York. If the situation demanded evacuation, however, we are organized to effect it. Routes and control of the flow of traffic are established. Private transportation would be expected, but mass transportation also would be available. Trucking, bus, and rail companies have plans for making their resources available for this, as well as other transportation needs. If evacuation is indicated, you will be given the necessary information by radio, and other available means, and local civil defense agencies have plans and resources to receive people evacuated from other areas. Unless you are specifically advised to evacuate, your safest place would be to remain where you have some protection from possible radiation.

This is what I consider the weakest point of our plans for civil defense: survival in fall-out. This is really the most difficult question to answer—protection from radiation—because nobody in this country or any other country quite knows the answer. I'm going to try to answer it, as well as I can, from the thousands of pages which have been written about it, as it applies to North Carolina today, with the understanding that we do not claim to have the perfect answer. We will do the best we can with what we have today, and we will improve later when we know more.

In North Carolina we can assume four things:

1) It would be very wise for everybody to know in advance where he and his family would go to avoid fall-out radiation.

2) There are many, many people who cannot afford even a fifty-dollar shelter.

3) People are unduly afraid of things they don't know much about, and they don't know much about fall-out.

4) It is hard to get people interested in shelters until they need one.

Now with these four understandings, let's see what is the best we can do.

First, what is fall-out, and what is the danger? They've written books about this, but let's try to boil it down.

Little particles of sand, water, and other material blown sky high by a nuclear explosion float down and are moved about by the winds. Because these particles were involved in the nuclear explosion they continue to give off radiation for a period, which will grow less and less as it burns out or "decays." The greatest danger would be for about twenty-four to forty-eight hours, but some danger might continue for a week or so. Obviously places very near the explosion would remain dangerous for many weeks. Our fall-out reporting service would keep you informed by radio and other means about local radiation.

While these particles are floating down they can fall out anywhere that dust or sand or rain can blow. Once they are settled, radiation from the particles is concentrated at the surface where they rest. Radiation travels in a straight line. So everything you can put between you and the surface of radioactive particles is that much more protection for you.

You will have some time between the warning and the danger, but this will depend on the distance, the wind, the size and the nature of the explosion. This time would range from less than an hour to several hours. We have the machinery to predict this with fair accuracy. This information would be passed on to you by CONELRAD radio stations, and other means.

You can stand some radiation like that from the sun throughout life and medium radiation for brief periods. Radiation can cause severe sickness but it is *not necessarily* fatal.

Fall-out cannot make things it falls on radioactive. Vegetables in the field, or exposed food anywhere, are contaminated only to the extent they might have particles on them and can be made safe by washing, brushing or peeling. Livestock will receive fair protection in barns under most circumstances. If particles get on you or your clothing they can be washed off.

You should make it your business to learn more about fall-out, and you can get an authoritative bulletin from your local or state civil defense office.

Now what kind of fall-out shelter do you need? You might have the right to use one of the marked, standard shelters in the urban areas. This varies so much from city to city that I suggest you see your mayor's civil defense director; and I urge all industry and building owners to co-operate in the marking of such shelters.

You may have built, or desire to build, a complete family

shelter, and plans for this may be obtained from your local civil defense office.

If you can't do this, as many North Carolinians cannot, here are some things to know:

Two feet of solid concrete or three feet of earth will give you almost absolute protection. Your imagination, a shovel, some boards or logs, can give you some pretty good protection, without spending any money. We called them foxholes in World War II. You can get a bulletin from your local civil defense office on different kinds of fall-out shelters.

Solid concrete blocks can be stacked for fall-out protection. If you aren't willing to build such a shelter now, at least let me urge you to have these materials ready.

If you get in the basement of an ordinary brick veneer home you will reduce your danger to one-tenth of the danger outside. A little fixing would give you better protection. One-tenth might still be too great. If you don't have a basement and get in the middle of such a home you will reduce the danger by about one-half.

Water is the number-one necessity to store. You should at least have some jugs or fruit jars on hand. You can be sure you have a faucet on your hot water tank, which is a ready-made emergency storage tank. You should have canned or packaged food, including juices which do not need to be refrigerated. You should have a radio which will run if the electricity goes off. You should have a flashlight. Other things you may need are listed in this civil defense pamphlet.

Some people will not take full protection in advance. I'm afraid human nature doesn't work that way. But you can take some of the protection, and you can get ready for additional action, even if for various reasons you do not make more complete preparations now. And you can understand the dangers better.

Let me make it clear that I think you should provide as much protection as you possibly can. Remember the first assumption: It would be very wise for everybody to know in advance where he and his family would go to avoid fall-out radiation.

This is not the complete story, but it is the heart of it.

We have people all over the state anxious to give you more information.

The best way not to need this protection is to have it.

I would hope that we never have any reason to recoil from any situation in fear. Civil defense is not based on fear. It is based on confidence in our strength, our knowledge, our ability to protect our nation and ourselves.

This nation, founded on freedom, holding aloft the banner for free people around the globe, with an abiding faith in God and His purpose for man, will endure so long as our spirit and our faith endure.

VETERANS DAY CEREMONY ON BATTLESHIP U.S.S. "NORTH CAROLINA"

WILMINGTON

November 11, 1962

In observance of Veterans Day, 1962, a ceremony was held on the battleship U.S.S. "North Carolina." The Governor referred to the Cuban crisis as a recent event but as a crisis which had subsided. He referred to areas of conflict and communism elsewhere: Berlin, the Himalayas of India, Viet Nam, the Congo, but the Governor said the order of the day was peace. The fact that the United States sought peace did not mean that its citizens would not fight for freedom. America, he said, "does not fear to negotiate" but would "never negotiate out of fear." Sanford expressed hope that Communists would see the lesson written in the blood of history. While military posts were necessary, the ultimate strength was in education. There was no question about America's willingness to fight and die but there was a question as to her willingness to take the leadership in defending America's "ancient heritage" on the education, industrial, and agricultural fronts. The battle of the free world was being fought in the United Nations; military might had to be kept strong, but it was also imperative for America to do her best in education, industry, and agriculture. Sanford said the veterans did not end their jobs when they removed their uniforms; their duty continued—"until all children have the chance for education, until all people everywhere have enough to eat and enough clothes to keep them warm; until mankind is free from fear, from want, and from dictatorship."

FOUNDERS DAY CELEBRATION AT
METHODIST COLLEGE

FAYETTEVILLE

November 15, 1962

[Speaking in his home town of Fayetteville, Governor Sanford took the opportunity to present his program in the field of higher education for the 1963 General Assembly. He explained that he planned to emphasize quality education on the college level. This speech, entitled "Education Is the Only Path to Progress," was considered the administration's blueprint for the years ahead; it was later issued as a pamphlet.]

Several days ago a friend asked me, "What can a poor man do for his children when it is time to send them to college? I can't afford it," he said, "but college is what they need and deserve."

My answer is that North Carolina must say to the young people of the state, "If you have the will and the skill you can go to college." We must make it our policy to provide the classrooms, to establish the loan funds, to employ the college teachers, and to have the teaching facilities and everything needed to match the ambitions of our youth.

We could pose this question another way, asking, "What can a state, one which is not as rich as most others, do about education beyond the high school?" Quality education costs money, yet it is what the state needs and deserves, what it must have if it is going to get ahead. Education is the way we have of climbing upward, one generation after another. It is the best hope we have that our children will be better able to make a better living and have a good life and meet the needs of their own day.

We go about this through use of teachers, books, pencils, Bunsen burners, educational television, blackboards, and countless other things. What we are going about, however, is a matter of the mind and wealth of each individual, and of us all as members of a family of man called North Carolinians.

There are other families of man scattered throughout the world who have not given their people the chance for education, and they are poor and depressed as a people. They have been left behind in technology, in statesmanship, in all development. Their people live in poverty and some of them actually are starving. Millions of these people live in hovels and shacks and slums, beyond the attention of doctors and beyond the protection of laws. The efforts of some of these people to rise from this condition are among the most dramatic and painful of our time.

We in the South, and in North Carolina, were in a state of poverty once, too. We have all heard that our country has never lost a war; that's so, but North Carolina has. We lost the bloodiest war in this country's history, and one of the bloodiest wars ever fought anywhere. Today stories of that war seem incredible to us. I was reminded of that recently when I made a talk in Florida on the subject of education. When I returned to Raleigh, a friend asked me if I realized that in December, 1903, Governor Charles Brantley Aycock had made a talk in Florida on the same subject. I had not remembered that, and I got down a biography of Aycock and found the text. In 1903, Aycock was two generations closer to the pain of that war than we, and I found he was obliged to be much more gloomy about the South than I had been in my Florida talk. "Today it seems to me," he said back then, "that we have less effect upon the thought and action of the nation than at any period of our history." His was a day when the South was trying to rid itself of the squalor of the Reconstruction period, when, as he said, "lawlessness stalked the State like a pestilence, death walked abroad at noonday, sleep lay down armed. . . ." We had lost a war, then had lost control of our government, and during it all we had lost our sense of well-being as a people. All this had happened to a people who before had often been distinguished. We had not been wealthy, but we had sometimes known outstanding leadership. Many a schoolboy can recite the great, grave names of the southern men who stood at the head of this nation in days when their leadership was not only the distinguishing mark of our country but a distinguishing mark of their time in the world. In our own state, poor as it was, we had at Chapel Hill the second largest university in America, second to Princeton. We had a public school system which stayed open even during the war. We had 50,000 students in attendance during the height of the fighting.

The war left North Carolina with sons to bury and others to mend; it left us with fallen houses and fences and sheds and cribs, and with the sense of despondency which inevitably follows the failure of a cause. Then came the bitter days of sorry leadership, a period of poverty, and of bad feelings between the races.

Finally, out of this unwholesomeness, near the turn of the century, came a group of progressive men. One of them was Charles Brantley Aycock. He said that North Carolina had a great destiny ahead. He told them what many of them didn't want to hear—that the people must tighten their belts and put their money into education, education for everybody. "You wealthy people may educate your son and daughter to the fullest extent possible," he said in his address in Florida, "giving them the learning of all the world, and after their education put them in a community where there are no other educated people, and they will fail to develop and grow as they would if they lived in a community where there was general culture. . . . We want the schools to find all of the strongest and best in competition one with the other until the fullest power of each shall be developed."

He fought for education, believing education to be the only basic way to build a state and prepare for a better life. For four years while he was governor, the state built schoolhouses on the average of one a day. He left office unpopular and died almost repudiated; but the people supported education, and because they did, North Carolina began to move forward. Progress came grudgingly and painfully, but it came, until now, two generations later, we have before us opportunities for leadership such as North Carolina has not known in decades.

The nature of these opportunities was suggested while I stood in Florida a few weeks ago, watching a rocket fired into space. This is symbolic of the time and place we have inherited. Our farms and cities are changing so fast that often the changes cannot be followed. Brick by brick, concrete on steel, wood and glass, pressed wood and plastic—we are building houses and factories, barns and cities that are better, cleaner, stronger, safer. And as this new age comes on, our country is turning to the South more and more. Our state finds itself with labor ready to go to work, with raw materials ready to be used, with power lines and gas lines in place; our roads are in; our railroads are ready. We have space here for expansion. We have a sound public school system. We have ports and are near markets. We are today ready for progress of a new order if we have the people educated to today's needs. To move into the mainstream of American life is our present calling, the newborn challenge.

The way we have to follow to make the best of this challenge is the way Aycock suggested to our grandfathers: the way of education for all the people. Education is the one way proved solid and firm and ready for the use of this state. There is only one way we in our history have found fully dependable, education for all people to the limits of their ability.

So the message of Charles Brantley Aycock of fifty-nine years ago is the message of today. The only difference is that our new world demands more education than did his.

Going from school district to school district, in recent months, talking to young people, and listening, I hear from them that they understand the challenges of our time, often better than we adults do. Most of them want to develop themselves well enough not only to keep up, but to contribute to the making of the future. Even little children have caught the breath of ambition.

More of our students realize that they must finish high school and go on to college. Their ambition, which is one of the most valuable resources of this state, is one reason the college tide is swelling. Another reason is that we simply have more young people of college age today than ever before. We have almost twice as many students in college now as only ten years ago, and the choices for study and the subjects of study are twice as complex.

In order to try to keep ahead of the growing, complex need for education, well over a year ago I appointed twenty-five citizens to a commission—the Commission on Education Beyond the High School, with able and experienced Irving E. Carlyle as chairman. A few weeks ago the members turned in to me their report, a comprehensive document, based on study and deliberation of many months.

From this study we can devise the North Carolina Master Plan for education beyond the high school.

PRIVATE COLLEGES

It is fitting and appropriate that I speak of advances in public education on the campus of a private church-related college.

The Commission *Report* is careful to point out that "nothing that we are proposing is calculated to impair the ability of the private institutions to serve the purposes for which they exist. We want to see the private institutions flourish and increase their capacity to provide their own unique contribution to the task of educating the people of North Carolina."

Indeed it is the sound policy of the state of North Carolina to encourage private institutions in every way. Except for the university, higher education began in the church-related colleges in the first half of the last century at Guilford, Trinity, Wake Forest, and others. I do not want to see their influence diminished in any degree, and I hope that all churches will increase the financial support they give their colleges.

Personally, I have long and strongly believed that America would not have grown great in moral strength had it not been for the influence of the church colleges. To this mission I have done all that I know how to do, and when I put down the official duties of my present office I intend to occupy a major part of my spare time to the building of this private, church college on whose campus we meet today and whose Board of Trustees I am honored to serve as chairman.

We need the influence of these private colleges and we need their advice. I was asked to create the mechanics whereby the private colleges could work together with the state, to give the benefit of their ideas to the Governor and the Board of Higher

Education, as to how we might improve the total of education and how we might assist in proper ways the development and operation of the private colleges. This we are doing, and we look forward to a fruitful partnership.

COMMUNITY COLLEGES

By the end of this decade young people seeking admission to college in North Carolina will exceed the present capacity of public colleges plus the planned capacity of private colleges by more than 31,000. This means that the majority of these young people will have no college opportunity unless we plan and act now. This figure might be disputed, and indeed has been disputed, but it cannot be denied that the figure, whatever, will be staggering; neither can it be disputed that the figure would be even higher if we did what we should do to encourage the percentage of our high school students to attend college which equals the national percentage. The *Report* reminds us: "In a day when some kind of post-high school training is essential to any sort of profitable employment, North Carolina cannot afford the 'economy' of sending a smaller percentage of our young people to college than do four-fifths of the 50 states."

How can we provide the college opportunities for these young North Carolinians, without which both they and the state will wither? Our problem today might be summarized as too few classrooms, too little money, too little time. We cannot build adequate colleges in the traditional pattern; we don't have the money. If we did, too many students could not attend college in the traditional pattern; they don't have the money. We need college opportunities, in large numbers, of high quality, preparing students for additional college, or preparing students for life and work without additional college. We need this at low cost, quickly, and the students need low tuition charges.

With this need, what can we plan? We already have in our state the community college concept, and we have the industrial education center concept, having tried the former on a limited basis and the latter on a rapidly expanding basis. We know how these work, what they can do, whom they will reach.

There is consensus among outstanding educators with extensive experience in the community junior college field that, on principle, the community college should be comprehensive, incorporating in an institution three things: appropriate technical-vocational work, college parallel studies, and adult education curriculums, all three being responsive to the changing needs of the area served by the college. These should be in commuting distance, and we should never anticipate building dormitories at these institutions.

We have the framework and the experience. It could be done rapidly, it would be relatively low in cost, and it would reach the greatest possible number of students. It would be less costly to the student.

This, then, will be our plan: One system of public two-year post high school institutions offering college parallel studies, technical-vocational-terminal work, and adult education instruction tailored to area needs, subject to state-level supervision by the State Board of Education, and advised by a proposed State Community College Advisory Council (consisting of at least seven persons, appointed by the State Board of Education).

The details will be arranged by the members of the 1963 General Assembly, and for this purpose I commend to them Chapter VIII of the *Report of the Commission on Education Beyond the High School,* which chapter I endorse *in toto.*

This broad recommendation needs a word of caution. We will require more comprehensive community colleges than we can immediately establish. It will take several years to do the job properly because we cannot start everywhere at once. Priority should be given to communities where there is a demonstrated need, where there is clearly demonstrated community interest, and where public schools are already adequately supported by local supplements.

I am suggesting to the State Board of Education that there be prepared immediately "tentative criteria and procedures" for establishment of these colleges, so that interested communities might know what they can do to establish one of these colleges.

I would trust that the General Assembly would provide the legislative standards for the establishment of these colleges, leaving the locations to the Board of Education.

With a system of comprehensive community colleges we will be able to meet the total need, to challenge even more high school graduates to continue their learning, to raise the technical competence of our people, to improve the level of an educated citizenry, to increase our income, to provide enrichment for the lives of those who otherwise would be passed by, and to grow in stature as a state and a people.

THE PUBLIC SENIOR COLLEGES

We now have nine public senior colleges located from Cullowhee to Pasquotank. In addition, we have three other institutions, ready and able—or almost able—to become public senior colleges in Asheville, Charlotte, and Wilmington.

It would be difficult to measure the tremendous contributions made today by our senior colleges. Traveling many times to many places across the state, you can begin to realize the enrichment given by them as you visit the schools in the mountains, and see leader after leader, teacher after teacher, sent out by Western Carolina; as you talk to the graduating class of Appalachian and experience the wholesome enthusiasm of these young people going out to add to the hope and progress of the education of their state; as you feel the surge of new intellectual life at Greenville; as you see obstacles battered down and barriers overridden at Winston-Salem, and Fayetteville, and Elizabeth City; as you see new and needed leadership emerging from the Agricultural and Technical College and North Carolina College; as you sense the promise at Wilmington, Pembroke, Charlotte, and Asheville. These things and more demonstrate daily the faith and vision of the people who have poured their lives into the making of our state colleges. Our colleges, public and private, need to obtain a new and higher mark of excellence as they train teachers and others who in turn will lead us to greater excellence.

We have not been able to support the acquisition of adequate faculties at those institutions, but we are financially able now and we are on the road to correcting this.

These institutions are the great hope for the majority of our students who will earn degrees, and they must be equal to the best in quality and excellence.

The institutions understand, as Davidson College understands, that you do not need to become gigantic, nor do you need to cover the field with graduate and professional training, to achieve distinction.

There is sometimes an inclination to make every junior college a four-year college and every college a university, but this is vain and foolish. A good college is far better and of far more influence than a sorry university. We cannot do without our four-year colleges and we cannot afford to have them second-rate.

The future plans of Asheville-Biltmore, Charlotte, and Wilmington are that they expand to four-year colleges. The need is there and they have the academic strength for such expansion. As to when, I would hope the General Assembly would delegate this to the judgment of the Board of Higher Education, based solely on educational considerations. As to how, the commission has thought through this and has outlined excellent procedures in the *Report*. It would seem to me that each should be given target dates as soon as possible so that they might start the sound approaches required.

I hope the General Assembly, the Board of Higher Education,

the college trustees, administration, and faculties will consider carefully the many concrete recommendations of the Commission on Education Beyond the High School, covering standards, admissions, finances, training teachers, research, counseling, student costs, remedial noncredit programs, dropouts, endowments, academic freedom, student loans, the trimester, co-operation, and general improvement.

THE UNIVERSITY

North Carolina has always appreciated its university, now a threefold campus, whose presence has spurred such institutions as Wake Forest and Duke to greater achievement and in turn has been spurred on to greater effort by their achievement.

It has attracted industry, developed our mental hospitals, discovered improved products of agriculture, nourished our schools, enriched our lives, and made us money.

The *Report of the Commission* recommends two things. First it points out that "the statutes do not contain an adequate definition of Consolidated University purposes." It would clarify the definition and this makes sense. This recommendation will be presented to the General Assembly as suggested in the *Report*.

Second, the commission also recommends "that the statutes be amended to authorize the Consolidated University Board of Trustees to establish additional campuses of the University under conditions prescribed" by the Board of Higher Education, subject to applicable statutory procedures. I think this is going to be necessary in a growing, complex industrial state, and probably we should make a start next year. This proposal will also be presented to the General Assembly.

It is worth repeating "two observations about the Consolidated University and the future. First, as a simple matter of economics, the State now and for the foreseeable future can afford only one university, *and that one should be the best that intelligent leadership can build.* . . . [Emphasis mine.]

"Second, new campuses of the Consolidated University should be established only where there is a clear need for the University programs in graduate and professional fields that only a university should offer."

The university is moving forward in many ways. There are things to be done, plans to be accomplished which have been spelled out by the president and the chancellors, the Commission *Report*, the trustees, the Board of Higher Education, the Advisory Budget Commission. These plans and this interest promise new advancement and new rewards to North Carolina. They deserve active support from all, because they will play a major role in meeting our state's need for education of the finest order. This is no time for division, for jealousy, for disunity.

The trustees of the University of North Carolina need to make some basic decisions. The wise vision of Governor O. Max Gardner in consolidating our university facilities over thirty years ago needs reaffirmation by us today. Our system of university education will be best met by unity of purpose, pooling in a more meaningful way the great resources which have been assembled at Raleigh, Chapel Hill, and Greensboro, with one function, one board of trustees, one president, one name. Should it be the University of North Carolina at Raleigh adding arts and sciences and taking leadership in the space age? Should it be the University of North Carolina at Greensboro broadening its purpose to include more graduate work and men students? These changes with the University of North Carolina at Chapel Hill expanding its purpose of interest in the total state, along with the flexibility to expand graduate and professional training to one or more new additional campuses over the next decade, is a concept which will make our educational leadership worthy of comparison with the best in the world.

I trust that the partisans of each of these great institutions will have the broad-mindedness to set us upon this course.

CONCLUSION

This *Report of the Commission* is perhaps the most thorough study of education beyond the high school made by any state. Along with the Southern Regional Education Board's "Goals Report" we have pointed out for us the sound path of progress. I hope we will use these studies and use them well. I hope the copies in the hands of educators, legislators, trustees, will become dog-eared with daily use.

Our mastering the complex potential for the development of the human resources will determine how well our state moves into the coming important years. This is the hope of the individual. It is the hope of North Carolina. It is the hope of the South. It was not without reason that Robert E. Lee, when he put away his uniform, accepted an appointment to head a small Virginia college. He recognized the need of the South then to be what all of us see the need to be in our own day.

We need an increase in strength in our state, for the weak and the wealthy, for farm and city people. Every one of us will prosper, and our children and their children, if we make the right decisions now. Our history has shown us what the right decisions are.

We have this plan; we have the resources, and now is the time to act together—to take the bold new steps which can give our state its time of highest achievement, its finest hour.

DEDICATION OF NORTH CAROLINA NATIONAL BANK BUILDING

CHARLOTTE

November 26, 1962

Speaking at the dedication of the North Carolina National Bank Building in Charlotte, the Governor said the bank was built by people who saw the potential of North Carolina's greatness and who were willing to risk investments for future gain. The story of the North Carolina National Bank and the story of North Carolina were one and the same, in that both were "built by boldness and faith." Some mistakes would be made, but mistakes were better than not taking a chance on the future. This philosophy had moved North Carolina from defeat and despondency at the turn of the century to a new day of new opportunities. The Governor summarized activities and achievements which showed the vitality of the state, but he said that not all were sharing in the prosperity. Though North Carolina had done much, much remained to be done. The state had to invest in the future by providing for community colleges, more paved roads, industrial technical training, educational TV, student loans, better ports, and many other needs not met. Full concern should be given to rehabilitating the needy, those in prison, the disabled, the mentally ill, the retarded. "Let us continue to dare, continue to strive, continue to move to make North Carolina the most prosperous and the most wholesome state in the union."

COMMISSION ON SECONDARY SCHOOLS OF SOUTHERN ASSOCIATION OF COLLEGES AND SCHOOLS

DALLAS, TEXAS

November 28, 1962

[Governor Sanford, who was then serving as Chairman of the Southern Regional Education Board, addressed the Commission on Secondary Schools of the Southern Association of Colleges and Schools meeting in Dallas, Texas. He described the deficiencies of southern education in contrast to the region's vast resources and urged members of the association to "make sacrificial efforts to catch up and assume the lead." Warning against a provincial approach to education, Sanford explained that southern education had to prepare children to face competition from all areas of the nation and the world.]

When I was a boy a group of us sometimes visited a farmer who lived out near the Lumbee River. He had been everywhere, it seemed to us, and he would tell us about his adventures. You didn't see quite as many magazines then, and there wasn't any such thing as television, so he was our eyes into the far corners of the world. He had crossed the Mississippi River. He had been all the way to the great hills of San Francisco. He had worked on a fishing boat off the coast of Canada. He had been all the way across the continent on a freight train, he said.

He had gone to school catch-as-catch-can, attending the type of school existing in North Carolina back before your organization was quite born. He knew a little about reading and writing, but he could talk about the continent of America, and Canada, and about Mexico, which he claimed to have seen, and Panama. We boys absorbed all that he told us. On dusty summer afternoons we sat on his porch listening.

One August day I recall one of the boys got to talking about being tied down to Scotland County, said he believed he wouldn't go back to school but would go on out to Seattle or even to Canada to get a job on a fishing boat.

The old man crossed that porch, took that boy by the front of his shirt, pulled him from the bannister to his feet and said firmly, "Listen here, don't you know you have to live in the world you're born to!"

There are signs that we in the South at last are taking hold of our own shirt fronts, shaking ourselves, and are saying to ourselves as southerners: "Listen, don't you know you have to live in the world you're born to?"

I'm not suggesting that we forsake the past, the good things of the past, but we do need to free ourselves of the weakening bondage which has held us down. The South, and the rest of the nation for that matter, needs to take a long, hard look at itself to see where it stands now, and to see where it hopes to stand twenty years from now.

The material assets of the South are many. It is the only region in the United States that fronts the sea on two sides. It has one-third of all the good farm land in the nation. The South has two-thirds of all the land in our country where the annual rainfall is more than forty inches, providing water in abundance for industry, for crops, for transportation, and for recreation. The

South produces up to 65 per cent of the nation's petroleum, 48 per cent of the usable clay, 53 per cent of the coal, 76 per cent of the natural gas, and 100 per cent of the bauxite and naturally occurring sulphur.

In addition to these assets the South is industrializing rapidly, and this fact constitutes one of our most dynamic potentials. There is evidence of this all the way from the Piedmont Plateau to the Gulf shores of Beaumont and Corpus Christi. Textile mills dot the streams of the Piedmont Plateau; paper mills gulp short leaf, loblolly, and other pines from Virginia to the Texas plains; flame and smoke point out the steel mills at night; and regional plants of big corporations spring up almost overnight.

Our public school system is southern, and we have no desire to make it northern or anything other than southern. But that does not require us to be provincial in our efforts to prepare our children to take part in life. The sheer impact of the change taking place in this modern-day America places our children in competition with children from every section of the country.

The present day businessman cannot rely on competition solely from his own county or even his own state. Products from all over America, and indeed all over the world, flow in daily to compete against the products he is selling. If he is a manufacturer, he can rest assured that a new industry from outside the South will soon come in and he will have to meet the new demands for labor and other resources.

If the child is setting out to become a lawyer, he can no longer plan to make a living on criminal cases and a few actions in the JP courts. He may be practicing in what we think of as a one-horse town, but he still must match wits with bond attorneys from Wall Street, tax attorneys trained by the federal government, and corporation lawyers sent out by General Electric and Standard Oil.

In all professions and businesses the child from the South can no longer think in terms of how good he might be in his own community. He must be trained to compete on equal terms with children schooled across the nation.

A friend told me once that he would rather live in the present than in the past, but he sure did like the past better. I understand that and I revel in the stories of the Old South, but whether the old folk stories of a never-never land were entirely true or not does not matter any longer.

My old man near the river lived in a world so different it's not easy for us to reckon with it today. Take the element of time itself. He farmed by spring, summer, fall. I don't remember his ever mentioning the month of a year; rarely did he refer to a day. He had no specific concept of how long an hour was. He would tell us to sit a spell. How long that was, nobody knew, and nobody cared.

These were the ways of another time, leisurely times, and we all like the memory of them. He liked them too, but at the same time he sensed that we boys were in for a change, and maybe he even knew that time and space were in for some changes too— more than in any other generation in world history. He perhaps was aware that the boys on his porch would come to know time by hours and minutes and seconds and split-seconds; that for one of them a fraction of a second would stand between him and death in planes powered by thousand-horsepower motors. He didn't know anything either about the speed of sound or how far it was to the moon. For him, the moon was just over the corn field. But he knew change was natural. And he sensed, perhaps because of his travels, that the changes in the future were not routinely mapped out, would not be repetitious, as spring, summer, fall, winter, follows spring, summer, fall, winter.

And so to them some thirty or thirty-five years ago he said that the training which had served him, which he had moved along with, just as he moved along in companionable style with time and space, would not serve them, and that they were the boys of a new day.

Now, a generation later, we can see that our own children are to be a part of a new day too, of still another new day. We can't see its face, can't tell much about it from this distance, can only judge that it will be far different from ours. We can know, however, that our children must prepare themselves to be part of the world, part of the dynamic new South, part of their own new day.

I don't think we are doing a good job of this in the South. For that matter I don't think the schools across America are doing what they are capable of doing. I think we are beginning to see what we must do; in some places we are getting a start, but we are not quite fully under way.

We are far behind the rest of the country, generally speaking; and while the distress and poverty of Reconstruction explains this, now is no time for explanations. Because we are behind it is required of us that we make sacrifical efforts to catch up and assume the lead.

We need our own and a new kind of emancipation proclamation which will set us free to grow and build, set us free from the drag of poor people, poor schools, from hate, from demagoguery. It has to be a bold dream for the future, realistic in terms of our whole country, and aware that the South is entering upon the mainstream of American life. This kind of proclamation can be written in one word: "education." It must be the kind of education which seeks excellence, reaches all, looks to the future. We simply have a difficult job to do, so let's get on with it.

About half of our students do not finish high school. Not half enough of our able students go to college or technical schools. We have too few teachers—not enough pay, not enough security, not enough freedom, not enough standing. Our classes are generally too large. Our libraries are generally not large enough. Our local governing bodies say too frequently that they don't have the money. Our state legislatures frequently do not have the money, and more frequently have not been given the information they need if they are to see the urgency of school needs.

In most of our schools we don't offer a selection of studies wide enough to cover the varied talents and skills the students have. By not challenging our gifted students we lose their interest, they lose their ambition, the region and nation lose their leadership which we need more than ever. In having too few programs for the very slow child, we deny happiness, leave too many unproductive, and make more burdens for society.

In school administration, not all of our principals and superintendents measure up to the professional standards we would set, but this too is a reflection of public attitudes and money shortages.

Not nearly enough people have nearly enough understanding of schools and the meaning education has for every part of our lives and every hope of our nation, and therefore not nearly enough citizens have the necessary commitment to building and paying for public education.

These are our problems—some of them. What do we do?

Well, we can think about our own individual schools, do a good job, and let it go at that. But you wouldn't be at this meeting if you believed that way. The critical need today in education for the South is for a universal belief in education, what it can do for a people, its power and its importance. Even in 1962 we need obedience to Jefferson's command to "preach a crusade against ignorance." And who can best preach this crusade? Those who are at the top in the region. And who are they? Members of the Southern Association. You must show the way.

Who knows better than you the drag of underdeveloped talent manifested by youth who quit school before completion? Who knows better than you the barrenness and dullness of the school programs characterized by a lack of appeal, lack of imagination, and lack of adequacy to meet the needs of 1962 youth? Who knows better than you what happens when graduates of high school are not prepared for college, or jobs, or in all cases to fill the obligations of citizenship?

Because you possess the knowledge, because you occupy the position, because education in the southern region is crying for leadership and direction, you have the responsibility for showing the way.

Educational leadership involves more than executive detail. It involves courage and concern, imagination and flexibility of mind, tolerance and the ability to receive and turn criticism to improvement.

If North Carolina has demonstrated nothing else, the events of the past two years have demonstrated that the people will support education, that they do understand the need, that they do believe in preparing for the future of their boys and girls, and that they will make the necessary sacrifices to support their schools.

Too often the trouble is that the public, busy with its many undertakings, doesn't know the shortages, is not aware of the needs, and therefore fails to insist on appropriate school improvement.

And too often the trouble is that the educators do not tell the story, do not get the public's attention, do not let the people know the needs of the schools. It is easy to understand that the educator has his problems, his daily routines, his own doubts about what his role in public appeal should be. Is it his duty to tell the full story, to suggest that there are shortcomings? Is it his duty to "sell" education? Is it his duty to ask for more than he knows lies within the present range of the public revenues?

I think you can afford to tell the full story. I think you can afford to say to your public that you are doing the best job you can with what you have. I think your people would like to know what you could do if you had more support. I think they would like to have you picture for them just what kind of school system your state, or county, or city could have. I think they should have goals for better schools, and I think no one is better qualified to define the goals than the professional educators.

True you cannot fight the battle alone. But you will not have to because among those responding to your call will be legislators, county commissioners, governors, and others in a position to take decisive action.

The South has its problems, but the South has the answer. Time and circumstances charge you with the duty of delivering the answer to all the people.

We know enough about our section to know that the future can be told in terms of the educational emphasis we establish in our own day. We know that the social, economic, scientific, and cultural progress of our people is dependent on education. We know the future of commerce, industry, agriculture, society in all its facets, and human happiness in most of its ways, are tied to education.

We know that many of our people are doing something about it and the South, this rich, great, storied, proud region is beginning to stretch, to grow, to expand to lead, to serve.

SHAW UNIVERSITY

RALEIGH

December 3, 1962

North Carolina made more progress in the twentieth century than any other state, starting from nothing and rising to leadership and recognition, but the state had not gone far enough, Governor Sanford said in an address at Shaw University. Because of faith, pride, belief in fair play, confidence, and co-operativeness, the state had moved forward. North Carolina had had little class or racial strife, had seen little of labor fighting management, had experienced few episodes involving section against section. Sanford said the program had only begun, and that schools and colleges and universities offered opportunities for all. He predicted that the state could have the best schools anywhere within ten years if groups continued to work together and did not deal in prejudices and did not repeal the school tax program for political reasons. He called on North Carolinians "to take the time to understand, to have the courage to hold what we have, to have the vision and faith to move forward in new boldness."

SOUTHERN ALBEMARLE CONVENTION

PLYMOUTH

December 8, 1962

Storms in the eastern part of the state were a cause of concern, and Sanford urged that that concern be carried further than temporary alleviation of loss and suffering. He discussed the impending danger of losing the coast line and showed the disastrous consequences if steps were not taken to prevent destruction. With the region rapidly developing in the areas of tourist attractions, new processing industries and better transportation facilities, the value of maintaining the coast line was greater than ever before. Plans to eliminate the threat were being developed through efforts of the Department of Water Resources and other state agencies and the federal government through its Corps of Engineers. Conservation measures had been recommended for certain areas. Sanford emphasized the urgency of the situation. He commented that "Meetings and blueprints and good intentions are not going to hold back the Atlantic Ocean." Though the federal government would provide much of the money and the state would provide additional funds, local sources would have to furnish money. Sanford urged the people "to meet that responsibility with the determination that is traditional with eastern North Carolinians and with the enthusiasm that has characterized your efforts to move forward in the past few years."

FACULTY CLUB OF THE
UNIVERSITY OF NORTH CAROLINA AT CHAPEL HILL

Chapel Hill

January 8, 1963

The Governor began his remarks with references to his student days at Chapel Hill and to his impressions and feelings concerning the university. He said that the age of the university—young in European terms—gave a sense of history because it was the first university of the people. New buildings and new programs, however, gave a feeling of the frontier. Though North Carolina had a lengthy history, it was still a frontier state, with its unexplored Coastal areas, its rapidly expanding Piedmont cities, and its undeveloped Mountain region. The Governor pointed out that North Carolina had more students in college than were enrolled in the entire British Isles, a consequence of the outburst of democratic feeling which followed the American Revolution and led to the founding of a state university and a state-wide system of public instruction. During succeeding generations changes in physical surroundings and in attitudes had taken place, and the university had instilled a sense of responsibility in many who later became the state's leaders. Despite this fact, 20 to 25 per cent of the adults in North Carolina were illiterate, and a democracy's survival depended on a literate citizenry. Public schools required improvements in budgets, curriculum, trained teachers, instruction. The Governor called upon "the faculty of our most distinguished university" to train more teachers and to study new methods of learning aids, to put more emphasis on extension work, to help keep professional people informed of changes in their fields, to expand the use of educational television, to help make possible a unified university system. Sanford reaffirmed the policy of closer ties between the state and the university. "Just as our problems are immense, our opportunities are great. Our people are ready to move ahead. We will need your help every step of the way, your help as thinkers, as teachers, as citizens." The Governor warned that the relationship between the university and the state would likely change, because in a frontier situation the relationship binding the two had not been finally defined. Though "the university must insist on its right to be free of political nagging and pressure, at the same time it must be bound by loyalty to the life of a people." Sanford expressed the belief that the university could be bound to a people and at the same time participate fully in the world society of scholars and learning, that a balance between the old concept of universities and the need for the university to serve the people could be achieved. The Governor ended by inviting the faculty of "the first university of the people" to seek "solutions which must be found for our people in the state and the South as we move toward the twenty-first century."

BRIGHT LEAF TOBACCO STATES CONFERENCE

RALEIGH

January 28, 1963

[Governor Sanford called this meeting in an effort to bring about regional action to counteract the growing threats to the southern tobacco industry. About 150 persons, representing the tobacco states of North Carolina, South Carolina, Georgia, Florida, and Virginia, attended the Raleigh meeting. Though the Governor's address touched on many facets of the tobacco industry, the hope for a regional research laboratory subsidized by federal funds was the closing suggestion.]

The flue-cured tobacco producing area of this great country has been recognized for years throughout the entire world for its superior flue-cured leaf. Two acres out of every five of our flue-cured tobacco crop move into foreign markets, either in the form of leaf tobacco or tobacco products. A decline in this export market would not only reduce the incomes of individual flue-cured tobacco producers but would also have an adverse effect upon the entire economy, every businessman, every citizen in the tobacco-producing states of Florida, Georgia, South Carolina, North Carolina, and Virginia.

We welcome you to this meeting to discuss a means of determining the way to insure the production of a high quality flue-cured tobacco which will be in demand by both foreign and domestic users alike.

In working toward this goal, we must recognize that survival of the tobacco industry demands that we not only develop desirable qualities in our leaf but that once these qualities are attained, we must also maintain the proper management of them.

Until recently, our tobaccos have been universally recognized as the "hallmark" of quality. As we have basked, complacently, in the sunshine of past achievements of a high-quality product, we have failed to capitalize on our leading position. During the period 1950 to 1954, our flue-cured crop represented about 67 per cent of the free world's flue-cured tobacco output, but the 1962 crop represented only 52 per cent—a drop of around 15 per cent.

During this same period, major gains have taken place in other flue-cured tobacco-producing countries such as Rhodesia-Nyasaland, our biggest competitor in world trade, where the 1962 harvest was double its average for the years 1950 to 1954. Substantial increases have also been recorded in Canada, India, Japan, Brazil, Pakistan, the Philippines, and Australia.

World demand and purchases are growing, but actual exports of flue-cured tobacco from the United States have not changed significantly from the level recorded in the early 1950's. During the same period, Rhodesia increased her exports by approximately 270 per cent. Exports from India and Canada have also risen sharply since 1950.

This indicates trouble. It indicates that we have failed, and failed miserably, to maintain our relative position in the world export market. These developments are of major concern to us and should sound a warning that the future for our flue-cured tobacco is in jeopardy. Flue-cured tobacco interests are confronted with an uncertain, hazard-laden future; yet if this problem is admitted and then met with determination, intelligence, and collective action, we can move back into the market and regain for the southeastern states the leading and increasing place in supplying quality tobacco for both the foreign and domestic markets.

No other country in the world has better soil, climate, and know-how for producing highly competitive flue-cured tobacco. The only catch is that we have not been taking full advantage of all our potentials. Since we have neglected to capitalize on these potentials, we now find ourselves confronted with the urgent need to regroup, evaluate our present position, develop plans, and take immediate steps toward regaining our proportionate share of the world's flue-cured tobacco market.

Foreign and domestic purchasers have recently called our attention to the quality deterioration in our flue-cured leaf. These complaints have particularly mentioned the lack of aroma in our leaf of recent years. Several important factors have been stressed on numerous occasions, as contributing to the deterioration of our flue-cured quality. Many of these complaints appear to be related to, or associated with, the natural and strong incentive in the past few years toward producing higher per-acre yields. The factors often mentioned include the use of certain high-yielding varieties which do not, under most farm conditions, produce leaf of desirable flavor and aroma; the excessive use of fertilizers; the production of an excessive number of leaves per acre either through spacing too closely or too-high topping or a combination of the two; excessive irrigation; harvesting immature tobacco; and many other such factors.

I do not know how much merit there is to be found in any of these complaints, but it is my firm conviction that this problem will not be solved until we have an understanding and clear definition of *quality* in tobacco.

People in the flue-cured tobacco-producing states of Florida, South Carolina, Georgia, North Carolina, and Virginia can share in the expanding world tobacco market if they improve the quality of their flue-cured tobacco leaf and widen the gap between the quality of their tobaccos and that of their competitors. We, of the southeastern states, can be effective in promoting our flue-cured leaf and insuring its future, both at home and abroad, only if we make sure that it possesses those characteristics for which consumer demand is greatest.

Our answer is research. Research provides a means through which we can obtain a knowledge of the visual, physical, and chemical factors that are indicative of quality in flue-cured tobacco.

I solicit your assistance and co-operation in obtaining a regional flue-cured tobacco quality research laboratory for seeking answers regarding tobacco quality—its definition and how it can be maintained and even enhanced in the future.

FIRST INSTITUTE FOR PAROLE BOARD MEMBERS

CHAPEL HILL

February 11, 1963

[In a news release in January, 1961, Governor Sanford noted that North Carolina's rank of fifth in prison population "imposes a great responsibility on the state of North Carolina and its people." As one means of meeting the challenge, the National Parole Institutes planned a series of national conferences; North Carolina held the initial meeting. The Governor's address opened the week-long conference which was held at the Institute of Government. The speech went beyond professional lines in an effort to further community co-operation and understanding of the penal system.]

I understand that this is the first in a series of institutes for parole board members to be held at different places across the United States. North Carolina is proud of her growing list of "firsts." I consider this one a highly significant addition. Adding to its significance is the fact that this is the effective beginning of two complementary programs.

The National Parole Institutes Program is administered by the National Council on Crime and Delinquency. Sponsors include the Association of Paroling Authorities, the United States Board of Parole, and the Interstate Compact Administrators Association of the Council of State Governments. Each succeeding institute in the N. P. I. series may have a different theme, but all will be designed to provide parole authority members and administrators with the opportunity to meet as you are meeting, to learn new concepts and techniques, and to review experiences related to parole. The N.P.I. program is an outstanding example of the short-term institutes receiving federal support under the Juvenile Delinquency and Youth Offenses Control Act of 1961.

Support from the same source and under the same authority has helped us to establish the Training Center on Delinquency and Youth Crime at the University of North Carolina's Institute of Government. This is one of a number of such centers so established at universities throughout the country. These centers provide a concentration of resources, knowledge, staff, and facilities on a long-range basis for the training of all categories of personnel who work with youth.

Thus, national and local endeavors are here joined for greater strength and enduring benefits. This is a commendable example of the co-ordination encouraged nationally by the President's Committee on Juvenile Delinquency and Youth Crime and in this state by a committee I have appointed to promote the same purposes. By co-ordinating these two programs in this way, the immediate and long-range impact of this particular institute is greatly increased. I believe we are here engaged in an endeavor of immense and lasting value.

The aim of the American system for the administration of justice is the protection of the public by measures consonant with our concepts of due process and individual dignity. This aim has at least three elements.

The first is the swift, certain, and impartial imposition of sanctions against individual lawbreakers. This requires sound laws and effective agencies of apprehension and prosecution.

The second element is the provision of proper controls for those who are unable to live a law-abiding life in a free community. Society has a right to expect protection against repeated crime by convicted persons.

More than apprehension, imposition of sanctions, and provision for controls is required, however, if the administration of justice is to be successful. Each year millions of offenders are convicted in our criminal courts. The vast majority of these never leave free society or are released after a relatively short confinement. Therefore, the third element must be a concern with developing self-control among those who break the law. Only when this is done can we claim success for our efforts to prevent repeated crime.

The experience of being apprehended and penalized is sufficient to develop self-control in some violators. For another relatively small group of offenders, neither penalties nor present knowledge about human behavior seems sufficient. We must provide for identifying and holding in safe custody for extended periods these offenders whose early release would endanger free society.

The overwhelming mass of law violators are vocationally unskilled, mentally or emotionally impaired, alcoholic, or simply socially untrained. Penalties and custody alone are not going to remove the root cause of their criminality. They require the attention of skilled persons who can bring to bear on these individual problems the scientific knowledge which we do have about human behavior. They need help to develop the vocational and social skills and the self-control required for law-abiding life in free society.

General public support for sound measures to prevent and control criminal and delinquent behavior is needed as never before. Each year we see the number of law violators increasing at a more rapid rate than our population is growing. Since the eighteen to twenty-five years old age group contributes heavily to our crime burden, we are faced with the high probability of a further rise in the crime rates as the youngsters born during the postwar "baby boom" reach this age of difficult adjustments.

We seem to be spinning in an inflationary spiral of institutional failure. Home and community inadequacies contribute to the development of juvenile delinquency. Too many delinquents pass uncorrected through the juvenile courts and correctional agencies into the courts and correctional services for adult offenders and out again with their criminality confirmed.

Clearly the confirmed criminal is the least hopeful prospect for shaping into a self-respecting and responsible citizen, willing and able to contribute constructively to the progressive development of a free society. We must not abandon all hope and cease our efforts to develop self-control and proper attitudes and aims among even the most hardened maximum-custody prisoners. But we should place the greatest stress upon programs designed to stop the growth of criminality as close to the seed stage as we can get.

The seeds for crime are large in number and varied in form. The vexing complexities of crime causation call for complete mobilization, proper co-ordination, and full utilization of many resources to meet the ominous threat to the stability of our social order posed by the accelerating growth of this agelong social problem.

Effective to cope with this challenge, public and private local resources, as well as state and federal programs, must be mobilized to move vigorously and imaginatively on a wide front. Even if all agencies directly connected with our system of criminal justice work harmoniously together, the system will fail to accomplish its mission if forced to operate in a hostile and inadequate society.

Therefore, when you consider your responsibilities as parole board members, you should not limit your concern to passing upon the cases officially before you. Your responsibilities as high office holders in a constitutional democracy include the exercise of leadership in the struggle of the people toward the realization of their full potential for a productive, healthy, and free society of self-respecting and responsible citizens.

The need for bold and imaginative leadership was never greater. Improvements must be made in our correctional methods, and the general public must be brought to understand and support constructive changes. You have a special responsibility to explain the nature and need for parole, and correctional innovations related to parole. But in your role as a citizen leader, you also have a responsibility to promote full mobilization and effective co-ordination of all resources for the prevention and control of crime and delinquency.

The public schools may well be the place where we can first discover and correct the criminal tendencies before their manifestation multiplies the problems of correction. The behavioral scientists are beginning to push back the frontiers of ignorance about the mental and emotional makeup of man. There is basis for belief that criminal characteristics can be detected in the formative stages when habit patterns are easier to alter.

I am not claiming that it is possible for us to eliminate the criminal element from our population by improving our public schools. I am not suggesting that we have reached the point where we can single out for correctional treatment every incipient criminal while still a school child. I am not asserting that we can correct every child believed to be headed toward a life of crime. What I am saying is that we must make fuller use of advancing knowledge for these purposes. By developing and using the full potential of our educational resources, I am confident that we can appreciably reduce the incidence of delinquency and crime.

One consequence of our failure to provide adequate schools is revealed by the appalling rate of unemployment among out-of-school youth between sixteen and twenty years of age. This rate is more than double the rate for all age groups.

School inadequacies are at least partly to blame for the growing number of school dropouts. Youngsters with inadequate schooling have great difficulty securing and retaining satisfactory employment. Unemployed and dissatisfied young people are much more likely to become delinquents or youthful offenders than are young people with worthwhile jobs. Stating the obvious serves to point up the importance of doing all that we can to provide our youth with the education and training they will need to find satisfying employment in the labor market of today and tomorrow.

Here in North Carolina we are developing a very good vocational training program in the industrial education centers located throughout the state. I am confident this program could meet the training needs of many young people who are not participating because they are not aware or not appreciative of the training available to them at these centers.

I have recently established the North Carolina Good Neighbor Council whose mission is to urge youth to become better trained and qualified for employment and to encourage the employment of qualified people without regard to race. I have asked all mayors and chairmen of boards of county commissioners to establish local Good Neighbor Councils. While the Good Neighbor program is not primarily directed toward the prevention of crime and delinquency, this will be an important consequence of its success.

Unfortunately, we are not going to be completely successful in our efforts to prevent crime and delinquency. I accept the regrettable probability that we shall continue to be confronted with a large number of young people whose misbehavior will extend beyond the correctional capabilities of family, church, and school. But I believe we can provide better services to help them find their way back to the path of rectitude as soon as possible after their first departure from it.

Several years ago I served as chairman of a commission appointed by Governor William B. Umstead to study the juvenile courts and correctional institutions of North Carolina. Throughout our study we adhered wholeheartedly to the concept that the proper function of a juvenile court and correctional system should be to correct unbalanced behavior patterns through guidance and training rather than to serve as a tribunal and instrument of punishment. That concept still guides my thinking in this area.

We must broaden and strengthen our programs for prevention, our juvenile and criminal court services, and our systems of community treatment, such as probation. But for the foreseeable future, we will be forced to deal with a number of offenders who will need to be removed from the community for a time. We must never cease our search for ways to keep this number as small and the time as short as we can without unjustifiable risk to the public. Major dependence must be placed upon you members of full-time parole boards to provide the requisite leadership.

Today there are more than 200,000 persons confined in penal institutions for adult felons in the United States. Each year more than 100,000 are admitted to these institutions. Over 95 per cent of these will eventually be released into our communities, probably half in two or three years.

If their prison experience has taught them respect for law, has increased their chances for successfully competing in our economic system, has given them a more healthy attitude toward themselves, and has instilled a sense of responsibility toward others, then we can feel that they have benefited from time in prison. The real test comes in the free community. Parole is a service that provides essential assistance at the time of crucial need.

Unfortunately, parole has too often been confused with the sentimental approach toward the offender. There is a compelling logic for a wisely operated parole program as part of a system of justice which seeks to protect the public while maximizing concern for individual dignity. This is not sentimentality.

Parole is a sensible way of retaining needed controls and providing rehabilitative assistance to persons released from prison during the period required for them to complete the difficult change from inmate to parolee to citizen. But there continues to exist major misunderstanding of its purpose, great variations in its use, and serious shortages of adequately trained personnel.

National prison statistics show that only 60 per cent of those released each year in the United States are released on parole. The other 40 per cent are turned loose with no controls or assistance. Variance in use of parole is very great. The five states using it most release over 90 per cent of their prisoners under parole supervision while the five using it least release only 25 per cent by parole.

Failure to exploit fully the potential of parole reflects a need for better public understanding of the vital role played by parole in the community's security and welfare. Public support is essential if parolees are to have a fair chance to succeed. A parolee denied a reasonable opportunity for a decent job and the self-respect that goes with it is highly likely to return to crime as the only life open to him. Public attention should be called to the fact that tens of thousands of parolees are living in the free community and making an acceptable adjustment. We should not permit the glare of publicity to be focused only on the relatively small percentage who fail.

The inmate population of the North Carolina prison system started to climb at the close of World War II. From less than 6,000 in 1945, the number grew at an alarming rate, passing 12,000 early in 1961, the year I became Governor. By a co-ordinated attack along the lines I have been advocating in this speech, we have succeeded in stopping the growth of our prison population. The Prison Department's budget requests for the next biennium are based on an inmate population estimate which represents a reduction of more than a thousand inmates from what the figure would have been if the average inmate population had continued to grow as it did from 1945 through 1961.

I do not discount the importance of tax dollar savings when I affirm that the savings in human resources and the reduction in heartbreak and mental anguish are the most significant gains realized by stopping the growth of our prison population.

Increased use of probation and parole for appropriate cases contributed significantly to the reduction of the prison population. Considerable credit is also due to prison rehabilitation programs. Perhaps the most significant single factor explaining the greater success of these programs is closer involvement of the free community.

Close co-operation between the Prison Department and free community agencies and citizens in aiding alcoholics has helped to remove many from the list of repeated offenders. Not so readily measurable but clearly considerable are the immediate and long-range benefits of the mental health clinic at Central Prison, which was established and is operated co-operatively by the Prison Department and the Hospitals Board of Control.

The rapid growth and remarkable success of our work release program has attracted national and international attention. Since the original enactment in 1957 of the Work Release Law, each session of the North Carolina General Assembly has produced modification broadening the law's application. Basic provisions have remained unchanged. These authorize the Prison Department to grant certain inmates of the State Prison System the privilege of working at regular employment in the free community and spending only their leisure time in confinement. Inmates granted these privileges surrender their earnings to the Prison Department. After deducting the cost of the inmate's keep, the Prison Department arranges for paying through the appropriate county department of public welfare such part of the balance of the inmate's earnings as is needed to support his dependents. The remainder is kept in trust and paid to him when he is paroled or discharged from prison.

Possession of money and productive employment on final release from prison are two positive factors contributing importantly to the low rate of recidivism for inmates granted work release privileges. Less tangible but probably even more important are the increased self-respect and self-confidence frequently found in those inmates who serve all or the final part of their prison sentences on work release.

Although the growth of the prison population has been halted, it will begin again unless we continue to develop alternatives to imprisonment for appropriate cases and unless we expand and improve programs for reducing the number of prisoners who return to crime after their release. We need more probation officers better to serve the courts so that judges can keep out of our prisons those offenders whose rehabilitation can be effected under supervision in the free community. We need more parole supervisors so that the public may be better protected by timely release of prisoners under supervision. We need to have the Work Release Law modified so that its proven value as a pre-parole program can be extended to prisoners serving sentences longer than five years. We need to expand and extend the programs and measures conducted co-operatively by the Prison Department and the Hospitals Board of Control to determine what can and should be done for prisoners who are mentally ill or inebriates. We need to make a comprehensive study of alternatives for treating the alcoholic offender. We need to provide our courts with diagnostic services to aid them when they are uncertain as to appropriate disposition of an offender, and with facilities to which they may send convicted offenders who should not be in prison but who cannot profit from probation until they have been given special preparation. We need to encourage and facilitate co-ordination of the programs of all agencies concerned with crime prevention and control.

Since Mr. Johnson Matthews, Chairman of our Board of Paroles, and Lee Bounds, Director of the Training Center on Delinquency and Youth Crime,[106] will be with you all of this week, I can depend upon them to provide you with more details about our programs and our plans.

I shall also depend upon them to gather for us the fruits of your deliberations at this institute. We need to help each other by free and full exchange of information, ideas, and experience. None of us can afford the luxury of complacent isolation. I am confident none of us desires it. I believe you all share my feelings about the importance of what you are doing this week. Thank you for the privilege of participating in this pioneering program.

AMERICAN ASSOCIATION
OF SCHOOL ADMINISTRATORS

ATLANTIC CITY, NEW JERSEY

February 19, 1963

Speaking in New Jersey to a group of school administrators from all over the United States, Governor Sanford told his audience that he had visited schools in 66 of North Carolina's 100 counties during the preceding year and a half. He said he had tried to impress upon the students the importance of education, but that he himself was impressed with all that was not being done. "In a government by, of, and for the people, public education is supported by political action," the Governor declared, and he called on those in the fields of politics and education to lead. Politicians had too often failed to provide funds, and educational leaders had failed to provide the desire in students to read and to develop their ability to think. Education, the Governor said, was fundamental to military defense, to increasing economic skills, to health and strength. For children from homes which were "culturally dispossessed," schools were an impossible challenge; these students dropped out only to accept menial jobs and to live in slums. Illustrating his talk with the "North Carolina Story," the Governor said that the lesson learned in his state was that people would support school improvement if the issue was put to them squarely. The North

---

[106] Vernon Leland Bounds, Assistant Director at the Institute of Government at Chapel Hill. *University Record, 1962-1963,* 300.

Carolina General Assembly appropriated funds to put into effect a program of quality education, thus making education the "first order of business." Immediately morale improved among school personnel, and all worked harder to justify the confidence placed in them. The state of North Carolina, with over a million students, provided 80 per cent of the support for the schools. The Governor told his audience of special classes for gifted students, of summer training programs for talented boys and girls, and of other specialized programs. He said some areas were not so fortunate as others, that ideas were strangers in those places, and that ways had to be worked out for helping this culturally deprived group. "Too long we have put most of our best teachers in the classrooms of the privileged children. . . . How in the world can we continue the present system of favoritism and not eventually split our society down the middle," the Governor asked. After quoting the credo on the Statue of Liberty, Sanford described America's disadvantaged segments of society as "our tired, our poor, our huddled masses yearning to breathe free." The golden door for this group of people was education, declared Governor Sanford, and "Special, understanding education is the lamp that will light their way." The schools had the responsibility of lighting the lamp, and the school administrators had to hold it high.

"NORTH CAROLINA DAY"
AT SALES EXECUTIVES CLUB OF NEW YORK

NEW YORK, NEW YORK

February 26, 1963

[Governor Sanford's trip to New York to "sell North Carolina industry" was reminiscent of his week-long trip in 1961 to the Ohio Valley. In attendance at this luncheon meeting were 800 Tar Heels accompanying the Governor, approximately 500 members of the Sales Executives Club, and 150 North Carolinians living and working in metropolitan New York. Color slides of North Carolina industry were shown and more than 5,000 "Made in North Caaolina" products were distributed to members of the club and guests. Sanford ended his talk with a proclamation of faith in the people of North Carolina and the value of the state's educational program.]

Your organization is of people in the business of selling, which is at the heart of the free enterprise system, and your club is designed to promote and to gain new knowledge about this fundamental process of commerce.

At first glance there may not be much similarity in your undertakings and the methods of "selling a state."

In the first place why sell a state? Why is it necessary? What is all of this business about salesmanship and state government? Are those of us in government getting too far afield when we think about selling?

The Raleigh *News and Observer* had this to say in an editorial: "What then is our duty? It is to go to work earnestly to build up North Carolina. . . . And what nobler employment could enlist the energies of a people than the developing of the great resources . . .?"

It so happens, this was written November 9, 1880. And indeed the energies were turned to developing the resources. It wasn't easy. The devastation of the war, little capital, the best of the youth killed or maimed, and sorry government made survival, much less advancement, difficult.

By the turn of the century, the size of the textile industry had increased by ten times and was to lead the nation by the 1940's.

In 1865 Washington Duke[107] was manufacturing tobacco on his farm, and his son Buck[108] was peddling it from a wagon. In 1890 the American Tobacco Company, combining and absorbing numerous other companies, dominated the industry. The division of this company in 1911 left North Carolina in a leading position which has been enhanced to the present day.

In 1881 a plant was organized to manufacture spindles for the cotton mills, and it later evolved into a furniture factory, but not until several other furniture factories were built. From this beginning, North Carolina has become the largest manufacturer of wood furniture.

So it was tobacco, textiles, furniture products manufactured from products of the soil, the best that could be done.

There were many other related businesses springing up, and individual initiative here and there set up more sophisticated industries, but the giants of the economy remained farming, textiles, tobacco, and furniture.

The depression of the 1930's made everybody aware of the dangers of an economy no more diversified than ours; and the war years brought much diversification, with national companies, the

---

[107] Washington Duke (1820-1905), farmer, Confederate soldier from Orange County; entrepreneur of early tobacco industry; wealthy North Carolina philanthropist. Ashe, *Biographical History*, III, 84-93.

[108] James Buchanan Duke (1856-1925), son of Washington Duke, tobacco manufacturer and capitalist leader in power development; organizer and President of American Tobacco Company, 1889-1912; Chairman, Board of Directors, British-American Tobacco Company, 1912-1925. Ashe, *Biographical History*, III, 102-113; *Who Was Who in America: A Companion Biographical Reference Work to Who's Who in America* (Chicago: A. N. Marquis Company, 1960), I, 344, hereinafter cited as *Who Was Who in America*.

electronics business, and the chemicals industry reaching into North Carolina for locations and markets.

Here then, at the end of World War II, with the lifting of restrictions, with greater wealth, with ambitious returning veterans, with wider purchasing power, was the opportunity North Carolina had been waiting for, the need for diversification, the call of 1880 "for developing the great resources."

Some of the growth could come from home industries, and much has. But across the nation was a trend for industry to spread out to other areas.

Here was the need to let the message get to those who were looking for new markets, new places, and new profits. Here was the call to tell business and industry about a new and growing land, holding profits and promise for those who would come and invest and expand.

Here was the call for salesmanship. Here was the need and demand for salesmanship. We had the soil and the land. But there is much land. We had the warm and healthful climate, but so did many other states. We had people, but doesn't everybody? We had water, but this wasn't exclusive. How could we be different, and how could we be better?

First of all, we decided that our main interest had to be people. We did not want smokestacks just for the sake of statistics. We wanted jobs for people so that they might provide more for their families and find more fulfillment in life. We decided we should not be too materialistic but should seek development in all fields. This was a fortunate choice because today industry offers more and wants more for its people. We wanted to make ours the kind of state in which people and industries could grow and prosper.

The great demand today is for management leadership. Cheap labor is not a drawing card for most industry. We say frankly if you are looking for cheap labor, don't look at us. We can promise you honest, hard-working labor. We can find you people who can learn quickly the new skills you require. We have an outpouring every year of men and women capable of leadership in management.

Leadership ability and industrial skills are the business of the state because education is the business of the state, and it is through education that we develop the managerial ability and the skilled labor which will develop and attract the kind of new industry we seek.

How do you sell a state? Well, first of all, you look to your duty.

The State University located at Raleigh and at Chapel Hill joined with Duke University, and these three outstanding institutions, with the state government and leaders of private business, created the famous North Carolina Research Triangle, the Research Triangle Institute, and gave new emphasis to science to get ready for an age of science in industry.

Faculty salaries were increased and enrichment funds were provided for the other fifteen tax-supported colleges, while the forty-two private colleges in the state were improving their facilities and faculties.

Education was to be the key to our hopes.

We established twenty industrial education centers across the state with education beyond the high school available in an almost unlimited array of subjects, with flexibility to reach out to every town and county, and enrolling more than 26,000 students last year, the third year since the first was built.

Education in skills was to back up our education for science and management.

Plans are now before our legislature for the development of a system of comprehensive community colleges which will make education available to thousands of additional students each year, and educated leaders available each year to our expanding economy.

We have embarked upon the most ambitious program of public school improvement in the history of the state. At the last session of the General Assembly we provided new funds which rated North Carolina as the state making the greatest leap forward. Just last week, the chairman of the State Board of Education appeared before the legislature to say that he had no additional requests; that for the first time in the history of the state all of the school requests were contained in the recommended budget.

Education up and down the line, from the first grade through the graduate school, is the trademark of the product we are selling.

We built state port facilities for the first time at the natural and long used but mostly undeveloped ports of Wilmington and Morehead City. Now we cannot build fast enough to keep ahead of the business.

We paved more roads and highways than any other state in the union. This too, was getting ready for business, an investment in better living, the greatest system of rural roads in America supporting a labor force not crowded into cities but coming to work on all-weather roads the year round, providing a system of primary and interstate highways capable of supporting the

North Carolina trucking industry, which is the largest in the nation.

This kind of homework was essential to support our selling. There are examples of many other things, many other improved programs to make North Carolina more attractive.

We have the only state-supported art museum. It is a very good one. Is this important to new industry? I think so.

We have a state-supported symphony orchestra, and several creditable city orchestras. We have the three outstanding outdoor dramas: at Cherokee in the Indian country, at Boone in Daniel's country, and at Manteo, *The Lost Colony,* where Englishmen first set foot in the New World.

We have the unique Outer Banks and the seashore, the highest mountains east of the Rockies, the Sandhills with the greatest concentration of golf courses.

You can take a vacation right in your home state, a different kind every summer, and, in fact, the tourist business is our third largest business; and we call North Carolina the "Variety Vacationland."

As a matter of fact, you can work all day and fifteen minutes after quitting time you can be sitting in your garden or if you are more ambitious, you can be tending the tomato plants.

We expanded our parks, cleaned up our streams and rivers, developed our forests and woodlands, promoted our fishing and hunting, strengthened our community planning so that we might avoid slums, spread out our recreational programs. As you know, we gave the country Miss America in 1962.

I have talked about what we have done since the end of World War II. I do not mean the Governor. I do not mean just the past governors. I do not mean the state government. The great progress North Carolina has made, the success of our efforts to get new industry, to expand old industry, to build better schools, roads, to make a better state, to provide new opportunities for our people, has been due to people.

The promise to industry is people—people productive, capable of intelligent leadership, wholesome, determined, building, growing, taking advantage of their opportunities to build a stronger America and a better life. This is really what we are selling. There isn't anything else which will attract and sustain industry and business.

The business of North Carolina is people, and the attraction of North Carolina is people.

I promised I would bring you some samples from North Carolina, so I have here today samples of North Carolina's

Maria Beale Fletcher, from Asheville, was chosen Miss America in 1962.

Governor Sanford participated in many dedication ceremonies for new industries in North Carolina. Here Malcolm R. Hunt, General Manager of the Electronic Products Division, is explaining machinery at the Corning Glass installation in Raleigh on the day of the dedication of the new plant, October 12, 1962.

success—its people. Representing almost 5 million people, here are 800 of North Carolina's finest product.

We have trained people from our State Department of Conservation and Development roaming the nation, talking to businesses looking for expansion opportunities in the Southeast. They can talk engineering, rail and transportation rates, water supply, labor potential, markets, and anything else of interest to the businessman.

Almost every community in the state has a group, mostly unpaid, ready to show the resources to those who seek expanded opportunities. We have had missions to New York, to Chicago, to Philadelphia, to Europe, to the Ohio Valley, with 50 to 100 North Carolinians going at their own expense, to talk with business leaders about the advantages of North Carolina.

Admittedly, sometimes this is misunderstood. On my trip with fifty North Carolinians through five cities of the Ohio Valley, a newspaper referred to our group as "Terry and the Pirates." But here is what we told them: "In the last decade, more than $1.5 billion was invested in new and expanded industrial plants in North Carolina.

"In the first quarter of this year, our state broke all of its records in erecting new industry—more than $42 million worth.

"During the recession of 1960, North Carolina's economy expanded. A recent United States Department of Commerce report pointed out that business in North Carolina generally held firm during 1960 despite reported recessive downtrends in the nation.

"The truth of the matter is that during the recession year of 1960, North Carolina was compiling a new record of industrial growth.

"We intend to accelerate that industrial drive.

"That is why we are here.

"There is profit in North Carolina for new industry. North Carolina is the leading industrial state of the fastest growing new market in America, the Southeast.

"We have not come here to engage in plant piracy. We are here to encourage industrial expansion. We haven't come to steal, we've come to sell—to sell North Carolina as a profitable site for expanding industries."

.   .   .   .

After the trip, the *Indianapolis Times* wrote an editorial entitled "Let's Follow Suit." The *Journal Herald* of Dayton called the visit "nothing short of inspiring." The *Dayton Daily News* wrote that North Carolina "knows that modern industries look for a community that can attract and hold executives, engineers, and technicians. Industries now ask about schools, colleges, technical institutes—even about libraries, art galleries, symphony orchestras." The *Columbus Evening Dispatch* entitled its editorial "North Carolina Sets Example."

The missions are occasional, but the roving ambassadors are constant, going to every part of the nation, telling the story, furnishing information, consulting about the possibilities. Has this kind of salesmanship been effective? We are sure that it has.

Last year the economy of North Carolina reached an all-time high.

We once were called, by one of our native historians, "The Rip Van Winkle State." More recently, the *National Geographic* called North Carolina "The Dixie Dynamo."

We also like to talk about North Carolina's government, because this is one of the truest indicators of the quality of the product we are selling. We have a surplus. We have a balanced budget. We rank in the bottom five of the fifty states in taxes, debt, government employees, state and local combined, per capita. Our credit is the best given any state—AAA. We have been in North Carolina neither radical nor reactionary.

Since the year of 1900, there has not been so much as a breath of scandal in North Carolina's state government. Without any self-praise, I can report honestly that our people deserve the well-known native slogan, "Good Government Is a Habit in North Carolina."

If you go out to sell a washing machine, you can develop one of two approaches. If you must, you can sell it for a dollar down, easy payments, and because it is cheap. That is what you have to rely on if your product doesn't have character. I am sure that you would rather sell on the basis of your product's name, its reputation, its soundness, and the character of your company.

We don't offer any cheap way. We don't offer tax concessions. We don't believe this is fair to the existing taxpayers, and we don't believe a company willing to avoid fair taxes will make a very good citizen anyhow.

We offer all we have: our climate, our water resources, our transportation, our schools, our natural beauty, our conscientious people.

We are trying to improve all of these things. That is our first order of salesmanship.

We do not hesitate to put out the challenge made famous in salesmanship, "Ask the man who owns one." Our business leaders, our industrialists are our best salesmen, by their testimony, as you will learn today at your individual tables, but more important by their example. They add much to the character of our product.

What North Carolina has to sell is what America has to sell, the hope of free men around the globe—a great productive capacity manned by a creative, enterprising, and freedom-loving people.

Essentially, we are selling character—character of our people as expressed in their lives, their work, their industries, their government.

We hope to keep this ingredient in our product always. That is the best way to sell a state.

INTRODUCTION OF
VICE-PRESIDENT LYNDON B. JOHNSON

RALEIGH

March 30, 1963

In introducing Lyndon B. Johnson to those attending the Jefferson-Jackson Day Dinner, Governor Sanford said that North Carolina continued to progress through the Democratic party. He called Johnson a man who stood for progress, growth, and new opportunity, a man who played important roles in the Roosevelt, Truman, and Kennedy administrations, and a man who had served in politics for years. Faced with world peace and space problems, the nation could look to its "capable, able, productive Vice-President" for sturdy leadership. He welcomed Johnson to North Carolina, predicting "I am sure that in 1968 it will be Lyndon B. Johnson."

DEDICATION OF
SCHOOL OF PUBLIC HEALTH BUILDING
UNIVERSITY OF NORTH CAROLINA

CHAPEL HILL

April 7, 1963

At the ceremonies of dedication of a new public health building in Chapel Hill, the Governor commented on the presence of out-of-state guests as testimony to the significance of the occasion. He spoke of the development of public health in North Carolina and of the leadership in the field throughout the years. The School of Public Health, with its outstanding department of environmental health sciences, was cited as a reason for the establishment of the national center for environmental health in the Research Triangle area. Sanford said North Carolina's dedication to professional education was matched by its concern for the health of the citizens. He called the building "a monument to our determination to insure that the world will be a better place in which to live tomorrow."

FIRST NATIONAL CONFERENCE
NATIONAL COMMITTEE FOR SUPPORT OF THE
PUBLIC SCHOOLS

WASHINGTON, D. C.

April 8, 1963

Speaking in Washington, the Governor urged the adoption of education as a mission for the nation. He said that for 375 years since the birth of Virginia Dare all Americans had sought a chance for the individual; this goal meant that every child should have the opportunity to get the most out of life and to give the most back. Such opportunity could not be achieved except by action of the state because the needs were too broad and too diverse for central solution by the federal government. Education was essential if goals were to be met. "The fundamentals of self-fulfillment, responsibility of citizenship, success of democracy itself depend on the quality and scope of our education." Scientific advances, cultural progress, farm practices all depended on education. Stability of government was the result of education; education itself in the future was dependent on education of the present. Sanford called for attention to the individual and to his chance in life. North Carolina's goal was worth the effort, and the General Assembly was working to accomplish that goal; the Governor observed that citizens would support advances if the question was put to them fairly and directly. He urged the nation to adopt the North Carolina mission, which was education.

CHICAGO APPRECIATION LUNCHEON OF CHARLOTTE CHAMBER OF COMMERCE

Chicago, Illinois

April 17, 1963

Governor Sanford, after describing links between North Carolina and Chicago, pointed out the fact that trade was a two-way street. Major business interests of Chicago had discovered that the road from North Carolina led to Chicago; the same road led from Illinois to North Carolina. Representatives of numerous companies had plants or offices in Charlotte because Charlotte and North Carolina had much to offer national companies; the Governor invited business people to attend the Trade Fair. Though North Carolina and Charlotte were late entering the era of industrial development, the state did not intend to be late in the atomic and space age. The South was the fastest-growing region in the United States; North Carolina was the fastest-growing state in education, industry, highways, and farming in the South; Piedmont North Carolina was the fastest-growing section of the state and Charlotte one of its most rapidly expanding centers. Sanford proceeded to cite the financial and commercial assets of Charlotte but concluded that the people were the greatest asset. He ended with an invitation to the citizens of Chicago to visit North Carolina for business and for pleasure.

ANNUAL SIXTH DISTRICT MEETING OMEGA PSI PHI FRATERNITY, A & T COLLEGE

Greensboro

April 27, 1963

[Governor Sanford's administration was noted for leadership in race relations during a period of unrest and actual violence in parts of the country. His positive stand was reflected over and over again. The establishment of the Good Neighbor Council was announced on January 18, 1963 (see statement on page 579); the Governor's handling of situations arising from student demonstrations during the spring resulted in favorable comment throughout the nation. In this address to students at A & T College, Sanford called on Negroes to meet their responsibilities to match their privileges.]

I am deeply honored by the recognition you have given me this afternoon. I would prefer to think that the honor is less a personal one than an endorsement of the position I have taken regarding the future of this state and all its people.

If this be the case, and I sincerely hope that it is, then I am happy that I can share this recognition with growing numbers of North Carolinians.

Simply stated, this position is nothing more and nothing less than an effort to meet the responsibilities of my office by reacting honestly and realistically to the challenge facing North Carolina at this critical moment in its history.

Facts cannot be denied, and in North Carolina today they can be stated simply. We must move forward as one people or we will not move forward at all. We cannot move forward as whites or Negroes or merchants or farmers or candlestick makers. We can only move forward as North Carolinians.

Another fact, simply stated, is that North Carolina has a fantastic potential. Much of this potential is obvious, and it is entirely probable that much of it has not become apparent to us yet. In any event, it cannot be argued that we have all the resources needed to give our people a standard of living that will be envied across the nation.

The most obvious fact, however, is that this prosperity will not just happen. It must be made to happen. And the only way we can make it happen is by developing and using to maximum advantage the knowledge and skills of all our citizens.

The answer doesn't lie in just finding jobs for all our people who can work and want to work. This is only a beginning. We have to look far beyond this point. Our goal—and the goal to which we must dedicate ourselves today—is to create in North Carolina the kind of business atmosphere that will give us the prosperity we seek, and more importantly, equip our own people to contribute to and derive maximum benefit from this new and dynamic society.

Both of these things must be accomplished at the same time. If we develop the skills of our people without developing the kind of economy that rewards those skills, we will have achieved nothing. Our young, productive citizens will leave us, as more than 300,000 of them did in the last decade and as an equal number are likely to do in the present decade.

On the other hand, if we struggle with the mechanics of economic growth—with making our cities more attractive, with building industrial plants, with making investment capital available, with developing our water resources—without training our people to be a vital part of this growth, then we have again defeated our own purpose.

The point is that we must have balance. We must develop the

opportunities and, at the same time, make sure that our people have the skills to take full advantage of those opportunities. We have not had this balance in the past. We do not have it now. But, and this is the important thing, we are much nearer acquiring that balance than we have ever been before. We are nearer because more of our people understand its importance and because more of them are working to make it a reality.

We will not reach this goal overnight. It is a long-range operation—long-range because the key is education. And, as all of you here know, there is no such thing as instant education. There is no magic wand that we can wave over the uneducated and unskilled men or women to equip them for productive roles in this fast paced and highly competitive society.

Unfortunately, there are a lot of these people in North Carolina. They are largely responsible for the fact that in 1962 our state dropped from forty-second to forty-fourth among the fifty states in per capita income. Actually, our per capita income rose 4 per cent, keeping pace with the national average. But this was not enough. Other states did better. This is the thing we are trying to do something about, and it is a thing we are going to do something about.

We are tackling the problem in two ways. In the first place, we are by no means writing off as losses those unskilled and poorly educated people who have passed what we normally consider the school age. We want these people to develop skills. We want them to have higher standards of living. We need them in our labor force, and we are sparing no effort to get them there.

In the past three years, for instance, we have established twenty industrial education centers at strategic locations across our state. More than 51,000 North Carolinians have been trained at these centers, many of them displaced farm workers and young people who dropped out of school before completing their education.

The second way in which we are tackling this problem is by building a public school system that will insure every boy and girl in North Carolina an opportunity to get a good education. And we are, whenever and wherever possible, encouraging our young people to take full advantage of this opportunity. We are speaking frankly to these youngsters. We are telling them that when they drop out of school at an early age they are, in this dynamic and highly technical day and time, dooming themselves to a life of failure. We hope we are getting this message across because, to a large extent, the future of North Carolina depends on it.

You have a special stake in what we are trying to do. You also have a special responsibility. The stake is the future of your people, not as Negroes, but as North Carolinians. The responsibility is to work with the members of your race to make absolutely certain that they understand all the factors involved and that they realize that they have a responsibility to themselves, their communities, and their state that transcends any responsibility relating to race.

In a speech in Little Rock, Arkansas, last week end I said frankly that we will begin to realize our great potential when, and only when, we give equal employment opportunities to Negroes. I said that in this country people of all races must have equal opportunities in life, that we cannot hold down one segment of our population without that segment holding us all down.

Old prejudices are being swept aside. There is a broader base of understanding between white and Negro citizens than has ever existed before. Your great-grandfathers were held in actual bondage. Your grandfathers and fathers had to contend with social and economic bondage imposed partly by custom, partly by environment, partly by prejudice, and partly by lack of educational opportunity. The vestiges of this bondage remain with us today, but they are being rapidly erased. The Negro of past generations could justify his lack of progress by pleading lack of opportunity, and his complaint was certainly a valid one. The complaint is still heard today, and in some instances it is still valid, but it becomes less and less so with each passing day.

Your generation will, in a very short time, see the day when the legitimate complaint becomes an excuse and the excuse becomes unacceptable to the thinking people of both races. Equal opportunity in all areas will be yours. And accompanying equal opportunity in all areas will be equal responsibility in all areas. The time for you to begin accepting this responsibility is now.

Negroes have fought a courageous fight in recent years to secure their rights as citizens. You have, in most instances, shown wisdom and patience and honest dedication to your purpose; and you have every right to be proud of what you have achieved.

But equality, in the truest sense, is not a thing that can be campaigned for in a picket line nor can it be decreed by a court. Voltaire once said: "They who say all men are equal speak an undoubted truth, if they mean that all have an equal right to liberty, to their property, and to their protection of laws. But they are mistaken if they think men are equal in their station and employments, since they are not so by their talents."

The point Voltaire is making is that equality under the law is one thing, but that equality in all other senses is a very personal thing with each individual. It is a thing that must be earned, not by petition, but by performance.

It is the God-given right of every man to compete in this world. But it is not his God-given right to win. This he must do for himself. In other words, it is the responsibility of every citizen of North Carolina to honor the Negro's right to equal opportunities in education and employment. But it is the responsibility of the individual Negro citizen to take full advantage of those opportunities. It is vitally important to the future of this state and all its people that our Negro citizens do just that.

North Carolina's potential is a challenge to every citizen. You have an important part to play in helping North Carolina meet that challenge. The job ahead is much too big for us to be sidetracked by differences that sap our collective strength. We must keep in mind that this battle which promises such rich spoils can only be won by all of us working together.

Destiny has handed the Negro citizens of North Carolina a new and imposing responsibility at easily the most demanding and most promising period in the history of our state.

I am confident this responsibility will be met.

NATIONAL ASSOCIATION OF HOSIERY MANUFACTURERS

Atlantic City, New Jersey

April 29, 1963

Governor Sanford told the National Association of Hosiery Manufacturers that one half of the hosiery industry was located in North Carolina, and he invited additional industries to join those already in the Tar Heel state. After this introduction, he spoke again on the theme of education as the mission of America. He reviewed the historical development of the United States, a country in which each individual was theoretically given a chance to develop his own capabilities to the fullest. He added that this dream could not become reality unless all states, communities, the federal government, and all citizens joined in making education the primary mission of the country. Sanford cited gaps, such as failure to provide opportunities for retarded children to develop their limited talents, concluding that the nation would progress only as individuals progressed.

CAPITOL PRESS CLUB DINNER HONORING
VICE-PRESIDENT LYNDON B. JOHNSON

WASHINGTON, D. C.

May 18, 1963

[Race relations had become a topic of major interest by the spring of 1963, and Governor Sanford took advantage of the opportunity of speaking in Washington to discuss the situation with this organization of Negro newsmen. His leadership in the time of turmoil had been outstanding. The formation of the Good Neighbor Council on January 18, 1963 (see statement on page 579) was one way in which economic opportunity was extended to Negroes in North Carolina. Later, on July 5, 1963, at the height of social unrest in the state, the Mayors' Cooperating Committee, composed of mayors of twelve cities and towns, was initiated to seek answers to various aspects of the problem. This address was indicative of the fact that North Carolina was meeting the challenge in a reasonable and fair way.]

I am happy to take part in a program honoring Vice-President Lyndon B. Johnson who has worked so tirelessly against discrimination because of race or religion or region. He is the sturdy, indomitable champion of fair play. His actions and successes contain a lesson for every American who believes that all men and women should have the broadest possible opportunity to make the most of their lives.

You know of course that he steered through the Senate the first civil rights legislation of this century, a personal triumph acknowledged by his colleagues. Today, with all of his duties, an aide recently told a national magazine, Mr. Johnson has made his work as chairman of the President's Committee on Equal Employment Opportunity his chief day-to-day responsibility. I have never heard him deliver a speech anywhere on any subject when there did not shine through his conviction that all men are entitled to fair play, his belief that the strong must help the weak, his ambition that this country must be the place where equal opportunity abounds.

He has done much, but the lesson for the rest of us is that he has done it in a manner which is lasting, that serves as a foundation for additional progress, in a spirit comprehending the true and broader goal we seek—good will among all men.

He hasn't sounded the bugle and declared war. He knows from the history of his own homeland that unwarranted militancy breeds prejudice and resistance, and that any victory is hollow if it arises out of bitter combat between brothers.

It would be a tragic denial of the lessons of civilized and Christian humanity for us to assume that progress in the

American democracy can come only from conflict and force. It will come more surely from good will, and it will be more lasting.

The press of America has ever championed the cause of liberty and human dignity. It can best do this by promoting broader understanding of the hopes of minorities, avoiding studiously the promotion of inflamatory situations. It also has the power to incite emotions of bitterness and blind rebellion. Restraint is difficult, but restraint is the mark of civilized man. Restraint is not weakness; restraint is courage. Restraint in the face of irresponsibility of others is great courage.

I happen to agree with the historians who argue that slavery could have been abolished without the fratricide of the Civil War and without the legacy of bitterness and impoverishment which that war left with us. The theory of peaceful abolishment never really got a chance because of hotheads. We suffered because the hotheads in all parts of the country and on all sides of the question prevailed then, and we will suffer if the hotheads prevail now.

In a place where we have reaped the bitter fruit of that needless conflict, North Carolina hopes to demonstrate to the world that prejudices can be erased and full opportunities can be opened up in a climate of restraint and a spirit of good will with "malice toward none." Others may fight, but we will reason. Others may operate out of inflamed passions, but we will proceed with a calm faith in the intrinsic goodness of the children of God.

This is not a time for impatient action even if impatience is justified. It is important for us to understand that inflamatory statements by demagogues purporting to work for the rights of minorities can hurt the cause of the minorities as much as irrational statements by demagogues who falsely claim to be speaking for the majority. This is a time for good faith and good will and a determination that we will help all men and women achieve their best chance in life because it is the right thing to do. That is the North Carolina story.

In this century, the leaders and the citizens of North Carolina have worked toward solutions to these difficult problems involving as they do deep-seated passions of human beings. At the start of this century Governor Charles Brantley Aycock, who turned a race campaign into a crusade for education, threatened to resign as Governor of North Carolina if the General Assembly did not provide schools for the Negro children as well as for the whites. In the early 1940's Governor R. Gregg Cherry sent North Carolina highway patrolmen into a community in which a race riot was threatened. In the next administration, Governor W. Kerr Scott broke color lines that had stood since Reconstruction by appointing a Negro to the State Board of Education. In the

late 1940's an attempt to revive the Ku Klux Klan in North Carolina was crushed with the full weight of the state and local government, and the Grand Kleagle was sent to prison. Under Governor
William B. Umstead, North Carolina refused to get into the
massive resistance business after the Brown decision of 1954.

It peacefully began desegregation of schools during the administration of Governor Luther Hodges, who now is Secretary of
Commerce. An incident on that touchy September day when,
without any court order and without any pressure, schools voluntarily and peacefully integrated in Winston-Salem, Greensboro,
and Charlotte—our three largest cities—is worth recalling here.
Some youngster or some adult, without an adult's mind, had
painted a "Negro go home" sign on the steps at R. J. Reynolds
High School. The white students, proud of their high school,
got down on their knees and scrubbed it off.

Since that time at the University of North Carolina at Chapel
Hill, one of the Negro law students has served in the highest
position possible for a law student to serve—as editor of the *Law
Review*.

More Negroes serve by appointment of the administration on
policy-making boards in North Carolina than, I suspect, in any
other state in the union. North Carolina, without demonstrations
and without court orders, peacefully integrated its state parks
in 1962. North Carolina, without demonstrations and without
court orders, abolished segregated rest rooms in state government
buildings in 1961. North Carolina, because of the votes of white
precincts as well as precincts in which Negro voters predominate,
has elected Negroes to the city councils of a good many of its
cities and towns.

Public order has been characteristic of North Carolina. As
you know there was practically nothing filed on the wire services
during the time the Freedom Riders were passing through North
Carolina in 1962. This was because there were no incidents. We
did have one mob scene. While the riders were in the Raleigh
bus station, we had a mob around the Pepsi Cola machine which,
through some quirk of mechanical fate, was putting out free
Pepsis.

We are now attempting in North Carolina to provide all
citizens the chance to make a better living. We have called on
the people to remove the barriers of discrimination in employment, and they are responding as we expected. We call this the
Good Neighbor Program, and we have enlisted some of the
outstanding citizens of the state to serve on this council. We are
doing this because we know we cannot prosper if a quarter of

our people cannot find adequate jobs, but we are also doing it because we believe in the dignity of the individual.

I report these things to you not to say that we have all of the answers. We don't. We do have a belief, however, that most people believe in fair play.

I think it important that the press of America report occasionally progress which is made as well as the difficult situations which inevitably occur in northern states as well as in southern states. Now, I fully appreciate the fact that a Boy Scout leading an old lady across the street is not as big news as a young juvenile delinquent running the same old lady down with a hot rod. But, I believe you will agree with me that you can sometimes get a highly distorted picture when you report only on the hot rods.

Americans have the opportunity for showing the newly freed nations of Africa and the Middle East and of Asia how to make democracy work. I think that we have to let these people know from time to time that while we have not achieved 100 per cent of our democratic goals that we are striving constantly to achieve those principles and that we *are* making significant headway.

North Carolinians, without a whole lot of ballyhoo, have been attempting for some years to achieve the ideals of the Declaration of Independence. We believe that negotiations, carried forward in good faith on both sides, serve a more lasting purpose and build a stronger foundation for good will between peoples than demonstrations.

We believe that rights are accompanied by responsibilities, *including responsibility of restraint.* It is a truism that sometimes discretion is the better part of valor. I would suggest that in this sensitive time in which we are now passing that the Negro leadership, which has long exhibited a high degree of responsibility, as well as determination for full freedom, can assist in the great progress of all citizens through good will. The exercise of mutual respect by both white and Negro citizens does not curtail the right of either.

We now are engaged in a long and bitter struggle with the Communist ideology which respects the rights of neither a majority nor the minority, which exploits on the international scene the natural resentments of newly freed peoples. As any one of you who covers the Department of State knows, America could win a lot of arguments with the big bomb.

As a nation, we are attempting to win this cold war without blasting. We are attempting to do it at the council tables of the United Nations and through the Organization of American States. We are, in short, committed to use force only as a last resort. Sometimes we don't always get all we seek. Sometimes we

have to tolerate a great deal from other countries whose philosophy is diametrically opposed to ours. We believe this patience
is justified. I would suggest that in the domestic struggles, you
might sometimes win a war and lose the peace.

The obstacles faced by Negroes in your generation and mine
are being removed. This cannot be done by force or by legal
rights alone. Our responsibilities are far more complex and
broader than that. Jobs and full rights cannot come except
through education. Education is the number-one job in America
today, and it requires our best efforts. Educational institutions,
no matter how good, cannot have full effect on the children of
slums and poverty. Our best efforts are required to remove these
blights.

North Carolina has based its hopes for the future, all of its
hopes, on a rapidly expanding and enriched system of schools and
colleges. We expect our educational opportunities to be the best
in the nation. This is the path to all of our goals for all races.
The education of our children is the best way to achieve their
rights and opportunities.

With you tonight, I salute the Vice-President of the United
States of America, a man of good will, a man of good faith, a
man of restraint, courage and understanding, a man of compassion
for the hopes of others.

I pledge my state to good will, good faith, restraint, courage,
understanding, and compassion.

1963 COMMENCEMENT EXERCISES
UNIVERSITY OF NORTH CAROLINA

CHAPEL HILL

June 3, 1963

Governor O. Max Gardner felt that his greatest contribution
to the state was the consolidation of the University of North
Carolina. Governor Sanford agreed that Gardner's appraisal was
correct, pointing out that the university had carried out its
primary purpose of educating men and women and thereby giving
them better and fuller lives. He said that the Chapel Hill university had been giving such advantages since 1795, the branch
in Raleigh since 1887, and the Greensboro institution since
1891. The demands and needs of 1963 required re-evaluation,
and Sanford referred to the study by the Commission on Education Beyond the High School, the trustees, and the General

Assembly. He said that a diploma from any branch of the University of North Carolina was a certificate of achievement and also a debt to the faculty, administration, and trustees of the university; to parents; and to all 4,600,000 citizens of North Carolina.

GOVERNOR'S SCHOOL OF NORTH CAROLINA

Winston-Salem

June 10, 1963

[The goal of offering each student the opportunity to develop his individual potential to the fullest was well known to educators and to the Sanford administration. With such a purpose in mind, the Governor's School, for gifted children, opened for its first eight-week session in the summer of 1963. In March, 1962, the Commission to Study the Public School Education of Exceptionally Talented Children had submitted its final report to the Governor. One of its seven recommendations was a summer program on a local or regional basis. With a grant from the Carnegie Foundation and other private sources, the school was authorized for three years with the expectation that it would be continued thereafter with state funds. The Governor addressed the 400 high school students at the opening on the Salem College campus in Winston-Salem on June 10, 1963. No credits or grades were given to these outstanding young people, the sole purpose of the school being to "stretch" the minds and abilities of those in attendance.]

I came here tonight to have supper with you and to say hello. It seemed to me that a school named the Governor's School ought to have a governor somewhere about.

Also I wanted to be sure that you students can still get your hats on. A friend warned me last week that your selection might have given you the big head.

I suspect it hasn't and hope it hasn't, and I am confident that by the time this faculty has finished with you, you'll all be as humble as can be.

Actually there are many other students who might be here, who weren't nominated or who in the judging didn't show up as well for one reason or another on a certain day. It's not our claim that we have the top 400 rising sophomore and junior high school students of the state; we do claim to have 400 *of* the top students, and each one has won fairly his right to be here.

Such a school as this has never been held, either here in North Carolina or anywhere else, and I believe you will learn a lot from being here, and from meeting with this excellent faculty and with each other. Gifted students doubtless learn not only from important ideas and gifted teachers but from working with other students of like ability and interests. It is democratic and fair to give them a chance to do so, to give every person we can the chance to develop fully his natural talents.

In preparing for this talk, I have tried to focus on the generation you students represent. You were born just after World War II, so you didn't know about the war firsthand. You have lived all your lives in the time of the cold war. This has been a dangerous period, too, and no doubt the tension has taken a toll on you, whether you realize it or not. If we could hook you 400 students up to a testing apparatus—and I'm just as glad we cannot—we might find that you are jittery by force of habit. You have been waiting for catastrophe all your lives. And here you are tonight, and it hasn't struck yet. The dangers still exist, however.

You have also lived in a period of social unrest. We are this summer in a peak phase of that unrest, and this state is certainly in the middle of things.

You live in a time which is unsettled in other ways. For example, when I was a boy the average American traveled in vehicles of some sort 350 miles to get here to school. You very likely travel many times that far in a year. The average salesman travels ninety or a hundred times that far a year. I don't know what the average governor travels, but it's a long way. And this is the different sort of world you are living in, and the only kind of world you have ever known.

By such statistics we see that we are going faster, we are going farther, we are moving more often. I believe we are more venturesome, too. This is the age of investigation. We are taking our chances and making discoveries.

The same exploratory spirit characterizes the arts, the sciences, and most of the other forms of work and learning. We are told that during the past twenty years, man's total knowledge has doubled. That is an astounding increase. Almost within the span of your lifetime we have doubled the findings of all previous generations. And the process continues. Not only that, but it accelerates, and today it is impossible for anybody to have as large a per cent of man's total knowledge as a brilliant scholar of a few decades back might have mastered.

We might add that this increase in knowledge is changing the balance among the disciplines, so that today many thoughtful people are concerned about the shift toward a technically-oriented society. They argue that the new knowledge should not replace the old, that what man has considered basic to education down through the years should not now be replaced by the sciences. They tell us that specialization will fragment our society and might produce men and women who cannot see the forest for trees.

The argument is not entirely on one side, however. The sciences have obviously improved our way of life. Not many of us would care to go back to the medical facilities of a previous generation, or abandon the many new powerful tools which are at our disposal. Also there has always been specialization; we find specialization to an advanced degree in the old-line disciplines which now seek to limit specialization in the sciences.

Beyond the range of this important debate, which is far more complex than my representation of it here, which is one of the most important debates of our time, we have the fact that the Russians have already decided. They have put technology at the center of their planned society. We will be in competition with that society, with their technology, and we will need to do what we must to preserve our freedom. That is a very practical consideration.

As you see, technological changes are pressing upon us changes in value judgments. We are making changes in value judgments all across the board. For example, when I was a boy, if a man traveled a lot, he was considered to be unreliable. He was not worth lending money to; he was not considered a safe risk. Today many of the best men in the country are traveling around a lot, including many of the bankers.

When I was young, a person could decide he would be a doctor, a lawyer, a farmer, a teacher, or whatever. Today he often must be more specific. What sort of doctor? What sort of lawyer? What sort of farmer? What sort of teacher?

When I was young, a person might train himself or herself for a profession and have assurance that the profession would offer a lifetime of productive work. Today the professions change rapidly, and new ones appear to challenge or replace some existing ones.

Meanwhile, as we move swiftly into a different sort of world, we drag behind us some old and costly problems. In our state, 25 per cent of the adults who go to take a driver's test cannot read the questions or write down their own answers. A high percentage of our people has never been given a chance to learn a technical skill. We have in our schools a high dropout rate, twice the national average. Half the students who enter our schools in the first grade never finish high school. We have much poverty in the state. Some of you who are here come from poor families, crumbling neighborhoods. We have a considerable amount of racial animosity and tension, which is particularly apparent at this time. All these lines which divide us into educated and uneducated, trained and untrained, rich and hungry, free and not-so-free must be examined, and the lines of communication between our different groups must be opened. We must seek solutions to our problems that are realistic and fair, and which admit that all of us are citizens of one state and that we will rise or fall together.

I was brought up to believe that change is abnormal and that a state of rest was normal. We come now to see that change is normal. Since World War II, since the time when you students were born, we have come in our country to change our ideas about that significant point. Change is normal, and we have to stay on our toes to keep up with it and do an adequate job of representing our society and our own best interests today. What is in a state of rest is in a precarious position.

There opened on Broadway this season a play titled *Stop the World, I Want to Get Off*. I like that title very well, but it doesn't suggest a solution to our problems. Nor does it reflect the fact that mankind has never had a day which is more interesting than this one, which offers greater opportunities than this one. We are today on a frontier. It is not a frontier of trees and new land, but it is a frontier just the same. It is in one sense a whole series of worlds to conquer. What we need are young men and women who can train themselves to explore and develop them. We need today men and women who can go deeper than men have thus far gone into the worlds of the mind and emotions. We need men and women to take their places on the moral frontiers of our age, which are the frontiers of ages past, as well. We need men and women who can work with the hard, tough problems of poverty and ignorance. We need men and women who can go into the worlds of music and the other arts, where so often are reflected the soul and temper of man. We need men and women who can keep this country in the lead in the race for outer space and the new worlds there.

I hope that each of you 400 young people will take your place in one or more of these frontiers. For eight weeks here in this school, each of you will be able to explore one of them, and at the same time each will be exposed to great ideas which have shaped the heritage of Western Man. You 400 students compose a most unusual community and are a composite of our needs; you reflect well the hopes we have for the future of our people here in our country and state.

I mention the state so often because I want you to find your lifework here. North Carolina is not a world unto itself, and I don't present it as such; at the same time, you are going to have to select a part of the world for your home, and I recommend this, your home state, to you. We are losing many of our best young people every year, and we ought not to continue to do so. We need you right here. North Carolina has made as much progress during this century as any state in the union. We are building solidly and we are doing good work. Maybe you can help us do better. You can help take North Carolina into the lead.

Therefore, I hope this school, as it helps to prepare you for the future, will emphasize challenges which face us here in our own part of the world. We got ourselves in a hole in North Carolina back about one hundred years ago. We have been in that hole for many decades, but we are winning our way out on our own terms and with our own resources and leadership. We have made more progress in the last fifty years than any other state in the union. Now we very much need your help and that of your friends back home.

You are to be here for only eight weeks, and that's much too short at time to solve all the problems of the universe or master all the techniques of your art or learn all the knowledge of your discipline. The school has been designed so that both students and teachers can choose what interests them most, and the school can become what you make it, as you work together and work it out. Next year perhaps a different design will evolve. The curriculum and schedule ought not to be locked down. Let the school change to reflect the interests and spirit of young people; let it change as the society changes and discovers new challenges; let it be responsive to its experimental nature and be for all its many students an adventure in education.

For you, I hope this summer is a memorable and enjoyable time.

SUMMER WORKSHOP
SOUTHERN REGIONAL EDUCATION BOARD

Chapel Hill

June 12, 1963

While not a legally required meeting of the Southern Regional Education Board, the summer workshops gave opportunities to review accomplishments, evaluate programs, and consider crises. Governor Sanford observed that educational attainment was a most important factor in economic growth, that areas with the highest average level of educational achievement were the centers of industry and commerce. He said that economic growth depended on technology which depended on science which depended on education. After reviewing progress made in North Carolina by the 1961 and 1963 legislatures, the Governor called attention to the opportunities made possible thereby. Groups of responsible leaders, such as the group attending the workshop, were called on to show citizens the way to fulfill the opportunity confronting them and to move forward with courage.

NORTH CAROLINA ASSOCIATION OF BROADCASTERS

DURHAM

June 17, 1963

[As he had done two years earlier, Governor Sanford used the occasion of his appearance before the North Carolina Association of Broadcasters to review the work of the General Assembly. He praised the 1963 legislators for refusing to "heed those voices of timidity and trepidation" and for adopting "the broadest-based and most far-reaching . . . higher education (program) in the nation." He concluded with a defense of the General Assembly which had been called a "do-little legislature" by some North Carolinians.]

When the Constitutional Convention of the United States met in 1787, there were critics both inside and outside of that hall in Philadelphia who despaired of the delegates ever doing anything that would last a year—much less the 174 years that it has lasted. Since the adoption of the Constitution, there have been cries of anguish against each of the Congresses.

In the history of North Carolina, there has never been a General Assembly which did not receive at least as much criticism as it received praise.

The 1963 General Assembly of North Carolina has been held up by certain critics for sins of commission as well as sins of omission. A disproportionally large amount of public discussion of the legislative bodies of our state has been devoted to what the members of the General Assembly were doing wrong. In this respect, our General Assembly is in the company of all legislative bodies of all time.

Criticism of a legislative body is expected in a democratic state. Under our guarantees of free speech and a free press, which includes the important media of radio and television, it is not necessary that that criticism always be valid or even that that criticism always be based on valid information. A member of the General Assembly of North Carolina is very much like the baseball player who bats .300 for the season and gets booed whenever he happens to strike out.

I might add, while we are talking about baseball, the Governor of North Carolina is something like the third base coach. The big difference is that the base runner usually pays attention to the third base coach.

The truth is that the writing of laws by a free assembly is one of the most unexpeditious methods of government ever devised. But there has never been a system devised which is a better way for all the people of all sections of a state to express their needs and their hopes. And, if it is not always so efficient, it is democratic and it is the best possible way known throughout the history of governments to get the will of the people put into the effect of laws.

I would like to discuss with you a few of the positive things that this General Assembly was doing while some critics were shouting it was doing nothing.

For example, here is the state budget for the next two years. This is the law. This is money. It is a requisition for the service needed and demanded by North Carolinians.

There are several thousand pages to this budget—and a good many dollars. The General Assembly has been through each line, item by item, and has given careful attention to these needs.

It is a fiscally-bound budget for a forward-bound state. This budget provides the means for a state on the go.

There has been talk of the increasing costs of government. This criticism, of course, deliberately overlooks the fact that North Carolina ranks in the bottom five of all the states in the nation in per capita taxation, in the number of public employees, and in indebtedness. I think this is a pretty good record.

Such criticism also deliberately ignores the twin facts of an ever-growing population. For example, every time we have thirty or more children coming up to the first grade, we need another teacher, books and equipment, and all of those things that support teaching. It also overlooks the fact that the cost of books, and asphalt and concrete, and the equipment, and all of the other items which are needed to serve the citizens of North Carolina have their own increasing costs.

Now let's look and see where our taxes are going because the most important single piece of legislation is the budget.

More than half of the $1.2 billion of state funds in this budget is devoted to the number-one obligation of the state government of North Carolina: education.

At the outset of the General Assembly, there was a clear determination that we would not heed those voices of timidity and trepidation. There was determination that we would not listen to the whispers that came from the fearful who have always opposed the accomplishments on which they would have rested in February of this year. This was not, and is not, the spirit of North Carolina. This was not the spirit of the 1963 General Assembly.

This General Assembly continued hard on the course set by the 1961 General Assembly—which provided more additional support for education of your sons and daughters than any General Assembly in the history of North Carolina and more than any General Assembly in the entire nation. The 1963 General Assembly held fast to this course for education as the number-one need for North Carolina and as the number-one hope for North Carolinians.

This year, for the first time in the history of our state throughout all the years, every red cent requested by the State Board of Education was approved by the Advisory Budget Commission and by this administration and sent forward to the General Assembly for its sympathetic consideration. The overwhelming majority of the members of the 1963 General Assembly approved close to 100 per cent those requests for public schools for our boys and girls. This included more than $500 million needed to maintain the services at their current level and almost $50 million more to enrich the educational opportunities of the children of our state. This is a lot of money. But the men and women of North Carolina have a lot of children—well over one million of these children are in the public schools today.

And although the cost was not nearly so great, the need to give a helping hand to retarded children was greater. Every citizen of North Carolina should applaud the action of the General Assembly during these last few weeks—when some have suggested it should be getting out of town—in appropriating the funds necessary for these forgotten children of North Carolina and providing the fullest and most far-reaching program we have ever had.

At the other end of the scale, this General Assembly provided for the expansion of special classes for the talented children, so that they might develop these greater talents to the fullest for their own benefit and the benefit of this state, of this nation, and our world in an age of technology and science.

A major addition in education came just last week when the State Senate approved extending the educational television system to the western and eastern corners of our state. I know that many of the stations represented here today have co-operated in the past with WUNC-TV in using television as a vast network for enlightenment. Now the children of the mountain coves and of the farm towns of eastern North Carolina and of the fishing villages along the Atlantic coast will have an opportunity for the first time to receive the best of instruction available through television.

In order to train students so that they may acquire skills needed for new and diversified industry, the General Assembly inserted into this budget major advancements for vocational training and for industrial education.

There was a time in the memory of some of us when a college education or any education beyond a high school diploma was something to be gotten through the school of hard knocks. We still have our school of hard knocks. But thanks to the work of the 1963 General Assembly, the boys and girls of this state in this generation and in future generations will have a better chance to get the educational equipment they need to turn those hard knocks into knocks of opportunity.

The General Assembly did this by adopting the Higher Education Act, which ranks among the broadest-based and most far-reaching pieces of legislation on higher education in the nation. In our state, this act will take its place along side the action of the 1931 General Assembly when it consolidated the university and with the provision of the Revolutionary Constitution of North Carolina which authorized the establishment of the university.

Now, what does this Higher Education Bill do? We could profitably spend several thirty-minute programs discussing this. But briefly to summarize the act, here are the three major accomplishments:

1. It authorizes a system of comprehensive community colleges across North Carolina when, where, and as needed. These community colleges will mean that young men and young women who never would have been able to go to Chapel Hill or to Raleigh or to Boone or to Greenville for college educations will now have the opportunity for college training. It means that these young men and women will be able to live and work at home and avoid the expense, which to all too many is prohibitive, of going away to college. This community college system also will benefit all the taxpayers of North Carolina for it will relieve some of the pressure for new buildings at our established colleges. Moreover, it is obvious that these community colleges will enrich the communities where they are located.

2. It authorizes an upgrading of the three campuses of the University of North Carolina, and especially those in Raleigh and in Greensboro. Because of this act, the University of North

Carolina at Greensboro will be able to award degrees that previously it had not been able to award, and it will be able to award them to men and women alike. North Carolina State of the University of North Carolina at Raleigh will be able to offer liberal arts and other programs which were unavailable there.

3. The Higher Education Act provided also for three new senior colleges at Wilmington, Charlotte, and Asheville. It might be interesting to note that in the three hundred years of North Carolina history, this state built twelve state-supported colleges. As an indication of the increased and rapidly increasing needs, in 1963 we have authorized the building of three additional senior colleges in three of the more populous areas of our state.

Does that sound like a "do-little legislature"?

I think it is the greatest advance in higher education in the history of the state, and I know that right now North Carolina is being looked to with envy by other states across this nation.

Where else is your tax money going? Well, for one thing, this General Assembly stopped additional diversions of highway funds and routed them to the purpose for which they were collected—the building and maintenance of roads and streets. Remember that North Carolina, because we have a single system, has 10 per cent of all the state-operated highways and roads in the nation and supports this 10 per cent on only 3 per cent of the total collection of road taxes in America. Remember also that North Carolina has more paved secondary roads than the great state of Texas. It has more paved state-operated roads per capita than any state in the nation.

Naturally, we want more roads, we want more roads paved, widened, and improved, but even in 1962, with all of these desires for better roads, with all of this record of the best road system in all of America, we built more secondary roads last year than in any year since Governor Kerr Scott's road bond issue, and we increased, while doing this, interstate and primary mileage by 10 per cent over any previous record.

We intend to see that the taxes paid by motorists are used for the benefit of the motoring public. We will do this because we want all-weather school bus routes, because we want the farmer to be able to get to town and the man in town to be able to get to the farm. We also will do it because we intend to keep on building our tourist and travel industry which already is producing almost $1 billion a year in North Carolina.

At least of equal importance to building good roads is the maintaining of safe roads. Every single day of the year, I get three or more slips of paper from the Motor Vehicles Department. These slips each represent deaths on the highways and streets of North Carolina.

It would have been easy simply to file these slips and forget them, because the members of the General Assembly understand no popularity contests have ever been won in North Carolina— or in any other state for that matter—by cracking down on drivers.

This administration could not ignore the 1,300 burials we had last year in North Carolina. That is why we proposed a major traffic safety program to the General Assembly.

The majority of the members of the General Assembly agreed on the majority of the safety bills introduced. We did not get all of the nine points through. But we did get more major traffic safety legislation passed in this General Assembly than in any General Assembly within our lifetimes. As you know, those acts include a chemical test for drinking drivers, driver training and probationary licenses for young drivers who have a disproportionately large number of accidents, and the requirements that seat belts be installed in all new cars. The General Assembly also provided for additional highway patrolmen and for the establishment of a permanent Coordinating Committee on Traffic Safety.

There has been increasing concern that the utilities laws of our state strike a fair balance between the public's right for fair prices and the companies' right for a fair return. Exhaustive studies have been made of the utility laws, and legislation is now pending in the House of Representatives; and I am sure that the utilities situation will be better when the General Assembly leaves than it was when the members arrived.

The most beneficial item in the new bill is the authorization for a public advocate to argue the public's side of rate cases and other cases, and a rate expert to represent the public in rate determinations.

In this age of atomic energy and the race in space, North Carolina's General Assembly has decided that we are not going to lag behind, as unfortunately we did during the Industrial Revolution.

Among steps upward taken by the General Assembly this year was the establishment of a space center at the Research Triangle and a significant strengthening of the schools of science at state-supported institutions of higher learning.

As we worked on the slide rules of space in the General Assembly, we have not forgotten the easel, the baton, and the pen of the creative talents of North Carolinians. The 1963 General Assembly moved to preserve one of the unique attractions of North Carolina when it gave legislative sanction and monetary support of the Outer Banks Commission. The administration and the General Assembly are vitally interested in this program of conservation and preservation, not only as a scenic wonderland but also because of the hard fact that the Atlantic Ocean could well flow into the streets of our coastal towns if we allow those banks to be destroyed.

A strong measure of support was invested in our deep-water ports at Morehead City and Wilmington. This money will be repaid to the people of the state many times over by additional international commerce.

At the other end of the state, the General Assembly provided for a major new agricultural research station in the mountains. And it substantially improved the campaign for the highly important food processing industry, both at State College and throughout the state.

North Carolina long has prided itself as a state where the weak could grow strong and the strong would grow great. There are many reasons for this state to devote more attention to helping the weak. The chief method we are using is education. But many other ways and means were considered by the 1963 General Assembly.

North Carolina is the only southeastern state with a state minimum wage law. After many years of defeat, it was adopted in 1959. It was extended to cover many additional people in 1961. In this session of the General Assembly, the minimum wage was raised from 75 cents to 85 cents per hour. This was 15 cents less than this administration sought, but it was 85 cents more than some lobbyists wanted.

It is an improvement. Counting both the additional wages for the lowest bracket and the consequent increases up the line, this improvement in the minimum wage act should mean more than $10 million in increased wages for North Carolinians.

The workmen's compensation benefits were increased. As in the minimum wage, many of us hoped these benefits would be increased more than they were. But if the amount was modest, the direction of the legislation by the General Assembly was right.

In other areas of humane legislation, greater protection was provided for migrant farm laborers, a new school for the deaf was implemented at Wilson, medical aid for the aged was set up, and additional medical aid for the indigent was authorized.

The General Assembly provided new funds for hospitals, especially mental hospitals. The General Assembly also approved a new Department of Mental Health which will continue the efforts to see that North Carolina not only cares for, but cures the mentally ill.

These then are a few of the achievements of the 1963 General Assembly.

The members have been working throughout this session at great personal sacrifice, leaving their work, leaving their families, coming to Raleigh to work long hours. The members have been working without pay this last week. They will work without pay all of this week, primarily on a fair redistricting bill. I am confident that they will adopt such a bill.

They are working overtime for you who are assembled here, and for you who are listening on your radio, and for those of you who are watching on television. They are working for all of the citizens of North Carolina.

You and I may not agree with everything they have done. But then you and your neighbors would not agree with each other on everything. And you and your cousins from the other end of the state certainly would not agree on everything.

They have been working hard. They have been working conscientiously. They have been working for the benefit of the future of North Carolina. They have been working with the desire to keep North Carolina moving forward, opening up new opportunities for all of our people, for our boys and girls, for people who are looking for a better chance in life.

In a democracy any citizen can criticize his legislature and his government any time he wants to. And he should. But the members of the 1963 General Assembly cannot honestly be critized for "doing little."

This General Assembly truly has compiled a record that is fiscally sound and forward bound.

Thank you.

STATE FUTURE FARMERS OF AMERICA CONVENTION

RALEIGH

June 27, 1963

Governor Sanford first expressed appreciation for the opportunity of discussing farming with the Future Farmers. Of all the problems surrounding agriculture—migration from the country because of mechanization, problems of disease, drought, and flood—the major one facing North Carolina was distribution. State College, the State Department of Agriculture, and research stations were working together in the field of food processing. The results of processing of tobacco, cotton, and forest products showed the value of this enterprise and pointed up the need of increased attention to processing other products. Other problems, the Governor said, were also of concern to future farmers. Surpluses, for example, should be used to feed the hungry; Sanford commended the idea of the World Food Bank and called on the Future Farmers to consider feeding and clothing people all over the world. Though there were many problems in the area of farming, the Governor expressed confidence that solutions would be found.

LEGISLATIVE WORK CONFERENCE
SOUTHERN REGIONAL EDUCATION BOARD

OKLAHOMA CITY, OKLAHOMA

August 8, 1963

Governor Sanford spoke on the value of life-long education when he addressed a group of the Southern Regional Education Board. He said that changing techniques required additional training and that men to whom continuing education was available were the lucky ones. The gradual shift from farm and blue-collar work to white-collar occupations meant a labor force inadequately trained; adult education was essential. Sanford mentioned television as one solution, but he encouraged the Southern Regional Education Board to find ways to measure the need for adult education successfully. He felt that each state would have to work out its own plans, but voluntary co-operation between institutions within the framework of the state system of higher education would have to be encouraged. He stressed the necessity of training with permanence rather than training with built-in obsolescence. The Governor, in his final remarks to the group, asked that citizens be offered "a lifetime of learning as the birthright for every man, to the end that he be an even more productive and effective member of society."

CONVENTION OF
ASSOCIATED MASTER BARBERS OF NORTH CAROLINA

DURHAM

September 2, 1963

[It is obvious to anyone reading this speech that Governor Sanford thoroughly enjoyed the occasion. The barbers, too, undoubtedly enjoyed the remarks of the Governor when he talked about "crew cuts, duck-tails, Elvis Presley sideburns," and about other down-to-earth aspects of barbering. As he often did, he devoted his remarks on the serious side to the subject of education, ending with the comment that to stop or to slow the "forward movement in education now would be as senseless as a barber putting down his clippers after he had trimmed just one side of a customer's head."]

I am happy for this chance to speak to the Master Barbers of North Carolina. I mean that. I have been listening to you for forty years and now you've given me a chance to say something back.

The cost of haircuts has gone up over the years since I first started getting them. But this is understandable.

In what other profession is a man required to be a master in his own work and also be able to predict with more accuracy than the U.S. Weather Bureau whether the weather will be good for golfing over the week end—tell the best kind of bait to use on the fishing trip—recite the Dow-Jones averages for the day—recall what Mickey Mantle batted in 1956 and in which round Joe Louis dropped Tony Galento—assess the megaton capabilities of the Russians—guide the salesman on the best route to the coast and the best place to stay and what to see once he gets there.

Who besides the barber is expected to do his primary duty and, as a fringe benefit for his customer, advise the college boy on how to make up with his girl friend, and the married man on the best store at which to buy an anniversary present. Who else carries an encyclopedia of information on matters so diverse as the current figures on the Gross National Product, tobacco prices on the Eastern Belt, and Jayne Mansfield?

But as heavy as the requirements of learning for master barbers are today, they are not as great as they once were. You know in olden days, barbers not only gave haircuts and shaves, but they also pulled teeth and did certain surgical work.

Your profession has a long and useful and honorable history. The strength of barbering is shown by the fact that you have survived crew cuts, duck-tails, Elvis Presley sideburns, electric razors and do-it-yourself barber kits, Steve Canyon streaks and peroxides, that "greasy kid stuff," and Yul Brynner.

Your profession has made great progress over the years. I know it has had a great effect on my profession of law. English lawyers and those on the continent started wearing wigs centuries ago. And they wear them until this day. I suspect that the reason American lawyers don't wear wigs like their European counterparts is that American barbers do a much better job of shaping a dignified and judicial head of hair.

The art of barbering has properly been memorialized in songs—all the way from Barber Shop Quartet ditties like "Shave and a haircut, two bits. Who's the barber, Tom Mix," to Rossini's great opera, *The Barber of Seville*.

The Marshall Plan and the Truman Doctrine and the Korean Conflict may have contained creeping communism, but it took the Master Barbers of North Carolina and other states to contain creeping dandruff.

I'm sure you enjoyed the poem by Dennis the Menace in the comics the other day: "Clip, clip, scissors and snip; spare my ear and button your lip!" But seriously, I have always agreed with that old barber shop sign that says: "There is nothing that costs so little and improves a man's appearance so much as a haircut." Let me add, that maybe besides hitting a hole in one, there is nothing that makes a man feel so good.

I would like to discuss with you for a little while tonight something that concerns you as barbers and as citizens and, most of all, as parents. I am speaking, of course, of education.

In 1961, thanks to the courage of the overwhelming majority of the members of the General Assembly, North Carolina appropriated more new funds for the education of your sons and daughters than ever before in the history of this state. In doing so—in adopting the quality education program—these legislators gave North Carolina's public school system the greatest rate of increased support of any of the fifty states in the entire nation.

But they didn't stop there. In 1963 most of those same legislators were back. And the 1963 General Assembly adopted almost 100 per cent of the money asked by the State Board of Education to keep our children going up the ladder.

Besides the program of progress for the public schools, the 1963 General Assembly also adopted one of the broadest-based and one of the most far-reaching programs for higher education ever adopted in America.

Under this Higher Education Act, North Carolina will build three new senior colleges—at Wilmington in the East, at Charlotte in the Piedmont, and at Asheville in the Mountains. Under this act, a system of comprehensive community colleges has been authorized. These comprehensive, two-year institutions will provide the first two years of college work for those who will be going on to the university or one of the state's senior colleges. But just as important as that, these community colleges also will offer courses in vocational and technological training for the young men and women who are not seeking college degrees. These will be courses designed to prepare young men and women for jobs. The community colleges will work closely with the twenty industrial education centers which we now have across the state.

The third major step in the Higher Education Act of 1963 was the upgrading of the University of North Carolina. And when I speak of the university, I mean, of course, all three branches of the university: the university at Chapel Hill, the university at Raleigh, and the university at Greensboro.

The 1963 General Assembly also approved a pilot program for greater vocational and industrial education in the high schools of our state. In other areas, it provided funds for especially bright students, and it provided funds for those whom we call "average" students, and it provided funds to launch a program for the retarded children. These programs cost money. Your money. Your tax money. The cost of education has gone up.

And as long as North Carolina's men and women keep getting married and keep having babies, and as long as inventors keep inventing new machines that require greater skills and greater knowledge, and as long as our society keeps getting more complex with human problems, and as long as fathers and mothers want a better chance in life for their children, the cost of education is going to rise.

The cost of education has risen just as the price of food has risen—although not nearly so much; the cost of education has gone up just like the price of cars has gone up—but not nearly so much; the cost of school buildings has jumped just like the wages of carpenters and electricians and plumbers and painters have jumped; the cost of learning has risen just like the cost of cutting hair.

I believe you gentlemen here tonight who work on heads will agree that we need to keep a boy's head trimmed and combed on the outside and his brain trained and keen on the inside.

We in North Carolina have just gotten started well on our quality education program. When the 1961 General Assembly adjourned, it had made more progress for our children than any legislature in the history of our state. But the job wasn't done.

The 1963 General Assembly adopted one of the greatest higher education acts ever adopted by a General Assembly in this or any other state. But the task isn't completed. To stop or even to slow our forward movement in education now would be as senseless as a barber putting down his clippers after he had trimmed just one side of a customer's head.

NORTH CAROLINA STATE EMPLOYEES ASSOCIATION

DURHAM

September 7, 1963

The slogan, "Good Government Is a Habit in North Carolina," was true because of the day-in and day-out work of state employees, the Governor told a group of employees at their annual convention. He said that a governor's job was temporary, but the employees stayed on year after year, providing for a strong continuity and for efficiency. Many helped to make good government a habit in the state—the General Assembly members, the Council of State, department heads and supervisors—but the average state employee was the single most important individual in upholding the tradition of good government. Sanford referred to periodic complaints about the cost of government, but he said it was impossible to go back to the days when every individual built his own water line and took care of his own garbage. North Carolina citizens could find no bargain greater than that of local and state governmental services, which cost less than those in forty-eight other states. The number of employees was lower than any state in proportion to population. Government costs rose with the rise in population, though the increase was not so great as in other areas. The Governor, outlining the accomplishments of the first two years of his administration, said that "all of these services of State Government are there because the citizens . . . want them, expect them, and need them." He expressed appreciation to the employees, on behalf of their employer, for efficient and economical government.

STATE-FEDERAL CONFERENCE ON
MENTAL RETARDATION

WARRENTON, VIRGINIA

September 19, 1963

[Governor Sanford addressed a White House-sponsored conference on mental retardation which was held in Warrenton, Virginia. He outlined the recent accomplishments made in North Carolina and expressed the hope that further progress would result from interstate co-operation on the problems of prevention and cure of mental retardation. His participation in this conference was characteristic of the Governor's vigorous campaign on behalf of "forgotten children."]

Of all the inventions down through the centuries, of all the discoveries since the time of Eden, of all of the miracles of nature, there is none that approachs the magnificence, the intricacies, or the potentials of the human mind.

I am happy to join with experts of psychology, social work, medicine, and government in seeking ways to turn on lights and to open doors for those whose mental capacities have, through some quirk of heredity or environment, failed to develop fully.

It is an indictment of our society and the society of other nations that while learning to open canned foods electrically, to broadcast voices and pictures electronically, to manufacture cars with automatic gears and power steering and power brakes and without cranks, to dam the greatest of our rivers, to irrigate the most arid of our lands, to travel safely under the polar cap, to fire missiles across oceans and continents, and to reach toward the stars themselves—that while doing all these things, we have failed to find the solution to the problems of mental retardation.

But it is a significant and a happy commentary that the President and his advisers should take time from the awesome responsibilities of world peace and of the myriad problems of the domestic scene to hold this conference and to seek ways to prevent and cure mental retardation.

This is a problem that must be of concern to all Americans, and it is a problem for which all of us must bear the blame if the solutions are not found. It is not a problem solely of the federal or the state or the local government. It is a problem of humanity, and therefore, it is a problem for us all—those in government and out, those at every level of government, those in all hospitals and medical schools, those in all churches in all regions.

The size of the problem of mental retardation is shocking. In North Carolina alone we have some 140,000 persons who are classified as mentally retarded. Until very recent years, the best a person afflicted with mental retardation could hope for in my state was custodial care. And much of that was of questionable standards.

Most of us here today well remember some mentally retarded boy who was locked away, fed like a vegetable, and treated like an animal. Later on the boy might be turned loose long enough to be sent to reform school. And still later, he might be sent to prison. Fortunately, those days largely have passed, just as the days when a mentally ill person was consigned to a "snake pit" are gone.

In recent years, North Carolinians have labored hard to provide better educational facilities for the great majority of the children who might, for want of a better term, be called "average." We have invested heavily to raise the standards of excellence of the public schools of North Carolina and of the institutions of higher learning of our state. The General Assemblies of North Carolina have raised teachers' salaries by more than 25 per cent in the last three years; they have cut the size of classes; they have provided guidance counselors; they have provided for assistant superintendents; they have provided for more adequate library services; they have provided for more clerical assistants to free the teachers for the fundamental duty of teaching; and they have provided many other needs of the public schools.

The General Assembly, with the support of the people of the state, has levied new taxes to improve the educational opportunities of our boys and girls.

We also have attempted to provide more adequately for the especially gifted children. We have done this through special classes in the public schools and, with the support of the Carnegie Foundation and North Carolina businessmen, through a special summer school for the academically and the artistically gifted.

North Carolina's recent endeavors and its twentieth century commitment to education were set down at the start of this century by Governor Charles Brantley Aycock, who set the theme by proclaiming that North Carolina would seek to give every child the opportunity "to burgeon out the best that is within him."

To honor this twentieth century commitment to education, we were obligated to provide education for the blind students. And we did. We had to provide education for the deaf. And we have. We also had to provide education for the mentally retarded. And that we are trying to do. As we have built ladders for the minds of the average and gifted children to climb, we finally have remembered these forgotten children.

We knew that these North Carolinians, who cannot because of intelligence limitations, learn, earn, produce, and live to the same extent as the majority of their fellow human beings, needed ladders also. We knew that the rungs on these ladders had to be closer together and had to be fashioned in shapes and materials different from the other educational ladders which we are building. We knew that these children needed the constant, guiding hand of a teacher who had been carefully trained to develop to the fullest the retarded capabilities.

To meet the awesome problem of mental retardation, the state of North Carolina has mobilized its public agencies, and we have sought to tie together the efforts of these agencies and other groups and organizations.

Early in 1962, we established the Governor's Commission for the Mentally Retarded, composed of outstanding lay and professional leaders from across the state. This commission was charged with the obligation of making a thorough study of the problem and of coming up with recommendations on ways to meet that problem. From this study commission came the idea, enacted by the 1963 General Assembly, of a continuing Advisory Council on Mental Retardation, financed by the state.

Other agencies of government which are directly involved in working with the mentally retarded include the State Mental Health Department, which is a redefinition of our mental hospital system as established by our 1963 General Assembly; the State Department of Public Health; the public schools; and the state and local departments of welfare; the Prison, Probation, Parole, and Correction departments.

Services for the mentally retarded might be placed in eight major categories.

The first is maternal, preventive, and diagnostic services, which are largely public health in nature. The chief problem, of the entire question of mental retardation and the greatest hope for solving the problem, is prevention.

There has been gradual progress for many years in the various preventive, diagnostic, and treatment services offered by our public health department as well as private practitioners. Four part-time child development clinics staffed by pediatricians, psychologists, social workers, and nurses have been developed in recent years in widely separated areas of the state. Three comprehensive full-time clinics for the retarded have been established in the past two years. One of these is in a state residential center for the retarded and the other two are at university medical centers under public health department support. Our legislature has appropriated $354,000 to be additional full-time developmental evaluation clinics during the coming biennium. A fourth clinic at the new western residential institution will begin functioning early next year. These clinics also carry out a major teaching function for various professionals working with retardates.

Five speech and hearing centers have been developed under the auspices of our Public Health Department during the past

seven years. Crippled children's orthopedic and other diagnostic
and treatment programs continue gradual expansion. The
mentally retarded are fully eligible for these programs and form
a substantial fraction of the patients served. Public health nurses
have become increasingly interested and involved in helping and
teaching parents to care more satisfactorily for their retarded
children in their own homes. The Public Health Department also
has placed major emphasis on the development of programs for
improved care of premature infants. Evidence is growing that
more adequate prenatal care and improved care of prematurely
born infants will prevent or reduce resultant mental retardation
in many cases. Seven primary centers for premature care have
been developed. These centers have assisted development of
training programs, particularly in improved nursing care, for
other hospitals.

Along with treating the mentally retarded child, we need to
provide parents with the knowledge to care for the retarded.
Such counseling is now available to a limited extent in our
comprehensive clinics, at the residential centers and from public
welfare workers. It is our hope that the incorporation of community mental health clinics and centers under the Department
of Mental Health will greatly increase the counseling available to
parents of the retarded.

In order to provide the greatest possible training for mentally
retarded children who are above the custodial level, we have
increased the number of special classes that are operated within
the public schools. Classes for the retarded have been increased
from 150 during the school year of 1957-1958 to 553 during the
current school year. We plan to raise that number to 663 for the
school year of 1964-1965. If we can continue this rate of growth,
special education classes will be available to all of North Carolina's educable and trainable children by 1968.

Some developments in the educational sphere planned for the
immediate future are as follow: Early this summer, our legislature
appropriated $241,000 for the coming biennium to establish a
training program for public school teachers for the retarded at
the State University of North Carolina. In addition, $100,000
was appropriated to establish a scholarship program to support
these special education teachers during their training. Ninety
thousand dollars was appropriated to the State Board of Education for the employment of a curriculum specialist in mental
retardation, for the development of a curriculum library and to
provide an adequate supply of appropriate textbooks for the
retarded in our public schools.

Now we in the state administration and the members of the

North Carolina General Assembly recognize that it is in the self-interest of the average citizen and of the above-average citizen to provide education and training for retarded citizens.

We know of the 1,578 retarded persons in the United States in 1958 who completed training under the Vocational Rehabilitation Program. Before rehabilitation, their total annual earnings were $70,000. This means that each of these people was averaging $34.36 a year—just about enough to feed and to clothe and to house them for one week a year. We know that the other fifty-one weeks of the year they had to be supported by their families, their churches, and the taxpayers. After these 1,578 persons had completed the Vocational Rehabilitation Program, their earnings jumped to $2.5 million, or $1,584 per person per year.

In order to provide greater vocational opportunities, the 1963 General Assembly appropriated approximately $500,000.

At present there are three facilities for the vocational training of the mentally retarded in North Carolina: a young, small program in our largest city, Charlotte; a thriving Good Will Industries day program in Winston-Salem, which includes training and sheltered workshop facilities for a limited number of mental retardates; and a large, vocational training unit operated at our eastern institution for the retarded. The number of mentally retarded adults successfully trained by our public rehabilitation facilities and placed in productive community employment has grown from seven in 1959 to ninety-three in 1962. Our legislature appropriated a total of $222,000 for this biennium to plan and construct two additional vocational rehabilitation centers for trainable and educable retarded persons. We have made progress but, obviously, we have a long way to go.

We need "half-way houses" for the mentally retarded. We plan to set up four such centers during the coming biennium and to employ additional rehabilitation counselors for work with retarded people in the communities. We are seeking through this program to provide for vocational training nearer the homes of the mentally retarded with consequent savings to the families of the retarded, and to the state.

In addition, $230,000 was appropriated to begin operation of two vocational rehabilitation programs in local residential institutions, to create four half-way community houses, and make possible the employment of additional rehabilitation counselors for retardates in the community. When added to matching federal funds, more than $1.1 million will be utilized in this biennium for new vocational resources for North Carolina's retardates.

Ten years ago North Carolina had a single residential insti-

tution for the retarded with a budget of $1.7 million per year
and a bed capacity of 1,850. Five years ago, two additional
residential institutions were in operation. The bed capacity had
been doubled and appropriations had been tripled—to $4.5
million a year.

In the current fiscal year, our institutional appropriations have
risen to $9.4 million. Later this year, a new 600-bed residential
center for the retarded will begin receiving patients. A 100-bed
facility for blind retardates will be under construction in the near
future.

It is impossible in a brief speech to translate progress into
detailed and human terms, but we are convinced that real
progress has occurred in our residential programs. I will only
mention four areas where marked progress has occurred:

1. Preadmission and diagnostic services.
2. Recreation and vocational training programs.
3. Medical care.
4. Habilitation and physical therapy programs for the severely
   handicapped.

A sum of $390,000 was provided for the next fiscal year for
the planning and construction of an in-patient facility for the
diagnosis and short-term treatment of mentally retarded and
emotionally disturbed children at the state university medical
center in Chapel Hill. One primary purpose of this facility is
the training of medical students and residents in the diagnosis
and treatment of these conditions. A sum of $156,000 was ap-
propriated to Murdoch Center for the purpose of expanding
programs of training personnel to work more effectively with
the mentally retarded in both institutional and community programs. A substantial beginning on such liaison and educational
endeavor already has been made by our state centers.

Research is one of the overriding needs in this fight against
mental retardation. This is the area of most rapid expansion
among all of our programs for the retarded. Our developmental
evaluation clinics have important research projects under way.
New major research programs in hereditary, metabolic, and
other causes of mental retardation are under way at two of our
university medical centers and at one state residential center.

Active continuing research by university sociologists is continuing at two of our residential centers. The Psychology Department at the University of North Carolina has undertaken
responsibility for program development in psychology at the
nearby residential center at Butner. This is a unique and exciting
venture. Basic research on learning and retardation is being
carried out as part of this program.

Programs of the county departments of public welfare have a very important part to play in North Carolina's services for the mentally retarded and their families. These overlap many of the headings previously mentioned, particularly diagnostic and treatment services.

The State Department of Public Welfare played a pivotal role in co-operative committee planning for licensure and supervision of private facilities for retarded children that began two and one-half years ago.

The Welfare Department now licenses eleven private facilities with a total of 191 beds for the retarded. Many of these are for severely retarded infants and young children. There has been steady gradual progress in child welfare and other casework services in most of North Carolina's 100 counties. An important fraction of these services are to the retarded and their families.

North Carolina has pioneered in homemaker services. This program began in three counties in 1947 and has spread to twenty counties with over fifty homemakers in 1962. A number of other counties are planning to initiate this program during this biennium. Homemaker services have often enabled families with retarded children to remain together during serious illnesses of one of the parents. They have helped families with retarded members in many other ways. The need for such services far outstrips available resources but, as in other areas, progress is being made.

More than 4,300 examinations by psychologists employed by the Department of Public Welfare were carried out in North Carolina last year; 82 per cent were carried out on children. This represents a 50 per cent increase in the past five years. Approximately half of these examinations were carried out on patients suspected of mental retardation. The largest share was seen for educational planning, the next largest because of behavior problems, and a significant number for consideration of placement in a state residential center.

The last session of the North Carolina General Assembly passed sweeping revisions of our statutes dealing with the mentally retarded and passed a number of constructive new laws to initiate, expand, and improve programs. I have mentioned most of these developments. Procedures for admission to state residential facilities were greatly simplified and the requirement for commitment was removed. A unified State Department of Mental Health was created with responsibility for mental hospitals, community mental health programs, and residential centers for the retarded. The Commissioner of Mental Health was provided deputy directors over each of these three divisions.

Graphic evidence of the hopeful and positive attitude of the North Carolina General Assembly toward the mentally retarded is the statute entitled "Objects and Aims of Centers for Mentally Retarded."

The residential centers shall have the following general aims and objects:

(1) To provide facilities and programs for those who cannot be contained in the community because of medical or psychosocial reasons;

(2) provide conditions which allow those admitted full development—emotionally, physically, and intellectually;

(3) provide medical care, educational opportunities, training in social and occupational skills, and opportunities for freedom and happiness to minimize the effects of the mental handicap;

(4) maintain facilities for evaluation and diagnosis, for cooperating with other agencies in instructing the public in the care of the mentally handicapped at home, and for aftercare of discharged residents from the centers;

(5) develop a therapeutic residential program that will be coordinated with an over-all state program;

(6) disseminate knowledge concerning the causation, prevention, nature and treatment of the mentally handicapped;

(7) engage in training and research in the field of the mentally handicapped;

(8) cooperate with all agencies—federal, state, or local in the further attainment of these objects.

Recognizing that states can help one another in meeting this problem, North Carolina and other southern states joined in a "Commitment to Health" at a meeting of the Southern Regional Education Board held in conjunction with the National Governors Conference this summer. We adopted a program for interstate co-operation between the states running from Delaware to Oklahoma to Texas on the problems of mental illness and mental retardation.

That commitment assumed by the southern states promises "to push back the curtain of ignorance which cloaks the causes of these disorders . . . to give us the energy to apply this information aggressively in programs for prevention of disorders and for strengthening the health-building resources of our society."

As we know, the most retarded aspect of the problem of mental retardation is not the people who suffer from it. We who have let this problem slide because it was so awesome are the ones who are most guilty of retardation. It would be my hope that this conference would be the first of many at developing the tools, the knowledge, and the desire to overcome this problem.

SOUTHEASTERN REGIONAL CONFERENCE OF THE AMERICAN PUBLIC WELFARE ASSOCIATION

ASHEVILLE

September 25, 1963

Governor Sanford, speaking on the subject of welfare, referred to the Constitution's preamble which gave as one purpose of government the promotion of the general welfare. He said the term "general welfare" was broader than the North Carolina Department of Public Welfare, that it meant concern at all levels of government for the lives and well-being of all citizens. In its broad definition, the term could include education, rehabilitation of citizens needing such service, co-operation in the drive for industry, conservation of natural resources. The welfare departments were asked to co-ordinate various activities for people they served. Sanford continued by saying that the North Carolina Fund was a program endeavoring to break the cycle of poverty by proper training of children so that they would not become parents of poverty. The state's official toast called North Carolina a land "where the weak grow strong and the strong grow great"; Governor Sanford concluded by saying "that the strong grow greatest by helping to lift up the weak."

SOCIETY OF AMERICAN ARCHIVISTS AND AMERICAN ASSOCIATION FOR STATE AND LOCAL HISTORY

RALEIGH

October 3, 1963

Addressing a joint meeting of the Society of American Archivists and the American Association for State and Local History, Governor Sanford commented on North Carolina's contribution to the archival profession. He mentioned the Tar Heels who had served as founders and leaders of the society. After welcoming the group to Raleigh, to help observe the three hundredth anniversary of the Charter of 1663, Sanford traced briefly the development of the State Department of Archives and History from the time of its beginning in 1903 as the North Carolina Historical Commission. He paid tribute to R. D. W. Connor, a pioneer in state archival pursuits who served as the first Archivist of the United States. Sanford called the new Archives and History—State Library building "North Carolina's birthday present to her own people." He observed that North Carolinians liked to study the past and preserve the best of it without worshiping it and that North Carolina was determined to move forward. The past would serve as a chart to the future.

LEGISLATIVE WORK CONFERENCE OF NEW ENGLAND BOARD OF HIGHER EDUCATION

PORTSMOUTH, NEW HAMPSHIRE

October 8, 1963

Governor Sanford compared New England to the South in his opening remarks, saying that the rising fortune of education in the New England area could be seen in the organization of a regional Board of Higher Education. Though New England was more fortunate than the South in its abundance of educational resources, certain benefits would accrue to both areas. The Governor suggested that the South was a pioneer when it pooled its educational resources on a regional basis by bringing together governors, legislators, and educators in the establishment of the Southern Regional Education Board. The theme of this conference was "Education and Economic Development." Sanford commented on the slow recovery of the South from the Civil War as compared with the rapid reconstruction of western Europe after World War II. He speculated on changes which might have been brought about had the southerners had more of their number educated. The close ties between economics and education were obvious. Through the SREB the South expressed its major educational goals: to give full educational opportunity to all people; to build southern institutions of national renown· to promote education which would produce a fine quality of public service and citizenship. Realizing fully that the South did not meet the national quality in education, the SREB took positive steps to strengthen the position of the region. As a result, the South was doing more planning for future needs than any other area. Sanford concluded with the opinion that the outlook, for the South and for New England, was optimistic so long as there were conferences such as this one.

RALEIGH HOME BUILDERS ASSOCIATION

RALEIGH

October 9, 1963

Speaking in Raleigh, the Governor referred to the many changes which had taken place in the city during the past few years. Construction of new homes in new developments had changed the landscape in a short span of time. Sanford reminded the builders and realtors that they tried to sell a young couple a three-bedroom house, that the extra rooms were soon filled with two boys and two girls, that the children were soon grown and buying homes of their own. Thus the need for new homes continued to increase. Sanford said that the relationship between business and government was sometimes pictured as one of conflict, but that the spirit of co-operativeness prevailed as a matter of fact, and free government and free enterprise together accomplished much. At the local level, water and sewer systems, streets, zoning ordinances, fire and police protection were all beneficial. Counties provided school buildings. The state government helped provide teachers, highways, and numerous services to the people. The cost to the citizen for all of these services led to a discussion of the state's low-cost operation and its top financial rating. Though the costs in the federal government were high, the provision of armed forces, postal service, farm programs, and numerous other services made for an expanding economy. The Governor showed specifically ways in which various groups benefited builders. He mentioned the rise in the cost of government, but he added that the cost of building was also rising. Parallel with increased costs was the fact that the quality of building and the quality of services also rose. Though the government was always subject to criticism, Sanford urged that there be "constructive, not distorted" criticism. He said government was not the enemy of free enterprise; evidence of this could be seen every time a foundation was poured. The chief executive praised the builders for their help in building a better Raleigh, a better North Carolina, a better America.

TWENTIETH ANNUAL TEACHERS INSTITUTE

RALEIGH

October 10, 1963

Governor Sanford expressed pleasure at the opportunity of discussing education with the teachers of the Roman Catholic schools of North Carolina. The state had, he said, long appreciated the partnership between the state and the churches in the cause for education. Approximately 40 per cent of all North Carolina college students were enrolled in church-related colleges. The education of 13,000 children by the Catholics was equivalent to $3.5 million yearly in state funds. The Governor added that the state would continue to rely heavily on church-related schools and colleges to assist in youth education. Regardless of the number involved in education, the bulk of work continued to be with teacher and pupil. Sanford described the teacher as "the number-one leader in molding our citizens." The need for education increased in direct proportion as the day of the unskilled worker and the undereducated man waned. Teachers had the responsibility of educating boys and girls, of building a better nation and a better world. In closing Sanford summed up his personal attitude with these words:

"As a Methodist, I commend you for your devotion.

"As a public official, I thank you for the job you are doing.

"As a parent, I wish you godspeed."

MARYLAND STATE TEACHERS ASSOCIATION

Baltimore, Maryland

October 17, 1963

[This address to teachers in Maryland was a strong indictment of the failure of Americans to provide the education which was essential for children growing up in the modern world. He called on those in his audience to measure, and where lacks were found, to fill the gap. He concluded that "the success of the classroom will determine the success, and even the survival of this America of ours."]

Last week end the road to free Berlin was blockaded, and we were ready to fight if necessary in order to keep it open. In the world scheme of things it is obvious that access to Berlin is vital to the free world. But access to the highest quality of education, less obvious to many people, is far more important to the free world.

In the defense of freedom, education is the ultimate weapon. In the reach for the stars, education provides the greatest power of thrust, and in the effort to increase our gross national product, to give every person a better chance to make a better living and to enjoy a better life, education is the index of our success or of our failure.

The results of the tests you give in your classrooms are more vital to the defense of democracy than the tests of weapons at the Aberdeen Proving Grounds. And what the economy of our nation will be in 1980 will be better judged by the report cards from the public schools of America than by the Dow-Jones average from Wall Street.

For most of our lives it has been necessary for us to be concerned with the threats against our free government and against our ideals of human worth—threats both from without and within. But I would argue that the troops stationed along the 38th Parallel in Korea and those stationed along the Iron Curtain in Europe and those stationed in Viet Nam are no more important in stopping Communism than the teachers stationed in the classrooms.

And I would contend that the greatest force for subversion in this land of ours is not the extremists of the far left or the extremists of the far right. The greatest force for subversion of our democratic ideals and our human aspirations is ignorance, resulting from dropouts, from those who stayed in but got only shoddy schooling, from the failure of the schools to find a way to encourage every child to make the most of his talents.

In this year of 1963, the most pressing domestic conflict in America has been the conflict over civil rights. I would not minimize the aspirations of anyone by saying that the greatest violation of civil rights is not the denial of the ballot. Nor is it the denial of the right to eat in a restaurant nor to see a movie nor to spend the night at a hotel. The greatest infringement on civil rights is the denial of the best educational opportunities a rich nation can provide for the boys and girls of America.

White and Negro children alike have been the victims of this denial. Children in farm areas and children in towns and cities have suffered. This infringement is true not only in southern states, but it is true also in the states of New England, the Middle Atlantic, the Midwest, and the Far West.

For too long, the citizens of America have given too little support to the public schools—and this goes for the wealthy states as well as for the poor. We have hesitated in erecting new and modern schools—even as we have added second and third baths to our homes, put down patios in our backyards, installed automatic dishwashers, automatic washing machines, automatic stoves, automatic disposals, and the myriad of other appliances that accompany our new homes.

Along our streets and roads, we run into frustrating traffic jams. But the worst those traffic jams can do is to make us late to work or late to supper. The traffic jams in our overcrowded classrooms will make us, as a nation, late in history.

For too long we have felt ourselves able to afford new automobiles but have been miserly in our appropriations for new school equipment. For too long we have put teachers' salaries too low on the totem pole. As a result we have not attracted enough of the bright young men and women to the teaching profession. And in most places we have not paid them enough to hold these good teachers once they go into the classrooms. There is no excuse for such short-sighted public policy.

It is my firm belief that a nation that can afford to send ships under the polar ice, a nation that can afford to grasp for the moon and the stars themselves, and a nation that can enjoy the standard of living that we in America enjoy today can also afford to provide the educational faculties and facilities that the children of this modern age need.

There are direct correlations between the educational attainments of people and the crime rate. There is a direct correlation between the earnings of a man and the number of years he spent in school—and what he learned during those years in school. There is a direct correlation in the investment people make in education and the over-all welfare of their community, state, and nation. There certainly is a correlation between education and human tolerance. There is a direct correlation between education and the economy. What a change in our nation a significant increase in the support of education could make.

We can see the great need for education in the farm field as we watch one tractor plowing in a single day the acreage that used to require half a dozen men and six mules to do in two days. We can see the need for education in the industrial plant as great automatic machinery does the labor that used to require hundreds of workers. We can see the need for education when we drive along the new highways of our nation as we watch a single steam shovel move more dirt in one swoop than a hundred men with shovels once did.

We know that the day of the unskilled worker and the under-educated man is fast waning. At the same time, we know that the need for technically skilled and highly educated men and women is growing rapidly. We know that in Raleigh, North Carolina, and that in Baltimore, Maryland, there are men and women on the unemployment rolls; at the same time jobs for highly trained and highly educated men and women go begging.

We certainly can see the need for education in the under-developed areas of North Carolina, and I suspect you can see the need for education in some under-developed areas of Maryland. We can see the terrible need for education in the prisons of our states where you can go by cell after cell of men who drifted to crime because they did not have skills or education needed for employment. We can see all too painfully the need for education in the underprivileged homes and neighborhoods of Baltimore and Raleigh and of every other city in this nation of ours.

You have a job as a teacher to teach, and this is the fundamental part of all this business of education. But there is more. It is your job as teachers to help inspire the support of the communities and the states and the nation to education. It is your job as teachers to provide the type of instruction which will interest boys and girls enough so that they will remain in school rather than dropping out of school and missing out on their best chance in life. It is your responsibility to teach in a way that you *will* be understood rather than to teach in a way that you *may* be understood.

As a parent, I recognize the competition that you face in your important task of imparting instruction. I realize that the teacher cannot be as entertaining to teen-agers as Elvis Presley or Sandra Dee. I realize that an elementary teacher cannot easily be as amusing to youngsters as Andy Griffith. And I realize that there is no packed stadium of fans to cheer the teacher as she breaks through a wall of ignorance as there is when a football player goes through the wall of the defense for a touchdown.

But certainly your classes in science and current events can be fascinating. Surely the voyage of submarines under the polar cap can be exciting. And surely the stories like those of Calvert and Francis Scott Key can be inspiring.

What kind of education do we need to provide in this ever changing and increasingly complex society of ours? Generally, we need a greatly strengthened public school system. We need a public school system with special attention for the gifted and with special consideration for the "slow" learners. And we need a public school system designed to bring out the best from that great majority of students whom we call average.

We need teachers who will hold out their hands of understanding to the slow and who will raise high the goals for the bright. We need a school system concerned with all hopes, all needs, all abilities. We need support from the public, financial and moral, in a degree far beyond anything we have ever known.

Where is America's heart? Is it her army and navy, her industrial might, her space ships in paths to the moon? Is it her wealth, her forests and streams, her minerals in the ground? Is it her broad prairies, her rich farmlands, her great cities? Or, is it the intelligence, the energy, the creativeness of her people?

These things make up the muscle, the sinews, the bone, but the heart that continually pumps new life, keeping these things useful and active, is the classroom. The classroom determines the strength of the armed forces, the success of the space conquest, the output of the industrial establishment. The classroom determines the accumulation of the wealth, the beneficial use of the water and trees, the value of the minerals in the ground. The prairies, the farmlands, the cities would perish without the nourishment of the classroom. The classroom unleashes the human resources.

Indeed all of our hopes, all of our achievements, all of our endeavors depend on education. If we are to seek effective endeavor, we must start with effective education. If we are to seek quality in American life we must start with quality in our education. If we are to know excellence in our undertakings, it can spring only from excellence in education.

This nation must understand that the first national purpose must be education. What else should stand ahead? Nothing. For all other purposes find their fulfillment through education.

To our detriment, this nation does not understand that the first national purpose is education. In our communities we do not recognize and appreciate properly the teaching profession. We border on stinginess in our financial support. We indulge a drop-out rate of disgraceful proportion.

We disregard too many individual needs. Curriculums are standardized at mediocrity, leaving too many young people unchallenged, untrained, and unproductive. We do not seek out vigorously enough the excellent minds. We do not begin to discover all the talent.

The space gap was nothing compared with the education gap. In the space gap, we measured our achievement against our guess of the achievements of our adversary. In the education gap, we measure what we have done against what we might have done. We measure what we are against what we might have been. We measure what we are to be against what we ought to be. It is time to measure. And having measured, it is time to fill the gap. What goes on in the classroom between the teacher and the student is the criterion by which we must judge our educational system. And the success of the classroom will determine the success, and even the survival, of this America of ours.

It is time to put education first.

QUARTERLY CONFERENCE OF
THE BOARD OF CONSERVATION AND DEVELOPMENT

ASHEVILLE

October 22, 1963

Addressing the quarterly conference of the Board of Conservation and Development, the Governor discussed the food processing industry. He mentioned the Food Industries Section of the Division of Commerce and Industry and the Department of Food Science at North Carolina State as steps in the direction of encouraging food processing. He said plans were made to promote the location of branch plants by out-of-state firms and to encourage established firms to expand, initiate new food processing operations, help introduce new products and processes, and co-ordinate production programs for various commodities. New interest had been shown in utilizing basic crops for various products, and North Carolina was in the forefront in the field of food preservation. Sanford said the stage was set for North Carolina to build plants and process foods in the same way that she built textile mills to process cotton and tobacco factories to process tobacco and furniture plants to process forest products.

NORTH CAROLINA ASSOCIATION OF REALTORS

ASHEVILLE

October 24, 1963

[Approximately 500 realtors and their wives heard Governor Sanford applaud the real estate industry as "an old and honorable profession," and he used the occasion to defend the oft-criticized partnership between government and free enterprise. This address was one of some sixty business and recreational features which were crowded into the three-day convention.]

I am happy for this opportunity to meet with the realtors of North Carolina. In traveling across our state and in seeing the thousands upon thousands of new homes going up, I know that yours is one of the fastest growing businesses in North Carolina.

I was interested, and I know that you were interested, in the latest figures on building permits in North Carolina: $22.6 million of building permits—of which residential permits constituted an important portion—were issued in the thirty-six largest cities of this state in September alone. This was a gain of 3.4 per cent over the building permits issued for the same cities in the same month in 1962. And similar growth figures hold true for all the cities and towns in the state as a whole. The growth in the real estate industry is indicative of the growth of business generally in North Carolina.

We have reached an all time high in employment: More than 1,300,000 persons are now gainfully employed in nonfarm jobs in North Carolina. New and expanding industry continues to build new plants and to provide more jobs in our state. The economy of our state, judged by every major index, is continuing a solid and steady growth.

The real estate industry is a vital part of this over-all economy. As any husband who has gone through the experience knows, when you close the papers on a new home, you are not just buying a house. The wife must have new furniture, and this means more sales for the furniture manufacturers of our state. The wife also is quick to advise the husband that she must have new mattresses, new sheets, new pillowcases, and new bedspreads for the new beds, and new drapes for the new windows. This means more sales for the department stores and more sales for the textile industry of our state. The husband quickly learns that new drapes require new rugs and new rugs require new lamps and new lamps require new tables on which to set the new lamps.

Of course, if the new home owner buys one of the houses that you realtors are developing in the suburbs, the wife often prevails on the husband for a second car. This not only means additional business for the car dealer, but it also means twice as much business for the fender repairman.

The new house which you sell means more business for the hardware merchant because the husband quickly finds that the wife has a multitude of jobs requiring hammers, saws, hatchets, pliers, and a multitude of other tools for the inside, and a regular supply room of tools for the yard and the garden. Unfortunately for the husband, one of the major purchases that he has to make is a lawnmower.

So you realtors are not only a major industry yourself, but you are a generator of business for many other industries.

Yours is an old and honorable profession.

Perhaps you have heard the story of the three men who were arguing over who belonged to the oldest profession in the world. There was a realtor, an architect, and a lawyer.

The realtor argued: "Now you know in the beginning they didn't have any homes in which to live and it had to be realtors who had those homes built and who sold those homes."

But the architect said: "Well, who do you think drew the blueprint for those houses if it weren't an architect? The architect had to create a design from all of that chaos."

But the lawyer had the last word: "Well, now who do you think was responsible for all of that chaos?"

From time to time, some critics of government try to portray the relationship between business and government as one of mortal conflict. These people paint government as a dangerous enemy to the hard-working businessman. Now this sort of criticism has been going on ever since our forefathers gained independence. And that's all right. A democracy thrives on criticism. There has never been an age in our nation's history when some unhappy soul wasn't predicting the demise of our democracy because of activities of government.

In this century, critics of government repeatedly have sounded the alarm. For years they have called up the ghosts of early patriots like Thomas Jefferson as an indictment against the present government. Of course, what these critics conveniently overlook is the big government act by Mr. Jefferson at the time of the Louisiana Purchase—the biggest real estate deal ever closed in America. What these critics also forget is the fact that during the twenties we had in this country the sleepy government that they seem to admire so much. And you and I both know what happened at the end of that decade. Some of you here this afternoon will remember how sorry the real estate market was in 1930. You remember the foreclosures. You remember that there weren't many new houses started in 1930 or 1931 or 1932. None of us want to return to "good old days" like those.

Now let's look and see just how free government and free enterprise work together. I believe that as realtors, you gentlemen will be among the first to recognize the importance of the cooperative partnership between private industry and government. At the local level, municipal government provides the water and sewer systems, the streets, the zoning ordinances which protect both the home builder and the home buyer. The municipal government provides police and fire protection. County government provides such vital services as school buildings. State government helps provide the teachers for those schools and the highways that serve an ever growing population, to mention just two of the thousand or so services of state government.

What is the cost of these state and local government services to you and to the other citizens of North Carolina? North Carolina ranks next to bottom in the nation in the cost of state and local government services. The number of governmental employees is in the bottom five in the nation. Our state government credit rating on Wall Street is the highest in the nation—Triple A.

A dramatic example of what the big investment brokers think

of the way government has been conducted in North Carolina during the twentieth century was offered a few weeks ago. North Carolina sold more than $21 million in state bonds at an interest rate of 2.8 per cent. Wouldn't we build some houses if we could borrow money that cheaply!

Now what about that federal government in Washington? It is costly—although it won't be quite so much so if the Senate approves the President's tax-cut bill. By far, the largest single expense of the federal government is the armed forces. But what do you suppose would happen to real estate values if we didn't have those armed forces?

The postal service is costly. But I don't know of any realtor or home owner who wants it discontinued.

The farm programs are supported by tax funds. But I don't have to tell an audience of businessmen in North Carolina what would happen to the balance sheets of the merchants, the bankers, and the builders in the city if we let the farm economy of this state and nation go to seed like we did in the twenties.

Some critics of government approve these fundamental services. But, they hasten to add, government has started meddling in too many things that are none of its business. There were critics saying the same thing about Teddy Roosevelt's conservation programs. But aren't we glad we still have an adequate supply of timber when we start to build houses?

Similarly, critics used to say government had no business interferring with the money market. In fact, critics of big government were certain that Andrew Jackson was turning this nation into a despotism in the 1830's when he decided that the federal government rather than a private corporation should control the currency.

And on that black day in 1929, some of these proponents of sleepy government were having second thoughts about the need for government regulation of the stock market.

I don't believe anyone here today feels that housing has been socialized because of the FHA and GI home loan programs. On the contrary. Those programs have acted as a catalyst to the private housing industry, to the finance industry, and to industry generally.

But I know that you realtors recognize these facts.

The cost of government, like the cost of houses, has gone up. You have increased the quality and quantity of appliances in homes. The services of government have increased with a growing population.

The day should never come when government and government

officials are not criticized by the citizens. Judging by some of the "letters to the editor," I see no danger of such a day.

But let the criticism be constructive, not distorted. Those who attempt to portray government in this nation as an enemy of free enterprise and as an oppressor of the people are doing a disservice to free enterprise and to free government.

I know you realtors are not buying any of it. You show your contempt for those cries of creeping socialism every time you list a piece of property. Every time you sell a house, you disprove the mournful warnings that our economy is weak.

You are helping to build a better North Carolina and a better America. And I am happy to have had this opportunity of meeting with you.

DEDICATION OF SATELLITE TRACKING AND DATA ACQUISITION FACILITY

ROSMAN

October 26, 1963

The space station at Rosman "was put here because the surrounding mountains shield it from electronic interference, so we can't claim much credit for getting it," Governor Sanford told the audience present at the dedication of the facility. It represented an opportunity, however, for the citizens of western North Carolina. The station, with its sixty-five scientists and technicians, would be an asset to the community. With high standards of education and the type of communities sought by scientific industries, western North Carolina could serve the industrial Piedmont and Tennessee Valley with scientific and technical know-how. The space program brought with it great potential for whole new industries, but the Governor predicted that North Carolina would not derive maximum benefits if the state did not remain alert. He reminded the audience that the Tar Heel state wanted to be a full partner and was preparing for this goal by emphasizing quality education, by its legislative blueprint for growth of higher education, and by the creation of the North Carolina Board of Science and Technology to work toward introducing scientific knowledge into the state. Sanford expressed confidence that North Carolina could be a leader in the scientific development.

DEDICATION OF KERR SCOTT DORMITORY
EAST CAROLINA COLLEGE

GREENVILLE

November 3, 1963

Governor Sanford compared East Carolina College, which had created for itself an unchallenged role of leadership in the field of higher education, with Kerr Scott, who worked for the advancement of rural North Carolina. He discussed briefly the growth and accomplishments of the school, saying that the influence of East Carolina could not be measured in tangible terms and that the potential of the state would not be achieved in eastern North Carolina without this institution. He called Scott a leader who helped pave the way for the work done at East Carolina. Scott, a far-sighted thinker, believed that every boy and girl had a God-given dignity of individual worth. Sanford commended a study of the life and work of Kerr Scott to those who would live in the dormitory named for him. "If you plow into your studies like Kerr Scott plowed into the soil and the soul of North Carolina," Governor Sanford said in conclusion, "our state will reap a rich harvest."

STATE PRINCIPALS CONFERENCE

GREENSBORO

November 7, 1963

Governor Sanford told North Carolina principals that the state had made a beginning, "but only a beginning." He said that the citizens were more aware than ever of education and its meaning, but that they were looking to the principals for leadership. He defined principal as "chief or main, highest in rank, the principal teacher, the main teacher." After asking how those in attendance filled the role of principal, the Governor stressed the importance of creative and instructional leadership. He discussed the problem of dropouts at some length, calling attention to the necessity of adjusting the school program to fit the needs of each individual and reviewing ways in which the dropout problem could be studied. "Vision, boldness of action, and even a radical departure might be called for," and the Governor continued by suggesting that obstacles could be overcome. Knowledge being power, Sanford reminded this group of educators that their

Because of his admiration and close association with Governor W. Kerr Scott, it was fitting that the Governor present the address at the dedication of the Kerr Scott Dormitory at East Carolina College in Greenville on November 3, 1963.

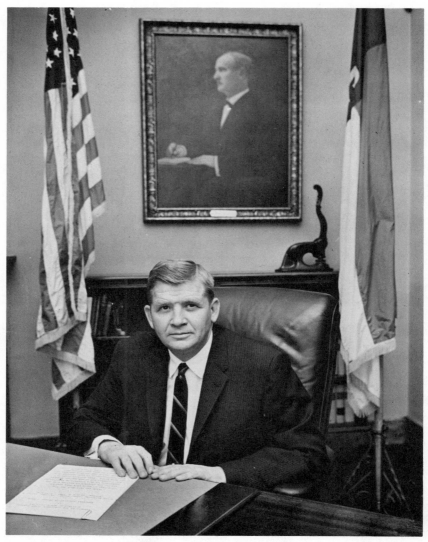

Governor Sanford followed in the footsteps of Governor Charles B. Aycock in stressing education during his administration. Governor Aycock's portrait in Sanford's office is in the background.

"knowledge of educational problems, strengths and weaknesses" empowered them to act, and he closed with an expression of confidence in the principals of North Carolina schools.

[At the conclusion of the speech, Baxter R. Ridenhour, president of the State Division of Principals, presented the Governor with a diamond-centered gold pin in the shape of North Carolina, saying that "We feel that for the past three years we've had a diamond in Raleigh."]

OHIO ASSOCIATION OF SCHOOL ADMINISTRATORS, OHIO SCHOOL BUSINESS OFFICIALS, AND THE OHIO SCHOOL BOARDS ASSOCIATION

COLUMBUS, OHIO

November 12, 1963

Sanford observed that children ask many questions, some of them hard to answer, but the real answer to the "whys" of this, that, and the other was education. Educated minds made planes fly, transmitted sound and pictures thousands of miles, and performed other wonders of everyday living. The theme for the conference, "Economic Growth through Quality Education," was appropriate, and Sanford said this theme was "not just a catchphrase . . . [but] a fact of life." He proceeded to discuss the idea that education was basic to economy as he traced the historical development of the North Carolina educational system. He stressed the contribution made by Governor Aycock, who promised every child "the equal right to burgeon out all that there is within him." He ended his sketch with a summary of 1961 and 1963 legislative accomplishments, commenting that action such as that taken in North Carolina would be supported by the people. Many industrialists, looking at prospective sites for expansion, were principally interested in the question of educational facilities and standards, realizing that there were direct correlations between education and the caliber of the worker, education and tolerance, and education and the crime rate. Sanford called for a greatly strengthened school system, one "concerned with all hopes, all needs, all abilities." The space gap was as nothing compared to the education gap, and the North Carolina Governor concluded by urging the group to put education first.

NORTH CAROLINA ASSOCIATION
FOR RETARDED CHILDREN

Raleigh

November 13, 1963

In discussing retardation, Governor Sanford said that of all the miracles and achievements of the ages, nothing approached the human mind in magnificence and potential. He expressed happiness in working with the members of the North Carolina Association for Retarded Children who were seeking to open doors for those whose minds did not fully develop. The Governor called mental retardation a problem of concern to all Americans and to all humanity. Some 140,000 mentally retarded people lived in North Carolina. The state had invested heavily in the education of the average child, the gifted child, the blind and the deaf; it was at last remembering the mentally retarded. Early in 1962 the Governor's Commission for the Mentally Retarded, made up of outstanding leaders in the field, was established. The idea of a continuing Advisory Council on Mental Retardation evolved. As a result the 1963 General Assembly provided new support for mentally retarded citizens, including appropriations for training of teachers and other personnel in this field. Though the state was appropriating almost twice the amount spent four years earlier, the Governor said North Carolina would have "done enough only when we discover the cause, provide the care, and offer a cure for the mentally retarded."

HARVARD UNIVERSITY

Cambridge, Massachusetts

November 15, 1963

[The fact that Governor Sanford was invited to lecture at Harvard University was testimony to his leadership in the field of education. The Alfred Dexter Simpson Lecture, sponsored jointly by the Harvard Graduate School of Education and the New England School Development Council, was established in 1961, to provide "an opportunity to explore the implications of policy decisions relating to education as well as the effect of education on national and international developments." This address, with the ensuing discussion period questions and answers, was published in pamphlet form by the New England School Development Council.]

Although I never had the pleasure of knowing Professor Alfred

Dexter Simpson,[109] I am honored to speak here tonight under the aegis of your remembrance of him. His investment in his Harvard classroom pays dividends to the children of today. His founding of the New England School Development Council demonstrates his conviction that our schools will never achieve their fullest potentialities unless educators and laymen, public officials and private citizens, combine their energy and share their understanding, and work together for improvement which now becomes both more difficult and more urgent each year. I flatter myself in feeling a kinship with him because of his faith in the worth of regional efforts to improve the region and to give example to the rest of the country. Although I had no part in founding the Southern Regional Education Board, I have served for two years as its chairman, and this participation has brought home to me clearly the new strength to be found in such regional enterprises.

I am here this evening, however, under two impressive auspices. At Harvard for the first time, I come with a sense of great respect. I remember reading of another North Carolinian, the young Tom Wolfe, who was counseled by Harvard graduate and University of North Carolina Philosophy Professor Horace Williams to go to Harvard for additional study. Wolfe, on the mere mention of the name of Harvard, tells us that to him—Wolfe the autobiographical narrator—it was "not the name of the university—it was rich magic, wealth, elegance, joy, proud loneliness, rich books and golden browsing; it was an enchanted name like Cairo and Damascus." And he felt somehow that it gave a reason, a goal of profit, to his wild ecstasy.

It is perhaps difficult for you here in Cambridge to comprehend the full meaning which the word "Harvard" has for people all over the world. Founded within two decades of the landing of the Mayflower, Harvard was the first-born child of the American pioneers. John Adams has written of them:

The Puritans transmitted to their posterity . . . a hereditary ardor for liberty and thirst for knowledge . . . [whose] civic and religious principles . . . conspired to prompt them to use every measure and take every precaution in their power to propagate and perpetuate knowledge. For this purpose they laid very early the foundations of colleges and . . . made an early provision by law that every town consisting of so many families should be always furnished with a grammar school. They made it a crime for such a town to be destitute of a grammar schoolmaster for a few months, and

---

[109]Alfred Dexter Simpson (1891-1955), author and educator from Vermont and Massachusetts; history teacher, principal; visiting lecturer on education at Harvard; Professor of Education at Harvard from 1941 until his death. *Who Was Who in America*, III, 788.

subjected it to a heavy penalty. So that the education of all ranks of people was made the care and expense of the public, in a manner that I believe has been unknown to any other people, ancient or modern.

In the same way that the influence of Harvard must have been instrumental in the enactment of the 1641 law to which Adams referred, Harvard has been from its birth a vital moving force in the nation's history. In education, Harvard means excellence, the closest approximation on this earth to the platonic idea of a community of scholars. In government and education also, Harvard means dynamic leadership, the kind of vision exemplified by Conant and Keppel and Kennedy.

The texts used nationwide are written at Harvard. The new curriculums and devices employed across the land are often devised at Harvard. Today's Horace Williamses are still trained at Harvard, and their inspiration sheds its warmth and light on many young minds all across the land.

And in these exciting and dangerous times when the mind's freedom is itself besieged, Harvard means courage in act as well as word, and by her courage she inspires determination to prevent the circumscription of liberty anywhere.

Indeed, Harvard, in so many ways, is the beacon of excellence and vision and the bulwark of liberty.

You did not, however, invite me here to tell you about yourself. Neither could you have invited me here to speak as an educator. I am not that, and perhaps I can redeem both you and me by making no such pretensions.

I do believe with John Fischer and Francis Keppel that it is time to put education first in American endeavors, and that school administrators have therein a responsibility for leadership to a degree beyond that generally acknowledged or expected.

I believe also that elected officials have a responsibility for promoting education and supporting, upholding, and encouraging school leaders to a degree beyond that generally acknowledged or expected. Thus a governor can have a part in school administration, "broadly conceived," without pretending to become an educator. In fact, he must take a part, because he is charged with the promotion of the general welfare, and directly responsible for schools or not, I am certain that nothing more greatly influences the general welfare than does education.

Sometime ago a newly-elected governor told me that he realized there was much to be done in education in America, that he wanted to get ahead of other states by strengthening his educational system. He reaffirmed this hope in his inaugural address.

Then, only recently, he asked me a question to which I have found no clear answer. "Where in the world," he wondered, "do you go to find out what needs to be done, what is important, what is urgent, what is good and what is at best harmless? How do you determine priorities; it is obvious we couldn't do everything needed all at once even if we had all the money on earth."

He told me his story of budget requests, from his state chief school administrator for help in teacher pay, free books, equipment supplements, and general support; from county officials wanting state bonds for school construction; from various boards and groups for industrial training, schools for the blind, for retarded children, for educational television, for adult education, for retraining and rehabilitation, for community colleges, for the university itself; and, from someone, for something, for money, everywhere he turned.

"You get the impression," he concluded, "that money will solve all of our problems in education, when indeed it will not. At best it is only the instrument, and the question of how to use this instrument, how to invest wisely the limited amounts we can obtain, what plan, program, and priorities to follow with what money we have, this question lingers on."

The delay and confusion experienced by this governor in being able to find the problem, the central need, the urgent first steps are disappointing because his state has long needed a governor with such dedication. The broader implications are that no state has clearly defined its goals, its purposes, it steps for advancement in education—total education. The truth of the matter is that education and its priorities are complex in a complex world and that it is not simple to find clear answers.

This complexity doesn't justify a failure to try, and indeed compels trying as hard as we can.

Education is going to be tremendously expensive over the next twenty years. This is not because "the cost of everything is going up," but rather because we are now engaged in a process which is drastically different. In the first place everybody will require an education, and that education must be beyond that previously considered adequate in variety, extent, and quality. We cannot afford duplication because we have hardly enough money available to do the essential. We cannot afford the continuance of gaps or countenance long delays in bridging them, because our society depends for its success on the leadership of its educated members. Neither can we afford the many soft spots, the neglect, the failure to draw a large population into the community of the educated.

Just as you have experienced severe drought in New England, so have we. Three weeks ago there came to my office a man who lives about three counties in from our coastline. This was the time when Hurricane Ginny was trying to decide if it wanted to attack North Carolina's coast or go on out to sea. I recounted the steps of preparation we had taken: the readiness of the highway patrol, civil defense, the Highway Commission, the Red Cross, and people alerted and buildings battened down. At that point, I commented, there was nothing left to do but to say a little prayer.

My visitor looked up sharply, as if I had offended him by referring so piously to prayer. "Did you really pray?" he asked.

"I did," I said.

"Well I want you to know I don't appreciate it," he said, "My crops needed the rain."

I told this gentleman not to blame me for his problem, that I really had very little influence up there.

Let me say first that we need a good siege of rain in American education. We might even get a small hurricane in American education if we don't begin to pray and seek our own souls, because I believe that there are few other endeavors which are no more than 50 per cent effective in which the people involved are so complacent about themselves.

Let us suppose a situation during the Battle of the Bulge of World War II in Belgium. The enemy had gained many advantages by surprise and maneuver. The weather was deplorable and the whole battle situation was tense and crucial. If the Germans could maintain the force and press of their surprise attack, they were on the way to at least a negotiated peace. The allied troops could see in defeat frustration, delay, and a tremendous disadvantage of position in spite of overwhelming superiority and earlier gain.

All in all, on a miniature scale, it was a prelude to the confusion and frustration, the surprise maneuver of the enemy, the crucial importance of every move, which we find in the world today.

Now if you had been with a particular battalion during that battle, you might well have seen orders come down to attack and take a wooded hill which, by the very nature of the flow and fluidity of the battle situation, could have been crucial to the holding of the battle lines and the repelling of the Germans.

There weren't many battle-worthy units capable of full effort immediately available, so this battalion was, in strength and experience, in a position of leadership at the moment, even if in a small way in the total sweep of a war, crucial to the hopes of freedom-loving people the world over. The task was theirs. Failure could have been costly. General Eisenhower, General Bradley, General Ridgeway, the allied Army, the American people, the

British Commonwealth, the French, looked, even if unaware, to this battalion at this point and at this critical moment to hold that part of the line and stem the attack and save the battle.

Let us suppose that the battalion commander, in consultation with his staff and company commanders, and for reasons known only unto themselves, had failed to understand the seriousness, or the purpose, or the urgency of their role in the sweep of history.

Let us suppose that they had said that half of the men will be armed, half of the men will be put into action, half of the men will make the effort, half of the men will at this time and place and spot protect the free world and the over-all and broad cause of mankind. Let us suppose that they had said to the other half: "You go your own way; do what you want to do; we are not going to use you; and whether or not you have guns and ammunition and move into position is of no moment to us."

This is hard to imagine because it would not have happened and in fact did not happen. The battalion took the ground and did its part in the cause of the free world. The supposition itself is ridiculous.

As ridiculous as it is, it has its parallel in the world today. America stands in the position of holding the line against the attack and maneuver of the totalitarian world. Its place and spot in history may be relatively small in the sweeping events of the total history of mankind, but its position is crucial, and the battle can be lost, and the advantage can be dissipated, and free men can be the loser of many gains. Every day is the most important day.

For in America, where every man is needed, where every talent is essential, where every resource must be mobilized, the word is out that we are not going to use half of the troops. They will be unarmed. They will not be in the fight.

For in America today, when brain power, and only brain power, will hold the line and product the gains and establish free man in a position of dominance, half of the brain power is not being used.

It is as if we did not understand the crucial nature of our responsibility. It is as if we did not understand that the battle is dangerous and that every man is needed, and needed fully armed. America, the leader of the free world, is sending into battle not more than half. To paraphrase Abraham Lincoln, America cannot exist half educated and half ignorant.

Do we not know that it is no longer the rifle but the brain that defends the nation? Do we not know that the cause of freedom is to be fought and won by the educated mind? Do we not know that the free world looks to America and that the freedom of man demands trained and skilled people, every person available and that we cannot afford to dissipate our strength by dismissing a full one-half of the troops?

In too many of our school districts only five, or fewer, out of ten children finish high school. And of those who finish most are not qualified or ready to do anything productive, either for themselves or society. In too many schools the preparation has been solely or primarily for college, and if you believe this has been accomplished either thoroughly or successfully, ask any college instructor.

At colleges we have all too many situations described so well by a college president about three years ago who, half serious, said, "I get 'em illiterate and I graduate 'em illiterate." By no means is that comment descriptive of all of American higher education, but it does describe far too much of what passes for American education, and the statement was made by the president of a teacher's college. So the school administrator points the finger back to teacher training, with some justification in most places.

Considering these conditions, some of our more reckless colleagues want to see the small hurricane descend on American education. I am one who only prays for rain.

In any event, the storm which is hovering around will insist that we part with a few cherished notions and make certain changes.

For one thing we need to get into our heads a clear understanding of the proper relationship between people and schools: that schools exist for people, and not people for schools. For example, we must abandon the notion that genius will win out on its own, that the talented child will find his own way through the educational system. The assumption is made that it is not the duty of the school system to pay special attention to the gifted and the talented—that they might even be harmed by such attention. They might be weakened, the theory goes, because the world belongs to those who compete for their places in it.

Competition we believe in, but if we really believe in the validity of this concept, we would revert to the log cabin and the unsupervised study by firelight. The thesis simply doesn't stand up in fact as applied to the talented children, and it doesn't stand up for any group or program either. The schools cannot design a program and content themselves simply to hope that it meets every modern need and that every child will be able to make out somehow.

If it is only the accident of birth and circumstance which is responsible for genius, why is it that far more geniuses are born and reared in some places than in others? I contend instead, that it is birth and circumstance plus one other element, educational opportunity. Genius develops where the educational ground has been plowed for the talented, the crop has been nurtured, the plants have been protected, the sun has been allowed to get through to them, and the harvest is more plentiful. There are exceptions, of course, but where this kind of cultivation of genius has not taken place, we find bare, caked, eroded fields in which talent simply will not mature. There is a certain toughness to the plants that grow here, a fibrous toughness, but they are scattered and warped.

It can be observed in almost any state that there is not, to say the least, enough mental discipline in most of the schools and that there is not enough demanded of those students who are capable of exceptional and superior work. To continue to let off the student of such capabilities with the easy path of the average is to deny him fulfillment and to deny society a resource it must have.

The challenge given the gifted student should be that he make the most of the rich sustenance made available to him. The challenge to school administration is to provide the sustenance. The sooner the student knows what he can accomplish, and the more he is persuaded that he is falling short when he does not exert his full effort, the stronger will be his development, provided nourishment is available.

I do not know the answer and have no idea that there is one answer. Testing, national or regional standards, and entrance requirements all have a place in providing motivation, but these are at best artificial. There are many other ways to strike the spark.

In my state we had the advantage of reviewing from across the country a number of programs for the gifted student. Some of them work; some fit a situation and some do not; some are very good, some are not so good; and none can be considered as fixed and final.

A commission authorized when Luther Hodges was governor of North Carolina studied, reviewed, set up pilot programs, and recommended several alternative approaches. These are being adopted by local school systems, and depending on size, situation, and other factors, you will find today special groupings, special classes, advanced programs, additional assignments, and other devices to add to the challenge of those capable.

Three years ago we had 2,500 students, last year 5,000, this year 7,500, and in a few years we hope to reach an enrollment of about 50,000 in these local programs. They should be, and I hope are, subject to constant re-evaluation, because so much is yet to be learned. This has been one of the softer spots in education, and I am simply saying we must seek, as we are seeking, ways to firm it up.

This past summer, as a capstone for this program, but also for the more important purpose of seeing how students can work and accomplish when both unlimited and unpressured, the Governor's School was created. With the help of a grant from the Carnegie Foundation and other private sources, this school was authorized for three years with the expectation that it would be included in the state budget after that time if its worth is demonstrated. It is directed by the State Board of Education, and accepts 400 students without any costs to them for an eight-week period during the summer. Selection is made from two groups, the intellectually gifted and the artistically talented.

Now we are not as good as we want to be and expect to be. The Governor's School taught us many lessons, but even with its shortcomings, it was received by students, parents, teachers, and the public with unbounded enthusiasm. I expect it will be even better next summer.

I do not suggest that we have any final answers, but we have, as a matter of broad public policy, determined that the school program should give the utmost effort to challenging children of ability all the way to the limits of that ability.

We found that children whose talents are artistic are different from those whose gifts are intellectual; but both are included, and this interweaving of art and intellect made the Governor's School all the richer. We found the use of the arts stimulating to the academic pursuits of the group, creating an atmosphere of pleasure in learning and doing.

The High School of Performing Arts in New York should receive careful attention in any planning. In its basic approach this is another vocational school, but there are some lessons to be drawn for general use in teaching the talented, and teaching the average, and, perhaps, in teaching the limited. Graduates of this school, where only three hours a day are devoted to academic work, did well enough on their SAT scores to cause their school to rank third in the entire New York City school system.

Right now we are designing a state-wide school for the performing arts, which will admit artists of high school and college age. This was authorized by the last session of our General Assembly. There were some good-natured jokes about the "flute-tooters bill" and the "toe-dancing bill"; nevertheless the legislators granted the authority and voted the funds, and that progress is the best evidence of a broad and humane vision.

Let us hope that, as the hurricane hovers near us, some rain will fall on the intellectually gifted and the artistically talented and on the programs for them.

Some rain ought also to fall on our programs for the disadvantaged, the retarded child, the physically handicapped, and the environmentally and culturally handicapped.

There are so many soft spots in our school program, but I do not think we need to get too discouraged when we remember that it was a very few years ago when most school administrators paid only scant attention to the physically handicapped, and stoutly declined to assume any responsibility for our mentally retarded.

Who doesn't remember poor little Willie following his older, or younger, brothers and sisters to school, attending whatever class would tolerate him, the butt of schoolyard jokes (unless the older brother was large enough to defend him), entering a race which he could never win or even finish. That a warm-hearted and generous society could have forgotten these children for so long is disgraceful. But that is being changed, and it is indeed time for generous rains to fall on the programs and hopes for the retarded child. These children are the concern of national emphasis now, and gone or going is the public school policy which ignores their needs.

Let me quote from our own Superintendent of Public Instruction, Dr. Charles F. Carroll:

There is no better evidence of North Carolina's attitude toward the education of its youth than that revealed in its provisions for exceptional children. As all of you know, this program is relatively new. In fact, on a statewide basis it is only in its 15th year. I glory in the opportunity afforded me from time to time to relate the record of achievements. . . . From 1949 through last school year, our Special Education Program has grown from one serving 2,161 pupils to a program serving 27,484 . . . [in] Speech and Hearing Handicapped Program . . . classes for the visually handicapped . . . for the crippled . . . for the educable mentally retarded . . . for trainable mentally retarded. . . . The number of Special Education teachers increased from a total of 54 in 1949-50 to 766. . . . During the current school year, 1963-64, we estimate that nearly 35,000 children will be enrolled in Special Education classes. . . . The number of Special Education teachers employed in this service this year is approximately 924, an increase of 155 over last year. . . . [Of those] 884 are employed from State funds, while 40 teachers are locally financed.

I cite this to indicate total commitment to this responsibility. No one knows the answers here, but we are learning about causes, teaching and learning possibilities, rehabilitation, counseling for parents, and we even have some hope of finding the means of prevention. Not only must the school pick up its share of the responsibility for the education, but it must share with other agencies the total responsibility. I noted with great satisfaction our superintendent's talking just last week about "a co-ordination of efforts" and also the use of "more of the resources of a total school program for retarded students." This is "administration, broadly conceived" applied to the needs of retarded children: complete concern, complete co-operation, constant effort to improve.

There is another kind of disadvantaged child who has been suffering from educational drought for at least forty years, to my knowledge; one we have hardly been willing to recognize, much less set about helping. Recognizing his disadvantage is part of the education of school administrators and public officials as they become committed to a program of education which embraces all special needs. I have a hunch that his may be the largest single group in need of special consideration.

I remember a little girl, with golden blonde hair, in the second grade of a school in the Great Smoky Mountains of my state. She couldn't read. I noticed her particularly. Whereas most children welcome a governor much as they would a brown bear or some other unusual creature, not so this child. She simply looked at the floor, shy and silent. The teacher said she didn't fit in and didn't like school.

This was the same expression I had seen in many other places, and I thought it might tell us something. When I got back to Raleigh, I asked an assistant to look into the situation. He told me later that he had learned that while her family was well respected, neither of her parents could read or write. This little girl had entered school without ever having seen a book opened. She was unprepared to understand how in the world meaning could be got onto or off of a piece of paper.

She was now unhappy at home just as she was at school, and her parents couldn't understand this for she had once been a bright and happy child, with a sense of humor and a delightful way of singing songs.

I am not convinced that the child is the one who is responsible for her early failure. I'm not sure her family is, either, for they carry on a culture which is respected and respectable, and they would like to see this little girl fit in and "do the right thing." The fault is not the teacher's, for she had all she could do to keep track of some thirty children. It was not the principal's fault, it is said, for the school had always operated on the assumption that it had a program that children must fit into.

As I see it, the fault is this assumption. This is the main reason for all the soft spots. The school administrator cannot be content unless he has a program which can be made to fit the needs of all the students. In the mountains, as well as in other sections, and even—indeed particularly—in the gray areas of the great cities, are many children who are from a culture that is now out of date, in fact, never was up to date. These people are not verbally minded.

This little blonde girl had seen her grandfather and father carve wooden toys, hook up the horse and go out to plow, cut wood; she had seen her mother weave and make pepper relish and bake a wonderful apple pie. She was brought up in such a friendly world and couldn't understand that which was a completely different world. Why is it that the school cannot take time to find something which this little girl can do well, and thus give her the confidence to do better all the other things the school will offer? Why is it that the school can find no way to introduce her to the strange world of school? Why is it that we are not paying attention to these children who are truly disadvantaged, who will never quite comprehend school, who will fall further and further behind, eventually to become one more dropout statistic?

It is, of course, all right to say we do not have the money, and let it go at that. But I don't think money is the chief problem. I think a false sense of toughness and an inclination toward obstinacy are our chief problems in too many schools.

In North Carolina we have just received a grant of $2 million from the Ford Foundation, and we've matched it with state funds, to run experiments in some of our schools, in the first three grades, to find out how we can do a better job of teaching reading, writing, and arithmetic. There is much support for free public kindergartens to get children ready for the first grade, and I do not rule out this approach; but it seems to me that we should do a satisfactory job with six-year olds in the first grade before branching out to take on five-year olds in kindergarten. We are not getting first graders ready for the second grade, nor third graders ready for the fourth grade. With this grant we expect to try ungraded classes, teacher aides, team teaching, preschool classes, greatly reduced class sizes; also we might experiment with the use of music, art, and handicrafts, because it is not inconceivable that these things might help the child to read.

In the case of the little mountain girl, our problem is with a child who comes from what is essentially a healthy environment. We have other children in our schools all across America who come from unhealthy environments. Their problems are not going to be solved easily. If the school is going to educate them perhaps it had best go out into their neighborhoods. Getting school, welfare, and public agencies to work together is not the easiest thing in the world to do; but New Haven and Oakland, as well as other locations, are wrestling with this. In our state, we have just launched a determined, planned attack on what we call "the cycle of poverty," because we observed that these disadvantaged children of poverty were coming into our schools, finding them a strange world indeed, and ultimately slipping out to become, in turn, the parents of poverty.

To do this we have set up the North Carolina Fund with over $10 million in project money, including large grants from the Ford, Z. Smith Reynolds, and Mary Reynolds Babcock foundations. We expect to say to the superintendents of schools, to the directors of welfare, officials of public health, city and county government, social agencies, that we need to work together; let's pick out a few neighborhoods to see what we can do to stop the cycle of poverty which blights the lives of so many of these young people.

This will be a tremendous effort, but the ultimate purpose will be to show us how the schools and other agencies can work together to do the total job. We cannot operate forever on foundation grants, and in time the schools and other agencies must find their way to achieving these goals as a part of their routine functions.

Certainly on these disadvantaged children of poverty must fall some of the beneficial rains of education.

All across our country we need to carry on such experiments. We must see what will happen if we get the school out into the arena where living and decision-making are going on. No doubt some of the schools in disadvantaged neighborhoods will need to be made into community centers with employment, welfare, health, and recreational activities in them, with classes for parents as well as children. Maybe we will even get radical enough to start assigning some of our better teachers to these schools.

Certainly school people will need more often to discuss their programs with employment people. In San Francisco there is an imaginative program which we are adapting to the needs of our state. Called the Richmond Project, it involves a team-teaching method in high schools. Each of four teachers has a given class for one or more hours a day. One teacher is from math, one from physics, one from English, one from the shop. The students take up a main topic; one week it might be the diesel engine. In physics and math they study the principles; in English they write about it and learn not only new words but the reason for being able to write clearly; in shop they will build some part of the engine.

The inescapable fact is that the students respond to school. As one of them said to a representative of mine, "Mister, this is the first time school ever made any sense to me."

Many of them discover college ambitions; others plan to go on to technical schools. Their work in English and other subjects improves.

This is not cited as the only way to develop a more meaningful curriculum, but rather as an example of creativeness in providing for the total needs of the students. We expect this year to adapt this program to the needs of the students in some of our schools.

In addition to the programs for the children with all their varying needs, we also should have better programs for adults. Often a person who didn't do so well in school later in life realizes his handicap and wants another chance. Also, a man often realizes that he isn't trained for new jobs, and he needs training, or re-training. Sometimes a person wants to know more about literature, science, history, the ways of the world. With increasing leisure, with changing technologies, adult education becomes more and more a concern of a comprehensive policy of total education.

We have twenty industrial education centers across the state concerned primarily with education beyond the high school. In addition we have the blueprint and the appropriations for community colleges which will be comprehensive in approach and will offer mostly adult education along with college parallel work. Some of the industrial education centers will be merged or expanded into comprehensive community colleges. We expect to have this kind of education beyond the high school, but not necessarily requiring a high school diploma, within easy reach of every citizen of the state.

We need to improve programs for all of the people in all of these ways, and many more, and in planning priorities we cannot overlook the colleges because they in turn determine the quality of secondary education. We need special attention for the colleges used primarily by Negro students. At one time it was urged that these schools be abandoned, but that is not realistic. We need to improve them.

The other day we received a call from an official of a great university in the Midwest who wanted to know which was our best state college with a high Negro enrollment; he said his institution might want to develop some kind of co-operative program. We sent back word we would rather have his university help the worst, but if he didn't want a real problem he could take the best. Already the University of North Carolina has such a co-operative program with one of our colleges originally organized for Negro students. We would welcome such an interest by colleges and universities in New England and other parts of the country.

With all of these efforts, we need to keep our eye on the quality at the topmost level, the university. We now have three campuses: Chapel Hill, North Carolina State at Raleigh, and Greensboro. It would be a mistake to have special programs for the gifted which deprive the average child of his rights; it would be a mistake to help the poor child at the expense of the opportunities of others. It would be a drastic mistake to reduce support of the university in order to help the colleges, or to expand secondary education, or to do anything else in education. We cannot try to elevate our general condition by pulling down our leadership.

We need other efforts, and must invest money where the need is, and must direct it squarely at the need. All of these many other needs will not automatically be fullfilled just because we have an outsanding university. But we cannot meet them adequately unless we do have a university of excellence; and indeed to reach our total effort with good sense and with accuracy will require the leadership of all our universities.

I had a talk about this kind of leadership two weeks ago with the president of the University of North Carolina, the president of Duke, and the chairman of the State Board of Education. We are trying to find a way to start a center of educational research and evaluation. It is astounding that we have not done much of this in America. I note that Dean Keppel told you two years ago that the educational enterprise "is now conducted with a bare fraction of one per cent devoted to research and development." The emphasis should be on the word "bare."

In addition to a lack of total public policy, there are so many things we do not know. What about the proper teaching of reading? I sense in the public a growing frustration; but calm comparison and evaluation of the several techniques—not name-calling—is what we need. I suspect all methods have some virtue, but in any event we cannot spare the specialists a generation to resolve their differences. What about an ungraded primary school? When should we commence teaching foreign languages? How many languages? Do English teachers have too many students? Do junior high school teachers have enough preparation in subject matter they teach?

Are science laboratory specifications proper? Is television in education being developed properly? Are visual aids used properly? When and how long should we teach participation in our appreciation of the arts? Is there any merit in homogeneous grouping in academic subjects and heterogeneous grouping in nonacademic subjects? What kind of vocational training, and when?

We cannot have a total program of education without having the answer to these and hundreds of additional questions.

We need to look at everything, contemplate all, study what is studied, look at total needs, establish priorities, seek the best, develop our full capacity, and reach everybody. With this research and development we must constantly refine educational policy, making this the strong force in state progress, a policy which will use all we have available for the best development of the state.

I anticipate that such a center of research and evaluation would work with the Governor's School, with other specialized schools, with programs all over the state, with the high schools and with schools below and beyond the high school, and indeed with total education. We are also thinking about setting up what we will call the "Advancement School," where students who have fallen behind might come for concentrated study, using the best techniques, the best devices, so that they might catch up rather than quit. This would serve not only as a means of reclaiming lost students but would provide the subjects for additional research.

I have had nothing to say about the devices of teaching, but neither have I had much to say about the methods of teaching. I was tempted, I will admit, but this is not the role for a governor to play. Both of these subjects will see much improvement and refinement, and both are challenging to public and school officials. Our research center, working with the universities, could evaluate and refine and apply the best.

Neither have I said anything about the bulwark of our civilization, the average student. I have not forgotten him. Rather I have assumed that every school administrator recognizes the need for general improvement, and every school administrator is engaged in seeking such improvement. As we start special projects, and as we reach for the soft spots in the total program, we must concern ourselves with across-the-board improvement of the quality and excellence of our schools. We have these many needs, and we must not, like Hamlet, allow the conflicting alternatives to puzzle our will to act.

Obviously a total program will cost much more than we have ever spent for education. But any way you look at it this money is an investment and will be returned to us many times over. It is more than just an investment for rich dividends, it is the price of survival.

We will need a more effective partnership with the federal government. Federal efforts have developed historically in a patch-

work and overlapping fashion which is as detrimental to education generally as it is beneficial to the specific favored programs.

We cannot, however, sit around waiting for Congress to do its
part. In each state, county, city, and school district we must issue a
call to arms. Leadership will respond to such a call and the people
will respond to leadership.

It is time we put education first in America, and in a way and
manner which is total.

Why should we be content with 50 per cent effectiveness? Why
not 70 per cent? Indeed, why not 100 per cent?

I have reviewed with you a number of things, similar to
progress being made across the nation, all showing that perhaps
the rains are beginning to fall. They are falling on the poor as
well as the rich, on the Negro as well as the white, on the forgotten as well as the average. We are making progress, you are
contributing to progress, and more is ahead for all of us.

I urge you who wish to honor Professor Simpson to memorialize
him by continuing to assume and exert leadership, leadership
broadly conceived, in order that the ideal of America may be
made as real and meaningful and far-reaching as possible.

Together, in this spirit, you can work toward the time when,
as a future John Adams might point out, the education of all
ranks of people was made the care and expense of the public, in
a manner unknown to any other people ancient or modern, and
by so doing we fulfill the old dream of an older day, adapted to
our own challenges.

Then all the places of our country, as a future Tom Wolfe
might point out, will be places of rich magic.

KENTUCKY ASSOCIATION FOR MENTAL HEALTH

Louisville, Kentucky

November 19, 1963

Governor Sanford observed that sometimes people acted as if
the world had gone mad; he gave examples of speeders and of
great nations "flexing their atoms and other armaments," but he
added that meetings of those interested in mental health proved
otherwise. With half the hospital beds in America filled by people
with mental problems, the seriousness of the situation was evident.
The Governor gave statistics concerning mental illness and said
that a cure had to be found. Though support in the field of
mental health had begun, much remained to be done. Regional

effort by southern states to fight mental illness and retardation resulted in a plan called "Commitment to Health." Sanford encouraged support for this plan, a plan agreed to by Kentucky and North Carolina and other southern states. The "Commitment to Health" set forth several goals: to seek ways to prevent mental disorders from occurring and to prevent needless disabling; to work for the best care of the mentally ill and retarded; and to strengthen forces "from which we derive the capacity to live productively and tolerate the stress and strain of living." Mental health leaders were called upon to improve services; to provide essential services for diagnosis, treatment, and rehabilitation; to provide emergency psychiatric treatment on a 24-hour a day basis; and to set up a network of local mental health services. Sanford reminded the group of the necessity of changing the attitude of the public toward the mentally ill. He urged state officials to cooperate and to provide funds to meet the needs for personnel, equipment, and research. He said North Carolina was spending twice as much that biennium as had been spent in the 1959-1961 period on hospitals for the retarded and for the mentally ill, but the amount was still insufficient. "We will have done enough," Sanford concluded, "only when we have done to mental illness and mental retardation what we did long ago to small-pox, tetanus and the other dread diseases."

NATIONAL CONFERENCE ON GOVERNMENT OF THE NATIONAL MUNICIPAL LEAGUE

DETROIT, MICHIGAN

November 19, 1963

The importance of cities was stressed by Governor Sanford, who stated that "Our cities are the command posts and the communications centers of our technological society. Even the nerve ends of agriculture come together in the market place." The power to create nations was derived from cities; states were indebted to their urban ancestry. State governments too often rebuffed city leaders in requests for legislation to help meet problems; consequently, they had to turn to the federal government. The Governor called attention to legislative apportionment, which was tied in with this philosophy; he referred to blights on urban areas and on the lives of men, saying blights thwarted the spirit and soul of men. Sanford urged that visions for cities be made realities, describing the "Piedmont Crescent" in this connection and adding that states would have to assume their share of responsibility in planning growth of cities as many problems extended beyond the boundaries of a single city. Stronger cities, the Governor concluded, would mean stronger states.

ALBEMARLE AREA DEVELOPMENT ASSOCIATION

Edenton

December 13, 1963

Governor Sanford told the Albemarle Area Development Association that state government was ineffective if it had to operate alone. He proceeded to make the statement particularly applicable to the area development program, calling the association a fine example of the value of local initiative and solutions supplemented by the state's technical assistance. With travel increasing, North Carolina could become a goal of vacationers. The Coastal Historyland Trail was a notable example of the way history could be used effectively as a natural resource. Sanford commented that when people got together and decided what they wanted, the state could support them along similar lines. In other areas of mutual concern, such as the development of food processing industries, the Albemarle group had taken the lead. Sanford observed that education was important to the area, that roads and bridges were vital to the economy, and that through local leadership and appropriated money these and other projects would move ahead. He said the state was happy to work with the Albemarle area in its many development opportunities.

DEDICATION OF FIRST FLIGHT AIRPORT

Kill Devil Hills

December 17, 1963

[In a two-day celebration on the Outer Banks, the sixtieth anniversary of the air age was celebrated. The dedication of the First Flight Airport was the climax, and Governor Sanford's address was followed by a colorfully-staged air parade and display. The ribbon-cutting ceremony was unusual and memorable; Governor Sanford and former Governor Luther H. Hodges boarded a twin-engine plane, which severed the ribbon on take-off. Some 300 dignitaries attended the celebration, including several visitors from Ohio, the home state of the Wright brothers.]

On behalf of all the citizens of North Carolina, I am happy to welcome each of you to this ceremony commemorating the sixtieth anniversary of the first airplane flight.

This section of North Carolina has marked three of the historic firsts of American heritage. Just across the Roanoke Sound is the site of the first English settlement in the New World. A few miles west of here is the town of Halifax where the first declaration for independence for this nation was adopted.

So, in this small area here in northeastern North Carolina a new nation was begun, a people declared for freedom, and man began his reach for the stars.

When Orville Wright flew the first airplane flight in history here sixty years ago today, his plane rose 10 feet high and traveled 120 feet before a forced landing. The flight lasted twelve seconds. Two weeks ago we had the Faith 7 Mercury Spacecraft capsule on exhibit at the State Capitol in Raleigh. Faith 7 was in orbit thirty-four hours. It traveled 546,000 miles— circling the earth twenty-two times. It reached a height of 165 miles.

This is indicative of the advances man has made in scientific and technological fields in this century.

As one of the astronauts rose in his spacecraft from Cape Kennedy, he mentioned on his radio that he had an excellent view of the Outer Banks of North Carolina. It seems appropriate that after sixty years of flying that space-bound flyers should note this narrow strip of land where man first raised himself from the ground.

On the monument to the Wright brothers are the words, ". . . conceived by genius, achieved by dauntless resolution and unconquerable faith."

Those words, reflecting the action of the Wright brothers, and reflecting also Sir Walter Raleigh's settlement on Roanoke Island and the Halifax Resolves for "Independency," are tributes to man's determination and man's capabilities to do "impossible."

Sometimes in this day of missiles, it is easy to wish that man had never left the ground. But we know that should man cease to seek to soar, the qualities which made him dare the seas to come to this land would be gone, too.

Airplanes have been used to blitz great cities and rain death upon the people in them. But they also have been used and are being used and will be used to speed people to their loved ones, to rush food and clothing and life's blood itself to the devastated, to encourage and expedite commerce, and in hundreds of other ways to make life better.

It is an unhappy commentary on the human race that we always have made advances faster and farther in physical sciences and in technology than we have in the social sciences and the humanities.

But, it is my firm belief that if man can raise a plane in the air, he also can raise the opportunities for all the children born in this land of ours, and in every land.

If we can fly a plane fast enough to break the natural boundaries of the sound barrier, surely we can break the boundaries of the cycle of poverty.

If we can develop fuel that raises tons of metal into the air, surely we can distribute food to feed the hungry.

If we can invent systems to land planes by instruments, certainly we can overcome physical and mental diseases.

If we can overcome the barriers of space itself, surely we can overcome the barriers to true peace on earth and good will toward all men.

I'll admit these problems of human relations are more difficult.

It used to be said that it would be as easy to go to the moon as it would be to relieve suffering and poverty or to teach people how to live with one another peacefully. But we are well on the way to the moon. It is just possible that the ratification of the nuclear test agreement means that we are on the way toward abolishing war.

The Wright brothers taught us much more than the fundamentals of aerodynamics. They taught the lesson that all things are possible.

If we are willing to dedicate to the problems that still stalk the earth as much attention and effort as we are now putting in the drive to conquer space, then we will begin to overcome the problems of ignorance, illness, poverty, bigotry, and oppression.

It would seem to me that in the dedication of this First Flight Airport, we should dedicate ourselves to the goal of using the genius of man, the dauntless resolution of man, and the unconquerable faith of man to send the hopes of man soaring just as the Wright brothers sent a plane soaring.

DEDICATION OF W. W. HOLDING INDUSTRIAL EDUCATION CENTER

RALEIGH

January 8, 1964

Speaking at the dedication of the W. W. Holding Industrial Education Center, the Governor reiterated that "brain power has replaced back power," and that North Carolinians were willing to make sacrifices for educational opportunities. After mentioning a number of programs in the field of education, the Governor said that unemployment and underemployment could be reduced only through education. The Department of Conservation and Development, the Department of Agriculture, the Board of Science and Technology, and the Research Triangle were working to produce new wealth through new jobs and new projects. All efforts would be to no avail, however, without educated minds, and industrial education centers provided the means of training craftsmen and technicians. These groups had been neglected in that training had not been provided for them with the result that jobs often went unfilled. The industrial education centers were called by the Governor "an integral part of our answer to unemployment, underemployment, and poverty. . . ." The center was dedicated "to the education of the people of Wake County and to the growth of North Carolina."

NORTH CAROLINA PRESS ASSOCIATION

Chapel Hill

January 16, 1964

The Governor reviewed with editors and reporters some of the achievements of 1963. He discussed advances in education, both in the public schools and in the area of higher education, concluding that the true payoff would come with the increased ability of children. He spoke of new industries, meaning new jobs; of new food processing programs; and of the motto "1.6 by '66," which meant farm income of at least $1.6 billion by 1966. The Governor also mentioned the highway improvements made in 1963; the decrease in prison population brought about through the co-operative efforts of the Probation, Paroles, and Prisons departments; and the boost given the mental health program through the establishment of the Department of Mental Health and new appropriations for the mentally retarded. Though state government had grown with the population, the number of state and local governmental employees, in proportion to population, was among the lowest in the nation. The credit rating of North Carolina was the highest in the nation. Governor Sanford expressed confidence in the ability of the citizens of the state to meet problems of 1964 and in the willingness of the press to help the state build on its past to achieve a richer future.

DISTINGUISHED SERVICE AWARD
AND BOSSES' NIGHT BANQUET

HICKORY

January 30, 1964

Taking as his theme the matter of economy in government, Sanford gave examples from state operations. He said that a recent survey of state agencies to determine ways to save showed that agencies had already practiced economy, that reversions each quarter saved a million dollars or so, and that waste was eliminated by use of the state-wide systems of roads and prisons and the state-supported schools. The Executive Budget Act provided controls whereby money appropriated did not have to be spent unless adequate justification existed, and the budget had always to be balanced. Sanford ended by reminding his audience that economy and efficiency were daily watchwords through North Carolina's governmental agencies.

ANNUAL WORKSHOP FOR COTTAGE COUNSELORS

SAMARCAND MANOR, EAGLE SPRINGS

February 4, 1964

Meeting with counselors at one of the state training schools, Governor Sanford commented that over 90 per cent of the young people going through the training schools had no further behavior problems. He said North Carolina was giving people who had not had advantages a better opportunity so they could have a better life. Though problems existed, and needs were great, the state had to remember that every child was important and that the 10 per cent creating further problems needed help. Sanford observed that between a fifth and a third of the people lived in conditions of poverty, and the cycle of poverty had to be broken. The opportunity existed for institutions to work with those from poor homes, to give them needed vision and spark. Children in training schools needed educational services, employment services, health services. Governor Sanford commended the leaders for the role they were playing and expressed appreciation from the state for the job being done.

INDUSTRIAL DEVELOPMENT CONFERENCE

RALEIGH

February 6, 1964

The Governor advocated adoption of the slogan, "Be Proud of North Carolina," for industrial development workers and for all North Carolina citizens. The state had a population of efficient people, an abundance of rich land, a good water supply, a temperate climate, an excellent transportation system with tracks of twenty-eight railroads and excellent airline service, and the asset of an outstanding educational system. Sanford said industrialists were interested in good schools, in good government, and in a sound fiscal system. North Carolina's soundness was demonstrated by its low per capita long-term indebtedness, its high credit rating, its reversions from appropriations. New individual and corporate citizens of North Carolina were proud of the state, and those born in the state had many reasons to share in that pride.

TARHEEL ELECTRIC MEMBERSHIP ASSOCIATION

RALEIGH

February 11, 1964

Sanford began by recalling the days without electricity and without telephones, days in which communication was difficult. He expressed thanks to the Rural Electrification Authority and organizations like the Tarheel Electric Membership Association which had worked with private companies to light the countryside. All of the state's economy had benefited as the REA and free enterprise had worked together. Governor Sanford was critical of remarks such as those made by Senator Barry Goldwater, who had charged the program with being socialistic. With nearly every political philosophy represented at this meeting, the Governor expressed doubt that there was a single socialist in the audience and said that there was need and room for both co-operatives and private utility companies. He added that he looked forward to the healthy operation of both.

ROTARY DISTRICT 769

Southern Pines

March 7, 1964

Speaking to a group of Rotarians, Governor Sanford proposed a partnership against poverty. Members of Rotary were affiliated with an organization which put "service above self." The Governor then discussed the North Carolina Fund, which was endowed by private funds to fight poverty. Only a fraction of the fifty-one proposals from sixty-six counties could be accepted, and Sanford expressed hope that the rejected programs could be implemented. He called attention to reasons for low income, including overdependence on agriculture and on one or two crops, late industrial development, and the ravages of the Civil War. The cycle of poverty had to be broken, and the responsibility lay with government at all levels and with civic leadership. The biggest instrument to change the course of poverty was education. Though the North Carolina Fund had only scratched the surface, it was hoped that it would show communities how to act to break the cycle. Local groups were being urged to initiate efforts to implement local projects, either with or without North Carolina Fund support. North Carolina had the resources, the knowledge, the people to overcome the existing situation and could set the pattern for America. Sanford said Tar Heels had "the courage and the compassion to do it."

TRAVEL COUNCIL OF NORTH CAROLINA

Raleigh

March 16, 1964

Travel and recreation were no longer for the few, Governor Sanford told the Travel Council. He stated that mechanization and automation had created time for leisure and recreation, making the tourist trade big business. He urged the group to help North Carolina attract tourists who would spend their entire vacations in the state rather than stop by overnight on their way elsewhere. Good accommodations, meals, recreation programs, and special attractions were essential, as was the preservation of the state's beauty. A resort training and research institute, which would look into new ideas and methods in the areas of food, lodging, and recreation, was being planned. Sanford

The Governor found little time for recreation, but he did take brief periods away from the office for hunting, fishing, and other outdoor sports. Here he and his son are shown water-skiing off the North Carolina coast.

Concern with tobacco problems remained with Sanford throughout his administration. The tobacco health scare created unusual worry in addition to normal
agricultural problems relating to North Carolina's number-one farm product.
Sanford is here inspecting tobacco in the field in July, 1962.

commented that travel and recreation meant money—which should be going into the pockets of North Carolinians.

TESTIMONY BY GOVERNOR SANFORD TO THE FEDERAL TRADE COMMISSION

WASHINGTON, D. C.

March 18, 1964

After the tobacco health scare, various proposals were made with regard to the labeling of cigarettes and other tobacco products. The Governor appeared before the Federal Trade Commission in Washington to give testimony on the issue. He commented that the proposed ruling would directly affect the economic welfare of North Carolina, that the controversy over tobacco and health was based on circumstantial evidence. While the health hazard should not be minimized, the fact remained that further research was needed; the evidence was indicative, but it did consist of assumption, and did not prove that moderate smoking was harmful. The Governor expressed the hope that cigarettes would not be labeled "a health hazard." He said that those who grew tobacco and manufactured tobacco products were concerned for public health and wanted safe tobacco products. Tobacco manufacturers were, in fact, the largest contributors to research being sponsored by both the Tobacco Industry Research Committee and the American Medical Association. The true problem was not cigarette smoking; rather, it was the cause and cure of cancer. The Governor mentioned North Carolina's three-member co-ordinating committee of scientific administrators who were to draw together all resources for cancer research. Sanford went on to tell the commission members that the tobacco economy in North Carolina was of great magnitude and that the government at all levels was a partner in the tobacco business through the imposition and collection of taxes. For example, tobacco contributed, in 1963, $2,030,304,000 to the federal government, a sum more than twice the total income of all tobacco farmers for their crop. The Governor continued with facts concerning the significance of tobacco to the economy of the country. He observed that the problem was many-sided, that automobiles and whisky could easily be considered potential dangers, and that excessiveness in any area was dangerous. He concluded by asking for moderation from the Federal Trade Commission, appealing for fairness.

FORTY-FOURTH ANNUAL CONVENTION
OF AMERICAN ASSOCIATION OF JUNIOR COLLEGES

BAL HARBOUR, FLORIDA

April 1, 1964

Having attended a junior college himself and having supported a comprehensive community college system in North Carolina, Governor Sanford was well qualified to speak to the American Association of Junior Colleges. In 1921 America had 207 junior colleges with some 16,000 students; in 1964 the number had grown to 694 with over 900,000 students. Junior colleges, originally patterned on the first two years of senior liberal arts colleges, had expanded their role and were constituting "a bridge in the American educational system . . . a bridge from high school to senior colleges . . . a bridge to better jobs . . . a bridge to a better living and a better life." By 1970, 42,000 more students in North Carolina would be wanting to go to college than in 1962. Of that number, 10,000 would be provided for by private institutions, but of the remaining 32,000, many would be unable to go away to college. The state would not have sufficient revenues to meet the needs for dormitory space. To insure post-high school studies to those who should continue their education, the system of comprehensive community colleges was recommended to the 1963 General Assembly. The Governor referred to the community college as "an excellent vehicle to carry education to the people at the lowest possible cost to the students, the parents, and to the taxpayers." The attempt to "diversify and decentralize . . . [the] state-supported college system" was made in hopes of overcoming the severe shortage of space in senior colleges and of providing college parallel work and vocational-technical training for many more of the state's youth than would otherwise be possible. If such plans were to succeed the support of all levels of government and of all citizens was needed. Sanford ended his address by referring to the community colleges as "the outstanding new educational development in America . . ." in this century.

NATIONAL ASSOCIATION
OF TOBACCO DISTRIBUTORS

MIAMI BEACH, FLORIDA

April 6, 1964

[In January, 1964, Governor Sanford cited statistics showing that nearly half of North Carolina's cash farm receipts came from tobacco, that Tar

Heel factories turned out 61 per cent of the nation's cigarettes, that 120,000 of the state's farm families grew tobacco, and that more than $2 billion was paid in annual federal tobacco taxes. These statements show why the state reacted with alarm to the unsettled legal allotment issue with Georgia, foreign competition, declining leaf quality, and particularly the Surgeon General's report on smoking as a health hazard. In this major policy speech, Sanford went beyond the bounds of narrow sectional interests and encompassed the physical, mental, and economic needs of all America. His insistence on reason over fear was typical of his earlier testimony before such bodies as the Federal Trade Commission in Washington. For a summary of the testimony of March 18, 1964, see page 405.]

As a governor, I am charged with many responsibilities for protecting the health of my people. I take those responsibilities seriously. I also am given many responsibilities to protect the economic health of my people, and I do not minimize these responsibilities.

Evidence has been presented that excessive smoking is injurious. We also have some evidence, far more than we need, that some people who believe smoking is harmful would take steps which would destroy tobacco farming and the tobacco industry. I believe there is a better way to protect the total health of our people.

As Governor of North Carolina, I am concerned with the physical health, interested in the economic health, and charged with promoting both. Therefore, I am compelled to examine carefully the *Report of the Advisory Committee to the Surgeon General,* and to enter conscientiously the effort to clarify the findings and to answer the questions raised, and to do it in a way which does not affect adversely either physical or economic health.

I have neither direct involvement nor financial interest in farming, manufacturing, or distributing tobacco; but I have a direct concern for all of the people involved in all of these activities. And whether we call it health or economic life, we are talking about people, and people are my immediate responsibility.

My state has more than its normal ratio of *people* vitally interested in the future of tobacco. Their interest is shared by millions of other American people, including you.

People grow tobacco—some three million of them—in twenty-one states reaching from Florida and Puerto Rico as far north as Massachusetts and as far west as Kansas and Minnesota.

People process tobacco—some 100,000 of them working in auction warehouses, handling plants, and factories.

People distribute tobacco products—you people—some 4,500 of you around this nation. And on the backbone of tobacco products, thousands of other low-cost consumer items piggy-back into the market place, providing a distribution system for hundreds of small manufacturers of non-tobacco products.

People sell tobacco products—in every town, village, and crossroads of America; in tobacco shops, groceries and supermarkets; in drug stores, restaurants, and service stations. We know there are plenty of people—small independent retailers—with nothing more than a stand in a hotel lobby who depend on tobacco sales for their livelihood.

People supply goods and services for the tobacco industry. Fertilizer and lime, cloth and twine, machinery and equipment, cellophane and aluminum foil, packages and cartons, distribution services by trucks, railroads, and airplanes. Literally millions of people are engaged in supplying thousands of needed goods and services.

All together there are some 21 million people involved to some degree in growing, manufacturing, and distributing tobacco. Most important of all—*people* use tobacco. These people are a large proportion of the adult population in this country, and they are consumers by their own free choice. It is for these millions who use and enjoy tobacco that the tobacco industry exists, in all its component parts.

The people of my state, you people here, other millions elsewhere in the tobacco business, are all committed to serving such customers as the secretary who relaxes for a few minutes with a smoke at her coffee break, the active business executive who finds his constant pace eased by his cigarette or pipe, the fisherman who just couldn't enjoy the sport without his tobacco, the contemplative scientist who sees formulas in smoke rings, the inspirational creative artist who visualizes his ideas with the aid of a puff, and the soldier in the training grounds or battlefield who at times prefers cigarettes to medals.

There is not any room for doubt that smoking brings pleasure, enjoyment, and contentment to millions of people each day. This is the best evidence that there is neither reason for our farmers to become discouraged nor any reason for your industry to panic.

I see for the tobacco industry new levels of growth and prosperity, once it is freed from the cloud of health considerations by scientific research and discovery into the basic causes of cancer and diseases of the heart and respiratory systems.

I do not in any way discredit the report to the Surgeon General; but when I am asked if it doesn't pin down the condemnation of tobacco, once and for all, my answer is, emphatically, that it does not.

But, someone may ask, doesn't the *Report of the Advisory*

Committee to the Surgeon General say smokers are harming themselves, that smoke is "dangerous to the lungs?"

And, doesn't the report say that smoke "causes inflammatory condition of the mucous membrane of the larynx, trachea, and bronchus and affects the circulatory organs of the body"?

It may surprise you, but the fact is that these quotations did not come from the *Report of the Advisory Committee to the Surgeon General*. The first one is lifted from King James' *Counterblast to Tobacco*, written 360 years ago, in 1604. The second one came from a British medical magazine, published 107 years ago, in 1857.

It is, I suppose, only small comfort that the pleasurable uses of tobacco have gone through repeated cycles of attack and condemnation of varying extremes.

Each century has had its dedicated forces, who were positive that the world's ills could be traced to tobacco and that immortality and the millenium would somehow be achieved if tobacco were abolished.

Within the past month in New York City, the cornerstone of the famous New York Times Tower was opened to disclose some newspapers put there in 1904. Here are some problems reported in the press of that day: Box office practices of Broadway theaters were being criticized—even as today; the police were hot after the Mafia organization—as they are today; bloody uprisings were being reported from Africa; New York commuters were complaining of delays on the railroads; and, sure enough, prominent on the front page of one major newspaper Ella Wheeler Wilcox, the poetess, was writing, "All statistics go to prove that the cigarette habit"—really, that is a direct quotation about statistics—they go to prove, she wrote, that cigarette smoking is injurious, "physically, mentally and morally—one or all three ways without exception."

That was sixty years ago and, along with international unrest and late trains, statistics are still with us.

My major purpose in relating some historical background is to bring into focus the fact that tobacco use spread among the peoples of the world is an enjoyable and relaxing custom in spite of the voices raised all along the way in notes of doom about its use. And it spread among the peoples of the world long before there were modern newspapers or radio commercials or television. As one student of tobacco history has observed, "Tobacco has always been its own best salesman."

The truth is that tobacco filled a need—call it psychological or social or tranquilizing or what you like. The New World's new plant filled a need and want among many millions of people for several centuries before our modern-day cigarette industry. This truth appears to be ignored by those who would try to stifle cigarette advertising as the only reason why people smoke. They simply are ignoring facts.

What has happened in the past sixty years, since Miss Wilcox wrote about her statistical link between cigarettes and the physical, mental, and moral ills of the nation?

We are bombarded today with the statistics of human troubles: social, economic, and some in the field of health. At the same time, there are more cheerful statistics, if we but pause to appreciate them.

Since the days of Miss Wilcox, the average life expectancy of the United States citizen has been extended from a little more than forty-seven years to over seventy years today—a gain of twenty-three years or about half the life span of the early 1900's. This is a fine tribute to medical science and its success in finding ways to save people in their early years who might otherwise have died with life unfulfilled.

Even more specifically, the death rates for major respiratory diseases—or diseases of the lung—have literally plummeted from about 430 per year per 100,000 of population at the turn of the century to slightly over sixty deaths per 100,000 population today. This is only 14 per cent of what it was sixty years ago. Again, this reflects the progress in our standards of living and medical care.

It is a fact, although I give it no significance, that there is a strong statistical correlation between these cheerful trends in vital statistics and statistics showing that it was in this same period that cigarettes grew in popularity to become the most predominant form of tobacco use.

In passing, let me observe that if the health trend had been in the opposite direction, with such a statistical correlation available, the blame almost certainly would have been heaped upon the cigarette! This seems to me to be a reasonable assumption because the campaigns against tobacco today are being waged primarily with statistical correlations of one kind or another.

Here is an example of how statistics are used to indict tobacco, and how difficult it is to get at the facts behind the statistics:

We know there is great headline potential in trying to link cigarette smoking with almost any phenomenon that is of human interest. In recent years, considerable attention has been given, with all manner of insinuations, to studies saying that smoking by expectant mothers results in a higher percentage of premature babies than among nonsmoking mothers. These reports were given public attention with the strong suggestion that something terrible was happening because of smoking.

What are the facts? In the first place, the word "premature" is often applied to any baby under a certain weight and doesn't really mean what most people assume. More importantly, when a thorough-going study of some 6,800 babies of both smoking and nonsmoking mothers was made, a completely different conclusion was reached.

Published earlier this year, this study found that the death rates among the underweight infants of *nonsmoking* mothers were actually higher than among those born to *smoking* mothers. The conclusion is that while smoking mothers are more likely to have the smaller or premature babies, these babies are much less likely to die at birth than similar babies of nonsmokers. *The reporting scientist noted that these relationships were not likely to be either causal or direct.*

I wonder how long it will be before this study of real babies and what happens to them will replace the legend of the statistics? The moral is that it is easier to spread a slander than to overcome its damage, even when truth and fact are the weapons of rebuttal.

I became interested in some items of an article carried by an important publication concerning the Advisory Committee's report on smoking. So I enlisted some help to have the matter looked into. Even now, I find it difficult to straighten out the misinformation as a result of the report and the dramatically staged press conference of last January 11.

I'll start by citing the gist of the statements in the article and then what we were able to find out was actually so.

Here are some of the items:

First, the press report referred to findings of "a population study of over one million men, since 1951. . . ."

The fact is, there was no such study. Several different studies were conducted. The largest population study mentioned in the report to the Surgeon General covered 448,000 men and only twenty-two months—not some thirteen years. The actual number of deaths studied was 11,600—or about 2.5 per cent of the number of men involved, and about 1 per cent of the million men which the article indicated were studied.

Also, the statement in the *Report of the Advisory Committee* that lung cancer deaths total 41,000 a year calls for some technical clarification. The Advisory Committee's report did not give the slightest recognition to the uncertainties involved in such a flat use of the 41,000 figure.

The fact is that deaths from lung cancer are recorded in two ways. In 1961, the latest year for which figures are available to me, there were 19,662 deaths recorded for primary cancer of the lung, which means the doctor said the lung was the site of origin.

In addition, there were 19,467 lung-cancer deaths recorded for which the doctor didn't say whether the disease began in the lungs or spread there from some other part of the body—which, I am told, quite frequently happens. And when the cancer originates somewhere else and spreads to the lungs, it's ridiculous to blame cigarettes. And yet these two different figures are lumped together, without explanation.

Is it any wonder that persons who enjoy the custom of cigarette smoking are dazzled by the statistics thrown at them? How can you or I quickly get the facts that can clarify a misleading statement, imperiously tossed out without qualification as to authenticity?

Here is another item reported in the publication: "Seven hydrocarbons found in cigarette smoke have been proved to be carcinogenic [cancer-causing] in laboratory animals. . . ." This, too, comes from the Advisory Committee's *Report*.

But what else does the *Report* say? It says that the "amount of known carcinogens in cigarette smoke is too small to account" for activity seen on laboratory animals.

The further fact is that this *Report* does not specify any substance in tobacco smoke that would account for causing a disease. And yet how many people realize this, among the millions of Americans to whom the *Report* was conveyed as an official finding on the smoking and health question?

Without going into detail, it is possible to tick off a number of other important points that might be made about this *Report*, to show that this particular dubious line isn't quite long enough to reach to the bottom of the puzzle of human ailments.

1. The *Report* says in at least two places that "statistical methods cannot establish proof of a causal relationship in an association." And yet, as far as I can determine, the *Report* proceeds to rely on statistics to arrive at its conclusions which condemn smoking.

2. The *Report* says that "no simple cause-and-effect relationship is likely to exist between a complex product like tobacco smoke and a specific disease in the variable human organisms." This to me says exactly what many others believe: The *Report* raised a lot of questions but it didn't find the answers.

3. The *Report* admits the existence of other factors, such as viruses, genetics, and previous lung ailments, but says the role of these can't be fully explained. Certainly, by giving only passing notice to these and by brushing aside such possible factors as air pollution, the *Report* does not give a full picture of the diseases that were studied.

4. The *Report* admits that the populations covered in the statistical studies are not representative of the U.S. male population. And it goes on to say that to apply the results of these studies to general populations involved "unverifiable judgment" —which in my language means simply opinions that can't be proved.

5. The *Report* concedes that animal experiments have failed to show any mechanism by which tobacco smoke could cause cancer or other diseases. And it admits that inhalation of tobacco smoke by experimental animals has failed to produce lung cancer, even though other substances inhaled by such animals have resulted in lung cancer.

There are other areas of the *Report* which also pose questions which tobacco's opponents find it is convenient to ignore.

Many critics of tobacco continue to cite nicotine as a suspect substance. The *Report* examined existing research and concluded that nicotine "probably does not represent a significant health problem" for smokers and other users of tobacco products.

Be sure to remember that one, the next time someone sounds off against nicotine.

I make no claim to the competence which would be necessary to attempt a scientific analysis of the *Advisory Committee Report to the Surgeon General*. It is becoming clearer every day, however, that the *Report* is by no means satisfactory to many doctors and scientists, either in its consideration of questions concerning tobacco use or in its contribution to scientific understanding of the diseases to which it addresses itself.

Writing in the *Virginia Medical Monthly*, Dr. Harry J. Warthen said: "Despite the general impression to the contrary, this *Report* falls short of proving the relationship between smoking and cancer." Incidentally, Dr. Warthen explained that he was not defending cigarettes but saying "that the *Report* bears out what physicians have known for a long time—namely, that the causes of cancer are complex and the present survey has done little to clarify the subject."

It is gratifying—and in some ways surprising—to observe that so many doctors and scientists have dared to express skepticism in public print about the *Report*, which initially was received so authoritatively.

Dr. Frank Figge, a well-known cancer research scientist at the University of Maryland, said: "I know these views are in disagreement with the statistics, but I believe individual susceptibility to cancer must be taken into account. . . . If not susceptible to lung cancer—and apparently 90 per cent of the population isn't—a person can smoke till doomsday and it won't hurt."

Author of a recognized textbook on lung cancer, Dr. Milton Rosenblatt, chief of medical clinics at New York Metropolitan Hospital, was quoted as saying: "It appears from the *Report* that the Surgeon General's Committee was greatly influenced by the statistical studies. . . . The fact is that we have no evidence that there has been an actual increase in the incidence of lung cancer during the past few decades because we have no reliable comparative data. . . . The cause of lung cancer and other cancers are still an enigma requiring much additional research."

And there are others, such as the doctor from Idaho who wrote the *Wall Street Journal* and said that by using the same statistical methods, it could be stated that tuberculosis "might have ceased to become a major cause of death due to the beneficial effects of smoking cigarettes."

Then there is the attitude expressed by Dr. Irvine Page of Cleveland, a former president of the American Heart Association who doesn't go along with the gloomy outlook that everything you like is bad for you.

"It's just that we are continuing to become aware of a large number of things that can be dangerous," says Dr. Page. "Automobiles, alcohol, smoking—and a lot of other things—can be harmful if you don't use them properly." Dr. Page recently gave some ten guide points in a report issued in February, and one guide was: "Avoid excesses in *everything* but don't miss *anything.*" From the ancient Greeks came the admonition, "Nothing in Excess." I believe that most Americans with any horse sense will recognize that in all things of life excesses should be avoided, and this applies to our speed in automobiles, to our eating, drinking and smoking habits, to our pleasures, to our exercises, and to our work.

I do not believe that those who enjoy tobacco should suffer an excess of slings and arrows at the hands of excessively dedicated regulators of our individual manners and customs. And yet this appears to be the desire of many of tobacco's critics.

One of North Carolina's most illustrious sons was the late Josephus Daniels,[110] Tar Heel editor, statesman, and cabinet member. Ambassador Daniels was no advocate of smoking, but his ire was directed chiefly at liquor because, as he put it, he never knew a man who beat his wife because he smoked.

Since the world-wide publicity given to the *Report of the Advisory Committee,* I have received letters from all parts of the

---

[110] Josephus Daniels (1862-1948), editor and publisher of the *News and Observer* in Raleigh, 1894-1948; Secretary of the Navy in Wilson's cabinet, 1913-1921; Ambassador to Mexico, 1933-1942. *Who Was Who in America,* II, 143.

world and a good many of them record that some doctors suggest cigarettes as a means of relaxation.

Whether smoking of tobacco, especially cigarettes, contributes to the health risk of smokers, or whether smokers are, in general, the type of persons who live the kind of life that increases their health risk is still a valid and unanswered question. Even the *Report of the Advisory Committee* admits there must be many constitutional and psychological elements involved in the statistical association upon which the *Report* is largely based.

Here is another area worthy of attention from competent researchers. If there is a special health risk in use of tobacco for some people, why is this so? The *Report of the Advisory Committee* does not offer any solid suggestions on the question. The *Report* fails to name a substance, or specify a mechanism, that will fully explain the decision to accept the statistical association. In fact, the committee specifically avoided any estimates of what the statistics really meant in terms of the general population.

On this point, I refer to testimony given a couple of weeks ago, before the Federal Trade Commission, by Assistant Surgeon General Hundley. He was asked if he could give some idea of what the statistics meant in terms of the general population. He replied that the Advisory Committee debated whether—in Hundley's own words—"to try to make some statistical computations and derive some sort of a figure. . . ." But, Dr. Hundley continued, it was decided not to try this because "so many assumptions had to be made that it was feared that the statistic would be as misleading as it was informative."

He then went on to say that the figures used to claim a risk among smokers "are not representative of the U.S. population as a whole and how you can translate that to the U.S. population as a whole is the difficulty."

It should be kept in mind that the committee did not do any of its own research in this area, but merely worked with previous reports based on the study of cigarette smoking in relation to various diseases.

What happens when the disease is studied, instead of cigarettes, is indicated by a recent report in Germany, where a group of distinguished physicians and pathologists studied actual lung-cancer cases over a period of many years. In their report, just issued, they determined that the evidence did not support the claim that cigarette smoking was an important factor . . . in fact, most of the lung-cancer cases were found among the groups with the least smoking.

And this report also cited another German study—sometimes overlooked by smoking critics—in which it was found that less than one-third of the lung-cancer patients under observation were cigarette smokers. What about the other two-thirds? Regardless of which percentage is valid, what about all the nonsmokers who develop lung cancer? What about the victims of cancer other than lung cancer? The fundamental question remains. What causes cancer? No report has given us the answer to that.

I suggest two constructive courses of action:

1. The continuing study of tobacco and smoke to identify or eliminate the suspected health risks.

2. The more intensive study of cancer and heart ailments— which strike smokers and nonsmokers—to see if we can crack the question of what causes these diseases. This will answer the questions about tobacco. More important, we will be in a position to find the cures for dread diseases which strike those who smoke, and those who do not.

That progress is being made in such research is encouraging. The American Heart Association just last month reported that, for the ten years of the 1950's, the cardiovascular death rates among men between forty-five and sixty-five have actually been going down. This is most welcome news, coming as it does in a period when cigarette smoking has been steadily climbing and when there have been accelerating efforts by tobacco critics to associate cigarette smoking with ailments of the heart.

Farmers and tobacco people have no desire to injure anyone's health. The desire of the tobacco industry to expand and hasten research into all phases of these health problems is well known. Individual companies carry on extensive programs of product research. The industry has supported for ten years a program of independent health research, to the extent of $7.25 million so far, through continuing support of the Council for Tobacco Research. The companies also have pledged a five-year total of $10 million to the American Medical Association's new research program on the health problems that have been associated with tobacco.

This is just one element of the tobacco-interested public that is contributing to such activities.

As I have reminded officials in Washington, there is another element of the public that is contributing public funds, more of which should be put to use in intensive research. I am speaking of the tobacco-consuming public, and its payment into the federal treasury of a sum in excise taxes which now totals well over $2.2 billion a year. And this doesn't include over $1 billion that is paid in taxes by tobacco users to states and municipalities.

Nor does it include the local taxes wholesalers pay because you are in a business that depends upon tobacco products. You bring to every community in the nation hundreds of needed items. Without you, an important river in our transportation of goods and services would be dried up completely. And without the tobacco products that are the backbone of your businesses, the flow of these other goods and services would also cease.

In the final analysis, I think all of us should give more thought to a challenging question posed by the *Report of the Advisory Committee to the Surgeon General.*

The *Report* asks, "What would satisfy the psychological needs of the 70 million Americans who smoked in 1963 if they were suddenly deprived of tobacco?"

Then the *Report* proceeds to admit that there is "no definitive answer to this question," but *Life* magazine quoted one psychiatrist as saying, "We might well have a nation of more alcoholics, more fat people who eat too much, more gum-chewers, more nail-biters, more people who simply talk too much."

So, in closing, I submit to you that the hour has its needs for action, but certainly the need for any more people who talk too much is not among them.

Thank you.

DAVIDSON COUNTY NCEA BANQUET

LEXINGTON

April 8, 1964

Again Governor Sanford spoke on education in general and on specific types of education in particular. He made reference to the Higher Education Act adopted by the 1963 General Assembly and to plans made for the expansion of higher education in North Carolina, to the Governor's School, to special training for the mentally retarded, to the Learning Institute of North Carolina, to Operation Second Chance, and to other programs which he mentioned briefly. Though North Carolina had made an outstanding start, much remained undone. The Governor pledged to continue his efforts "until the last hour of the last day I occupy this office." He said that Governor Hodges had helped prepare the first budget of the Sanford administration and he would help with that for the 1965-1967 biennium. To make the program for children the best in the nation was a ten-year project, and Sanford promised to do all he could to see that the program was continued. He said he felt that the people were in favor of quality education and that North Carolinians "have

the courage to go out and face the future and to grasp the opportunities of that future." Progress up the education ladder had
been made, but not enough progress to permit a standstill. Because North Carolinians had always supported education when
given an opportunity to do so, Governor Sanford felt confident
that they would continue to invest in their children's future.

EDUCARE

LOS ANGELES, CALIFORNIA

April 10, 1964

Speaking to a California audience, Governor Sanford said
that North Carolina had followed the example of California in
many respects. A committee had gone from North Carolina to
study the California system when work was begun on the Higher
Education Act. The Governor declared that neither North Carolina nor California was satisfied and that there would be no
need for an organization such as Educare if there was satisfaction.
The purpose in mentioning North Carolina was to emphasize
the point that people did understand education and would support it. The program in his state, Sanford told the group, was
possible because of the work and support of thousands of citizens.
Education was the first goal in North Carolina, a goal which had
also been put first by the legislature. With a system of state support of schools, legislative backing was imperative. The Governor went on to express the opinion that education and classrooms were vital if communism was to be stopped, because
ignorance was the greatest force for subversion. The greatest
infrigement of civil rights was the denial of the best educational
opportunities. All over the United States there was too little support for schools. The Governor commented on the correlation between education and crime; between education and earnings;
between education and the over-all welfare of the community,
state, and nation; between education and human tolerance; and
between education and the economy. Many questions were raised
by Sanford, all of which could be answered with the word "education." He called on Americans to put education first because
the "extent of the advance of education will determine the
success, and even the survival, of this America of ours."

WESTERN CAROLINA COLLEGE ASSEMBLY

Cullowhee

April 14, 1964

The Governor spoke on the topic, "Opportunities Provided by the State of North Carolina to College Students." He stated that the state afforded the chance "to build something worthwhile in an exciting land." The Appalachian program was to be the beginning of a new, enriched, and rewarding era for western North Carolina. In discussing reasons for the slow economic growth in that section, Sanford went into some detail concerning transportation and education. Federal funds for roads were formerly allotted on the basis of the number of people who used them, but this system was detrimental to certain areas. After a "development factor" was proposed, more highways were constructed in the Appalachian region than ever before, but the number was still insufficient. The Governor reminded graduates that they could be part of this growth and development. In commenting on education, the Chief Executive continued his talk by calling college graduates the leaders, adding that schooling had to be adequate to enable children to compete with people from all parts of the nation. He urged the conservation of natural resources and the development of recreational areas to attract new wealth, new people, and new ideas. He concluded that many opportunities for a bright career were open and that the state needed college graduates. "Stay with us—the future is here." The answer to the question of what North Carolina could do for college students was summed up when Governor Sanford told the group that the state could give them "life and opportunity."

MEETING OF COUNTY CHAIRMEN OF
JOHN FITZGERALD KENNEDY LIBRARY DRIVE

Chapel Hill

April 16, 1964

Governor Sanford spoke of the many reasons North Carolinians wanted to honor President Kennedy by helping to erect the Kennedy Library. The death of the President was a loss to North Carolina, to America, and to the free world. The Governor stated that veterans would want to contribute because Kennedy was a Purple Heart veteran; mothers because he fought for better educational opportunities for their children; older citizens because he led the campaign to help them; businessmen because he led the fight for an equitable tax reduction; farmers because of his support of farm programs; and many parents and grandparents because of his devotion to the fight against mental retardation. North Carolina's goal of $230,000 was less that the amount the state received from the Kennedy Foundation for programs to combat mental retardation. Sanford remarked that this was the one memorial in which Kennedy himself had expressed an interest during his lifetime. The Governor thanked the county chairmen, from both political parties, who had joined in this campaign for the Kennedy Library.

STATEMENT BEFORE THE UNITED STATES HOUSE OF REPRESENTATIVES, AD HOC SUBCOMMITTEE ON THE WAR ON POVERTY PROGRAM OF THE COMMITTEE ON EDUCATION AND LABOR

WASHINGTON, D. C.

April 17, 1964

Because North Carolina had pioneered with its own antipoverty program, Governor Sanford was invited to share the experiences of his state with congressmen studying the possibilities of a federal program of a similar nature. The Governor began with a summary of the economic situation in North Carolina and the fact that poverty did exist throughout the state. The idea of the North Carolina Fund emerged and private foundations were convinced of the validity of the suggestion that they support the new program on a trial basis. Sanford said that charity and relief were not answers, that people needed a means to work themselves out of poverty and to become self-supporting. With a $14 million grant from the Ford Foundation and the Reynolds-Babcock Foundation, the program was implemented. The Governor continued by showing how this program would fit into the proposed Economic Opportunity Act by reviewing various provisions of the federal bill. His belief in education as the ultimate key to the eradication of poverty was confirmed by the provisions of the federal bill for such programs as the Job Corps. The Governor explained how the North Carolina Fund had worked, with communities surveying their own needs and submitting their own proposals for projects which would operate under the fund. He said that fifty-one projects from sixty-six counties were submitted. Even those which were rejected had been of value in that they had pointed out specific needs in local communities; the federal plan would supplement the North Carolina Fund and would help fulfill those needs. Governor Sanford discussed and expressed approval of various aspects of the federal act in some detail. In his concluding remarks he reminded the committee members that poverty existed in the midst of plenty, that children of poverty would become the parents of poverty, and that the cycle had to be broken. "That is what the North Carolina Fund is about and that is what the President's poverty program is about."

FOUNDATIONS GROUP

New York, New York

April 21, 1964

Speaking on the subject "A North Carolina Renaissance: A State's Strategy for Human Development," Governor Sanford observed that many foundations which had turned eyes and funds toward North Carolina had representatives present. The motto of the state, "To be rather than to seem," was the American dream; to help all citizens redeem this legacy, the state had set up a series of developmental programs and experiments. Governor Sanford said he entered office in 1961 with a mandate for progress. Though North Carolina did not industrialize as soon as other sections, the state was catching up and was experiencing industrialization and automation in one period. Because too many North Carolinians remained on the outskirts of the great American dream despite progress, action was imperative; this action resulted in a close partnership between public and private leadership. Private foundations participated, thereby enabling the state to use an imagination not possible within the limits of public budgetary restrictions. "Foundations can use states to achieve their purposes of betterment. States can use foundations to seek the fulfillment of human needs, aspirations, and possibilities." The Governor listed fourteen projects financed by foundations and briefly explained the purpose of each. The influence and support permitted a new flexibility which enabled North Carolina to see dramatic educational and cultural results.

GOVERNOR'S CONFERENCE ON OCCUPATIONAL HEALTH

GREENSBORO

April 23, 1964

The adult working age group was the one which had had its health neglected more than any other, but North Carolina was interested in measures to promote and protect the health of all. The Governor stated that part of this interest had developed to the extent that the Occupational Health Council, organized in 1958, worked co-operatively with the State Board of Health, the Industrial Commission, the Department of Labor, and in some areas, the Utilities Commission. It also sought participation of the medical profession. Even with the co-operative work, however, the council would be helpless without the backing of management. Sanford observed that many employers were unfamiliar with resources available to them. Absenteeism was a critical problem, with 75 or 80 per cent being caused by nonoccupational illness. The Governor reminded the group that much of the responsibility for the health of the worker rested with the worker himself, which called attention to the need for basic health facts such as could be taught by the occupational health program. In twenty or more counties the Medical Society's Committee on Occupational Health had made available facts about physicians willing to serve full time or part time in an industry's occupational health program. Specific programs of help to industry had also been implemented in local health departments in several areas.

NORTH CAROLINA PRODUCTS WEEK LUNCHEON

RALEIGH

April 24, 1964

Governor Sanford called the grocery industry a vital link in the system which relayed food from the farm to the dinner table. He favored an expanded food industry, which would mean new jobs, saying that state agencies were working co-operatively along this line. The tobacco scare showed that North Carolina should not put all its eggs in one basket or all its investments in one crop. An intensive research program would find the cause and cure of cancer, the Governor predicted, but tobacco farmers should also diversify. Citing the dairy industry as one which had grown in a few years, Governor Sanford continued by calling attention to North Carolina foods which were being processed in the state: pickles, country hams, sweet potatoes, poultry, and peanuts. With 62 cents of every food dollar going for processing, packaging, and advertising, North Carolina stood to gain by expansion in this area. The Governor expressed pleasure at being able to join in the promotion of North Carolina Products Week.

DEDICATION OF HERBERT C. BONNER BRIDGE

OREGON INLET

May 2, 1964

This bridge, a link to the Outer Banks and a monument to the early colonists, was dedicated in a ceremony in which Sanford spoke of the spirit of the Roanoke Island settlers. Though the colonists were lost, their spirit lived on and was the same spirit which pushed to the west and which had served all America in times of stress and advancement. Pride and spirit were evident in North Carolina as programs to strengthen education, to curtail diversion of gasoline taxes from highway purposes, to build and pave roads and bridges were provided for by the legislature. Sanford spoke briefly of the history of support for roads and highways from the 1920's to recent years, pointing out that roads paved the way to industry. As population increases occurred, many roads had to be resurfaced or rebuilt. This bridge, which spanned Oregon Inlet for nearly 2.5 miles, was built to withstand winds of over 120 miles per hour. The Governor gave statistical information about the bridge and stated that it had cost just under $4 million. It was named for a great American, Herbert C. Bonner, who served in Congress for over a quarter of a century. Governor Sanford paid tribute to Bonner, saying that the spirit and the courage of the first colonists were exemplified in Congressman Bonner.

GROUND-BREAKING CEREMONIES
NORTH CAROLINA JEWISH HOME FOR THE AGED

CLEMMONS

May 3, 1964

The Governor began with a brief review of the contributions

made by the Jewish people to the state and commended the group on the establishment of a home for the aged. He observed that "an individual human being is the be-all and end-all of all our own institutions. Nothing is worthwhile which is not directed at the liberation of the individual human spirit, the strengthening of a man making it possible for every human being to develop himself to the ultimate bounds of the talents which God put in him, enabling every human being to live life to the fullest." He expressed the opinion that government existed to aid the individual, adding that his administration was "founded on the conviction that there were too many people in North Carolina who did not have at their disposal the tools with which to build their lives." Lack of educational opportunities, mental retardation, physical handicaps, crime, and lack of roads were all conditions which existed and which needed correcting. The Governor then reviewed efforts made during his administration to remedy the defects in the state of North Carolina.

INSTITUTE OF RELIGION

RALEIGH

May 5, 1964

Speaking to the Institute of Religion at the United Church in Raleigh, the Governor referred to the concern of the institute with the promise of America. He went on to discuss North Carolina's anti-poverty program, which was also about the promise of America, saying that that promise was the spirit with which President Johnson had proposed the attack on poverty. Those from tenant farms, slums, and blighted areas were seeking the opportunity to become self-supporting. This was the reason North Carolina paid so much attention to education, the reason for the accelerated drive for industry, the reason for the North Carolina Fund. Sanford cited progress in those areas and others, but he added that more remained to be done. All of the state's human resources needed to be developed. While the state as a whole was in the midst of prosperity, there were those who were hungry, those with no skills, those "whose dreams . . . [would] die." The cycle of poverty had to be broken; this was the purpose of the North Carolina Fund. Children of poverty became parents of poverty unless citizens, through government, civic organizations, and churches took positive action. Governor Sanford observed that many of those critical of Johnson's program were the same ones who benefited because of President Roosevelt's programs. In closing, he said, "If we are to reach the moon and the stars, and we are, surely we can reach also the man and the woman and the boy and the girl on the wrong side of the tracks."

WELCOME TO PRESIDENT LYNDON B. JOHNSON

ROCKY MOUNT

May 7, 1964

[In connection with the campaign against poverty, President Johnson visited several areas of the country including North Carolina. At Rocky Mount he spoke to an estimated crowd of 175,000; during the day he visited a farm family whose income and education were below average. Governor Sanford, in his speech of welcome to the President, showed that the program to break the cycle of poverty was not a government handout but was a sincere effort to help those who would help themselves.]

Mr. President, we welcome you to North Carolina.

You are not in a section of poverty, but you are in a section where there is poverty.

You have been concerned about the millions of Americans who are now living in poverty without any reasonable prospect of help or hope.

We in North Carolina likewise have been concerned about those of our people who cannot provide for themselves and their children the basic necessities of life.

We know that, in the midst of plenty and prosperity, there are people who have been displaced from the farm and the factory by machines, and lack the education and technical training to find other jobs; there are people who are eking out a bare existence on the land with no future in sight for their children to make a living on that land; there are people who have been living in poverty for generations, who, with their children, now are locked in a cycle of poverty.

Some of this poverty is deserved; some of it is undeserved. But we cannot stand by and let apathy and despair destroy the new generation of children now headed for a life of poverty.

Mr. President, all of these kinds of people are represented in this courtroom today.

Our aim in North Carolina is to make it possible for every child to receive a good education, to develop his talents, to acquire the skills needed in the factory and on the farm, and to go out into the world with the odds in his favor.

To make this possible we have provided more teachers, more guidance counselors, and better supervision in our schools. We are seeking better ways of teaching reading to the very young and giving vocational education to our high school students. We have developed a new system of industrial education centers and community colleges to offer every person, whether or not he is a high school graduate, the training or retraining he needs to get a job.

But better education is not enough. Children must *want* to learn. They must also understand that good jobs and decent incomes depend on education. And they must see down the road ahead of them job opportunities that will give them a chance to use what they have learned.

The children of poverty will find neither motivation nor opportunity if we can't find ways to encourage their parents. We must insure that the family has the necessities of life: a decent house, ample food and clothing, and good health care. We must kindle the desire to succeed on the ashes of frustration.

For centuries men have tried to find answers to the paradox of great need in the midst of plenty. Recognizing that we had to try again to find new and realistic answers to these basic problems, we went out and secured some "risk capital" from private foundations. We established the North Carolina Fund to make grants to a few communities that were willing to pull together their leaders, to sit down and define the problems faced by those living in poverty, and to work together to find ways in which these people could be helped to break out of the cycle of poverty. Our hunch was that we could not help people help themselves if the community did not focus its health, education, welfare, housing, and employment resources in their support.

Mr. President, we announced that we could help about ten communities launch an experimental program. We asked which communities were interested. In response to the invitation, thousands of North Carolinians—public officials, civic leaders, and representatives of those who needed help—sat down to take hard looks at their communities. The measure of the heart and conscience of this state lies in the fact that the North Carolina Fund received fifty-one proposals, involving sixty-six of our 100 counties. They came from the Mountains, from the Coastal Plain you are now visiting, and from the cities in our Piedmont. The North Carolina Fund's limited moneys will enable a few communities, representing a good cross section of the state, to start these action programs immediately. But in all of these counties, and more, we have the people and the leadership who already have done the type of thinking that you asked for under

Title II of the Economic Opportunity Act. These communities are ready to go to work.

We have an excellent example in the community you are visiting today. Nash and Edgecombe counties are in the midst of a prosperous agricultural area, specializing in tobacco, cotton, corn, peanuts, and lumber. More than 30 per cent of the residents of these counties work on farms. In Rocky Mount and the surrounding towns you will find tobacco processing industries as well as textile and furniture manufacturing.

The median family income in this area is about $3,000, which is not bad on the average for a farm area. But I am suspicious of averages. I look beyond them to see not only the prosperous farmer with a higher than average income, but also the farmer who has been made obsolete by the tractor and the mechanical cotton harvester. I see the tenant farmer who has little education and a large family. He makes a bare living but his children find no hope on the farm. I see the families who, in rural and urban areas alike, never have been able to break out of poverty. I see the father who migrates to the city with no skills and no education with which to compete for skilled employment.

This picture is what the leaders in Nash and Edgecombe counties and the city of Rocky Mount saw as well. They were not content with a community where an increasing stream of tenant farmers moved to town equipped with less than five years of education. They were not content to mechanize the farm and neglect the displaced sharecropper and laborer.

For more than a year the leaders in these two counties have been working on a community action plan. With state help they are establishing an industrial education center. They have worked hard to open up new job opportunities. And they have submitted a comprehensive plan to the North Carolina Fund— a package of projects—intended to help children and their parents overcome the burdens of poverty. They want to help erase illiteracy, provide job training, improve the education of disadvantaged children, and strengthen the family and the home environment.

The North Carolina Fund has responded by selecting Nash and Edgecombe counties as a site for one of seven comprehensive, experimental programs to be supported by the fund during the next four years.

Mr. President, I want to ask Mr. W. W. Shaw,[111] as chairman, and the members of the Nash-Edgecombe Area Steering Com-

---

[111] William W. Shaw (1903-), bank president; insurance company president, business and civic leader, musician from Rocky Mount. Powell, *North Carolina Lives*, 1095-1097.

mittee on the North Carolina Fund to stand as I present to you a copy of their plan for action. This plan is not yet a complete blueprint. But with this dynamic leadership we are confident we will find here some answers for eastern North Carolina.

You can see that with our private, limited funds, we can work on not more than about 10 per cent of our opportunities. I think we have demonstrated that the people will respond, but I think also we have demonstrated that we cannot complete the job, and cannot reach all of our possibilities, without the co-operation of the government. The local people will provide the leadership, but they need financial support.

I know that the leaders in these counties and in all our counties are very hopeful that the federal poverty legislation soon will pass the Congress. They have provided the type of thinking you have asked for in Title II of that legislation. They recognize that no program aimed at the complex problems of poverty will get the job done without a partnership between the community, the state, and the federal government. I must add, also, that all other sections of your program, now pending in Congress, will support the purposes of this community effort.

Mr. President, again I welcome you. I wish that we had more time to show you all that we are doing in North Carolina. We are glad that you could come to a community that is typical of a desire throughout this state to marshal all our resources, with imagination and intelligence, so that today's children of poverty will not become tomorrow's parents of poverty.

STUDENT ACTIVITIES BANQUET

RALEIGH

May 12, 1964

Speaking at the Erdahl-Cloyd Union of North Carolina State, Governor Sanford referred to the state-wide leadership furnished by this university and its related branches. He commented that division within the consolidated university had to end and that there must be a unified effort to build a university comparable to the best in the nation. Consolidation had brought benefits to the state as a whole. Sanford remarked that the purpose of the university was to educate men and women and to give each individual the opportunity for a fuller life while at the same time giving the state and its citizens a richer future. The university, with its three branches—Chapel Hill since 1795, Raleigh since 1887, and Greens-

On May 7, 1964, President Lyndon B. Johnson visited North Carolina as part of an inspection of areas of poverty in the South. He and his party and Governor Sanford are shown at the Marlow farm near Rocky Mount.

On May 17, 1964, a service in tribute to President John F. Kennedy was held at Kenan Stadium in Chapel Hill. President William C. Friday of the University of North Carolina, Secretary of Commerce Luther H. Hodges, Senator Ted Kennedy, Mrs. Joseph Kennedy, Governor Sanford, and the Rev. Billy Graham were present for the occasion.

boro since 1891—had been doing this. The university was owned by the citizens of North Carolina, including those who never had the opportunity to study at any of its branches. The Governor observed that a diploma represented achievement but it also represented a debt to the faculty and administration and trustees, to parents, and to all citizens of North Carolina.

JOHN F. KENNEDY MEMORIAL TRIBUTE

CHAPEL HILL

May 17, 1964

[North Carolina citizens paid tribute to the late President Kennedy in a spring memorial program held at Kenan Stadium in Chapel Hill and by a significant monetary contribution toward the John F. Kennedy Library. In a state-wide effort to sell 23,000 tickets at $10.00 each, North Carolina was the first state to conduct its campaign for contributions to the library. Mrs. Joseph P. Kennedy and Senator Ted Kennedy were present for the addresses by Dr. Billy Graham, noted North Carolina evangelist, and Secretary of Commerce Luther Hodges. At the conclusion of the program, Mrs. Kennedy accepted the check for the state's donation toward the library. The remarks of presentation by Governor Sanford marked the solemnity of the occasion.]

Mrs. Kennedy, Ladies and Gentlemen:

This is a service in tribute,
on one Sunday afternoon,
in one American state,

But North Carolinians,
and other free people,
and freedom loving people
around the globe, in all places,
will always remember
President John Fitzgerald Kennedy.

This tribute today is our tangible contribution
to a place of memory,
But the memory of John Kennedy
Will never be housed in a single place;

Because his resolute and honest expression
of American aspirations for mankind,
and belief in man,
restored the hopes of men and women

on this side and beyond all the curtains of the world
that indeed
in the last half of the twentieth century
to the benefit of all peoples
We could "invoke the wonders
of science instead of its terrors."

Because no man in American history better demonstrated
to other countries
the goodness and high purpose of the American dream;

And because no man has surpassed
his steadying and reassuring influence
on a shaken world;

Because of these and many other things
The memory of John F. Kennedy
will be housed in the minds and hearts
of every nation
as long as man is free
as long as men hope to be free.

Therefore, on behalf of almost five million
North Carolinians, I am happy to present
a token of our admiration of President
John F. Kennedy to his mother,
Mrs. Joseph P. Kennedy, and to
present to our people a very
remarkable mother,
Mrs. Kennedy.

FARM-INDUSTRY DAY

WOODLEAF

May 19, 1964

Speaking at Farm-Industry Day in Woodleaf, Sanford said education, business, and agriculture were "the three basic numbers to the combination to unlock the future of North Carolina." The state had set the pace in education, and Sanford referred to 1961 and 1963 accomplishments. After discussing programs in the field of education, he discussed industry and cited statistics to show advances in that area. He hastened to say that industry included agriculture and that North Carolina was "planning to plant and not to foreclose its farms." Though doubt had been expressed in the past when rural roads were paved, those roads proved to be roads to prosperity. The Governor also praised state employees for their efficiency, saying that North Carolina was forty-eighth in the nation in the number of state and local government employees in comparison with the population. Statistics showed that *"North Carolina is both fiscally sound and forward bound."*

STATE DEMOCRATIC CONVENTION OF 1964

RALEIGH

May 20, 1964

[Sharing the platform with Governor Sanford at the 1964 State Democratic Convention was Senator Hector MacLean of Lumberton who gave the keynote address. The Governor's speech, in which he reviewed accomplishments of the Democratic party and voiced confidence in it, set the tone for an enthusiastic, harmonious convention.]

This administration is concerned with people and with giving them a chance to do better than they have before. This is the way to develop the economy. This is the way to develop free enterprise. This is the way to develop democracy. And we are determined to promote that concern with the greatest possible efficiency and the lowest possible cost. The record shows that the Democratic party has done just that.

This Administration has spent much money and it is glad of it. It undoubtedly appears cheaper to neglect the aged, the feeble, the infirm, the defective, to forget the children of this generation, but the man who does it is cursed of God and the state that permits it is certain of destruction. There are people on the face of the earth who take no care of the weak and infirm, who care nought for their children and provide only for the gratification of their own desires, but these people neither wear clothes nor dwell in houses. They leave God out of consideration in their estimate of life, and are known to us as savages.

These words are highly appropriate today, but they were delivered by Governor Charles Brantley Aycock sixty years ago at the State Democratic Convention of 1904.

The Republicans said Charles Brantley Aycock would bankrupt the state with his education program. They said Cam Morrison would bankrupt the state with his good roads program in the twenties. They said Angus McLean and Max Gardner would ruin us with money put in colleges and the university. They were certain that Kerr Scott was bankrupting the state with his farm-to-market roads in the forties. They said Luther Hodges had grifters and grafters milking the state dry in the fifties.

Like every other Democrat here today, I am proud to be in company with men like Aycock, Morrison, McLean, Gardner, Scott, and Hodges, and to have the Republicans accusing me like they did other Democratic governors of this century.

After sixty-three years of this kind of Democratic "spending" and "bankruptcy," do you know how North Carolina's credit rating stands? Any investment broker can tell you. After sixty-three years of Democratic government, North Carolina's credit rating stands Triple A. That's where it stands today!

North Carolina ranks forty-eighth among all the states in the union—third from the bottom—in the number of state and local governmental employees. North Carolina ranks second from the very bottom in the per capita expenditures for state and local governmental services. We provide the services but we don't waste money in doing it.

North Carolina does not operate with deficit budgets. Red ink in the budget-making process of North Carolina is illegal and it is unheard of.

But this frugality is not achieved at the expense of essential services. As Aycock enjoined the Democrats of 1904, we do care for the aged. We do care for the feeble. We do care for the infirm, both the mentally and physically ill. We do care about more jobs and better pay. We do, above all else, care for our children, and we are willing to invest our tax money in their future. In 1964 we do follow the principles of Charles Aycock of 1904 and of Thomas Jefferson of 1804. We agree with Jefferson that "If a nation expects to be ignorant and free, in a state of civilization, it expects what never was and never will be."

Democrats in Raleigh and in Washington do care about the causes of poverty. Democrats under Franklin D. Roosevelt cared and Democrats under John Kennedy cared and Democrats under Lyndon Johnson care.

The Democratic party always has been, is now, and always will be a party that cares for the weak, the infirm, the young, and the old. It will always be the party that looks for better opportunities for all the people.

It is a party that faces the future without fear; it is a party that votes yes to the future. That is why the people of this state will vote Democratic to keep progress flowing from the State Capitol and from the White House this year.

And that is why North Carolina and the Democratic party

will continue to look to the future and work for the future—in 1964 and in 1965 and all the years ahead.

TESTIMONY, SPECIAL APPALACHIAN COMMITTEE OF THE HOUSE PUBLIC WORKS COMMITTEE

WASHINGTON, D. C.

May 22, 1964

The Governor testified in support of House Bill 11065, concerning the Appalachian region. He explained that only 20 per cent of North Carolina's population was in this area and that North Carolina had only 6 per cent of those included in the Appalachian region as defined by the bill, but that the group was significant. The people of the area received the same services as those of other sections of North Carolina, which meant that the state put a disproportionately high share of money into the region because of the great difficulties and high costs. The people of western North Carolina had taken steps to remedy the situation in various ways. Outdoor dramas, such as *Unto These Hills,* had attracted tourists. The Western North Carolina Associated Communities, which sponsored the drama, also founded the Western North Carolina Regional Planning Commission which had made an economic analysis of the western part of the state and had outlined a development program. A development association in eleven counties in northwestern North Carolina and the Asheville Agricultural Development Council had both contributed to the welfare of the area. Sanford mentioned poor access in the area as a major problem. Though North Carolina ranked third in the percentage of highways paved, there was still not enough money. Roads had been built where traffic pressure was the greatest; the highway portion of the bill was, therefore, imperative for the North Carolina mountain section. North Carolina would raise matching funds, but help was needed to carry out all of the programs which had to be carried out to enable the region to be revitalized. Governor Sanford promised that investments made by federal and state governments would be returned many times over.

COMMENCEMENT EXERCISES OF 1964
UNIVERSITY OF NORTH CAROLINA AT CHAPEL HILL

Chapel Hill

June 1, 1964

Speaking to the 1964 graduates of the University of North Carolina at Chapel Hill, Governor Sanford did not give the usual commencement address. He reviewed the history of the university in some detail, reminding the graduates of the sacrifices made throughout its history by many dedicated citizens of North Carolina. He discussed the role of the school, pointing out its common functions shared with other great institutions of learning, but adding that the Chapel Hill school also had distinctive qualities. He praised the university for furnishing "creative, courageous leaders in virtually every area of endeavor. . . ." Sanford praised it also for its leadership in solving problems of each succeeding generation and for being the "chief instrument for the progress of North Carolina." Not only had the university served the past; it was serving the present generation. With so many roles to perform, some criticism was to be expected; to meet the criticism, it was imperative that the institution remain in full and constant communication with the people of North Carolina. Sanford reminded the audience that the school could not exist in "sterile scholasticism. . . ." In discussing some of the problems facing the university from within, the Governor said that the needs of the entire state had to be considered; competent faculty had to be recruited; the problem of how to provide excellent teaching and creative research had to be solved, though the necessity of good teaching had always to be given priority. The state had problems facing it, and the university would continue to provide leadership to meet those problems. Sanford closed with quotations from Archibald D. Murphey and Harry Woodburn Chase concerning the mission of the University of North Carolina at Chapel Hill.

REPORT TO GOVERNORS CONFERENCE

Cleveland, Ohio

June 8, 1964

[The Sheraton-Cleveland National Hotel in Cleveland, Ohio, was the scene of this annual Governors Conference. Governor Sanford discussed the report of the Interim Study Committee on Federal Aid to Education with those in attendance. While not offering any ready answers to the problem of federal aid to education, recognition was given to the complexities involved, and the way was paved for objective thinking and valid decisions in the future.]

The great historian Edward Gibbon summarized one period as follows:

The reign of Antonius is marked by the rare advantage of furnishing very few materials for history; which is indeed little more than the register of the crimes, follies and misfortunes of mankind.

On the other hand, Herbert George Wells, the noted British novelist and historian, concluded, "Human history becomes more and more of a race between education and catastrophe."

Our own Henry Adams said, "Practical politics consists in ignoring facts."

With that prelude, I propose that we, a group of practical politicians, shall in the next fifteen or twenty minutes summarize and consider almost two hundred years of the facts of educational history.

I was very happy when our Chairman, Governor Anderson, and the Executive Committee agreed to appoint an Interim Study Committee on Federal Aid to Education. Education is the largest single area of governmental expenditure in our states. In the average state in 1961, 36.6 per cent of *all* state and local revenues were expended for education. Needless to say, a program of this magnitude is of importance to all of us.

There are shortcomings in American education and many soft spots which need to be firmed up. Whether the federal government should take a more meaningful part is the object of this discussion, but regardless of what the federal government does, or what the governors might ultimately recommend that the federal government do, the states have a challenging obligation. There is much to be done, regardless of how the financial burden is shared.

We have been too long in determining how we should proceed. We have been too long in waiting, in some places, for the federal government to act, and, in some other places, of simply failing to take necessary action. If federal participation in education is to remain at its present level, or if federal participation is to be reduced in any area, then all the more strongly must the states step up to meet educational needs.

A strong educational system is vital to us as individuals, as states, and as a nation. The educated individual can live a fuller and more meaningful life in that he will be better able to support himself and contribute to the social, political, and economic welfare of the nation. All of our states are competing with one another to develop industry and increase the income of our people. A strong educational system is necessary to provide the skilled labor force which industrialization requires. An educated citizenry will also enable our states to gain the maximum in social progress from whatever economic advance we achieve. Finally, education is essential to national survival in these prolonged years of cold war. The productive potential which we require to remain strong cannot be achieved without education. Perhaps most important of all, the quality of statesmanship necessary to preserve the peace in these troubled times can be developed only through liberal education.

The public schools are a state-local partnership in every state, although the relative importance of the partners varies from state to state. At the two extremes, the state of Delaware provides over 81 per cent of the cost of local schools, and Nebraska furnishes 6 per cent. This comparison serves merely to illustrate the diversity of arrangements for education in our states. Each of us, I am sure, has had experience in this state-local partnership. In many of our states, the state education association is quite able to make its influence felt in public affairs.

We sometimes ignore the third partner in the education enterprise: the federal government. Activity of the federal government in education actually began with the federal land grants which preceded the ratification of our present constitution. Although no general federal aid bill has ever been enacted, new programs of aid to specific educational activities have gradually increased in number through the years.

Argument regarding the pros and cons of federal aid has been fairly constant since the establishment of the land grant colleges in 1862. I feel that one of the greatest contributions which our Interim Study Committee can make is to describe the issues of federal aid in a manner which will enable you to make your own objective decisions regarding these questions. That is what we have tried to achieve in the study which we place before you today.

I suspect that the question of whether or not we should have federal aid to education is almost moot by now. The federal government in 1962 provided 19 per cent of the cost of all higher education. This expenditure makes it almost an equal partner with the state and with parents in the support of higher education. True, much of this money was for contract research services, but it still provided support of education, particularly at the graduate level. The federal share in the public schools was less, about 2 per cent, if the school lunch program is excluded. The percentage ran much higher in states which have a great many federal installations. School districts in these states obtain federal help in meeting school problems intensified by federal activity.

The statement is often made that history repeats itself. This has certainly been true in federal aid to education. Some national crisis has repeatedly led to consideration of direct federal aid to general education, opponents have been able to block the passage of general legislation, and a new program of special assistance to education has been enacted as a solution, or partial solution, to the original problem.

The economic and social aftermath of the Civil War produced a general federal aid debate which continued from 1870 to 1890. During this period, the Senate passed federal aid bills on three occasions and the House once. Never, however, was the concurrence of both houses obtained. The passage of the Second Morrill Act in 1890, providing continuing appropriations to support agricultural, mechanical, and military education in the land grant colleges, closed this period of debate. Congress then turned its attention to support of vocational education at the secondary level.

The rate of selective service rejections in World War I, resulting from illiteracy and physical defects which could have been remedied if discovered in school, again created a demand for general aid. This debate was to continue from 1918 through 1925. Another proposal in 1929 would have provided direct assistance to education in rural areas. The depression intervened and necessitated emergency federal aid to the schools, as well as as giving renewed emphasis to demands for more permanent federal support. Federal aid bills were continuously before the Congress through 1939. The Lanham Act was passed in 1940 to provide some assistance to school districts affected by expanding federal activity.

World War II, starting in 1941, again brought to light illiteracy and remedial physical defects, as well as deficiencies in technical education. A critical teacher shortage developed and lasted through the 1940's. General federal aid remained a lively issue until the defeat of the Taft bill in 1949. In 1950 Public Laws 815 and 874 were enacted to provide federal assistance for both school construction and current operating expenses in districts affected by federal activities.

The baby boom of the 1950's and the suburban dispersal of population continued to present serious educational problems. Proponents of federal aid shifted their approach to a quest for school construction aid, in an effort to avoid the bitterness of the religious issue, as it had manifested itself in 1949. School construction aid was the issue through 1957.

The successful launching of the Russian Sputnik on October 4, 1957, focused the attention of the American people, as never before, on education. The result was the enactment in 1958 of the National Defense Education Act, providing an extensive program of federal support, both of higher and secondary education, primarily, but by no means exclusively, in the fields of science and modern languages.

The continuing cold war emphasizes the importance of education to our national survival. Both houses of the Congress passed federal aids bills in 1960, and the Senate passed a bill in 1961. This period of struggle reached a climax in 1963. General federal aid was decisively defeated. The Congress, however, enacted an unusually large number of categorical programs to meet the needs of education. These included aid for construction of higher education facilities, expansion of vocational education, medical school construction, library services, and extensions of the National Defense Education Act and the programs of aid to federally-affected areas.

What are the issues which have prevented the enactment of general federal aid legislation for almost a century? The major points of controversy are fear of federal control of education, treatment of private schools, and race relations. Some groups have also exerted great influence with their contention that federal aid is unnecessary, and that education needs can be met by state and local governments. Advocates of federal participation also disagree among themselves as to the precise form it should take.

The congressional hearings and debates are replete with examples of speakers who listed a half dozen or more objections and then concluded that the federal aid bill would provide aid to parochial schools, would deny aid to parochial schools, would result in integrated schools, would continue segregated schools, or would bankrupt American business. This is not to say that sincere state rights adherents and those who believe in local school autonomy do not oppose federal aid on principle. They have a lot of company, though.

The present programs of federal participation in education have not resulted in overt federal control of curriculum, employment of teachers, choice of textbooks, or general school administration. Such programs have, of course, influenced the administration of local schools and institutions of higher education by causing changes in program emphasis. Without the federal programs, I doubt that we would have as many courses in vocational education, the sciences, or military subjects. These changes in emphasis, however, are in accord with national goals as defined by the Congress.

Although precise policy positions have been modified from time to time, the Catholic Church has consistently opposed federal aid proposals which did not include assistance for private schools. Protestant groups have as consistently opposed direct aid to parochial schools. Private schools are eligible under several of the present federal programs, perhaps the most significant being the Higher Education Facilities Act of 1963. Current efforts at a solution to the religious issue lie in the areas of defining and assisting secular elements of private school education and in the construction of "shared time" facilities, which could be used by both public and private school pupils in an area.

The major issue dividing federal aid advocates has been that of flat grants versus equalization of educational expenditures and program. Many northern congressmen favor flat grants in which their states would share. Most southern and western congressmen, who accept the principle of federal aid, prefer equalization grants which could be used to bring educational expenditures in their states closer to the national norms. Most bills have contained some combination of flat grants and equalization payments, in an effort to obtain enough votes for passage.

This treatment of the facts of federal aid to education has, of necessity, been sketchy. I hope it serves to introduce the report now before you. As you have seen, the issues of federal aid are not simple.

In the words of the Woonsocket, South Dakota, *News*:

People come in three classes: the few who make things happen, the many who watch things happen, and the overwhelming majority who have no idea what happened.

As the governors of our respective states, and as a conference, we have a responsibility to "make things happen" in this area so vital to all of us. I have not attempted to give you the answers today, not even *my* answers, but we owe the quest for them to our people, to our states, and to our nation.

NORTH CAROLINA ASSOCIATION OF COUNTY COMMISSIONERS

MOREHEAD CITY

June 15, 1964

In his address to county commissioners, Governor Sanford

stressed the importance of state-county co-operation. He said his
administration had worked well with counties; that new industry had meant new jobs, resulting in an increase in the tax
base; that the 1961 program for improvement in the public
schools was a giant step forward and that during that same year,
fifty-two counties had increased their support to the schools; that
in the next three years over eighty counties had given increased
support to schools, and that this co-operation was beneficial to all
children. The educational program and its support had drawn
national attention, and the Governor stressed the importance of
continuing it. Sanford continued with brief comments on welfare programs, the need for additional hospital care for older
people, and the vital necessity of breaking the cycle of poverty so
as to prevent the need for welfare assistance. Before closing he
made several statements concerning roads in the state. He also
urged the continuation of research in the light of the tobacco
health scare and asked that price-support programs be continued.
After discussing these several areas of mutual concern, he told
the commissioners that North Carolina had a challenge to show
the rest of the nation "how to go about building the Great
Society."

AMERICAN SYMPHONY ORCHESTRA LEAGUE AND COMMUNITY ARTS COUNCILS

DETROIT, MICHIGAN

June 20, 1964

[In his address to two national cultural organizations, Governor Sanford
reviewed the cultural progress made in North Carolina, beginning with
events of the sixteenth century. He painted a bright picture for the state's
future and in so doing, defended state support of the arts.]

I am particularly happy to talk to you tonight about state
support of the arts—specifically North Carolina's role—for two
reasons. First, I think the proper relation of a governmental
unit to the arts is generating much discussion, even controversy,
at the present time. This is true, whether the city, state, or
federal government is involved.

Second, I think this will be the first time that the role North
Carolina has played in fostering the arts has even been fully
and publicly told.

It was in 1780, while he was in Europe as Minister Plenipotentiary negotiating treaties of peace and commerce with Great Britain, that John Adams wrote to his wife:

I could fill volumes with descriptions of temples and palaces, paintings, sculpture, tapestry, porcelain, etc., if I could have the time, but I could not do this without neglecting my duty. My duty is to study the science of government that my sons may have the liberty to study mathematics and science. My sons ought to study geography, navigation, commerce and agriculture in order to give their children a right to study philosophy, painting, poetry, music, architecture, sculpture, tapestry and porcelain."

Today, we are several generations past John Adams' grandsons, and I think we are doing much to fulfill his prophecy.

North Carolina, although not many people may realize it, has an artistic tradition that can be traced back to 1585, when John White came over to Roanoke Island with the ill-fated Lost Colony. While he was in the colony, before he returned to England to get desperately needed supplies, he did numerous water colors of the area, including the Indians, birds, animals, fishes, and reptiles that he encountered.

From these paintings, a series of engravings was made in 1590. They remain today the classic illustrations of sixteenth century America. The paintings themselves disappeared until they were discovered in 1865 in the library of an Irish nobleman. The following year they were acquired by the British Museum.

Now, I am happy to say that these paintings have been made available to the public after ten years of work by the University of North Carolina Press and the British Museum in facsimile reproductions of all the surviving White paintings. Only several months ago the first set was presented to the White House by the state of North Carolina.

If some of the first art in America was created on the coast of North Carolina, some of its first chamber music was written in the Piedmont area, in Salem, the Moravian settlement that is now a part of Winston-Salem. There in 1789 John Frederick Peter composed a half dozen quintets that are still played today and have been recorded. Peter was only one of a group of composers who provided music for Old Salem, its Collegium Musicuum and its church. Today, the Moravian Music Foundation in Winston-Salem is hard at work getting this music out of the archives and having it published for modern performance.

Back on the seacoast at Wilmington, the Thalian Association was organized in 1788 and is the oldest Little Theater organization in the United States. It presents its plays today in a theater that was built in 1858, on the site of an even earlier theater.

I would not be so rash as to say that North Carolina's modern artists, writers, and composers come from direct lines that extend back to 1585, or even the eighteenth century. What I do mean to say is that North Carolina has long provided fertile soil for our artists, composers, writers, and musicians, and it continues to do so today. Nor would I say that the state of North Carolina itself has always been the patron of the arts that it is today. But I do say that without this tradition, I am sure it would have been much more difficult, not to say impossible, to get our legislators to appropriate money for things cultural. This they have done willingly these past few decades.

Perhaps North Carolina's most spectacular venture into the arts was made in 1947, when the General Assembly appropriated $1 million to establish a State Arts Museum on the condition that the North Carolina State Art Society secure an equal amount to be added to the original grant. The S. H. Kress Foundation of New York, as a part of its program of establishing galleries throughout the United States, pledged a collection of art of a value to be as least $1 million. The state then provided and renovated a four-story building. On April 6, 1956, the North Carolina Museum of Art opened its doors, and North Carolina became the first state to set aside public funds to found a state art collection.

Today, the North Carolina Museum of Art boasts a collection of more than 1,000 works of art valued in excess of $7.5 million. State support of the museum continues at the rate of some $150,000 a year. Since this sum is hardly enough to provide money for acquisitions, the museum depends on donations of art. North Carolina residents, foundations, and businesses have been most generous.

One of the more intriguing plans to get art for the museum was organized last year in Winston-Salem, when a Collectors' Choice Show was sponsored by local citizens. Fine works of art were selected from many New York galleries and displayed at the Forsyth County-Winston-Salem Library. All the works were for sale, either for the purchaser's own collections or for gifts to the museum. The museum was assured that the donated art would be acceptable because the director passed on each painting and sculpture before it was sent to the exhibit. As a result of this project, some truly fine art valued at more than $300,000 now graces some North Carolina homes, as well as the walls of the State Art Museum.

If there is one art that is indigenous to North Carolina, it is probably the symphonic drama. To tell the story of the first British colony in America, which so mysteriously disappeared nearly four hundred years ago, Paul Green,[112] North Carolina's

---

[112] Paul Eliot Green (1894-   ), professor and playwright from Chapel Hill; alumnus of the University of North Carolina and Cornell; Pulitzer Prize winner in 1927 for his play, *In Abraham's Bosom*. Powell, *North Carolina Lives*, 511.

own Pulitzer Prize-winning playwright, wrote *The Lost Colony*. It was produced in 1937 on Roanoke Island, the very site of the colony. *The Lost Colony* is running today, as it has every summer since 1937 with the exception of the war years. *The Lost Colony*, and the others which have followed in its wake, combine drama, music, dancing, and spectacle. The association which produces *The Lost Colony* has had its vicissitudes. It is not a money maker, but rather a labor of love. While the weather generally has been good to it—surprisingly few performances have been rained out over the years—a hurricane did sweep away the waterfront theater one time. It has since been rebuilt better than ever.

While a quasi-private organization is responsible for producing *The Lost Colony,* the state of North Carolina, recognizing it as not only a cultural asset but a tourist attraction as well, has underwritten it and since 1947-1948 made small grants to it to insure its continuation. These grants in recent years have amounted to no more than $10,000 annually.

The success of *The Lost Colony* has led to many other outdoor dramas throughout the country, as well as in North Carolina. *Horn in the West,* at Boone in the mountains of western North Carolina, has received state financial help over the years. *Unto These Hills,* the Cherokee story told right in the Cherokee country of western North Carolina, is the most successful of them all. It actually makes a profit, and although state funds helped get it on its feet, it now needs no state financial help.

Because the interest in the symphonic drama is so widespread, and because the main source of know-how in producing these dramas is located in North Carolina, the Outdoor Drama Institute was founded at the University of North Carolina in 1963. This institute advises producers, writers, directors, managers, and sponsors of outdoor dramas from all over the United States. I might add that the institute is on friendly ground at the University of North Carolina, since it is the home of the Playmakers, one of the older and more famous college drama organizations.

Also in the field of drama, the Parkway Playhouse in Burnsville, a summer stock group, received a state subsidy. Although it does not receive state money, the Flat Rock Playhouse at Flat Rock has been designated by the legislature as the North Carolina State Theater.

In order to bring good theater closer to young people, the state and a private foundation joined forces in 1963 to finance a group of touring professional actors who presented Shakespearean scenes in schools throughout the state. This year, the state alone financed a similar tour, as well as one by the Flat Rock Playhouse players, who appeared in *The World of Carl Sandburg*. Sandburg, incidentally, is a resident of North Carolina.

Nor has North Carolina neglected the films. In 1963 the North Carolina Film Board was set up by this state with a grant of money from the Richardson Foundation. This board produces documentary films about the human, natural, and economic resources of the state, and seeks to do the same type of work done for Canada by the National Film Board of Canada. In fact, when we set up the film board, we got the best man in the business of documentary films to head it up. He is Jim Beveridge,[113] formerly of the National Film Board of Canada. The first three films have now been finished and several more are almost ready.

In the field of music, North Carolina has long been active. I think most of you people here are well aware of the Brevard Music Center, in western North Carolina, which was organized and is run by one of your own well-known members, Jim Pfohl.[114] Over the years, the state has made financial grants to Brevard.

But it is the North Carolina Symphony, founded in 1942 and the first state symphony orchestra in the nation, that has probably received more direct aid over a longer period of time than any other group, with the exception of the museum. The North Carolina Symphony and its Little Symphony tour the state giving both adult and youth concerts. In 1963, for instance, they visited fifty-two communities, and, under the conductor, Benjamin Swalin, gave 125 concerts. Truly, no part of North Carolina is without its opportunity to hear good music. Out of a budget of around $200,000, the state provides $75,000 for the symphony.

There are other symphonies in North Carolina: in Charlotte, Winston-Salem, Asheville, Greensboro, and the Triangle Little Symphony of Raleigh, Chapel Hill, and Durham. These groups are supported locally and do not receive state grants.

In 1963 North Carolina celebrated the tercentenary of the grant of land by King Charles II of England. A commission to plan the celebration was set up by the 1959 legislature. Naturally, the celebration included a few speeches, and the issuance of a stamp to commemorate the occasion, but the main emphasis was on uncovering the heritage of North Carolina and on educating

---

[113] James Beveridge, former producer and executive producer for the National Film Board of Canada; experience in film-making in England and India; Director of North Carolina Film Board while on two-year leave of absence from Canadian Film Board. Statement of Governor Sanford of February 6, 1963.

[114] James Christian Pfohl (1912-   ), musician from Charlotte; student at Cincinnati Conservatory of Music; founder and Director of Transylvania Music Center at Brevard since 1936. *Who's Who in America*, XXXIII, 1580.

citizens of the state regarding the state's heritage. Prizes were given in a literary competition for the best poem and the best book written on the theme. An opera was commissioned, *The Sojourner and Molly Sinclair*, composed by Carlisle Floyd;[115] its premier performance was conducted by Julius Rudel[116] of the New York City Opera Company. The leads were sung by Patricia Neway and Norman Treigle, both members of that company.

The North Carolina Museum put on a large show of art of the period; and a large trailer, containing an exhibit of state history, toured the state.

No account of the arts in North Carolina would be complete without a mention of another event, which I believe is unique. That is what has come to be known as "Culture Week," celebrated annually in Raleigh, the capital, at the end of November.

Basically, "Culture Week" encompasses the annual meeting of twelve state-wide cultural societies and organizations. These groups meet to hear concerts and lectures and to award prizes and scholarships to creative North Carolinians for painting, novels, poetry, and works of nonfiction. Included in these groups are the North Carolina Federation of Music Clubs, the North Carolina Literary and Historical Association, the State Art Society, the North Carolina Folklore Society, the North Carolina Symphony Society, the North Carolina Society of Local and County Historians and others. While there is no state money involved in the support of these organizations, they all have the blessing and support of the state government, which takes a back seat in the news during this one week.

North Carolina, with both state and private support, has accomplished major restoration programs at Tryon's Palace, the home of the Royal Governor of North Carolina, and at Old Salem which was a well-established town when President George Washington came through during his tour of the nation in the eighteenth century. Our interest in history is also demonstrated by our support of the North Carolina Department of Archives and History—one of the outstanding agencies of its kind in the nation.

And now I want to mention two things which are of particular interest to me. These are two schools: one just now getting its

---

[115] Carlisle Floyd (1926-   ), composer of musical dramas; native of South Carolina; 1956 winner of the New York Critics Award; composer of *Susannah* and *Passion of Jonathan Wade*. *News and Observer*, September 15, 1963.

[116] Julius Rudel (1921-   ), Austrian-born conductor; with New York City Opera since 1943; appointed General Director, 1957; recipient of various awards for musical endeavors. *Who's Who in America*, XXXIII, 1731.

second summer session under way; the other, in the planning stage looking toward its opening in September, 1965. Several years ago, while surveying the educational opportunities of North Carolina, it was suggested to me that we should do something extra for the gifted and talented students in North Carolina's high schools. Out of these discussions came the idea of what was later to be known as the Governor's School of North Carolina.

What we proposed to do was inaugurate a summer school for 400 of the state's most academically and artistically gifted students, a school that would stretch the minds of these students, that would develop their general and specific abilities, so that from those gifted and talented youngsters would some day emerge adults who would improve—by inventing, discovering, reasoning, or reconstructing—our practical and aesthetic worlds.

With a grant of $225,000 from the Carnegie Corporation of New York and a like sum from eleven foundations and industries in Winston-Salem, the first session of the Governor's School was held last summer on the campus of Salem College in Winston-Salem. The students were chosen on the basis of recommendations from their principals, or, in the case of the artistically gifted students, on the basis of auditions. For eight weeks last summer, these 400 students studied in one of the following fields: English, foreign language, mathematics, natural science, social science, art, choral music, instrumental music and piano, drama, and dance. Eighteen of the students concentrated in art, thirty-five in dance, twenty-seven in drama, forty-one in choral music, fifty-four in instrumental music, and five in piano. The others were in the academic disciplines. Each student spent eighteen classroom hours a week in his major interest area; three hours a week in a minor area; and four hours a week in a class entitled "Essential Ideas."

It was a thrilling experience for these students, and for those of us who were able to see these students in action in the seminar rooms or on the stage or concert platform.

Under its present financial grants, the Governor's School is to run for three years. We hope the school can be made a permanent part of the state's educational structure, if tests we are making show we are accomplishing our aims.

The second school, of which I wish to speak and which I think will be of some interest to you, is the North Carolina School for the Performing Arts, which will open its doors, also in Winston-Salem, in September, 1965.

The school was authorized by last year's session of the North Carolina legislature, thus making possible a dream long held by people like Jim Pfohl and Vittorio Giannini[117]—who is scheduled to be its first head. To this school will come students, not only from North Carolina but from all over the Southeast. They will receive academic instruction, and the very finest professional training in their respective fields, whether it be music, drama, or dance.

There is not another school exactly like this anywhere in the country, although we would like it to be somewhat similar to the High School of the Performing Arts in New York City. We realize we are entering unchartered territory, but we have high hopes for its success.

You might be interested to know how the school happened to be located in Winston-Salem, already the home of the Governor's School.

When the legislature authorized the establishment of the school, it did not appropriate enough money to build a campus. As a result, the school was offered to the city or town making the most attractive proposition. The decision was made by the school's advisory committee, among whose members are Peter Mennin,[118] Agnes De Mille,[119] Jose Limon,[120] Paul Green, Julius Rudel, Leontyne Price,[121] Zelda Fichlandler,[122] Sidney Blackmer,[123] Eugenie Ouroussow,[124] Frederic Franklin,[125] Richard Adler,[126] and

---

[117] Vittorio Giannini (1903-   ), composer, conductor, teacher from Pennsylvania; scholarship student in Milan, Italy, in New York and Cincinnati; associated with Transylvania Music Center at Brevard; chosen Director of the North Carolina School of the Performing Arts, 1964. Who's Who in America, XXXIII, 732; Governor Sanford's statement of May 13, 1964.

[118] Peter Mennin (1923-   ), composer, music conservatory administrator from New York; member of faculty, Julliard School of Music since 1947; Director of Peabody Conservatory of Music; recipient of many national and international awards. Who's Who in America, XXXIII, 1372.

[119] Agnes De Mille, choreographer from New York; student, University of California; student of dance, London; arranger of dances for Oklahoma, Carousel, and Brigadoon; assisted in organization of London Ballet Company. John Parker (ed.), Who's Who in the Theatre: A Biographical Record of the Contemporary Stage (New York: Pitman Publishing Corporation [Twelfth Edition], 1957), 440, hereinafter cited as Parker, Who's Who in the Theatre.

[120] Jose Limon (1908-   ), concert dancer, choreographer, born in Mexico; art and dance student in New York, 1930-1940; choreographer for various Broadway shows, 1933-1940; member of various college faculties in the dance department. Who's Who in America, XXXIII, 1204.

[121] Leontyne Price later declined the appointment.

[122] Zelda Fichlandler later declined the appointment.

[123] Sidney Blackmer (1898-   ), actor, native of Salisbury; law student at the University of North Carolina at Chapel Hill; made stage debut in New York, 1917, film career, 1914. Parker, Who's Who in the Theatre, 284-285.

[124] Eugenie Ouroussow, Director, School of American Ballet, New York City. Information supplied by Bill Herring, School of the Performing Arts.

[125] Frederic Franklin later declined the appointment.

[126] Richard Adler (1921-   ), musical comedy writer from New York; member of Dramatists Guild and American Guild of Authors and Composers. Who's Who in America, XXXIII, 24.

Jan Peerce.[127] After a tour of the cities seeking the school, the committee recommended Winston-Salem. Winston-Salem offered the
school a whole high school campus, which the local school board
was planning to convert to other uses. But a million dollars was
needed to renovate the campus and add living quarters for the 400
students expected eventually to attend. In a three-day period a
group of the younger leaders in Winston-Salem raised more than
$900,000. Now Winston-Salem, already a cultural center, will be
the home of the North Carolina School for the Performing Arts.

I have purposely ended my catalog of North Carolina's participation in the state's cultural life with two examples of education. When a state makes financial grants, it should, and often
must, justify its actions in the eyes of the people.

If I were called upon to justify North Carolina's participation
in the arts, I could easily do it on educational grounds alone. With
its financial help to arts, music, drama, and dance, as well as historic restoration, North Carolina, I believe, is building an
audience that will in the future demand and get the finest in all
those fields.

The arts are supported in many ways at our state-supported
universities and colleges, but I haven't space to document these
expenditures.

North Carolina's participation in the arts is not that of direct
support of the artists themselves. Rather, North Carolina is, I
believe, creating a climate where the artist—amateur and professional—in whatever field, can flourish.

Finally, I would say that most of North Carolina's participation
in the arts has come about because people at the local level have
demanded it. They are the ones who best see the cultural needs
of their communities and act to fill those needs. The state's role
is one of encouragement and some financial help where it is
needed. The financial help comes, not because the state wants
to force anything on the people, but only after the people have
asked for help.

I make no grandiose claims for North Carolina's participation
in the cultural life of the state. Other states have perhaps done
more. Certainly, others have done it differently. But our way, so
far, has suited us fine.

I know that the state's participation is bound to increase over
the years. The forms it will take will probably be different from
those at present. But I can say that the climate of North Caro-

---

[127] Jan Peerce (1904-   ), operatic and concert tenor from New York; violinist
with dance orchestra, 1920-1932; performer in Radio City Music Hall, Carnegie
Hall, and the Metropolitan Opera; on radio broadcasts and recordings and in
numerous concert series. *Who's Who in America*, XXXIII, 1563.

The Governor, on a visit to Transylvania Music Camp in Brevard, took time to display his musical talents. With him is the Director, Dr. James Christian Pfohl.

A group leaving for the celebration of North Carolina Day at the New York World's Fair is pictured in front of the Legislative Building on June 1, 1964. Cherokee Indian Chief Richard Crow is with the Governor.

lina—which is a moderate one any way you look at it—will be healthy and progressive, whether you think of commerce, industry, tourism, or the arts.

DEDICATION OF
WAYNE COUNTY TECHNICAL INSTITUTE

GOLDSBORO

June 24, 1964

Speaking at the dedication of the Wayne County Technical Institute, Sanford observed that an excellent place to see North Carolina's constant need for improving education was at the air base in Goldsboro. To make planes fly took a lot of things, the Governor said, but the main thrust of power was education. He said that "Brain power has replaced back power as the number-one need in our economy." Sanford then launched into a discussion of the necessity for quality education, saying that new industry and new programs were assuring North Carolina's participation in the space age and that these programs could not work without educated minds. The Wayne County Technical Institute was called an answer to poverty, near-poverty, and low income in that it would provide adult education courses and vocational training which would afford an opportunity for many to acquire technical knowledge and skill. The age of automation required change; facilities of the Goldsboro institution would help Wayne County and North Carolina bridge the chasm of change.

DEDICATION OF STANLEY POWER TOOLS PLANT

NEW BERN

June 25, 1964

Since this event was being held in the home county of Conservation and Development head, Robert Stallings, Governor Sanford began his speech by acknowledging the work of this leader and his department. He then spoke of eastern North Carolina's great progress, saying the income of the area had increased by $93,655,000 in new industrial salaries alone during the preceding three and one-half years. Thanks to Stanley Power Tools and other companies the potentials of North Carolina in general and of the eastern section of the state in particular would be realized.

The Stanley company had joined others in this section for a number of reasons: available resources; increased interest in having industry; and work by local governments, the Chamber of Commerce, and state agencies. Industrial growth came about also because of attention paid to the things that counted most such as education, the welfare of the people, and a heritage of historical lore. This company was not the only one to realize what eastern North Carolina had to offer in the way of industrial location. From 1961 until May, 1964, 161 new plants and 297 expansions of plants were organized in this area, representing investments of $240,682,000 in new plants and $72,314,000 in expansion. After reviewing further achievements and progress of North Carolina, Governor Sanford closed by saying, "North Carolina is a good site on which to manufacture and a good market in which to sell . . . [but] most important of all, . . . [it] is a good place to live."

STATE-WIDE TELEVISION ADDRESS
ON POLITICAL CAMPAIGN

CHARLOTTE

June 26, 1964

[Governor Sanford made it clear on a number of occasions that he intended to stay out of active politics in the gubernatorial primaries at which his successor would be nominated. Three contenders—I. Beverly Lake, Dan K. Moore, and L. Richardson Preyer—conducted long and arduous campaigns prior to the first primary. After Lake had been eliminated, the second-primary contest between Moore and Preyer was nearing its close when Sanford reversed his "no statement" policy and publicly endorsed Richardson Preyer as the man he personally felt most capable of carrying forward North Carolina's progressive programs.]

I haven't been taking an active part in this campaign, but I don't think I would feel right about it five years from now, or next year, or right now, if I didn't tell you how I feel about it, and how I see what it will do to our future. After all, the people of North Carolina have been pretty good to me, couldn't have been better.

We have worked together in building a better state, in making the improvement of our school system the wonder of the nation, in making our state one of the most favored by industrialists looking for new sites, in exhibiting an enthusiasm and excitement about the things we can do, working together as the people of North Carolina.

I don't mean you have all agreed with me all of the time. Of course you haven't. I haven't agreed with myself some of the time. But you have had the spirit and the willingness to believe that North Carolina could be the best. Nobody could ask for any more, and I am grateful.

I am not coming here tonight to tell you how to vote. Your judgment is just as good as mine, and your combined judgment is a whole lot better than mine. But since we have been so far together, I want to tell you how I feel about this election—what I think it will do to our future.

I have stayed out of any active part in the campaign, not because I have been afraid to take a stand, not because I have had the least doubt for the past three or four months about which candidate could do the job that needs to be done.

I stayed out because I didn't see how I could get into day-to-day debate, answering charges, clarifying misleading statements; in effect, replying to those candidates who, it seemed, really wanted to argue with me rather shape up their own program.

I think they knew they had me at a disadvantage, and I made the mistake of saying that I didn't intend to get into any argument, answer any charge, or get involved. This seemed to give them their chance. They became more bold and stepped up their charges, so day in and day out they hammered away at me.

My reasoning was that I had a job to do. For example, I couldn't have cleared up the Chapel Hill demonstration situation if I had been burdened and saddled with day-to-day debate about the next governor.

For another example, we were right in the middle of putting together the Learning Institute of North Carolina. You haven't even heard much about this, but if you have got a boy or girl, smart but not getting much out of school, if you have a child who had trouble learning to read, if you are worried about your teenager dropping out of school, then LINC will probably be the greatest thing you have ever heard of. It is the first organization of its type in America, bringing the best minds of our whole state and country to bear on the problems of the schools and the children.

This is an example of the kind of thing we have been trying to do. You have seen other newspaper reports, almost every day, about fresh ideas, new ideas, strong ideas, coming from people all over the state and nation, which involve vocational education in our high schools, preschool training for children from deprived neighborhoods, new training programs in cold war citizenship education for our social science teachers, programs in high schools all across the state for the gifted student. These and many other ideas will give boys and girls, all people, a better chance to get ready, to grow stronger, to be able to build better. I would have had to drop most of these things, at least de-emphasize them, if I were going to spend several months to answer every campaign charge, every political exaggeration.

I did suggest finally that I might save up all the charges and answer them all at once, at the end of the campaign. Now it is the end of the campaign, now I can answer them all, by saying that they are all—you know it—politically inspired, and everybody will have forgotten about them a month from now. I can answer by saying that I have always, whatever the decision or the action, tried to do what I thought would be best for the state and the people, not only now, but ten years from now.

What worries me about all these charges is not that they have been directed against me, but that it now becomes very difficult, if not impossible, for those who have made those charges to serve adequately as governor. They have condemned roundly almost every program the people of the state now have going; they have promised to change everything; they have actually said that education no longer comes first in the budget, and that is the main place it must come first—in the budget. It's easy to put it first in other places. I know from firsthand experience, both in the legislature and the Governor's Office, that if the governor doesn't take a strong and determined position, the schools will not make the progress that they must make if our state is to be what it must be and our boys and girls are to have the chance they must have.

And frankly, I don't understand their criticism of our handling of the difficult race situation, or their lack of appreciation for the Good Neighbor Council, called by one national commentator "the most creative approach in America." How then would they do it? Of course, nobody is completely happy about the situation, but we do not have closed schools as they do in Virginia communities where the Byrd plan was followed; we don't have business afraid to come into the state as we have seen under the Arkansas plan; we don't have bloodshed and violence and riots and daily fear as they do under the Mississippi plan and in some northern cities. What would they substitute for the North Carolina plan? This might very well be the most important issue of the campaign, and I think they have put themselves in an impossible position to operate on the basis of fairness and calmness, which are the keynotes of the North Carolina plan.

Why, also, would anybody want to upset our industrial development? Along with a vigorous approach to our multitude of tobacco problems, our creative food processing program, our total assistance to the textile workers and industry—this is the economic future of the people of our state. I have been thoroughly berated about most of these things, yet only two or three weeks ago, based on a national survey, *Business Week Magazine* found that of all the fifty states, North Carolina was in the top five of the states where industrialists from across the nation would rather move new plants. We were the top in our region, with no other state even close. Why would anybody want to tear up this program, and what would they put in its place?

It's no wonder, then, that I want to talk with the people and let them know what I feel. I think these are good programs. I want to see them continued.

When I was a boy, every Sunday afternoon at Jack Roper's farm, we used to have relay races. We drew two lines, one down under a big oak tree at the end of the yard, and another line next to the front porch. We picked our runners, and each man had to run down the front path to the far line and back, and then pass the stick on to his teammate. Each man had to run his own race, but the success of the team depended on how well each man ran.

I have been running as fast as I could and the best I could. Here is one runner, however, who says, "Give it to me and I am going to walk to the finish line. I don't like the way you have been running. Look, you're out of breath. I'm going to walk, and then I won't be out of breath, and besides, I won't take the chance of stumbling." He may be right, but he wouldn't win for us either. He wouldn't even get to the finish line, at least not in time to make any difference. It is no wonder that I say, "Let's don't use that kind of runner on our team. Let's give it to this other runner, who says, 'Let me have it and I'll run faster and better than you did.'"

That is the way I feel about this election. You, the people, choose who will run your race. I am pleading that we let the great race for progress in North Carolina be run by the candidate who wants to run—not walk—and is willing to run hard, who wants to win for North Carolina. My interest is not in personalities, not in personal glory, not personal at all. It's certainly not in political machines. In fact, it's a new experience for me to be labeled as a political machine, because all of the time that I've been working in politics, first for Kerr Scott and then in my own election, I've been fighting what I thought was the old machine. And now, suddenly, I'm supposed to have a machine of my own. The truth of the matter is that one candidate has a group of loyal supporters, and his opponent will always charge that he is run by a machine.

Certainly there are people united behind each of these candidates, and one group of supporters favors the programs I've been talking about, and the other group does not. My interest is in these programs. I think our future depends on them. I think these programs are in danger unless we have Richardson Preyer[128] in there running hard for us.

I think with Judge Preyer we have a man who has the individual wisdom to move us forward. I think with Judge Preyer we have the honesty and integrity to take the courageous action and make the tough decision. I think in Judge Preyer we have the boldness and the imagination to give us four years of exciting and beneficial progress. At the end of his four years, I'm sure our children will have a better chance to make something of themselves. I think we will have more jobs for our people. I think our road system will be attracting even more industry because it will be the best road system in America. I think our people will be living in peace and not in a fearsome situation of extremists—of citizen against citizen. I think our tobacco farmers will have more security. I think our workers will have the better wages. I think we will all be proud to be from North Carolina and that people everywhere will be saying, "I wish we could do things like the people of North Carolina do them."

I believe this with all my heart, and I'm taking nothing away from any other individual when I say for our times, for this point in our developing history, for our own hopes and needs right now, Richardson Preyer is the man we should choose.

You alone make the decision—you choose the runner. I have one vote and I'm not telling you how to vote. But I'm saying, please put in the man who is willing to run the race all of the way.

STUDENT NEA NOTABLES DINNER

SEATTLE, WASHINGTON

July 2, 1964

Because of his intense interest in education, it was appropriate that Governor Sanford deliver the notables dinner address at the Student National Education Association convention. He began with a discussion of the need of teachers to have concern

---

[128] Lunsford Richardson Preyer (1919-   ), lawyer and former United States judge from Greensboro; alumnus, Princeton and Harvard; civic and educational leader; unsuccessful candidate for the Democratic nomination for governor of North Carolina, 1964. *Who's Who in America*, XXXIII, 1618; *News and Observer*, June 28, 1964.

because progress in government, economic development, national defense, and the world situation had to rely on education as a foundation stone on which to build objectives. Educators were also responsible for developing concern in public officials. Teachers were called on to feel concern for every individual child; without education, Sanford reminded the audience, a child was helpless. North Carolina's story was then cited as illustrative of what could happen when both educators and public officials were concerned. The response of the General Assembly in providing funds for advancement and the imaginative leadership on the part of state leaders had combined to make for progress. Governor Sanford outlined various programs which were being carried out in North Carolina. After discussing these, he concluded that the job was waiting to be done and that North Carolina would proceed to do it.

DEMOCRATIC UNITY DINNER

CHARLOTTE

July 31, 1964

[On June 27 Dan K. Moore was elected winner of the Democratic gubernatorial nomination after a heated campaign prior to the second primary. Governor Sanford, having publicly supported the losing candidate, stated clearly that he would support the Democratic candidate in the November election and urged all Democrats to back the choice of the party.]

Democrats:

I am for Dan Moore.[129]

I don't need to get united. I stay united in the Democratic party. I stay united in the Democratic party, in rain or shine, when we are in and when we are out.

I was Democratic, all the way, when Harry S. Truman and Kerr Scott were our candidates. I don't regret that and I am proud of it.

I was Democratic, all the way, when Adlai Stevenson and William Umstead were our candidates. I don't regret that and I am proud of it.

I was Democratic, all the way, when Adlai Stevenson and

---

[129] Daniel Killian Moore (1906-), lawyer, corporation official, former judge from Canton; member of North Carolina House of Representatives, 1941; county attorney, 1931-1943; Governor of North Carolina, January 1965—. Powell, *North Carolina Lives*, 875; *News and Observer*, January 9, 1965.

Luther Hodges were our candidates. I don't regret that and I am proud of it.

I was Democratic, all the way, when John F. Kennedy (along with, I might add, another pretty good candidate) was our candidate. I certainly don't regret that, and all of North Carolina can be proud of the fact forever that North Carolina went for John Kennedy.

So, this year, I am Democratic, all the way, when Lyndon B. Johnson and Dan K. Moore are our candidates. We can be proud of that and we will never regret it.

North Carolina needs Lyndon B. Johnson. He is fair to all people, not just to some of the people. He is firm with all nations, but he holds up the true spirit of the United States of America. He is sane and restrained, careful but determined, and while from Texas, he knows that this is not the wild West and you can't shoot 'em up just because you don't like them.

North Carolina is growing, going, moving upward, reaching for new opportunities long held out of our reach by history. The time is at hand when new jobs, new schooling, new advancements are coming our way.

North Carolina cannot afford to have a national leader who doesn't understand anything about the great American mechanism except the rear view mirror and the brakes.

Now is our time, most of all in North Carolina, to look ahead, plan ahead, move ahead. So we must have Lyndon B. Johnson.

And the Democratic party cannot fly on one wing. This is a time for all who believe in the orderly progress the Democratic party has brought to America to unite, across the board, up and down, regardless of primary preferences, to go all the way for all the Democrats.

Indeed, all the way is not enough. We need to go all the way with Lyndon B. Johnson and Moore. And all the way with Lyndon B. Johnson and Dan K. Moore is the only path for those who believe in the Democratic party.

I renew my pledge to support all the way President Lyndon B. Johnson and Dan K. Moore.

RALEIGH FOOD BROKERS DINNER

RALEIGH

August 12, 1964

Sanford began with the comment that Raleigh, as the largest food distribution center between Washington and Atlanta, was an appropriate place to have a "kickoff" dinner for Food Brokers Week. He said food processing had been stressed by his administration, and he asked the group to marshal its resources behind him. North Carolina had approximately 1,200 food processing plants, employing 31,000 persons with an annual payroll in excess of $147 million. The firms bought approximately $390 million worth of farm produce every year, and processors added $350 million worth of value to the commodities before they were sold. North Carolina's opportunity for additional food processing was great in that it did not produce enough to meet the demands of the citizens. To help this situation a Department of Food Science had been established at North Carolina State; a Food Industries Section existed as part of the Division of Commerce and Industry in the Department of Conservation and Development; and the North Carolina Department of Agriculture was cooperating in this field. The big need of existing food processors was an adequate merchandising program. Sanford mentioned an awards program which would recognize annually the merchant doing the most to promote the use of North Carolina products. He told the food brokers they held "the key that . . . [could] unlock the gate to opportunity. . . ."

PIONEER CORN COMPANY OPEN HOUSE

LAURINBURG

August 29, 1964

Addressing the group attending the open house of the Pioneer Corn Company, the Governor talked about agriculture, observing that it was likely to be overlooked in the scientific age. Science and technology had been applied to the field of agriculture, which was of vast importance to the Tar Heel state. Reviewing briefly the historical developments which had occurred, the Governor reminded those in attendance that at the beginning of the century one farm worker produced a sufficient amount for seven people; in 1963 the number had grown to twenty-three. Machinery, fertilizers, marketing all played a part. The improvement in seed had been spectacular, and the Pioneer Corn Company had had a major role in the production and selling of hybrid corn in twenty states. The company's twenty geneticists and fifty assistants worked throughout the United States to achieve the breeding of new and better hybrids. The Governor discussed in some detail the history of the company and its achievements. He said that

North Carolina, too, worked in numerous ways to better agriculture, and he reminded his audience that farmers bought some $9.7 million worth of seed each year, had almost $469 million invested in tractors and $171 million in trucks, owned farm equipment, bought fertilizer and liming material annually, purchased feed for the dramatically increased number of livestock they owned, and kept some $250 million in insurance in force. The agricultural picture continued to change and improve. Governor Sanford ended with the statement, "We are proud of our heritage in agriculture and launch out confidently to a greater harvest."

CARNEGIE AWARDS BANQUET
OF WINSTON-SALEM OPTIMIST CLUB

Winston-Salem

September 5, 1964

Labor Day week end was an appropriate time to consider the never-ending job of reducing death, damage, and disability from automobile accidents, the Governor told a Winston-Salem group on September 5, 1964. The estimate was that twenty-two—more than would die in Viet Nam battles—would be killed on North Carolina highways. Deadly were the "High-powered cars and low-conscious drivers." Race riots in Harlem, Rochester, and Philadelphia produced headlines as to injuries and property destruction. More people were killed and more property damage was done by drivers, however, than by rioters. The Governor said he hoped for the elimination of faulty safety equipment on cars. The 1963 General Assembly adopted more safety legislation than had been enacted in North Carolina since the coming of the T-Model, but no provision was made for safety inspection. Despite the stress on safe driving, the toll continued to mount. Sanford expressed the opinion that ultimately a way would be found to decrease wreckage on the highways, but the cure would be hard because it had to be found in the drivers of the vehicles using the roads.

DINNER HONORING THE DUKE ENDOWMENT

Charlotte

September 24, 1964

At a dinner honoring the Duke Endowment, Governor Sanford said that James B. Duke regarded the Duke Endowment as the outstanding achievement of his career. His second greatest achievement, he felt, was the assembling into the American Tobacco Company of men able to operate successfully the large companies resulting from the dissolution of the parent company. The Duke Endowment had benefited all of North Carolina. Appropriations to orphanages, hospitals, colleges, universities, and industries had been made, resulting in better lives, finer leadership, deeper Christian faith. Its contribution to education was of particular interest. Three of the four educational beneficiaries of the Duke Endowment were in North Carolina: Duke, Davidson, and Johnson C. Smith University. They had received over $118 million of the $206 million distributed by the endowment since its beginning. The Duke Endowment stood as a monument to one of North Carolina's ablest men, the Governor told the group in closing.

CAROLINA TEXTILES, INC., PLANT DEDICATION

MONROE

September 24, 1964

The Governor welcomed a company making quilts, sheets, and 35,000 other items, saying that population growth would mean a greater demand for such goods. The company was cited as an excellent example of the growth of industry in North Carolina, but Sanford reminded the audience that a large proportion of the "new" industry in the state was really an expansion of the old. He said that the Department of Conservation and Development had done much to encourage and assist business firms, that conferences with buyers from the federal government had helped establish the fact of what was needed, and that provision of information concerning financing had also been of help. From January, 1961, through June, 1964, over $1 billion was invested in new plants in North Carolina. There were 624 "new" industries and 1,383 expansions of established ones, meaning a total of almost 103,000 jobs as a result. Leading in the industrial expansion was the textile industry, which was vital to North Carolina's economy. Nearly half of all manufacturing employees in the state were textile employees and one-fifth of all Tar Heels depended on the textile industry for their economic well-being. The textile industry paid more than $839 million each year in wages in North Carolina. The new plant at Monroe was part of that growth and showed that the state's future was "limited only by . . . vision for the future and . . . work to make that vision a reality."

FORTY-SECOND ANNUAL
WESTERN DISTRICT NCEA MEETING

Asheville

September 29, 1964

The theme, "Education for World Understanding," was called an excellent choice by Governor Sanford, who felt that peace and understanding could only come through education. He called education "the foundation of economic opportunity . . . the foundation of democracy . . . [and] the foundation of the needs and hopes of the nation." He then discussed North Carolina's quality education program, but he emphasized the incompleteness of the program. He urged parents and educated leaders to vote for bonds for needed classrooms, adding that the issues were nonpartisan. He cited statistics and facts to support his plea, pointing out the necessity of classrooms "in which to teach our children who will be the statesmen, the scientists, the industrialists and the citizens of a free, prosperous, and peaceful world."

STATE-WIDE PLANNING MEETING
ON SCHOOL CONSTRUCTION

Raleigh

October 1, 1964

[The 1961 defeat of proposed bonds was not easily forgotten. After approval by the General Assembly of a $100 million school bond issue, nonpartisan forces went to work to convince the citizens of the need for an affirmative vote when the bond election was held. The efforts of the Governor and his supporters resulted in an overwhelming vote in favor of the bonds of November 3.]

If there is a single theme that has run through the record of North Carolina in the twentieth century, it has been that North Carolinians are unafraid of the future.

The citizens of this state have never trembled at the future. North Carolinians have never fallen faint at a challenge. And the state of North Carolina has not shirked her duty to her posterity.

That is why I am confident that North Carolinians will vote on

November 3 for bonds to build the classrooms needed by the boys and girls of this state.

If we are true to the record thus far achieved by our state in this century, we can do no less.

At the very start of this century there were many arguments against the building of public schools. There were many who thought Charles Brantley Aycock was being overly optimistic when he said North Carolina could provide universal public education. But the overwhelming majority of the citizens of North Carolina agreed with Aycock and built a school every day of his administration.

In the twenties when the state was getting into the road-building business, there were many who feared that Governors Cam Morrison and Angus McLean were being unduly extravagant by recommending multimillion dollar road-bond issues. But the majority of the citizens of North Carolina determined that they would link the county seats of our state. As a result we got a running start throughout the nation and as a consequence North Carolina has been known as the "good roads state" ever since.

In 1949 there were questions raised as to whether the road bonds and the school bonds advocated by Governor W. Kerr Scott would not bankrupt the state. The majority of North Carolinians didn't share those fears. They voted for the Scott-tops and for the new schoolrooms. As a result, North Carolina has reaped economic and human benefits ever since.

In 1953 there were some who failed to see the need for the bonds recommended by Governor William B. Umstead for building schools and mental hospitals. But the overwhelming majority of North Carolinians agreed with Governor Umstead that this state did need adequate classrooms and that we did need better mental hospitals. And the majority of the adult citizens agreed with Governor Umstead that we could afford those investments.

There are not many of you in this audience here today, and there certainly are not many in the entire state of North Carolina, who did not attend a public school that was built through a bond issue—either a local bond issue or a state bond issue.

On November 3 the adult citizens of North Carolina will determine if we want to risk as much for our children as our fathers and grandfathers risked for us.

On November 3 we will have the opportunity of voting on a $100 million program to build the schoolrooms which are so badly needed across North Carolina.

It should be stressed that the state is not rushing into this matter. When the public schools opened across our state earlier this month, North Carolina needed more than 11,000 additional new or renovated schoolrooms. The need is definite. The only question that we face on November 3 is whether we will begin to meet that need with state aid.

We know that if we want to provide our sons and daughters with adequate educational facilities, we are going to have to build these 11,000 schoolrooms.

There are many excellent reasons for our approval of this bond issue.

We know that from an economic point of view this proposed $100 million investment is a blue chip stock.

We know that North Carolina's credit rating ranks Triple A on Wall Street—and you can't get any higher than that.

We know from past experience that money invested in the education of our sons and daughters returns itself to the state's economy many times over.

We know, as pointed out in the fact sheet prepared by Dr. Charles F. Carroll, that the majority of classrooms built before 1930 are obsolete.

We know that many counties have reached or are approaching the limit of their bonded indebtedness. And this includes the large, well-to-do counties as well as the small ones.

We know that we have a mobile population and that the population of the state is shifting, thus creating additional school needs in various parts of our state.

Another reason that we need to approve this bond issue is the fact that many of our current classrooms are overcrowded. Teachers presently have too large a number of pupils to give adequate attention to individual students.

There are many, many reasons for adopting the school bond issue.

In fact, there are 1.2 million reasons. That's how many boys and girls we have in public schools of North Carolina today. And that number is increasing each year.

If there ever was a program for education that arose from the grass roots, this school bond program is it. The reason that it was introduced in the General Assembly was not because someone at the top said it should be introduced. It was introduced because the people at the local level—people like you and your neighbors—saw the urgent need for more classrooms. Some parents saw their children going to school in double shifts. Other parents saw their children being taught in trailers. Still many others saw their children attending classrooms that were outdated years ago. That is the reason that organizations like the United Forces for Education, the North Carolina Association of County Commissioners, the North Carolina School Boards Association, and many others got behind this bill and helped put it through the General Assembly.

Anyone who doubts that this is a nonpartisan issue needs only to read the vote in the State House of Representatives and in the State Senate. In the State House of Representatives, 104 members, representing both parties, voted for the bond issue. In the Senate this bond issue was approved by a two to one margin. It is easy to understand why members of both parties supported the school bond bill in the 1963 General Assembly. It is easy to understand why elected representatives of every section of our state supported this act. There is not a single school unit in North Carolina that does not need additional school space. That's why the legislators gave this bond issue overwhelming approval.

And that's why I am confident that when parents and grand-parents and other citizens go the polls on November 3, they will overwhelmingly approve this bond issue. I believe the adult citizens of North Carolina will decide the children of our state are worth it.

SOUTHERN ASSOCIATION OF STATE PLANNING AND DEVELOPMENT AGENCIES

RALEIGH

October 5, 1964

The greatest industrial story since the industrial revolution was probably written in the southern states after World War II, according to Governor Sanford. Formerly the South, overly dependent on agriculture, exported young people to other sections and imported manufactured goods. After World War II, the section was ready to move forward. Sanford said there was no excuse for the low economic status of the South because natural resources were abundant and problems and handicaps of the past had been overcome. There was no question but that the last part of the twentieth century belonged to the southern section of the United States.

DEDICATION CEREMONIES FOR NEW DORMITORIES AT CHOWAN COLLEGE

MURFREESBORO

October 17, 1964

Speaking at the dedication of new buildings at Chowan College,

Governor Sanford told of the deep regard for the past prevalent in the Chowan area, adding that there was even greater regard for posterity. He said North Carolina built on the past but did not rest on the past. To prove his point, he reviewed some of the history of the area and of Chowan College. The true value of Chowan would, he felt, be seen in the future as its graduates assumed position of leadership. The Governor continued with a discussion of the significance of all church-related colleges. He said he favored the proposal that these schools receive their fair share of funds coming into North Carolina under the Higher Education Facilities Act. Such a proposal would not violate the principle of separation of church and state but would represent a marked saving to the taxpayers and would not be charity. The Governor suggested that the state pay to each student attending a private college a tuition grant equal to half of what it would cost if the student attended a state-supported institution. He also recommended unlimited loan funds from the state. In conclusion, Sanford expressed the opinion that new frontiers would be conquered in Chowan College and across North Carolina by putting faith and work and money into education.

PIEDMONT CRESCENT TOUR BANQUET

CHARLOTTE

October 20, 1964

[The Piedmont Crescent Tour, which originated in Raleigh and terminated in Charlotte, had as its theme the importance of planning for the Piedmont Crescent area of North Carolina. A special nine-car Southern Railway train carried civic leaders and businessmen from cities and towns in the area. The climax of the trip was the address by Governor Sanford at the banquet held at the Myers Park Country Club in Charlotte.]

The Piedmont Crescent of North Carolina is probably a unique area in the nation. It is in the mainstream of East Coast commerce. It has a good mixture of industry, services, and agriculture. It has a good mixture of developed land and open space. It already operates as an economic region. It has 2 million people— as big as a "metropolis"—yet not a "mother city." It has a string of livable size, sister cities.

It has tremendous potential if regionalism is promoted to exercise economic power; to have cultural, business, and recreation facilities usually found only in a metropolis (concert halls, major league baseball, banking services, markets); to attract payrolls; to preserve identity of cities by keeping them from fusing together; to make the nation conscious of the area (America will remember "powerful Piedmont Crescent" when it may not remember "Burlington" or "Greensboro" or "Concord" or "Charlotte") and to spread benefits throughout North Carolina.

Modern commerce requires concentration of business, services, and people.

The Crescent may be the compromise between Frank Lloyd Wright's "Broadacres," a rural city—and LeCorbusier's concept of the super-city with very high density.

If we "follow the path of least resistance" as Lewis Mumford warned us fifteen years ago, "the cities of North Carolina will lose their regional characteristics, instead of developing them further, and will take on the worst features of metropolitan areas everywhere, with blight and bankruptcy as their final portion. In fifty years, if North Carolina does not plan to maintain its present decentralized pattern, Charlotte, Raleigh, and High Point will be indistinguishable from Detroit; and the surrounding countryside will become merely a real-estate speculators' annex to the growing metropolis."

He went on to point out that we would be "wealthier in all the things that money can buy, and poorer in all the things that are beyond price or purchase: neighborly association, friendly intercourse, home life, intimate contact with nature, the spiritual values that cannot be mechanized, standardized, or wholly institutionalized."

If we force the thinking on development of these cities into the traditional molds, we will make the traditional mistakes.

Since the area is different, since it is not blighted, since there is a special opportunity to create a new type of city, it will require *new* thinking. Let us throw away the book on cities and take a fresh approach. Why not? Very few have the chance we have to *create* the good life as we build an urban region. Most other cities are preoccupied with undoing mistakes.

Our task will take thought and action by thousands of people to get the job done. Someone has to start, someone must organize and lead.

To provide the leadership I have started by appointing the Executive Committee on the Piedmont Crescent 2000 Commission. The members will recruit the 2000 good citizens whose thought and action will be needed. They will plan for the year 2000.

Their charge, as I have told them in giving them their commissions, is:

The promotion of the proper development of the Piedmont Crescent of North Carolina, which is that group of cities and related rural areas from the vicinity of the city of Raleigh to the vicinity of the city of Charlotte.

The stimulation of the growth of jobs, income, and capital investment in the Crescent.

The giving of advice on the proper growth of the Crescent to the end that it may be economically efficient, culturally rich, and aesthetically attractive.

The education of the people on the problems, potentials, and programs of the Crescent.

That is a staggering assignment in four sentences. It is for them and for you and for the people of the Crescent to translate it into programs, into action, and into the finest region of cities in the United States. [The Governor concluded by naming the members of the commission. See list of appointments, pages 747-748, for these names.]

GOVERNOR'S TRAVEL INFORMATION CONFERENCES

GREENVILLE, WINSTON-SALEM, ASHEVILLE

October 28, 29, 30, 1964

Three day-long conferences were held in October, 1964, to promote the travel industry in North Carolina. North Carolinians who were in the business of serving tourists and other travelers were invited to attend. The Governor asked his audience if each thought he was getting his share of this billion-dollar industry, which was estimated to grow to $2 billion by 1974 and to $3 billion by 1984. With 27 million people visiting North Carolina in 1963, the need for good service was obvious. Sanford urged the group to be prepared for future visitors and to remember that there was no longer any such thing as "in-season" because tourists were taking trips at all times of the year. Increased incomes and leisure were predicted for the future, meaning more business for service stations, motels, and restaurants. North Carolina's advertising campaign would mean business for North Carolinians. Sanford complimented the TV stations and other news media for their co-operation in giving free advertising to the state, but he reminded his audience that competition for the travel dollar would increase. "By more closely co-ordinating the activities of all segments of the travel industry—restaurants, service stations, hotels and motels, travel and historical attractions, cities and counties—we can present a unified promotion punch that other states can't touch. The spirit is here—the opportunity is here." Thus did the Governor sum up the requirements for expansion. He concluded by saying that "travel is a big and growing business in North Carolina. Every community can share in its benefits. To what extent can be determined by how well we recognize our assets, develop them, and market them. Together, let's make the most of North Carolina's fabulous travel future."

OPENING OF ADVANCEMENT SCHOOL

WINSTON-SALEM

November 8, 1964

[The Advancement School, made possible by financial investments on the part of the state, the city of Winston-Salem, the Department of Health, Education, and Welfare, and the Carnegie Foundation, was established to give specialized training for three months to eighth graders whose achievements were below the level of their potential. At no cost to them, seven students and a teacher attended from each school represented. Three hundred and fifty students were present for this opening address by Governor Sanford.]

Those who come to this place, students and teachers alike, are explorers pioneering into new and exciting frontiers.

North Carolina is a leader in education and I would have us become *the* leader in American education.

We know there are better ways of teaching and quicker ways of learning than we are now using. You students are prospecting for those ways.

You were chosen because you have the intelligence and ability, and because we had confidence in your willingness to help us seek the answers to the riddles of learning.

The Advancement School is one path to these discoveries about learning and teaching we expect to make. What we discover here will be sent out into the schools of the nation for the enlightenment of those who are charged with the education of the nation.

So what you do here is not limited to you, and it is not limited to the Advancement School in Winston-Salem. The work you do here, if you do it well and conscientiously, can become universal.

We seek to become the best in the nation in the system of education we offer our boys and girls. The Advancement School is one of the means of achieving this ambition. It is a part of the broad plan of the Learning Institute of North Carolina, which we have come to call "LINC."

LINC joins together all the forces of education, to seek, to test, and to evaluate all that is known or to be known about learning and education. LINC joins together all the forces of education to apply and put to us all of the profitable lessons learned by this joint and massive effort of research and development.

Sponsored by Duke University, the University of North Carolina in all of its campuses, the State Board of Education, and the North Carolina Fund, joined in by the Superintendent of Public Instruction and the Department of Public Instruction and the Board of Higher Education, advised and counseled by our school superintendents, principals, and teachers across the state, LINC truly belongs to everybody who has anything to do with the schooling of our youth.

LINC is the most significant factor in the improvement of education in America. This is our means of leadership. As we do a better job in education, North Carolina becomes the leader and North Carolinians become the contributors to and the beneficiaries of an advancing civilization.

You are a part of the frontier of improved education.

I am grateful to Gordon McAndrew[130] and faculty, to city officials and all you have planned, to Harold Howe[131] and LINC and to you.

This school is the spirit of North Carolina.

GOVERNORS CONFERENCE ON EDUCATION

ATLANTA, GEORGIA

November 11, 1964

Meeting in Atlanta, Governor Sanford began with a reference to Veterans Day, commenting on the appropriateness of celebrating the occasion with a conference concerned with the improvement of educational opportunities. Challenges to maintain peace and freedom remained. The South was rising in the fields of education, industry, commerce, and agriculture; the South was rising as a

---

[130] Gordon L. McAndrew, native of Oakland, California, participant in teaching and experimental programs; former Director of Interagency School Project of Oakland Public Schools; appointed Director of North Carolina Advancement School, 1964. *News and Observer,* July 31, 1964.

[131] Harold Howe, educator from Scarsdale, New York; served in capacities of teacher, principal; trustee of Yale, Vassar; named Director of Learning Institute of North Carolina, 1964. *News and Observer,* May 1, 1964.

region; and each state of the South was also rising as a unit. In the past southerners had blamed the lost cause, discriminatory freight rates, lack of capital, a disease-prone climate, and other external factors for their troubles, but such factors could no longer be used as excuses. The South had come to realize that ignorance and freedom would not work together, that farming was becoming increasingly mechanized and required skilled workers, that cheap labor would not attract industry in the future though expensive education would, and that investments in education were vital to economic growth. The need for skilled craftsmen, scientists, and engineers had to be met in order to attract top industries. Sanford commented that the time had come for the South to stop crawling and walking and to begin running. He added that too small a proportion of southerners were engaged in occupations which required a high degree of education and training. The South, which needed to get the most out of educational efforts at all levels, also needed long-range plans. The Governor referred to North Carolina's study of education beyond the high school and Georgia's Educational Improvement Council, commenting that North Carolina's educational and government officials would watch Georgia's effort with interest. Education was crying for leadership; Sanford urged the South to answer the call and serve in the role of leader in this vital area.

NEW JERSEY EDUCATION ASSOCIATION

ATLANTIC CITY, NEW JERSEY

November 13, 1964

Governor Sanford spoke to a group of New Jersey educators, again speaking on the theme of education. He said the greatest force for subversion of democratic ideals and human aspirations was ignorance. The greatest infringement on civil rights was the denial of the best educational opportunities. Rural and urban children, children from all sections and of all races were the victims of this denial. Education determined progress. "It embraces all the hopes that the government fosters, including world peace. . . ." Educational support was a requirement for industry and business growth; a "child is helpless without education." North Carolina's story was summarized to illustrate the results when both educators and public officials were concerned. Concern was needed, however, beyond the legislative halls and beyond monetary support. School people had to have an active concern.

The Governor described North Carolina programs for retarded children; he discussed the investment of $4 million to find better ways of teaching the first three grades; he told the group about the "Operation Second Chance" program for dropouts; and he briefly explained the Learning Institute of North Carolina, LINC, which was set up to do research on education. These examples showed what could be accomplished when there was concern and conviction that the job could be done. Sanford stated that the job was waiting to be done and that there was no need for delay in getting to work on it.

DEDICATION OF STATE LEGISLATIVE BUILDING

RALEIGH

November 20, 1964

[Governor Sanford's statements concerning the new Legislative Building revealed clearly the significance of the occasion. The building, designed by Edward Durrell Stone, of New York City, and Holloway-Reeves, of Raleigh, was the first state-owned structure to be planned and used solely for legislative fuctions. Its architecture attracted much attention, and thousands of citizens visited Raleigh to see the new State House. The formal dedication ceremony, held two years after the Legislative Building had been completed and put in use, was attended by dignitaries from all parts of North Carolina. Because the plane bringing him from New Haven, Connecticut, especially for the dedication ceremony was delayed by bad weather, the Governor's remarks were read by Mr. Hugh Cannon, Director of Administration.]

The most eloquent dedication that could be given for any building was written during the first six months of 1963. It was written by the members of the 1963 General Assembly when they wrote one of the most forward-looking legislative records of any General Assembly in the long history of North Carolina.

This is a magnificent building, and we could spend hours discussing its beauty. This is a fascinating building which has attracted tens of thousands of people from each of the 100 counties of North Carolina and from each of the fifty states and from many foreign lands. In the future years it will attract millions more.

But more magnificent and fascinating even than the architecture and setting of this building is the action for progress of North Carolina that already has taken place within these halls.

From this Legislative Building already have come $100 million worth of new classrooms for the boys and girls of North Carolina. From this building have come the blueprints and funds for three new senior colleges—one in the East at Wilmington, one in the Piedmont at Charlotte, and one in the West at Asheville. From this building also have come many new laboratories and classrooms and dormitories for our university and each of the state-supported colleges. In this building the authorization and the financing of a system of comprehensive community colleges across North Carolina have been made.

Here the legislators of North Carolina already have built new port facilities, new highways, new industries, new educational television stations, provided for new opportunities for the talented and new chances for the retarded, another new building which will be located near here for the cultural agencies of state government, new mental hospitals, and a new school of the arts.

Within this building also has been written more traffic safety legislation than in any session of the General Assembly since the coming of the T-Model Ford.

This has come about not as a Governor's program, but as a program for all the citizens of North Carolina. This record of achievement for North Carolinians resulted from the courage of the members of the 1963 General Assembly. We had a strong General Assembly in 1963, and we will have a strong General Assembly in 1965. North Carolina is proud of its past. And, therefore, it is appropriate that you can see from this building the old State Capitol where for more than a century legislators worked for the betterment of North Carolina.

North Carolinians are even prouder of their future, and it is to that future that we are dedicating this remarkable building today. The record already compiled here will be written large in the history of our state. The future of North Carolina will be tied closely to what goes on here in 1965 and 1967 and 1969 and all the years ahead.

Here then is a building which embodies consensus of the needs and the dreams and the potential of North Carolinians from the Atlantic to the Appalachians.

DEDICATION OF SANDHILLS COMMUNITY COLLEGE

SOUTHERN PINES

November 25, 1964

The orbit into space did not just happen. "Man built upon man's knowledge. Frontiers of new knowledge were forged. Brain power had long before been put to work." Thus did Governor Sanford begin his address at the dedication of a new community college in Southern Pines. He called the new institution a pioneering one, a status which could also be applied to the entire comprehensive community college system in North Carolina. The system was not being established, without prior knowledge, however, as other states had had experience in this field. Sanford said the goal of his administration had been quality education and that hopes had become realities. He outlined major achievements in the field of education, concluding with the prediction that a new day was being realized through education and that the door of opportunity was being opened.

CONVENTION OF THE NATIONAL COUNCIL OF TEACHERS OF ENGLISH

Cleveland, Ohio

November 26, 1964

During the last weeks of his administration, Governor Terry Sanford continued to speak on the topic of education, both in addressing groups in North Carolina and in speaking to out-of-state audiences. After outlining progress made in America, Governor Sanford told an Ohio audience that there were still gaps in many areas, such as education, peace, and mental retardation. He concluded that teachers had a vital role in remedying existing defects and that the sum total of efforts in the classroom was more important to the continuing defense than the total sum of efforts at military bases. Education, the key answer to overcoming poverty, trained young people to use their brains rather than their backs. Sanford stressed the strong correlation between a state's investment in education and its income. Experience showed that "as we have invested more in schoolhouses, we have been obligated to invest less in the poor houses." Experience further showed "that the lines at the Welfare Department decrease in direct proportion to the increase in lines at commencement time." The success of the Economic Opportunity Act would be determined by the educational opportunities action taken.

DEDICATION OF GASTON COLLEGE

Dallas

December 6, 1964

Governor Sanford began by commenting on landmarks calling attention to the emerging state of North Carolina, such as smokestacks, silos and barns, highways, and most significantly, schools and colleges. He referred to Gaston County as an outstanding one, but one in which too many of the people had not had an opportunity for education to equip them for higher paying jobs. Because of this situation, the decision was made to build a comprehensive community college, with financing being made possible because the citizens of the county were willing to vote a new tax on themselves. Sanford said funds thus spent would be repaid as they were returned in the form of "higher salaries, greater trade, more bank deposits and in a thousand other ways." Gaston College was cited as an example of co-operative endeavor of local, state, and federal governments. The 1963 General Assembly approved the system of community colleges, schools which would bring education beyond the high school to every section of North Carolina. In dedicating Gaston College, Governor Sanford charged the students of the county and neighboring counties "to take full advantage of new and exciting educational opportunities."

DEDICATION OF SITE FOR FOOD SCIENCE BUILDING NORTH CAROLINA STATE OF THE UNIVERSITY OF NORTH CAROLINA AT RALEIGH

RALEIGH

December 11, 1964

The dedication at which Governor Sanford spoke represented, he said, a potential investment which would bring a rich return. Teaching and research would take place, and this Department of Food Science was part of the plan to lift North Carolina farm income to $1.6 billion by 1966. Despite cancer scares, boll weevils, black shank, and other problems, the goal would be met. Despite the know-how of farmers, they had to eat food products produced all over the country, a fact which led the Governor to stress the need for North Carolina to process food. He said education had been emphasized but there were still limited opportunities and many of the educated children were moving elsewhere. Industrial expansion, including that in the field of food processing, would provide incentive which was badly needed. Since the establishment of a special food processing program in 1961, an average of one new food processing plant, or expansion, had occurred every week. Sanford mentioned the co-operative endeavors of the Department of Conservation and Development, the Department of Agriculture, the North Carolina Rural Rehabilitation

Corporation, and the Business Development Corporation, along with North Carolina State. With local co-operation added, North Carolina could produce its own food. "And if we fret that our waistlines are getting larger, we will know that the income of North Carolina is getting larger with every mouthful we eat."

PRODIGAL SONS AND DAUGHTERS OF NORTH CAROLINA LUNCHEON

WASHINGTON, D. C.

December 21, 1964

[The Prodigal Sons of North Carolina was an organization established by Governor Sanford for native Tar Heels who, working and residing outside the state, maintained close ties with their home state and with each other. Speaking to a luncheon meeting of the Washington group, Governor Sanford told the members of news "back home."]

Looking around these tables today, you can see why North Carolinians are not scared of the federal government as some folks are in other states. We are not afraid of Washington and we are not going to secede from the union because a good portion of the people running things up here are our kinfolk.

We are proud of the Tar Heels who work in the White House, in the other executive offices, in the Congress, in business and industry, the arts and the professions.

In fact, we are just as proud of you as we are of those earlier Prodigal Sons like Andrew Jackson, James K. Polk, and Andrew Johnson, who began in North Carolina their journeys to Washington.

For those of you who have not had the opportunity to get back home lately, I want to report to you that North Carolina is changing—and we believe that it is changing for the beter. Over the years North Carolina has moved from the south end of a mule to the topside of a computer. We still have our "chitlin" struts like we always did, but we now also have a fast growing food processing industry. Those pine trees still stand as tall as they did when you lived in North Carolina, but they now share the landscape with skyscrapers and smokestacks and even a NASA tracking station.

I don't have to remind the members of this audience that North Carolina was the site of the first English settlement in the New World. But you will be interested in the fact that North Carolina in the last few years has been establishing sizable colonies of immigrants from New Jersey and New York and Illinois and other states as new industries move into our state.

Of course, you know that North Carolina was first in the union to open a state university. But you may be interested in knowing that in the last General Assembly we authorized three new senior colleges—one in the East at Wilmington, one in the Piedmont at Charlotte, and one in the West at Asheville. Perhaps even more important we authorized construction of a system of comprehensive community colleges that is designed to extend universal public education for two additional years.

North Carolinians are proud of our past. But we are prouder still of our potential. That's why when we celebrate, as we did last week, the anniversary of the first airplane flight at Kitty Hawk, we celebrate even more the production of missiles at places like Western Electric and Douglas Aircraft Company.

Tar Heels traditionally have boasted of the fact that the first declaration for independence was adopted at Halifax a month or so before the Philadelphia Convention in 1776. We also are proud of the fact that North Carolina refused to ratify the United States Constitution until the civil rights contained in the first ten amendments were added.

But it occurred to us that if the men at Halifax had the courage to declare for independence back in 1776 and if North Carolinians of the eighteenth century were so democratic that they would not ratify the Constitution until the Bill of Rights was added, then we of the twentieth century should show some of the same sort of courage. That's why in recent years North Carolina towns from the old plantation country of the East to the communities of the mountains have established Good Neighbor Councils to encourage employment without regard to race, color, or creed. That is why the 1963 General Assembly took the color bar from around our National Guard. And that is why state agencies have been encouraged and instructed to hire people without regard to race.

North Carolinians have been doing these things because down through the generations the citizens of our state have sought to hand their sons and daughters two things: a rich past and an even richer future.

I was interested in 1963 to read of a high level debate between Gerald Johnson and Arnold Toynbee. It was Toynbee's theory that the reason for North Carolina's modern progress was the fact that prior to the Civil War we didn't have nearly as much as other southern states. Therefore, we didn't lose as much in the Civil War, and we didn't spend as much time worrying about the past.

I am inclined to agree with Gerald Johnson's theory that it has been since 1900 that North Carolina has forged ahead and that the big reason for whatever progress our state has made in this century can be credited to Charles Brantley Aycock. Aycock proposed "the equal right of every child born on earth to have the opportunity to burgeon out all there is within him."

Now that was a right tall order for a mighty poor state when Aycock uttered those words. It was an extremely hard order for North Carolinians in the depression thirties. It certainly was not an easy goal to fulfill when schools in other states were closing after the Supreme Court decision of 1954.

But during the depression, North Carolina kept faith with Aycock's goal by adopting an unpopular tax to keep the school doors open. And in the fifties responsible leaders in both the white and Negro races kept faith with that goal by refusing to permit the closing of the school doors. I believe North Carolinians of this decade are keeping faith with that goal, as evidenced by the overwhelming approval in both houses of our General Assembly of an unpopular tax to finance the greatest advance made in public education in the history of North Carolina.

If you think about Aycock's words a minute, you will see that they are pregnant with problems as well as with potentials. How do you build an educational system that gives a child of an IQ of 142 the opportunity to burgeon out all that is within him? On the other end of the scale, what do you do for the child who through a quirk of nature is mentally retarded? What sort of school opportunities do you present the child who is artistically gifted? What do you do for the young man who, having finished high school, does not have the money to go on to college? How do you provide for the child who is talented with his hands but doesn't do too well with "book learning"? What sort of educational opportunity do you offer the child from the underprivileged neighborhood who comes from a home where there are no books?

It seemed to us that if we found the solutions to these questions we would be finding solutions to the continuing problem of how to end the cycle of poverty under which the children of poor parents grew up to be the parents of poor children. We also knew that through building schools we would be building the much needed new industries in our state. It was obvious to us that as mechanization continued on the farm and as automation continued in the factories brain power would replace back power as the chief need for employment. So first, we turned our attention to the so-called average child who constitutes the great bulk of the population. We added $100 million in enrichment funds to the public school budget in 1961, and we added another $50 million in 1963.

Now these enrichment funds went to many different channels. One of the largest of these channels, of course, was the pay of school teachers. Without any disrespect to Senators Ervin[132] and Jordan, I would say that I agree with Admiral Hyman Rickover when he says that teachers should be paid more than United States Senators. (Rickover said senators because they make more than governors.) Yet for too long in North Carolina, and in most states, we have tried to pay teachers off with red apples and year-book dedications. The enrichment funds for the public schools also meant smaller class loads. They meant more books in libraries. Those funds meant clerical assistance for the teachers so that the teachers could spend their jobs with the students rather than reports. These enrichment funds meant that students in every school could have a wider range of courses. For example, students in some schools would have a chance to study physics for the first time.

To effect these improvements, we had to pay for them. And we are paying for them through what is popularly known back home as "Terry's Tax." I've never been sorry that I recommended that tax and I have yet to meet a legislator who was sorry that he voted for it. I might add, the vast majority of those legislators were re-elected not only in 1962 but were re-elected also in 1964.

Now according to NEA figures North Carolina made the greatest advance of any state in the union in 1961 in improving its public schools. It would have been easy to stop right there. But North Carolina was too far behind the rest of the nation. And our nation was too far behind where it should be in public education.

It seemed to us that if we took care of the average child that we also should take care of the especially talented child. Therefore, we greatly increased the special classes for the bright students within the public school system of North Carolina, and we established a special school to provide superior instruction for 400 talented children every summer at Winston-Salem.

At the other end of the scale we were interested in the mentally retarded children. For too many years the only thing we had to offer the mentally retarded was a chain and filthy clothes at worst, or, at best, custodial care. We knew from experience that many of these children were trainable and educable. Therefore, the 1963 General Assembly of North Carolina adopted a broad

---

[132] Sam J. Ervin, Jr. (1896-   ), lawyer, judge, and civic leader from Morganton; Congressman in United States House of Representatives, 1946-1947; Associate Justice of State Supreme Court, 1948-1954; successor to Clyde R. Hoey in the United States Senate. *North Carolina Manual, 1963,* 499-501.

program which seeks to help such children to become self-respecting and self-supporting.

Then, we looked at the children who had average or above-average intelligence but who, for one reason or another, just do not learn. This fall we opened what we call the Advancement School of North Carolina. In this school students will live in dormitories and receive intensive instruction from teachers from across the state. We hope in this school not only to help the students chosen to take a semester of work there to catch up, but also to take the lessons that we learn there and supply them in each of our 100 counties and offer the lessons that we learn to schools in other states.

Now what about the young people who are artistically gifted? Should they have to go to Julliard or to Europe to develop their talents? We thought not. Therefore, we established the North Carolina School of the Arts which will open next year.

In looking over the educational needs of North Carolina we saw a statistic that we did not like: We found that about 50 per cent of the children who started in the first grade never got through high school. We found that those who did get through high school often did not have the education that they needed to move successfully into adult life. To examine this question and many others related to education our state established the Learning Institute of North Carolina. No industrialists operating on a budget of more than a half billion dollars a year would neglect his research department the way that we have neglected research into education. We hope and we believe that LINC will be successful in learning some new things about education.

Once a boy or girl has finished high school where does he or she go? In our ever increasing labor market no less an authority than Secretary of Labor Willard Wirtz has suggested two additional years of compulsory education. That is the reason that we have established a blueprint for a system of comprehensive community colleges to be built as and where needed across our state. In these comprehensive community colleges, we have included the industrial education centers to provide the instruction for young people to acquire the skills so badly needed by our increasingly skilled industries. We also have included college parallel work so that students may live at home and commute to college. Many of these students could never have afforded to go to Chapel Hill or to Boone or to Greenville to college. Then we have assigned these comprehensive community colleges the large task of providing adult education courses to help grown people learn how to read and write. We have dedicated two of these new colleges within the last two weeks. And we hope that there will be twenty-two when this decade is over.

North Carolinians have made these and other advances in education because:

We believe education is more important in breaking the cycle of poverty than all the handouts combined.

We believe the report cards from the schools are more important to the economy than the Dow Jones averages.

We believe that sitting in schools will more rapidly assure equal rights than sitting in restaurants and that education is our best cure for bigotry.

In our reach for the stars, education provides the greatest thrust power.

REPORT TO THE PEOPLE OVER STATE-WIDE RADIO AND TELEVISION NETWORKS

RALEIGH

January 4, 1965

[In this last gubernatorial report to the people, Governor Sanford discussed his administration, its accomplishments, and its aspirations for North Carolina, in a thirty-minute broadcast over the facilities of WTVD-TV and WPTF radio. As a final gesture to the student population of North Carolina, Governor Sanford invited students from Raleigh's Needham Broughton High School to be with him in the studio. The Governor did not speak from a formal address but delivered his remarks "off the cuff." This transcription of his remarks was made from a tape recording at Radio Station WPTF in Raleigh.]

During the past four years, I've been traveling about the state, visiting schools, and talking to students about what I hoped we could do in North Carolina and what I hoped we could do in the schools. I had a very real feeling that the students could do about as much as any other group in setting high standards of quality, in achieving those standards by better performance in school, and by insisting to their elders, their parents, their leaders, their school people, and the people in government who vote money, that they wanted to have the best school system in all the world. I believe that the students, working together and catching this spirit, have done much to contribute to the improvement of education in this state, and because of that, to help in the total effort to improve education all across the country. So on this last day, as I had a chance to talk to the people of the state, and again to the students of the state, I thought that we might have a final

conference on where Norh Carolina has been, and where we hope
it will continue to move in the future.

I grew up in Laurinburg, a town about 100 miles south of
Raleigh, and on the wall of the house I lived in was a framed
drawing, "The Toast to the Old North State." As you know, it
goes something like this:

> Here's to the land of the long-leaf pine
> The summer land where the sun doth shine,
> Where the weak grow strong, and the strong grow great,
> Here's to down home—the Old North State!

That's what we've been trying to do in North Carolina: to make
it a place where the weak grow strong and the strong grow great.
And that's what it's all been about; that's what everything that
we've done in government in the past four years has been measured
against. Can we make North Carolina the kind of a community
where all the people can have their best chance to grow strong,
and to grow still stronger, and then grow great? Measure everything we've done against that ideal, that hope, and that challenge,
and you'll find that we have tried to follow that light.

Now I don't mean physically strong and physically great, alone,
though that's important too. You know something about our
physical fitness programs. Some of you have participated in those
programs, and a couple of you obviously haven't. You know something about the wonderful climate that we have here— the attractions for people who are facing retirement.

That kind of physical climate is good, and we are proud of it
and glad to have it. But when we talk about growing strong and
growing great we're talking about something of far greater
significance and fuller meaning than just physical well-being and
physical strength. This business of growing strong begins with
you, because I think we must start with people who are developing, who have their chance now to get ready for whatever they
are going to do. This whole business starts with you, your attitude and your belief, how you look at the state, and how you hope
for the future.

Let's take your jobs, for example. This state has been trying
to do a great deal about providing jobs. We don't want you to
finish school, go to college, and then to leave the state never to
return, except maybe for visits at Christmas time. We want our
skilled young people to use their knowledge and brains and talents
here at home. We want to create the kind of jobs right here that
can give you as good a challenge as you get anywhere else. That's
why the state is engaged in the business of trying to provide better
jobs and broader economic opportunity—not just to have jobs,

but because jobs give people a chance to grow stronger, and ultimately, the whole people a chance to grow greater.

We can't create jobs—the state can't make jobs—but what we can do is to make this the kind of place that will be attractive to people who can create jobs—to industry. And so we've spent a lot of time trying to get industry to come here. The father of one of you in this studio is a good example. He came here with a whole new system of plants because North Carolina looked attractive to him as a place that his company could come and make a profit and do well in the community. We've been trying to appeal to industry in that way so jobs will be created, not by the state, but because of the efforts the state has been making.

Now you can measure, also, our hope to grow stronger and greater by what we've done in highways. You might think that highways don't have much to do with people, but they do. Governor Scott's secondary roads, giving us the finest system of secondary roads anywhere in the country, have contributed so much to industrial development. People who live out in nonurban areas can drive in to work and out in all kinds of weather. So we have a tremendous working force without having to crowd them all in relatively unwholesome living conditions. Roads contribute much to jobs, which, in turn, contribute to a better life. This administration has spent a lot of time on roads, not because we wanted to say we have the best road system—though I think now we perhaps have the third best road system in the country—but because we wanted to create a stronger economic base. In this administration we have spent more money, invested more money, and I think wisely invested it, in roads—interstate roads, primary roads, and secondary roads—than any other administration in the history of the state. We've done it as our hope for the future, as another means, you see, of growing stronger.

You've probably heard this story or read it in the paper, but I think it helps illustrate the point that no matter how good we get we still need to do more. We still have people who are living on unpaved roads, and we still have very dangerous sections of primary roads. We badly need interstate roads or four-lane limited highways in some sections of the state, including an east-west highway. I had been in office less than two years when I had a man call on me who wanted a little piece of road paved. I couldn't very well do it—the priority system simply wouldn't allow it—and I was trying to let him down as easily as possible. And I explained to him that in terms of all the miles and the miles paved that we ranked behind only New York and Ohio. If you throw in the automobiles as a factor we probably rank number one, because we have fewer automobiles per mile in North Carolina as compared to those states. So we probably have the best road system in the country. I said, "But in any event, Kerr Scott paved more roads in the time he was in office than have ever been paved in Texas. California, a tremendous state, has about the same number of paved secondary roads as we have, but they have about twice as many unpaved." Happening to look at some figures there, I added, "In the eighteen months I've been in this business, I've paved more secondary roads that have ever been paved in the whole state of Louisiana." And I could see that I was really getting to him—he was nodding and agreeing with everything I was saying. "Now what do you think about that?" I asked.

And he said, "I'll tell you what I think about that—I don't live in Texas or California!"

So you see, in spite of the fact that we are getting good all the time, when you measure it against what we can do, we still haven't gone nearly far enough. We need to continue to make our road and port systems, our rails and airways, the very best possible because all of these things help make this a state on which we can build a stronger economic base. And all of these things go together to provide jobs, which in turn provide you with a better opportunity to use your education.

Governor Hodges gave this whole idea of creating new jobs a new outlook. He traveled all over the country, in fact, to other parts of the world, to tell people about North Carolina. "Here is a good place to come and build a plant," he would tell them. And we've carried that on. I visited in Los Angeles, Chicago, Cleveland, Pittsburgh and New York, and a number of other places to talk to industrialists. I told them that North Carolina has what it takes, and that we have a growing state, a state where you can make a profit, a state where industry can do well. Therefore we attract their attention, they come to North Carolina, and they build up a reservoir of opportunity for you. That's what all this industrial development is about. It's not so we can cite statistics and say we're doing well and growing. We're growing for a purpose—to help you to have a better chance in life, to grow strong and then to grow great through opportunities.

Now we've got a record of which you can be proud. In the last four years we've seen more economic growth, more new jobs, and more new investment than at any time in our history. We are moving upward, and we ought to continue to move upward if we continue to drive. During the past four years we've seen invested in this state in new plants—new plant facilities which includes of course expansion of old plants— $1.3 billion in new capital investment. That means at least 120,000 new jobs. Those are the jobs we can count with this new investment, with this new industry; but if you were to consider all the grocery clerks and other people that service those 120,000 paying positions, you would realize how many new jobs are really created. Out of these new jobs alone at least $400 million in new payroll has been brought to North Carolina in the last four years. So that's what we're all about—seeking jobs is simply to seek better opportunities.

And we haven't just been seeking jobs, but because we want the best kind of jobs, we've been putting emphasis on several new kinds. For instance, we've been putting special emphasis on food processing. Food processing not only means something to the manufacturer and the person working in the processing, but it means something to the farmer, and in turn to the small town bank, the small town merchant, and the small town businessman, because farm income plays back into the smaller communities. So you see, we've tried to put emphasis on a specialized kind of new industry. With the efforts of the Food Science Department at State College, of our Commerce and Industry Division, and the Department of Agriculture, we're selling people on the idea that food processing has a great opportunity for North Carolina. In these four years we have seen a new food processing industry— or an expanded food processing industry—on the average of one a week. We're now really beginning to move.

We are anxious, not just to have any kind of industry, but to develop our scientific potential. Here we are, living in an age of technology; naturally we want to take advantage of it. The 1963 legislature, which did so many good things, created the Board of Science and Technology. This board, made up of professors and businessmen, is charged with the responsibility of relating the new technological achievements in the country and in the world to North Carolina industry. This question of how to make science come here and create new jobs and new opportunities for you is another example of specialized interest.

There are a lot of other things that can be done to create economic opportunity—planting trees, for example. The state's engaged in the business of growing seedlings that in turn are made available at cost to land owners who plant trees. During the past four years we've cut and processed more timber, and therefore drawn more wealth from the land, than any other four-year period. We have a very fine forestry division. Well, that's good, but what have we done, along with growing more and cutting more than ever before? We've ended up this four-year period with more timber still in the ground than when we began. So we're getting more out of it, but we're keeping more there as we build up a resource for the future.

The same kind of conservation may be observed with our water resources. We've impounded more water, or provided for the impounding of more water than ever before, and we need to preserve this resource. We've developed the mineral resources, again drawing wealth from the land; and we've done it in such a way that the land is not destroyed and scarred as was done fifty or a hundred years ago in other parts of the country. The new phosphate mines in Beaufort County, for example, not only will bring in a new chemical complex to that part of the state and create many, many new opportunties, but it is being mined in such a careful way that the countryside remains unspoiled. In fact, the developers are going to clean it over so well and plant it that it will be far prettier than it was when they began. They may even start cattle raising on the old phosphate grounds as they develop them. So you see how careful planning can use the resources for wealth and still protect your future.

Now those are just some of the examples of state progress—I can't possibly tell you everything that ought to be told in the brief time that's available. But there's another thing that maybe people haven't always understood. You may say, "I can build a house any way I want to or I can build a business anywhere I want to." Well, I think you should be able to do with your property essentially anything you want to do. But somehow we've got to plan our growth and zone it. To decide on a particular kind of community is simply to say we aren't going to build houses in a way that they are destined to turn into slums. Part of this business of bringing in new industry is what kind of a community environment our state offers.

Consequently we have a greatly-expanded Community Planning Section in state government. It doesn't go out and tell local communities how to do, but it does advise the local officials, and it gives them expert advice. Since most of our small towns can't hire planning departments of their own we provide this service. Every small community now has a chance to become the kind of attractive community which will be appealing to new industry, and perhaps more important, will become more wholesome for the people already there.

But in bringing in new jobs and providing these opportunties for you, maybe the most important single factor has been what I like to call the spirit of the people. When folks come looking around and thinking about investing their money they want to know something about the people. North Carolina has given the impression that it's a state on the go, that it's ambitious, looking to the future, the kind of state that has good government as we do, the kind of state that says that we're going to be fair to everybody and not spend all our energy in group fighting. If we try to give the spirit of North Carolina the tone of being one that's fair to everybody, that's wholesome in its outlook, that believes that prejudice has no place in our lives, that has an optimistic faith in the future and what we can do, then that spirit of North Carolina is going to do more than anything else to create the jobs and the opportunities to help us grow strong and help us then grow great. It's this spirit that you can be a part of, and can mean so very, very much to what we're doing. And we need to keep this a state on the go, a state that's fair to everybody, and a state where we have to keep good government—honest, clean government—a habit that it's been so long.

But I wouldn't want to give you the impression that jobs are our only purpose. Jobs are important only because jobs help people have a better chance in life. That's why we're seeking them and that's why we're spending the time on it. Our main purpose, of course, is to help people help themselves. By helping people help themselves we create a stronger community, and ultimately, a greater community.

This goes straight back to the state's business of keeping people in prison. It's not enough just to punish them—that has been the traditional approach—but North Carolina says we're going to help them help themselves. We don't want them coming back to prison. If we've got them there one time that's one time too many; we want to help them. So we have now a high school in the woman's prison, and a high school and a technical school in Central Prison for men. We have a deliberate program designed to say to every prisoner, "All right, you're in here, you're going to pay your penalty, but at the same time we don't want you ever to come back." And so we're trying to train them and to help them and to move them along. Because of our expanded prison, probation, and parole systems, we are now one of the few states with a decreasing prison population. In view of rising crime rates and rising population, this effort to look out for people and give them a better chance in life has certainly paid dividends for the state and her citizens.

We also have a responsibility to look out for people who can't look out for themselves—those people who are mentally ill. This is another part of the responsibility of the state to be concerned with people, and we've greatly expanded this. We are considered to have one of the half-dozen best mental health systems in the country, and we're improving all of the time. We have an excellent system of hospitals now, with a general hospital within reach of every citizen of the state of North Carolina. Again, a responsibility is met to help people grow strong and to be in a position to take advantage of their opportunities.

We have many special groups that need our special attention. The retarded children have never gotten much of a break in getting an education and getting a skill and getting ready for life. The 1963 General Assembly approved a broad program that covers all of this, and we are going to see that they aren't neglected.

Then we looked at another group of children—children caught up somehow in poverty. You probably remember some of them came into school around the first grade and maybe lasted through the third or the fourth or the fifth, but somehow they never seemed to have a chance in life, because they were just caught up in poverty. Well, we said that this is too great a drag on the economy; this doesn't give the child a fair break in life. What can we do about it? We started a program that said not a handout, but a helping hand. And we want to give these children, through what now has been called the War on Poverty, a chance to break out of this situation through many, many ways. I think it can be done. I think it's the first time in the history of civilization that it can be done. And as a result of the new, broad opportunities for these people, the level of the entire state will be raised.

Now what's our principal weapon in the fight on poverty? It's education. If you educate people, people will create their opportunities. If you seek these things, you can best obtain them by education. So first of all we set out to improve the general standard of education. In 1961, the whole level was raised— across-the-board improvement of education for the average student which makes up the great bulk of the population. Then with our special programs for the gifted children, the Governor's School, we said that if they have unusual talents they ought to be given a chance to develop them. The School of the Arts, which will be open next fall, helps us to lead the advance of civilization, and to create the best of the talents. We have hoped to make our schools the best in the nation; we'd like first of all to see that our schools have the highest standards. We'd like to see that our schools miss nobody, that they take into account all kinds of talent and abilities and limitations. And we'd like to see the kind of a system that is not static—we don't know what's best and we'll not know what's best tomorrow. We need to keep on growing and improving and seeking better ways of doing our job of education. To do some of that, we have looked at the failures and the dropouts, and we've set up what has been called the Advancement School. This is established and will be developed at Winston-Salem. Here, bright students, average and above

The Governor was presented an award, May 25, 1964, by the National Education Association for his work with the drop-out problem. Shown with him are Dr. A. C. Dawson, Dr. Charles F. Carroll, Mr. Daniel Schreiber of the NEA, and Dr. Lois Edinger, a North Carolinian who served as national president of the NEA, 1964-1965.

"Stones for the House that Terry Built" illustrates vividly the tremendous impact of the Sanford administration on the state of North Carolina.

average in intelligence, who haven't been learning, but who have been dropping out, are going to come together for a quarter at a time in residence. In this Advancement School we're going to try to find out why they haven't been learning and how we can do a better job of teaching. This is our great laboratory of learning, and we hope to find better ways.

Then we've set up a program with private funds that we call the ABC Program, or the "Three R's Program." Four hundred schools across the state are experimenting in how to do a better job of teaching reading and writing in the first three grades, because about 50 per cent of the students weren't learning to read and therefore ultimately weren't doing very well or were dropping out.

Then we've established something you will hear much about and the nation is looking at; we call it the Learning Institute of North Carolina, LINC. It's over in the Research Triangle at Quail Roost, and it's the most significant research project in the country. It's going to tie together all there is to be known about education, with Duke University and the University of North Carolina, the North Carolina Fund, and the Board of Education all working together for the first time to find the best possible answers to improvement of learning and then to apply them to the system of education in the state. So this is our hope for the future; this is our means of continuing to improve in the future, as we find better ways to make our school system the best in the nation.

All of these things, I think, sum up without a lot of dry statistics, the aims of this administration. I hope you begin to catch the spirit that in North Carolina we have great faith in the future. In North Carolina we believe that we can lead in the advancement of civilization, and as I've said before, I hope we can become the most civilized community in all the world. We're going to do it by concerning ourselves with people, working with people, and providing for them a better opportunity in life. And I believe if we put our trust in people, and if our weapon against poverty and bigotry is education, we can conquer all battles and make North Carolina a leader of all the rest of the nation. You can be a part of that leadership. That's what this administration has been about.

LIST OF OTHER SPEECHES
AND ADDRESSES

LIST OF OTHER SPEECHES AND ADDRESSES

[This list contains the speeches, addresses, and other talks made by Governor Sanford during 1961-1965 in addition to those printed or summarized in the preceding sections of this volume. An asterisk following the date on which a speech was made indicates that the Governor spoke without manuscript and there was no copy to be preserved.]

January 9, 1961	MAHOGANY ASSOCIATION AWARDS DINNER, Chicago, Illinois
January 12, 1961	GROUND-BREAKING CEREMONIES FOR W. F. FANCOURT COMPANY (delivered by Hargrove Bowles, Jr.), Greensboro
January 25, 1961*	EDUCATION RALLY, Asheville
January 26, 1961*	GOVERNOR'S COUNCIL ON OCCUPATIONAL HEALTH, Raleigh
January 30, 1961	RURITAN NATIONAL CONVENTION, Washington, D.C.
February 1, 1961	DEDICATION OF CHEMSTRAND RESEARCH CENTER, Research Triangle Park
February 1, 1961	DISTRICT FIVE, NORTH CAROLINA STATE SCHOOL BOARDS ASSOCIATION, Teachey
February 8, 1961*	FARM CONFERENCE OF NORTH CAROLINA BANKERS ASSOCIATION, Raleigh
February 12, 1961*	METHODIST DISTRICT RALLY, Garner
February 13, 1961	EDUCATION RALLY, Rocky Mount
February 17, 1961	ANNUAL MEETING, NORTH CAROLINA ASSOCIATION FOR MENTAL HEALTH, Raleigh
February 24, 1961*	IN COMMEMORATION OF FIFTH ANNIVERSARY OF GENERAL ELECTRIC OUTDOOR LIGHTING DEPARTMENT PLANT, Hendersonville
February 24, 1961	ANNUAL MEETING OF HENDERSONVILLE CHAMBER OF COMMERCE, Hendersonville
March 3, 1961*	DEMOCRATIC CLUB, Charlotte
March 6, 1961	CAMPBELL COLLEGE FOUNDERS DAY, Buies Creek
March 8, 1961	RALEIGH WOMAN'S CLUB, Raleigh
March 8, 1961	NORTH CAROLINA MERCHANTS ASSOCIATION, Raleigh

March 8, 1961*	COUNTY COMMISSIONERS ON FOOD SURPLUS PROGRAM, Raleigh
March 10, 1961*	WILMINGTON CHAMBER OF COMMERCE, Wilmington
March 11, 1961	ANNUAL MEETING, NORTH CAROLINA MEAT PACKERS ASSOCIATION, Raleigh
March 11, 1961	INTRODUCTION OF ADMIRAL HYMAN G. RICKOVER AT YOUNG DEMOCRATIC CLUB RALLY, Raleigh
March 12, 1961*	DEDICATION OF GREENSBORO COMMUNITY CENTER, Greensboro
March 13, 1961	CONTEMPORARY ISSUES CLASS, NORTH CAROLINA STATE COLLEGE, Raleigh
March 13, 1961	"KICK-OFF" DINNER, RALEIGH CONCERT MUSIC ASSOCIATION, Raleigh
March 15, 1961	INTRODUCTION OF DR. JERROLD R. ZACHARIAS, CHAIRMAN, PHYSICAL SCIENCE STUDY COMMITTEE, TO THE NORTH CAROLINA JUNIOR SCIENCE SYMPOSIUM, Raleigh
March 18, 1961	INAUGURATION OF DR. SAMUEL D. PROCTOR, A & T COLLEGE, Greensboro
March 18, 1961	SANFORD PROGRESS DAYS CELEBRATION, Sanford
March 18, 1961	NORTH CAROLINA ASSOCIATION OF CERTIFIED PUBLIC ACCOUNTANTS, Chapel Hill
March 21, 1961	ROBESON COUNTY SCHOOLMASTERS CLUB, ROWLAND
March 22, 1961	O. MAX GARDNER AWARD DINNER, Raleigh
March 22, 1961	INTRODUCTION OF FREDERICK R. KAPPEL, PRESIDENT OF AMERICAN TELEPHONE AND TELEGRAPH COMPANY, TO NORTH CAROLINA CITIZENS ASSOCIATION, Raleigh
April 4, 1961*	NATIONAL SPORTSWRITERS AWARDS BANQUET, Salisbury
April 9, 1961	NORTH CAROLINA FOOD DEALERS ASSOCIATION, Chapel Hill
April 10, 1961	NATIONAL SECURITY SEMINAR, Winston-Salem

April 10, 1961*	SOUTHERN STATES PROBATION, PAROLE, AND PRISON ASSOCIATION MEETING, Durham
April 11, 1961	WESTWOOD BAPTIST CHURCH BROTHERHOOD (LADIES NIGHT), Durham
April 12, 1961*	WAKE COUNTY DEMOCRATIC WOMEN, Raleigh
April 13, 1961*	NORTH CAROLINA ELECTRICAL CONTRACTORS, Raleigh
April 14, 1961	INGLIS FLETCHER DAY, Edenton
April 17, 1961	ORDER OF THE GOLDEN FLEECE, Chapel Hill
April 19, 1961	MEETING OF FORSYTH COUNTY AND WINSTON-SALEM TEACHERS, Winston-Salem
April 20, 1961	THE OPENING OF SELIG MANUFACTURING COMPANY, Siler City
April 20, 1961*	OPENING OF PITTMAN PLAZA SHOPPING CENTER WITH GOVERNOR LINDSAY ALMOND, Lynchburg, Virginia
April 20, 1961	WENDELL CHAMBER OF COMMERCE, Wendell
April 24, 1961*	CONSERVATION AND DEVELOPMENT BOARD AND GUESTS, Sanford
April 27, 1961*	OPEN HOUSE AT MASLAND DURA-LEATHER COMPANY, Mocksville
May 1, 1961*	GROUND - BREAKING CEREMONY, NORTH CAROLINA BAR CENTER, Raleigh
May 1, 1961	TWENTY-SIXTH ANNUAL CONVENTION, NORTH CAROLINA AUTOMOBILE DEALERS ASSOCIATION, Pinehurst
May 1, 1961	DEDICATION OF NORTH CAROLINA EDUCATION ASSOCIATION HEADQUARTERS BUILDING, Raleigh
May 4, 1961	SAVINGS BONDS LUNCHEON, Raleigh
May 6, 1961*	ANNUAL SOUTHERN PHOTOGRAPHER-OF-THE-YEAR BANQUET, Durham
May 11, 1961*	INSURANCE COMPANY EXECUTIVES ON NORTH CAROLINA TRAFFIC SAFETY COUNCIL, New York

May 12, 1961*	MEREDITH COLLEGE ALUMNAE, Durham
May 15, 1961*	HOKE COUNTY GOLDEN JUBILEE CELEBRATION, Raeford
May 18, 1961	MOUNT OLIVE JUNIOR COLLEGE APPRECIATION DAY, Mount Olive
May 20, 1961*	PAST MASTERS NIGHT OF LAURINBURG MASONIC LODGE #305, A.F. & A.M., Laurinburg
May 21, 1961	EAST CAROLINA COLLEGE COMMENCEMENT EXERCISES, Greenville
May 26, 1961*	ROANOKE RAPIDS CHAMBER OF COMMERCE, Roanoke Rapids
May 27, 1961*	NORTH CAROLINA STATE COLLEGE COMMENCEMENT, Raleigh
May 30, 1961	MEMORIAL DAY SERVICES, NATIONAL CEMETERY, Raleigh
June 5, 1961	INTRODUCTION OF JOHN B. SWAINSON, GOVERNOR OF MICHIGAN, AT THE UNIVERSITY OF NORTH CAROLINA LAW SCHOOL, Chapel Hill
June 6, 1961	BELMONT ABBEY, Belmont
June 9, 1961	FORTY-THIRD ANNUAL CONVENTION, NORTH CAROLINA AMERICAN LEGION, Charlotte
June 10, 1961	NATIONAL CONVENTION OF BENEVOLENT, PATRIOTIC ORDER OF DOES (delivered by Mrs. Margaret P. Foxworth), Asheville
June 12, 1961	NORTH CAROLINA CHAPTER OF THE ORDER OF THE EASTERN STAR, Raleigh
June 16, 1961*	DEDICATION OF MOUNTAIN HORTICULTURE CROPS RESEARCH STATION, Fletcher
June 17, 1961	THIRTIETH INFANTRY DIVISION ANNUAL REVIEW, Fort Bragg
July 11, 1961	SWEARING-IN CEREMONIES FOR NEW STATE HIGHWAY COMMISSION, Raleigh
August 3, 1961	FORTIETH ANNIVERSARY MEETING OF NORTH CAROLINA ASSOCIATION, ORDER OF DeMOLAY, Charlotte
August 8, 1961	ANNUAL DINNER OF FRANKLIN CHAMBER OF COMMERCE, Franklin

August 11, 1961	DEDICATION OF NUTRENA FEED MILL, Wilson
August 15, 1961*	NATIONAL CONVENTION OF COUNTY COMMISSIONERS, Chicago, Illinois
August 17, 1961*	MIDDLE ATLANTIC ASSOCIATION OF PRESS NEWSPAPER PUBLISHERS AND MANAGING EDITORS, White Sulphur Springs, West Virginia
August 18, 1961	COMMENCEMENT EXERCISES, GEORGE PEABODY COLLEGE FOR TEACHERS, Nashville, Tennessee
August 19, 1961	"CONSOLIDATED UNIVERSITY DAY" AT *THE LOST COLONY*, Manteo
August 31, 1961*	SPECIAL SHOWING OF EXHIBIT ON "YOUR STATE AND THE ATOM," Raleigh
September 8, 1961	ANNUAL MEETING, NORTH CAROLINA PEANUT GROWERS ASSOCIATION, Lewiston
September 8, 1961*	NORTH CAROLINA DEBUTANTE BALL, Raleigh
September 14, 1961*	SOCIETY OF INDUSTRIAL REALTORS, Charlotte
September 15, 1961	INTRODUCTION OF SECRETARY OF AGRICULTURE ORVILLE FREEMAN AT BREAKFAST SPONSORED BY FARMERS COOPERATIVE EXCHANGE AND NORTH CAROLINA COTTON GROWERS COOPERATIVE ASSOCIATION, Raleigh
September 15, 1961	ANNUAL MEETING, FARMERS COOPERATIVE EXCHANGE AND NORTH CAROLINA COTTON GROWERS COOPERATIVE ASSOCIATION, Raleigh
September 15, 1961	PENDER COUNTY AGRICULTURAL FAIR, Burgaw
September 16, 1961	TENTH ANNIVERSARY CELEBRATION HONORING BERKSHIRE KNITTING MILLS, Andrews
September 20, 1961	DINNER HONORING JOHN MOTLEY MOREHEAD, Chapel Hill
September 23, 1961*	WYOMING YOUNG DEMOCRATIC CLUBS CONVENTION, Cheyenne, Wyoming
September 27, 1961	COMMUNITY MEETING ON EDUCATION, Chattanooga, Tennessee

September 29, 1961*   STATE HIGHWAY AND PRISON EM-
PLOYEES ASSOCIATION, Durham

October 2, 1961   DEDICATION OF R. J. REYNOLDS TO-
BACCO COMPANY'S WHITAKER PARK
PLANT, Winston-Salem

October 3, 1961*   LUNCHEON OF SUPERINTENDENTS,
PRINCIPALS, AND DIRECTORS OF IN-
STRUCTION, Kannapolis

October 4, 1961*   DEDICATORY ADDRESS AT MACON
JUNIOR HIGH SCHOOL, Warrenton

October 8, 1961*   DEDICATORY ADDRESS AT NEW ASHE-
VILLE BILTMORE COLLEGE, Asheville

October 9, 1961*   NORTH CAROLINA ASSOCIATION OF
INSURANCE AGENTS, Pinehurst

October 11, 1961*   WADESBORO MERCHANTS ASSOCIA-
TION, Wadesboro

October 15, 1961   DEDICATION OF WEST MONTGOMERY
HIGH SCHOOL, Troy

October 15, 1961*   DEDICATORY ADDRESS AT CHARLOTTE
COMMUNITY COLLEGE, Charlotte

October 16, 1961*   LAND GRANT COLLEGE CENTENNIAL
AT STATE FAIR, Raleigh

October 20, 1961*   DEDICATION OF MADISON-MAYODAN
SCHOOL, Mayodan

October 22, 1961   DEDICATION OF WRENN STREET WING,
SOUTHERN FURNITURE EXPOSITION
BUILDING, High Point

October 23, 1961*   REMARKS AT UNVEILING OF TOWN
CLOCK, Ahoskie

October 23, 1961*   AREA DEVELOPMENT ORGANIZATION,
Ahoskie

October 24, 1961*   CONFERENCE OF NORTH CAROLINA
SOLICITORS CONCERNING TRAFFIC
SAFETY PROGRAM, Raleigh

October 25, 1961   TWELFTH ANNUAL FALL FESTIVAL, Red
Springs

October 26, 1961   GREENSBORO KIWANIS CLUB, Greensboro

October 31, 1961*   BRUNSWICK COUNTY EDUCATION RAL-
LY, Shallotte

October 31, 1961*   COLUMBUS COUNTY EDUCATION
RALLY, Whiteville

October 31, 1961*	BLADEN COUNTY EDUCATION RALLY, Elizabethtown
October 31, 1961*	ROBESON COUNTY EDUCATION RALLY, Lumberton
November 1, 1961	METHODIST COLLEGE FOUNDERS DAY PROGRAM, Fayetteville
November 2, 1961*	HALIFAX COUNTY EDUCATION RALLY, Roanoke Rapids
November 4, 1961*	NORTH CAROLINA STATE COLLEGE SCHOOL OF AGRICULTURE OPEN HOUSE, Raleigh
November 5, 1961*	SURRY COUNTY EDUCATION RALLY, Dobson
November 7, 1961*	ORGANIZATION MEETING OF ECONOMIC DEVELOPMENT COMMITTEE OF NASH, EDGECOMBE, MARTIN, WILSON, PITT, AND BEAUFORT COUNTIES, Rocky Mount
November 10, 1961*	WELCOMING ADDRESS AT DREYFUS LABORATORY, Research Triangle Park
November 10, 1961*	YOUNG DEMOCRATIC CLUBS CONVENTION, Durham
November 12, 1961	NORTH CAROLINA JOINT COUNCIL ON HEALTH AND CITIZENSHIP (delivered by Graham Jones), Greenville
November 14, 1961*	PIEDMONT AREA DEVELOPMENT ASSOCIATION, Charlotte
November 15, 1961*	GRAHAM COUNTY EDUCATION RALLY, Robbinsville
November 15, 1961*	CLAY COUNTY EDUCATION RALLY, Hayesville
November 15, 1961*	CHEROKEE COUNTY EDUCATION RALLY, Murphy
November 17, 1961*	GATES COUNTY EDUCATION RALLY, Gatesville
November 17, 1961*	HERTFORD COUNTY EDUCATION RALLY, Ahoskie
November 17, 1961*	NORTHAMPTON COUNTY EDUCATION RALLY, Jackson
November 19, 1961*	DEDICATION OF WILMINGTON COMMUNITY COLLEGE, Wilmington
November 21, 1961*	DURHAM DIVISION OF RESEARCH TRI-

	ANGLE, AT HOME SECURITY LIFE IN-SURANCE COMPANY, Durham
November 22, 1961*	GOLDEN AGE THANKSGIVING BAN-QUET, Raleigh
November 28, 1961*	SECOND ANNUAL FARM POLICY RE-VIEW CONFERENCE, Raleigh
November 28, 1961	MUSIC DAY OBSERVANCE, NORTH CARO-LINA FEDERATION OF MUSIC CLUBS, Raleigh
November 30, 1961	SPECIAL CONFERENCE OF SOUTHERN REGIONAL EDUCATION BOARD, Louis-ville, Kentucky
December 2, 1961*	THIRTEENTH ANNUAL CONFERENCE ON EDUCATION FOR EXCEPTIONAL CHILDREN, Winston-Salem
December 3, 1961*	DEDICATORY ADDRESS AT CHARLES B. AYCOCK SCHOOL, Pikeville
December 5, 1961*	REMARKS TO AMERICAN GOVERNMENT CLASSES FROM DUKE UNIVERSITY, Ra-leigh
December 14, 1961*	UNIVERSITY OF NORTH CAROLINA ALUMNI BANQUET HONORING DR. FRANK P. GRAHAM, New York City
December 15, 1961*	NORTH CAROLINA SOCIETY OF NEW YORK, New York City
December 21, 1961*	CHARLOTTE CHAMBER OF COMMERCE, Charlotte
January 3, 1962*	INTRODUCTION OF ALLEN H. SEED, JR., TO RALEIGH GARDEN CLUB, Raleigh
January 5, 1962*	REMARKS TO TEEN-DEMS, Raleigh
January 31, 1962*	CHAPEL PROGRAM AT METHODIST HOME, Charlotte
January 31, 1962*	FORMAL DEDICATION, NORTH AND SOUTH CAROLINA REGIONAL OFFICE, ALLSTATE INSURANCE COMPANY, Char-lotte
February 9, 1962	OPENING OF LINDSAY C. WARREN BRIDGE ACROSS ALLIGATOR RIVER FROM TYRRELL COUNTY TO DARE COUNTY, East Lake
February 9, 1962*	NORTH CAROLINA CEMETERY ASSOCI-ATION, Pinehurst
February 10, 1962	OPENING DAY CEREMONIES, BASF COLORS AND CHEMICALS, INC., Charlotte

February 12, 1962*	COMMENTS TO THE MEN OF THE EDENTON STREET METHODIST CHURCH, Raleigh
February 16, 1962	DEDICATORY ADDRESS AT FAYETTEVILLE AREA INDUSTRIAL EDUCATION CENTER, Fayetteville
February 18, 1962*	THE CONGREGATION OF WRIGHTSVILLE METHODIST CHURCH, Wrightsville Beach
February 20, 1962*	EDUCATION RALLY, HORTON HIGH SCHOOL, Pittsboro
February 20, 1962*	EDUCATION RALLY, PITTSBORO HIGH SCHOOL, Pittsboro
February 20, 1962*	EDUCATION RALLY, CHATHAM HIGH SCHOOL, Siler City
February 20, 1962*	EDUCATION RALLY, JORDAN MATTHEWS SCHOOL, Siler City
February 20, 1962*	EDUCATION RALLY, CHATHAM CENTRAL HIGH SCHOOL, Bear Creek
February 20, 1962*	EDUCATION RALLY, ELISE HIGH SCHOOL, Robbins
February 20, 1962*	EDUCATION RALLY, PINCKNEY HIGH SCHOOL, Carthage
February 20, 1962*	EDUCATION RALLY, CARTHAGE HIGH SCHOOL, Carthage
February 20, 1962*	EDUCATION RALLY, ABERDEEN HIGH SCHOOL, Aberdeen
February 20, 1962*	EDUCATION RALLY, LEAK STREET SCHOOL, Rockingham
February 23, 1962*	DINNER FOR CHARLOTTE YWCA BUILDING CAMPAIGN, Charlotte
February 24, 1962*	PHI ALPHA DELTA DISTRICT CONVENTION, Winston-Salem
February 27, 1962*	AGRICULTURE COUNCIL JOINT PROGRAM, Raleigh
March 2, 1962*	EDUCATION RALLY, WEST EDGECOMBE SCHOOL, Rocky Mount
March 2, 1962*	EDUCATION RALLY, TARBORO HIGH SCHOOL, Tarboro
March 2, 1962*	EDUCATION RALLY, CARVER HIGH SCHOOL, Pinetops

March 2, 1962*	EDUCATION RALLY, ELM CITY HIGH SCHOOL, Elm City
March 2, 1962*	EDUCATION RALLY, SPEIGHT SCHOOL, Saratoga
March 2, 1962*	EDUCATION RALLY, SARATOGA CENTRAL SCHOOL, Saratoga
March 2, 1962*	EDUCATION RALLY, GREENE COUNTY CENTRAL SCHOOL, Snow Hill
March 2, 1962*	EDUCATION RALLY, GREENE COUNTY TRAINING SCHOOL, Snow Hill
March 3, 1962*	NORTH CAROLINA AFL-CIO MEETING, Raleigh
March 6, 1962*	CUMBERLAND COUNTY BAR ASSOCIATION, Fayetteville
March 7, 1962*	COMMENTS AT OPEN HOUSE, BURLINGTON-ALAMANCE INDUSTRIAL EDUCATION CENTER, Burlington
March 7, 1962	ANNUAL MEETING, WINSTON-SALEM TRAFFIC CLUB, Winston-Salem
March 8, 1962	ELON COLLEGE FOUNDERS DAY PROGRAM, Elon College
March 8, 1962*	STATE STUDENT LEGISLATURE AT NORTH CAROLINA STATE COLLEGE, Raleigh
March 9, 1962*	GREETINGS AT AMERICAN LEGION ORATORICAL CONTEST, Lexington
March 12, 1962*	DEMOCRATIC RALLY, Asheboro
March 14, 1962*	CLAYTON WOMEN'S CLUB, Clayton
March 16, 1962*	EAST CAROLINA COLLEGE ALUMNI BREAKFAST, Raleigh
March 17, 1962*	NORTH CAROLINA JUNIOR CHAMBER OF COMMERCE OUTSTANDING YOUNG FARMER AWARD PRESENTATION, Wilson
March 18, 1962*	NORTH CAROLINA B'NAI B'RITH CONVENTION, Fayetteville
March 19, 1962*	MEREDITH COLLEGE STUDENTS, Raleigh
March 19, 1962*	EDUCATION RALLY, E. E. SMITH SCHOOL, Kenansville
March 19, 1962*	EDUCATION RALLY, KENANSVILLE ELEMENTARY SCHOOL, Kenansville

March 20, 1962*	EDUCATION RALLY, POPE HIGH SCHOOL, Burgaw
March 20, 1962*	BURGAW HIGH SCHOOL, Burgaw
March 20, 1962*	PENDERLEA HIGH SCHOOL, Willard
March 20, 1962*	EDUCATION RALLY, UNION HIGH SCHOOL, Clinton
March 20, 1962*	EDUCATION RALLY, CLINTON HIGH SCHOOL, Clinton
March 20, 1962*	EDUCATION RALLY, SAMPSON COUNTY HIGH SCHOOL, Clinton
March 20, 1962*	EDUCATION RALLY, ROSEBORO-SALEMBURG HIGH SCHOOL, Salemburg
March 20, 1962*	EDUCATION RALLY, HOBBTON HIGH SCHOOL, Newton Grove
March 20, 1962*	MEN OF THE CHURCH OF THE GOOD SHEPHERD, Raleigh
March 21, 1962*	NORTH CAROLINA ELECTRIC MEMBERSHIP ASSOCIATION, Raleigh
March 21, 1962	NORTH CAROLINA CITIZENS COMMITTEE, Raleigh
March 22, 1962*	O. MAX GARDNER AWARD DINNER, Greensboro
March 24, 1962*	GOVERNOR'S CONFERENCE FOR FOREIGN STUDENTS, Raleigh
March 27, 1962*	EDUCATION RALLY, NEWBOLD HIGH SCHOOL, Denver
March 27, 1962*	EDUCATION RALLY, JASPER HIGH SCHOOL, New Bern
March 27, 1962*	EDUCATION RALLY, BARBER HIGH SCHOOL, New Bern
March 27, 1962*	EDUCATION RALLY, NEW BERN HIGH SCHOOL, New Bern
March 27, 1962*	EDUCATION RALLY, PAMLICO TRAINING SCHOOL, Bayboro
March 27, 1962*	EDUCATION RALLY, PAMLICO HIGH SCHOOL, Bayboro
March 27, 1962*	EDUCATION RALLY, FARM LIFE HIGH SCHOOL, Vanceboro
March 27, 1962*	EDUCATION RALLY, SAMPSON ELEMENTARY SCHOOL, Kinston

March 27, 1962*	EDUCATION RALLY, GRAINGER HIGH SCHOOL, Kinston
March 28, 1962*	EDUCATION RALLY, JONES HIGH SCHOOL, Trenton
March 28, 1962*	EDUCATION RALLY, JONES CENTRAL HIGH SCHOOL, Trenton
March 28, 1962*	EDUCATION RALLY, RICHLANDS HIGH SCHOOL, Richlands
March 28, 1962*	EDUCATION RALLY, JACKSONVILLE HIGH SCHOOL, Jacksonville
March 28, 1962*	EDUCATION RALLY, GEORGETOWN HIGH SCHOOL, Jacksonville
March 28, 1962*	EDUCATION RALLY, SWANSBORO HIGH SCHOOL, Swansboro
March 28, 1962*	EDUCATION RALLY, HAVELOCK HIGH SCHOOL, Havelock
March 28, 1962*	EDUCATION RALLY, BEAUFORT HIGH SCHOOL, BEAUFORT
March 29, 1962	VIRGINIA PUBLIC RELATIONS CONFERENCE, Williamsburg, Virginia
March 31, 1962	STATE CONVENTION, NORTH CAROLINA ASSOCIATION OF FUTURE HOMEMAKERS OF AMERICA, Raleigh
March 31, 1962	INTRODUCTION OF ROBERT F. WAGNER, MAYOR OF NEW YORK CITY, AT JEFFERSON-JACKSON DAY DINNER, Raleigh
April 2, 1962	QUARTERLY MEETING OF BOARD OF CONSERVATION AND DEVELOPMENT, New Bern
April 4, 1962*	VANCE COUNTY NCEA BANQUET, Henderson
April 4, 1962*	VANCE COUNTY EDUCATION RALLY, Henderson
April 5, 1962	CAROLINAS UNITED FUND REGIONAL MEETING, Raleigh
April 5, 1962*	DEDICATORY ADDRESS AT LAURINBURG ARMORY, Laurinburg
April 5, 1962*	SOUTHERN REGIONAL TRAVEL COUNCIL, Charlotte
April 5, 1962*	INTRODUCTION OF ORVILLE FREEMAN, SECRETARY OF AGRICULTURE, AT MECKLENBURG COUNTY DEMOCRATIC RALLY, Charlotte

April 8, 1962*	DEDICATION C E R E M O N Y, MECKLEN-BURG COLLEGE, Charlotte
April 9, 1962*	HIGH POINT COLLEGE YOUNG DEMO-CRATIC CLUB, High Point
April 12, 1962*	INAUGURAL CEREMONIES FOR PRESI-DENT OF ST. ANDREWS COLLEGE, Laurinburg
April 13, 1962*	PAMLICO-ALBEMARLE SCHOOLMASTERS CLUB, Pantego
April 14, 1962*	NORTH CAROLINA VOCATIONAL AS-SOCIATION, Raleigh
April 16, 1962*	EDUCATION RALLY, SHELBY SENIOR HIGH SCHOOL, Shelby
April 16, 1962*	EDUCATION RALLY, CLEVELAND HIGH SCHOOL, Shelby
April 16, 1962*	EDUCATION RALLY, SHELBY JUNIOR HIGH SCHOOL, Shelby
April 18, 1962	GRAND LODGE PAGEANT, Raleigh
April 19, 1962*	FARM CREDIT DISTRICT MEETING, Raleigh
April 19, 1962*	SOUTHERN MUNICIPAL AND INDUS-TRIAL WASTE CONFERENCE, Chapel Hill
April 26, 1962	DEDICATION LUNCHEON FOR FUTOR-IAN-STRATFORD FURNITURE COMPANY PLANT, Rocky Mount
April 26, 1962	FORSYTH COUNTY SCHOOL BANQUET, Winston-Salem
April 27, 1962	DEDICATION OF THE ASHEVILLE IN-DUSTRIAL EDUCATION CENTER, Asheville
May 4, 1962*	INTERNATIONAL ASSOCIATION OF EM-PLOYMENT SECURITY COMMISSION PER-SONNEL, Raleigh
May 4, 1962*	DISTRICT CONVENTION OF OPTIMISTS CLUBS, Durham
May 9, 1962	A N N U A L INSTALLATION BANQUET, HENDERSON JUNIOR CHAMBER OF COMMERCE, Henderson
May 10, 1962	DEDICATION OF LINDSAY C. WARREN BRIDGE, Columbia
May 10, 1962	PERQUIMANS COUNTY DEMOCRATIC RALLY, Hertford

May 12, 1962*	ANNUAL DINNER OF NORTH CAROLINA SOCIETY OF WASHINGTON, D.C., Washington, D.C.
May 14, 1962*	CONFERENCE ON JUVENILE DELINQUENCY, Chapel Hill
May 14, 1962*	DEDICATION OF NEW CREDIT UNION BUILDING, Raleigh
May 15, 1962	GREETINGS AT BUSINESS AND INDUSTRY'S SALUTE TO CAMPBELL COLLEGE, Raleigh
May 15, 1962*	ANNUAL AGRICULTURE EXTENSION CONFERENCE, Asheville
May 17, 1962	INTRODUCTION OF JAMES E. WEBB, ADMINISTRATOR OF NATIONAL AERONAUTICS AND SPACE ADMINISTRATION, AT DUKE UNIVERSITY SYMPOSIUM ON SPACE RESEARCH, Durham
May 25, 1962*	CATHEY CLUB OF NORTH CAROLINA STATE SCHOOL FOR THE BLIND, Raleigh
May 27, 1962*	HOMECOMING SERVICE OF MOUNT ZION METHODIST CHURCH, Cornelius
May 29, 1962	HIGHWAY SAFETY MEETING ON PROJECT IMPACT, Raleigh
June 2, 1962	NORTH CAROLINA STATE COLLEGE COMMENCEMENT, Raleigh
June 4, 1962	GREETINGS AT UNIVERSITY OF NORTH CAROLINA COMMENCEMENT EXERCISES, Chapel Hill
June 10, 1962*	ANNUAL CONVENTION OF NORTH CAROLINA REGISTER OF DEEDS ASSOCIATION, Hendersonville
June 12, 1962	FUNERAL DIRECTORS AND MORTICIANS ASSOCIATION, Raleigh
June 12, 1962*	INSTITUTE FOR MENTAL HEALTH BUSINESS ADMINISTRATORS, Raleigh
June 16, 1962*	INTRODUCTION OF SARGENT SHRIVER, DIRECTOR OF PEACE CORPS, AT TEEN-DEMS CONVENTION, Raleigh
June 23, 1962	DEDICATION OF WILMINGTON CAUSTIC SODA TERMINAL, Wilmington
June 26, 1962	NORTH CAROLINA A.B.C. LAW ENFORCEMENT OFFICERS ASSOCIATION, Carolina Beach

June 29, 1962	ANNUAL MEETING OF ROANOKE-CHOWAN AUTHORS, ARTISTS, AND MUSICANS, Pendleton
July 6, 1962	DEDICATION OF IDEAL CEMENT COMPANY PLANT, Castle Hayne
July 14, 1962	DEDICATION OF NEW WATERSIDE THEATER, Manteo
July 16, 1962	CONVENTION BANQUET, NORTH CAROLINA SEEDMEN'S ASSOCIATION, Blowing Rock
July 17, 1962	OPENING OF CANTRELL, AND COCHRANE, LTD., PLANT, Charlotte
August 1, 1962*	ANNUAL MINERAL AND GEM FESTIVAL, Spruce Pine
August 2, 1962*	NORTH CAROLINA TRADE FAIR LUNCHEON, Charlotte
August 8, 1962	CONFERENCE ON CHRISTIAN EDUCATION AND CHRISTIAN YOUTH COUNCIL, Salisbury
August 10, 1962*	AGRIBUSINESS CARAVAN LUNCHEON, Raleigh
August 20, 1962*	ORGANIZATIONAL MEETING OF OUTER BANKS SEASHORE PARK COMMISSION, Nags Head
August 27, 1962	FOOD BROKERS DINNER, Raleigh
August 29, 1962*	"MADE IN NORTH CAROLINA" DAY, EXHIBITION OF PRODUCTS FROM 100 NORTH CAROLINA MANUFACTURERS, Hollywood, Florida
September 4, 1962*	EDUCATION RALLY, KNOTTS ISLAND ELEMENTARY SCHOOL, Knotts Island
September 4. 1962*	DEDICATION OF KNOTTS ISLAND FERRY, Knotts Island
September 4, 1962*	EDUCATION RALLY, KNAPP HIGH SCHOOL, Currituck
September 4, 1962*	EDUCATION RALLY, CAMDEN HIGH SCHOOL, Camden
September 4, 1962*	EDUCATION RALLY, MARIAN ANDERSON HIGH SCHOOL, Belcross
September 4, 1962*	ELIZABETH CITY STATE TEACHERS COLLEGE, Elizabeth City
September 5, 1962*	EDUCATION RALLY, PASQUOTANK ELEMENTARY SCHOOL, Elizabeth City

September 5, 1962*	EDUCATION RALLY, ELIZABETH CITY HIGH SCHOOL, Elizabeth City
September 5, 1962*	EDUCATION RALLY, P. W. MOORE HIGH SCHOOL, Elizabeth City
September 5, 1962*	EDUCATION RALLY, PASQUOTANK CENTRAL HIGH SCHOOL, Elizabeth City
September 5, 1962*	EDUCATION RALLY, PERQUIMANS UNION HIGH SCHOOL, Winfall
September 5, 1962*	EDUCATION RALLY, PERQUIMANS HIGH SCHOOL, Hertford
September 5, 1962*	EDUCATION RALLY, EDENTON HIGH SCHOOL, Edenton
September 5, 1962*	EDUCATION RALLY, CHOWAN HIGH SCHOOL, Tyner
September 5, 1962*	EDUCATION RALLY, WHITE OAK ELEMENTARY SCHOOL, Tyner
September 7, 1962*	REMARKS TO DEMOCRATIC NOMINEES FOR NORTH CAROLINA GENERAL ASSEMBLY, Raleigh
September 8, 1962	CHARLES M. GOLD APPRECIATION NIGHT, Rutherfordton
September 12, 1962	DEDICATION OF CAROLINA POWER AND LIGHT COMPANY STEAM ELECTRIC GENERATING PLANT, Goldsboro
September 14, 1962*	EDUCATION RALLY, FARMVILLE HIGH SCHOOL, Farmville
September 14, 1962*	EDUCATION RALLY, H. B. SUGG HIGH SCHOOL, Farmville
September 14, 1962*	EDUCATION RALLY, EAST CAROLINA COLLEGE AND GREENVILLE CITY SCHOOLS, Greenville
September 14, 1962*	EDUCATION RALLY, ROBINSON HIGH SCHOOL, Winterville
September 14, 1962*	EDUCATION RALLY, WINTERVILLE HIGH SCHOOL, Winterville
September 14, 1962*	EDUCATION RALLY, AYDEN HIGH SCHOOL, Ayden
September 14, 1962*	EDUCATION RALLY, SOUTH AYDEN HIGH SCHOOL, Ayden
September 16, 1962*	DEDICATION CEREMONIES FOR WILKESBORO DAM AND RESERVOIR, North Wilkesboro

September 17, 1962*	EDUCATION RALLY, WEST WILKES HIGH SCHOOL, North Wilkesboro
September 17, 1962*	EDUCATION RALLY, LINCOLN HIGH SCHOOL, Wilkesboro
September 17, 1962*	EDUCATION RALLY, WILKES CENTRAL HIGH SCHOOL, North Wilkesboro
September 17, 1962*	EDUCATION RALLY, SPARTA HIGH SCHOOL, Sparta
September 17, 1962*	EDUCATION RALLY, PINEY CREEK HIGH SCHOOL, Piney Creek
September 17, 1962*	EDUCATION RALLY, ASHE CENTRAL HIGH SCHOOL, Jefferson
September 17, 1962*	EDUCATION RALLY, BEAVER CREEK HIGH SCHOOL, West Jefferson
September 17, 1962*	EDUCATION RALLY, APPALACHIAN STADIUM, Boone
September 18, 1962*	BOARD OF DIRECTORS, NORTH CAROLINA NATIONAL BANK, Raleigh
September 18, 1962	FOURTH ANNUAL BANQUET OF APEX CHAMBER OF COMMERCE, Apex
September 24, 1962*	EDUCATION RALLY, GRANITE FALLS HIGH SCHOOL, Granite Falls
September 24, 1962*	EDUCATION RALLY, HUDSON HIGH SCHOOL, Hudson
September 24, 1962*	EDUCATION RALLY, LENOIR HIGH SCHOOL, Lenoir
September 24, 1962*	EDUCATION RALLY, FREEDMAN ELEMENTARY SCHOOL, Lenoir
September 24, 1962*	EDUCATION RALLY, BANNER ELK SCHOOL, Banner Elk
September 24, 1962*	EDUCATION RALLY, CROSSNORE SCHOOL, Crossnore
September 24, 1962*	EDUCATION RALLY, HARRIS HIGH SCHOOL, Spruce Pine
September 24, 1962*	EDUCATION RALLY, BOWMAN SCHOOL, Bakersville
September 24, 1962*	EDUCATION RALLY, EAST YANCEY HIGH SCHOOL, BURNSVILLE
September 25, 1962*	EDUCATION RALLY, MARION HIGH SCHOOL, Marion

September 25, 1962*	EDUCATION RALLY, GLEN ALPINE HIGH SCHOOL, Glen Alpine
September 25, 1962*	EDUCATION RALLY, OLIVE HILL HIGH SCHOOL, Morganton
September 25, 1962*	EDUCATION RALLY, MORGANTON HIGH SCHOOL, Morganton
September 25, 1962*	EDUCATION RALLY, VALDESE HIGH SCHOOL, Valdese
September 25, 1962*	EDUCATION RALLY, MONROE AUDITORIUM, Hickory
September 25, 1962*	EDUCATION RALLY, ST. STEPHENS HIGH SCHOOL, Catawba
September 25, 1962*	EDUCATION RALLY, ROSENWALD HIGH SCHOOL, Catawba
September 26, 1962*	EDUCATION RALLY, TAYLORSVILLE GYMNASIUM, Taylorsville
September 26, 1962*	EDUCATION RALLY, HAPPY PLAINS GYMTORIUM, Taylorsville
September 26, 1962*	EDUCATION RALLY, HIDDENITE HIGH SCHOOL, Hiddenite
September 26, 1962*	EDUCATION RALLY, STATESVILLE HIGH SCHOOL, Statesville
September 26, 1962*	EDUCATION RALLY, UNITY HIGH SCHOOL, Statesville
September 26, 1962*	EDUCATION RALLY, HARMONY SCHOOL, Harmony
September 26, 1962*	EDUCATION RALLY, YADKINVILLE SCHOOL, Yadkinville
September 26, 1962*	EDUCATION RALLY, BOONVILLE SCHOOL, Boonville
September 26, 1962*	EDUCATION RALLY, YADKIN HIGH SCHOOL, Boonville
September 26, 1962*	NEWTON LIONS CLUB, Newton
September 27, 1962*	OPENING OF NORTHWESTERN MUTUAL INSURANCE COMPANY BUILDING, Raleigh
September 27, 1962	ANNUAL MEETING, NORTH CAROLINA PUBLIC HEALTH ASSOCIATION, Raleigh
September 28, 1962*	EDUCATION RALLY, MERRICK-MOORE HIGH SCHOOL, Durham
September 28, 1962*	EDUCATION RALLY, HILLSIDE HIGH SCHOOL, Durham

September 28, 1962*	EDUCATION RALLY, DURHAM HIGH SCHOOL, Durham
September 28, 1962*	EDUCATION RALLY, NORTHERN HIGH SCHOOL, Durham
September 28, 1962*	EDUCATION RALLY, PERSON COUNTY HIGH SCHOOL, Roxboro
September 28, 1962*	EDUCATION RALLY, ROXBORO HIGH SCHOOL, Roxboro
September 28, 1962*	EDUCATION RALLY, HILLSBORO HIGH SCHOOL, Hillsboro
September 28, 1962*	EDUCATION RALLY, CENTRAL SCHOOL, Hillsboro
September 28, 1962*	EDUCATION RALLY, CHAPEL HILL HIGH SCHOOL, Chapel Hill
October 4, 1962*	STATE AFL-CIO CONVENTION, Raleigh
October 6, 1962*	NORTH CAROLINA DEMOCRATIC WOMEN'S LUNCHEON, Asheville
October 6, 1962*	INTRODUCTION OF BERT COMBS, GOVERNOR OF KENTUCKY, AT VANCE-AYCOCK DINNER, Asheville
October 7, 1962*	NORTH CAROLINA BOTTLERS ASSOCIATION, INC., Asheville
October 7, 1962*	NORTH CAROLINA ASSOCIATION OF INSURANCE AGENTS, Pinehurst
October 10, 1962*	THIRD CONGRESSIONAL DISTRICT DEMOCRATIC RALLY, Beaufort
October 11, 1962*	FOURTH CONGRESSIONAL DISTRICT DEMOCRATIC RALLY, Lexington
October 12, 1962*	DEDICATORY ADDRESS AT CORNING GLASS PLANT, Raleigh
October 12, 1962*	SIXTH CONGRESSIONAL DISTRICT DEMOCRATIC RALLY, Greensboro
October 13, 1962*	REMARKS TO INDUSTRIAL ENGINEERS AND CONSULTANTS, Asheville
October 14, 1962*	HOMECOMING DAY SERVICES, EDGERTON MEMORIAL METHODIST CHURCH, Selma
October 15, 1962*	YOUNG DEMOCRATIC CLUBS RALLY, Statesville
October 15, 1962*	GOVERNOR'S COMMITTEE ON EMPLOYMENT OF THE HANDICAPPED, Asheville

October 17, 1962*	GOVERNOR'S TRAFFIC SAFETY MANAGEMENT CONFERENCE, INSTITUTE OF GOVERNMENT, Chapel Hill
October 18, 1962*	FIFTH CONGRESSIONAL DISTRICT DEMOCRATIC RALLY, Dobson
October 22, 1962*	NINTH CONGRESSIONAL DISTRICT DEMOCRATIC RALLY, Concord
October 23, 1962*	EIGHTH CONGRESSIONAL DISTRICT DEMOCRATIC RALLY, Rockingham
October 24, 1962	DEDICATION OF NUCLEAR POWER PLANT, Parr, South Carolina
October 24, 1962*	ELEVENTH CONGRESSIONAL DISTRICT DEMOCRATIC RALLY, Asheville
October 25, 1962*	TENTH CONGRESSIONAL DISTRICT DEMOCRATIC RALLY, Hickory
October 26, 1962*	DEDICATION OF NORTH CAROLINA BAR CENTER, Raleigh
October 27, 1962	DEMOCRATIC PRECINCT RALLY, STANLY COUNTY, New London
October 28, 1962	REMARKS TO TRAFFIC SESSION, NATIONAL SAFETY CONGRESS (delivered by telephone), Chicago, Illinois
October 30, 1962*	SEVENTH CONGRESSIONAL DISTRICT DEMOCRATIC RALLY, Lumberton
October 31, 1962*	DEDICATION OF FARMERS COOPERATIVE EXCHANGE MILL, Farmville
October 31, 1962*	SECOND CONGRESSIONAL DISTRICT DEMOCRATIC RALLY, Roanoke Rapids
November 1, 1962	NATIONAL CONVENTION OF LITTLE PEOPLE OF AMERICA, INC., Asheville
November 1, 1962*	GOVERNOR'S CONFERENCE ON AREA REDEVELOPMENT, Asheville
November 3, 1962*	GOVERNOR'S CONFERENCE ON AREA REDEVELOPMENT, Raleigh
November 8, 1962	DEDICATION OF COOPER D. CASS BUILDING, Winston-Salem
November 13, 1962	PROCESSED FOODS LUNCHEON, Raleigh
November 14, 1962	ANNUAL MEETING OF THE NEW YORK CHAPTER, UNIVERSITY OF NORTH CAROLINA ALUMNI ASSOCIATION, New York City

November 16, 1962	DEDICATION OF HOSPITAL CARE ASSOCIATION OFFICE BUILDING, Durham
November 16, 1962	THIRTY-FIFTH ANNUAL CONVENTION OF THE CONGRESS OF COLORED PARENTS AND TEACHERS, Gastonia
November 17, 1962*	DEDICATION OF WILLIAM D. CARMICHAEL GYMNASIUM, NORTH CAROLINA STATE COLLEGE, Raleigh
November 21, 1962	ANNUAL RADIO AND TELEVISION AWARDS LUNCHEON, Raleigh
November 26, 1962	ANNUAL MEETING, NORTH CAROLINA FARM BUREAU, Asheville
December 1, 1962*	VIRGINIA MILLS, Swepsonville
December 5, 1962*	DUKE UNIVERSITY POLITICAL SCIENCE STUDENTS, Raleigh
December 6, 1962*	ROUGHEDGE FARMERS CLUB ANNUAL LADIES NIGHT BANQUET, Roughedge
December 7, 1962	WINGATE COLLEGE, Wingate
December 7, 1962	CAROLINAS-VIRGINIA PURCHASING AGENTS ASSOCIATION, Pinehurst
December 12, 1962*	DEDICATION OF PARKWOOD SHOPPING CENTER, Raleigh
January 12, 1963*	ANNUAL INSTALLATION MEETING, STATE YOUNG DEMOCRATIC CLUBS OFFICERS, Goldsboro
January 18, 1963	NORTH CAROLINA PRESS ASSOCIATION, Chapel Hill
January 18, 1963	INTRODUCTION OF JAMES E. WEBB, ADMINISTRATOR OF NATIONAL AERONAUTICS AND SPACE ADMINISTRATION, AT EIGHTY-THIRD ANNUAL BANQUET OF THE CHARLOTTE CHAMBER OF COMMERCE, Charlotte
January 28, 1963*	ADDRESS TO CONSERVATION AND DEVELOPMENT BOARD, Durham
January 30, 1963*	NORTH CAROLINA TRAFFIC SAFETY MEETING, Raleigh
February 9, 1963	SECOND HEALTH CAREERS CONGRESS, Durham
February 10, 1963*	RECEPTION HONORING AVRAHAM HARMAN, AMBASSADOR FROM ISRAEL, Durham

February 11, 1963*	INSTITUTE FOR PAROLE BOARD MEMBERS, INSTITUTE OF GOVERNMENT, Chapel Hill
February 11, 1963*	LAURINBURG NCEA BANQUET, Laurinburg
February 12, 1963	SIR WALTER CABINET, Raleigh
February 14, 1963*	DISTRICT BETA CLUB MEETING, Murfreesboro
February 22, 1963*	DEDICATION OF CUTLAR MOORE BRIDGE, Lumberton
February 22, 1963*	DEDICATION OF ED J. GLOVER FIRE STATION, Lumberton
February 24, 1963*	BROTHERHOOD DAY SERVICE, WHITE ROCK BAPTIST CHURCH, Durham
February 28, 1963*	EDUCATION RALLY, CHAPEL HILL HIGH SCHOOL, Chapel Hill
February 28, 1963*	EDUCATION RALLY, LINCOLN HIGH SCHOOL, Chapel Hill
February 28, 1963*	YOUNG TURKS DINNER, Greensboro
March 1, 1963*	EDUCATION RALLY, ROSEWOOD HIGH SCHOOL, Goldsboro
March 1, 1963*	EDUCATION RALLY, Fremont High School, Fremont
March 1, 1963*	EDUCATION RALLY, NEW HOPE HIGH SCHOOL, Goldsboro
March 1, 1963*	EDUCATION RALLY, GOLDSBORO HIGH SCHOOL, Goldsboro
March 1, 1963*	EDUCATION RALLY, DILLARD HIGH SCHOOL, Goldsboro
March 1, 1963*	EDUCATION RALLY, CARVER SCHOOL, Mount Olive
March 1, 1963*	EDUCATION RALLY, MOUNT OLIVE HIGH SCHOOL, Mount Olive
March 1, 1963*	SCIENCE FAIR, GOLDSBORO JUNIOR HIGH SCHOOL, Goldsboro
March 1, 1963*	WAYNE COUNTY UNIT OF NCEA, Goldsboro
March 2, 1963*	WELCOMING JAYCEES TO RALEIGH, Raleigh

March 7, 1963*	NORTH CAROLINA MENTAL HEALTH ASSOCIATION BANQUET, Raleigh
March 8, 1963	NORTH CAROLINA MENTAL HEALTH LEADERSHIP CONFERENCE, Raleigh
March 8, 1963*	NORTH CAROLINA CITIZENS COMMITTEE FOR BETTER SCHOOLS, Chapel Hill
March 12, 1963*	LENOIR COUNTY INDUSTRIAL EDUCATION CENTER BANQUET, Kinston
March 13, 1963*	SEVENTH ANNUAL CONFERENCE ON OCCUPATIONAL HEALTH, Charlotte
March 14, 1963*	WOMAN'S NATIONAL DEMOCRATIC CLUB, Washington, D.C.
March 21, 1963	REMARKS ON FORTHCOMING ANNIVERSARY OF THE BATTLE OF GETTYSBURG, Raleigh
March 23, 1963*	DINNER HONORING H. CLIFTON BLUE, SPEAKER OF THE HOUSE OF REPRESENTATIVES, NORTH CAROLINA GENERAL ASSEMBLY, Carthage
March 26, 1963*	JOSEPHUS DANIELS JUNIOR HIGH SCHOOL PTA, Raleigh
March 27, 1963*	STATE COUNCIL MEETING OF HOME DEMONSTRATION CLUBS, Raleigh
April 9, 1963	WHITE HOUSE MEETING ON THE APPALACHIAN REGION (presented by George M. Stephens, Jr.), Washington, D.C.
April 20, 1963*	THE ARKANSAS YOUNG DEMOCRATIC CLUBS, North Little Rock, Arkansas
April 22, 1963	DEDICATION OF CRAVEN COUNTY HOSPITAL, New Bern
April 22, 1963*	QUARTERLY MEETING OF THE CONSERVATION AND DEVELOPMENT BOARD, Greenville
April 23, 1963*	STATE SCHOOL FOR THE BLIND, Raleigh
April 24, 1963*	DEDICATION OF RANDOLPH INDUSTRIAL EDUCATION CENTER, Asheboro
April 27, 1963*	LAW DAY BANQUET, Winston-Salem
April 30, 1963*	NORTH CAROLINA AUTOMOBILE DEALERS ASSOCIATION, Pinehurst
April 30, 1963*	GOVERNMENT PROCUREMENT CONFERENCE, NORTH CAROLINA INTERNATIONAL TRADE FAIR, Charlotte

May 2, 1963*	SOUTHERN TRUST CONFERENCE, Charlotte
May 3, 1963*	NORTH CAROLINA SCHOOL FOOD SERVICE ASSOCIATION, Raleigh
May 8, 1963*	EDUCATION RALLY, NORTH ROWAN HIGH SCHOOL, Spencer
May 8, 1963*	EDUCATION RALLY, DUNBAR HIGH SCHOOL, Spencer
May 8, 1963*	EDUCATION RALLY, EAST ROWAN HIGH SCHOOL, Salisbury
May 8, 1963*	EDUCATION RALLY, BOYDEN HIGH SCHOOL, Salisbury
May 8, 1963*	EDUCATION RALLY, SETZER SCHOOL, Salisbury
May 8, 1963*	EDUCATION RALLY, PRICE HIGH SCHOOL, Salisbury
May 10, 1963	DIAMOND JUBILEE CELEBRATION, PEMBROKE STATE COLLEGE, Pembroke
May 16, 1963*	DEDICATION OF GORDON FOODS PLANT, Raleigh
May 17, 1963*	SECOND STATE CONFERENCE ON PROGRAMS FOR EXCEPTIONALLY TALENTED CHILDREN, Charlotte
May 22, 1963*	POULTRY PROCESSORS ASSOCIATION, Raleigh
May 26, 1963	ELIZABETH CITY STATE TEACHERS COLLEGE, Elizabeth City
June 1, 1963*	GRADUATION EXERCISES, NORTH CAROLINA STATE COLLEGE, Raleigh
June 2, 1963*	GRADUATION EXERCISES, WOMAN'S COLLEGE, Greensboro
June 8, 1963*	STATE CONVENTION OF VETERANS OF FOREIGN WARS, Asheville
June 16, 1963*	NORTH CAROLINA BOYS STATE, INSTITUTE OF GOVERNMENT, Chapel Hill
June 18, 1963*	WESTERN ELECTRIC AWARDS CEREMONIES AND LUNCHEON, Greensboro
June 19, 1963*	DEDICATION OF PEDEN STEEL BUILDING, Raleigh
June 21, 1963*	STATE AMERICAN LEGION CONVENTION, Charlotte

June 24, 1963*   CITIZENS SCHOLARSHIP FOUNDATION AWARDS CEREMONIES, Smithfield

June 25, 1963*   GOVERNOR'S YOUTH FITNESS CONFERENCE BANQUET, Raleigh

June 26, 1963*   DEDICATION OF VIRGINIA ELECTRIC AND POWER COMPANY'S GASTON DAM, Roanoke Rapids

July 1, 1963*   REDEDICATION OF NORTH CAROLINA MONUMENT AT GETTYSBURG BATTLE-GROUND, Gettysburg, Pennsylvania

July 17, 1963*   REMARKS AT PERFORMANCE OF *THE LOST COLONY* (ATTENDED WITH ALBERTIS S. HARRISON, JR., GOVERNOR OF VIRGINIA), Manteo

July 23, 1963*   SOUTHERN REGIONAL EDUCATION BOARD LUNCHEON, Miami, Florida

August 19, 1963   SOUTHERN GOVERNORS CONFERENCE ON SPECIAL SOUTHERN REGIONAL EDUCATION BOARD REPORT ON MENTAL HEALTH, White Sulphur Springs, West Virginia

August 19, 1963   ANNUAL CONVENTION OF THE NORTH CAROLINA ASSOCIATION OF COUNTY COMMISSIONERS (delivered by Revenue Commissioner W. A. Johnson), Raleigh

September 6, 1963* LUNCHEON WELCOMING SPRING MILLS TO NORTH CAROLINA, Laurinburg

September 18, 1963 GOVERNOR'S COMMITTEE ON EMPLOYMENT OF THE HANDICAPPED, Raleigh

September 25, 1963* FORTY-FIFTH ANNUAL CONVENTION OF THE NATIONAL ASSOCIATION OF STATE DEPARTMENTS OF AGRICULTURE, Chapel Hill

October 1, 1963*   NORTH CAROLINA MOTOR CARRIERS ASSOCIATION, Pinehurst

October 3, 1963   REMARKS AT SYMBOLIC GROUNDBREAKING CEREMONIES FOR NORTH CAROLINA ARCHIVES AND HISTORY—STATE LIBRARY BUILDING, Raleigh

October 11, 1963*   WELCOMING ADDRESS TO NORTH CAROLINA DEMOCRATIC WOMEN, Raleigh

October 15, 1963*   CHAPEL SERVICE, SOUTHEASTERN BAPTIST THEOLOGICAL SEMINARY, Wake Forest

October 22, 1963	INDUSTRY APPRECIATION DAY, Mebane
October 23, 1963	UNITED NATIONS WORKSHOP, NORTH CAROLINA STATE OF THE UNIVERSITY OF NORTH CAROLINA, Raleigh
October 24, 1963*	TEACHERS APPRECIATION NIGHT, Elkin
October 25, 1963*	EDUCATION RALLY, MORRESVILLE HIGH SCHOOL, Mooresville
October 25, 1963*	EDUCATION RALLY, DUNBAR HIGH SCHOOL, Mooresville
October 25, 1963*	EDUCATION RALLY, ROCK SPRINGS HIGH SCHOOL, Denver
October 25, 1963*	EDUCATION RALLY, NEWBOLD HIGH SCHOOL, Lincolnton
October 25, 1963*	EDUCATION RALLY, LINCOLNTON HIGH SCHOOL, Lincolnton
October 25, 1963*	EDUCATION RALLY, WEST LINCOLN HIGH SCHOOL, Lincolnton
October 25, 1963*	EDUCATION RALLY, CHERRYVILLE HIGH SCHOOL, Cherryville
October 25, 1963*	EDUCATION RALLY, CHAVIS HIGH SCHOOL, Cherryville
November 1, 1963*	BERTIE COUNTY TERCENTENARY CELEBRATION, Windsor
November 3, 1963*	COLLEGE DAY AT CENTENARY METHODIST CHURCH, Smithfield
November 6, 1963	THE ANNUAL MEETING OF WAKE COUNTY RED CROSS CHAPTER, Raleigh
November 14, 1963*	STUDENT BODY AND FACULTY OF BRANDEIS UNIVERSITY, Waltham, Massachusetts
November 20, 1963*	CONFERENCE OF A.M.E. CHURCH, NORTH CAROLINA COLLEGE, Durham
January 10, 1964	INTRODUCTION OF DOUGLAS MacARTHUR II, AMBASSADOR TO BELGIUM, AT FOURTH ANNUAL FARM POLICY REVIEW CONFERENCE, Raleigh
January 11, 1964*	INTRODUCTION OF HENRY HALL WILSON, ADMINISTRATIVE ASSISTANT TO THE PRESIDENT, AT STATE YOUNG DEMOCRATIC CLUB MEETING, Southern Pines
January 15, 1964	VIRGINIA ASSOCIATION FOR MENTAL HEALTH, Richmond, Virginia

January 21, 1964*	FOOTBALL HALL OF FAME DINNER, Durham
January 23, 1964*	MOBILE HOME PARKS CONVENTION, Raleigh
January 29, 1964	TESTIMONY BEFORE THE AGRICULTURE SUBCOMMITTEE OF THE HOUSE OF REPRESENTATIVES CONCERNING NEED FOR TOBACCO RESEARCH, Washington, D.C.
January 29, 1964*	ACHIEVEMENT AWARDS DINNER, MONTGOMERY COUNTY INDUSTRIAL SCHOOL, Troy
January 31, 1964*	RALEIGH DISTRICT CONFERENCE OF THE METHODIST CHURCH, Raleigh
February 3, 1964*	ADDRESS TO BOARD OF CONSERVATION AND DEVELOPMENT, Charlotte
February 16, 1964*	COVENANT UNITED PRESBYTERIAN CHURCH, Durham
February 18, 1964*	COLLEGE OF WILLIAM AND MARY, Williamsburg, Virginia
March 2, 1964*	UNIVERSITY OF MASSACHUSETTS, Amherst, Massachusetts
March 4, 1964*	PRINCETON UNIVERSITY, Princeton, New Jersey
March 7, 1964	NORTH CAROLINA JUNIOR CHAMBER OF COMMERCE, Raleigh
March 11, 1964*	MEETING OF GREENSBORO UNITS OF NCEA AND NCTA, Greensboro
March 15, 1964*	METHODIST YOUTH FELLOWSHIP, HAYES BARTON CHURCH, Raleigh
March 17, 1964	CHARLOTTE ROTARY CLUB, Charlotte
March 30, 1964	INTRODUCTION OF DR. BILLY GRAHAM AT SPECIAL RECOGNITION DINNER FOR CITY OF CHARLOTTE AND MECKLENBURG COUNTY OFFICIALS, Charlotte
April 7, 1964	REMARKS TO NATIONAL SPORTSCASTERS AND SPORTSWRITERS ASSOCIATION, Salisbury
April 8, 1964	AGRICULTURE EXPORT EXPANSION WORKSHOP, Raleigh
April 8, 1964	DRIVER EDUCATION CONFERENCE, Raleigh

April 14, 1964*	SOUTHEASTERN CHILD CARE ASSOCIATION, Asheville
April 15, 1964*	"ALL-AMERICA CITY" CIVIC LUNCHEON, Gastonia
April 16, 1964*	MOCK POLITICAL PRESIDENTIAL ELECTION, Chapel Hill
April 18, 1964	JEFFERSON-JACKSON DAY DINNER, Raleigh
April 24, 1964	DEDICATION OF NATIONAL HEADQUARTERS BUILDING OF AMERICAN ASSOCIATION OF TEXTILE CHEMISTS AND COLORISTS, Research Triangle Park
April 25, 1964*	INAUGURATION OF DR. S. P. MASSIE, JR., AS PRESIDENT OF NORTH CAROLINA COLLEGE, Durham
April 25, 1964*	VIRGINIA'S NINTH CONGRESSIONAL DISTRICT JEFFERSON-JACKSON DAY DINNER, Abingdon, Virginia
April 26, 1964	FAYETTEVILLE STATE COLLEGE FOUNDERS DAY, Fayetteville
April 26, 1964*	SOUTH ATLANTIC REGIONAL DRIVE-IN CONFERENCE OF SCHOOL ADMINISTRATORS, Durham
April 27, 1964*	BOARD OF CONSERVATION AND DEVELOPMENT DINNER, Wilson
April 28, 1964*	AMERICAN SOCIETY FOR PUBLIC ADMINISTRATION, Raleigh
April 29, 1964*	CONFERENCE ON COMMUNITY DEVELOPMENT PROGRAMS, Washington, D.C.
April 30, 1964*	EDUCATION RALLY, NEW LONDON ELEMENTARY SCHOOL, New London
April 30, 1964*	EDUCATION RALLY, NORTH STANLY HIGH SCHOOL, New London
April 30, 1964*	EDUCATION RALLY, ALBEMARLE SENIOR HIGH SCHOOL, Albemarle
April 30, 1964*	EDUCATION RALLY, BADIN UNION SCHOOL, Badin
April 30, 1964*	STANLY COUNTY NCEA UNIT, Albemarle
May 1, 1964*	NORTH CAROLINA RURAL SAFETY COUNCIL, Raleigh
May 4, 1964*	SOUTHERN CONFERENCE ON TEACHERS RETIREMENT, Raleigh

May 11, 1964	TWENTY-MILLIONTH VISITOR CEREMONY, JOHN H. KERR DAM AND RESERVOIR, Boydton, Virginia
May 14, 1964	PRESENTATION OF WORLD PEACE AWARD OF THE AMERICAN ASSOCIATION TO PAUL G. HOFFMAN, MANAGING DIRECTOR OF UNITED NATIONS SPECIAL FUND, Chapel Hill
May 21, 1964*	DEDICATION OF GUY PHILLIPS SCHOOL, Chapel Hill
May 24, 1964*	DEDICATION OF 4-H CLUB CENTER, CHINQUA-PENN PLANTATION, Reidsville
May 29, 1964	NORTH CAROLINA STATE OF THE UNIVERSITY OF NORTH CAROLINA COMMENCEMENT, Raleigh
June 2, 1964*	COMMENCEMENT EXERCISES AT CHRISTIAN COLLEGE, Columbia, Missouri
June 14, 1964	EAST CAROLINA COLLEGE COMMENCEMENT EXERCISES, Greenville
June 24, 1964	WAYNE COUNTY INDUSTRIAL COMMITTEE OF 100, Goldsboro
July 20, 1964*	CONSERVATION AND DEVELOPMENT BOARD MEETING, Morehead City
August 11, 1964*	NORTH CAROLINA ASSOCIATION OF COUNTY ACCOUNTANTS BREAKFAST, Washington, D.C.
August 11, 1964*	TWENTY-NINTH ANNUAL CONFERENCE OF NATIONAL ASSOCIATION OF COUNTIES, Washington, D.C.
August 13, 1964*	EIGHTY-FOURTH ANNUAL MASONIC PICNIC, Mocksville
August 30, 1964	DEDICATION OF WILSON MEMORIAL HOSPITAL, Wilson
September 1, 1964	DEDICATION OF DILL DIVISION OF EATON MANUFACTURING COMPANY, Roxboro
September 14, 1964	NORTH CAROLINA CIVIL DEFENSE ASSOCIATION, Raleigh
September 17, 1964*	DEMOCRATIC WOMEN'S CONVENTION, Charlotte
September 29, 1964	DEDICATION OF COWANS FORD STATION AND LAKE NORMAN, Cowans Ford Dam, Charlotte

October 5, 1964   DEMOCRATIC RALLY, Parkersburg, West Virginia

October 6, 1964*   INTRODUCTION OF PRESIDENT LYNDON B. JOHNSON AT DEMOCRATIC RALLY, Raleigh

October 8, 1964*   DEMOCRATIC RALLY, Hopkinsville, Kentucky

October 9, 1964*   DEMOCRATIC RALLY, Louisville, Kentucky

October 12, 1964   REPORT FOR THE COMMITTEE ON INDUSTRIAL DEVELOPMENT, SOUTHERN GOVERNORS CONFERENCE, San Antonio, Texas

October 17, 1964*   BLOUNT COUNTY DEMOCRATIC RALLY, Maryville, Tennessee

October 26, 1964*   DEMOCRATIC RALLY, Columbia, Kentucky

October 26, 1964*   DEMOCRATIC RALLY, Morganfield, Kentucky

October 27, 1964*   FAMILY LIFE COUNCIL LUNCHEON, Durham

October 27, 1964*   STUDENTS FOR JOHNSON-HUMPHREY RALLY, DUKE UNIVERSITY, Durham

October 29, 1964*   FORSYTH COUNTY DEMOCRATIC RALLY, Winston-Salem

November 4, 1964*   PHI DELTA KAPPA BANQUET, Chapel Hill

November 12, 1964*   TRENTON ROTARY CLUB, Trenton, New Jersey

November 17, 1964*   PRODIGAL SONS OF NORTH CAROLINA LUNCHEON, New York City

November 17, 1964*   COUNCIL OF CHIEF STATE SCHOOL OFFICERS, New York City

November 30, 1964   DEDICATION OF AEROGLIDE CORPORATION PLANT, Raleigh

December 1, 1964*   CHAMBER OF COMMERCE TRAFFIC AND TRANSPORTATION COMMITTEE LUNCHEON, Winston-Salem

December 2, 1964*   EDUCATION RALLY, ROBERSONVILLE HIGH SCHOOL, Robersonville

December 2, 1964*   EDUCATION RALLY, WILLIAMSTON HIGH SCHOOL, Williamston

December 2, 1964*   EDUCATION RALLY, SOUTHWESTERN HIGH SCHOOL, Windsor

December 2, 1964*	EDUCATION RALLY, BERTIE COUNTY HIGH SCHOOL, Windsor
December 2, 1964*	EDUCATION RALLY, NORTHAMPTON HIGH SCHOOL, Conway
December 2, 1964*	REMARKS AT PRESENTATION OF ECONOMIC STUDY OF NORTHAMPTON COUNTY HIGH SCHOOL, Conway
December 5, 1964*	DEDICATION OF SCHIEFFELIN & COMPANY PLANT, Apex
December 8, 1964*	YOUNG DEMOCRATIC CLUB, Chapel Hill
December 9, 1964*	DUKE UNIVERSITY LAW SCHOOL, Durham
December 11, 1964	TEXTURED FIBRES, INCORPORATED, OPEN HOUSE, Liberty
January 5, 1965*	GOOD NEIGHBOR COUNCIL, Winston-Salem
January 6, 1965*	EDUCATION RALLY, FRANKLIN HIGH SCHOOL, Franklin
January 7, 1965*	EDUCATION RALLIES IN CUMBERLAND, HOKE, LEE, AND HARNETT COUNTIES

PROCLAMATIONS

DISASTER AREA

EXECUTIVE DEPARTMENT
RALEIGH

A PROCLAMATION BY THE GOVERNOR

March 8, 1962

[This was the first of several state of emergency proclamations issued during the Sanford administration as a result of severe storms, or as was the case in October, 1963, a severe drought. In this instance, President Kennedy responded favorably, on March 16, to the state's request for federal aid to recover from the coastal disaster.]

WHEREAS, On Wednesday, March 7, 1962, a devastating storm struck the coastal counties of Dare, Currituck, and Hyde, causing great damage and destruction resulting in major disaster conditions;

AND WHEREAS, Ocean tides three to four feet above normal high tides and extremely high winds caused great damage to homes, streets, highways, public utilities, and facilities;

AND WHEREAS, State and local agencies, including the Civil Defense organizations, have been actively engaged in rendering assistance and all available state and local governmental funds are, or will be, committed to this purpose;

AND WHEREAS, Serious damages were suffered as a result of this storm involving a primary federal aid highway along the Outer Banks, with the result that emergency relief funds are badly needed for repair of said highway under the provisions of Section 13-A U. S. Code annotated;

NOW, THEREFORE, I, Terry Sanford, Governor of North Carolina, do hereby declare a state of emergency to exist in the counties of Dare, Currituck, and Hyde, as a result of this storm, in witness whereof, I have hereunto set my hand and caused the Great Seal of the State of North Carolina to be affixed.

(Seal)

Done at the City of Raleigh this eighth day of March in the year of our Lord, nineteen hundred and sixty-two.

Terry Sanford, *Governor.*

By the Governor:
Graham Jones, *Press Secretary to the Governor.*

THANKSGIVING DAY

EXECUTIVE DEPARTMENT
RALEIGH

A PROCLAMATION BY THE GOVERNOR

November 22, 1962

WHEREAS, Americans, blessed by a generous Creator, have set aside a day of Thanksgiving since the early days of this nation to return thanks to God and to share our blessings in a feast of brotherhood;

AND WHEREAS, North Carolinians from Nags Head to Nantahala, like our fellow Americans from the Atlantic to the Pacific, have much for which to be grateful in this year of 1962;

AND WHEREAS, Since the last Thanksgiving, the freedoms of man, gained over the period of thousands of years, and indeed, the very existence of man, have been gravely threatened and greatly defended, it is especially timely to render thanks to our Creator;

AND WHEREAS, North Carolinians have reaped bountiful harvests in 1962 from their farmlands, their factories, and their schools to the end that we can face the winter with confidence;

AND WHEREAS, North Carolinians and all Americans can demonstrate the true spirit of Thanksgiving by sharing our surplus of prosperity with less fortunate neighbors through our Thanksgiving offerings:

Now, THEREFORE, I, Terry Sanford, Governor of North Carolina, do hereby proclaim Thursday, November 22, 1962, a legal holiday in North Carolina and request that all North Carolinians observe this day as one of Thanksgiving to the God who has been so generous to us.

(Seal)

In witness whereof, I have hereunto set my hand and caused the Great Seal of the State of North Carolina to be affixed. Done at the City of Raleigh, this the twenty-first day of November in the year of our Lord nineteen hundred and sixty-two.

Terry Sanford, *Governor.*

By the Governor:

Graham Jones, *Press Secretary.*

Special Session of the General Assembly

Executive Department
Raleigh

A Proclamation by the Governor

October 10, 1963

Whereas, The General Assembly of 1963, by Resolution No. 90, requested the Governor of North Carolina "at his discretion, to call an Extra Session of the General Assembly of North Carolina, reciting as the reason therefor that the General Assembly of North Carolina has been unable to agree on the provisions of an Act to redistrict the State Senate, as required by the Constitution of North Carolina."

Now, therefore, I, Terry Sanford, Governor of the State of North Carolina, do, by and with the advice of the Council of State, proclaim that the General Assembly of the State of North Carolina shall meet in Extraordinary Session at Raleigh, North Carolina, at Noon, on Monday, October 14, 1963, for the purpose of considering and enacting legislation to redistrict the State Senate, as required by the Constitution of North Carolina. I do hereby call upon, notify, and direct all members of the said General Assembly to meet at the Legislative Building in the City of Raleigh at Noon, on Monday, October 14, 1963, in such General Assembly as provided by the Constitution.

(Seal)   In witness whereof, I have hereunto set my hand and caused the Great Seal of the State of North Carolina to be affixed. Done at the City of Raleigh, this the tenth day of October, in the Year of our Lord one thousand nine hundred and sixty-three.

Terry Sanford, *Governor.*

By the Governor:
Graham Jones, *Press Secretary.*

PRESIDENTIAL ELECTORS

EXECUTIVE DEPARTMENT

RALEIGH

A PROCLAMATION BY THE GOVERNOR

December 9, 1964

WHEREAS, The State Board of Elections of the State of North Carolina has canvassed the returns of the votes cast for electors for President and Vice-President of the United States at the General Elections held on November 3, 1964;

AND WHEREAS, Said State Board of Elections has prepared and certified an abstract of same to the Secretary of State of the State of North Carolina;

AND WHEREAS, Said Secretary of State has, under his hand and the seal of his office, certified to the undersigned Governor of the State of North Carolina the names of as many persons receiving the highest number of votes for electors of President and Vice-President of the United States as the State of North Carolina is entitled to in the Electoral College:

NOW, THEREFORE, I, Terry Sanford, Governor of the State of North Carolina, pursuant to the power and authority vested in me by the provisions contained in the General Statutes of North Carolina, Section 163-110, do hereby proclaim that the following persons have been duly elected as electors for President and Vice-President of the United States:

ELECTORS AT LARGE

Robert E. Williams

Angus McKellar

ELECTOR	CONGRESSIONAL DISTRICT
C. Don Langston	First
Dr. Badie T. Clark	Second
Dr. John D. Robinson, Jr.	Third
Brantley Poole	Fourth
Allen H. Gwynn, Jr.	Fifth
Carl T. Durham	Sixth
Sam C. Morris	Seventh
C. C. Randall	Eighth
Mrs. Stella Anderson	Ninth
Mrs. Lester Gifford	Tenth
E. L. Loftin	Eleventh

and each of the electors above named is hereby enjoined to attend a meeting at the Capitol in the City of Raleigh, North

Carolina, at noon, on the fourteenth day of December, 1964, for the purpose of voting for the President and Vice-President of the United States, as required by law.

(Seal) Done at our Capital City of Raleigh, this ninth day of December, in the year of our Lord one thousand nine hundred and sixty-four, and in the one hundred and eighty-ninth year of our American Independence.

Terry Sanford, *Governor.*

By the Governor:

Graham E. Jones, *Press Secretary.*

INAUGURATION OF DAN K. MOORE

EXECUTIVE DEPARTMENT
RALEIGH

A PROCLAMATION BY THE GOVERNOR

January 7, 1965

WHEREAS, The Constitution of North Carolina provides that the supreme executive power of the State shall be vested in a Governor and stipulates that his term of office shall be for four years, commencing on the first of January next after his election by the qualified electors of the State and shall continue until his successor is elected and qualified;

AND WHEREAS, In the general election of November 3, 1964, the Honorable Dan K. Moore was elected Governor at the same time that other constitutional state officers were chosen, and the results of this election have been certified by legally prescribed authority;

AND WHEREAS, The Honorable Dan K. Moore and other elected constitutional officers will take their oaths of office in a ceremony beginning at noon on January 8, 1965;

AND WHEREAS, The Constitution has been amended to defer the beginning of the biennial session of the General Assembly from January to February, thus preventing the General Assembly from performing customary functions in connection with the inauguration of the Governor and other constitutional state officers:

NOW THEREFORE, I, Terry Sanford, Governor of the State of

North Carolina, do hereby proclaim Thursday and Friday, January 7 and 8, 1965, as the period for the festivities and ceremonies pertaining to the inauguration arranged by the Governor's Inaugural Committee.

(Seal)

> Done at our capital city of Raleigh, this seventh day of January, in the year of our Lord one thousand nine hundred and sixty-five, and in the one hundred and eighty-ninth year of our American Independence.

Terry Sanford, *Governor.*

By the Governor:
Graham Jones, *Press Secretary.*

EXECUTIVE ORDERS

ESTABLISHING THE GOVERNOR'S COMMISSION ON EDUCATIONAL TELEVISION

May 15, 1962

WHEREAS, The General Assembly established in 1953 the State Educational Radio and Television Commission for the purpose of making recommendations concerning the uses proposed for television facilities for educational and cultural purposes with particular reference to the development, financing, operation, and management of television facilities for educational and cultural purposes; and

WHEREAS, This Commission, in accordance with Chapter 1204 of the 1953 Session Laws, completed its work and reported its findings to the Governor, thereby in the opinion of the Attorney General, terminating its existence; and

WHEREAS, As a result of the work of the Commission, and with the generous assistance of a number of individuals and corporations, the University of North Carolina established WUNC-TV on Channel 4; and

WHEREAS, There is today a pressing need to expand the service of educational and cultural television throughout the entire State; and

WHEREAS, Recent legislation in the United States Congress provides for the granting of federal funds for educational and cultural television equipment; and

WHEREAS, In view of the growing importance of television as an educational medium, it is imperative that North Carolina take advantage of this legislation in the most efficient and fruitful fashion:

There is hereby established the Governor's Commission on Educational Television.

COMPOSITION:

The Commission shall be composed of so many members as the Governor sees fit to appoint, with balanced representation of professional and educational interests as well as geographical distribution. Persons shall be appointed to membership by the Governor for terms of two years.

DUTIES:

It shall be the duty of this Commission to consider all requests originating in North Carolina for federal grants to be used for educational and cultural television purposes within this State, and to advise the Governor as to which proposals should receive

the official support of the State, and in what order of priority.
The Commission is also charged with the responsibility of advising the Governor as to the most efficient, fruitful, and expeditious way in which the benefits of educational television can
be provided to all the people of North Carolina. It shall be the
duty of the Commission to report to the Governor on October
1, 1962, and every six months thereafter.

MEETINGS:

Meetings of the Commission shall be held at the call of the
person designated by the Governor as Chairman of the Commission.

Done in Raleigh, North Carolina, this the fifteenth day of
May, nineteen hundred and sixty-two.

Terry Sanford, *Governor.*

ESTABLISHING THE NORTH CAROLINA OUTER BANKS SEASHORE PARK COMMISSION

August 3, 1962

WHEREAS, There is an urgent need to preserve the outer banks
of North Carolina from the forces of nature threatening their
destruction and endangering inland waters and land areas of
the State; and

WHEREAS, There is increasing need for more public recreational areas which afford all of the advantages of water sports
and fishing; and

WHEREAS, That reach of the North Carolina ocean shore line
known as the outer banks contains a large part of the remaining
undeveloped and unspoiled areas available for development in
the interests of all the people; and

WHEREAS, It has become increasingly clear that concerted action is necessary in order to plan carefully for the conservation
and development of this area;

There is hereby established the North Carolina Outer Banks
Seashore Park Commission.

COMPOSITION:

The Commission shall be composed of so many members as
the Governor sees fit to appoint. Persons so appointed shall serve
for terms of two years. The following persons shall serve on this

Commission by virtue of the offices which they occupy: The Chairman of the Board of Water Resources; the Director of the Property Control Division of the Department of Administration; the Chairman of Parks Committee of the Board of Conservation and Development; the Director of Civil Defense of the State of North Carolina; the Director of the North Carolina Recreation Commission; the Chairman of the North Carolina State Highway Commission or his nominee.

DUTIES:

It shall be the duty of this Commission to examine the North Carolina outer banks from Shackleford Banks to the Virginia state line, and to plan and assist in the preservation of the shore line and the establishment of public parks in that area. It will be the responsibility of this Commission to decide how the outer banks can best be protected and how the coastal areas can best be preserved from great damage. The Commission is also charged with the responsibility of planning for the soundest development of the outer banks area, keeping in mind the advancement of tourism, business, and industry as well as necessary conservation practices. The Commission is specifically charged with the duty of developing a comprehensive plan of co-operation among related state and federal agencies in order to carry out its responsibilities as assigned herein. Once this plan has been devised, this Commission shall be that State agency charged with co-ordinating the implementation of the comprehensive plan. It shall be the duty of the Commission to report to the Governor so often as seems desirable to the Commission, but at least every six months.

ORGANIZATION:

The Governor will designate a chairman, a vice-chairman, a secretary, and an executive committee. The North Carolina Outer Banks Seashore Park Commission shall be furnished office space and staff assistance by the Department of Water Resources.

MEETINGS:

Meetings of the Commission shall be held at the call of the Chairman of the Commission.

Done in Raleigh, North Carolina, this the third day of August, nineteen hundred and sixty-two.

Terry Sanford, *Governor.*

ESTABLISHING THE GOVERNOR'S COMMISSION ON THE STATUS OF WOMEN

October 11, 1963

WHEREAS, The women of this State have served with distinction in their roles as homemakers, participants in cultural and civic affairs, and working contributors to governmental and economic progress; and

WHEREAS, The full realization of the rights and potentials of women is of vital importance to the advancement of our State; and

WHEREAS, Measures that contribute to strengthening family security and home life will advance the general welfare; and

WHEREAS, Measures that strengthen full and effective participation in cultural and civic affairs are important to continuing progress in our State; and

WHEREAS, It is in the interest of our State to promote the economy and security of our people through the most efficient and effective utilization of the skills of all persons; and

WHEREAS, Women should have the opportunity to develop in their varied capacities and fulfill their aspirations on the basis of individual merit; and

WHEREAS, A Commission should be charged with the responsibility for developing recommendations to overcome discrimination in employment and other outmoded limitations based on sex, and to provide services to enable women to continue in their family role while making maximum contributions to the world around them:

NOW, THEREFORE, By virtue of the authority vested in me as Governor of the State of North Carolina by the State Constitution and Statutes, it is ordered as follows:

PART I

ESTABLISHMENT OF THE GOVERNOR'S COMMISSION ON THE STATUS OF WOMEN

Sec. 101. There is hereby established the Governor's Commission on the Status of Women, referred to herein as the "Commission." The Commission shall terminate not later than January 1, 1965.

Sec. 102. The Commission shall be composed of twenty members appointed by the Governor from among persons with a competency in the area of women's activities and public affairs, and from among such officials of state agencies as are considered necessary to carry out the work of the Commission. The Governor shall designate a Chairman, Vice-Chairman, and Executive Vice-Chairman from among the membership.

Sec. 103. The Commission shall meet at the call of the Chairman.

Sec. 104. Necessary facilitating assistance, including the provision of suitable office space, shall be furnished the Commission by appropriate state agencies designated by the Department of Administration. An Executive Secretary shall be detailed by the Governor to serve the Commission.

Sec. 105. The Commission is authorized to use the services of consultants and experts as may be found necessary and as may be otherwise authorized by law.

Sec. 106. All executive departments and agencies of the State are directed to co-operate with the Commission in the performance of its duties.

Part II

Duties of the Governor's Commission on the Status of Women

Sec. 201. The Commission shall review the progress, consider the potential, and make recommendations as needed for constructive action on problems in the following areas:

(a) The employment policies and practices of the State of North Carolina, with reference to additional affirmative steps which should be taken through legislation, executive or administrative action to assure nondiscrimination on the basis of sex and to enhance constructive employment opportunities for women.

(b) Employment policies and practices, including those on wages, under State contracts.

(c) State Labor laws dealing with such matters as wages, hours and working conditions, to determine whether they are accomplishing the purposes for which they were enacted and whether they should be adapted to changing technological, economic, and social conditions.

(d) Differences in legal treatment of men and women in regard to legal and property rights, and family relations.

(e) Policies and practices with respect to education, including counseling.

(f) Policies and practices with respect to vocational training and retraining.

(g) Health and welfare programs as they affect women in the performance of their varied capacities.

(h) The general welfare of disadvantaged groups.

(i) New and expanded services that may be required for women as wives, mothers, volunteers, and workers, including home services and arrangements for care of children during the working day.

Sec. 202. The Commission shall submit a final report of its recommendations to the Governor by January 1, 1965.

Done in Raleigh, North Carolina, this eleventh day of October in the year of our Lord one thousand nine hundred and sixty-three.

Terry Sanford, *Governor.*

ESTABLISHING THE NORTH CAROLINA STATE ARTS COUNCIL

December 3, 1964

1. There is hereby created "The North Carolina State Arts Council."

2. The purpose of said Council shall be to advance the interests of the arts, to survey the status and the needs of the Arts of North Carolina, to develop the influence of art in education, to encourage professional training and standards in the performing and fine arts in North Carolina, and to represent the State of North Carolina in matters relating to the provisions of the National Arts and Cultural Development Act of 1964, and in national and regional meetings and conferences of similar councils.

3. The Council shall consist of twenty (20) members, appointed by the Governor of North Carolina for a term which shall expire on September 1, 1966, unless the existence of the Council is sooner terminated as herein provided.

4. No member shall receive from the State compensation or reimbursements for expenses, and no State funds shall be expended or obligated by the Council or in behalf of the Council.

5. The Council shall report recommendations to the Governor of North Carolina on or before July 1, 1966, relating to the permanent organization of a North Carolina Arts Council

and other matters deemed appropriate by the Council; and this Council shall cease to exist when a permanent Council is established, or in any event no later than September 1, 1966, unless its existence is reserved by the Governor of North Carolina.

6. The Council may accept gifts, and may expend any funds received in any way that the Council shall determine so as to accomplish the objects of the Council.

Done at Raleigh, North Carolina, this 3rd day of December, 1964.

Terry Sanford, *Governor.*

STATEMENTS AND ARTICLES

STATEMENTS AND ARTICLES

[Literally hundreds of statements, press releases, public announcements, and articles were issued from the Governor's Office during the Sanford administration. It is obvious that only a limited few could be included in this volume. Over forty short articles in a series entitled "Be Proud of North Carolina," special articles for newspapers and magazines, and transcripts of press conferences would all add interest to a volume of Sanford material, but space limitations prohibit the use of most of this material. Statements on various subjects would fill a book in themselves. Selection was made on the basis of significance in most instances, though some statements were included as being representative of a larger number on the same or related topics. In many instances the statements relate closely to addresses made by the Governor and should be read in connection with the speeches for complete clarity and meaning. Where addresses adequately cover the subject, statements have been omitted. Subjects such as the tobacco health scare, civil rights and race relations, the Job Corps, and retarded children are examples in this category. Many, many special "days," "weeks," and "months" are observed in North Carolina and elsewhere; statements on such subjects as "Gasoline Retailers Day," "Beauty Career Days in North Carolina," "Corn Bread Week," "Apple Week," "Sweet Potato Week," "Women in Construction Week," "Play Tennis Week," "North Carolina Beauty Salon Week," "PBX Operators Week in North Carolina," "Music Month," and "American History Month" are examples picked at random from the numerous omitted statements.]

DESIGNATING NORTH CAROLINA'S OPENING OF THE CIVIL WAR COMMEMORATION

January 6, 1961

The President of the United States, acting on the request contained in a joint resolution of the Congress, has proclaimed Sunday, January 8, 1961, as the official opening of the one hundredth anniversary of the Civil War.

North Carolinians were "First at Bethel, Farthest at Gettysburg, and Last at Appomattox." North Carolinians also were among the first to strive to bind up the wounds of the nation and to defend the nation in subsequent wars.

It is therefore fitting that North Carolina should join in prayer with her sister states—North, South, East and West—in opening the Civil War Centennial observance.

In recognition of this, I am happy to designate Sunday, January 8, 1961, as the official opening of

NORTH CAROLINA'S COMMEMORATION OF THE CIVIL WAR

and call upon all citizens of our state to join with citizens of all of the other United States in observing Sunday, January 8, 1961, as a day of prayer.

DESIGNATING BROTHERHOOD WEEK

February 6, 1961

The annual celebration of Brotherhood Week, to be held February 19-26, 1961, is sponsored by the National Conference of Christians and Jews.

The National Conference of Christians and Jews is diligently working to establish a social order in which the religious ideals of brotherhood and justice shall become the standards of human relationship.

The purpose of Brotherhood Week is to symbolize renewed dedication to the ideals of greater tolerance, understanding, friendship, and co-operation among all our citizens, and greater respect for the difference and beliefs of our people.

Our strength as one nation under God depends on our unity and informed vigilance as a free people.

Brotherhood Week is in the tradition established by our forefathers and enunciated in the Declaration of Independence and the Constitution and deserves the wholehearted co-operation of all the people of our state.

Therefore, I am happy to proclaim the week of February 19-26, 1961, as

BROTHERHOOD WEEK

in North Carolina, and urge the people of this state to observe this week with full awareness of their responsibility to increase that spirit of brotherhood so essential to the progress of our state and our nation.

REGARDING STATE PERSONNEL

April 12, 1961

I think the state employees are generally doing an outstanding job. I have not been surprised but I have been pleased to find that they are conscientious and are earning their pay. I am happy to be associated with them.

Two bills are being prepared and will be introduced shortly on subjects dealing with state employees.

First, a bill is being prepared to provide for longevity pay. This will be enabling legislation that will permit the Governor and Personnel Council to set up a system for state employees to receive an additional increment based on length of meritorious service when they can no longer receive ordinary merit increments.

Second, legislation is being prepared to increase the size of the State Personnel Council from five to seven members with at least two members on the council to come from the ranks of state employees.

I am quite aware of the financial needs of all state employees. It is my hope that more money will be available to take care of those needs. At the present time the joint finance committees are working on numerous revenue bills, and we are giving careful consideration to additional financial compensation for state employees in addition to the recommendation of the Advisory Budget Commission.

CONCERNING ECONOMIC LEGISLATION

April 24, 1961

Make no mistake where this administration stands. I chose my company with the man who stood with the "branch head boys." I still covet their confidence. But I want to make it clear that my whole purpose, town and country, is to serve the people who in this rich time still seem lost on dead-end streets.

I have talked much about schools. I mean to go on stressing education—quality education for our children. But that is not all. Quality education is only the best, the essential, the shining example of the full opportunity North Carolinians must have. And in terms of opportunity we do not deal merely with children. Indeed, regardless of the quality of the schools we provide, our children may be denied the best chance if the opportunities of their parents here and now are stifled.

There are three legislative proposals which will help open up the dead-end streets.

First, I favor a fair and adequate minimum wage. We haven't gone as far as we can, but it seems to me the least we can do right now is to adopt Representative Kennedy's bill expanding coverage.

Two years ago when North Carolina first and in limited fashion adopted a minimum wage law, we heard dire predictions from the lobbyists that a state which paid its poorest people a minimum wage would bankrupt businesses. The truth is that there has not been a single failure honestly due to minimum wages we have paid in the past two years. The least we can do is to extend it to thousands of others whose pitiful wages help keep all North Carolina poor.

Second, the poorest must find credit when they are pressed for funds without mortgaging their hopes and lives to money lenders, loan sharks, and usurers. I don't want to see us become so involved in the fight between "big" small lenders and "little" small lenders that we forget our purpose is to protect the least of our people who are in no position to protect themselves.

The present expansion of this business, like flies around a honey pot, indicates that there is still a profit in oppression. And there has been oppression of the poor in the small loan business in North Carolina. It should be our business to stop it in terms of both good business and good heart.

Third, I endorse without reservation the bills to improve sanitation requirements of migrant labor camps and to require safeguards on motor vehicles used in transporting migrant workers.

This group of people constitutes the most hopeless and helpless element of wealthy America. The ultimate answer perhaps lies in a greater development of mechanical harvesting equipment and an expanding economy making it possible for these migrant workers to find employment not requiring nomadic existence. But for the present, we should do everything possible to lessen the misery, the health hazards, the dangers to which we have too long closed our eyes.

North Carolina cannot afford to continue its dead-end streets.

ANNOUNCING THE NORTH CAROLINA INTERNATIONAL TRADE FAIR

April 27, 1961

This autumn the state of North Carolina will hold the first state-sponsored International Trade Fair for the purpose of showing people from all over the world North Carolina's manufactured goods and the international trade potential of our state.

The International Trade Fair in North Carolina will offer management, salesmen, and buyers the unique opportunity of seeing the products of thousands of North Carolina manufacturers, ranging from textiles and tobacco to furniture and electronics.

We are inviting industrial, commercial, and governmental

leaders from Europe, Latin America, and the Orient to come to North Carolina on this occasion. We expect this to be a fair where sales are made and orders taken for quality North Carolina goods which will be on exhibit.

The International Trade Fair in North Carolina, and the resulting increase in international trade which we firmly expect from the fair, will have beneficial effects on North Carolina's production and trade.

While minor in itself, we believe it will be an important step in the right direction for the solution of the problem on the gold imbalance. We trust this fair will set a pattern for selling American goods and spreading American good will abroad.

In view of the importance of this fair to the United States, generally, and to North Carolina, in particular, I have asked President Kennedy to give it his attention, his interest, and his assistance. The United States Department of Commerce is cooperating in many ways.

North Carolina has accepted the President's challenge: We are not asking what the federal government can do for us. Rather, we are, with this International Trade Fair in North Carolina, seeing what we can do for the United States through the exchange of trade, ideas, and good will.

The North Carolina International Trade Fair is to open October 12. We are hoping President Kennedy will come to North Carolina to help us open it. That is Columbus Day and we are inviting our friends overseas to rediscover America and North Carolina.

COMMENDING THE NORTH CAROLINA SENATE ON PASSAGE OF THE REVENUE ACT

June 8, 1961

I admire and appreciate the courage and the vision so clearly demonstrated by the members of the Senate this afternoon.

APPLAUDING THE PASSAGE OF THE
APPROPRIATIONS ACT BY THE
STATE HOUSE OF REPRESENTATIVES

June 8, 1961

This was excellent! Such overwhelming support of quality education and the other programs for advancing North Carolina is a credit to the leadership and membership of the House. I thank them.

ON THE SETTLEMENT OF THE MARS HILL SCHOOL
CONTROVERSY

June 13, 1961

[A long-standing case of political rivalry in Madison County mushroomed into a dramatic controversy in the spring of 1961 when the school board failed to re-elect Ralph Neill as principal of Mars Hill School. Faculty and parents protested, alleging that politics and education were mixed by the action. Concern of state officials increased when students staged an eight-day boycott of classes. After a series of futile conferences among leaders and an attempt by State Superintendent of Public Instruction Charles Carroll to settle the argument, Governor Sanford intervened. This statement marked the formal settlement of the controversy, an arbitrary solution which both groups agreed in advance to accept.]

On May 21, I agreed to serve as arbitrator in the dispute then existing between the Madison County School Board and patrons and faculty members at Mars Hill School. While it was an unusual step to "borrow trouble" in this manner, I consider it justified because it appeared to be the only means possible at that time of ending a student boycott at the school. The boycott was ended that day and almost all the students who had been absent from the school for more than a week returned to class. The school time lost has been made up.

As their part of this agreement, parties involved in the dispute —the Madison County Board of Education, the Mars Hill School District Committee, representatives of the faculty and of the Citizens Committee—agreed and bound themselves in all good faith to accept the solution which I, as Governor of North Carolina, should present. They further agreed to co-operate with each other in all good faith to the end that such solution should have a reasonable opportunity for resolving the dispute. Subsequently, my assistant, Hugh Cannon,[133] went to Madison County and reduced this understanding to writing.

On June 2, I directed Tom Lambeth,[134] my administrative assistant, to go to Madison County for the purpose of investigating the situation and reporting back to me the facts surrounding the dispute. Earlier I had discussed the dispute with representatives of the various parties involved.

On June 2 and 3, my administrative assistant was in Madison County. In meetings which lasted for more than thirteen hours, he met with approximately 600 citizens of the county. He talked individually with sixteen members of the faculty, most of the members of the Madison County Board of Education, the county superintendent, the principal of the Mars Hill School, students, and parents. In group meetings, he met with fourteen other members of the faculty, members of the Mars Hill School District Committee, and the Mars Hill Citizens Committee. He conducted a public hearing, attended by approximately 500 citizens of the county.

On the basis of information gathered in the talks which I have held with the parties involved and on the basis of the investigation, I have arrived at several conclusions which I feel should be cited as the basis for my recommendations.

1. The action of the Madison County Board of Education in not re-electing Ralph Neill as principal of Mars Hill School was action legally taken by a properly constituted board with full authority to make decisions in such matters.

2. I would also point out that Mr. Neill had failed to receive the recommendation of the superintendent of schools for re-election in 1960, but he had been continued as principal by action of the board, overruling the action of the superintendent. Friction has been evident for several years, but friction is difficult to define and no good purpose would be served by attempting to document the many differences of the past.

3. There is no evidence of recent coercion being exerted on members of the school faculty to obtain political contributions. Teachers were specifically questioned as to this point. With one exception, they indicated that any such contributions, at least in recent years, had been made voluntarily. Finally, on this point, I have carefully investigated the inci-

---

[133] Hugh Cannon (1931-   ), lawyer from Raleigh; Rhodes Scholar, 1955; member of staff of Institute of Government, 1956; gubernatorial assistant, 1961; Director of Administration, 1961. *North Carolina Manual,* 1963, 459.

[134] Thomas Willis Lambeth (1935-   ), member of news staff of *Winston-Salem Journal,* 1959-1960; administrative assistant to Governor Sanford, 1961. *North Carolina Manual, 1963,* 457.

dent cited in the press (when Mr. Neill was reported to have
refused to allow solicitation of campaign contributions during school hours) and find that such a request was made.
This was in 1958. Mr. Neill properly refused permission for
solicitation at the school. I must add that his action was endorsed at that time not only by the County Board of Education but also by the executive committee of the majority
party. Mr. Neill reports that there have been no attempts
since that time to make such solicitations. I have concluded
that this incident had nothing to do with the failure of the
board to re-elect Mr. Neill.

4. While the Madison County Board of Education has absolute
authority to make such decisions, reasons given for failure to
re-elect Mr. Neill are nebulous and seem insufficient in light
of the overwhelming support of his administration by patrons
of the school. It also seems significant to me that his re-
election this year was recommended by the superintendent of
Madison County schools.

5. I find almost unanimous agreement on the point of all parties
involved in this dispute that both Mr. Neill and Mr. Anderson are capable and dedicated school administrators.

6. Mr. Neill has the support and respect of almost all members
of the Mars Hill School faculty. I would point out that even
members of the faculty who failed to sign the statement op-
posing the board's action in Mr. Neill's case register no
criticism.

7. I find that Mr. Neill and members of the faculty must share
a great deal of the responsibility for the student boycott
which interrupted normal activity at the Mars Hill School
for a period of eight days. The boycott did nothing to relieve
the tension surrounding the dispute and was an expensive
and unfortunate incident in this affair. While there is no
evidence that Mr. Neill encouraged the boycott, it is obvious
that he made it possible through his refusal to demand that
students return to the school. One of the student leaders of
the boycott clearly demonstrated Mr. Neill's lack of positive
action when he publicly stated, "When Mr. Neill says jump,
we jump. We would have walked back in the school the minute he said come." The actions of certain members of the
faculty are also to be criticized both before and during the
boycott. Teachers left classrooms unattended to hold meetings in which their protests could be discussed and strategy
determined. There seems little doubt that some teachers actively encouraged students to participate in the boycott.

School bus drivers in some cases told students not to board buses during the boycott; and, in at least one incident, forcibly removed students from buses.

8. I find that members of the Mars Hill School faculty expressed great concern as to the security of their jobs. While most of them have been teaching for a number of years at the school, they indicate that they have done so most of the time uncertain about their tenure. For a number of years, the practice existed of not notifying teachers of their re-election for an unusual length of time. This, however, has not been true in recent years. Last year, teachers were notified before the end of the current school year and this year would have been notified at such a time had not the boycott interrupted the normal operation of the school.

9. As a matter of policy, the state cannot condone student "walkouts" as a solution to any difficulty. Staying out of school is a violation of law.

CONCLUSIONS

After carefully considering all of the factors involved, including the necessity for maintaining respect for properly constituted authority, the obviously overwhelming sentiment of the school patrons, and, finally but primarily, the best interests of the children at Mars Hill School, I recommend the following:

1. That Mr. Neill be re-elected for the coming school year.

2. That those protesting action of the County Board of Education confine their protests in the future to the appellate machinery provided by law. They will be given an opportunity later this year to express their opinions to a commission set up by the General Assembly, at my request, to study carefully the many and varied ways of school board selection and to make appropriate recommendations. This is the proper, lawful method of effecting the will of the majority.

3. That the children be advised by the principal, the teachers, and the parents that force is not a proper method of relief, and while legal process may be slower, it is nevertheless the method adopted by those nations believing in the principle of the rule of law.

ON EXECUTIVE CLEMENCY

July 4, 1961

[In the spring of 1959, a textile strike at the Harriet-Henderson Cotton Mills in Henderson grew to violent proportions with the dynamiting of a power plant which served the mill. Several labor leaders, including Boyd Payton, Carolinas Director of the Textile Workers Union of America, were later convicted of participating in the conspiracy and were sentenced to four to ten years. A fifteen-month legal battle to avoid prison sentences proved futile as did an appeal to Governor Hodges for executive clemency. The defendants began their prison terms in November, 1960. The Boyd Payton case continued to receive much publicity, and Governor Sanford's July 4 statement expressed his views on executive clemency and revealed his decision to reduce sentences in a number of cases. Three and one-half years later Payton was granted a full pardon by the Governor. See page 638.]

The courts of our state and nation exercise in the name of the people the powers of administration of justice. The Executive is charged with the exercise in the name of the people of an equally important attitude of a healthy society—that of mercy beyond the strict framework of the law.

The use of executive clemency is not a criticism of the courts, either express or implied. I have no criticism of any court or any judge. Executive clemency does not involve the changing of any judicial determination. It does not eliminate punishment; it does consider rehabilitation.

To decide when and where such mercy should be extended is a decision which must be made by the Executive. It cannot be delegated even in part to anyone else, and thus the decision is a lonely one.

It falls to the Governor to blend mercy with justice, as best he can, involving human as well as legal considerations, in the light of all circumstances after the passage of time, but before justice is allowed to overrun mercy in the name of the power of the state.

I fully realize that reasonable men hold strong feelings on both sides of every case where executive clemency is indicated. I accepted the responsibility of being Governor, however, and I will not shy away from the responsibility of exercising the power of executive clemency.

After careful consideration, I have today signed orders granting executive clemency of some degree to twenty-nine prisoners.

These are all a matter of public record, but I would call your attention to seven of them because of widespread public interest.

I have reduced the sentences of seven of the men involved in the Henderson strike by three years each. Thus four are eligible for parole immediately, and Auslander, Payton, and Gore will be eligible for parole later this summer. (The eighth, Malcolm Jarrell, was released on parole in April.)

The prison record always has been one of the considerations, and outstanding work has been done by one of these men in teaching illiterates at Central Prison how to read and write.

ON EMPLOYMENT OF EX-PRISONERS

July 27, 1961

The highest purpose of our entire system of criminal justice is to return convicted offenders to free society willing and able to meet the responsibilities and to earn the rewards of citizenship in a democracy. This system will fail to accomplish its high purpose if forced to operate in a society that rejects the released prisoner. This should be an obvious truth. It apparently is not. Far too many good citizens fail to appreciate the effect of their open and automatic hostility toward persons who have served time in our prisons.

When a prisoner is ready to return to free society, he too frequently finds the doors to the prison open to let him out, but the doors of opportunity for constructive living are closed to him in the free community. Some employers automatically reject applicants who are ex-prisoners. This unfortunate policy places a frustrating obstacle in the paths of those who sincerely desire to rise above their mistakes and live as law-abiding citizens.

Put yourself in the position of a person who has committed an offense and found himself in prison. You behave yourself, acquire good work habits and useful skills, learn how to use idle time constructively, become a member of Alcoholics Anonymous, receive and profit from religious and social counseling, learn how to study, and rediscover the value of reading good books. You are released. You go home to your wife and children ready and willing to act the part of a good husband, father, and citizen. Then no one will hire you because you have served time in prison. How would you react?

This week, Director J. Edgar Hoover reported F.B.I. statistics showing that our country's crime rate is growing four times faster than our population. The public is and should be alarmed by this fact. Yet it is not enough to press for apprehension and conviction of a criminal. Tax money spent to put an offender into prison and keep him there will be largely wasted if he does not leave prison ready and *able* to make an honest living in free society. It is important to remember that 97 per cent of those committed to prison are released. We believe our Prison Department's varied programs are preparing our prisoners for constructive citizenship. Whether they will be *able* to take their proper place in free society will depend in large part upon the willingness of employers to give them fair consideration for employment. Anything that can be done to reduce the difficulties ex-prisoners face in finding gainful employment will lessen the dangers of their slipping back into crime and returning to swell the population of our prisons. A repeater back in prison is a burden on the taxpayers. An ex-prisoner employed in the free community is a taxpayer contributing to the support of governmental services. Prisoners' families swell the welfare rolls. Employed ex-prisoners support themselves and their families. Therefore, every employer who finds it possible to hire an ex-prisoner is serving his own self-interest as well as contributing to the good of society as a whole.

Many employers have told us how pleased they are by the job performance of the ex-prisoners they have hired. They also comment favorably on the fact that the Prison Department provides them with useful and comprehensive information about prisoners seeking employment. These employers have found that they can rely upon the Prison Department's statements concerning the applicant's physical condition, attitude, special problems, as well as particular abilities. We hope our reporting of the favorable results obtained by the employers who have used ex-prisoners trained by the Prison Department will convince many other employers that they have been missing out on a good deal.

I believe state government should take the lead in giving fair consideration to job applicants who are ex-prisoners. We can hardly expect to convince private enterprise of the merits of an enlightened employment policy concerning ex-prisoners unless we demonstrate the courage of our own declared convictions. I have asked that a study be made of the employment policies and regulations of state agencies in order to find and test the validity of any that bar ex-prisoners.

I am proud of the teamwork exemplified by the presence here of officials representing the Employment Security Commission, State Board of Public Welfare, Board of Paroles, and the Prison Department. I am pleased that the press, radio, and television representatives are giving wide publicity to our intensified efforts to expand and improve the prisoner job placement program. I hope that these efforts and this publicity will bring to our program additional support from representatives of industry, business, farm groups, civic clubs, churches, and interested individuals. I am here and now appealing for such support. Please send to me or to the Director of Prisons any suggestions you may have for improving this vital program.

ON THE DEATH OF LIEUTENANT GOVERNOR H. CLOYD PHILPOTT

August 19, 1961

This is a shattering blow to the state and to Mrs. Sanford and me personally. No one could have asked for a dearer or a better friend, and no one could have expected more conscientious and able service to the state he served so well in so many ways.

I have said on numerous occasions, and I must emphasize again now, that there would have been no quality education program except for Cloyd Philpott. He endorsed it in the heat and danger of his own campaign, and he sustained it and me in the legislative battles.

School children, and indeed all of North Carolina, will be the beneficiaries of his life's service for generations to come.

STATEMENT OF FRIENDSHIP WITH MEXICO

September 10, 1961

[Governor and Mrs. Sanford and Press Secretary Graham Jones flew to Mexico to promote the Alliance for Progress and to create interest in the North Carolina International Trade Fair to be held in Charlotte the next month. The party visited President Lopez Mateos, toured housing developments, the university, visited medical centers and industrial plants, conferred with public officials, and enjoyed a state dinner at the United States embassy.]

I deem it an honor to be in Mexico as a guest of your government and to have the opportunity to meet, to know, and better to understand the people of this country of freedom and friendship.

I think that misunderstanding stems from lack of knowledge and personal contact with people. You can read history books and sociology treatises, which naturally help, but nothing compares to personal communication with the men who are working actively to better the condition of their own people.

I look forward with special interest to meeting President Lopez Mateos, whose speeches I have read with great interest. He is a strong leader in Latin America and, indeed, in all of the Americas. He has greatly manifested his ideas in international politics with understanding and respect for all countries within freedom and a democratic form of life.

I believe that only within the framework of law and democracy can we achieve the goal of higher standards of living that this restless time of ours is challenging us to attain.

Our two countries are good friends working together for peace and progress. Mexico and the United States can be even better friends in the future and more effective partners in the efforts that have to be permanent for the achievement of progress in the alliance to which we belong.

ON THE GOVERNOR'S COMMISSION ON EDUCATION BEYOND THE HIGH SCHOOL

September 15, 1961

Education, more than any other service of the state, enables us to build the foundation of the future.

After considering the recommendations of the State Board of Higher Education and after conferences with representatives of the board and other educational leaders, I have decided to appoint a Governor's Commission on Education Beyond the High School.

The purpose of such a commission at this time is (1) to identify and define the State's needs in higher education, and other education beyond or in lieu of the high school, and (2) to recommend the most efficient plans and methods of meeting those needs.

The use of such a commission is a part of our determination to see that the taxpayers get maximum returns in both quality and quantity of education for their dollars.

The commission will be charged with the responsibility of making a comprehensive study of the state's entire system of public supported higher education, including all institutions and agencies offering educational and instructional curriculums and services beyond the high school.

No limitations will be imposed upon the commission's broad powers because it is deemed wise that it shall work as an independent agency of the state and with complete freedom to exercise the collective judgment of its members in making its final recommendations. Without limiting the broad authority of the commission, I am suggesting that specific attention be given to the following questions:

A. *Enrollments:*

1. For maximum progress in North Carolina, what are the numbers of students who should be enrolled for education beyond the high school by types of institutions and by years for the next several decades?

2. What is the optimum growth plan for existing institutions?

3. What should be the basis of selection and distribution of students among institutions of different types and purposes?

4. What policies should we employ to get a larger percentage of our high school graduates in college?

5. What policies should we employ to reduce the high percentage of student "dropouts"?

B. *Faculties:*

1. How many faculty members will be needed to provide instruction at desired levels and standards?

2. What salary levels must be provided for the faculties?

C. *Improved Utilization:*

1. What principles should be established to promote greater utilization of physical facilities and faculties of individual institutions?

2. To what extent might joint use of libraries, physical plants, equipment, and personnel be feasible?

D. *New Institutions:*

1. Is the present Community College Act an adequate instrument of policy for the development and operation of an effective system of public supported community or junior colleges, and what amendments, if any, are desirable?

2. What standards should be adopted in determining the need for the establishment of additional four-year colleges?

3. Should the need for resources and facilities of higher education in the more populous areas be met by establishing additional branches of the university or existing four-year colleges in those areas?

E. *Allocation of Functions:*

1. What policies should be adopted in the allocation of

educational functions among existing and future institutions to avoid unnecessary duplication?

2. What is the best system for co-ordinating the two-year educational programs and the technical programs of the community colleges with the educational and technical programs of the industrial educational centers?

3. How may the state-supported institutions of higher education and the privately supported and church related institutions co-ordinate their efforts and resources in meeting the educational needs of our people?

F. *Financing:*

1. How much will a reasonable program of education beyond the high school cost during the next fifteen years in capital improvements and operating expenses?

2. Is the present system of line item budgeting for institutions of higher education adequate and desirable, and, if not, what changes should be made?

3. What should be the distribution of costs as between the state and the students?

4. What is the trend of tax resources in North Carolina? What is the state's ability to pay?

5. What are prospective outside sources of financial support?

G. *Co-ordination:*

1. What should be the pattern of relationships among all types of publicly supported institutions beyond the high school? Specifically, what should be the relationship among the two-year academic and technical programs of college grade and the programs offered by the industrial education centers; the undergraduate program of the senior colleges and the university?

2. What is the best structure for public policy control and co-ordination of publicly supported institutions?

3. What means for consultation and co-operative planning may be devised whereby private and public institutions in the state may contribute most effectively in meeting the needs of the state?

H. *Specialization:*

What should be the plan of development of specialized, professional, and post-baccalaureate education such as medicine, law, graduate education; extended education, including educational television, adult education, and off-campus centers? [Here followed a list of persons appointed to the commission. See list of appointments, pages 741-742.]

I am asking Irving Carlyle to serve as chairman. I recommend that the commission employ a full-time secretary. Expenses must be approved in advance by the Council of State.

I am requesting that interim reports be furnished, and that the final report be filed no later than September 1, 1962.

URGING ECONOMY IN GOVERNMENT

November 25, 1961

Every time I go to Washington, I come away with the feeling that a far more efficient job could be done with fewer people. Bogged down in an overly-protective civil service system, it is almost impossible for the Congress and the executive to do anything about it. This has been true equally of both parties.

In state government across the nation we have fewer problems, but nevertheless some of the same influences are working against efficiency. Generally in North Carolina we do have able, conscientious, and hard-working state employees, and all citizens should be proud of the way these employees have served the state.

Still I have always been convinced that there are many ways we can save money, employ fewer people, and improve the essential services.

There are certain services where personnel cannot be reduced but must indeed increase as the population grows. One example is that every time we have approximately thirty more pupils in school, we will have a need for one more teacher.

But there are other services where we need not increase personnel in line with the population in order to provide the services needed for the people.

I have today written all department and agency heads, asking them to look actively for ways to save on their budgets. I have asked them to furnish us a memo at the end of each month on any actions they have taken to save money. I have reminded them to realize that the General Assembly, in formulating the budget, set a limit to which they could go, not to which they must go. These people are conscientious and economy-minded, but the purpose of my letter is to emphasize active efforts to save money.

I call on all state employees to join in an effort to demonstrate that we can make our government more effective while saving money for the taxpayers.

We have an obligation to tighten our own belts when so much of the national resource must go to essential national defense.

We have an opportunity to demonstrate that governments, state and federal, can be made effective and economical.

We also have a duty, which we will not forget, to make state services adequately fulfill the proper needs of the people.

CHRISTMAS STATEMENT

December 20, 1961

It is in keeping with the heritage of men of good will the world over to pause from their work to commemorate Christmas. In this year of Our Lord, 1961, when a godless ideology challenges the peace, the freedom, and the very existence of men and nations of good will, it is especially appropriate that we should honor the birth of the Prince of Peace.

The spirit of Christmas is universal. In our small part of the universe, here in North Carolina, we join fellow pilgrims the world over in turning our attention to the manger and the hope which rose from it for persons of all races, colors, creeds, and nations.

We will pray that we may celebrate next Christmas and the succeeding Christmases in peace. We will also pray for the strength and the courage that, in peace or war, future Christmases shall be celebrated in freedom.

We will pray finally that neither rockets, nor satellites, nor the mushroom clouds of nuclear bombs will ever obscure our sight from the Star in the East which heralded peace on earth, good will to men.

ON THE BURCH-BREWER CASE

January 7, 1962

[This initial statement issued by Governor Sanford marked the beginning of a year-long legal drama centering on Robert Burch, career highway engineer for twenty-two years; Bobby Burch, his son, and Kidd Brewer, Raleigh businessman and political aspirant. The two men were convicted in July of conspiring to divert highway funds. The defendants lost in their appeals of the decision and began serving prison terms in 1963. Bobby Burch, convicted of "influencing agents" and fined, was pardoned by the Governor in November, 1963.]

Investigation completed this week end has confirmed that Highway Department engineer Robert A. Burch has for several years been too closely associated with Mr. Kidd Brewer in connection with funds received from companies selling sign materials to the State Highway Commission. Mr. Burch has the responsibility for procurement of signs.

Apparently these funds were paid by sign companies to a company organized by Mr. Brewer, Interstate Services, Inc., and in turn paid by Mr. Brewer's company to the college-age son of Mr. Burch.

Therefore, Mr. Burch has been fired today, effective at the close of business last Friday.

Our investigative files have been turned over to the Attorney General.

Since 1958 Mr. Brewer's company has been paid approximately $80,000 by certain sign companies receiving state business, and approximately $40,000 of this amount was paid over by Mr. Brewer's company to Mr. Burch's son. This company's operating expense for this period amounted to about $1,500.

The companies making payments to Mr. Brewer's company will be suspended from doing further business with the state, and additional action will be determined by the additional investigation now being conducted.

At least the following companies are involved: Traffic and Street Sign Co., Newark, New Jersey; Pfaff and Kendall, Newark, New Jersey; Wald Industries, Huntingdon, Pennsylvania; NSE Signs and Stampings division of National Safety Engineers, Inc., Birmingham, Alabama [and subsequently Minnesota Mining and Manufacturing Company, St. Paul, Minnesota.]

[On January 18 the following summary of the S.B.I. preliminary report was released through the Governor's Office.]

(It will be understood that the purpose of making this report public is to reveal the pertinent facts resulting in the discharge of Robert A. Burch, but that certain proof, details, and correspondence should remain confidential pending determination of legal action.)

In addition to the approximately $85,000 already reported, Mr. Kidd Brewer also received an additional amount of $148,000 from a company selling products on specifications prepared by Mr. Robert A. Burch. This amount was paid in a round-about manner.

Between August, 1955, and December 15, 1961, Minnesota Mining and Manufacturing Company paid approximately $148,-000 to Parkway Company, Inc., a small retail hardware store operated in Boone by Mr. Paul Armfield Coffey, Brewer's nephew. Parkway Company in turn paid this money in full over to Underwriters Insurance Company of North Carolina, an insurance business operated by Brewer in Raleigh, North Carolina. The payment checks going from Parkway to Underwriters were then endorsed "for deposit only to the account of Kidd Brewer." Apparently this Brewer account was drawn on for college payments on behalf of Robert M. Burch.

According to the Highway Department, "Mr. Robert A. Burch wrote specifications for all sign projects for the entire state. The Bridge Department or roadway contractors on various projects had nothing to do with the sign projects. That some time after a project was underway and Mr. Burch's employees (i.e., those under his supervision) thought the erection of signs would not interfere with the construction of the highway, the sign specifications would be written. Other departments and contractors working on the roadway or bridge had nothing to do with where signs were placed or what specifications were written."

Mr. Burch also had the responsibility of drawing specifications for products utilizing reflective materials. All of these specifications must conform with interstate standards, but one material could be favored, while still conforming.

Officials of Minnesota Mining and Manufacturing Company state that Mr. Brewer's services were retained by them because of "people" he knew in state government, but they explained that Robert A. Burch was the only state official they knew was contacted. There is no evidence that anyone else was contacted about signs or sign materials by Mr. Brewer, and no one else would have been in a position to determine specifications.

There is no evidence that the Minnesota Mining and Manufacturing Company knew that anything was paid to Mr. Burch's son, but there is a notation in the company files: "As you may know, in his capacity as traffic engineer for North Carolina, Mr. Burch has been very influential for a number of years in getting our products used by that state."

Interstate Services, Inc., received payments as follows. This money was split between Mr. Brewer and Mr. Robert M. Burch.

Pfaff and Kendall	$41,192.46
Traffic and Street Sign Company	31,032.60
Prismo Safety Corporation	3,062.31
Wald Industries, Inc.	2,444.37
National Safety Engineers	6,043.02
Southern Aluminum and Steel Corporation	500.00
Union Metal Manufacturing Company	754.85

ON PRIDE IN NORTH CAROLINA'S PROGRESS

January 11, 1962

[On January 10 Governor Sanford had casually stated that the governorship had put an end to further political ambitions. Later, when asked to face the question of his future in a more serious context, he admitted the earlier statement was somewhat exaggerated. This statement, made the next day, confirmed the Governor's strong interest in North Carolina and his desire to be of service.]

I call your attention to the February issue of *National Geographic*. The lead article, entitled "North Carolina, Dixie Dynamo," is a forty-three page story and contains about four dozen attractive illustrations. Malcolm Ross, who has spent a great deal of time in North Carolina, has done a wonderful job. I hope that every North Carolinian will read it.

I have great enthusiasm for what can be done in North Carolina. After having been in office for one year, that enthusiasm has grown even more. There is nothing more interesting than the Governor's Office. I have enjoyed every hour of every day.

People in this state, as in other states, have always been divided between those who are willing to rock along, and those who are willing to plan and work for better things for the people. It was this way in Governor Aycock's day and it has been this way ever since.

I plan to continue to work with those who believe in progress, who have faith in our capacity, who want to make the opportunities for people in North Carolina just as great as opportunities people have anywhere else in the country.

These are the people I've always been with, and these are the people I intend to work with for the rest of my life.

Let not a casual statement about my future plans to run for office be interpreted as a diminishing interest in North Carolina.

ON THE PORTS AUTHORITY BONDS MATTER

March 2, 1962

Several proposals to purchase revenue bonds have been made to the North Carolina State Ports Authority, the proceeds of the sale to be used to continue a much needed expansion program. The idea of financing port expansion by issuing revenue bonds has been before the ports policy-makers since 1959. This is a sound method of financing, and a businesslike approach to meeting our needs.

When the North Carolina legislature created the Ports Authority, it specifically granted powers to operate without restrictions for the purpose of stimulating trade and commerce throughout North Carolina, and the undertaking has been profitable in many ways. The idea of allowing seaport authorities to operate as a business rather than an institution is "as old as the Port of London" itself.

The intention of the legislature when creating the Ports Authority was to allow the financing of operations and expansion without risking the full faith and credit of the state or obligating the taxpayers. Issuing of revenue bonds does not obligate the taxpayers.

The same policy exists at other ports along the Atlantic. Recently, for example, Norfolk has sold $27 million worth of revenue bonds, $15 million of which will be expended on one facility. The Georgia Ports Authority just sold $11.5 million worth of revenue bonds, which was in addition to an expansion of $5.5 million from revenue bonds completed recently. None of those pledged the credit of the state.

With all this expansion up and down the eastern seaboard financed by revenue bonds, there is considerable interest by private capital in financing the North Carolina State Ports Expansion Program through the revenue bonds of the North Carolina State Ports Authority.

Recently, D. Leon Williams, Executive Director of the North Carolina State Ports Authority, said: "If we are to keep pace with expanding foreign trade and continue to discharge our duty to the utmost to stimulate the commerce of North Carolina, we must keep pace with our neighbors and we should not put off any longer the opportunity of financial and useful gain that our present momentum of expansion is producing."

We are developing these possibilities of revenue bonds. We will have additional information very soon.

DESIGNATING PEACE CORPS DAY

March 12, 1962

The United States has sent young men overseas to fight for democracy in three wars during the last fifty years.

On March 1, 1961, under the leadership of President John F. Kennedy and with the approval of the Congress, this nation began sending a new kind of corps to other lands to fight for freedom—the Peace Corps.

Members of the Peace Corps go armed with the education and the training and the talents of America. They carry textbooks instead of rifles and medical kits rather than ammunition bandoleers.

The enemies these young Americans are fighting are disease and ignorance and poverty.

On March 16 and 17, a conference on the Peace Corps will be held at the University of North Carolina at Chapel Hill.

Therefore, I am happy to designate Saturday, March 17, as

PEACE CORPS DAY IN NORTH CAROLINA

ON PER CAPITA INCOME

May 1, 1962

I am happy to note that North Carolina has moved upward two notches in per capita income as compared with other states. In 1960 we moved from forty-fifty to forty-fourth and in 1961, to forty-second. This shows progress.

If we counted the per capita income of only the white citizens we would rank thirty-second instead of forty-second.

This is some indication that the inability of the qualified Negro to find adequate employment drags down the economy of the entire state.

This is our problem and it requires our best minds and biggest hearts. It is not the problem of government as much as it is the problem of all citizens.

This lack of adequate opportunities has long been on the conscience of many people of the state, but we can be sure it is also a detrimental force on our joint and many efforts to raise the economy of the state.

ON THE DEATH OF CHARLIE GOLD

June 28, 1962

In the death of Charlie Gold, thousands of North Carolinians have lost a personal friend and all North Carolinians have lost an outstanding public leader and servant.

He spent most of his adult life in the service of his state and nation.

As Commissioner of Insurance, Charlie Gold constantly put the public interest first. The citizens of North Carolina returned that faith by demonstrating their overwhelming confidence in him in 1956 and again in 1960.

I have ordered state flags to be flown at half-mast in respect to the service he rendered to North Carolina.

ON THE DEATHS OF NORTH CAROLINA OFFICERS IN VIET NAM

July 19, 1962

As we go about our daily lives in a free and peaceful land, we sometimes forget there are many nations in which war—hot war —is being waged and in which freedom is yet to be won.

The death last Saturday in Viet Nam of Captain Don J. York of Asheville, and the deaths of Captain Robert D. Larson of Fayetteville, Chief Warrant Officer Joseph Goldberg of Sanford, and Specialist-5 Harold Lee Guthrie of Route 7, Burlington, are a grim reminder that there are jungles of despotism yet to be cleared and that these jungles still threaten to encroach on lands of those who would be free.

Captain York, Captain Larson, Warrant Officer Goldberg, and Specialist-5 Guthrie did not have to be in Viet Nam. The United States does not have to concern itself with Viet Nam.

We could let the Communists have it by default.

But our nation learned at Pearl Harbor that the only isolation which is possible is the isolation of the grave—where dictators periodically attempt to assign us.

Captain York, Captain Larson, Warrant Officer Goldberg, and Specialist-5 Guthrie, like so many Americans before them, died in a strange place, halfway around the world from their homes, in a conflict that seems very remote and of little significance.

But their stand in Viet Nam is as near to us in fact as the stand of the men of Kings Mountain during the Revolution or the fight against enemy submarines off the coast of North Carolina during World War II.

All North Carolinians and all Americans owe these men a salute.

In recognition of the fact that they died for the freedom of North Carolina as well as for the freedom of Viet Nam, I am ordering the state flag on the Capitol to be flown at half-mast on Friday, July 20.

ON THE SAVING OF TAX FUNDS

August 4, 1962

During this past year, we have saved $17,078,149 of appropriated funds, and this amount has reverted to the General Fund. This reversion is the largest saving since the enactment of the Executive Budget Act of 1925.

This saving of tax funds compares favorably with the unexpended appropriations from the General Fund for the last six preceding fiscal years which have averaged $8,452,040 a year.

This saving has been a result of our determined policy to keep the state on the go while being extremely careful about spending money. These two goals are not incompatible as the record of this first fiscal year demonstrates.

It is in keeping with our record of a relatively high degree of services while ranking next to the bottom, forty-ninth, in per capita state and local tax expenditures.

It is a result of co-operation by every state department head and proof of the eagle eyes of Hugh Cannon and David Coltrane.

I congratulate all of the agency heads and state employees who have made this record possible. Their results have been outstanding. They have clearly demonstrated that they are dedicated to giving our citizens a sound return on the tax dollar.

ON THE PROPOSED ENVIRONMENTAL HEALTH CENTER

September 5, 1962

[This statement, prepared in the Governor's Office, was delivered by Congressman Horace Kornegay before the House Appropriations Subcommittee considering location of the proposed Environmental Health Center. During Governor Sanford's last week in office, he announced the federal government's choice of the Research Triangle as the site of the future research facility.]

Chairman Thomas and Members of the Subcommittee:

I have requested Congressman Kornegay to read the following statement on behalf of the state of North Carolina, which statement is endorsed by the undersigned members of Congress.

The state of North Carolina invites the attention of the Deficiencies Subcommittee of the House Committee on Appropriations to the Research Triangle Park of North Carolina as a desirable site for the proposed Environmental Health Center of the United States Public Health Service.

The Research Triangle Park is a body of land located within a triangle formed by the University of North Carolina in Chapel Hill, Duke University in Durham, and North Carolina State College of the University of North Carolina in Raleigh. Already a number of nationally known concerns have established research laboratories in the area. These three great institutions have on their faculties outstanding leaders of academic and professional talent, some of whom are expert in the field of environmental health. These universities can make invaluable contributions to the center's work.

The Environmental Health Center is a project that has been initiated by the United States Public Health Service. That service is recommending that the center be located in the Washington area. This project was submitted to Congress last year but was rejected by the Senate Appropriations Committe on the ground that "the contemplated site is an extremely poor selection and that inadequate justification was presented in support of the request." This year the Public Health Service revived the project and has again recommended a site in the Washington area.

In March of this year, the state of North Carolina decided to make known to the proper federal authorities the advantages of locating this center in the Research Triangle Park of North Carolina. A representative of mine accordingly made inquiries early in March as to the stage to which the project had developed at that time.

We then presented to Secretary Abraham Ribicoff and the Deputy Director of the Budget, Mr. Elmer Staats, the many advantages to the United States government of locating the center in the North Carolina Research Triangle rather than in the

Washington area, including the fact that adequate land for the center would be given to the government without cost.

It seems to me that there are some very compelling reasons for locating the Environmental Health Center in the Research Triangle Park rather than in the Washington area or in fact any other area within the United States. Some of these reasons are as follows:

1. Locating the center in the Research Triangle Park would save the government and the American taxpayers initially a sum of $1,300,000 which the present supplemental budget proposes for land acquisition.

2. Construction costs in the Research Triangle are reported by the F. W. Dodge Company to be 80 per cent of construction costs in the Washington area. These lower construction costs in the Research Triangle area apply not only to public buildings, but would also reduce building costs for private dwellings and all other projects that would have to be built, such as roads, utilities, etc. I understand that the long-range plans for the Environmental Health Center contemplate eventual construction costs of several hundred million dollars. Locating the center in the Research Triangle Park would, therefore, effect a saving to the federal government in construction costs alone possibly in excess of $50 million over those in the Washington area.

3. In the event of enemy attack, the risk of damage to the center is much less if it is located in the Research Triangle rather than in the Washington area. The Washington area, with its concentration of governmental operations, is certain to be a prime object of enemy attack. The continuing operation of the center, after enemy attack in any part of the country, may be of vital importance to survival. No matter how conscientiously its advance planning may be, unforeseen problems will almost surely arise. In such event, the fact that an Environmental Health organization of experts is in existence and functioning may mean the saving of thousands of lives.

4. The foregoing considerations would seem to outweigh any arguments in favor of the Washington area based on its proximity to the administrative branches of the Public Health Service, the research activities of the National Institutes of Health and the related programs of other departments of the government. Decentralization has been highly successful in the cases of the Communicable Diseases Center in Atlanta, Georgia, and the various laboratories of the Atomic Energy Commission, among others. It would likewise be successful if the proposed Environmental Health Center is located in the Research Triangle. There

would not appear to be the same need for a research facility's proximity to the administrative offices of the various related government agencies that there is for the ordinary kind of operational agency. Administrative control of the center will be largely by telephone wherever the center is located. Furthermore, with the Washington National Airport approximately sixty minutes from the Research Triangle and with eight flights daily in each direction, the Research Triangle will be practically as accessible to administrative offices in Washington as a Maryland site, which must be reached through Washington traffic.

5. If placed in the Research Triangle area, the facilities of the center will be located in a planned research park, designed to function properly and to be attractive even when filled to capacity. Likewise, the surrounding region's development is completely supervised by a regional planning commission and enjoys the full co-operation of all local governments.

6. It seems to me that there is a great need for research facilities to be related to educational institutions. The government draws off far too many scientific personnel who, if close to universities, could assist in the training of additional young scientists.

The foregoing statement is simply a concise summary of our position, which has been more fully stated in the presentation made last spring. It is hoped that the members of the subcommittee will use their influence to suggest that it would be to the advantage of the government to locate this facility away from the crowded Washington area.

DESIGNATING YOUTH APPRECIATION WEEK

November 9, 1962

The America of tomorrow will be largely dependent upon the capabilities, the initiative, and the moral and religious fiber of the youth of today.

Today's climate of world affairs confronts our youth with a multitude of decisions, uncertainties, and frustrations heretofore unexceeded.

Publicity has been given to crimes committed by, and the delinquency of, a small percentage of our youth to the extent that there has resulted in some areas a widespread doubt as to the quality and integrity of the nation's youth.

To the contrary, statistics show that approximately 5 per cent of them are delinquent.

The delinquency of the 5 per cent reflects no discredit on the remaining 95 per cent, many of whom are engaging, of their own initiative, in wholesome and constructive civic and religious activities to the betterment of our nation and its communities.

Therefore, I am happy to designate the week of November 12-18, 1962, as

YOUTH APPRECIATION WEEK

in this state and call upon the parents and other citizens in the state to join with Optimist International in recognizing the qualities and merits of our youth and to make our appreciation known to them.

ON MEDICAL CARE FOR INDIGENTS

December 26, 1962

The 1961 General Assembly transferred the administration of funds for the hospitalization of medically indigent patients from the Medical Care Commission to the Department of Public Welfare. This transfer made federal matching funds available for the medically indigent for the first time.

Our state also has taken advantage of the Kerr-Mills Act which increased the federal matching formula for medical care of persons sixty-five and over.

In these two ways, medical care through hospitalization to people who cannot pay for it has been greatly extended in North Carolina in recent months.

In spite of this progress, I am not satisfied with medical care for the aged. I believe that people, especially older people who have worked hard all of their lives and have only meager savings, are entitled to know that they are not going to suffer needlessly because of inadequate medical care.

I am asking a special committee to study the wider use of Kerr-Mills, and other available means of assuring proper medical care for older people. I am sure that they can have ready the necessary legislation to provide adequate hospitalization, outpatient services in hospitals or other qualified facilities, drugs, and possibly dental services and home nursing care. [The statement concluded with a list of persons appointed to serve on the committee.]

DESIGNATING CARL SANDBURG DAY

December 27, 1962

January 6, 1963, will mark the eighty-fifth birthday anniversary of Carl Sandburg, poet of devotion, biographer by work, and Tar Heel by choice.

Carl Sandburg was a son of the Midwest whose poetry gave us a definition of the new values of the urban industrial society.

Carl Sandburg had written most of his poetry and his classic, *Abraham Lincoln,* when he decided to come East, to relax and write his autobiography.

In 1940 the Sandburgs roamed up and down the eastern seaboard to look for "the place," and they came to the Connemara Farms at Flat Rock, North Carolina. They decided to look no further. In sight of Mount Mitchell, Carl Sandburg put on his eye-shade and wrote the first volume of his autobiography, *Always the Young Strangers,* and soon, in his speeches across the country, he began to say: "I am a Tar Heel," and in a speech in Los Angeles during the presidential campaign of 1960, he told the audience: "I am just a North Carolina mountain boy. . . ."

It is therefore fitting that the state of North Carolina honor this great American on his eighty-fifth birthday as testimony to the spiritual wealth he has created for us and for our youth and for Americans yet unborn.

Therefore, I am happy to designate January 6, 1963, as

CARL SANDBURG DAY

and on behalf of his four and one-half million fellow citizens of North Carolina, I wish him many more years of good health and good fortune in the sapphire hills of North Carolina.

DESIGNATING JOB CORPS WEEK

January 2, 1963

Twenty per cent of the families in America have incomes of less than $3,000 a year. These Americans are deprived of many of the benefits and even necessities which are part of an adequate standard of living. The young men and women born in these families are severely handicapped in their efforts to get a good education and to learn the skills which will permit them to move into a better world.

Thousands of these deprived Americans live in North Carolina. We are now using every resource of the state, county, and municipal governments to help these families—and their youngsters—break out of this cycle of poverty.

A new federal program, the Job Corps, holds unusual promise for helping us with this problem. The Job Corps will provide away-from-home training centers for young men and women from sixteen to twenty-one. At these centers these youngsters will have a chance to improve their basic educational skills, and receive vocational training to help them find and keep work when they return home. While they are in training, they will receive food, clothing, shelter, pocket money, and severance pay upon completion of their Job Corps program. They will also be able to send family allotments home while they are in training.

I want to be sure that every one of these youngsters has a chance to escape from the cycle of deprivation in which they live. I want to be sure that every young man and woman in North Carolina who can use Job Corps training finds out about it.

During the week of January 3, 1965, the Job Corps will conduct a nation-wide effort to bring its message to the attention of needy youngsters. Job Corps recruiting materials are being distributed throughout our country by private and governmental organizations. An all-out effort is being made to get the youth—those whom the Job Corps can best help—to respond by sending in cards showing their interest.

To make sure the Job Corps news is spread, state agencies which come in close contact with these youngsters—the State Board of Public Welfare, and the State Employment Security Commission—will give priority to distributing Job Corps recruiting news to the young men and women who need it. I urge that local governmental agencies make a similar effort, and I hope that the news media of our state participate in this campaign to broadcast the Job Corps story.

Finally, in order to insure that these efforts are co-ordinated with the national efforts of the Job Corps, I designate the week of January 3-9, 1965, as

JOB CORPS WEEK IN NORTH CAROLINA

PROCLAIMING THE TERCENTENARY OF THE CAROLINA CHARTER OF 1663

January 4, 1963

This year, 1963, is the tercentenary of the Carolina Charter of 1663 and is so proclaimed here today at the beginning of the year to mark a time when all citizens of our state should educate themselves regarding the significant events of North Carolina's early Colonial history.

The year 1963 marks the three hundredth anniversary of the charter by which King Charles II of England granted to the eight Lords Proprietors "all that territory . . . in America . . . within six and thirty degrees of northern latitude and to the west as far as the South Seas, and so southerly as far as . . . one and thirty degrees of north latitude. . . ."

The century that followed this event witnessed the successful outcome of the colony's struggles to overcome obstacles to its growth by the application of its God-given resources and the determination of its people. The century 1663-1763 saw the reinforcement of the early English settlers by the migrations of Highland Scots, Scotch-Irish, and Germans of the Moravian Brethren, so that a population of less than 5,000 at the start of the period grew to more than 200,000 by its close. The character of those peoples has shaped the attitudes of North Carolinians throughout their history.

This charter is a major landmark in the early history of North Carolina and America, because it conferred upon its settlers the rights enjoyed by Englishmen under the laws of England.

This is a year to know more about North Carolina, and our history, and the contributions made by early Carolinians to the development of the American character, with a pride in our rich past, and with a new strength to develop a richer future.

ON INDUSTRIAL PROGRESS

January 10, 1963

North Carolina was the fastest growing state in the nation's fastest growing region in new industry in 1962.

The economy of North Carolina reached an all-time high during the past year. This is indicated by all major indexes of business and personal economic growth including the following:

To observe the beginning of the tercentenary of the granting of the Carolina Charter of 1663, a "birthday party" was held at the Governor's Mansion. Costumes of the Colonial period and a cake depicting the outline of the original grant to the Lords Proprietors called attention to the tercentenary year in a dramatic way. The Governor and Mrs. Sanford, Cherokee Chief Osley Saunooke, and Mr. and Mrs. Julian Oneto of Nags Head participated in the cake-cutting.

Two international trade fairs were held in Charlotte during the Sanford administration. Here the Governor and Nat Carson are shown at the fair sitting in the world's largest upholstered chair, April 28, 1963.

1. North Carolinians gainfully employed in all nonagricultural jobs numbered 40,200 above the same period in 1961. For the first eleven months of 1962—the latest period on which tabulations have been completed—an average of 1,249,300 persons were employed in nonagricultural jobs. For the same period in 1961, the average was 1,209,100.

2. Retail and wholesale activity in North Carolina reached record levels in 1962.

3. The travel-serving industry in North Carolina, the third largest money-producing industry in the state, set a new record in 1962, exceeding $900 million in income last year.

4. Bank debits for North Carolina's banks were excellent. In the nine key cities in North Carolina, bank debits rose 15.5 per cent for the first nine months of 1962. The last quarter, due to seasonal activity, is expected to be substantially above the first three quarters of the year.

5. New businesses incorporated in North Carolina in 1962 reached a record high.

6. Construction of new homes and new office buildings and new industrial plants continued to grow. In thirty-six key North Carolina cities in 1962, building permits were up 4.2 per cent. The permits for those cities totaled $221,254,558 in the first eleven months of 1962.

In brief, business in North Carolina was never better.

Many people and many organizations from Raleigh west to Asheville and Sylva, and east to Wilmington and the Outer Banks are responsible for this record year in economic growth.

Local development groups, chambers of commerce, county and local government leaders deserve much of the credit.

At the state level, the Board of Conservation and Development, under the leadership of Hargrove "Skipper" Bowles, Bob Stallings, and Jim Hinkle have worked around the clock.

They have worked with the Board of Conservation and Development to attract new industries and, more important, to help expand established industries.

The success of their work is reflected in the following figures:

1. The industrial gains in North Carolina in 1962 were the highest in the Southeast, which is the fastest growing region in America.

2. North Carolina had 567 new and expanded industrial plants in 1962, compared to 503 new and expanded plants in 1961. Of this total, 182 were new companies and 385 were expansions of established industries.

3. Total capital investments in new plants in 1962 amounted

to $229,562,000. Of this total $95,001,000 was for new companies and $134,561,000 was for expansions. The capital investments for the record year of 1961 were $279,447,000.

4. Additional new industrial jobs totaled 24,697 in 1962. In the record year of 1961, new industrial jobs totaled 35,000.

REPORTING SCHOOL IMPROVEMENTS

January 17, 1963

I am happy to furnish the Goldsboro *News-Argus* a report on school improvement during the first two years of this administration. I have constantly emphasized that we can expect no overnight miracles, that we must sustain our efforts and interest for at least ten years, and most of the work must be done locally. But so far the results have been even more rewarding than expected.

The increased public school appropriations made by the 1961 General Assembly are buying full value in improved education for the children of North Carolina. The vision and courage of these legislators will be long remembered in the history of North Carolina progress.

The firm conviction of local school superintendents is shown in a report to the State Board of Education's Department of Curriculum Study and Research.

Asked to list the constructive changes they can identify in local school units as having resulted from action taken by the 1961 General Assembly and from increased local interest and support, the following improvements are reported as taking place all over North Carolina:

1. Improvement in the effort, interest, and attitude of teachers, including improvement in the quality of applicants for teaching positions. Many faculty groups have voluntarily gone on an eight-hour day at school for teachers in addition to the many hours overtime teachers work.

2. Concentration on instruction during the school day with more emphasis on serious study and a reduction of time and effort spent on extracurricular activities.

3. Improvement in libraries and library services, especially in the elementary schools.

4. Reduction in class size.

5. Improvement in supervision by principals, supervisors, and assistant superintendents.

6. Improvement in guidance services.

7. Provision of more teachers for special education classes.

8. Improvement resulting from clerical services for principals and teachers.

9. Addition of needed vocational and college preparatory courses to the high school curriculum.

10. More co-operative attitude on the part of the community, especially in relation to eliminating interruptions of school time.

11. More serious study by students.

In the important areas of school consolidation, this state is making marked improvement.

Accreditation of the public schools is climbing. This is important not so much because of a certificate on a principal's wall but because accreditation is a yardstick to measure the quality of education being offered to our sons and daughters.

More than 500 teachers have returned to North Carolina from teaching positions in other states since the 1961 General Assembly had the courage to raise the salaries of teachers in our state.

A longer lasting effect of the quality education program has been the increase in the number of teachers who are trained in North Carolina colleges who have been able to afford to stay in North Carolina to teach.

Moreover, the number of young men and women entering the teaching profession has risen noticeably.

There are fewer teachers with substandard certificates now than we had before adoption of the quality education program.

This improvement in the quality of instruction has had an obvious effect on the quality of learning—and the interest by students in learning. A considerably higher percentage of students who enter high school now are completing their high school work, rather than dropping out.

Of course, the greatest effect of the quality education program will be in the pay envelopes, the homes, and the minds of the children, your sons and daughters, and of mine, when they have grown up.

The pay checks we will be able to measure. And it is an easily proved fact that the better a boy's education, the higher his salary will be as a man.

To some extent we will be able to measure the effects of quality education on the future homes of North Carolina. I would imagine that there would be better homes, more books, more newspapers, better furnishings.

But the greatest result of all from the quality education program will be one that we cannot measure on an adding machine, or a slide rule, or even a Univac. What happens in the minds of the young people will be the greatest result of the quality education program.

The improved education received by Tar Heel boys and girls will be the highest monument to the courage of the legislators who adopted the program—and to the taxes to pay for that program.

What happens in the minds of the boys and girls will pay the richest dividends to the adults of North Carolina who are investing their tax dollars in their children's education.

What happens to the mind and to the spirit of North Carolina is what the quality education program is about. And the mind and the spirit of North Carolina will be the final judge of the success of the quality education program.

OBSERVATION FOR A SECOND CENTURY

January 18, 1963

[Governor Sanford's leadership in the field of race relations was well known throughout the United States. In an address to the North Carolina Press Association, on January 18, 1963, the Governor issued two statements. In the first, he called on North Carolinians to give up their unfair discrimination practices and provide economic opportunities for Negro citizens. In the second, he established the Good Neighbor Council which was to provide economic opportunities for qualified Negroes and which was to encourage young people to take advantage of opportunities for education and training. These statements prompted letters from within the state and from other states. A letter from Virginia stated: "It is good news that at long last a Southern Governor has had the courage and decency to advocate fair and equal treatment for the Negroes. Let us hope that other Southern political leaders will be encouraged to follow your fine example. My commendation and highest respect." Another congratulated the Governor on his "courageous stand for equal job opportunities for Negroes in North Carolina. Your action can certainly be hailed as a pioneer effort in the racial field at a most crucial time. . . . The type of leadership you exemplify can be fully appreciated." Another told the Governor that his statement "made me very proud to be a North Carolinian."]

The American Negro was freed from slavery one hundred years ago. In this century he has made much progress, educating his children, building churches, entering into the community and civic life of the nation.

Now is a time not merely to look back to freedom but forward to the fulfillment of its meaning. Despite great progress, the Negro's opportunity to obtain a good job has not been achieved in most places across the country. Reluctance to accept the Negro in employment is the greatest single block to his continued progress and to the full use of the human potential of the nation and its states.

The time has come for American citizens to give up this reluctance, to quit unfair discriminations, and to give the Negro a full chance to earn a decent living for his family and to contribute to higher standards for himself and all men.

We cannot rely on law alone in this matter because much depends upon its administration and upon each individual's sense of fair play. North Carolina and its people have come to the point of recognizing the urgent need for opening new economic opportunities for Negro citizens. We also recognize that in doing so we shall be adding new economic growth for everybody.

We can do this. We should do this. We will do it because we are concerned with the problems and the welfare of our neighbors. We will do it because our economy cannot afford to have so many people fully or partially unproductive. We will do it because it is honest and fair for us to give all men and women their best chance in life.

ON ESTABLISHING THE GOOD NEIGHBOR COUNCIL

January 18, 1963

In North Carolina we will attempt to provide leadership for the kind of understanding America needs today.

To carry out these hopes we will do five things right now:

1. We have established the North Carolina Good Neighbor Council.

It will consist of twenty-four outstanding citizens of the state. David S. Coltrane will be chairman; Dean James T. Taylor will be vice-chairman. Coltrane is the former Director of Administration and presently Special Consultant to the Governor. Taylor is former Dean of Men at North Carolina College.

We will also name an additional advisory committee to reach more sections of the economy and the state.

The council will have a twofold mission: to encourage employment of qualified people without regard to race; and to urge youth to become better trained and qualified for employment.

2. We are asking all mayors and chairmen of county commissioners to establish local Good Neighbor Councils.

3. We have issued a memorandum to heads of state agencies, departments, and institutions, asking them, if they have not already done so, to examine and formulate policies which do not exclude from employment qualified people because of race.

4. Being aware that complete success cannot be achieved without wise and vigorous leadership from private business and industry, we will conduct a conference this spring, inviting leading industrialists and businessmen to participate.

5. We call on church leaders, pastors, and civic organizations to support the objectives of the Good Neighbor Councils in their own effective ways.

[The statement was concluded with the names of members of the Good Neighbor Council. For a list of these people, see page 743.]

ON THE DEVELOPMENT OF THE
CAPE FEAR RIVER BASIN

March 14, 1963

[This statement was made before the House Flood Control Subcommittee in Washington at the time it was conducting hearings on a proposed Cape Fear River Basin project. In addition to gubernatorial support, the long-range project under discussion also received the backing of the majority of the state's congressional delegation.]

Thank you for the chance to appear before this committee. I am here in support of a 100-year plan for the comprehensive development of the water and land resources of the Cape Fear River Basin in North Carolina.

This is a plan recommended by the U. S. Army Corps of Engineers for developing this great river and tributaries for flood control, water supply for municipalities, industries, and agriculture, water quality control and recreation. The foundation stone of this plan is the New Hope Reservoir. I am asking that you authorize this project so that development of the Cape Fear River Basin can proceed.

The need of the basin is great. Its people have waited a long time to develop and use their land and water resources at their full potential.

This project was started by Senator Kerr Scott and is being carried on by a number of people under the able leadership of Senator Everett Jordan. I have been interested in this project since the days when Kerr Scott was governor. Speaking in Fayetteville on September 25, 1950, Governor Scott said:

> . . . with the entire Cape Fear Valley pulling together for the development of the Cape Fear River as a whole for the benefit of all, the voice would have been much louder. . . . I say, here and now, that if we do not look forward, plan wisely, and conserve and protect these resources which are now wasting, we will not only be breaking faith with future generations, but also cheating ourselves.
>
> The valley of the Cape Fear, stretching as it does more than 150 miles from the piedmont to the sea, is potentially one of the richest regions of our state. It is rich in agricultural possibilities and offers great opportunities to diversified industry. All that is needed is vision and a singleness of purpose to bring about its development.

The truth of that is more apparent today than ever before.

This long broad valley reaching from the Piedmont area of our state down to the Atlantic Ocean has contributed greatly to the progress of North Carolina from Colonial days to modern times. In this pleasant land live 922,599 people, 20 per cent of our population. They have built up considerable industries, a strong agriculture, and attractive tourist facilities that are all known far beyond our borders.

The people of the Cape Fear River Basin have achieved these things despite a great handicap. Too many times, destructive floods have hurt the area. These can occur at any season of the year and in a large part of the basin. The threat of floods is hindering the greater economic development which is the right of its people.

We are told that the Corps of Engineers' plan will protect only the lower part of the basin and do nothing for the upper area. Yet the corps' plan would permit the building of these smaller dams for local benefit; in fact, the corps recommends that its own project be supplemented by upstream improvements and land treatment measures, as provide by P. L. 566, Eighty-third Congress.

I am in favor of building them all, because in the future we will need all the water we can get. This is one of the best investments we can make in the future. We should impound all the water we can at every feasible place. It will serve us well over the years. In North Carolina we are stepping up our soil conservation and sound watershed program. The state legislature doubled the survey teams so we might accelerate the whole program. We are determined to save our water reservoirs.

The alternative plan of nothing but small dams of and by itself cannot control flooding throughout the basin. Existing federal legislation, in any event, is not adequate to put such an undertaking into effect.

Flood protection is needed now. We have waited too long. The Corps of Engineers' plan, keyed by the New Hope Reservoir, can come into being almost at once.

Unfortunately, dislocations will occur to some extent each time a public works program is placed in effect, and I regret this. We cannot continue to progress as a nation, however, unless we utilize our natural resources to their fullest extent and in the best interest of the greatest number of our citizens.

I concur in the recommendations contained in the report of the U. S. Army Corps of Engineers. As the initial step in the development of the basin, I strongly urge that authorization for the immediate construction of the New Hope Dam be given favorable consideration by your committee.

I assure the committee that the state administration will do everything within its capability to meet any nonfederal participation and co-operation that may be required in the construction of the New Hope Dam.

Thank you very much.

ON THE FUTURE OF RECREATION
IN NORTH CAROLINA

March 15, 1963

[The "Land and Living" report referred to in this statement was a thirteen-page study of recreation trends in North Carolina. The report also contained proposed state action to meet the growing demands for recreational facilities.]

The quality of our living is inescapably related to land and its conservation, and I am happy to release the "Land and Living" report made by the North Carolina Recreation Commission.

Conservation includes the preservation of our land and water, its scientific analysis as to best use, and a plan of action as to its wise use for the full life in North Carolina and for the greatest of economic advantage to people.

In my efforts to follow good conservation practice and best to apply its advantages to land and water for living in North Carolina, I have directed various state agencies to review the past, to look ahead, to take inventory, to analyze, and to plan for the future.

This report is the first of a series of such reports from North Carolina state agencies. It is a preliminary report, done by our North Carolina Recreation Commission. I have studied this report and find well-selected data, some excellent analyses, and some basic suggestions of great importance to North Carolina's future.

This report predicts that:

by 1980, unless the state immediately sets a high priority on the acquisition or other form of reservation of land holdings of scarcity value (ocean, beaches and adjacent lands; State parks; lake and stream shores; unique natural, historic, and scenic areas) all such lands will be lost to the North Carolina public. These recreation areas and other resources can be conserved and their maximum economic and other advantages assured to North Carolina only if their use is programmed under competent recreation and conservation leadership. By 1980, unless remedial steps are undertaken at once, there will be an overwhelming deficiency of recreation land and water and open space in and near population centers of North Carolina.

A state-wide, long-range master plan for recreation is needed.

Recreation is big business. The recreation market last year was $47 billion, 12 cents of every consumer dollar.

In North Carolina, travel alone accounted for $888 million of state business, in much of which recreation purposes were the impelling factors.

North Carolina is strategically equipped to gain vast economic benefits from recreation and its supplementary effects in business and industry. We have a variety of wonderful natural resources, a hospitable and energetic people and the North Carolina Recreation Commission to render experience-directed advisory assistance and guidance to our recreation-economic efforts.

In recreation may be much of our hopes for a bright economic future in North Carolina. This report points the way to state action which can become the sound base upon which to rest our economic as well as our societal hopes for the future. It is through the wise use of land for living in North Carolina. As Governor, I commend this report to the area, county and city planning boards, and to the people of North Carolina for their study and consideration.

ON HIGHWAY CONSTRUCTION AND MAINTENANCE

March 29, 1963

I am aware of the importance of roads, highways, and city streets. These links of commerce help everybody and they are good investments.

I am most grateful for the members of the General Assembly who have deep interest in the progress of our road program.

I did not make a road bond or new road taxes a part of my program when I came into office because I felt my job was to stop the diversions from the highway fund in order to have more construction and maintenance money.

This we were able to do, and we have let to contract more highway and road construction than in any similar period in history. We have built more secondary roads than any administration except Kerr Scott's.

By additional steps against diversion now being taken, we should be able to continue this pace during the next two years.

Whether we should have bonds or operate on a pay-as-you-go basis is a matter for legislative decision. I have not asked for any additional funds because I believe we can meet the pressing needs of the people without bonds.

I do think that we should be thinking about the future—studying needs, trends in construction costs, in maintenance costs, in urban requirements, and looking for ways to keep North Carolina in front of all the states in highways and roads. I hope the General Assembly will call for this studying and planning.

Again I thank the members of the General Assembly, especially Senator Robert F. Morgan,[135] Senator Saunders,[136] Representatives Harris, Wallace,[137] and the many others, who have shown such a genuine interest in keeping our system the best.

Of course, we have needs now. We are meeting many of them.

So that there will be no feeling that we are not pressing as hard as possible, let me point out six facts about our highway system.

1. Because we have a single state system (only two or three other states work it this way), we are able to support 10 per cent

[135] Robert Foster Morgan (1922-   ), merchant and civic leader from Shelby; state senator, 1953-1963. *North Carolina Manual, 1963*, 541.

[136] William Preston Saunders (1897-   ), retired manufacturer from Southern Pines; mayor of Robbins, 1935-1950; state senator, 1963. *North Carolina Manual, 1963*, 543.

[137] Joseph Paul Wallace (1905-   ), automobile dealer and service station owner from Troy; state senator, 1943; member of House of Representatives, 1945-1949; 1955-1963. *North Carolina Manual, 1963*, 615.

of all state highway mileage on 3 per cent of road taxes collected in America and with the fewest highway employees.

2. We have the best road system in America, counting totals and percentage paved, except for New York and Ohio, and the use is so much greater in those two states because of the heavy population that we would rank well ahead of both of them in mileage of highways available to each resident or motorist.

3. The great state of Texas today has fewer miles of paved secondary roads to date than were paved in North Carolina by Kerr Scott alone.

4. In the brief time since I have been in office, we have paved more secondary roads than the total paved to date in Louisiana, Maine, Montana, Nevada, New Mexico, North Dakota, and Rhode Island.

5. California has 28,000 miles paved to our 27,000 miles but has almost twice as many miles unpaved as do we.

6. South Carolina has 4,372 paved secondary miles compared to our 27,000 miles, or 16 per cent compared to our 46 per cent. Georgia has 12,000 paved, or 18 per cent. Tennessee has 16,000 miles or 29 per cent.

During the remaining year and a half we intend to build roads as rapidly as possible, on existing revenue, and we will be able to keep up the pace by the legislative action in stopping diversions, and the administrative action in improving efficiency.

ON THE PROPOSED BREATHOLIZER BILL

April 26, 1963

[The so-called "breatholizer" bill, supported wholeheartedly by Governor Sanford, was enacted into law by the 1963 General Assembly. See *Session Laws, 1963,* c. 966, for "An Act to Amend the General Statutes of North Carolina to Provide for Breath Tests for Intoxication in Criminal Cases Involving Drunken Driving."]

The breatholizer bill is simple in concept, operation, and purpose.

We have always allowed a patrolman to testify in a drunken driver case that, "I smelled whisky on his breath."

This is a highly unscientific way. It is like limiting testimony of skid marks to evidence that it "looked like a considerable number of feet" instead of saying, "I measured the marks with a tape and they were precisely 32 feet and 10 inches."

The breatholizer bill would simply allow the officer to "smell" the breath of an offender in a scientific manner. It puts into use a scientific instrument which measures precisely the amount of alcohol consumed. It tells whether it is too much under our laws, or not enough to constitute a crime, and thus this scientific approach protects the individual as well as the public.

Other states have found that the use of the scientific test deters driving while drinking, and that is what we are trying to accomplish.

There is no longer any mystery concerning a chemical test for drunkenness. It is endorsed by the American Medical Association, American Bar Association, and the National Safety Council.

Thirty-four states and the District of Columbia have enacted legislation defining drinking and driving in the terms of alcoholic content of the blood.

The implied consent feature of the breatholizer bill repeatedly has been upheld in the courts. Opposition to the implied consent clause overlooks the fact that the requirement of fingerprinting long has been an established practice of American justice.

When the cry of the rights of drinking drivers goes up, we should remember the right of law-abiding citizens to live.

The greatest advantage of such legislation is not the number of people it would enable the courts to convict of drinking and driving, but the great psychological deterrent it has on those perons who are tempted to drink and drive. It also would protect the innocent and convict the guilty. It is conservatively estimated that in 50 per cent of all accidents alcohol is prevalent in one or more of the drivers and that one-third of all fatalities involved drivers who had been drinking before driving.

DESIGNATING LAW DAY

April 30, 1963

North Carolina and the United States were founded on the precept that all men are equal before the bar of justice and that all citizens should equally enjoy the rights established by law. That we in the state and nation have not always succeeded in exercising that precept to perfection does not detract one iota from the belief held by the vast majority of Americans in that principle. On this basis of law was founded our democratic government in North Carolina and in the United States. On the basis of law, we will make advances in economic and social and religious life.

As a lawyer and as a public official, it seems to me particularly fitting that Americans should pay their respect on May 1 to the law which guarantees their rights as free men. For this is the day when the advocates of the Communist ideology parade their might before the eyes of the world.

When man came down out of the trees and walked out of the jungle and first recognized the necessity for working together for the good of the individual and the community at large, he committed himself to a system of rules which we now refer to as law.

Without the law, the masses of men are mobs.

Without the law, the weak are helpless.

Without the law, might makes right.

Without the law, equitably written and fairly administered, there is chaos and there is an anarchy—an anarchy that does not connote freedom from restrictions but an anarchy that connotes absence of reason and of orderliness and of rights and of life itself.

Therefore, I am happy to designate May 1, 1963, as

LAW DAY IN NORTH CAROLINA.

PROPOSAL ON BEHALF OF THE FORGOTTEN CHILDREN

May 5, 1963

[In placing emphasis on quality education, Governor Sanford did not overlook those children for whom special education was needed. Provision was made for the exceptionally talented and for the mentally retarded. In this statement, which was presented to the legislature, the Governor spoke feelingly in behalf of the latter group and outlined requests for appropriations totaling $1,822,052 for the biennium. The 1963 General Assembly actually appropriated $1,822,652 to provide for the programs and services requested by the Governor. Details of the appropriation are given in *Session Laws, 1963*, c. 845.]

We have made great progress in North Carolina during the past two years in quality and extent of the education available to all our people. As countless generations of North Carolinians climb the educational ladder which the present legislators and their predecessors in the 1961 General Assembly have strengthened, lengthened, and widened, they will be able to see farther, work more skillfully, and live life more fully—all because of what the people of the state have done. The silver talents which you have invested today will yield in the future polished talents of a value incalculably greater than that of precious metal. More youngsters will learn more; more adults will earn more; and the lamps of dynamic, prosperous, and cultured communities will burn ever more brightly.

Let us not forget, however, as we build these ladders for our children's minds to climb, that there are in North Carolina today at least 160,000 persons who cannot, because of intelligence limitations *alone,* learn, earn, produce, and live to the same extent as the overwhelming number of their fellow human beings of comparable age. I speak in their behalf; they cannot come to the legislature on their own behalf. These persons are not afflicted by mental illness, although the frustrations produced by their inability to communicate—brought on by our failure to educate and train them—do often complicate their intellectual slowness with mental illness. Chiefly, however, these are human beings who were born with marked deficiencies of recognizable intelligence—intelligence quotients of 70 or below. They are not sick; but the patient attention which their needs require is just as elaborate, painstaking, and expensive as if they were.

They need ladders, too; but the rungs on their ladders must be much closer together, and must be fashioned in shapes and materials different from the other ladders which we are building.

They need the constant, guiding hand of a teacher who has been carefully trained to develop all that is within them.

These people need to be identified, so that they are not confused with others whose afflictions do not consist of mental retardation. For this task, we will need the expert services of the psychologist, the psychiatrist, the social worker, the physician, the teacher. The knowledge of all of these practitioners is urgently needed if we are to succeed in attacking the baffling problems posed by a lone, retarded child. Yet we do not have even a minimal number of these specialists trained in the problems of retardation.

Now is the time to act. There are in North Carolina, below the age of thirty, at least 75,000 children and adults who are retarded, but who are considered either trainable or educable. To fail to give them education and vocational training suited specifically for their needs is to condemn them to a bleak, joyless, and unproductive existence in which their lives are but a drag on their families, on all North Carolinians, and chiefly on themselves. Here, then, is the personal tragedy of human waste. Keep in mind, however, that we are also talking about persons who, if made productive through education and vocational training, would contribute substantially to our gross state product. For example, there were 1,578 retarded persons in the United States in 1958 who completed training under the Vocational Rehabilitation program. Before rehabilitation, their annual earnings were $70,000; after rehabilitation, their earnings were $2.5 million.

There are many things which we do not know about retardation. We need research desperately which will tell us these three things about it:

1) What causes it and what steps might be taken to prevent its occurrence?

2) How can we identify those afflicted with it?

3) How can we reach into the minds of retarded persons and interest them in learning the skills for which their intellects are suited and the general knowledge which will immeasurably enrich their lives?

We need to get on with the tasks before us. Without action now, the number of retarded persons will continue to grow, as will this profound tragedy of personal waste. If we act now, simultaneously to provide training for personnel to work with retarded persons, to provide education and training for the retarded children and adults themselves—both within our institutions, the public schools, and the community—and to support the needed research, we will solve many of the problems created by retardation, and we will move much closer to knowledge about retardation itself.

To study the over-all problem of mental retardation, I appointed a Commission on Mental Retardation. This commission, under the able chairmanship of Mr. Charles Waddell of Asheville,[138] gave thorough and thoughtful consideration to all aspects of retardation and reported its findings to me last fall. That report has already been released to the public.

To continue studying the state-wide problem of mental retardation, and to co-ordinate the attack by all state and private organizations on this problem, I am recommending the creation of an Advisory Council on Mental Retardation. This will necessitate expenses in the amount of $20,000 per year.

In addition, I am recommending that the General Assembly appropriate funds this biennium for several specific programs designed to attack the problem of mental retardation on several fronts.

---

[138] Charles E. Waddell, banker from Asheville, and member of Council on Mental Retardation. Information supplied by Senator Herbert Hyde of Asheville.

First of all, we need a training program for teachers who will teach the retarded children in our school program. This should be centered at Chapel Hill but also should include all other state colleges engaged in training teachers. This will require $120,000 per year, but this is fundamental. This is where we start.

To train both specialists and nonspecialists for work with the retarded, we need to establish at Murdoch School a training program which will assure a supply of competent personnel for our community and institutional programs. The cost for the biennium will be $155,960.

To train medical students and residents in the diagnosis and treatment of mental retardation, we need a Center for Mental Retardation at the Psychiatric Center in Chapel Hill. We have such a woeful shortage. This will cost $780,000, but half of this is available from federal funds.

To attract teachers into training for the education of the retarded, I recommend the creation of a teacher scholarship program which will cost $100,000 for the biennium. As I pointed out above, the problems of teaching mentally retarded children are different from those involved in teaching normal children. Therefore, the teachers must be trained to use different techniques. I am convinced that the only way to attract a sufficient supply of trained teachers into this particular specialty is to provide for them the additional funds which the extra training will cost.

To provide the kind of vocational training which will enable trainable and educable retarded persons to become productive, useful citizens, I recommend the appropriation of a sum of $452,092 for the vocational rehabilitation program over and above the amount already requested by the Hospitals Board of Control. This sum, when matched with available federal funds, will allow us to establish vocational rehabilitation programs in all of our state institutions, will make possible the creation of eight rehabilitation houses in the next biennium, will permit the Department of Public Instruction to begin the establishment of vocational rehabilitation centers in several communities and to employ additional rehabilitation counselors for work with retarded persons in the communities. Think what it will mean to the many thousands of retarded human beings in North Carolina to be taught to earn their livelihood.

One of the most critical aspects of the retardation problem is the overwhelming lack of adequate facilities and personnel for the identification and evaluation of retarded persons. In a recent study of Alamance County children's handicaps, it was determined that there are roughly three times more retarded children in that county than had been known from all public and private agency records. I want also, at this time, to single out the Alamance County project as an example of close and generous cooperation of state, county, and city agencies, the university, the medical society, Alamance County Hospital, physicians, and many public-spirited citizens of Burlington, all of whom have increased substantially what we know about the prevalence of children's handicaps.

To help identify and evaluate retarded persons, I recommend the appropriation to the State Board of Health of the sum of $354,000 to establish and operate during this biennium evaluation and development clinics, spaced geographically around the state so that this kind of facility is accessible to all persons in North Carolina wherever they may live.

To permit the employment of a curriculum specialist, to develop and make available a curriculum library and special textbooks for the retarded children of North Carolina, I recommend the appropriation to the State Board of Education of the sum of $90,000.

I realize that these recommendations combine into a large sum, a total of $1,822,052 for the biennium. As large as it is, however, it does not approach the amount of money which adequately trained and educated retarded persons will contribute to the economy of North Carolina in an equivalent period of time. And you cannot measure the heartbreak in dollars and cents.

I am urging the General Assembly to take a giant step this session, thereby helping many thousands to take the many tiny steps which will enable them to join in the life of our dynamic state of North Carolina. These are the forgotten children. Ours is the opportunity to see that they are remembered.

ON NORTH CAROLINA'S PART IN THE SPACE AGE

May 5, 1963

[As early as December 2, 1961, the Sanford administration was thinking in terms of North Carolina's role in the space age. On that day the Governor announced at the Morehead Planetarium in Chapel Hill the organization of the 39-member Scientific Advisory Committee. The committee, he explained, would help meet the "rapid pace of scientific and technological change" within the state, and would be "still another valuable tool in attracting new industry." Largely because of the work of this nonstatutory committee, a proposal for the establishment of a permanent Board of Science and Technology was sent to the 1963 General Assembly on May 6, 1963, and was later adopted. It was in anticipation of the proposal to follow that Governor Sanford addressed his remarks in this statement.]

North Carolina does not have a real part in the space age.

I suggest we move boldly to carve ourselves a significant part.

We do not have a launching site so we cannot compete in launchings with Cape Canaveral.

We do not have the combination of adequate rail service and water transportation sites, so we cannot compete with the valley of the Mississippi River in the construction of the hardware of space flight.

California has the base of a great aircraft and electronics industry which we do not. They have made fabulous investments in higher education which in turn have attracted the scientists and industries which now attract nearly half of the national space funds.

Massachusetts has the MIT, Harvard, and Clark combination in education and a sophisticated combination in industry, which enable them to contribute mightily to the probe of space. We have much of this too, but we are not using it fully.

There are only forty members of the Association of American Universities, the elite of the American universities. Massachusetts has three members, but North Carolina has two, Duke and Chapel Hill. State, with proposed changes, can soon become eligible and I am convinced can qualify. Then we will be one of four states with three or more members of the Association of American Universities. We will have the added advantage of having our three within a very few miles of each other.

We have another advantage that perhaps no other state has. We have already tied these three great universities together in a working partnership, and have demonstrated that we can work closely together through the Research Triangle.

This is our great resource, giving us the power to do things in the space age enjoyed by very few other states.

Our question is to find the best way of using this resource.

This is not our only resource. We also have industries already working in space, atomic, and related sciences, capable of tremendous expansion.

What kind of a program can we have that will give us in North Carolina a leading position? A program is not just going to unfold before us. We cannot go to Washington and say give us some space projects, some space industries, and even if we could this would not be of much lasting value. We need to start something for ourselves, something bold and imaginative.

For two years now we have worked on many ideas, many suggestions, many plans for finding a more prominent role for North Carolina as the world advances into the age of space.

We have worked with the officials of the National Aeronautics and Space Administration, other federal agencies such as the Atomic Energy Commission, with our own university president and chancellors, with industry leaders, with the Department of Conservation and Development, the Research Triangle Institute, and with the Governor's Scientific Advisory Committee. We have invited in for discussion such outside authorities as Dr. William Baker, chief of Bell Laboratories.

Since we cannot build the space ships, and cannot launch them, and cannot even contribute very much to the design of them, what can we do to make a contribution to the national effort on the one hand and to reap the benefits for the people of our state on the other?

We can, through our scientists at our universities, engage in specific research projects, fitting piecemeal into the total effort across the nation. We are doing some of this, but we need to do more, and we need to broaden our approach.

The science of the space age cuts across the traditional academic disciplines, and chemistry, physics, biology become one, and indeed become one with all human knowledge in meeting the demands of space study. It is not enough that our efforts be limited to a good project in one subject, or a brilliant inquiry into another, but instead we must find the way to have all departments, all disciplines, all scientists, all faculty members working together to define and seek the broader goals.

And it is not enough to have such co-operation merely within our great universities. State must help Duke, and Duke must help Chapel Hill, and Chapel Hill must respond to both, and the best of each must furnish the leadership for all.

Even this is not enough. If we are to know what we seek, and if we are to make it a part of the economy, we must bring into partnership all of the industrial potential of the state and attract even more.

First then, we can achieve more broadly applied scientific research dealing with the countless opportunities of space-atomic technology, if we have the machinery to focus all departments of all three universities, plus appropriate industrial resources, on the total effort. This is one of California's secrets, and we can do it.

But this is not enough, and we can do more, and we can begin to make a unique contribution to the nation and to North Carolina. In the pursuit of space secrets across the nation it is obvious that many things will be learned which can be applied to everyday processes and activities and needs. Things are being learned which will help in the communications field, in the building field, in textiles, in the chemical industry, in food processing, in almost everything. There is probably not a single business which will not enjoy some of the "fallout" of space technology. In fact, Congress has specifically charged the space agency with the responsibility of seeing that such discoveries and advancements are applied to the private sector of the economy.

This is the place we can get aboard ahead of most other states. By tying together government agencies, universities, private industry, in research and development, oriented primarily toward using the discoveries of space technology, although not limited to this, we can assure much progress for our state and can make substantial contribution to the space-atomic age.

In terms of the future position of North Carolina in industry, commerce, and education, this achievement could be one of the most significant steps taken in this session of the General Assembly.

We have almost completed a sound and workable plan, and along with members of the Governor's Scientific Advisory Committee, we will be ready tomorrow to present our requests to the General Assembly and to the general public our concepts of what can be done to move North Carolina into the space age.

FAVORING A FAIR MINUMUM WAGE

June 2, 1963

[Governor Sanford, in this statement, spoke in favor of a law to increase the minimum wage to $1.00. An act ratified on June 11 raised the minimum wage to 85 cents. See *Session Laws, 1963,* c. 816.]

I cannot and do not go along with any feeling that the minimum wage will be satisfactory if raised to only 85 cents.

Senator Robert F. Morgan of Cleveland, who long has worked for a fair minimum wage, quoted Commissioner Frank Crane correctly. Mr. Crane simply said he was afraid it was going to be set at 85 cents. I am not. I have confidence in the members of the General Assembly.

Our minimum wage for industry and business should be $1.00. The Senate bill is fair and reasonable. It would do much to lift the economy of the state and it would do much to lift the individual chance of many men and women who are trying to support their families.

We should do no less. There are plenty of people with strength to fight the increase to $1.00. And they are fighting it. We need also more people of strength raising their voices for the man who does not know how and who cannot come to Raleigh to speak for himself and his family.

Our great task in North Carolina is to quit being poor. A decent minimum wage is one of the best ways to a better living for everyone.

A minimum wage has never wrecked any business, as we have heard predicted so direly for twenty-five years. A minimum wage of $1.00 would help everybody in North Carolina.

ON THE DEATH OF POPE JOHN XXIII

June 3, 1963

I join with North Carolinians of all faiths and of all denominations, and with millions the world over, in mourning the passing of Pope John XXIII.

It is left to future historians with the perspective of time to evaluate his place in the record of mankind.

But we who live now know that his pleas for peace and for human dignity and for brotherhood were a persistent and potent influence for the welfare of man.

Therefore, men of good will will spend not so much time mourning a transient death as they will in carrying forward the eternal labor for humanity for which he worked so faithfully.

ON THE PROGRESS AND POTENTIALS OF NORTH CAROLINA

June 5, 1963

Recently, I came across a familiar old speech. It was delivered by President Teddy Roosevelt, calling his nation to greatness.

"Far better it is," he said, "to dare mighty things, to win

glorious triumphs, even though checkered by failure, than to take rank with those poor spirits who neither enjoy much nor suffer much because they live in the gray twilight that knows neither victory nor defeat."

That is the philosophy which has moved North Carolina from the ashes of defeat and despondency at the turn of the century to a new day of new opportunity. Progress has always followed boldness.

We are today at the point of breakthrough in North Carolina. Never have the opportunities been so great.

Farming is not drying up; it is growing with new vitality.

New industry, home-grown and from other states, is breaking records every day.

Residential and industrial construction is continuing to rise.

Retail sales, personal income, and jobs have never been higher.

With all of this we are well aware that all people are not sharing in this new prosperity. We are also aware that unless we do certain things, make bold new investments, carry on strengthened programs, then this prosperity and these opportunities will not flow across the state to all people.

There are things to be done. We have invested much in education. We are receiving rich dividends. But we haven't done it all. As long as there is an inferior school, we haven't completed our responsibility. As long as a single child is denied an education beyond the high school for reasons of lack of funds or lack of classroom space, then we are failing the challenge. Unless we advance our colleges and university with advancing times, then we do not understand our destiny.

Without new taxes, without an increase in our bonded indebtedness, with one of the lowest per capita tax rates in the nation, we are for almost the first time in our history in a financial position to invest fully in the future of our people and our state.

We have made much progress. We have much to do.

ON BIBLE READINGS AND PRAYER IN THE
PUBLIC SCHOOLS

June 18, 1963

[On June 17, 1963, the United States Supreme Court ruled, 8 to 1, in the case of *School District of Abington Township, Pennsylvania et al. v. Schempp et al.* 374 U.S. 203 (1963), that state and local regulations requiring the recitation of the Lord's Prayer or Bible verses in the public schools were unconstitutional. Governor Sanford issued a statement on the subject the following day.]

We will go on having Bible readings and prayers in the schools of this state just as we always have. We do not require the Bible reading and praying, but we do these things because we want to. As I read the decisions, this kind of thing is not forbidden by the Constitution, and indeed, it should not be.

STATEMENT TO NEGRO LEADERS MEETING AT THE CAPITOL

June 25, 1963

[Civil rights demonstrations became more and more frequent during the spring of 1963. Governor Sanford invited Negro leaders to a mid-morning session at the Capitol to discuss their differences. With Capus Waynick, gubernatorial aide on racial matters, presiding and some 150 Negroes attending, the Governor asked the group to substitute negotiations for demonstrations. A rejection of his plea was clearly evident in the ensuing discussions, and many Negroes voiced intense dissatisfaction with the state's handling of civil rights issues and vowed to continue the demonstration movement. A gradual reduction in the number of demonstrations occurred, however, as the Governor continued to work with the Negro leadership in helping solve problems relating to race.]

You are here at our invitation to find a better way to express your hopes, desires, and aspirations. You must find a way not only which expresses the depth and breadth of your dissatifaction, but which also encourages people to assist in opening up jobs and other opportunities.

The device of the mass demonstration has largely served its purpose in North Carolina. It got across your message and the urgency that had not been fully understood prior to then.

A penetrating insight came from a soldier, who happens to be a North Carolina Negro, who wrote: "I am as much to blame for the riots on the streets of Lexington as those who were there. For it was I who stood aside, saying and doing nothing for many years, and all the while some white people thought I was happy and content when I knew it wasn't so."

The demonstrations have shown just how unhappy and discontented you are, how anxious you are to remove, and remove right now, the indignities and injustices which have been visited upon your parents and their parents.

These demonstrations have been followed by progress for you, but you would be making a mistake to assume that the demonstrations alone, as such, brought your progress. The demonstrations brought the message, and the message, in its truth and fullness, stirred the action which brought your progress. This may be a subtle distinction, but it is an important distinction, and it has great meaning for your future.

The mass demonstration awoke and jolted many people, but this method had reached the point of diminishing returns in its latter days, destroying good will, creating resentment, losing friends, and not influencing people.

There are thousands of North Carolinians with both the desire and the ability to start removing indignities and injustices, so the long-range response of good will, fairness, and full job opportunity depends on mutual respect, not intimidation.

These mass demonstrations also had reached the point where I, as head of the executive branch of government, responsible for law enforcement, peace and order, was required to establish a firm policy for North Carolina. My responsibility for public safety required that I take action before danger erupted into violence.

I do not intend to let mass demonstrations destroy us. It would be unfortunate if I were called on to prove this. As head of the executive branch, I am entitled to the support of all good citizens, and I call on you to join with others in holding down strife.

I hope you will not declare war on those who urge courses of reason at this time.

There indeed are people in the land today who say that the white man is your enemy and war is necessary.

Not so!

Emphatically not so in North Carolina!

Your enemy and mine is a system bequeathed us by a cotton economy, kindled by stubbornness, intolerance, hotheadedness, north and south, exploding into war and leaving to our generations the ashes of vengence, retribution, and poverty.

The way to fight this common enemy is education, up and down the line and across the board.

The way to fight this enemy is to open up job opportunities for everybody, everywhere, on the basis of ability and training, without regard to race. As a state we cannot afford to use only part of our human resources.

The way for you to fight this enemy is through dignity, clearly and forcefully stating your honest feelings, seeking understanding and accomplishment, through good will which is at hand in so many places. This kind of leadership and responsible example by you would be applauded and widely accepted across the nation.

That is why you are here. The story this morning is not the story of mass demonstrations. The real story is not beclouded by the story of possible violence, of the force, the danger, with failure to establish clearer understanding.

The story this morning is the reasonable story of what you think and why. I believe that is important.

General Capus Waynick is the representative of the Governor's Office. If this forum is of advantage, then we can hold others in other cities, as an alternative to potentially dangerous and generally misunderstood mass demonstrations. I am sure that North Carolina mayors and other leaders will co-operate fully. I am sure that they are willing to discuss all things with you and assist you in many ways.

Now is the time for men and women of good faith to put North Carolina above the distressing clamor of racial conflict.

Now is the time for reason to prevail.

ON THE NEED FOR A SPECIAL SESSION OF THE GENERAL ASSEMBLY

June 26, 1963

[Because the 1963 General Assembly failed to provide for redistricting, a special session of the legislature was called. The General Assembly, meeting October 14 to 17, ratified an act establishing senatorial districts and apportioning members on the last day of the special session. Another bill, to change the number of legislators and pattern the North Carolina General Assembly after the federal Congress, required ratification by the people as the Constitution would have had to be amended. This proposal, the "little federal plan," was defeated in a state-wide referendum held on January 14, 1964. See also statement of October 23, 1963, page 606.]

A special session of the General Assembly will be necessary.

Unfortunately, redistricting was put off until too late in the session, and then the complexity of it made a solution impossible. It is true that most of the members were primarily occupied until late in the session with other important subjects, including higher education, utilities, and highway safety. In retrospect it is easy to say that a bill should have been brought to the Senate floor earlier, but be that as it may, it is going to be necessary that the job be done.

I will withhold decision on the exact date. In the meantime, I will appoint a special committee to study the problem and prepare recommended legislation.

STATEMENT AT MEETING OF NORTH CAROLINA GOOD NEIGHBOR COUNCIL

July 3, 1963

We are just going to have to open up jobs for all people on the basis of ability and training and promotions on the basis of performance.

I believe this should be done, can be done, and will be done by North Carolina people because it is right morally and because economically we cannot afford to do otherwise.

I do not intend to try to force anybody. I do not believe in force. I do believe the conscience of North Carolinians will get this done.

The industrial education centers, training people in new skills, have the policy that there must be no racial discrimination in admissions to courses. We cannot have it any other way. These schools are supported by state, local, and federal funds and they are open to anyone who can qualify. We have had some suggestions that this policy is not being followed in all the centers. I have no evidence of this. In any event, we invite anyone to report any violations of this policy to D. S. Coltrane, chairman of the Good Neighbor Council.

There will not be any discrimination in state jobs. Such discrimination is both unconstitutional and undemocratic. Negroes are invited to apply, just as all other citizens, to Walter Fuller, State Personnel Officer, and their applications will be judged solely on merit and ability.

I hope private employers will continue to examine their employment policies, and will join with other citizens of good will in wiping away the last remnants of economic discrimination. In North Carolina we will do this, not in token degree because it is forced by law, but in full and fair degree because it is the proper and decent thing to do. I am pleased with the initial voluntary reaction of North Carolina employers, and I am sure we will soon see the general end of policies which deny full economic opportunity to citizens who have the training and ability to do the job.

The Good Neighbor Council, established on January 18, 1963, to better race relations in North Carolina, met on July 3. Seated to the Governor's right is David S. Coltrane, Chairman of the council.

The Governor is shown with projects, from sixty-six counties, submitted for consideration by the North Carolina Fund.

I also urge all leaders of the Negro communities to get across the message that jobs are being opened up and that it is important, yes urgent, that young people take advantage of all training to earn the qualifications which will fit them for these jobs. This advice, of course, applies to all youth.

ON THE FOUNDING OF THE NORTH CAROLINA FUND

July 18, 1963

I have joined today with three other citizens to found the organization which will administer the Ford Foundation money we expect to get and the money from state foundations which might come in, too.

The name of the new organization is the North Carolina Fund. It is a nongovernment corporation, and it will have offices in Durham. Its purpose is to find new and better ways to improve education, economic opportunities, living environment, and general welfare of the people.

Four of us signed the incorporation papers: Charles H. Babcock [139] of Winston-Salem, John H. Wheeler[140] of Durham, C. A. McKnight [141] of Charlotte.

I am inviting twelve other citizens to serve with me on the Board of Directors. [This paragraph ended with a list of members of the board. See page 745 for appointments to this board.]

Twenty or more rural and urban communities will be selected for special help by the organization. These communities will develop their own comprehensive programs for making improvements, using schools, welfare, public health, and other agencies.

The corporation also will support programs of state-wide interest. Initially, emphasis is likely to be placed on a program to improve the teaching of reading, writing, and arithmetic in the

---

[139] Charles Henry Babcock (1899-   ), stockbroker from Winston-Salem; Director of R. J. Reynolds Company, Security Life and Trust Company, and President of Mary Reynolds Babcock Foundation. *Who's Who in America*, XXXIII, 85.

[140] John Hervey Wheeler (1908-   ), lawyer, banker, Negro civic leader from Durham; Director of Mechanics and Farmers Bank; participant in U.S. South Africa Leader Exchange Program. Albert Nelson Marquis and Others (eds.), *Who's Who in the South and Southwest: A Biographical Dictionary of Noteworthy Men and Women of the South and Southwestern States* (Chicago, Illinois: A. N. Marquis Company, 1963), VIII, 897.

[141] Colbert Augustus McKnight (1916-   ), editor of the *Charlotte Observer;* civic and educational leader in North Carolina. *Who's Who in America*, XXXIII, 1350.

first three grades of over 100 of our schools and a new method of introducing vocational education into high schools.

This new method requires the use of a team of four teachers, one from math, one from science, one from English, and one shop teacher. The four will work together in order to offer a group of students academic-vocational, pre-technician's training. We have some teachers coming in for this project next week.

There is no telling how much money the fund will receive over the next four years, but we feel confident that we will have about $10 million in foundation money, some of it national and some of it state, and we expect most of it to be in hand by the first frost. We will get other money from Washington and elsewhere, as the need arises, and we expect the local communities to help pay.

The first meeting of the Board of Directors will be here in Raleigh in my office next Friday.

URGING STUDENTS BACK TO SCHOOL
(For Radio Station WKIX Back-to-School Program)

August 15, 1963

During the summer months some of you high school students have been working and earning your own money. Now you are faced with a hard decision: Should you go back to school or should you continue on your summer-time jobs?

The pay checks you have been getting every week seem large, and school may seem like hard work without pay. But the truth of the matter is that you will make more money in school this fall than anywhere else. Without a high school diploma, you soon will find yourselves on dead-end streets. Without at least high school diplomas, you will have trouble finding work, especially work with a future.

The state of North Carolina—through the quality education program in the public schools, the industrial education centers, the community colleges, and the state-supported senior colleges and university—has provided you with educational opportunities which your fathers and mothers never had.

I hope you will return to school and take full advantage of these opportunities. By returning to school you can help assure your own future. And you will help assure the future of our state and nation, because that future depends as much on what happens in the classrooms as it does on what happens on the launching pads at Cape Canaveral.

It's smart to go back to school—and it pays. I hope you will.

ON FUND APPROVED FOR ADVANCE PURCHASE OF RIGHT-OF-WAY

October 3, 1963

In approving a revolving fund for advance purchase of right-of-way today the Highway Commission took a very forward-looking action.

This has been an objective of my administration and has been under study and development by my office, the Department of Administration, and the Highway Department for some time.

The state can look toward the saving of many millions of dollars by getting the needed land before buildings are on it. It should save property owners trouble and money, too.

Very few other states have this kind of program. For North Carolina it is a logical development from the joint State-Cities Thoroughfare Planning Law of 1959. This state fund will in effect be a major state aid program for cities, because they share in right-of-way costs.

This fund will also allow us to get space for widening many two-lane highways to four. Without it we might have to relocate them in the future at much greater expense.

ON THE ELSIE WEBB CONTROVERSY

October 12, 1963

[James Elsie Webb, appointed highway commissioner at the beginning of the Sanford administration, completed his four-year term in spite of this 1963 controversy which precipitated repeated demands for his resignation. The dispute, centering in Commissioner Webb's home county of Richmond, involved generally the relocation of U.S. Highway 220 near Rockingham and specifically Webb's possible personal interests in the project. The relocation had been the subject of a long-standing controversy in the county, but it was not until two months prior to this statement that a conflict of interest was publicly suggested. After investigations by the Bureau of Public Roads, the SBI, and the Justice Department had produced no evidence of legal violation on the part of Mr. Webb, the *News and Observer* insisted that there still remained some question of "legal ethics" and "abuse of public position."

It was to erase this "cloud of doubt" over the head of the highway commissioner that Governor Sanford issued this Saturday statement. To placate newsmen who had asked for release of the SBI report on the matter, a summary of the report was granted at this time. Subsequently, after additional investigation, the Highway Commission of the Moore administration approved the same relocation route.]

The *News and Observer* suggested today editorially that the failure to release the investigative report pertaining to the relocation of Highway 220 in Richmond County left some doubt hanging over the head of Commissioner Webb.

Mr. Elsie Webb is a respected citizen. He has performed many civic services for his community. He has an excellent reputation. I do not want to see a cloud remain over his name and reputation.

It is difficult enough to get good men to serve in voluntary public offices without subjecting them to unfair charges.

I was advised some months ago that the report by the Bureau of Public Roads is a matter of public record so I assume I can release the exact wording of the three charges. These are the charges investigated by the State Bureau of Investigation. They are best reported in a letter from this office to the Secretary of Commerce [Luther Hodges], appropriate parts of which follow:

I have received from Mr. D. Grant Mickle, Acting Director, Bureau ,of Public Roads, a letter setting out charges against J. Elsie Webb, a member of our State Highway Commission. In addition, Mr. [W. F.] Babcock has carefully and at considerable length gone over the entire file with your Mr. Redwine. In addition, I have just examined thoroughly the entire file.

In addition, I have been looking into Mr. Webb's conduct in relation to the relocation of Highway 220 since I was first made aware of the anonymous letter from Rockingham to Senator John J. Williams of Delaware in which improper conduct on the part of Mr. Webb was charged.

Let me state, as a matter of policy, that we will not tolerate any degree of malfeasance, and intend to take appropriate administrative and legal action whenever we discover such action.

At the same time we will not take any action out of fear that some Congressional committee might make some unjustified charge, thereby placing us in a position of embarrassment. Mr. Webb's reputation is very good across the State and in his own home community, except possibly with his political opponents. I cannot and will not injure that reputation on mere suspicion. If that unjustified embarrassment comes, I will face it and absorb it before I will destroy a man's lifetime community standing.

The charges made in Mr. Mickle's letter are mere suspicions, and unsubstantiated although your best investigators have spent countless hours on this case.

The first charge did raise some question in my mind about the legal ethics of the transaction, although this has nothing directly to do with improper conduct for gain as a Highway Commissioner.

"(1) Commissioner Webb acquired property within the limits of a proposed improvement on a highway location, which was known to him in his official capacity, several months before the information concerning this proposed improvement was announced to the public."

"(2) Commissioner Webb, acting as attorney for the property owners in the sale of the above-mentioned property, did not disclose to the owners that the purchaser was acting at Webb's direction and as agent for him. In addition, these property owners did not know at the time of the sale of their property to Commissioner Webb through his agent, that the highway through this property was to be improved."

The evidence in the file, however, mitigates the cloud of unethical conduct as a lawyer. It is his story that he intended to buy it for his brother, who was not available, and that later his brother wanted him to take part of it. This is his story, the option was drawn to the brother, and the lack of guile in asking the grantors to execute a deed to him and the placing the deed on the public record substantiates this.

The fact that he already owned considerable land and highway frontage in that very vicinity, and that he informed the Highway Commission that he wanted no damages for the widening and relocation of the highway where it ran through his property, further negates any charge of desire for improper personal gain through the acquisition of the McNeill property.

Affidavits from Mr. Marshall and Mr. C. B. Deane[142] recently forwarded to the Bureau of Public Roads indicate clearly that Mr. McNeill was aware of the fact that US 220 was to be widened before the sale of the property took place. I enclose copies.

The next charge supplies no proof.

"(3) Our investigation shows that Sheriff Goodman[143] is associated as a business partner in the operation of a real estate venture with Commissioner Webb; that on or about September 8, 1961, Sheriff Goodman purchased property known as Shaw Woods; that thereafter Commissioner Webb in his official capacity as highway commissioner participated in the determination to relocate Highway Route 220 through the Shaw Woods property."

This allegation indicates that Commissioner Webb participated in the determination to relocate US 220 through the Shaw Woods property. It leaves the impression that Commissioner Webb used his influence to put the highway through Shaw Woods. This is incorrect and is not borne out by the testimony.

The testimony shows in many places that Commissioner Webb requested the Highway Department to study alternate locations with a view towards finding a line that would tie into US 1 north of the motels and businesses so that they would not be bypassed. These preliminary plans and cost estimates have been made available to the Bureau of Public Roads.

In addition, Bureau and State engineers analyzed these lines on the ground and found that they were not practical. The matter was discussed fully in an Advance Planning report and at a meeting of the Planning Board made up of State and Bureau engineers. It was the determination of these engineers that such a line was not feasible and therefore the only alternate line was to bypass the motels. The decision that the motels must be bypassed moved the line so that it touched the edge of Shaw Woods.

---

[142] Charles Bennett Deane, lawyer and civic leader from Rockingham, member of Congress, 1947-1957, Powell, *North Carolina Lives*, 353-354.

[143] Raymond W. Goodman, sheriff of Richmond County, close friend and political ally of Elsie Webb. *North Carolina Manual, 1963*, 692; *News and Observer*, August 11, 1963.

In my judgment Commissioner Webb was acting properly in his capacity because of the requests of Town officials and businessmen that every effort be made to construct the project so that it would not bypass the motels and business area south of the city.

I would suggest, indeed insist, that the route of relocation of Route 220 be re-studied. If the Bureau and State engineers were improperly influenced, then the first step should be to correct this.

In addition to the request made in this letter for a restudy of the location, I turned all of the material given to me over to the State Bureau of Investigation, with the request (request and not direction because the SBI does not operate under the Governor's Office) that they thoroughly investigate the matter. The Attorney General also reviewed this file and the report.

A summary of the SBI report (227 pages plus exhibits) is attached.

The conclusion of this report is " (17) *That the investigation made did not establish that Commissioner J. Elsie Webb influenced the locating of the proposed route through property owned by him or through property owned by Sheriff Ray Goodman.*"

ON THE REDISTRICTING OF THE STATE SENATE

October 23, 1963

I congratulate the General Assembly on meeting the constitutional duty of redistricting now. The 1965 senate will be as completely representative as we can make it, and I am gratified that the action was concluded in only four days. The members did what they were called into session to do, and they did indeed do it with dispatch.

So many governors have had so much trouble with this issue of redistricting, but getting it done in a proper manner in North Carolina has been relatively easy.

I had obligations which required me to leave Raleigh before the session was concluded, so I take this opportunity to express publicly my deep appreciation.

The fact that a constitutional amendment is to be submitted to the people should not detract from the outstanding accomplishment of redistricting now, according to population, and according to our Constitution. I shall have some comment about the amendment within the next several days.

ON DRIVER TRAINING REQUIREMENT FOR YOUTH
November 4, 1963

[By action of the 1963 General Assembly compulsory driver training was initiated for minors between the ages of sixteen and eighteen. See *G.S.* 20-11; *S.L., 1963*, c. 968, ss. 2, 2A.]

We are making some progress in traffic safety but not nearly enough.

I foresee the day when all new drivers will take courses in safe driving before being licensed. I also would predict that sooner or later all people who violate traffic laws would be required to take some kind of refresher course.

Driver mistakes and faults cause too many accidents, and most of these could be corrected by better training.

The driver training now required for new drivers in the younger ages is a step in the right direction.

We wouldn't undertake to fly an airplane, or operate a piece of industrial machinery, or do anything else as dangerous as driving without some training.

I think this new training program is going to do much good, and every parent should be able to breathe a little easier. Every young driver will be a little better protected. And I am sure this program of training will be improved year by year.

I hope the young people will accept it in the spirit in which it is offered, and I am sure they will. Here is a chance to learn how to drive for greater enjoyment and with greater safety.

REACTION TO THE ASSASSINATION OF PRESIDENT JOHN F. KENNEDY
November 22, 1963

The tragedy of the assassination of the President is overwhelming.

ON THE DEATH OF PRESIDENT JOHN FITZGERALD KENNEDY
November 23, 1963

North Carolinians mourn the death of John Fitzgerald Kennedy, President of the United States of America, and mourn the tragic and disgraceful cause.

This wholesome, courageous, warmhearted leader of the free people of the world spent most of his life, in uniform and out, in bold and intelligent attack on tyranny, bigotry, and oppression.

With a passionate concern for all people, often harassed from both sides and from behind, President Kennedy set his strength determinedly for human understanding and world peace, remaining always resolute in his faith, always undaunted and unafraid.

The valiant soldier of freedom is dead.

All mankind is less.

IMPRESSIONS RECEIVED DURING FIRST CONFERENCE WITH PRESIDENT JOHNSON

November 26, 1963

Last night I had the opportunity to meet with the new President of the United States, Lyndon B. Johnson. I was in the company of thirty-six other governors, of both parties, from Maine to Alaska to Hawaii.

Yesterday was a long and hard day for the President. He had invited the governors to stay over to meet with him at eight o'clock. As we left the hotel room, we were watching the television report of his greeting the heads of states and representatives of some eighty countries.

He came to our meeting thirty minutes late. He had been talking at great length to French President Charles de Gaulle and Canadian Prime Minister Lester B. Pearson and was delayed for extremely good reasons. He couldn't possibly have had time to eat supper.

I was impressed by a number of things.

First, he is working extremely hard.

Second, he has the capacity to take over. He has been in the middle of the Kennedy administration and has been in a position to keep well informed on everything. His background is one of the broadest possible experience. He already knows most of the heads of state. No Vice-President has ever been better prepared.

I was impressed again with what I have known a long time. He has a generous heart and a deep compassion for people, all people, especially those who need his help and concern.

I was impressed with his sincerity, his desire to measure up to the great traditions of the office. At the same time he is essentially a humble man. This was best expressed in his call for help from all governors, all congressmen, all people. He was talking about every single one of us in North Carolina.

He will continue to work for the programs now pending in Congress, which he helped to shape. At the top of the list he put education, civil rights, and tax reduction.

We must have the tax reduction to spur the economy to greater growth, he said. This is the only way to balance the budget and reduce the debt. This is the only sound long-range approach, he said. This makes a lot of sense, and he said he needed the understanding of everybody in North Carolina.

Civil rights is high on his list, he said, because the greatest democracy in the world cannot afford to have people held down, "be they Orientals in California, Mexicans in the Southwest, Negroes in Mississippi, or Johnsons in Johnson City, Texas." The President of a free people cannot condone second-class citizenship.

Education needs the support of the bills now pending, and more too. He has the same kind of faith in education the people of North Carolina have.

He told the governors, Democratic and Republican, that he needed right now the strength of every citizen. We must show the world democracy can remain strong in spite of the tragedy of last week. We have suffered a loss beyond words, he told us, and we need to join together in greater unity, ridding ourselves of fear and hatred and false accusations.

"There will be plenty of time for politics after the two national conventions," he told this group from both parties. "Until then, let's work together to show how strong and vital America can be."

He was talking to the citizens of North Carolina through me, and he said he needs the help of every one of you.

He made a tremendous impression on the governors. I believe he will make the same impression on the people.

ON NATURAL RESOURCES OF THE STATE

December 13, 1963

North Carolina has been blessed by an abundance of natural resources.

Our land is rich.

Our rainfall rate is excellent.

Our climate is mild.

The varieties of our topography are beautifully diverse, so much so that North Carolina is truly called "Variety Vacationland."

But the greatest natural resource of North Carolina is the people. North Carolinians have proved repeatedly that they are capable of doing anything they set out to do. Through the education programs the state now has under way for the boys and girls, we plan to achieve much more with the other natural resources with which we have been endowed.

ON HIS ROLE IN THE PRIMARY CAMPAIGN

January 26, 1964

I notice the candidates are calling names, including mine. I suppose this is natural, but I have something to say about it.

I have at least eighty-eight different irons in the fire, programs and projects and things ranging from special schools for dropouts to seafood research, to highway safety, to tobacco research, to inventorying ground water resources, to medical aid for older people, to the development of a phosphate industry, to meeting delegations from other countries, to widening Highway 17, to school visits, to mountain roads for development, to physical fitness programs, to finding loan funds for college students, to the regulation of the possum season, to entertaining industrial prospects, to bridges over the Roanoke, to reviewing requests for commutations and pardons, to arranging for a forty-hour week for employees, to advertising for tourists, to demonstrations, to development of historic sites, to court reform, to Good Neighbor efforts, to an Appalachian program, to employment of the handicapped, to the reduction of air pollution, to working for community development, to declaring special weeks and days, to extending the use of probation, to the improvement of teacher education, to deciding on more than eighty speaking invitations each week, to prison psychiatric treatment, to reforestation, to attracting science-based business, to a Southport ferry, to dedications, to rural telephones, to high dams and medium bridges, to reducing expenses, to civil defense preparations, to community college boards, to helping private colleges, to getting from Arapahoe to Cherry Point, to education in prisons, to planning for Piedmont Crescent growth, to naming members to several hundred commissions, to increasing exports of farm products, to Heritage Square and Capitol planning, to alcoholic rehabilita-

The Governor often spoke of people as North Carolina's greatest resource as he stressed the need for quality education for boys and girls of the state. Here he and a group of blind students are inspecting together the Faith 7 capsule in front of the Capitol.

The Learning Institute of North Carolina was one of the significant projects initiated by the Sanford administration. Its board of directors, at a meeting on March 13, 1964, is pictured here. Left to right, seated, are Mrs. Harry Horton, Dr. Guy Phillips, Governor Sanford, Dr. Douglas Knight; standing, Robinson Everett, Dr. Charles F. Carroll, Dr. Harold Trigg, Dr. Everett Hopkins, Dr. William C. Archie, Dr. Donald B. Anderson, Dr. William C. Friday, Dallas Herring, and John Ehle.

tion, to helping with sixth grade arithmetic, to answering 300 letters a day, to seeing people with problems, to presiding over the university trustees, to the surplus food program, to the protection of our textile industry, to worrying about N. C. Symphony funds, to remedial reading programs, to stopping dropouts, to obtaining foundation funds for special projects, to encouraging National Guard and reserve enlistments, to attracting qualified people to state employment, to maintaining equitable freight rates, to working with farm organizations, to studying library resources, to working for accelerated public works grants, to improving the status of women, to providing technical assistance for industry, to the preservation of the Outer Banks, to utilization of mineral resources, to cleaning up our rivers and streams, to expediting interstate highway construction, to choosing a band for the World's Fair, to flood control, to expanding opportunities for the retarded child, to honoring outstanding high school students, to promoting the Coastal Historyland Trail, to building secondary roads, to adult illiteracy, to the administration of welfare funds, to development of our ports, to understanding the causes of poverty, to recreation programs, to children with speech and hearing defects, to promoting the Research Triangle, to expansion of facilities for the mentally ill, to development of adequate industrial education, to extending educational television, to securing the Environmental Health Center, to explaining to dozens and dozens why I left their special interests, and mine, off of this list.

If the candidates will let me attend to these duties, I will gladly leave the campaigning to them.

ON ESTABLISHING THE LEARNING INSTITUTE OF NORTH CAROLINA

February 2, 1964

I have today joined with five fellow citizens in founding the Learning Institute of North Carolina.

LINC is a research and development center unlike any now existing in our country, combining the chief educational forces of a whole state in an effort to find ways to improve learning.

I was joined in this move by Dallas Herring, Chairman of the Board of Education, and Charles F. Carroll, State Superintendent of Public Instruction, who represent the public schools. I was joined by Bill Friday, President of the University of North Carolina, and Douglas Knight, the President of Duke University, who represent the university forces of our state. I was joined by Bill Archie, the Director of the Board of Higher Education, who represents the public colleges and teacher training centers of our state.

I signed the charter of LINC as Chairman of the North Carolina Fund.

LINC ought to delve into the very center of the problems of learning, to try to find out why some children do well and some don't live up to their potentials. For a long time we've maintained that the children who don't learn are at fault, but we ought to stop blaming such important matters on children and look to ourselves and our own systems for some of the blame. This might mean new teaching methods, new approaches, and almost certainly it is going to put the spotlight on community faults outside the schools themselves.

LINC will have a few demonstration projects, such as the North Carolina Advancement School, which we announced earlier when we received a $500,000 grant from Carnegie.

I am able to announce today, also, a grant from the federal government of about $80,000 to make it possible for LINC to hold a series of conferences involving top educators to help plan the Advancement School and LINC.

The staff for LINC has not been chosen. John Ehle of my staff will continue to co-ordinate this and the related projects. Among educators from out of state who are going to help us are Nicholas Hobbs of the Peabody Institute, Fred Jackson of the Carnegie Foundation, John Ivey of Michigan State, Paul Ylvisaker of the Ford Foundation, Francis Ianni and Edward Brice of the Office of Education in Washington, C. Ray Carpenter of Penn State, and Winfred Godwin of the Southern Regional Education Board. They will join educators from our public school system, from our universities, and from the colleges and will help us focus attention, devise action, seek improvement for the benefit of our children. These conferences will get under way in February.

I consider LINC to be a major development of our state. It is the result of many months of work, and now there are more months of work ahead.

There will be twelve directors for LINC. Duke University will appoint two, of whom one is to be the President; the University of North Carolina will appoint two, of whom one is to be the President; the Board of Education will appoint four, one of them to be the Chairman and another to be the Superintendent of Public Instruction; the Board of Higher Education will appoint two, one of whom is to be the Director; the North Carolina Fund will appoint two, one of whom is to be the Chairman. It is expected that these agencies will give financial support to LINC from their research budgets.

ON THE VOCATIONAL EDUCATION PROGRAM

February 12, 1964

Automation in the factories and mechanization on the farms is greatly accelerating the importance of vocational education in North Carolina.

Since brain power has replaced back power as the number-one need in our economy, the vocational education program of North Carolina is vital to the state as a whole and to thousands of individual citizens.

ON THE RESEARCH TRIANGLE
(STATEMENT MADE FOR THE ASSOCIATED PRESS)

February 12, 1964

The Research Triangle is an excellent example of the interdependence of industry and education in North Carolina. Including within its boundaries Duke University at Durham, the University of North Carolina at Chapel Hill, and the University at Raleigh, the Research Triangle is designed to utilize to the fullest possible extent for industry, commerce, and government, the brain power of those three outstanding institutions.

The businessmen of North Carolina have contributed millions of dollars for the development of the Research Triangle Park on which great new laboratories for science and technology are being built.

The Research Triangle of North Carolina is a striking example of the fact that North Carolina, which was late in getting in on the industrial revolution, will play an increasingly important role in the atomic revolution and the space age.

The presence of the Research Triangle has served as a strong magnet in our campaign for new industry. Some companies are attracted by it because they wish to establish a laboratory there. Other companies plan to have the Research Triangle Institute do contract work. All new companies are impressed with the Research Triangle's potential for the future.

ON THE NEW WESTERN RESIDENCE
FOR THE GOVERNOR

March 9, 1964

[The Governor's summer home, a gift of the Asheville Chamber of Commerce, is an eight-room rock and frame house situated high on Patton Mountain overlooking Asheville and the Blue Ridge Mountains. The state, in accepting the residence, agreed to maintain and staff it.]

I think having a residence for the Governor in western North Carolina is a wonderful accomplishment, and I am most grateful to the Asheville Chamber of Commerce for its initiative in making this gift possible. Although I have traveled into the western counties many times, I have not been there as much as I would have liked. I hope this will have the effect of linking the western part of the state more closely with the rest of the state.

More than two years ago the Department of Conservation and Development and I started looking for some place which could serve as a headquarters in the west for the governor. We need this so that people with ideas and needs can communicate more closely with the Governor's Office and state government.

I will be at this residence within the next few weeks. I invite the citizens of the western counties to come by, sign the guest book, have a cup of coffee, and tell me anything that might be on their minds. I also will schedule ten more official visits during the balance of this year and we will give adequate advance notice of the dates.

ON THE PRESIDENT'S ANTI-POVERTY PROGRAM

March 18, 1964

I like the President's message on poverty, and North Carolina is ready to march with him in this war on an enemy which has destroyed the spirit of so many of our citizens.

President Johnson's new program is designed to remove the

barriers to the exits from poverty. The objective is for us to remove the causes of poverty, rather than continuing to carry the burden of the people of poverty.

It gives hope to the hopeless.

First, there is education. The country will be given a new kind of school opportunity. These will be job training centers, residence schools where young people who haven't finished school can get education, training, and skills. North Carolina already has the facilities available, and we can move into operation today.

Also proposed is a work-training program, education along with part-time work, not in a residence school. The North Carolina Fund can administer this program through local communities, some of which already have submitted such proposals. This kind of productive part-time work would keep the young in our schools or industrial education centers, where they might get the education they will need.

In addition, there will be a self-help program for college students, which will enable colleges to provide jobs for students without adequate finances.

A second major proposal is community action.

Plans by communities willing to put their own money and effort to work on breaking the cycle of poverty will be given help.

Fortunately, we have a reservoir of such community action plans, fifty-one covering sixty-six counties, submitted to the North Carolina Fund the first week in February.

These are fresh and ready to go. Communities might well get in touch with the North Carolina Fund and get guidance on how to go about working up such an action program.

Third is the program of volunteers: the domestic Peace Corps to serve in the disadvantaged places of America. President Johnson said: "If the states request them, if the community needs and will use them" they will be provided. North Carolina will be ready to know how to use these volunteers effectively, because we have a program going. The North Carolina Volunteers, college students working under the North Carolina Fund during the summer, is a prototype of the national program, and we will gain some valuable advance experience.

In operation already are many other programs, private and public, designed to help those trapped in the prison of poverty.

Using these existing programs will be a part of any good community action program.

I agree with President Johnson that "for the first time in our history, it is possible to conquer poverty."

I also agree with him that as "we broaden the base of abundance, giving more people the chance to produce and consume, we create new industry, higher production, increased earnings and better income for all."

And I am also grateful that Lyndon B. Johnson is the kind of President who has a deep compassion for the least of his fellow citizens.

DESIGNATING SPECIAL TIME FOR THE AGING IN NORTH CAROLINA

April 17, 1964

One citizen out of every fourteen in North Carolina is sixty-five years of age or older. All of the rest of us will eventually reach that age if we are lucky and if we watch what we eat, where we drive, and our step.

For some, the age of sixty-five means a release from the duties that have bound them since their school days. It means fishing and hunting in the middle of the week. It means time to read the books for which there was no time in the hurried earlier years. It means an end to shrill alarms in the morning. It means naps in the middle of the day.

For many who are sixty-five and older, it means a time to do a lot of work of the kind that is preferred.

For most it is freedom from the need to rush, to challenge, to prove.

North Carolina is a greater state because of the achievements compiled by the 323,000 citizens of our state who are sixty-five or more. Those of use who have not yet attained that period of life can continually profit from the experience, the knowledge, and the wisdom of these senior citizens.

In return for the benefits we constantly enjoy from the past and present work of these senior citizens, it is incumbent upon the rest of us to assist them. To do so, we have the Governor's Co-ordinating Committee on Aging. Increasing efforts need to be made by governmental, religious, civic, business, and other organizations to help provide suitable housing, economic solvency, medical care, social services, and recreation.

In co-operation with the Governor's Coordinating Committee on Aging, all North Carolinians should recognize our deep debt to senior citizens and our responsibilities to their health, happiness, and welfare.

Therefore, I am happy to designate the week of May 3-9, 1964, as the

SPECIAL TIME FOR THE AGING IN NORTH CAROLINA.

ON COMMUNITY PROJECTS TO BE SUPPORTED BY FEDERAL GRANT

April 20, 1964

With the approval of the State Board of Public Welfare and in co-operation with the Director of the North Carolina Fund, the Commissioner of Public Welfare has filed a request with the Welfare Administration of the United States Department of Health, Education, and Welfare for necessary funds to carry out a demonstration project in the co-ordination of community services. We have just been notified today that this request, which involves a federal grant of over $400,000, has been approved.

Under this plan for a demonstration project, it is proposed to employ twenty-five community services consultants to be assigned to work with the planning committees in the communities which have submitted project proposals to the North Carolina Fund. These will be the community projects that have not been selected for the North Carolina Fund grants but where there is a keen interest in the community in continuing the projects which were submitted to the Fund. A great deal has been accomplished already in the process of examining the problems faced by the people in these communities, and it is this interest and momentum which we wish to support in this demonstration project.

By furnishing a staff person to the community committees we hope to broaden the base of co-operation between all agencies and organizations, private and public, in order that existing resources, or those which can be developed, will be used more effectively.

This will be an all-out effort in these communities chosen to help the people help themselves through the plans which they have developed. This plan in itself does not provide solutions to community problems, but it is anticipated that through such co-ordination of efforts solutions can be found which will assist in all-out efforts to "break the cycle of poverty." If one solution to a problem in the community rests in securing training and employment opportunities for the unemployed, then this staff person would help the community to mobilize the necessary resources to make the plan effective. This involves a close working relationship with the representatives of the Employment Security Commission, the State Board of Education, the Department of Public Instruction, the Labor Department, the Department of Public Welfare, and other state and local agencies. It will be the responsibility of the community services consultant to work not for the welfare department, but with this total group in an effort to co-ordinate the work of all agencies in a comprehensive community movement to help solve the problems with which the community is confronted. Funds are available for many smaller but valuable demonstration projects to show what can be done to develop and utilize community resources to meet specific problems. If the Economic Opportunity Act of 1964 becomes a reality, it is anticipated that the community services consultants will work with community committees in the development of projects to create opportunities for employment and training for eligible young people.

This is *not* a project through which any one agency is to attempt to run a comprehensive community services project but rather to promote the co-operation of all agencies in their efforts to help solve the problem of poverty. In other words, it is hoped that this will result in a single purpose approach with the support and co-operation of all the agencies concerned. It is anticipated that through this demonstration project the communities involved will receive the same sort of help that the communities selected by the North Carolina Fund will receive through the funds provided by the North Carolina Fund.

ANNOUNCING THE LOCATION OF THE STATE SCHOOL OF THE PERFORMING ARTS

April 30, 1964

The Advisory Board of the State's Arts School has spent these past days with hundreds of citizens, representing Winston-Salem, Greensboro, Hillsborough, Durham, and Raleigh.

They have been seeking two things: adequate quarters for the school, and the continued support of the school.

Never before has the state undertaken such an assessment of its cultural resources. Actually, never has any state done so.

The board which made our study is composed of professional artists representing many years of experience. Not only are they artists, but most of them are teachers as well. Last night I met with them and heard from them their report, and in their report were many fine tributes to North Carolina.

They unanimously recommended to the board of trustees and to me that the new school be placed in Winston-Salem.

The Winston-Salem offer consists of the Gray High School, which now is used by about 1,000 students. The entire facility will be turned over to the arts school. There is an auditorium, two gymnasiums, thirty-five or more classrooms, a cafeteria, and other accommodations. Also, there are twenty acres of playing fields. Some of the land will be used to build dormitories, and the money for the dormitories, about $1 million, is now being raised in Winston-Salem; most of the money is in hand and the rest of it is in sight. Over 4,500 people have already contributed.

The campus will be completed and ready for the opening of the school in September of 1965. At that time, it is expected that 400 elementary, high school, and college students will begin their work there.

I recognize with appreciation the co-operation of all the competing cities. I congratulate and express my appreciation to the representatives of these communities and regret that we have only one school. Certainly the state is indebted to hundreds of people in many places. I hope that all the places will now work to make this school an institution for the whole state and for the whole South and for the whole country. The children after all will come from every place, and they are the purpose and substances of what we are about.

CONCERNING HIGHWAY PATROL MATTERS

May 9, 1964

[This defense of the Highway Patrol grew out of months of criticism of the organization and charges that patrolmen were required to make arrests and were promoted on the basis of a quota system of arrests. During the time in which the question of arrests and quotas had been under discussion, the Governor's Office received hundreds of letters from troopers who defended the Highway Patrol.]

I think there is general agreement that it is time to wind up the investigation of the morale and quota system of the Highway Patrol. It has accomplished all it is going to accomplish, and it is doing more harm than good now.

The Patrol is in the executive branch, but I have co-operated with the inquiry and the hearings because, as always, I wanted to co-operate with the General Assembly. It is time to conclude this one.

I think the morale of the Patrol is hurt by two influences. There are always a few disgruntled people in any organization, and these do an organization no good.

Most patrolmen are proud of their organization. They love the Patrol, and they will do everything possible to improve it. The Patrol has built a wonderful reputation and its members have every reason for tremendous pride.

The other detrimental influence has been the effort by some legislators and some lawyers to discredit traffic law enforcement.

The legislative act to stop the use of an airplane to spot dangerous speeders is an example of this wrong attitude. We are not playing a sporting game of hounds and foxes. We are trying to save lives. We intend to catch violators. We intend to enforce the traffic laws. We intend to do everything we can to stop violations which cost lives. We are tough and we intend to remain tough. Our patrolmen are courteous and considerate, but also they have a lifesaving job to do.

A part of this wrong attitude is the false suggestion that some kind of artificial arrest quota was required of patrolmen. This isn't so, but we know that deaths go up as arrests go down.

Any time a lawyer asks a trooper on the witness stand if he has to make a certain number of arrests to fulfill a quota, you can be sure that lawyer is suggesting this simply to save a guilty client. This device ought to be recognized as such.

The members of the legislature who fell for this old line have done our people great harm.

All of this investigation of a quota system has made our patrolmen so sensitive that arrests have indeed decreased; and deaths have drastically increased.

I am reassuring our patrolmen that they will receive complete support for a tough arrest policy. We expect them to enforce all of the laws without fear or favor. They will receive absolute and complete backing.

If a trooper is asked about a quota system, I hope he will answer:

"Yes, we do have an official quota system. It is to arrest all of the people who are violating the traffic laws. It is to make all the arrests necessary to stop the killing, injuring, and destruction taking place on our highways."

This is the only kind of quota system we intend to have.

ON THE SUCCESS OF THE KENNEDY MEMORIAL DRIVE

May 17, 1964

[For details concerning the Kennedy Memorial service in Chapel Hill, see page 429.]

I am grateful to Hugh Morton, state chairman, and the 102 local chairmen who have made our drive for the Kennedy Memorial successful.

The treasurer, Andrew Jones,[144] does not have a final accounting, and will not have for two or three days. We do know that most of the counties have reached their quotas, and most of those which have not have asked for an additional week. We will work with these counties over the next several days. The quota we accepted is $230,000.

It is impossible to get an accounting from the local distribution because a free child's ticket could have been picked up with every adult ticket. Also we have received through the mail many contributions for less than $10.00 and no ticket requested.

In any event, we know the drive for the library to house the papers and records of President John F. Kennedy has been successful. This is the first in the country, and North Carolina becomes the first state to deliver its quota. It will take us at least a week to count everything and get all the county reports completed, but today I want the state committee, the local chairmen, and all the people who have worked and all the people who contributed to know we are most grateful.

APPEAL FOR RESPONSIBLE CAMPAIGN BEHAVIOR AND ATTITUDES

May 24, 1964

In the last week of the campaign I would like to express my belief that the state of North Carolina is more important than the Governor's Office. This statement is made to all citizens, Democrats and Republicans alike, as we face the end of a long and important campaign.

I hope we can avoid reckless and irresponsible charges.

---

[144] G. Andrew Jones, Jr. (1920-   ), lawyer from Raleigh, Assistant Attorney General, 1961-1963; veteran and retired Reserve Commander; State Budget Officer since 1963. *North Carolina Manual, 1965*, 479; Governor's Appointment Book.

I hope we can make our great decision with calmness and deliberation, befitting the intelligent people of an enlightened state.

I hope we will rise above unsigned leaflets, rumors, slanders, and fear tactics. I hope each citizen will vote for his choice, not against the other candidates. I hope each citizen will vote in confidence that his choice is good for the future of the state, not in fear because of rumors that are always spread during the closing days of a campaign but which invariably fade out when the election is over.

If you get a leaflet not authorized by the headquarters of a responsible candidate you can assume it is false.

If you hear a rumor repeated, you can know it is false, or it would have been issued officially by the headquarters of a responsible candidate.

I hope the voters will throw away the leaflets and turn away the rumor mongers. North Carolina does not need to do business that way.

We can indeed vote for a candidate, as we choose, who will do the most for the future of North Carolina.

URGING CITIZENS TO VOTE

May 29, 1964

The first and foremost duty of all of North Carolina voters on Saturday is to exercise our greatest right—that of voting.

I sincerely trust that all voters, whether they are Democrats or Republicans, will make a stop at their voting places the first order of business Saturday.

I fully appreciate the fact that many citizens like to go to the beaches or the mountains of our state on the week ends. Others like to get out in the country or go fishing.

I sincerely trust that before you go to any of these places that you will go to your polling place.

On Saturday all of us should remember that the right of the ballot is the foundation for all of our other rights.

And, we should remember that one of our great strengths over communism is the fact that we in America have free elections where the people can decide without intimidation who the elected officials will be.

A lot of men have spent a lot of time in foxholes for free government. I hope every registered voters of North Carolina will spend a few moments in the voting booth on Saturday for free government.

The progress and future of North Carolina depend on the decision the people make Saturday.

DENOUNCING ACTIONS OF THE KU KLUX KLAN AS ILLEGAL

June 22, 1964

[The growing civil rights movement and the anticipation of federal civil rights legislation perhaps did much to intensify Ku Klux Klan activity in North Carolina. With an increase of Klan aggressiveness across the state, Governor Sanford, in this and following statements, made his position quite firm.]

Because there is a growing concern across the state, I think it is necessary to remind the people involved that the Ku Klux Klan is not going to take over North Carolina.

Taking the law into their hands, running people away, burning crosses, making threats, wearing hoods, are all illegal practices and are not going to be permitted.

In 1953, the General Assembly, following the conviction of a number of members of the Ku Klux Klan, passed a law with teeth in it.

It was designed primarily by Clifton L. Moore, then the solicitor who prosecuted the Klan members, who now is Associate Justice of the North Carolina Supreme Court.

Here are the teeth, here is what is provided, here is what is against the law:

1. It is against the law to belong to certain kinds of organizations: "It shall be unlawful for any person to join . . . solicit members for . . . or assist in any way any secret political society. . . ." G.S. 14-12.3.

A secret society "shall mean any two or more persons . . . combined or united for any common purpose whatsoever, who shall use among themselves any certain grips, signs or password, or who shall use for the advancement of any of their purposes or as a part of their ritual any disguise of the person, face or voice or any disguise whatsoever. . . ." G.S. 14-12.1.

"The term 'secret political society' shall mean any secret society, as hereinbefore defined, which shall at any time have for a purpose the hindering or aiding the success of any candidate for public office, or the hindering or aiding the success of any political party or organization, or violating any lawfully declared policy of the government of the State or any of the laws and constitutional provisions of the State." *G.S.* 14-12.1.

"The term 'secret military society' shall mean any secret society . . . when members are illegally armed, or . . . have for a purpose the engaging in any venture by members thereof which shall require the illegal armed force. . . ." *G.S.* 14-12.1.

2. It is against the law to use "any signs, grips, passwords, disguise of the face, person or voice, or any disguise whatsoever in the furtherance of any illegal secret political purpose. . . ." *G.S.* 14-12.4.

3. It is against the law to permit such a secret society to meet. *G.S.* 14-12.5.

4. It is required that the regular meeting places be marked. It is against the law to meet elsewhere unless newspaper notice is given two days in advance. It is required that the membership lists be available. *G.S.* 14-12.6.

5. It is against the law for a person over sixteen years old to wear a mask, hood, or device whereby the person, face, or voice is disguised, to be in a public place, or demand entrance or go into someone else's residence. *G.S.* 14-12.8, 12.9.

6. It is against the law to burn a cross on the property of another without first getting written permission. *G.S.* 14-12.12.

The SBI has been asked to keep a running investigation.

The State Highway Patrol is being instructed to watch for violations.

Local law enforcement officers should also watch for violations.

Superior Court solicitors have the responsibility for bringing the indictments, and I am sure they will do so where they uncover violations.

Let the KKK get this clear. I am not going to tolerate their illegal actions, and the people of North Carolina are not going to put up with it.

I repeat, the KKK is not going to take over North Carolina.

ON THE CIVIL RIGHTS ACT

July 7, 1964

The Civil Rights Act is the law of the land, and the question confronting us now is what shall be our reaction to the law.

Every indication is that the citizens of North Carolina will obey the law. This is the result of a good climate of tolerance and understanding which exists here, and it is a wonderful credit to the people of the state.

Everybody can be sure this new law is going to be tested in the courts very soon, but in the meantime, as law-abiding people, we must rely on the established legal procedures in the courts and not on force of any kind.

Force and bitterness are not in keeping with the North Carolina tradition, and we must not let such feeling control our actions.

Before the enactment of the civil rights statute many of the cities and towns of North Carolina were making vigorous voluntary efforts to provide much greater opportunities which the Negroes sought. At the state level we had established the North Carolina Good Neighbor Council in recognition of the justice of the Negroes' plea for better economic opportunities. The council has been conducting a program planned to increase job opportunities for Negroes and to sharpen the skills of Negroes who might be available to fill better jobs. This work must continue if substance is to be given to the larger measure of freedom for all people.

I repeat a statement that I made some months ago to the following effect: Now is a time not merely to look back to freedom, but forward to the fulfillment of its meaning. Despite great progress, the Negroes' opportunity to obtain a good job has not been achieved in most cases across the country. Reluctance to accept the Negro in employment is the greatest single block to his continued progress and to the full use of the human potential of the nation and its states.

It is my hope that the spirit which has characterized much of the work that has been done in the interest of racial justice in the past several years in this state will survive and be strengthened and that the Negro leaders will manifest their own sense of increased responsibility. They should recognize that the federal statute cannot accomplish for them the economic advance they seek and that they will need the good will of employers to reduce the economic disparity they suffer now.

My appeal to our people of both races is unchanged, therefore. That appeal is that we honor the law—that we "deal justly, love mercy, and walk humbly with our God." That way we will find peace and the kind of progress that can enrich all our people both spiritually and materially.

ON THE DEATH OF L. Y. BALLENTINE

July 19, 1964

Mrs. Sanford and I join all North Carolinians in extending to Mrs. Ballentine our deepest sympathy.

Throughout his life, "Stag" Ballentine served the citizens of his state.

As a county commissioner of Wake County, as a state senator, as Lieutenant-Governor, and as Commissioner of Agriculture, "Stag" Ballentine devoted his energy and talents to making North Carolina a better state.

Because of his work, our farms are more productive. Our farmers are living better lives and our farm economy is stronger. Citizens both in the rural areas and in the towns have benefited.

His interest in improving education has benefited every young person in the state.

I am ordering all state flags to be flown at half-staff in respect to the record of service he compiled for North Carolina.

URGING SUPPORT OF THE DEMOCRATIC CANDIDATE FOR PRESIDENT

July 23, 1964

Since the Republican convention I have been listening to the arguments against President Johnson, and I am more than ever convinced that the people of North Carolina have everything to gain by supporting the Democratic party and President Lyndon B. Johnson in the national election this fall.

There are seven points around which the campaign seems to be shaping up, and all of these favor President Johnson.

1. The world is so strained and the daily stresses are so severe that our worries and fears at times almost overwhelm us. It is a temptation to be against everything, such are the times. But being against things doesn't improve the situation. The true anwers cannot come from the pressure of extremist groups who would destroy more than they improve. We need a President who will not trade on fears, but rather will work creatively and positively in the true tradition of the country. We need a President who looks to the future and works to make it better. We need a President with faith and confidence in what this country can do. President Johnson is that kind of man.

President Lyndon B. Johnson visited North Carolina during his campaign for the presidency in the fall of 1964. Governor Sanford appeared with the President on October 6 at Reynolds Coliseum in Raleigh. Shown with the two are Lynda Bird and Lady Bird Johnson; Congressmen Basil Whitener, Harold Cooley, and David Henderson; and State Democratic Executive Committee Chairman, J. Melville Broughton, Jr.

At the twentieth reunion of the 517th Parachute Combat Team's invasion of Southern France, Governor Sanford jumped from the training tower at Fort Bragg on August 15, 1964. He entertained his fellow paratroopers at the Governor's Mansion during the course of the reunion.

2. In North Carolina today race relations is the chief topic. This is a tough problem. Of course, we are all disturbed, but we cannot select the President on this issue alone. The problem is not going away regardless of who is President. We cannot afford the kind of leadership which would destroy the lines of communication and set race against race. That would indeed bring on problems that we couldn't handle. There is an even more important side. We need a President with the courage and the Christianity to try to develop human understanding in a world full of ferment. With the peoples of Africa and Asia emerging, with the freedom of civilization at stake, this great nation of freedom cannot afford to deny the full opportunities of life to all of her people. Mature people understand that. They understand that the President of the United States of America cannot condone second-class citizenship, no matter how unpopular that might make him at home. All of this is difficult for the President, and he needs our help and support.

3. The economy has never been better. The gross national product is at an all time high, personal income is up, profits are up, and unemployment is down. Business is good and getting better. The Kennedy-Johnson program of promoting the economy has paid off, and the program will be advanced under President Johnson during the next four years. We have strong growth and expansion without inflation. North Carolina especially needs this kind of economic climate, because we have so much to gain right now from economic growth. We need prosperity as never before, and we are in a better position to profit from it than ever before.

4. We need a President who can cut costs of government without cutting economic progress. This President Johnson has done. We need a President who understands that the strengths of the space age economy are complex, and who knows how to keep all of the elements in balance. We need a man like President Johnson, who comprehends that, unfortunately, there are no easy answers to complex problems. We can't abolish government. Right now in North Carolina we are making too much progress to turn our backs on the wise and comprehensive approach we are taking under the leadership of Lyndon Johnson.

5. We would like to have a President who has compassion for people. The foolish idea that it is a sign of weakness to be concerned about unfortunate people is no part of the American tradition. The charge that the poverty program is designed just to get votes hardly stands up. Not many of these people vote. Certainly the children of poverty, whom the President is trying to

lift up, do not vote. The poverty program is not a dole or a give-away. It is a creative way of getting away from doles and hand-outs. Anyone who will take time to read the bill will see this is a program of education, true new and unconventional educa-tion, but nonetheless education. The hopes of these children and parents caught up in a web of disadvantage cannot be dismissed by callous statements. We need a President with compassion and feeling who will improve our economy and our lives by lifting up these people so that they might help themselves.

6. Most of all the people of North Carolina need a President who can ease the tensions of the world. President Johnson has demonstrated that he is calm, mature, and a superb negotiator. The dangers in Cuba and Viet Nam have been with us more than the four years of this administration, and while we would like to find an easy clear-cut way out, we know we cannot "shoot 'em up" in the old wild west tradition. The constant pressures being applied by our government will win out. The President has the strength of character, the brave patience, as well as the patriotism, to see us through. He will take the intelligent path, not the foolhardy path.

7. In these times of national peril we need a President with stamina and stability and courage. President Johnson is that kind of man. He will not collapse after keeping the store for less than a week. He will stand strong and firm in any emergency.

REPLY TO FRIENDS DESIRING TO PROMOTE HIS CANDIDACY FOR VICE-PRESIDENT

August 18, 1964

Like anyone else I appreciate any and all kind words from friends, and I am grateful for their friendship in promoting me as a possible vice-presidential candidate.

At the same time I wouldn't want anybody to think I am vain enough to believe this is a possibility.

So I think I should make it clear that I am not running for the job and don't expect to get it, all the time remaining grate-ful for the generous efforts of Dr. John Dees, Ernest Parker, and the others.

COMMENT ON THE DEMOCRATIC TICKET
August 26, 1964

I think the Democrats have put together an outstanding ticket, made up of two of the most able men in public service today.

We had indicated in advance that we would be willing to go with President Johnson's choice, and we should be. It was his responsibility to suggest the name of the man he considered best suited to become President in event that was necessary.

I am well aware of the feeling that Senator Humphrey has been criticized for his role in the matter of promoting civil rights. I would hope all would remember that Senator Humphrey has led the fights for sounder agricultural programs, has worked for conservation and education measures which have greatly benefited all of the South as well as the country.

The Johnson-Humphrey Democratic ticket will be the best for the future and the progress of North Carolina.

ARTICLES ON SUBJECT OF "STRATEGY FOR STATE DEVELOPMENT"
September 22, 23, 24, 1964

[In a series of three articles, Governor Sanford reviewed North Carolina's lack of planning of the past, explained why and how key people had met to work out "a sound policy of planning," and summarized the report which had resulted from these efforts. Not only were a number of Dan K. Moore's supporters asked to participate in the initial planning sessions, but they were also appointed to the advisory committee named to implement the plan. This co-operative effort helped assure the translation of a report on paper to future reality.]

I

Veterans Day will be celebrated within a few weeks, and thinking back to the battles of World War II reminds me of what is going on in North Carolina today. The state government every day is fighting a battle to gain more employment and higher incomes for North Carolinians. We are in daily competition for a slice of the nation's economic wealth. The fight is intense and it gets fiercer every day. Furthermore, the conditions under which we fight change constantly with the rapid advance of technology.

This battle has been costly and difficult so far. In spite of the money the state and private enterprise have invested since World War II, the income of the average North Carolinian has remained at just about 70 per cent of the national figure. We have had to run hard just to keep up. Nor is the outlook for an easy victory. A competent, independent company has completed a study which predicted that, although North Carolina will grow in riches, in 1976 it can expect to be in forty-second place in per capita income. That is just where we are now. The report also suggests that we will have a decreasing share of the nation's wealth. This, however, is a projection of what we are expected to do. It definitely is not a measure of what we can do.

We might invest more public money in programs to promote growth. We will do some of this, but we can't always find enough money. There is an alternative which will help regardless of how much we invest. We can spend the money we have more effectively. To do this we need to know more about the current state of the state and the likely changes coming up in the future.

We are certain we can get a larger slice of the national economy if we plan ahead.

The economic battle is like a military battle. The commander groups his forces for action just as we group state employees into departments. He expects each group to be resourceful and to respond to the situation it finds in the field. No general, though, would send his troops into the field without an over-all strategy. Nor would he do so without pretty good information about the opposition and the terrain. State governments across this nation have traditionally operated without adequate information, and in most states there isn't even a strategy planning staff to assist the governor. The way to get ahead of the other states, to get a bigger slice of the economy, it seems to me, is to beat them on information and strategy.

Before I got the job, I thought I was a pretty good student of the Office of Governor. But I found that I had no conception of the demands upon it. One man cannot develop a co-ordinated program without staff planning assistance. I suspect every recent governor has come to realize this, but perhaps not until near the end of his term. I am resolved not to handicap the next man by ducking the issue and leaving him without this kind of help. A governor needs it most at the beginning of his term when he is shaping his program.

Private enterprise provides a comparison with the state, too. In industry the "research and development" function has become very important. No industry which expects to survive as a profitable enterprise would think of overlooking it. Many of them spend large percentages of their funds on research and on planning in order to be able to anticipate the conditions of the future. Any business which did not do so would soon have to surrender to the competition. Any state which does not do so may likewise have to surrender.

Although the money spent by North Carolina on research and information and on planning for the future has been somewhat haphazard, there has been some.

North Carolina had a State Planning Board in the 1930's and 1940's which did some excellent work. However, the initiative came from an agency of the federal government. With the board having been placed pretty much outside the mainstream of administrative decision-making, its program was terminated in 1947. Several of the state government's departments do a good job of planning their programs. There have also been some notable special studies, for instance the "Carlyle Report" which charted a new direction for higher education in North Carolina.

It is not simply that there has been no thinking about the future. The difficulty is that it has been spotty. There is not enough co-ordination between programs, either. All of our departments must look ahead, and the whole state government must become a single, co-ordinated instrument for development.

In 1961 I installed an assistant for economic development to take an over-all look at the economic situation and at our state programs. He has been a great help in shaping programs which require the co-operation of more than one state agency or which deal with the federal government or with local development groups. This helped a great deal, but more manpower is needed for proper planning. It can mean the difference between making the right or wrong decisions or spending tax dollars more efficiently, or less so.

I have been searching for the best way to go about systematic and intelligent planning for the future. To help me determine how a better job can be done I had a study conducted during the summer. I charged the group making the study with helping me find the way to organize, staff and budget for strategic development planning.

The next two articles will describe the findings and the recommendations.

II

All summer long we have been drawing up plans for a sound policy of planning for the state. Under a grant from the Housing and Home Finance Agency, we have brought together a number of very competent people to advise with us—they have come up with a good report.

"Strategy for Development" is an important report. It contains recommendations on how North Carolina's state government can organize, staff and finance for better program and policy planning. The immediate result could be better development of our state at less cost. The ultimate result could be that we would catch and pass the states we now trail.

The study was done by a small, special staff under the direction of George Stephens, Jr., my assistant for economic development; they were all experts in the subject of planning and government. If they had been lazy, they probably could have written a report after consulting each other. But they didn't.

First they talked with every department head about his program, his ideas for the future, and his contacts with other agencies. The relationship to federal agencies and local governments was discussed. An inventory was done on what information was collected by each agency and what the source was. The department heads got a chance to say what information and forecasting services they really need to do the best job.

Most agencies said that they get overwhelmed in dealing with work thrust on them. They noted that they seldom look beyond the biennial budget period. On the other hand some departments were found to be doing an excellent planning job.

The next step was to discuss these problems in groups. To give an example, all agencies concerned with economic development were brought together for a seminar. It was led by State Senator Gordon Hanes, a man experienced in government and in industry. Philip Hammer, a top ranked economic consultant sat in to question and to comment.

Similar meetings were held for those involved in natural resources, human resources, regional and metropolitan development, and for the experts in the use of data and forecasting.

Now, for the past two years or so we have held meetings at which we've asked each department to explain and discuss its past and future programs with other officials. These meetings stimulated a lot of thought. It was an eye opener, though, to discover that the seminars for the planning study provided the first occasion for many of these officials to meet to discuss programs of mutual interest.

Consider the problem of developing our tourist industry. It is one of the fastest growing parts of our economy—an increasing number of our citizens are drawing their livelihood from the tourist business. To develop it properly will require a co-ordinated effort by the State Recreation Commission; the Department of Conservation and Development's Divisions of Parks, Forestry, Travel Information, and Geodetic Survey (for mapping) ; the Department of Water Resources; the Wildlife Commission; the Highway Commission; and training through the Department of

Public Instruction, Community Colleges, Higher Education, and the Employment Security Commission. In addition there are several federal agencies and lots of local governments involved.

The tasks of industrial development, education, agricultural development, and other programs also require the co-operation of several agencies.

Complicated? It surely is! And they can't work together effectively without a common plan, program, policy, or whatever you want to call it. Furthermore, that plan must be under constant study to meet changing obligations and opportunities.

This summer state officials told us they want the opportunity to plan, to talk together more, to co-ordinate their efforts and to have access to useful data and good forecasts. Those meetings let a lot of fresh air into state government.

III

In two previous articles I have given the reasons for producing "Strategy for Development," a report on how North Carolina can do a better job of planning for the future. The way in which the study was produced was described, too.

At this point it is appropriate to let the report speak for itself through its summary of present shortcomings in respect to good planning:

The State lacks a staff responsible for focusing on problems affecting more than one agency.

The State lacks a staff capable of concentrating on special problems and providing immediate information to the Governor and department heads.

The State lacks a clearing house for collecting data and communicating information, programs and decisions.

The State lacks sufficient personnel to perform program planning functions within key agencies.

The State presently lacks adequate arrangements for coordinated assistance to metropolitan and regional planning efforts.

The State lacks a staff to plan for and coordinate federal programs.

"Strategy for Development" then follows with recommendations to plug the gaps and achieve a more businesslike approach in managing the affairs of the state:

It is recommended that a Long-Range Planning Division be activated within the Department of Administration as authorized in G.S. 143-337.

It is recommended that the Planning Division initiate comprehensive planning activities within three major areas of State responsibility: economic research and development, natural resources development and human resources development.

It is recommended that existing sources of information within State Government be improved by employing, in close cooperation with the Planning Division, the most advanced techniques of data processing, communication and forecasting.

It is recommended that key State agencies strengthen their planning activities by assigning full-time planning responsibility to agency personnel.

It is recommended that the Planning Division determine a system of planning regions and coordinate programs of assistance to aid the establishment of professionally staffed regional planning commissions.

It is recommended that the Planning Division become a center for information concerning federal assistance programs and coordinate planning for the most effective use of funds available to meet the State's needs.

It is recommended that the Planning Division be prepared to conduct special studies at the request of the Governor and department executives.

It is recommended that the planning process initiated by this study be continued by securing a professional staff and financial support by matching State personnel and financial contributions with federal funds."

In conclusion the report says: "North Carolina State Government must have the capacity to anticipate its problems, evaluate alternative paths to the future and make choices most conducive to sound development. A systematic state planning process can help provide the means to these ends. As the planning program reaches maturity, State officials will be assured of having the machinery, the information and the resources necessary to move North Carolina forward. Through this process North Carolina can shape its own destiny and most effectively serve its citizens."

I subscribe to the recommendations. Years of study of state government and almost four years as governor tell me they are sound. We are already moving to carry them out.

I have named an advisory committee to translate this plan into action. The chairman is George Broadrick, a banker from Charlotte; Watts Hill, Jr., an insurance executive of Durham; Thomas D. Bunn, lawyer and legislator of Raleigh; General J. R. Townsend, former city manager of Greensboro and Chairman of the State Water Resources Board; William F. Henderson, Executive Secretary of the Medical Care Commission; George Randall, Director of Prisons.

It will be the committee's responsibility to organize and get under way an effective strategy for development. This is our opportunity to gather the information, to make the plans, to look to the future, to leapfrog the state ahead.

ANNOUNCING "WHISTLE STOP TOUR" OF MRS. LYNDON B. JOHNSON

September 27, 1964

Mrs. Lyndon B. Johnson will be in North Carolina on Tuesday and Wednesday, October 6 and 7. Mrs. Sanford and I are honored to be her hosts and to accompany her on her trip through our state.

Her precise schedule will be announced within a day or so, but generally, she will come from Virginia to Raleigh and then to Charlotte, making stops at a number of places in between.

There is a fair chance that the President will join her at whatever point his schedule will permit, probably Raleigh.

Mrs. Johnson will come with a message that should appeal to the hearts and minds of all North Carolinians, and indeed to all southerners. She herself is a native of the South. . . .

Her message will be one of good will, of compassion for the problems of others, and of progress and understanding which has brought a new prosperity and broader opportunities to all North Carolinians.

The Johnsons are our people, serving in the most demanding position of leadership in all the world. As they serve the nation, and through the nation the hopes of freedom around the world, they deserve the support of their native region.

I hope that in North Carolina we can have the largest crowds and the warmest support for Mrs. Johnson.

All Democratic candidates for state leadership, our two distinguished senators and our congressmen, and party leaders will be on the train with Mrs. Johnson.

I hope all citizens of both parties will turn out to greet Mrs. Johnson on her trip through her native South.

STATEMENT MADE ON ELECTION EVENING

November 3, 1964

It already is obvious that President Johnson is the overwhelming choice of America.

He is carrying North Carolina by a significant majority.

North Carolina, the nation and the free world will benefit from today's vote.

Our state will continue its unbroken march of progress in this century under Dan Moore, Bob Scott, a Democratic General Assembly, and a Democratic Council of State.

It is deeply gratifying to see North Carolinians again demonstrating their faith and purpose in education by approving the nonpartisan school bond issue.

APPEAL FOR SUPPORT OF THE TOBACCO QUOTA REFERENDUM

December 3, 1964

The income of North Carolina's tobacco farmers is at stake on December 15.

If the tobacco quota referendum fails, there would be no support prices on tobacco.

Some of our tobacco leaders have told me that flue-cured tobacco prices would drop at least to 30 cents, and maybe even to 20 cents if we had no support prices. Such a price cut would bring on a deep depression for much of North Carolina.

There are more than sixty counties in the state where flue-cured tobacco provides a great deal of income to people in the county. These people are not just farmers but also the merchants and businessmen who sell to farmers.

Take Wake County, for example. Its tobacco income in 1964 was almost $21 million. Without support prices, that would have been reduced to less than $15 million. Such a cut would take many times $15 million from the incomes of service stations, clothing stores, oil dealers, hardware stores, farm equipment dealers, fertilizer firms—all the people who deal with farmers.

To get down to a personal basis, consider the case of a single tobacco farmer. Eliminating support prices would cut his tobacco income per acre in half or less. If he now grosses $1,200 an acre, he would get less than $600 without supports. That's hardly enough to pay for labor and supplies.

Losing the tobacco program would mean wrecking not only the farmer and people who sell to him; it would mean bankrupting our tobacco warehouse system, destroying our great tobacco organizations, turning many tobacco land communities and towns into ghost areas.

There is one thing about this referendum that everyone voting in it must understand:

The vote is only on whether to continue the tobacco program. If the necessary two-thirds majority is not gained, there will be no tobacco program.

The widespread controversy over the recently announced 19.5 per cent cut has a lot of people confused. They believe that they can vote down the acreage cut.

Now I realize that the cut hurts a lot of growers very much. It is not an easy thing to take, but it's vitally necessary to help line up supply and demand.

But the December 15 vote cannot reduce the cut without eliminating the whole tobacco program. That means growers would
have to take a far worse cut—in their tobacco incomes.

As one man said, "What's 20 per cent of nothing? That's what
we would have without a program."

The cotton quota program, too, is vital to the future of North
Carolina. Cotton would be supported at 50 per cent of parity
without price supports. Cotton income in the state would be
reduced drastically.

The structure of Tobacco Associates, which promotes sale of
flue-cured tobacco, is tied strongly to the over-all tobacco program. Without a tobacco program, there would be no basis for
financing the work of Tobacco Associates.

The North Carolina Peanut Growers Association, in its ten
years of existence, has done a remarkable job of marketing and
promoting our peanuts.

I urge farmers to vote "YES" on all of these programs which
are so vital to North Carolina.

WARNING TO THE KU KLUX KLAN

December 7, 1964

[Newspapers announced that the Christmas parade at Louisburg would
be integrated for the first time in 1964. Consequently, the Ku Klux Klan
made several threats against the staging of the event, thus provoking this
gubernatorial rebuke.]

It is the height of sacrilege for the Ku Klux Klan to try to
inject hatred into the Christmas parade at Louisburg.

I would urge all members of the KKK to read again the Christmas story and the message of good will to all men contained in
the Bible.

In the meantime, I am instructing the State Highway Patrol
to provide all aid necessary to insure that the citizens of Louisburg will be unmolested when they hold their traditional Christmas parade.

If there are illegal acts on the part of KKK members, they will
be prosecuted.

ON THE DECISION TO PARDON BOYD PAYTON

December 31, 1964

[Boyd Payton's original sentence was reduced by Governor Sanford in July, 1961. See statement and explanation on pages 552-553.]

The case of Boyd Payton and his associates has been before this office from time to time, and like all other cases it has received careful attention.

In January of 1963 seven of the jurors who sat on the case petitioned me, after reciting some facts and opinions, that they "recommend that each of the defendants now be granted a full pardon."

I have decided not to take action on all of them but I have decided to grant a pardon to Boyd Payton for two reasons:

First, the evidence against him was different, causing Mr. Justice Bobbitt to file a dissenting opinion saying, "In my view, the evidence, as to Payton, is insufficient to support the verdict."

Second, Payton has been unable to earn a living, having cut his ties with the union, and having found that this conviction has been a bar to other employment. I, for one, do not believe a conviction should be allowed to dog the tracks of a man for all of his life.

I have talked about executive clemency for Payton to a large number of people. They are split about fifty-fifty on whether I should grant a pardon.

I have decided, out of a sense of compassion, to grant a pardon.

NEWS CONFERENCES

[Throughout his term of office, Governor Sanford held regularly scheduled news conferences. A number of these were transcribed and distributed to North Carolina newspaper editors and radio and television news directors. Because they include a variety of topics and also show the ease with which the Governor answered questions of reporters, the news-conference transcripts are of interest. One is published here.]

August 10, 1961

ROY PARKER (*News and Observer*): Governor, what is the current status of the special session and the bond election for the bond that has already been authorized?

GOVERNOR SANFORD: We will issue a proclamation in a day or so calling for the election on November 7 for the bonds authorized by the General Assembly. This includes what might be called the usual types of bonds authorized by the session of the General Assembly which cover many of the items that are financed by bond issues—educational projects, buildings which are customarily financed by bond issues rather than out of current revenues. The self-liquidating port bonds will be in that issue and the others authorized by the General Assembly. So we will get on with that election and carry out the mandate of the General Assembly, and we will worry about other issues and other sessions and other elections at a later date. To put it specifically, there will be no special session prior to November 7.

BRANDT AYERS (*Raleigh Times*): Are you considering calling a special session next year?

GOVERNOR: Well, I'm not even considering what I am going to do in December. I've hardly thought about what I am going to do tomorrow.

PARKER: There'll be no special session . . .

GOVERNOR: Prior to this election.

SCOTT JARRETT (WFMY-TV): Governor, have you had a chance to study or read the State Civil Rights Committee report put out yesterday?

GOVERNOR: No.

PARKER: Governor, do you intend to keep Ed Scheidt on as Commissioner of Motor Vehicles?

GOVERNOR: Well, I haven't made a decision on that.

GEORGE PENNY (WRAL-Radio) : Governor, recently some of the other department heads of the state got an increase in pay. Was he not overlooked in that?

GOVERNOR: Did he get an increase?

PENNY: According to my recollection, I don't believe he did.

GOVERNOR: You want to know whether it was deliberate or accidental?

PENNY: Yes, that's what I want to know.

GOVERNOR: Well, I can't answer that question because I don't know.

PENNY: Who could answer it?

GOVERNOR: Well, I could, but I just don't have the facts today. I'm like you, I'm not sure whether he got a raise or not.

PENNY: I'm pretty certain he did not.

GOVERNOR: Well, I'll bet he would know.

MOTTE GRIFFITH (*Raleigh Times*): Governor, yesterday, you've probably seen it in the paper, I don't know, one of the clerks here . . .

GOVERNOR: What do you mean "the" paper? [Laughter].

GRIFFITH: I said "in the paper," a clerk here who had been a prisoner was arrested for peeping tom . . .

GOVERNOR: Yes.

GRIFFITH: And he was fired this morning. Do you have any comment on that? Several weeks ago you made some observations on prisoner rehabilitation.

GOVERNOR: Well, when you start trying to work with individuals and give people jobs, it's sort of like playing ball. You win some, you lose some, and some get rained out. I think that is so of individuals. You give people a break. Some people justify your confidence in them. Some people don't. It's just one of those things. It doesn't in any way change my opinion that we need a program which will in every possible way lessen repeaters in our prison system. I suppose that's the implication in any question relating to it. I would say that it does not, that people are going to continue to fall by the wayside, both those that have, and those who have not, prior to that had any difficulty with the law. It's just one of those unfortunate things about human nature. I'm very sorry that anybody got in difficulty and we hope that it will be kept at a minimum.

JERRY ELLIOTT (WPTF-Radio): Governor, have you had any late reports on the status of the price-fixing investigation?

GOVERNOR: No.

AYERS: Governor, have many ex-prisoners been hired by the state to your knowledge?

GOVERNOR: I don't have any figures on that. I doubt if very many have been hired.

AYERS: Does the firing of this man represent a policy that if . . .

GOVERNOR: Well, it represents a policy to this extent, that we are going to let most people go who are convicted of being peeping toms [laughter].

ELLIOTT: But not all of them [laughter].

PENNY: Why would you say that is a more serious offense than stealing typewriters and adding machines and that sort of thing?

GOVERNOR: Well, have we caught anybody stealing typewriters, adding machines?

PENNY: No, sir, but this man that was convicted of peeping tom had served time for stealing typewriters and adding machines and you've got a lot of them around here.

GOVERNOR: A lot of peeping toms or a lot of typewriter thieves? Well, it shows that he's versatile anyhow, he . . . [laughter]

PARKER: Governor, have you got any implication as to why they are still holding up Mr. Malcolm Seawell's appointment?

GOVERNOR: No, I'm not in on that policy level.

GOVERNOR: I noticed a paper, not the paper, had something to say about the ax falling today. I would say this, I appreciate the fact that a lot of people are probably wondering about the ax, but I remind all of you that I said that I wasn't coming into office to fire people just for the sake of firing them, I wasn't coming in here to upset the orderly administration of government simply to reward those people who have been of help during the elections, that my primary obligation was getting good people in office and keeping good people in office and seeing that this government is run most effectively and most efficiently, and that will be my attitude. Now I know it's pleasant to see the ax fall and it's entertaining for a lot of folks around Raleigh and maybe elsewhere, too. So I just want to clear that up. There will be no mass turnover simply for the sake of turnover. We will, from time to time, change people where we think that the job might be done more efficiently. We will change people where we think maybe a little new life or new spirit would do some good. But I made up my mind a long time ago that, number one, that in no way at any time would I ever be vindictive in replacing people or changing things around and that I would not change them around simply for the sake of changing, that the only way I thought I could improve the services to the state, I am going to take my time and be certain that when we keep people on who are now in office that we are keeping them on because that is for the best interest of the state. When we let them go, that, too, will be in the best interest and I'll have announcements from time to time about changes, but it will be in the light of this approach: to provide better state services for the people.

GRIFFITH: Governor, at least two lawmakers seem to think the ax might fall in the near future. Mr. Jackson has been reported as being in Raleigh on a permanent basis and so has Mr. Cohoon. Are you planning to appoint either of these two gentlemen in the near future?

GOVERNOR: I'll say this, that both of those gentlemen, or either one of them, would make mighty good men in state government. And I'd consider myself very fortunate if I got them to join this administration.

PENNY: Have you made any attempt to get them to join the administration?

GOVERNOR: Well, I'll say that I have had some preliminary conversations with them.

ELLIOTT: Would you include Mr. Herbert Hardy in that general statement, Governor?

GOVERNOR: Well, I . . . that I have had preliminary conversations with him and that he would make a good man?

ELLIOTT: Yes.

GOVERNOR: Well, there's no question about that. I could name 170 in the General Assembly.

GRIFFITH: Including the 13 or 14 Republicans too?

GOVERNOR: Oh, yes, in fact I'm appointing a couple of Republicans. Is that announcement ready, Graham?

GRAHAM JONES (Press Secretary) : Sir? [Laughter.]

GOVERNOR: Well, it's not ready, but . . . .

JONES: You have already announced several, Governor, including Mr. West of Cherokee, and I think you have two that you are planning to appoint to the Board of Elections.

GOVERNOR: Yes. Incidentally, those two appointed to the Board of Elections will be from a list submitted by the Republican Executive Committee and they will be people who will fairly represent the interest of the minority party as well as the overriding interest of the state. I think it is only fair if you put Republicans on a board that they be Republicans recognized as Republicans by that party.

AYERS: Will Mr. Voseburgh be one of them, Governor?

GOVERNOR: Who is Voseburgh?

AYERS: He is an almost attorney.

GOVERNOR: Did he pass the bar?

AYERS: No.

PENNY: Any comment?

GOVERNOR: All I'm glad is that I didn't flunk it when I took it. I'm sorry for anybody who does.

PHIL ELLIS (WPTF-Radio) : Would you mind amplifying on that bear incident you were talking about in Macon County the other night?

GOVERNOR: Oh, I had a little run-in with a bear up there in the mountains a couple of years ago. But that's a long story and it's better told by Dick Phillips or Pat Taylor because I am inclined to stick to the truth. At any rate, we were camping up there and a bear got our food in the middle of the night and in spite of the fact that I threw rocks at him, he wouldn't leave any of it. They are not vicious though, they tell me.

ELLIS: You going to take any chances?

GOVERNOR: Well, as Pat Taylor points out, that's the general rule, but how do you know when a bear will come along who is an exception?

PARKER: Governor, have you received an invitation to this next meeting of the Southern Governors?

GOVERNOR: No.

AYERS: Governor, although most of the migrants are now in New Jersey, I wonder if you would encourage in any formal avenue of correcting some of the situations that existed with the Employment Security Commission? They can, under certain conditions blacklist people from taking on migrants the next season and my question is, would you in the cases in thirty camps that have found to be in violation of the only state statute, would you encourage the ESC to blacklist these camps if something is not done to correct those situations in violation of the state law?

GOVERNOR: Would you repeat the question? [Laughter.]

AYERS: Should I start in the middle?

GOVERNOR: As I understand the question, you want to know if we will attempt to be more vigorous in enforcing the law. Now as I understand the question and as I understand the situation, on the state level, we have pretty well enforced the law. Possibly on the health situation on the local level, the camps have been at times inspected at the beginning of the season and then for various reasons, maybe a lack of adequate personnel or for other reasons, the local health authorities haven't been too vigilant in continuing inspection. Let me make this clear, though, as my attitude. I think the farmer has a responsibility for providing the kind of camp which can be kept clean. That goes to the early inspection and that's when the state and local agencies come in and look it over. But I think we ought to find a way to put the burden of keeping it clean, not on the farmer, who is out trying as best he can to make ends meet and to pay back his seed and fertilizer bills, and that's been the case in the last several years in most of the farm economy. I think we ought to find a way to put the burden on this straw boss, this group leader, to keep camps clean once that the camp is in proper shape in the first instance. I don't think it is fair to put all of this burden on the farmer. He contracts with the group leader to provide labor and I think he ought also to contract with him that he will keep the living conditions up to standard. So, as I have said before—and drew some criticism from your paper for not putting every farmer in jail—I don't intend to put every farmer in jail and I don't think that we ought to crack down in that way. I think that most of them have provided fairly good situations in the first instance. I think that our desire in the future ought to be that we put the burden on the person who is in a position to keep control of it and if he doesn't, we ought to outlaw him and not let him serve as a broker for labor anymore. I think that that would get at it right away. And, I think that you agree, from the articles I read that you wrote and which I think did a great deal of good in stirring up public interest, I think that you agree that the key man in this thing is the labor broker so to speak or the crew chief or whatever he is called. He has control of the people and I think it is only fair that the farmer put the burden on him and I think our laws ought to be directed in that manner.

AYERS: In other words, you would encourage Employment Security to blacklist certain crew chiefs.

GOVERNOR: I think that is the key to it. We can't blacklist the farmer and keep him from getting his potatoes out of the ground. That is part of the vital economy of the state and he is not the man in a position to do something about it. But the person who is making that middle man's profit is in a position, as I analyze it, to do something about it. And my efforts are going to be directed at making him an honest man.

AYERS: He is, Governor, but the farmer himself is the man who establishes . . .

GOVERNOR: Yes . . .

AYERS: . . . and in this case it was the law that required sanitary . . .

GOVERNOR: Yes, that sanitary conditions be provided. Whether or not they are kept sanitary, of course . . .

AYERS: Well, now if in certain cases according to the Board of Health there were not even privies provided.

GOVERNOR: Yes, well, I don't think those camps ought to be certified in the first instance. I think when you certify a camp as being in proper shape at the first of the season that the farmer has provided his essential responsibility at the point. From then on, it ought to be up to the crew chief.

AYERS: But in those instances in which they . . .

GOVERNOR: Well, if they don't, they can't be certified, they can't use them. If they aren't up to standard, they ought not to be certified, and I would not favor any closing of eyes as to the basic condition of the camp. It ought to be in a condition it could be kept in a sanitary state.

AYERS: If it is not, then you would favor not certifying those camps?

GOVERNOR: Of course not. If they are not up to standards, they ought not to be certified.

PENNY: Governor, you have been making some speeches that sound kind of like a taxpayer here recently on your quality education program. For instance, I believe . . .

GOVERNOR: I have been a taxpayer for a long time [laughter].

PENNY: I know, but you are expressing some . . .

GOVERNOR: I represent the taxpayers.

PENNY: . . . expressing some of the opinions of taxpayers, rather, on a 40-hour week for teachers. Do you mean that they work teaching 40 hours or that they are just on the school grounds or in the schools 40 hours?

GOVERNOR: They couldn't teach very well for 40 hours and do a good job. Most good teachers, the vast majority of good teachers, in North Carolina, work much more than 40 hours a week. I think any investigation of that would indicate to you that that is so. What I am saying is this, that those few teachers who might run over the children getting out when the last bell rings ought to be made to understand that they have a responsibility to do a full day's work and a full week's work and I hope that that will be a policy across this state adopted by local boards that we are talking about a minimum schedule when we talk about working eight hours a day at school and working 40 hours a week. That is the minimum any good teacher ought to do under our present system and our present salary scales, and I think most of them are now doing more than that. I am talking about those few that haven't taken seriously enough their responsibilities.

PENNY: Well, I understand in these additional state funds that money has been provided to take some of the clerical work and some of the other duties off the teachers which will free them to do more teaching.

GOVERNOR: Well, I pointed out that if you didn't, to do more teaching and to correct more papers so that they could give the kind of examination that would better reflect the child's ability instead of just giving a yes or no answer or multiple choice. I think that educators generally agree that one reason that children don't write better and compose better sentences is that too often they don't have the opportunity to do that in schools because they get away from the long, written answers because they simply haven't had time always to grade that many papers. This is especially so in the English courses and the social studies. There ought to be more writing, the educators think. Well, one of the objectives in taking some of the paper work off of the teacher was to give the teacher an opportunity to do a better job. My point is this. Why take it off, if the teacher is not going to understand that she must do much in addition to what she is now doing. Don't take any work off the principal if he is just going to sit in the office once that you have taken it off; and my statement to the superintendents last night was that it is not enough to relieve these people of the nonteaching duties, but let's go one step further and see that they understand fully what they can do now with that additional time.

PENNY: What would you say the reaction of the superintendents and teachers to these speeches is?

GOVERNOR: My impression is that the teachers and superintendents and the principals and the school people, including the school boards and the other people working with public education, now have a higher morale than they've had in my observation over many years, that they are ready to go, that they see that this is a challenge, that they understand that the burden of improving schools is not on me or the General Assembly but on them and that they take it very seriously, that they intend to do their best.

ELLIOTT: Have you had any indication that the filling of vacancies in the teaching ranks has become easier in light of this program?

GOVERNOR: Well, a good many superintendents have said so, though I am sure that situation varies with different parts of the state. I also made the point that I did not think we ought to fill a vacancy simply because we had a vacancy to fill. That's not limited to the school system. It would apply to any other state department. Just because we have a position that can be filled; I don't think we ought to fill it until we find the person that has the proper qualifications, I would hope that, and I think this is true, generally speaking, that the school people aren't going to be too hasty in doing it. That they are going to adhere to high standards and that the people who are put into these new jobs will be people who can add to the quality of the program. I would also say that I would hope that just because the state has come in now and created new positions to lessen the teacher load and ultimately to give the children more attention, the county officials would not take this as a signal to decrease their appropriations. I think this has not been the case but in one or two counties, but they defeat the whole purpose if they now diminish the county contributions to the school program just because the state has increased its attention to the school program and wherever I find that, I would hope to discourage it. You know now, a distressingly large number of our schools are not accredited by the Southern Association. If we are going to reach accreditation, we need not only to put this additional state effort in but we need additional local effort. One of the things I want to talk about this fall as I travel around the state is what do we need to do to get our schools property accredited, not for the sake of being accredited, but for the sake of the improvement of the schools. Accreditation is merely a goal that helps us improve and we are going to need additional effort, I have said all along, not only from the teachers and the professionals, but from people who give support at the county level as well as this wonderful new support provided by the General Assembly. So, if it is going to be done, all have got to increase their interests in assistance, not decrease their efforts, if we are going to do all that I think we can do.

Thank you.

APPOINTMENTS

APPOINTMENTS

This list includes only the appointments made by Governor Sanford during the years of his administration 1961-1965. It does not contain all the persons who served on the various boards, commissions, and other appointive agencies during this period. These may be found in the *North Carolina Manual, 1961* (pp. 275-330) and the *North Carolina Manual, 1963* (pp. 317-374), issued by the Secretary of State. The arrangement of the agencies here follows the order in which they appear in the *Manual*.

An asterisk by a name indicates that the person was appointed and reappointed by Governor Sanford. A dagger indicates appointment during a previous administration and reappointment by Governor Sanford.

COUNCIL OF STATE

Editor's Note: Although the members of the Council of State are elected and not appointed, it is appropriate that those who served in the major positions in the Sanford administration be included here.

Governor
Terry Sanford

Lieutenant Governor
H. Cloyd Philpott[1]

Secretary of State
Thad Eure

State Auditor
Henry Lee Bridges

State Treasurer
Edwin Maurice Gill

Superintendent of Public Instructio
Charles Fisher Carroll

Attorney General
Thomas Wade Bruton

Commissioner of Agriculture
Lynton Yates Ballentine
James A. Graham [2]

Commissioner of Labor
Frank Crane

Commissioner of Insurance
Charles Fortune Gold
Edwin Sidney Lanier [3]

---

[1] Deceased, August 19, 1961.
[2] Succeeded L. Y. Ballentine, deceased.
[3] Succeeded Charles Gold, deceased.

Name of Appointee	Address	Date Appointed	Date of Expiration
ADMINISTRATIVE ASSISTANTS TO GOVERNOR			
PRESS SECRETARY			
Graham E. Jones	Raleigh	1-1-61	At pleasure of the governor
ASSISTANT TO GOVERNOR			
Hugh Cannon[4]	Raleigh	1-1-61	At pleasure of the governor
ADMINISTRATIVE ASSISTANT			
Thomas W. Lambeth, *Private Secretary*	Raleigh	1-1-61	At pleasure of the governor
LEGAL ASSISTANT			
Joel L. Fleishman	Fayetteville	9-25-61	At pleasure of the governor
ADMINISTRATIVE OFFICERS			
ADJUTANT GENERAL			
Claude T. Bowers[5]	Warrenton	2-1-61	At pleasure of the governor
THE DEPARTMENT OF ADMINISTRATION [6]			
David S. Coltrane, *Director*†	Raleigh	1-6-61	At pleasure of the governor
Hugh Cannon, *Director*[7]	Raleigh	12-4-61	At pleasure of the governor
STATE BUDGET OFFICER			
G. Andrew Jones, Jr.	Raleigh	7-1-63	At will of the director, with approval of governor
STATE PROPERTY OFFICER			
Frank B. Turner	Raleigh	1-9-61	At will of the director, with approval of governor
DIRECTOR OF GENERAL SERVICES			
George B. Cherry	Raleigh	1-9-61	At will of the director, with approval of governor
STATE PURCHASING OFFICER			
W. H. White[8]	Raleigh	1-9-61	At will of the director, with approval of governor
John T. Henley[9]	Raleigh	7-16-63	At will of the director, with approval of governor

ASSISTANT DIRECTOR OF ADMINISTRATION

W. H. White[10] .... Raleigh .... At will of the director, with approval of governor

ASSISTANT STATE BUDGET OFFICER

John L. Allen, Jr.[11] .... Raleigh .... 3-1-63 .... At will of the director, with approval of governor

COMMISSIONER OF AGRICULTURE [12]

James A. Graham[13] .... Raleigh .... 7-30-64 .... General election, 1964

COMMISSIONER OF INSURANCE [14]

Edwin S. Lanier[15] .... Chapel Hill, Raleigh 7-5-62 12-31-64

GENERAL ASSEMBLY

SENATE [16]

Hector MacLean[17]	Lumberton	6-15-61	End, 1961 General Assembly
Chatham C. Clark[18]	Elizabethtown	10-19-61	End, 1961 General Assembly
Irwin Belk[19]	Charlotte	11-28-61	End, 1961 General Assembly
L. B. Hollowell [20]	Gastonia	9-25-62	End, 1961 General Assembly
Joe K. Byrd [21]	Morganton	8-28-63	End, 1963 General Assembly

[4] Resigned 12-4-61 to become director of administration.
[5] The adjutant general, who is appointed by the governor and serves at his pleasure, must have five years of commissioned military service. *General Statutes of North Carolina*, s. 127-12, hereinafter cited as *G. S.; Public Laws of North Carolina, 1917*, c. 200, s. 13, hereinafter cited as *P.L.* Bowers succeeded Capus Waynick, resigned.
[6] The director of the department is appointed by the governor and serves at his pleasure. Other division heads are appointed by the director with the approval of the governor, and are removable at will of the director with the approval of the governor. *G. S.*, 143-337, 143-338; *Session Laws of North Carolina, 1957*, c. 269, s. 1, hereinafter cited as *S. L.*
[7] Succeeded David S. Coltrane.
[8] Resigned to become assistant director of administration.
[9] Succeeded W. H. White; Henley resigned January 31, 1965.
[10] Resigned.
[11] Resigned to become personnel director, 12-31-63.
[12] An elective office, vacancies in this position are filled by the governor. His appointee serves until the next general election. *Constitution of North Carolina*, Art. III, Sec. 13.
[13] Succeeded L. Y. Ballentine, deceased.
[14] The commissioner of insurance is an elective official, but appointed by the governor when there is a vacancy during the term, as in this instance. *Constitution of North Carolina*, Art. III, Sec. 13.
[15] Succeeded Charles Gold, deceased.
[16] The governor follows the recommendation of the county executive committee of the political party to which the vacating legislator belongs in appointing a successor. *Constitution of North Carolina*, Art. II, Sec. 13; *G. S.* 163-6.
[17] Succeeded Cutler Moore.
[18] Succeeded Edward B. Clark, resigned.
[19] Succeeded J. Spencer Bell, resigned to become federal judge.
[20] Succeeded Miles Hoffman Rhyne, resigned and moved to California.
[21] Succeeded H. J. Hatcher, resigned.

Name of Appointee	Address	Date Appointed	Date of Expiration
HOUSE OF REPRESENTATIVES [22]			
John T. Randall [23]	Hendersonville	2-6-61	End, 1961 General Assembly
Hoyle T. Efird [24]	Gastonia	2-18-61	End, 1961 General Assembly
Claude M. Hamrick [25]	Winston-Salem	3-6-61	End, 1961 General Assembly
Mrs. J. M. Phelps [26]	Creswell	3-30-61	End, 1961 General Assembly
A. Myles Haynes [27]	Charlotte	12-18-61	End, 1961 General Assembly
William Johnson White, Sr. [28]	Columbia	12-1-61	End, 1961 General Assembly
Roberts H. Jernigan, Jr. [29]	Ahoskie	8-21-62	End, 1961 General Assembly
Mrs. Iona T. Hargett [30]	Trenton	12-18-62	End, 1963 General Assembly
Paul D. Roberson [31]	Robersonville	1-28-63	End, 1963 General Assembly
L. J. Phipps [32]	Chapel Hill	3-18-63	End, 1963 General Assembly
Edwin J. Hamlin [33]	Hillsboro	9-19-63	End, Special Session, 1963 General Assembly
Paul I. Ingle [34]	High Point	3-16-64	Beginning, 1965 General Assembly
JUDICIAL OFFICIALS			
JUSTICES OF THE SUPREME COURT OF NORTH CAROLINA [35]			
Emery B. Denny, *Chief Justice* [36]	Raleigh	3-9-62	Next general election
Susie Marshall Sharp [37]	Reidsville	3-9-62	Next general election
EMERGENCY JUSTICES OF THE SUPREME COURT OF NORTH CAROLINA [38]			
John Wallace Winborne	Marion	3-13-62	For life
JUDGES, SUPERIOR COURT [39]			
Eugene G. Shaw [40]	Greensboro	10-9-61	1-1-63
John D. McConnell [41]	Southern Pines	11-17-62	12-31-66
Elbert S. Peel, Jr. [42]	Williamston	1-23-63	12-31-70
William A. Johnson [43]	Lillington	4-21-64	12-31-66
SPECIAL JUDGES, SUPERIOR COURT [44]			
Harry Lee Riddle, Jr.*	Morganton	6-23-61-63	6-30-63-67
James William Copeland *	Murfreesboro	7-5-61-63	6-30-63-67
Hal Hammer Walker*	Asheboro	7-3-61-63	6-30-63-67
Edward B. Clark * [45]	Elizabethtown	8-10-61-63	6-30-63-67
John D. McConnell [46]	Southern Pines	7-7-61	6-30-63

J. Carlton Pittman[47]	Sanford	3-10-62	6-30-63
Harry C. Martin * [48]	Asheville	3-2-62-63	6-30-63-67
Walter E. Brock * [49]	Wadesboro	12-12-62-63	6-30-63-67
James MacRae[50]	Fayetteville	12-19-62	6-30-63
James Farr Latham * [51]	Burlington	1-8-63-63	6-30-63-67
Hubert E. May[52]	Nashville	1-20-64	6-30-67

[22] The governor follows the recommendation of the county executive committee of the political party to which the departing legislator belongs in appointing a successor. Constitution of North Carolina, Art. II, Sec. 13; G. S. 163-6.
[23] Succeeded Thomas B. Lockaby, resigned because of ill health.
[24] Succeeded Max L. Childers, resigned.
[25] Succeeded F. L. Gobble, deceased.
[26] Succeeded J. M. Phelps, deceased.
[27] Succeeded Irwin Belk, resigned.
[28] Succeeded William Charles Cohoon, resigned.
[29] Succeeded Roger R. Jackson, Jr., resigned.
[30] Succeeded John M. Hargett, deceased.
[31] Succeeded Elbert S. Peel, Jr., resigned.
[32] Succeeded John W. Umstead, retired due to health.
[33] Succeeded L. J. Phipps, resigned.
[34] Succeeded Hardy Carroll III, deceased.
[35] The Supreme Court is composed of six justices and one chief justice elected by the people for terms of eight years each. Vacancies are filled by appointment of the governor, and justices thus appointed serve until the next general election. Constitution of North Carolina, Art. III, Secs. 21, 25; S. L., 1961, c. 313.
[36] Succeeded John Wallace Winborne, who resigned to become emergency justice of the Supreme Court of North Carolina.
[37] Succeeded Emery B. Denny as associate justice.
[38] Serves for life upon retirement from the Supreme Court of North Carolina and upon commission by the governor. G. S. 7-39.7; S. L. 1955, c. 90, s. 7.
[39] Judges of the Superior Courts are elected for terms of eight years beginning in January following the general election. Vacancies are filled by appointment of the governor to serve until the next general election. Constitution of North Carolina, Art. IV, Sec. 21; S. L., 1955, s. 129; S. L., 1961, c. 730, s. 5.
[40] Succeeded L. Richardson Preyer who resigned to become a federal judge.
[41] Succeeded F. Donald Phillips, resigned.
[42] Succeeded Malcolm C. Paul, deceased.
[43] Succeeded Clawson L. Williams, deceased.
[44] The 1963 General Assembly provided for eight special judges of the Superior Court to be appointed for four-year terms by the governor. G. S. 7-54; S. L., 1963, c. 1170.
[45] Succeeded J. Braxton Craven; Clark resigned January 2, 1963, to become general counsel to Governor Sanford.
[46] Resigned as of December 31, 1962.
[47] Succeeded Susie Sharp; Pittman resigned December 27, 1962.
[48] Succeeded W. Jack Hooks, deceased.
[49] Succeeded John D. McConnell, resigned.
[50] Succeeded Edward B. Clark, resigned to become general counsel to Governor Sanford on January 2, 1963.
[51] Succeeded J. Carlton Pittman, resigned.
[52] Succeeded George M. Fountain.

Name of Appointee	Address	Date Appointed	Date of Expiration
SOLICITOR, SUPERIOR COURT [53]			
Max Lamar Childers [54]	Mt. Holly	2-7-61	General election, 1962
Ike F. Andrews [55]	Siler City	7-1-61	General election, 1962
Daniel Kramer Edwards [56]	Durham	9-8-61	General election, 1962
EMERGENCY JUDGES, SUPERIOR COURT [57]			
Walter J. Bone	Nashville	11-1-62	For life
Hubert E. Olive	Lexington	11-1-62	For life
F. Donald Phillips	Rockingham	11-1-62	For life
Henry L. Stevens, Jr.	Warsaw	11-1-62	For life

GOVERNMENTAL BOARDS AND COMMISSIONS

Name of Appointee	Address	Date Appointed	Date of Expiration
ADVISORY BUDGET COMMISSION [58]			
Ralph H. Scott [59]	Haw River	7-10-61	At pleasure of the governor
David S. Coltrane, *Chairman* [60]	Raleigh	11-23-61	At pleasure of the governor
E. D. Gaskins [61]	Monroe	7-22-62	At pleasure of the governor
William H. White [62]	Raleigh	7-16-63	At pleasure of the governor
BOARD OF DIRECTORS OF THE NORTH CAROLINA AGRICULTURAL HALL OF FAME [63]			
Mrs. Charles Graham †	Linwood	6-12-61	1-27-67
S. Glenn Hawfield [64]	Monroe	12-16-64	1-27-69
STATE BOARD OF AGRICULTURE [65]			
James Atwell Alexander †	Stony Point	7-3-61	5-4-67
Thomas O. Gilmore [66]	Julian	7-3-61	5-4-67
Thomas Ghio Joyner [67]	Garysburg	7-3-61	5-4-67
David Townsend, Sr. [68]	Rowland	7-3-61	5-4-67
Claude T. Hall †	Woodsdale	7-18-63	5-4-69
J. Hawley Poole †	West End	7-18-63	5-4-69
A. B. Slagle †	Franklin	7-18-63	5-4-69
David Townsend, Jr. [69]	Rowland	12-3-64	5-4-67

State Board of Alcoholic Control [70]

Cleon W. Goodwin [71]	Wilson	1-16-61	4-23-63
Claude J. Mabry, Jr. * [72]	Shelby	3-18-61-62	4-23-62-65
Thomas Victor Aldridge, Chairman * [73]	Raleigh	8-29-61-64	4-23-64-70
J. B. Spilman [74]	Greenville	7-2-63	4-23-66

At pleasure of the governor

North Carolina Aquatics Recreation Study Commission [75]

Turner W. Battle	Rocky Mount	2-28-64

[53] The 1961 General Assembly divided the state into twenty-four solicitorial districts in contrast to the former number of twenty-one. Solicitors, elected by the qualified voters of the state for a four-year term, hold office until their successors are qualified. Vacancies are filled by appointment of the governor until the next general election. Constitution of North Carolina, Art. IV, Secs. 23, 25; G. S. 7-40, 7-43, 7-68; S. L., 1961, c. 730.

[54] Fills newly appointed solicitorship in district 10-A.

[55] Fills unexpired term of Grady Stott.

[56] Fills unexpired term of William H. Murdock, appointed U.S. Attorney for the middle district.

[57] Any judge of the Superior Court who has attained the age of sixty-five years and has served fifteen years on the Superior Court bench may retire and become an emergency judge of the Superior Court. Constitution of North Carolina, Art. IV, Sec. 11; G. S. 7-51.

[58] This commission is composed of six members, of whom two are appointed by the governor and serve at his pleasure. The other four are the chairmen of the Appropriations and Finance Committees of the House of Representatives and the Senate. The governor is ex officio member. G. S. 143-4.

[59] Succeeded Joseph C. Eagles, Jr.

[60] Succeeded J. K. Doughton, resigned.

[61] Succeeded David S. Coltrane, resigned.

[62] Succeeded E. D. Gaskins.

[63] This board is composed of three members appointed by the governor for six-year terms and five ex officio members specified by the legislature. G. S. 106-568.14, 106-568.15; S. L., 1953, c. 1129, s. 3.

[64] Succeeded T. E. Brown.

[65] The board is composed of the commissioner of agriculture, who is ex officio, and ten members serving six-year terms, appointed by the governor with confirmation by the Senate. The members are to be so distributed as reasonably to represent the different sections and agricultural interests of the state, and all must be practical farmers engaged in their profession. G. S. 106-2.

[66] Succeeded W. I. Bissette, resigned.

[67] Succeeded Glenn Gilmore.

[68] Succeeded J. Muse McCotter.

[69] Succeeded David Townsend, Sr., resigned because of health.

[70] The board consists of three members—one chairman and two associate members—appointed by the governor. The 1963 General Assembly amended the provisions for the terms of office as follows: the chairman serves for six years; the associate members serve staggered terms of three years each. No member may have any financial interest in the alcoholic beverage industry and each must be well known for character, ability, and business acumen. G. S. 18-3; S. L., 1963, c. 916.

[71] Succeeded J. Irvin Morgan, Jr.

[72] Succeeded J. Clinton Newton, resigned.

[73] Succeeded William S. Hunt, deceased.

[74] Succeeded Cleon W. Goodwin.

[75] As established by the 1963 General Assembly, the commission consists of ten members, eight of whom shall be appointed by the governor, one by the president of the Senate from the Senate membership, one by the speaker of the House of Representatives from the House membership. One administrative official shall be appointed from each of the following agencies: the North Carolina Recreation Commission, the State Wildlife Commission, the State Board of Health, the State Wildlife Federation, the Department of Conservation and Development, the State Department of Water Resources, the attorney general's office, and the State Stream Sanitation Committee. S. L., 1963, Res. 83.

Name of Appointee	Address	Date Appointed	Date of Expiration
James F. Bullock	Raleigh	2-28-64	At pleasure of the governor
Thomas C. Ellis	Raleigh	2-28-64	At pleasure of the governor
J. Harry Cornell	Raleigh	2-28-64	At pleasure of the governor
J. D. Foust, *Chairman*	Raleigh	2-28-64	At pleasure of the governor
Walter E. Fuller	Raleigh	2-28-64	At pleasure of the governor
E. C. Hubbard	Raleigh	2-28-64	At pleasure of the governor
Marshall Staton	Raleigh	2-28-64	At pleasure of the governor

STATE DEPARTMENT OF ARCHIVES AND HISTORY EXECUTIVE BOARD [76]

Name of Appointee	Address	Date Appointed	Date of Expiration
Josh L. Horne †	Rocky Mount	6-12-61	3-31-67
Fletcher M. Green †	Chapel Hill	6-12-61	3-31-67
Edward W. Phifer, Jr.[77]	Morganton	7-16-63	3-31-69
Ralph P. Hanes †	Winston-Salem	7-16-63	3-31-69
Robert F. Durden[78]	Durham	5-8-64	3-31-65

STATE DEPARTMENT OF ARCHIVES AND HISTORY, SPECIAL PEACE OFFICERS [79]

Name of Appointee	Address	Date Appointed	Date of Expiration
Bennie C. Keel [80]	Mt. Gilead	2-1-61	At will of the governor
James E. Ivey[81]	Fremont	10-30-63	At will of the governor
Wayne Smith[82]	Burlington	10-30-63	At will of the governor
Willie G. Moore, Jr.	Bath	10-30-63	At will of the governor
Robert G. H. Crawford	Mt. Gilead	10-7-64	At will of the governor
William G. Faulk, Jr.	Southport	10-7-64	At will of the governor
Melvin Jack Rose	Four Oaks	1-17-64	At will of the governor

NORTH CAROLINA ARMORY COMMISSION [83]

Name of Appointee	Address	Date Appointed	Date of Expiration
Daniel K. Edwards[84]	Durham	2-14-61	At pleasure of the governor

BOARD OF TRUSTEES OF THE NORTH CAROLINA MUSEUM OF ART [85]

Name of Appointee	Address	Date Appointed	Date of Expiration
Mrs. Charles B. Aycock	Kinston	7-22-61	7-1-67
Egbert L. Davis, Jr.	Winston-Salem	8-14-61	7-1-67
Edwin M. Gill	Raleigh	8-14-61	7-1-67
Mrs. Charles Kistler	Fayetteville	7-22-61	7-1-67
Mrs. William Joslin	Raleigh	7-22-61	7-1-64
Robert Lee Humber, *Chairman* *	Greenville	8-14-61-64	7-1-64-70

Ralph C. Price *	Greensboro	8-14-61-64	7-1-64-70
Mrs. James H. Semans *	Durham	8-14-61-64	7-1-64-70
Mrs. Larry Cohen †	Greensboro	9-2-64	7-1-70

BOARD OF DIRECTORS OF THE NORTH CAROLINA STATE ART SOCIETY, INCORPORATED [80]

Mrs. W. Frank Taylor	Goldsboro	9-19-61	7-1-65
Harry Dalton	Charlotte	8-14-61	7-1-65
Robert Lee Humber	Greenville	9-19-61	7-1-65
Mrs. George W. Paschal, Jr.	Raleigh	8-14-61	7-1-65

ATLANTIC STATES MARINE FISHERIES COMMISSION [87]

Robert Ballance[88]	Manteo	9-23-63	6-20-66

[76] The board consists of seven members appointed by the governor for six-year terms. G. S. 121-3.
[77] Succeeded James W. Atkins.
[78] Succeeded D. J. Whitener, deceased.
[79] Upon application of the director of the Department of Archives and History, the governor is authorized to commission as special peace officers such of the employees of the department as the director may designate for the purpose of enforcing the laws, rules, and regulations adopted for the protection, preservation, and government of state historical or archeological properties under the department's control. G. S. 121-9; S. L., 1955, c. 543.
[80] Succeeded Helmuth J. Naumer.
[81] Succeeded Richard W. Sawyer, Jr.
[82] Succeeded Ava L. Honeycutt, Jr.
[83] The commission is composed of five members, two of whom are appointed by the governor and are federally recognized officers on the active list of the State National Guard. The remaining three are ex officio members as follows: the governor, who is chairman, the attorney general, and the adjutant general. G. S. 143-230; S. L., 1947, c. 1010, Sec. 2.
[84] Succeeded Edward F. Griffin.
[85] As created by the 1961 General Assembly, the board consists of fourteen members which include the following: four members elected by the board of directors of the North Carolina State Art Society, Incorporated, two ex officio members (the governor, the superintendent of public instruction), and eight members appointed by the governor. Four of the gubernatorial appointees shall serve initial terms of three years; four others for terms of six years. Thereafter, reappointments are for six-year terms. G. S. 140-2; S. L., 1961, c. 731.
[86] The board consists of sixteen members, four of whom are appointed by the governor for a term of four years, eight of whom are chosen by the members of the North Carolina State Art Society, Incorporated, and four of whom are ex officio members, as follows: the governor, the superintendent of public instruction, the attorney general, and the chairman of the art committee of the State Federation of Women's Clubs. The act inserting these provisions became effective July 1, 1961. G. S. 140-11; S. L., 1961, c. 1152.
[87] From each state which is represented on this commission, three members are appointed for three years. Of the members from North Carolina, two serve ex officio as follows: one designated by the Board of Conservation and Development and one a member of the legislature designated by the State Commission on Interstate Cooperation. The third member is appointed by the governor. G. S. 113-877.3; S. L., 1949, c. 1086, s. 3.
[88] Succeeded Walton S. Griggs.

Name of Appointee	Address	Date Appointed	Date of Expiration
	ATOMIC ENERGY ADVISORY COMMITTEE [89]		
Atwell Alexander †	Stony Point	9-1-61	7-1-67
Killian Barwick†	Elizabeth City	9-1-61	7-1-67
Agnew Bahnson, Jr., *Chairman* [90]	Winston-Salem	9-1-61	7-1-67
C. E. Boulware[91]	Durham	9-1-61	7-1-67
Wilbur H. Currie †	Carthage	9-1-61	7-1-67
Gerald Edwards[92]	Greensboro	9-1-61	7-1-67
John I. Hopkins †	Davidson	9-1-61	7-1-67
Forrest Shuford II [93]	Raleigh	9-1-61	7-1-67
M. I. Shuford [94]	Jacksonville	9-1-61	7-1-67
William L. Wilson[95]	Raleigh	9-1-61	7-1-65
Barnes Woodhall [96]	Durham	1-8-62	7-1-68
R. H. Goodman †	Williamston	4-3-62	7-1-67
John Victor Hunter III [97]	Greensboro	4-3-62	7-1-65
Lauchlin M. Currie[98]	Greensboro	4-3-62	7-1-63-69
Clifton E. Crandell * [99]	Chapel Hill	6-8-62-63	7-1-63
A. L. Jameson[100]	Williamston	9-20-62	7-1-68
Nello L. Teer, Jr.[101]	Durham	10-1-62	7-1-63
Emil T. Chanlett †	Chapel Hill	11-18-63	7-1-69
Henry T. Clark, Jr. †	Chapel Hill	11-18-63	7-1-69
William F. Henderson †	Raleigh	11-18-63	7-1-69
T. H. LeCroy†	Rocky Mount	11-18-63	7-1-69
Leo W. Jenkins†	Greenville	11-18-63	7-1-69
Robert J. Reeves †	Durham	11-18-63	7-1-69
H. B. Robinson †	Raleigh	11-18-63	7-1-69
E. Jack Story †	Raleigh	11-18-63	7-1-69
Charles H. Wheatley[102]	Charlotte	11-18-63	7-1-69
Charles D. Barbour[103]	Durham	3-27-64	7-1-69
Mrs. L. Graham Walton[104]	Whiteville	3-27-64	7-1-65
Charles J. Nooe	Leaksville	3-27-64	7-1-69
George Herbert[105]	Durham	1-5-65	7-1-67

NORTH CAROLINA AWARDS COMMISSION [105]

Henry Belk	Goldsboro	12-5-61	At pleasure of the governor
Gordon Cleveland	Chapel Hill	12-5-61	At pleasure of the governor
William D. Snider	Greensboro	12-5-61	At pleasure of the governor
Gilbert Stephenson	Pendleton	12-5-61	At pleasure of the governor
Richard Walser	Raleigh	12-5-61	At pleasure of the governor

CHARLES B. AYCOCK MEMORIAL COMMISSION [107]

Gertrude Carraway †	New Bern	7-22-61	5-24-67
Mrs. Charles G. Doak †	Raleigh	7-22-61	5-24-67
William T. Joyner †	Raleigh	7-22-61	5-24-67
Mrs. Charles Powell [108]	Goldsboro	7-22-61	5-24-67
D. J. Rose †	Goldsboro	7-22-61	5-24-67
Martha Stroud [109]	Goldsboro	7-22-61	5-24-67

[89] The committee consists of thirty-five members, of whom thirty-two are appointed by the governor and of whom three, the commissioner of agriculture, the state superintendent of public instruction, and the state health director, serve as ex officio members. Initial appointments are made as follows: ten members for two-year terms, eleven for four-year terms, and eleven for six-year terms. Reappointments are for six years. At least one member shall be specialized as a radiologist, one a nuclear physicist, one a radiation physicist, one a public health physician, one a dentist, and one a sanitary engineer. G. S. 104C-3; S. L., 1959, c. 481.
[90] Succeeded Fred C. Alexander, deceased.
[91] Succeeded William M. Peck, resigned.
[92] Succeeded R. H. Goodman.
[93] Succeeded J. W. Bean.
[94] Succeeded Sheldon P. Smith.
[95] Succeeded B. J. Romeo.
[96] Succeeded Wilbur C. Davidson, resigned.
[97] Succeeded Wilbur H. Currie, resigned.
[98] Succeeded William M. Whyburn, resigned.
[99] Succeeded John C. Brauer, resigned.
[100] Succeeded R. H. Goodman, deceased.
[101] Succeeded J. C. Cowan, Jr.
[102] Succeeded J. J. Hill.
[103] Succeeded E. Jack Story, resigned.
[104] Succeeded Lauchlin M. Currie, resigned.
[105] Succeeded Agnew Bahnson, Jr., deceased.
[106] As established by the 1961 General Assembly, the commission is authorized to administer the program of public recognition of creative North Carolinians. The board consists of five members who serve at the pleasure of the governor. S. L., 1961, c. 1143.
[107] Twenty-one members, three of whom serve as ex officio members (the director of the Department of Archives and History, the superintendent of the Department of Public Instruction, and the director of the Department of Conservation and Development), and eighteen of whom are appointed by the governor for six-year terms serve on this commission. S. L., 1949, c. 1021.
[108] Succeeded Jesse Aycock, Sr.
[109] Succeeded Martha Gold Borden.

Name of Appointee	Address	Date Appointed	Date of Expiration
	COMMISSIONER OF BANKS [110]		
F. Shelby Cullom[111]	Raleigh	7-16-63	4-1-67
	STATE BANKING COMMISSION [112]		
Charles M. Johnson, Sr. * [113]	Raleigh	2-16-61-63	4-1-63-67
Howard Marion Browning[114]	Charlotte	7-10-61	4-1-65
Jesse Clyde Johnson[115]	Mayodan	7-10-61	4-1-65
John Van Lindley †	Greensboro	7-7-61	4-1-65
Manly Emerson Wright [116]	Asheville	7-10-61	4-1-65
J. Ernest Paschall [117]	Wilson	7-17-61	4-1-65
Ralph T. Morris	New Bern	7-24-61	4-1-65
Edwin P. Brown †	Murfreesboro	7-16-63	4-1-67
E. D. Gaskins[118]	Monroe	7-16-63	4-1-67
Lewis R. Holding[119]	Charlotte	7-16-63	4-1-67
Paul H. Thompson[120]	Fayetteville	7-10-64	4-1-67
	STATE COMMISSION FOR THE BLIND [121]		
Frank C. King †	Brevard	8-11-61	5-21-66
Herbert C. Bradshaw †	Durham	1-21-63	5-21-67
Paul Alford [122]	Durham	10-7-63	5-21-68
Joe W. Hood †	Wilmington	10-7-63	5-21-68
Alston B. Broom[123]	Fayetteville	11-25-63	5-21-68
	NORTH CAROLINA BOARD OF BOILER RULES [124]		
Grover L. Dillon, Jr.[125]	Raleigh	7-4-61	6-18-66
Wilkes C. Price †	Asheville	8-1-63	6-18-68
W. E. Shuping, Jr. †	Charlotte	8-1-63	6-18-68
William C. Wallin †	Winston-Salem	6-20-64	6-18-69
	BUILDING CODE COUNCIL [126]		
Harley B. Foster †	Greensboro	10-24-61	7-31-67
Jack Covington[127]	Winston-Salem	10-24-61	7-31-67
Andrew Roth[128]	Charlotte	10-24-61	7-31-67

Rodney R. Breece[129]	Wilmington	10-24-61	7-31-65
J. J. Barnes[130]	Angier	10-24-61	7-31-65
John M. Council, Jr.[131]	Wananish	10-4-63	7-31-69
J. Sidney Kirk †	Raleigh	8-21-63	7-31-69
James A. Stenhouse[132]	Charlotte	8-21-63	7-31-69

BURIAL ASSOCIATION COMMISSIONER[133]

Currie Edwin Walker[134]	Columbia	7-4-61	6-30-65

---

110 The commissioner is appointed by the governor for a four-year term. G. S. 53-92, 53-96.

111 Succeeded Ben R. Roberts.

112 The commission consists of eleven members, ten of whom are appointed by the governor for four-year terms, and the state treasurer who serves as ex officio member. An amendment by the 1961 General Assembly increased the appointive membership from nine to ten and eliminated the attorney general from ex officio membership. Five of the members are to be bankers, and the remainder of them are to be selected so as fairly to represent the industrial, manufacturing, business, and farming interests of the state. G. S. 53-92; S. L., 1961, c. 547.

114 Succeeded G. Harold Myrick, resigned.

115 Succeeded E. D. Gaskins.

116 Succeeded Don S. Elias.

117 Succeeded Charles M. Reeves, Jr.

118 Succeeded John W. Spears.

119 Succeeded Edwin Duncan.

120 Succeeded John P. Stedman.

121 Succeeded Charles M. Johnson, Sr., deceased.

121 The commission consists of eleven members, of whom six are appointed by the governor to serve terms of five years. The superintendent of the State School for the Blind and Deaf, the state supervisor of vocational rehabilitation, the state health director, the director of the North Carolina Employment Service, and the commissioner of public welfare are ex officio members who serve while they hold their respective positions. G. S. 111-1, 111-2, 111-3.

122 Succeeded Howard E. Jensen.

123 Succeeded Joe W. Hood, deceased.

124 The board is made up of six members, of whom five are appointed by the governor for terms of five years each. The sixth member is the commissioner of labor, who serves ex officio and is chairman of the board. Of the five appointive members one is a representative of the owners and users of steam boilers within the state, one a representative of the boiler manufacturers within the state, one a representative of a boiler inspection and insurance company licensed to do business in North Carolina, and one a representative of the operating steam engineers in North Carolina, and one a licensed heating contractor. G. S. 95-54; S. L., 1953, c. 569.

125 Succeeded R. Gordon Thomas.

126 The council consists of nine members appointed by the governor for six-year terms. Members are chosen from the professions of architecture, engineering, and construction as designated by law. G. S. 143-136; S. L. 1957, c. 1138.

127 Succeeded Thomas C. Cooke.

128 Succeeded John Smith, Jr.

129 Succeeded S. W. Sanders, Jr., resigned.

130 Succeeded Jack H. Rogers.

131 Succeeded A. H. Jeffress.

132 Succeeded A. G. Odell, Jr.

133 The commissioner is appointed by the governor for a term of four years. G. S. 58-224.

134 Succeeded Shem K. Blackley, Sr.

Name of Appointee	Address	Date Appointed	Date of Expiration
COMMISSION TO STUDY THE CAUSE AND CONTROL OF CANCER IN NORTH CAROLINA [135]			
Seth M. Beale	Elkin	7-13-62	Report to the General Assembly 1963, 1965
Rachel D. Davis III	Kinston	7-13-62	Report to the General Assembly 1963, 1965
Ernest Fisher	Franklin	7-13-62	Report to the General Assembly 1963, 1965
William L. Flowers	New Bern	8-6-62	Report to the General Assembly 1963, 1965
Mrs. Lambeth Gibbs	Rutherfordton	7-13-62	Report to the General Assembly 1963, 1965
T. R. Hairfield	Lenoir	7-13-62	Report to the General Assembly 1963, 1965
Mrs. D. M. Jernigan	Raleigh	7-13-62	Report to the General Assembly 1963, 1965
J. Wesley Jones, Jr.	Statesville	7-13-62	Report to the General Assembly 1963, 1965
Donald B. Koonce	Wilmington	7-13-62	Report to the General Assembly 1963, 1965
Will H. Lassiter, *Chairman* [136]	Smithfield	7-13-62	Report to the General Assembly 1963, 1965
Hector MacLean	Lumberton	7-13-62	Report to the General Assembly 1963, 1965
Joe Nagelschmidt	Chapel Hill	7-13-62	Report to the General Assembly 1963, 1965
R. L. Pittman, *Chairman*	Fayetteville	7-13-62	Report to the General Assembly 1963, 1965
Mrs. Grace T. Rodenbough	Walnut Cove	7-13-62	Report to the General Assembly 1963, 1965
J. S. Simmons	Sanford	7-13-62	Report to the General Assembly 1963, 1965
Mrs. Marie Smathers	Canton	7-13-62	Report to the General Assembly 1963, 1965
Mrs. J. V. Whitfield	Wallace	7-13-62	Report to the General Assembly 1963, 1965
Mrs. Al Williams	Elizabeth City	7-13-62	Report to the General Assembly 1963, 1965
J. O. Williams	Concord	7-13-62	Report to the General Assembly 1963, 1965
Vivian E. Irving [137]	Raleigh	10-22-62	Report to the General Assembly 1963, 1965
J. Kempton Jones	Chapel Hill	12-17-64	Report to the General Assembly 1965
Richard M. Peters [138]	Chapel Hill	12-17-64	Report to the General Assembly 1965
NORTH CAROLINA CAPE HATTERAS SEASHORE COMMISSION [139]			
Aycock Brown †	Manteo	9-26-62	1-12-66
Miles Clark †	Elizabeth City	9-26-62	1-12-66
Carlos D. Oden †	Hatteras	9-26-62	1-12-66
Julian Oneto †	Nags Head	9-26-62	1-12-66
Theodore Rondthaler †	Ocracoke	9-26-62	1-12-66
STATE CAPITAL PLANNING COMMISSION [140]			
Mrs. John M. Abernethy	Newton	7-22-61	Serve until duties completed
Robert Lee Humber	Greenville	7-18-62	Serve until duties completed

Gordon Hanes	Winston-Salem	7-18-62	Serve until duties completed
O. Arthur Kirkman, *Chairman*	High Point	7-18-62	Serve until duties completed
John Parker	Chapel Hill	7-18-62	Serve until duties completed
Brian Shawcroft	Raleigh	7-18-62	Serve until duties completed
Pearson H. Stewart	Durham	7-18-62	Serve until duties completed
H. P. Taylor, Jr.	Wadesboro	7-18-62	Serve until duties completed
Mrs. Earl Teague	Statesville	7-18-62	Serve until duties completed
Thomas D. Bunn[141]	Raleigh	6-7-63	Serve until duties completed
George M. Stephens, Jr.[142]	Raleigh	12-17-64	Serve until duties completed

CAROLINA CHARTER TERCENTENARY COMMISSION [143]

Henry Belk †	Goldsboro	11-21-61	9-1-63
Mrs. Doris Betts[144]	Sanford	11-21-61	9-1-63
Chalmers G. Davidson †	Davidson	11-21-61	9-1-63
Lambert Davis †	Chapel Hill	11-21-61	9-1-63
Mrs. Ann B. Durham[145]	Burgaw	11-21-61	9-1-63
William Carrington Gretter, Jr.[146]	Louisburg	11-21-61	9-1-63
Grayson Harding †	Edenton	11-21-61	9-1-63
Mrs. James M. Harper, Jr.[147]	Southport	11-21-61	9-1-63

[135] The 1961 and 1963 sessions of the General Assembly provided for the continuance of the commission established in 1957. The group consists of twenty members appointed by the governor, ten of whom are chosen from the medical profession and ten of whom are not associated with the medical profession. Members are instructed to report to the governor and to the General Assembly in 1963 and 1965. S. L., 1961, Res. 70; S. L., 1963, Res. 46.

[136] Succeeded R. L. Pittman as chairman.

[137] Succeeded Mrs. D. M. Jernigan, deceased.

[138] Succeeded R. L. Pittman, deceased.

[139] Five members appointed by the governor for four-years terms each and four ex officio members consisting of the director of the Department of Conservation and Development and three members of the Board of Conservation and Development designated by the governor. P. L., 1939, c. 257.

[140] The commission was created by the 1961 General Assembly for the purpose of investigating present policies and future planning of governmental capital improvements and recommending a long-range plan. The group consists of nine members appointed by the governor, two of whom shall have served in the General Assembly. G. S. 129-26, 129-27; S. L., 1961, c. 361.

[141] Succeeded H. P. Taylor, Jr., who did not accept the appointment.

[142] Succeeded Thomas D. Bunn, resigned.

[143] As established by the 1959 General Assembly, the commission consists of twenty-two members appointed by the governor for two-year terms plus three ex officio members: the superintendent of the Department of Public Instruction, the director of the Department of Archives and History, and the director of the Department of Conservation and Development. The 1961 General Assembly authorized with new appropriations the continuance of the commission until June 30, 1963. S. L.,1959, c. 1238; S. L., 1961, c. 1065.

[144] Succeeded Mrs. Inglis Fletcher.

[145] Succeeded Gilbert T. Stephenson, resigned.

[146] Succeeded Ben Dixon MacNeill, deceased.

[147] Succeeded J. Emmett Winslow.

Name of Appointee	Address	Date Appointed	Date of Expiration
Mrs. Ernest L. Ives[148]	Southern Pines	11-21-61	9-1-63
Henry W. Jordan[149]	Cedar Falls	11-21-61	9-1-63
Mrs. Kauno A. Lehto †	Wilmington	11-21-61	9-1-63
James G. W. MacLamroc †	Greensboro	11-21-61	9-1-63
Mrs. Harry McMullan †	Washington	11-21-61	9-1-63
Paul Murray †	Greenville	11-21-61	9-1-63
Dan M. Paul [150]	Raleigh	11-21-61	9-1-63
Robert H. Spiro, Jr. †	Macon, Georgia	11-21-61	9-1-63
David Stick †	Kitty Hawk	11-21-61	9-1-63
J. P. Strother[151]	Kinston	11-21-61	9-1-63
Mrs. J. O. Tally, Jr. †	Fayetteville	11-21-61	9-1-63
Francis E. Winslow, *Chairman* †	Rocky Mount	11-21-61	9-1-63
Thomas H. Wright [152]	Wilmington	11-21-61	9-1-63
William C. Fields [153]	Fayetteville	1-16-62	9-1-63

GOVERNOR RICHARD CASWELL MEMORIAL COMMISSION [154]

Name of Appointee	Address	Date Appointed	Date of Expiration
R. Hunt Parker †	Roanoke Rapids	1-20-62	11-30-69
J. Lawrence Sprunt †	Wilmington	1-25-62	11-30-69
Mrs. W. H. Belk [155]	Charlotte	1-25-62	11-30-67
Mrs. Raymond E. King, Jr.[156]	Charlotte	1-25-62	11-30-65
Mrs. W. M. Bellamy †	Wilmington	2-5-63	11-30-69
Edmund H. Harding †	Washington	1-18-63	11-30-69
Sam N. Clark †	Tarboro	12-10-63	11-30-71
John G. Dawson †	Kinston	12-10-63	11-30-71
Thomas J. White †	Kinston	12-10-63	11-30-71
Mrs. George W. Knott †	Kinston	12-10-63	11-30-71

STATE CIVIL AIR PATROL AGENCY [157]

Name of Appointee	Address	Date Appointed	Date of Expiration
Samuel C. Hair * [158]	Charlotte	12-8-61-63	9-1-63-65
Stanhope Lineberry *[159]	Charlotte	12-8-61-63	9-1-63-65
Frank Odell Sherrill † *	Flat Rock	12-8-61-63	9-1-63-65

NORTH CAROLINA CIVIL DEFENSE AGENCY [160]

Name of Appointee	Address	Date Appointed	Date of Expiration
Edward Foster Griffin, *Director*	Louisburg	1-10-61	At pleasure of the governor

COMMERCIAL FISHERIES ADVISORY BOARD [161]

Garland F. Fulcher[162]	Oriental	8-2-61	7-1-65
Clyde R. Potter[163]	Belhaven	8-2-61	7-1-65
Lewis J. Hardee †	Southport	9-30-63	7-1-67
Ralph S. Meekins †	Wanchese	9-30-63	7-1-67
Rex S. Winslow, *Chairman*[164]	Chapel Hill	9-2-63	7-1-67
Monroe Gaskill †	Cedar Island	9-9-64	7-1-68
Percy G. Grant †	Holly Ridge	9-9-64	7-1-68
Robert McCotter[165]	Vandemere	1-6-65	7-1-65

COMMERICAL FISHERIES STUDY COMMISSION [166]

James T. Barnes	Southport	11-8-63	At pleasure of the governor
David Beveridge	Beaufort	11-8-63	At pleasure of the governor
Al Chestnut	Morehead City	11-8-63	At pleasure of the governor
Moncie L. Daniels, Jr.	Manteo	11-8-63	At pleasure of the governor

[148] Succeeded D. Victor Meekins.
[149] Succeeded George M. Stevens.
[150] Succeeded Mrs. Robert Grady Johnson.
[151] Succeeded Mrs. William Daniel Holmes.
[152] Succeeded Winston Broadfoot.
[153] Succeeded Paul Green.
[154] The commission consists of twenty members, sixteen of whom are appointed by the governor for eight-year terms and four of whom are ex officio (the director of the Department of Archives and History, the superintendent of the Department of Public Instruction, the mayor of Kinston, and the chairman of the Lenoir County Board of Commissioners). G. S. 143-204.1; S. L., 1955, c. 977, s. 1.
[155] Succeeded Mrs. Inglis Fletcher, resigned.
[156] Succeeded Mrs. Charles M. Johnson, resigned.
[157] The agency is composed of three members appointed by the governor and six ex officio members specified by the General Assembly. Appointive members serve terms of two years each, and vacancies are filled by the governor. G. S. 167-1; S. L., 1953, c. 1231, s. 1.
[158] Succeeded Charles T. Hagan, Jr.
[159] Succeeded Lloyd Griffin.
[160] The agency is composed of one member appointed by the Department of Motor Vehicles, who acts as executive vice-chairman; the governor, who acts as chairman; the commissioner of the Department of Motor Vehicles, who acts as executive vice-chairman; the executive secretary of the State Board of Health; the chancellor of North Carolina State University; the director of the State Bureau of Investigation; and the general counsel for the North Carolina League of Municipalities. G. S. 166-3, 166-4.
[161] The board is composed of seven members appointed by the governor for four-year terms: one from the Southport area, one from the New River Inlet area, one from the Morehead area, one from the Pamlico area, one from the Hatteras area, one from the Albemarle area, one from the state at large to be designated as chairman. S. L., 1955, c. 1031.
[162] Succeeded W. H. Mason.
[163] Succeeded Dick O'Neal.
[164] Succeeded A. W. Daniels, resigned.
[165] Succeeded Garland F. Fulcher, resigned.
[166] As established by the 1963 General Assembly, the commission consists of eleven members appointed by the governor to serve at his pleasure until the final report is made to the 1965 General Assembly. S. L., 1963, Res. 72. Governor Sanford chose not to fill all vacancies.

Name of Appointee	Address	Date Appointed	Date of Expiration
P. D. Midgett, Jr.	Englehard	11-8-63	At pleasure of the governor
Ottis Purifoy	Morehead City	11-8-63	At pleasure of the governor
Hugh Ragsdale, *Chairman*	Richlands	11-8-63	At pleasure of the governor
Frank Thomas	Raleigh	11-8-63	At pleasure of the governor
Karl M. Wilbur	Beaufort	11-8-63	At pleasure of the governor
NORTH CAROLINA CONFEDERATE CENTENNIAL COMMISSION [167]			
W. H. S. Burgwyn †	Woodland	11-21-61-63	9-1-63-65
Mrs. D. S. Coltrane † *	Raleigh	11-21-61-63	9-1-63-65
Mrs. G. W. Cover †	Andrews	11-21-61-63	9-1-63-65
H. H. Cunningham * [168]	Elon College	11-21-61-63	9-1-63-65
Hugh Dortch, *Chairman* † *	Goldsboro	11-21-61-63	9-1-63-65
Mrs. R. O. Everett * [169]	Durham	11-21-61-63	9-1-63-65
Mrs. William C. Friday[170]	Chapel Hill	11-21-61	9-1-63
Ernie Greup * [171]	Durham	11-21-61-63	9-1-63-65
Mrs. Charles U. Harris †	Raleigh	11-21-61-63	9-1-63-65
W. S. Jenkins † *	Chapel Hill	11-21-61-63	9-1-63-65
R. F. Van Landingham * [172]	Thomasville	11-21-61-63	9-1-63-65
James S. Lewis †	Goldsboro	11-21-61	9-1-63
Robert Long[173]	Statesville	11-21-61-63	9-1-63-65
Mrs. Mary Jane McCrary †	Brevard	11-21-61-63	9-1-63-65
Hector MacLean † *	Lumberton	11-21-61-63	9-1-63-65
R. Hunt Parker †	Raleigh	11-21-61-63	9-1-63-65
Mrs. Sadie S. Patton * [174]	Hendersonville	11-21-61-63	9-1-63-65
John R. Peacock † *	High Point	11-21-61-63	9-1-63-65
Mrs. Alvin Seippel * [175]	Winston-Salem	11-21-61-63	9-1-63-65
Glenn M. Tucker * [176]	Carolina Beach	11-21-61-63	9-1-63-65
Robert H. Woody † *	Durham	11-21-61-63	9-1-63-65
George Myrover * [177]	Fayetteville	1-16-62-63	9-1-63-65
Mrs. Earl Teague * [178]	Statesville	1-16-62-63	9-1-63-65
Mrs. Jessie Ruth Seagroves * [179]	Siler City	1-16-62-63	9-1-63-65
F. C. Salisbury * [180]	Morehead City	4-25-62-63	9-1-63-65
W. Cliff Elder	Burlington	12-11-63	9-1-65

BOARD OF CONSERVATION AND DEVELOPMENT [167]

Robert Emmet Bryan[182]	Goldsboro	7-21-61	6-30-65
Ila Green Campbell[183]	Waynesville	7-21-61	6-30-65
Edward Robert Evans[184]	Ahoskie	7-21-61	6-30-65
E. Hervey Evans, Jr.[185]	Laurinburg	7-21-61	6-30-65
E. D. Gaskins[186]	Monroe	7-21-61	6-30-65
Andrew Gennett[187]	Asheville	7-21-61	6-30-65
Luther Warren Gurkin, Jr.[188]	Plymouth	7-21-61	6-30-65
Charles E. Hayworth[189]	High Point	7-21-61	6-30-65
Roger Pierce Kavanagh, Jr.[190]	Greensboro	7-21-61	6-30-65
Lorimer Willard Midgett †	Elizabeth City	7-21-61	6-30-65
Eric Winfred Rodgers †	Scotland Neck	7-21-61	6-30-65

167 As established by the 1959 General Assembly, the commission consists of twenty-five members, each appointed by the governor for two-year terms, plus three ex officio members: the superintendent of the Department of Public Instruction, the director of the Department of Archives and History, and the director of the Department of Conservation and Development. The 1961 General Assembly authorized with new appropriations the continuance of this program through 1963. S. L., 1959, c. 328; S. L., 1961, c. 1064.

168 Succeeded R. F. Hoke Pollock.
169 Succeeded William B. Rodman, Jr.
170 Appears on the record to have succeeded James Stikeleather, Jr., but did not accept appointment.
171 Succeeded Henry S. Stroupe.
172 Succeeded Thomas H. Wright.
173 Succeeded H. Galt Braxton.
174 Succeeded Reed Sarratt.
175 Succeeded Hugh T. Lefler.
176 Succeeded Glenn Tucker.
177 Succeeded Robert R. Garvey, resigned.
178 Succeeded Frontis W. Johnston.
179 Succeeded Fitzhugh H. Lee.
180 Succeeded James S. Lewis, resigned.
181 The 1961 General Assembly increased the number on the board from fifteen to twenty-eight persons to be appointed by the governor. Under this law the terms of office of members expired on June 30, 1961, on which date fourteen were to be appointed for four-year terms and fourteen were to be appointed for two-year terms. Subsequent appointments were to made for four years. In selecting the membership the governor was to give proportionate representation to each function and activity of the department. Governor Sanford chose not to fill all vacancies. S. L., 1961, c. 197.

182 Succeeded Voit Gilmore.
183 Succeeded Scroop W. Enloe, Jr.
184 Succeeded Miles J. Smith.
185 Succeeded W. J. Damtoft.
186 Succeeded Orton A. Boren.
187 Succeeded Edwin Pate.
188 Succeeded H. C. Kennett.
189 Succeeded Hugh Morton, resigned.
190 Succeeded Max Watson.

Name of Appointee	Address	Date Appointed	Date of Expiration
Robert Walter Scott [191]	Haw River	7-21-61	6-30-65
James Abraham Singleton [192]	Red Springs	7-21-61	6-30-65
J. Bernard Stein [193]	Fayetteville	7-21-61	6-30-65
John McCorkle Akers † *	Gastonia	7-21-61-63	6-30-63-67
Mott Parks Blair * [194]	Siler City	7-21-61-63	6-30-63-67
Gladys Strawn Bullard *	Raleigh	7-21-61-63	6-30-63-67
Daniel David Cameron *	Wilmington	7-21-61-63	6-30-63-67
John T. Dees *	Burgaw	7-21-61-63	6-30-63-67
William Perry Elliott, Sr. *	Marion	7-21-61-63	6-30-63-67
Woody Robert Hampton *	Sylva	7-21-61-63	6-30-63-67
Gordon Coble Hunter *	Roxboro	7-21-61-63	6-30-63-67
Ryan Walker Martin † *	Lexington	7-21-61-63	6-30-63-67
Carl Greaves McCraw *	Charlotte	7-21-61-63	6-30-63-67
Ernest Elbert Parker, Jr. *	Southport	7-21-61-63	6-30-63-67
R. A. Pool *	Clinton	7-21-61	6-30-63
Walter Eugene Simmons †	Tarboro	7-21-61-63	6-30-63-67
Charles Byrd Wade, Jr. *	Winston Salem	2-6-62-63	6-30-63-67
Paul H. Thompson * [195]	Fayetteville	7-23-62	6-30-65
Hargrove Bowles, Jr., *Chairman* [196]	Raleigh	3-5-64	6-30-65
G. C. Robbins, Jr. [197]	Blowing Rock	7-16-64	6-30-67
Charles C. Ervin [198]	Charlotte	7-17-64	6-30-67
John L. Fraley [199]	Cherryville		

DIRECTOR OF CONSERVATION AND DEVELOPMENT [200]

Name of Appointee	Address	Date Appointed	Date of Expiration
Hargrove Bowles, Jr. [201]	Greensboro	1-9-61	At pleasure of the governor
Robert L. Stallings, Jr. [202]	New Bern	7-31-62	At pleasure of the governor

SPECIAL PEACE OFFICERS FOR DIVISION OF PARKS, DEPARTMENT OF CONSERVATION AND DEVELOPMENT [203]

Name of Appointee	Address	Date Appointed	Date of Expiration
Tracy R. Wallace	Lake Warden	3-21-61	At pleasure of the governor
Jerry G. Thompson	Park Attendant	8-29-61	At pleasure of the governor
John R. Wilson [204]	Park Ranger II	8-29-61	At pleasure of the governor
Charles W. Brown [205]	Park Ranger I	12-21-61	At pleasure of the governor
Stanley H. Johnson [206]	Assistant Lake Warden	3-29-62	At pleasure of the governor
James M. Carey [207]	Assistant Lake Warden	5-3-62	At pleasure of the governor

Name	Position	Date	Term
Henry T. Hood	Lake Warden	5-3-62	At pleasure of the governor
William D. Hill, Jr.[208]	Park Ranger I	8-24-62	At pleasure of the governor
Ottie J. Carroll, Jr.[209]	Park Ranger I	1-18-63	At pleasure of the governor
Lauris K. Joyner[210]	Park Ranger I	3-20-63	At pleasure of the governor
Willie A. Shaw[211]	Park Ranger II	5-14-63	At pleasure of the governor
Van A. Pierce[212]	Park Ranger I	6-20-63	At pleasure of the governor
Lester M. Goodwin, Jr.	Assistant Lake Warden	3-17-64	At pleasure of the governor
Phil Ray McCorkle[213]	Park Ranger I	5-27-64	At pleasure of the governor
Ebert Gerald Guyton[214]	Assistant Lake Warden	6-18-64	At pleasure of the governor

STATE BOARD OF CORRECTION AND TRAINING [215]

Name	Place	Date	Term
Mrs. John L. Frye[216]	Robbins	8-16-61	7-1-67
Mrs. C. L. Gilliatt †	Shelby	8-16-61	7-1-67
Joseph W. Nordan †	Raleigh	8-16-61	7-1-67
Clyde Auman †	West End	8-8-63	7-1-69

---

201 Succeeded B. C. Trotter.
202 Succeeded Floyd J. Boiling.
203 Succeeded W. B. Austin.
204 Succeeded Amos Kearns.
205 Succeeded W. Eugene Simmons, resigned.
206 Succeeded E. D. Gaskins, resigned.
207 Succeeded Robert Walter Scott, resigned.
208 Succeeded Paul H. Thompson, resigned.
209 Succeeded Ryan Walker Martin, resigned.
200 The director is appointed by the governor and serves until the end of the governor's term or until a successor is appointed. G. S. 113-9.
201 Succeeded William P. Saunders.
202 Succeeded Hargrove Bowles, Jr., resigned 7-23-62.
203 These officers are employees of the Department of Conservation and Development, designated by the director of that department, and commissioned by the governor to serve at his pleasure. S. L., 1947, c. 577.
204 Succeeded Allen R. Conley, Jr.
205 Succeeded John D. Barnett, transferred.
206 Succeeded Rushian J. Gibson, transferred to State Lakes Division.
207 Succeeded Rushian J. Gibson, commission canceled, 6-20-63.
208 Succeeded Clyde H. Miller, transferred.
209 Succeeded James H. McQueen.
210 Succeeded Oren D. Hawkins, transferred.
211 Succeeded Charles O. Lucas, transferred.
212 Succeeded James M. Carey.
213 Succeeded Charles W. Brown.
214 Succeeded Van A. Pierce
215 The board consists of nine members appointed by the governor for six-year terms, plus the commissioner of public welfare who serves ex officio. The 1963 General Assembly changed the name of the board to the State Board of Juvenile Correction. G. S. 134-90; S. L., 1947, c. 226, S. L., 1963, c. 914, s. 4.
216 Succeeded Charles F. Strosnider, retired.

Name of Appointee	Address	Date Appointed	Date of Expiration
Elton Edwards †	Greensboro	8-8-63	7-1-69
Steed Rollins †	Durham	8-8-63	7-1-69
	THE COURTS COMMISSION [217]		
David M. Britt	Fairmont	7-25-63	12-31-70
Stephen B. Dolley, Jr.	Gastonia	7-25-63	12-31-70
J. J. Harrington	Lewiston	7-25-63	12-31-70
A. D. Folger, Jr.	Madison	7-25-63	12-31-70
Wilbur M. Jolly	Louisburg	7-25-63	12-31-70
Leonard W. Lloyd	Robbinsville	7-25-63	12-31-70
Karl W. McGhee	Wilmington	7-25-63	12-31-70
John Alexander McMahon	Chapel Hill	7-25-63	12-31-70
James B. McMillan	Charlotte	7-25-63	12-31-70
Dickson Phillips	Chapel Hill	7-25-63	12-31-70
J. Eugene Snyder	Lexington	7-25-63	12-31-70
H. Patrick Taylor [218]	Wadesboro	7-25-63	12-31-70
Lindsay C. Warren, Jr.	Goldsboro	7-25-63	12-31-70
Staton P. Williams	Albemarle	7-25-63	12-31-70
A. Augustus Zollicoffer, Jr.	Henderson	7-25-63	12-31-70
	THE ROBERT LEE DOUGHTON MEMORIAL COMMISSION [219]		
Mrs. R. S. Ferguson	Taylorsville	11-14-61	At pleasure of the governor
J. Harry Miller	Stony Point	11-14-61	At pleasure of the governor
A. Vance Chaote	Sparta	11-14-61	At pleasure of the governor
J. Kemp Doughton	Sparta	11-14-61	At pleasure of the governor
R. Austin Jones	West Jefferson	11-14-61	At pleasure of the governor
William B. Austin	Jefferson	11-14-61	At pleasure of the governor
Mrs. Stella W. Anderson	West Jefferson	11-14-61	At pleasure of the governor
C. A. Cannon, Chairman	Kannapolis	11-14-61	At pleasure of the governor
M. Smoot Lyles	Concord	11-14-61	At pleasure of the governor
Harold Coffey	Lenoir	11-14-61	At pleasure of the governor
Dennis S. Cook	Lenoir	11-14-61	At pleasure of the governor
Mrs. Margaret B. Moore	Lenoir	11-14-61	At pleasure of the governor
J. Gordon Bush	Lenoir	11-14-61	At pleasure of the governor

J. Sam Holbrook	Statesville	11-14-61	At pleasure of the governor
James V. Johnson	Statesville	11-14-61	At pleasure of the governor
Joe Knox	Mooresville	11-14-61	At pleasure of the governor
Jim Graham	Raleigh	11-14-61	At pleasure of the governor
John Kesler	Salisbury	11-14-61	At pleasure of the governor
Walter Woodson, Sr.	Salisbury	11-14-61	At pleasure of the governor
Leslie M. Weisiger	Salisbury	11-14-61	At pleasure of the governor
Mrs. E. G. Harwood	Albemarle	11-14-61	At pleasure of the governor
W. H. Morrow	Albemarle	11-14-61	At pleasure of the governor
Gordon H. Winkler	Boone	11-14-61	At pleasure of the governor
Robert C. Rivers	Boone	11-14-61	At pleasure of the governor
Fred M. Morrison	Shelby and Washington, D. C.	11-14-61	At pleasure of the governor

STATE BOARD OF EDUCATION [220]

Guy B. Phillips	Chapel Hill	4-13-61	4-1-69
W. Dallas Herring†	Rose Hill	4-13-61	4-1-69
John M. Reynolds[221]	Asheville	4-13-61	4-1-69
John A. Pritchett†	Windsor	7-5-63	4 1-71
Barton Hayes†	Lenoir	7-5-63	4 1-71

COMMISSION ON THE STUDY OF THE MANNER OF SELECTION OF MEMBERS OF THE SEVERAL BOARDS OF EDUCATION OF THE COUNTY AND CITY ADMINISTRATIVE SCHOOL UNITS OF THE STATE [222]

Lawson Brown	Lexington	7-20-61	Report to the 1963 General Assembly
Ben E. Fountain, Jr.	Chapel Hill and Elizabeth City	7-20-61	Report to the 1963 General Assembly
Herman H. West	Marble	7-20-61	Report to the 1963 General Assembly

[217] With the amendment of the state constitution in 1962, the new judicial article required changes in the courts. This commission, charged with drafting legislation to implement the article, consists of fifteen members to be appointed jointly by the governor, the president of the Senate, the speaker of the House of Representatives, and the chairman of the House and Senate judiciary committees. At least eight of the members shall have served in the General Assembly. All serve until work is completed or not later than December 31, 1970. S. L., 1963, Res. 73.

[218] Deceased April 12, 1964.

[219] By action of the 1961 General Assembly the commission consists of twenty-five members who are appointed by the governor and who serve at his pleasure. S. L. 1961, c. 1079, s. 1.

[220] The board is composed of thirteen members, ten of whom are appointed by the governor and confirmed by the General Assembly for eight-year terms. The lieutenant governor, the state treasurer, and the superintendent of public instruction serve as ex officio members. Constitution of North Carolina, Art. IX, Sec. 8; G. S. 115-16.1.

[221] Succeeded Gerald Cowan.

[222] As established by the 1961 General Assembly, the commission consists of nine members, three of whom are named by the governor, three by the lieutenant governor from the Senate membership, and three by the speaker of the House from the House membership. S. L., 1961, Res. 21.

Name of Appointee	Address	Date Appointed	Date of Expiration
NORTH CAROLINA BOARD OF HIGHER EDUCATION [223]			
N. Elton Aydlett†	Elizabeth City	7-1-61	6-30-69
Charles M. Reeves, Jr.[224]	Sanford	7-1-61	6-30-69
Mrs. Doris Goerch Horton[225]	Pittsboro	1-26-62	6-30-65
Mrs. Harry B. Stein[226]	Fayetteville	9-19-62	6-30-69
William A. Dees, Jr.[227]	Goldsboro	7-3-63	6-30-71
Joseph W. Grier, Jr.[228]	Charlotte	7-3-63	6-30-71
Allen H. Gwyn, Jr.[229]	Reidsville	7-9-64	6-30-67
John R. Jordan, Jr.[230]	Raleigh	7-15-64	6-30-71
W. Dallas Herring[231]	Rose Hill	7-22-64	6-30-65
Gordon H. Greenwood[232]	Black Mountain		
DIRECTOR OF HIGHER EDUCATION			
William C. Archie	Georgia	2-22-61	
BOARD OF CONTROL FOR THE SOUTHERN REGIONAL COUNCIL FOR EDUCATION [233]			
Charles F. Carroll†	Raleigh	6-12-61	6-30-65
W. Lunsford Crew†	Roanoke Rapids	7-20-62	6-30-66
William C. Archie[234]	Raleigh	8-13-61-64	6-30-64-68
William C. Friday[235]	Chapel Hill	6-14-63	6-30-67
STATE BOARD OF ELECTIONS [236]			
Robert S. Ewing[237]	Southern Pines	8-17-61	5-1-65
Dan S. Judd[238]	West Asheville	8-17-61	5-1-65
David M. McConnell†	Charlotte	8-17-61	5-1-65
Warren Williams†	Sanford	8-17-61	5-1-65
Joseph Zaytoun[239]	New Bern	8-17-61	5-1-65
C. B. Hawkins[240]	Bryson City	5-30-62	5-1-65
William Joslin[241]	Raleigh	7-31-62	5-1-65
Hiram H. Ward[242]	Lexington	6-9-64	5-1-65
THE GOVERNOR'S COMMITTEE ON EMPLOYMENT OF THE HANDICAPPED [243]			
C. A. McKnight	Charlotte	9-14-62	At pleasure of the governor
R. O. Evans	Charlotte	9-14-62	At pleasure of the governor
J. D. Hofler	Asheville	9-14-62	At pleasure of the governor

William F. Dowdy, Jr.	Shiloh	At pleasure of the governor	9-14-62
Marvin Zerden	Hickory	At pleasure of the governor	9-14-62
Earl H. Tate	Lenoir	At pleasure of the governor	9-14-62
Burke H. Taylor	New Bern	At pleasure of the governor	9-14-62
W. C. Grier	North Wilkesboro	At pleasure of the governor	9-14-62
Allen C. Mims	Rocky Mount	At pleasure of the governor	9-14-62
J. Frank Efird	Salisbury	At pleasure of the governor	9-14-62
Clyde Rhyne	Sanford	At pleasure of the governor	9-14-62
J. O. Thomas[244]	Leaksville	At pleasure of the governor	9-14-62
Ben McDonald	Wilmington	At pleasure of the governor	9-14-62
John T. Brandon	Winston-Salem	At pleasure of the governor	9-14-62
Thomas M. Mullen	Charlotte	At pleasure of the governor	9-14-62
Leslie Brady	Newton	At pleasure of the governor	9-14-62
R. C. Godwin	Raleigh	At pleasure of the governor	9-14-62

[223] The board is composed of nine members, all appointed by the governor for eight-year terms. One appointee must be a member of the State Board of Education and no member shall be an officer or employee of the state. The director is appointed by the Board of Higher Education with the approval of the governor. G. S. 116-156, 116-163; S. L., 1955, c. 1186, s. 2.

[224] Succeeded Charles H. Reynolds, resigned.

[225] Succeeded Mrs. Thomas R. Easterling, resigned.

[226] Succeeded Charles M. Reeves, Jr., resigned.

[227] Succeeded John P. Kennedy, Jr., resigned.

[228] Succeeded L. P. McLendon.

[229] Succeeded William F. Womble.

[230] Succeeded Oliver C. Carmichael, resigned.

[231] Filled the unexpired term of Allen H. Gwyn, Jr., resigned.

[232] Filled the unexpired term of W. Dallas Herring.

[233] The North Carolina membership of this board consists of the governor, who serves ex officio during his tenure of office, and four additional members appointed by the governor for four-year terms. At least one of the gubernatorial appointees shall be selected from the field of education and at least one shall be a member of the legislature. S. L., 1949, Res. 26; S. L., 1957, Res. 27.

[234] Succeeded H. Harris Purks, resigned.

[235] Succeeded Alfonso Elder.

[236] The board consists of five members appointed by the governor for terms of four years each. Not more than three of the members may be of the same political party. G. S. 163-8.

[237] Succeeded William T. McShane.

[238] Succeeded Mrs. Charles W. Tillett.

[239] Succeeded Joseph M. Bryan.

[240] Succeeded Dan. S. Judd, resigned.

[241] Succeeded David M. McConnell, resigned.

[242] Succeeded Robert S. Ewing, resigned.

[243] As created by the 1961 General Assembly, the committee consists of an indefinite number of state leaders and representatives of industry, business, agriculture, labor, veterans, women, and religious, educational, civic, welfare, and scientific groups, and all other interested groups or individuals approved by the governor's executive committee. G. S. 143-283.4; S. L., 1961, c. 981.

[244] Declined the appointment.

Name of Appointee	Address	Date Appointed	Date of Expiration
H. A. Wood	Raleigh	9-14-62	At pleasure of the governor
Walter Fuller	Raleigh	9-14-62	At pleasure of the governor
John Kennedy	Fayetteville	9-14-62	At pleasure of the governor
Francis W. Mulcahy	Winston-Salem	9-14-62	At pleasure of the governor
A. H. Zealy, Jr.	Goldsboro	9-14-62	At pleasure of the governor
Philip Belt	Raleigh	9-14-62	At pleasure of the governor
Thomas A. Bateman	Washington	10-1-62	At pleasure of the governor
S. Marvin Burton	Raleigh	2-4-64	At pleasure of the governor
Robert Lassiter	Chapel Hill	2-4-64	At pleasure of the governor
Milton N. Hinnant	Charlotte	6-10-64	At pleasure of the governor
Benjamin G. Runkle	Raleigh	9-20-64	At pleasure of the governor
Mrs. Lou E. Culbreth	Southern Pines	9-16-64	At pleasure of the governor
Herbert L. Hawley	Chapel Hill	9-16-64	At pleasure of the governor
S. Thad Cherry	Fayetteville	9-16-64	At pleasure of the governor
Charles A. Burgess	Raleigh	9-16-64	At pleasure of the governor
Thomas H. Ward, Jr.	Greensboro	9-16-64	At pleasure of the governor
James E. Filipski	Greensboro	9-16-64	At pleasure of the governor
Mrs. Jewel P. Osborne	High Point	11-20-64	At pleasure of the governor
Robert M. Smith	Mt. Airy	11-20-64	At pleasure of the governor
Philip R. Penland	Asheville	11-20-64	At pleasure of the governor
Mrs. Bert G. Tyson	Greenville	11-20-64	At pleasure of the governor
Crayton E. Rowe	Charlotte	12-15-64	At pleasure of the governor
C. Coleman Cates	Burlington	12-15-64	At pleasure of the governor
Robert Pace	Chapel Hill	12-15-64	At pleasure of the governor
Ronnie Shavlik	Raleigh	12-15-64	At pleasure of the governor
Herbert O. Sieker	Durham	1-4-65	At pleasure of the governor

THE GOVERNOR'S EXECUTIVE COMMITTEE ON EMPLOYMENT OF THE HANDICAPPED [245]

Name of Appointee	Address	Date Appointed	Date of Expiration
Al Bechtold*	Charlotte	1-17-62	6-30-62-65
Gary C. Davis*	High Point	1-17-62	6-30-62-65
Stanley Frank*	Greensboro	1-17-62	6-30-62-65
William H. Ruffin*	Durham	1-17-62	6-30-62-65
James Semans*	Durham	1-17-62	6-30-62-65
James A. Babcock	Raleigh	1-17-62	6-30-63

Henry Belk*	Goldsboro	1-17-62-63	6-30-63-66
Robert Hess	Durham	1-17-62	6-30-63
Hugh Chatham	Elkin	1-17-62	6-30-63
Mrs. Charles Norwood	Goldsboro	7-22-61	6-30-63
W. C. Boren III, Chairman*	Greensboro	1-17-61-64	6-30-64-67
John B. Hatfield*	Greensboro	1-17-61-64	6-30-64-67
Maurice Hill*	Morganton	1-17-61-64	6-30-64-67
Arthur H. Jones	Charlotte	1-17-61	6-30-64
Louie Woodbury, Jr.*	Wilmington	1-17-61-64	6-30-64-67
Stephen H. Van Every[246]	Charlotte	8-12-63	6-30-65
Mrs. George Nicholson†	Chapel Hill	8-12-63	6-30-66
Mrs. Lucille Clasz†	Asheville	8-12-63	6-30-66
James Allen[247]	Louisburg	12-10-63	6-30-66
Robert William Watkins[248]	Boone	12-10-63	6-30-66
John A. Tate, Jr.[249]	Charlotte	11-25-64	6-30-67

EMPLOYMENT SECURITY COMMISSION [250]

Henry Eli Kendall, Chairman†	Raleigh	7-8-61	7-1-65
Thomas Bernard O'Connor[251]	Forest City	7-8-61	7-1-65
James Ward Seabrook[252]	Fayetteville	7-8-61	7-1-65
Maurice T. Van Hecke†	Chapel Hill	7-8-61	7-1-65
Billy Earl Andrews[253]	Durham	2-11-64	7-1-67
Horace E. Stacy, Jr.[254]	Lumberton	2-17-64	7-1-65
Charles L. Hunley[255]	Monroe	9-28-64	7-1-67
Charles T. Kivett[256]	Greensboro	9-28-64	7-1-67

[245] As organized by the 1961 General Assembly the committee consists of fifteen members to be appointed by the governor. Five members are initially appointed for one year, five for two years, and five for three years; thereafter terms shall be set for three years each. Ex officio members include the governor, the commissioner of labor, the commissioner of insurance, the chairman of the Employment Security Commission, and the director of vocational rehabilitation. G. S. 143-283.5; S. L., 1961, c. 981.
[246] Succeeded Al Bechtold, resigned.
[247] Succeeded Hugh Chatham, resigned.
[248] Succeeded Mrs. Charles Norwood.
[249] Succeeded Arthur H. Jones.
[250] The commission consists of seven members appointed by the governor and by the governor for four-year terms. The chairman, appointed also by the governor for a four-year term, shall not engage in any other business, vocation, or employment. G. S. 96-3.
[251] Succeeded Mrs. Quentin Gregory.
[252] Succeeded Crayon C. Efird.
[253] Succeeded Bruce E. Davis.
[254] Succeeded Maurice T. Van Hecke, deceased.
[255] Succeeded W. Benton Pipkin.
[256] Succeeded R. Dave Hall; Kivett's term ended with his resignation 12-10-64.

Name of Appointee	Address	Date Appointed	Date of Expiration
EMPLOYMENT SECURITY COMMISSION ADVISORY COUNCIL [257]			
Mrs. W. Arthur Tripp[258]	Greenville	4-3-64	At pleasure of the governor
BOARD OF TRUSTEES OF THE NORTH CAROLINA FIREMEN'S PENSION FUND [259]			
Clifton Blue[260]	Aberdeen	11-24-64	6-30-67
Berry C. Gibson†	Charlotte	11-24-64	6-30-67
I. Miller Warren†	Plymouth	11-24-64	6-30-67
BOARD OF DIRECTORS OF THE FLUE-CURED TOBACCO COOPERATIVE STABILIZATION CORPORATION [261]			
E. Y. Floyd†	Raleigh	8-27-63	7-1-66
GENERAL STATUTES COMMISSION [262]			
Robin L. Hinson* [263]	Rockingham	7-14-61-63	6-1-63-65
James L. Woodson[264]	Salisbury	7-14-61	6-1-63
Richard S. Clark[265]	Monroe	5-29-63	6-1-65
STATE BOARD OF HEALTH [266]			
Mrs. W. Kerr Scott [267]	Haw River	2-13-61	5-1-61
Lenox D. Baker†	Durham	9-21-61	5-1-65
Glenn Hooper[268]	Dunn	9-21-61	5-1-65
David Townley Redfarn[269]	Wadesboro	9-21-61	5-1-65
B. W. Dawsey†	Gastonia	10-4-63	5-1-67
S. G. Koonce[270]	Chadbourn	10-4-63	5-1-67
HEALTH INSURANCE ADVISORY BOARD [271]			
Joseph E. Barnes*	Raleigh	12-14-61-63	9-15-63-65
Watts Hill, Jr.*	Durham	12-14-61-63	9-15-63-65
Hubert F. Ledford*	Raleigh	12-14-61-63	9-15-63-65
Frank W. Jones*	Newton	12-14-61-63	9-15-63-65
John T. Manning*	Chapel Hill	12-14-61-63	9-15-63-65
O. F. Stafford*	Greensboro	12-14-61-63	9-15-63-65
Mrs. Stella Spencer*	Lenoir	12-14-61-63	9-15-63-65
John C. Williamson*	Knightdale	12-14-61-63	9-15-63-65

Gerard de Trafford Worthington	Greensboro	12-14-61	9-15-63
C. Cecil Duncan[272]	Charlotte	11-17-63-63	9-15-63-65

HERITAGE SQUARE COMMISSION [273]

O. Arthur Kirkman, *Chairman*	High Point	7-18-62	6-30-67
John Parker	Chapel Hill	7-18-62	6-30-67
Gordon Hanes	Winston-Salem	7-18-62	6-30-67
Robert Lee Humber	Greenville	7-18-62	6-30-67
H. P. Taylor, Jr.	Wadesboro	7-18-62	6-30-67
Mrs. John Miles Abernethy	Newton	7-18-62	6-30-65
Brian Shawcroft	Raleigh	7-18-62	6-30-65
Pearson H. Stewart	Chapel Hill	7-18-62	6-30-65

[257] Membership is composed of an equal number of employers and employees who are representative of their vocation, employment, or affiliation, and such public members as may be designated. G. S. 96-4 (e).

[258] Succeeded Mrs. R. C. Lewellyn, resigned.

[259] The board consists of five members, three of whom are appointed by the governor for four-year terms, and two of whom are ex officio: the state insurance commissioner and the state auditor. Of the appointive members, one must be a paid fireman, one a volunteer fireman, and one a representative of the public at large. S. L., 1959, c. 1212.

[260] Succeeded Clyde Carter.

[261] One member of this board is appointed for a three-year term by the director of the Agricultural Extension Service or any other public official or commission, in this case, the governor. G. S. 54-146 (b); S. L., 1963, c. 1168, s. 11.

[262] The commission is made up of nine members appointed for two-year terms as follows: one each by the presidents of the North Carolina State Bar and North Carolina Bar Association, one each by the deans of the law schools of Duke University, Wake Forest College, and the University of North Carolina, one each by the president of the Senate and the speaker of the House of Representatives of the General Assembly, and two by the governor. G. S. 164-14 (a).

[263] Succeeded Fred W. Bynum, Jr.

[264] Succeeded Carl V. Venters.

[265] Succeeded James L. Woodson.

[266] The board is composed of nine members serving terms of four years each, five of whom are appointed by the governor and four of whom are elected by the North Carolina Medical Society. One of the members appointed by the governor shall be a licensed pharmacist, one a reputable dairyman, one a licensed dentist, and one a licensed veterinarian. G. S. 130-4, 130-5; S.L., 1957, c. 1357, s. 1.

[267] Succeeded Mrs. J. E. Latta, resigned.

[268] Succeeded Zeno L. Edwards, Sr.

[269] Succeeded Mrs. W. Kerr Scott, resigned.

[270] Succeeded Jasper Carlton Jackson.

[271] As authorized by the 1961 General Assembly, the board consists of ten members, nine of whom are appointed by the governor for two-year terms and one of whom is the commissioner of insurance of North Carolina who serves as ex officio member. Five of the appointive members must be from the public at large and four are appointed from the insurance industry upon recommendation of the commissioner of insurance. G. S. 58-262.1, 58-262.2; S. L., 1961, c. 1044.

[272] Succeeded Gerard de Trafford Worthington, resigned.

[273] The commission was created by the 1961 General Assembly for the purpose of planning and providing suitable buildings for the North Carolina State Library, the State Department of Archives and History, the North Carolina Museum of Art, and the State Museum of Natural History. It consists of nine persons appointed by the governor for initial terms of six and four years, and for subsequent terms of six years. At least two members shall have served in the General Assembly. G. S. 129-18, 129-19; S. L., 1961, c. 385.

Name of Appointee	Address	Date Appointed	Date of Expiration
Mrs. Earl Teague	Statesville	7-18-62	6-30-65
Thomas D. Bunn[274]	Raleigh	6-7-63	6-30-67
George M. Stephens, Jr.[275]	Raleigh	12-17-64	6-30-67
STATE HIGHWAY COMMISSION [276]			
Merrill Evans, *Chairman* * [277]	Ahoskie	2-6-61-61	6-30-61-65
Clifton L. Benson * [278]	Raleigh	5-29-61-63	6-30-63-65
Yates Randolph Bennett	Burnsville	7-11-61	6-30-65
Cyrus Watson Brame	North Wilkesboro	7-11-61	6-30-65
Daniel G. Bell	Morehead City	7-11-61	6-30-65
Arthur Graham Elliott	Washington	7-11-61	6-30-65
Duncan McLauchlin Faircloth	Clinton	7-11-61	6-30-65
James Kirk Glenn	Winston-Salem	7-11-61	6-30-65
William Edwin Horner	Sanford	7-11-61	6-30-65
David Worth Joyner	Rocky Mount	7-11-61	6-30-65
Ted Jordan	Robbinsville	7-11-61	6-30-65
Jackson Bristol Kirksey	Morganton	7-11-61	6-30-65
John Clinton Newton, Jr.	Shelby	7-11-61	6-30-65
James Gwaltney W. MacLamroc	Greensboro	7-11-61	6-30-65
Thomas Rodwell McLean	Fayetteville	7-11-61	6-30-65
E. Murray Tate, Jr.	Hickory	7-11-61	6-30-65
John Gilliam Wood	Edenton	7-11-61	6-30-65
James Elsie Webb	Ellerbe	7-11-61	6-30-65
Paul Reid Younts	Charlotte	7-11-61	6-30-65
Andrew W. Nesbitt [279]	Fairview	7-11-62	6-30-65
H. Graham Phillips[280]	Jacksonville	10-11-62	6-30-65
John O. Buchanan[281]	Asheville	8-17-64	6-30-65
DIRECTOR OF HIGHWAYS			
Willard Farrington Babcock	Raleigh	7-1-62	6-30-66
CONTROLLER OF STATE HIGHWAY COMMISSION			
E. T. Aiken, *Acting Controller*	Raleigh	4-1-62	6-30-66
DIRECTOR OF SECONDARY ROADS			
Benjamin E. Roney	Rocky Mount	7-20-61	At pleasure of the commission

HISTORIC BATH COMMISSION [276]

Name	Location	Date	
Mrs. Luther H. Hodges	Washington, D. C.	5-4-61	At pleasure of the governor
Elizabeth Thompson	Raleigh	5-4-61	At pleasure of the governor
Mrs. George Maurice Morris	Washington, D. C.	5-4-61	At pleasure of the governor
Mrs. Samuel N. Clark	Tarboro	5-4-61	At pleasure of the governor
Mrs. William T. Old	Norfolk, Virginia	5-4-61	At pleasure of the governor
Mrs. Edward Pryor	Bath, England	11-29-61	At pleasure of the governor
James A. Stenhouse	Charlotte	12-6-61	At pleasure of the governor
Mrs. Charles A. Cannon	Kannapolis	12-6-61	At pleasure of the governor
C. Wingate Reed	Washington	12-6-61	At pleasure of the governor
William W. Studdert	Washington	12-6-61	At pleasure of the governor
Mrs. Claude E. Venters	Bath	12-6-61	At pleasure of the governor
Mrs. Emily H. Warren	Washington	12-6-61	At pleasure of the governor
Mrs. Harry McMullan	Washington	3-9-62	At pleasure of the governor
Mrs. John A. Tankard	Bath	12-6-61	At pleasure of the governor
Mrs. Marjorie S. Charles [283]	Norfolk, Virginia	1-2-63	At pleasure of the governor
Herbert R. Paschal, Jr.	Greenville	5-31-63	At pleasure of the governor
Mrs. Taylor B. Attmore, Jr. [284]	Washington	5-5-64	At pleasure of the governor
Milo Gibbs [285]	Washington	5-5-64	At pleasure of the governor
Mrs. G. W. Marsh	Bath	5-5-64	At pleasure of the governor

[274] Succeeded H. P. Taylor, Jr., who did not accept appointment.

[275] Succeeded Thomas D. Bunn, resigned.

[276] The commission as set up by the General Assembly of 1957 consisted of seven members appointed by the governor for four-year terms. The governor designated one member to be chairman for two years. The 1961 General Assembly reorganized the commission, effective on July 1, 1961. Under the new law a chairman and eighteen members were appointed by the governor for four-year terms. Commissioners under both provisions were chosen to represent all interests of the state, both geographic and economic, and not to represent any particular area. The director of highways and the controller of the Highway Commission are appointed by the commission with the approval of the governor for four-year terms. The director of secondary roads is appointed by the commission with the approval of the governor and serves at the pleasure of the commission. S. L., 1957, c. 65, s. 1; S. L., 1961, c. 232, s. 1; G. S. 136-1, 136-4, 136-4.1, 136-4.3.

[277] Succeeded J. Melville Broughton, Jr.

[278] Succeeded Lee White, resigned.

[279] Succeeded Yates Randolph Bennett, retired.

[280] Succeeded Daniel G. Bell, deceased.

[281] Succeeded Andrew W. Nesbitt, resigned.

[282] The commission is composed of at least fifteen members who are appointed by the governor and who serve at his pleasure. Three others serve as ex officio members: the director of the Department of Archives and History, the chairman of the Beaufort County Board of Commissioners, and the mayor of Bath. S. L., 1959, c. 1005.

[283] Succeeded Mrs. Oscar Smith, deceased.

[284] Succeeded Mrs. John A. Tankard, resigned.

[285] Succeeded Lindsay C. Warren, resigned.

Name of Appointee	Address	Date Appointed	Date of Expiration
Mrs. Roscoe Tankard	Bath	5-5-64	At pleasure of the governor
Mrs. William Rumley, Jr.	Washington	5-5-64	At pleasure of the governor

HISTORIC EDENTON COMMISSION[296]

Name of Appointee	Address	Date Appointed	Date of Expiration
Mrs. Edward G. Bond	Edenton	2-26-62	At pleasure of the governor
Irwin Belk	Charlotte	2-26-62	At pleasure of the governor
S. N. Clark	Tarboro	2-26-62	At pleasure of the governor
Jonathan Daniels	Raleigh	2-26-62	At pleasure of the governor
Mrs. Carrie M. Earnhardt	Edenton	2-26-62	At pleasure of the governor
Mrs. Frank P. Graham	New York City	2-26-62	At pleasure of the governor
Mrs. Inglis Fletcher	Edenton	2-26-62	At pleasure of the governor
Richard H. Howland	Washington, D. C.	2-26-62	At pleasure of the governor
Robert Lee Humber, Chairman	Greenville	2-26-62	At pleasure of the governor
Mrs. J. Harold Lineberger	Belmont	2-26-62	At pleasure of the governor
Dan M. Paul	Raleigh	2-26-62	At pleasure of the governor
Mrs. K. S. Trowbridge	Plymouth	2-26-62	At pleasure of the governor
James Webb	Greensboro	2-26-62	At pleasure of the governor
Mrs. J. Emmett Winslow	Nags Head	2-26-62	At pleasure of the governor
A. C. Boyce	Edenton	8-28-62	At pleasure of the governor
Albert Byrum	Edenton	8-28-62	At pleasure of the governor
Richard D. Dixon, Jr.	Edenton	8-28-62	At pleasure of the governor
Mrs. F. B. Drane	Edenton	8-28-62	At pleasure of the governor
Mrs. E. N. Elliott	Edenton	8-28-62	At pleasure of the governor
B. Warner Evans	Edenton	8-28-62	At pleasure of the governor
John W. Graham	Edenton	8-29-62	At pleasure of the governor
J. Welch Harriss	High Point	8-28-62	At pleasure of the governor
Mrs. John A. Kramer	Edenton	8-28-62	At pleasure of the governor
Mrs. Leon G. Leary	Edenton	8-28-62	At pleasure of the governor
Elizabeth Vann Moore	Edenton	8-28-62	At pleasure of the governor
Mrs. Trent Ragland	Raleigh	8-28-62	At pleasure of the governor
Mrs. W. B. Rosevear	Edenton	8-28-62	At pleasure of the governor
Marie Thomas	Charlotte	8-28-62	At pleasure of the governor
David M. Warren	Edenton	8-28-62	At pleasure of the governor

Gilliam Wood	Edenton	8-28-62	At pleasure of the governor
Mrs. Joseph C. Mason	Winston-Salem	9-26-62	At pleasure of the governor

HISTORIC HILLSBOROUGH COMMISSION[287]

Mrs. Lyman A. Cotten	Chapel Hill	6-24-63	5-1-69
Mrs. D. St. Pierre Du Bose	Chapel Hill	6-24-63	5-1-69
Mrs. Alfred G. Engstrom	Hillsboro	6-24-63	5-1-69
Edwin J. Hamlin	Hillsboro	6-24-63	5-1-69
Frank H. Kenan, Jr.	Durham	6-24-63	5-1-69
L. J. Phipps	Chapel Hill	6-24-63	5-1-69
Mrs. L. Richardson Preyer	Greensboro	6-24-63	5-1-69
C. W. Stanford, Jr.	Raleigh	6-24-63	5-1-69
Richard Walser	Raleigh	6-24-63	5-1-69
Victor S. Bryant, Sr.	Durham	6-24-63	5-1-67
E. Wilson Cole	Hillsboro	6-24-63	5-1-67
Mrs. John W. Labouisse	Durham	6-24-63	5-1-67
James G. W. MacLamroc	Greensboro	6-24-63	5-1-67
Henry W. Moore	Hillsboro	6-24-63	5-1-67
Robert J. Murphy, *Chairman*	Hillsboro	6-24-63	5-1-67
Mrs. J. C. Webb	Hillsboro	6-24-63	5-1-67
James M. Johnston	Washington, D. C.	6-24-63	5-1-67
John A. Kellenberger	Greensboro	6-24-63	5-1-67
Mangum Weeks	Alexandria, Virginia	8-5-63	5-1-67
Mrs. Ernest L. Ives	Southern Pines	8-5-63	5-1-67
Mary B. Forrest	Hillsboro	6-24-63	5-1-65
Voit Gilmore	Southern Pines	6-24-63	5-1-65
A. H. Graham	Hillsboro	6-24-63	5-1-65
Mary Henderson	Chapel Hill	6-24-63	5-1-65
William S. Powell	Chapel Hill	6-24-63	5-1-65
Mrs. S. R. Prince	Reidsville	6-24-63	5-1-65

[286] As established by the 1961 General Assembly, the commission consists of not less than fifteen members to be appointed by the governor, as well as three ex officio members: the mayor of Edenton, the chairman of the Board of Commissioners of Chowan County, and the director of the Department of Archives and History. The governor's appointees serve at his pleasure. *S. L. 1961*, c. 1009, s. 1.

[287] As established by the 1963 General Assembly, the commission for the preservation and restoration of historic Hillsborough consists of not less than fifteen members appointed by the governor. Initial terms are as follows: one-third of membership appointed for two years; one-third, for four years; and one-third for six years. Reappointments are for six years. Ex officio members include the mayor of Hillsborough; the chairman of the Board of Commissioners, the register of deeds, and the clerk of Superior Court of Orange County; and the director of the State Department of Archives and History. *S. L., 1963*, c. 196, s. 1.

Name of Appointee	Address	Date Appointed	Date of Expiration
Ralph H. Scott	Mebane	6-24-63	5-1-65
Mrs. A. B. Stoney	Morganton	6-24-63	5-1-65
James Webb	Greensboro	6-24-63	5-1-65

HISTORIC SITES ADVISORY COMMITTEE[288]

Name of Appointee	Address	Date Appointed	Date of Expiration
James McClure Clarke	Asheville	4-22-63	7-1-67
Mrs. P. P. McCain	Wilson	4-22-63	7-1-67
James A. Stenhouse	Charlotte	4-22-63	7-1-67

HISTORIC SWANNSBOROUGH COMMISSION[289]

Name of Appointee	Address	Date Appointed	Date of Expiration
Mrs. Clara P. Baker	Swansboro	4-10-64	At pleasure of the governor
Mrs. W. Carroll Bryan	Jacksonville	4-10-64	At pleasure of the governor
Martha Bell Conway	Richmond	4-10-64	At pleasure of the governor
Lyman A. Cotten	Chapel Hill	4-10-64	At pleasure of the governor
Percy G. Grant	Holly Ridge	4-10-64	At pleasure of the governor
Harry V. Hamilton	Cedar Point	4-10-64	At pleasure of the governor
J. L. Huff	Swansboro	4-10-64	At pleasure of the governor
Mrs. B. B. C. Kesler	Richlands	4-10-64	At pleasure of the governor
Tucker R. Littleton	Swansboro	4-10-64	At pleasure of the governor
Mrs. Daisy S. Moore	Swansboro	4-10-64	At pleasure of the governor
Alice Noble	Chapel Hill	4-10-64	At pleasure of the governor
Percival Perry	Winston-Salem	4-10-64	At pleasure of the governor
F. C. Salisbury	Morehead City	4-10-64	At pleasure of the governor
Mrs. MaBelle Smith	Raleigh	4-10-64	At pleasure of the governor
Mrs. Mary Ward Smith	Swansboro	4-10-64	At pleasure of the governor
Mrs. J. O. Tally, Jr.	Fayetteville	4-10-64	At pleasure of the governor
Carl E. Weeks	Swansboro	4-10-64	At pleasure of the governor
W. G. Womble, Jr.	Raleigh	4-10-64	At pleasure of the governor

NORTH CAROLINA HOSPITALS BOARD OF CONTROL[290]

Name of Appointee	Address	Date Appointed	Date of Expiration
H. W. Kendall†	Greensboro	7-25-61	4-1-65
C. Wayland Spruill [291]	Windsor	7-25-61	4-1-65
David W. Royster, Sr.[292]	Shelby	7-25-61	4-1-65
Mrs. W. Kerr Scott	Haw River	7-25-61	4-1-65

Name	City		
W. Lunsford Crew* [293]	Roanoke Rapids	7-25-61-62	4-1-62-66
William L. Thorp [294]	Rocky Mount	7-25-61	4-1-63
Yates Palmer†	Valdese	7-25-61	4-1-65
William Austin McFarland	Columbus	8-3-61	4-1-65
N. Cortez Green†	Williamston	5-14-62	4-1-66
William P. Kemp†	Goldsboro	5-14-62	4-1-66

NORTH CAROLINA INDUSTRIAL COMMISSION [295]

Name	City		
John Robbins McLaughlin [296]	Statesville	8-24-61	5-1-67
Forrest H. Shuford II [297]	Raleigh	12-6-62	5-1-67
J. W. Bean, Chairman†	Raleigh	9-9-63	5-1-69

INSURANCE ADVISORY BOARD [298]

Name	City		
J. Leslie Atkins, Jr. [299]	Durham	12-14-61	9-1-65
Harry E. Bray†	Providence	12-14-61	9-1-65
L. M. Buchanan†	Greenville	12-14-61	9-1-65
H. Ralston Thompson [300]	Yanceyville	2-20-62	9-1-65
Robert G. Deyton†	Raleigh	10-2-63	9-1-67

[288] As created by the 1963 General Assembly the committee consists of seven members, which include the following ex officio members: the state budget officer, the chairman of the department of history of the University of North Carolina, dean of the school of design of North Carolina State College, and the director of the Department of Conservation and Development. Of the three gubernatorial appointive members who serve four-year terms, one must reside in the eastern section of the state, one in the piedmont, and one in the western section of the state. G. S. 121-8.1; S. L., 1963, c. 210, s. 2.

[289] As created by the 1963 General Assembly, the commission consists of not less than fifteen members who are appointed by the governor and who serve at his pleasure. In addition to the gubernatorial appointees, three others serve ex officio: the mayor of Swansboro, the chairman of the Board of Commissioners of Onslow County, and the director of the State Department of Archives and History. S. L., 1963, c. 607.

[290] The board consisted of fifteen members appointed by the governor for terms of four years each. One member was chosen from each of the twelve congressional districts and three were selected at large. In 1963 the board was incorporated in the State Board of Mental Health. G. S. 122-7. See footnote 339 for further information.

[291] Succeeded J. F. Strickland, resigned.
[292] Succeeded Mrs. Reba Gavin, resigned.
[293] Succeeded Wayland Spruill.
[294] Succeeded I. D. Thorp.
[295] The commission is composed of three members, including the chairman, appointed by the governor for six-year terms. G. S. 97-77.
[296] Succeeded R. Brookes Peters.
[297] Succeeded John Robbins McLaughlin, resigned.
[298] The board is composed of seven members, six of whom are appointed by the governor and one of whom, the commissioner of insurance, is an ex officio member and chairman. Appointments and reappointments are for four-year terms. The governor appoints members to fill any unexpired term of office and may remove members when he feels the public interest requires such action. G. S. 58-27.1.
[299] Succeeded W. H. Andrews, Jr.
[300] Succeeded Harry E. Bray, resigned.

Name of Appointee	Address	Date Appointed	Date of Expiration
H. P. Mobley†	Williamston	10-2-63	9-1-67
Max O. Welborn†	Yadkinville	10-2-63	9-1-67
North Carolina Commission on Interstate Cooperation[301]			
T. Wade Bruton†*	Raleigh	8-24-61-63	6-30-63-65
David S. Coltrane†*	Raleigh	8-24-61-63	6-30-63-65
George W. Randall†*	Raleigh	8-24-61-63	6-30-63-65
Charles L. Wheeler[302]	Raleigh	5-19-64	6-30-65
Judicial Council[303]			
Louis W. Gaylord, Jr.*[304]	Greenville	7-6-61-63	6-30-63-65
John C. Kesler†*	Salisbury	7-6-61-63	6-30-63-65
John H. Kerr Reservoir Development Commission[305]			
Edwin W. Woodhouse[306]	Raleigh	2-8-62-63	Term of office
G. Ernest Beal†[307]	Red Oak	2-8-62	Term of office
Robert W. Scott[308]	Haw River	2-8-62	Term of office
Charles F. Blackburn	Henderson	2-8-62	7-26-67
William B. Tarry	Oxford	2-8-62	7-26-67
Robert Clyde Mitchell	Manson	2-8-62	7-26-67
Charles Bradshaw[309]	Raleigh	2-8-62	7-26-67
W. R. Lawrence†	Colerain	2-8-62	7-26-67
John T. Church[310]	Henderson	12-18-64	7-26-67
J. C. Cooper, Sr.†	Henderson	8-9-63	7-26-69
Tom Harrington, Sr.†	Henderson	8-9-63	7-26-69
N. Warren Weldon†	Stovall	8-9-63	7-26-69
Special Police for the John H. Kerr Reservoir Development Commission[311]			
Paul M. Anderson	Henderson	8-29-61	At will of the governor
Lemuel P. Eastwood	Henderson	8-29-61	At will of the governor
Jesse J. Stem, Jr.	Henderson	8-29-61	At will of the governor
Willim L. Twisdale	Henderson	8-29-61	At will of the governor
Board of Commissioners of the Law Enforcement Officers' Benefit and Retirement Fund[312]			
Jay Charles Rumple[313]	Statesville	11-14-61	At pleasure of the governor

W. B. Lentz†	Raleigh	4-17-62	At pleasure of the governor
William A. McCall [314]	Charlotte	4-17-62	At pleasure of the governor
Travis Clement [315]	Durham	10-9-62	At pleasure of the governor

STATE LEGISLATIVE BUILDING COMMISSION [316]

Oliver R. Rowe	Charlotte	8-24-64	To serve until completion of duties

COMMISSION ON THE DEDICATION OF THE STATE LEGISLATIVE BUILDING [317]

John W. Green	Raleigh	7-9-64	At pleasure of the governor
Richard Peyton Woodson III	Raleigh	7-9-64	At pleasure of the governor

[301] The commission is composed of three administrative officials appointed by the president of the Senate, and three representatives designated by the speaker of the House of Representatives. G. S. 143-178, 143-182; S. L., 1961, c. 1108.

[302] Succeeded T. Wade Bruton, resigned.

[303] The council consists of fourteen members, of whom two are appointed by the governor for two-year terms, three senators designated by the president of the Senate, and three representatives designated by the speaker of the House. The 1961 General Assembly provided for a tenth member, the speaker of the House of Representatives. Other members consist of the chief justice of the Supreme Court, two judges of the Superior Court designated by the chief justice, the attorney general, and eight additional members. Appointive members are selected on the basis of their interest in and competency for study of law reform. G. S. 7-448, 7-449.

[304] Succeeded Ike E. Andrews.

[305] The 1961 General Assembly increased the total membership on this board from ten to twelve to be appointed by the governor. One person representing the Board of Conservation and Development, one from the North Carolina Recreation Commission, and one from the Wildlife Resources Commission serve as ex officio members also appointed by the governor and serve only during their terms of office in the respective commissions. The remaining nine who serve for six years are chosen as follows: two residents of Granville County, two residents of Warren County, and three at large. G. S. 143-284: S. L., 1951, c. 444, s. 1; S. L., 1961, c. 650.

[306] Succeeded Charles L. McCullers as the representative of the Recreation Commission.

[307] Representative of the Wildlife Resources Commission.

[308] Succeeded W. Eugene Simmons as the representative of the Board of Conservation and Development.

[309] Succeeded John P. Swain.

[310] Succeeded W. R. Lawrence, deceased.

[311] An indefinite number of qualified persons serve at the will of the governor or until the termination of their employment with the John H. Kerr Reservoir Commission. G. S. 143-286.

[312] The board consists of the state auditor, chairman ex officio, the state treasurer, the state insurance commissioner, and four members to be appointed by the governor to serve at his will. One of the appointive members shall be a sheriff, one a police officer, one a state law enforcement officer, and one a representative of the public at large. G. S. 143-166.

[313] Succeeded W. Boman Sanders, resigned.

[314] Succeeded C. C. Stoker, resigned.

[315] Succeeded M. E. Cavendish, resigned.

[316] The commission consists of seven members as follows: three appointed by the governor, two who have served in the state Senate appointed by the president of the Senate, and two who have served in the House of Representatives appointed by the speaker of the House. S. L., 1959, c. 938.

[317] The commission, as created by the 1963 General Assembly, consists of members of the State Legislative Building Commission, members of the Legislative Building Governing Commission, and a representative of the architects and builders. Two persons are to be appointed by the president of the Senate, two by the speaker of the House of Representatives, two by the chief justice of the Supreme Court of North Carolina, and two by the governor of the state. S. L., 1963, c. 297.

George Carrington†	Burlington	7-5-63	7-1-67
Royster Chamblee	Raleigh	7-5-63	7-1-67
Dwight W. Quinn[331]	Kannapolis	9-24-63	7-1-65
William R. Stanford†	Durham	7-29-64	7-1-68
Paul W. Bumbarger, Jr.†	Hickory	9-29-64	7-1-68
B. Lee Mootz[332]	Winston-Salem	7-29-64	7-1-68

ADVISORY COUNCIL TO THE NORTH CAROLINA MEDICAL CARE COMMISSION[338]

Mrs. Virginia Foglia[334]	Albemarle	7-22-61	7-1-65
W. T. Armstrong[335]	Rocky Mount	10-19-61	7-1-65
Charles A. Cannon[336]	Kannapolis	10-19-61	7-1-65
W. Ralph Deaton[337]	Greensboro	10-19-61	7-1-65
James P. Richardson†	Charlotte	10-19-61	7-1-65

[318] The board is composed of eight members, six of whom are appointed by the governor, and two of whom are ex officio (the state superintendent of public instruction and the librarian of the University of North Carolina). The governor's appointees serve overlapping terms of six years. G. S. 125-3; S. L., 1955, c. 505, s. 3.

[319] The commission consists of nine members, five of whom are appointed by the governor for two-year terms, and four of whom are ex officio (the state treasurer, the state auditor, the secretary of state, and the commissioner of revenue). G. S. 159-3.

[320] Succeeded Walter A. Coble.

[321] Succeeded W. T. Moss.

[322] Succeeded C. W. Roberts.

[323] Succeeded Earl H. Tate, resigned.

[324] The board consists of the eight members of the board of trustees of the Teachers' and State Employees' Retirement System and two local governmental officials appointed by the governor to serve four-year terms. One of the appointive members must be a full-time executive officer of a municipality participating in the retirement system and the other must be a full-time officer of a participating county. G. S. 128-28 (c), 135-6 (b); S. L., 1961, c. 515, s. 3.

[325] The commission consists of twenty members who serve four-year terms. Of this number, eleven are appointed by the governor, seven are nominated by the various medical associations for appointment by the governor, and two are ex officio (the state health officer and the commissioner of public welfare). The 1963 General Assembly eliminated the nomination of a member by the State Dental Society and provided that this member should be appointed by the governor. G. S. 131-117; S. L., 1963, c. 325, s. 1.

[326] Succeeded W. M. Rick.

[327] Succeeded Mrs. Worth Yount, deceased.

[328] Succeeded Eugene G. Shaw, resigned.

[329] Succeeded Earl H. Tate, resigned.

[330] Succeeded Agnew Bahnson, Sr.

[331] Succeeded J. B. Lee, Jr., resigned.

[332] Succeeded Sample B. Forbus; Mootz resigned on December 3, 1964.

[333] The council consists of five members appointed by the governor for four-year terms. G. S. 131-120.

[334] Succeeded Fred Hubbard.

[335] Succeeded Eugene A. Hargrove.

[336] Succeeded Claude F. Gaddy.

[337] Succeeded Joe M. Cox.

Name of Appointee	Address	Date Appointed	Date of Expiration
MEDICAL CENTER STUDY COMMISSION[338]			
James M. Alexander	Charlotte	2-26-64	Report to the 1965 General Assembly
Walter R. Berryhill	Chapel Hill	2-26-64	Report to the 1965 General Assembly
Addison G. Brenizer, Jr.	Charlotte	2-26-64	Report to the 1965 General Assembly
Henry T. Clark, Jr.	Chapel Hill	2-26-64	Report to the 1965 General Assembly
Mrs. George L. Carrington	Burlington	2-26-64	Report to the 1965 General Assembly
William F. Henderson	Raleigh	2-26-64	Report to the 1965 General Assembly
John W. Rankin	Charlotte	2-26-64	Report to the 1965 General Assembly
Joseph C. Hinsey	New York City	4-9-64	Report to the 1965 General Assembly
Vernon W. Lippard	New Haven, Connecticut	4-9-64	Report to the 1965 General Assembly
STATE BOARD OF MENTAL HEALTH[339]			
John W. Umstead[340]	Chapel Hill	1963 General Assembly	For Life
William L. Thorp†	Rocky Mount	10-3-63	4-1-67
R. P. Richardson†	Reidsville	10-3-63	4-1-67
Frank Graham Umstead[341]	Chapel Hill	10-3-63	4-1-67
Samuel L. Elfmon[342]	Fayetteville	7-23-64	4-1-67
R. V. Liles†	Wadesboro	7-23-64	4-1-67
Jimmy V. Johnson[343]	Statesville	9-23-64	4-1-69
MEDICAL ADVISORY COUNCIL TO THE STATE BOARD OF MENTAL HEALTH[344]			
Edgar T. Beddingfield *	Statonsburg	12-2-63-64	6-30-64-67
Mason Meads *	Winston-Salem	12-2-63-64	6-30-64-67
John S. Rhodes *	Raleigh	12-2-63-64	6-30-64-67
Bennie Brooks Ward *	Shallotte	12-2-63-64	6-30-64-67
Roy S. Wynn *	Charlotte	12-2-63-64	6-30-64-67
Amos N. Johnson	Garland	12-2-63	6-30-65
W. C. Davidson[345]	Roaring Gap	12-2-63	6-30-65
Issac M. Taylor	Chapel Hill	12-2-63	6-80-65
Thomas G. Thurston	Salisbury	12-2-63	6-30-65
Barnes Woodhall	Durham	12-2-63	6-30-65
Andrew Best	Greenville	12-2-63	6-30-66
George C. Ham	Chapel Hill	12-2-63	6-30-66

John R. Kernodle	Burlington	12-2-63	6-30-66
John L. McCain	Wilson	12-2-63	6-30-66
John C. Reece	Morganton	12-2-63	6-30-66

COUNCIL ON MENTAL RETARDATION[346]

Joe K. Byrd	Morganton	12-5-63	6-30-65
Ralph H. Scott	Haw River	12-5-63	6-30-67
Jyles J. Coggins	Raleigh	12-5-63	6-30-65
M. Glenn Pickard	Burlington	12-5-63	6-30-67
Louis G. Christian	Raleigh	12-5-63	At pleasure of the governor
Samuel O. Cornwell	Raleigh	12-5-63	At pleasure of the governor
James F. Donnelly	Raleigh	12-5-63	At pleasure of the governor
Nile F. Hunt	Raleigh	12-5-63	At pleasure of the governor
Blaine M. Madison	Raleigh	12-5-63	At pleasure of the governor
Taylor R. Kennerly	High Point	12-5-63	6-30-67
Mrs. M. P. Bailey	Greenville	12-5-63	6-30-66
Charles Waddell	Asheville	12-5-63	6-30-66
Mrs. Rufus W. Reynolds	Greensboro	12-5-63	6-30-65
Emil Cortes	Burlington	12-5-63	6-30-65

[338] Created by the 1963 General Assembly to study the feasibility of establishing a medical training center at Charlotte, the commission consists of nine members to be named by the governor. At least three of them shall be medical doctors in good standing in North Carolina. S. L., 1963, Res. 53.

[339] By action of the 1963 General Assembly, the powers and duties of the State Hospitals Board of Control, the State Board of Health over the operation of mental health clinics, and the State Board of Public Welfare over the licensing of private mental hospitals and institutions were transferred to the newly created State Board of Mental Health. Persons serving on the Hospitals Board of Control prior to the enactment of this act continued to serve the duration of their terms. Thereafter membership consisted of fifteen members, one from each of the eleven congressional districts and four at large, appointed by the governor for initial terms of three, four, five, and six-year terms. In contrast to previous four-year terms, reappointments are made for six years. At least two shall be licensed to practice medicine. G. S. 122-1.1; S. L., 1963, c. 1166, s. 3.

[340] Made Chairman Emeritus for life by the 1963 General Assembly. S. L., 1963, c. 712.

[341] Succeeded John W. Umstead, retired to become Chairman Emeritus for life.

[342] Succeeded Dewey H. Bridger.

[343] Succeeded George R. Uzzell.

[344] As authorized by the 1963 General Assembly, the council is composed of fifteen members appointed by the governor. Initial appointments are made as follows: five for three-year terms, five for two-year terms, five for one-year terms. Thereafter all appointments are for three years. G. S. 35-70; S. L., 1963, c. 668, s. 1.

[345] Resigned, December 10, 1964.

[346] As created by the 1963 General Assembly, the council is composed of eighteen members appointed by the governor. Two members each shall be chosen from the House of Representatives and the Senate to serve two- and four-year terms. Representatives of the State Board of Health, the Department of Mental Health, the State Board of Public Welfare, the State Board of Education, and the State Board of Correction and Training shall serve at the governor's pleasure. Eight other persons who shall be selected without regard to employment or professional association shall serve initial appointments of one, two, three, and four-year terms, with reappointments for four-year terms. G. S. 35-73; S. L., 1963, c. 669.

Name of Appointee	Address	Date Appointed	Date of Expiration
Courtland H. Davis, Jr. *	Winston-Salem	12-5-63-64	6-30-64-68
Laura Harbison *	Raleigh	12-5-63-64	6-30-64-68
Harrie R. Chamberlin	Chapel Hill	12-5-63	6-30-67
Harold L. Trigg	Salisbury	12-5-63	6-30-67
MERIT SYSTEM COUNCIL[347]			
Fred S. Royster †	Henderson	9-8-61	4-8-67
Mrs. Peggy Warren Satterfield *[348]	Hillsboro	9-8-61-63	4-8-63-69
Carson Bain[349]	Greensboro	12-9-63	4-8-69
Perry White[350]	Sanford	11-24-64	4-8-65
Mrs. Stella Spencer[351]	Lenoir	11-24-64	4-8-65
B. Paul Woodard[352]	Princeton	11-24-64	4-8-65
NORTH CAROLINA MILK COMMISSION[353]			
Charles McLawhorn[354]	Winterville	8-17-61	8-6-65
D. L. Paul †	New Bern	8-17-61	8-6-65
Oliver A. Swaringen †	Concord	8-17-61	8-6-65
Ophelia W. Needham *[355]	Graham	3-22-62-63	8-6-63-67
W. M. Buck[356]	Warsaw	1-9-63	8-6-66
Wade M. Hobson[357]	Yadkinville	3-10-64	8-6-67
J. Everette Flora *[358]	Charlotte	5-20-64-64	8-6-64-68
Andrew W. Nesbitt[359]	Fairview	8-13-64	8-6-67
BOARD OF DIRECTORS OF THE NORTH CAROLINA MILK PRODUCERS COOPERATIVE, INCORPORATED[360]			
J. H. Hundley †[361]	Norlina	9-20-61	2-8-64
JOHN MOTLEY MOREHEAD MEMORIAL COMMISSION[362]			
Mrs. Huger S. King †	Greensboro	9-1-61	7-1-67
Arnold A. Schiffman †	Greensboro	9-1-61	7-1-67
A. Earl Weatherly †	Greensboro	9-1-61	7-1-67
COMMISSIONER OF MOTOR VEHICLES[363]			
Edward Scheidt †	Raleigh	9-8-61	At will of the governor

NORTH CAROLINA NATIONAL GUARD ADVISORY BOARD[304]

Wallace J. Dickens*	Whiteville	2-22-62-62	12-31-62-64
Junius H. Millard*	Fayetteville	3-20-61-62	12-31-62-64

NORTH CAROLINA NATIONAL PARK, PARKWAY AND FORESTS DEVELOPMENT COMMISSION[305]

Walter F. Osborne†	Sparta	8-11-61	7-1-67
Robert Sloan[306]	Franklin	8-11-61	7-1-67
Paul W. Warlick[307]	Asheville	9-20-62	7-1-65
Frank H. Brown, Jr.†	Cullowhee	8-7-63	7-1-69
W. Ralph Winkler, Sr.†	Boone	8-7-63	7-1-69

[347] The council is composed of five members appointed by the governor for six-year terms. No member shall have held political office or have been an officer in a political organization during the year preceding his appointment, nor shall he hold such office during his term. G. S. 126-1.

[348] Succeeded Charles Wade, resigned.

[349] Succeeded J. O. Wells.

[350] Succeeded Fred S. Royster, resigned.

[351] Succeeded Katharine Jocher, resigned.

[352] Succeeded R. B. Justice, resigned.

[353] The commission consists of nine members, eight of whom are appointed by the governor. The members must include a producer, a producer-distributor, two distributors, three representatives of public interests, and a retailer; the ninth member, ex officio, is the commissioner of agriculture. Terms of office of the appointive members are for four years. G. S. 106-266.7; S. L., 1953, c. 1338; S. L., 1955, c. 406.

[354] Succeeded Fred M. Eagles.

[355] Succeeded W. W. Fitzpatrick.

[356] Succeeded Mark Goforth.

[357] Succeeded William C. McIntire, Jr.

[358] Succeeded H. G. Strom, resigned.

[359] Succeeded I. B. Julian.

[360] One member of this board is appointed for a three-year term by the director of the Agriculture Extension Service or any other public official or commission, in this case, the governor. G. S. 54-146 (b); S. L., 1963, c. 1168, s. 11.

[361] Resigned.

[362] Nineteen members compose this commission, of whom nine are appointed by the governor, three are appointed by the Board of County Commissioners of Guilford County, three are appointed by the City Council of Greensboro, and four serve ex officio (the director of the State Department of Archives and History, the superintendent of the Department of Public Instruction, the director of the Department of Conservation and Development, and the state treasurer). Initial appointments were for two, four, and six-year terms. Reappointments are for six years. S. L., 1959, c. 1308.

[363] G. S. 20-2 provides that the commissioner serve at the will of the governor.

[364] This board is composed of the adjutant general, the general officers of the active National Guard, and two other members of the active National Guard appointed by the governor for two-year terms. S. L., 1957, c. 136.

[365] The commission is composed of seven members appointed by the governor for terms of six years. In addition, there are two ex officio members as follows: the chairman of the State Highway and Public Works Commission and the director of the Department of Conservation and Development. One member must reside in each of the following counties: Buncombe, Haywood, Jackson, and Swain; three members must be residents of counties adjacent to or affected by the Blue Ridge Parkway, the Great Smoky Mountain National Park, or the Pisgah or Nantahala National Forest. G. S. 143-255, 143-256.

[366] Succeeded John Archer, resigned.

[367] Succeeded Robert I. Presley, deceased.

Name of Appointee	Address	Date Appointed	Date of Expiration
ADVISORY COMMISSION FOR THE STATE MUSEUM OF NATURAL HISTORY[308]			
Linville L. Hendren *	Elkin	9-20-61-64	8-31-63-65
Roy Parker, Jr. *	Raleigh	9-20-61-64	8-31-63-65
R. M. Schiele *	Gastonia	9-20-61-64	8-31-63-65
BOARD OF COMMISSIONERS OF NAVIGATION AND PILOTAGE FOR THE CAPE FEAR RIVER[369]			
Oliver Carter[370]	Wilmington	9-6-61	4-15-65
Louis A. Hanson †	Wilmington	9-6-61	4-15-65
Prince O'Brien †	Southport	9-6-61	4-15-65
J. E. L. Wade[371]	Wilmington	9-6-61	4-15-65
R. M. Williams †	Wilmington	9-6-61	4-15-65
BOARD OF PAROLES[372]			
Howard Hepler †	Raleigh	8-7-61	7-1-65
N. F. Ransdell[373]	Varina	7-20-62	7-1-66
William H. Gibson[374]	Winston-Salem	12-19-63	7-1-66
STATE PERSONNEL COUNCIL[375]			
Frederick Dale Graham[376]	Raleigh	9-8-61	7-1-67
Victor Emsley Jones	Greensboro	9-8-61	7-1-67
Perry White	Sanford	9-8-61	7-1-67
Fred Charles Norman[377]	Elkin	9-8-61	7-1-67
William Melvin Shuford[378]	Asheville	9-8-61	7-1-65
Fred Stovall Royster, Chairman †	Henderson	9-8-61	7-1-63
Mrs. Peggy Warren Satterfield[379]	Hillsboro	9-8-61	7-1-63
William W. Wells, Jr.[380]	Asheville	9-20-62	7-1-65
NORTH CAROLINA STATE PORTS AUTHORITY[381]			
James Farr Latham	Burlington	7-21-61	6-30-63
John Mercer Reeves †*	Pinehurst	7-21-61-63	6-30-63-69
Edward Nelson Richards *[382]	Raleigh	7-21-61-63	6-30-63-69
Cooper D. Cass[383]	Winston-Salem	7-21-61	6-30-65
William G. Clark, Jr. †	Tarboro	7-21-61	6-30-65
Louis Stuart Ficklen[384]	Greenville	7-21-61	6-30-65

E. G. Anderson[385]	Robersonville	7-21-61	6-30-67
Joseph Orchard Foil[386]	Greensboro	7-21-61	6-30-67
William James Pharr[387]	McAdenville	7-21-61	6-30-67
Frank Howard Ross, Jr. *[388]	Charlotte	1-23-63-63	6-30-63-69

EXECUTIVE DIRECTOR

James W. Davis	Baltimore, Maryland	11-9-62

STATE PRISON COMMISSION[389]

Linn D. Garibaldi, *Chairman* †	Matthews	8-3-61	6-30-65
M. B. Davis †	High Point	9-6-61	6-30-65

368 As created by the 1961 General Assembly, the commission shall consist of at least nine members, which shall include the director of the Museum of Natural History, the commissioner of agriculture, the state geologist, the state forester, the director of the Institute of Fisheries Research of the University of North Carolina, the director of the Wildlife Resources Commission, the superintendent of public instruction, or any qualified repre-entative of any or all. The three members appointed by the governor for two-year terms must represent the three geographical areas of the state. G. S. 143-370; S. L., 1961, c. 1180, s. 1.

369 The board consists of five members appointed by the governor for four-year terms. At least four of these members shall be residents of New Hanover County and none shall be licensed pilots. G. S. 76-1.

370 Succeeded H. S. McGirt.

371 Succeeded R. W. Cantwell.

372 The board is composed of three members appointed by the governor for four-year terms each. Members are prohibited from using their positions to influence political activities. G. S. 148-52, 148-52.1.

373 Succeeded W. A. Brame.

374 Succeeded N. F. Ransdell, who moved into position of chairman of board, succeeding Johnson Matthews.

375 The 1961 General Assembly enlarged this council from five to seven members to serve initial terms as follows: two for a two-year term, two for a four-year term, and three for a six-year term. Thereafter all members serve for six years in contrast to the former term of four years. G. S. 143-35; S. L., 1961, c. 625.

376 Succeeded Mrs. Grace M. Hartzog.

377 Succeeded R. B. Justice.

378 Succeeded Wade Barber.

379 Succeeded John Harden.

380 Succeeded William Melvin Shuford, resigned.

381 The authority consists of nine members appointed by the governor. The 1961 General Assembly increased the terms from four years to six years and provided for initial terms to be staggered ones of two, four, and six years. The executive director is appointed by the authority with the approval of the governor. S. L., 1961, c. 242; S. L., 1959, c. 523; G. S. 143-216, 143-218 (5).

382 Succeeded Harvey C. Hines.

383 Succeeded Earl N. Phillips.

384 Succeeded Charles Gray, Sr.

385 Succeeded Collier Cobb, Jr.

386 Succeeded Kirkwood Floyd Adams.

387 Succeeded Thomas M. Evins, resigned.

388 Succeeded James Farr Latham, resigned.

389 The commission consists of seven members appointed by the governor for four-year terms. The governor designates one of the members of the commission as chairman. The director is appointed by the commission with the approval of the governor to serve a four-year term. G. S. 148-1, 148-1 (c).

Name of Appointee	Address	Date Appointed	Date of Expiration
Jack Moody * [390]	Siler City	9-6-61-63	6-30-63-67
Wilson W. Woodhouse [391]	Raleigh	9-6-61	6-30-65
Mrs. Eunice Ayers [392]	Winston-Salem	7-22-61	6-30-65
Edgar Gurganus †	Williamston	6-19-63	6-30-67
Ruben J. Dailey [393]	Asheville	10-31-63	6-30-65
Carl W. Meares [394]	Fair Bluff	10-31-63	6-30-67
Charles M. Johnson, Jr. [395]	Raleigh	12-1-64	6-30-65
DIRECTOR OF PRISONS			
George W. Randall	Raleigh	7-2-62	7-1-66
SPECIAL OFFICERS, STATE PRISON DEPARTMENT [399]			
John H. Baker, Jr.	Raleigh	2-16-62	At will of the governor
K. C. Barnette [397]	Knightdale	2-8-63	At will of the governor
N. H. Byrd [398]	Nashville	2-8-63	At will of the governor
J. R. Sears [399]	Raleigh	6-13-63	At will of the governor
C. S. Hawley [400]	Raleigh	8-21-63	At will of the governor
Clinton D. Vernon †	Raleigh	5-8-64	At will of the governor
A. F. Wadford	Raleigh	5-25-64	At will of the governor
Holly M. Britt †	Raleigh	11-8-64	At will of the governor
STATE PROBATION COMMISSION [401]			
Allen H. Gwyn, Sr. [402]	Reidsville	10-3-61	5-28-66
Thomas D. Stokes * [403]	Lexington	5-15-62-63	5-28-63-68
W. H. S. Burgwyn, Jr. [404]	Woodland	6-19-62	5-28-67
John I. Anderson †	Brevard	7-21-64	5-28-69
DIRECTOR			
William Charles Cohoon *	Columbia	10-3-61-63	7-1-63-66
STATE BOARD OF PUBLIC WELFARE [405]			
Edwin N. Brower, Sr. †	Hope Mills	7-12-61	4-1-67
J. Gordon Bush [406]	Lenoir	7-12-61	4-1-67
Samuel E. Duncan [407]	Salisbury	7-12-61	4-1-67
Mrs. Neil Goodnight * [408]	Charlotte	7-22-61-63	4-1-63-69
Robert O. Ballance [409]	Manteo	9-24-63	4-1-69

Mrs. Annie Ruth Kelly[410]	Albemarle		4-1-65
John C. Carlton[411]	Pinetops		4-1-67
Mrs. Isobel Young Martin[412]	Raleigh		4-1-67

COMMISSIONER OF PUBLIC WELFARE

Roy Eugene Brown[413]	Raleigh		8-2-63

COMMISSION TO STUDY PUBLIC WELFARE PROGRAMS[414]

Dallas Alford	Rocky Mount	12-15-61	Report to the governor by December 1, 1962
Mrs. J. B. Chase	Eureka	7-22-61	Report to the governor by December 1, 1962
I. P. Davis	Winton	12-15-61	Report to the governor by December 1, 1962
Worth Gentry	King	12-15-61	Report to the governor by December 1, 1962
L. Stacy Weaver, Jr.	Fayetteville	12-15-61	Report to the governor by December 1, 1962
Jack Wofford	Forest City	12-15-61	Report to the governor by December 1, 1962
W. C. Reed	Kinston	1-2-62	Report to the governor by December 1, 1962

390 Succeeded Harley C. Shands, resigned.
391 Succeeded Mrs. J. Melville Broughton.
392 Succeeded W. W. Shope.
393 Succeeded M. B. Davis, deceased.
394 Succeeded James M. Parrott, Jr.
395 Succeeded Wilson W. Woodhouse, resigned.
396 The governor is authorized to appoint officers upon recommendation by the Prison Department for the purpose of transferring prisoners from place to place in the state. The officers also are to be commissioned specifically or generally to return escaped prisoners or other fugitives from outside the state. G. S. 148-4.
397 Succeeded William Carter Smith.
398 Succeeded Holly Britt.
399 Succeeded William O. Upchurch.
400 Succeeded Clinton D. Vernon.
401 The commission consists of five members appointed by the governor for five-year terms, one member's term expiring each year. The director is appointed by the commission with the approval of the governor. G. S. 15-201.2, 15-202.
402 Succeeded L. Richardson Preyer.
403 Succeeded W. Jack Hooks, deceased.
404 Succeeded William J. Bundy.
405 The board consists of seven members, at least one of whom must be a woman, appointed by the governor for six-year terms. The commissioner is appointed by the board subject to approval of the governor. G. S. 108-1, 108-3; S. L., 1945, c. 43.
406 Succeeded Tom Cornwall.
407 Succeeded Jack Kirksey.
408 Succeeded E. H. Evans, resigned.
409 Succeeded Mrs. Robert E. Stratford.
410 Succeeded Irving E. Carlyle, resigned.
411 Succeeded J, Gordon Bush, resigned.
412 Succeeded Edwin N. Brower, Sr., resigned.
413 Succeeded Ellen B. Winston.
414 As created by the 1961 General Assembly, the commission consists of not less than three nor more than seven members appointed by the governor. Members serve until they make their report to the governor and to the 1963 General Assembly. S. L., 1961, Res. 66.

THE NORTH CAROLINA RECREATION COMMISSION[415]

Name of Appointee	Address	Date Appointed	Date of Expiration
Charles L. McCullers †	Kinston	10-20-61	7-1-65
Edwin W. Woodhouse[416]	Raleigh	10-20-61	7-1-63
Eric B. DeGroat[417]	Boone	7-9-62	7-1-66
William L. West, Jr.	McAdenville	7-19-62	7-1-66
Eric B. DeGroat	Boone	1-13-64	7-1-66
Charles S. Hubbard †	Wilson	1-13-64	7-1-68
Mrs. Harriet B. Pressly †	Raleigh	1-13-64	7-1-67
Augustus Buchanan Purcell	Charlotte	1-13-64	7-1-69
Leonard H. Robinson	Greensboro	1-13-64	7-1-65
William L. West, Jr.	McAdenville	1-13-64	7-1-64

NORTH CAROLINA RECREATION COMMISSION ADVISORY COMMITTEE[419]

Name of Appointee	Address	Date Appointed	Date of Expiration
Charles Milner, Chairman †	Chapel Hill	11-10-61	7-1-63
Sigmond Bear *[420]	Wilmington	11-10-61-63	7-1-63-65
C. Walton Johnson †	Weaverville	11-10-61	7-1-63
Harold Hipps[421]	Greensboro	11-10-61	7-1-63
W. Paul Lyman †*	Raleigh	11-10-61-63	7-1-63-65
Nick Hondros *[422]	Charlotte	11-10-61-63	7-1-63-65
Mrs. Earleen Pritchett[423]	Boone	11-10-61	7-1-63
Blaine M. Madison †	Raleigh	11-10-61	7-1-63
Alex McMahon †	Chapel Hill	11-10-61	7-1-63
Floyd T. Siewart[424]	Cullowhee	11-10-61	7-1-63
Mrs. George Perrin, Jr.[425]	Greensboro	11-10-61	7-1-63
Mrs. Frances Cleary †	Chapel Hill	11-10-61	7-1-63
Ray Smith †	Roanoke Rapids	11-10-61	7-1-63
Mrs. Miles A. Hughey †	Raleigh	11-10-61	7-1-63
Ottis Mabe †	Greensboro	11-10-61	7-1-63
James T. Barnes *[426]	Raleigh	11-10-61-63	7-1-63-65
Hugh Hines †	Raleigh	11-10-61	7-1-63
Mrs. T. Frank Suggs *[427]	Rocky Mount	11-10-61	**7-1-63**
Mae Crandall[428]	Gastonia	11-10-61-63	7-1-63-65
	Raleigh		

R. Phil Hanes, Jr.* [429]	Winston-Salem	11-10-61-63	7-1-63-65
Pearson Stewart* [430]	Raleigh	11-10-61-63	7-1-63-65
A. C. Snow †*	Raleigh	11-10-61-63	7-1-63-65
Frank Jarmon [431]	Durham	11-10-61	7-1-63
Taylor Dodson †*	Winston-Salem and Pfafftown	11-10-61-63	7-1-63-65
Ruth Current †*	Raleigh	11-10-61-63	7-1-63-65
Mrs. Gertrude White *[432]	Durham	11-10-61-63	7-1-63-65
Howard Pullen †*	Raleigh	11-10-61-63	7-1-63-65
T. Ed Pickard *[433]	Charlotte	11-10-61-63	7-1-63-65
Cecil Lee Porter [434]	North Wilkesboro	11-10-61	7-1-63
Roland McClamroch [435]	Chapel Hill	11-10-61	7-1-63
J. O. Bell, Jr.	Tuxedo	1-10-64	7-1-65
Mrs. Vida K. Bryant	Charlotte	1-10-64	7-1-65

[415] The commission originally consisted of eleven members, seven of whom were appointed by the governor for four-year terms. The 1963 General Assembly reduced the membership to ten, six of whom are initially appointed by the governor for terms of one, two, three, four, five, and six years. Reappointments are for six years. The four ex officio members prior to 1963 (the governor, the superintendent of public instruction, the director of the Department of Conservation and Development, and the commissioner of public welfare) were changed under the new law to include three new ones (the chairman of the Recreation Advisory Committee, the representative of the Governor's Coordinating Council on Recreation, and the president of the North Carolina Recreation Society), with the governor retaining his position. Members must be persons who understand rural, urban, governmental, private, and commercial recreation interests of North Carolina and the nation. G. S. 143-207; S. L., 1945, c. 757, s. 3; S. L., 1963, c. 542.

[416] Succeeded W. D. James, resigned.
[417] Succeeded Ralph F. Johnson.
[418] Succeeded R. W. Watkins.
[419] Thirty members appointed by the governor for two-year terms compose this committee. The governor designates the chairman. Members must represent, insofar as feasible, all groups and phases of beneficial recreation in the state. G. S. 143-210. Note: With the reorganization of the Recreation Commission by the 1963 General Assembly the sequence of appointments was begun anew. This fact explains the lack of explanatory footnotes concerning who succeeded whom in the 1964 appointments.
[420] Succeeded Mrs. Maurice Honigman.
[421] Succeeded Josephine Gallagher.
[422] Succeeded Anne W. Tillinghast.
[423] Succeeded Richard Pierce.
[424] Succeeded Donald Capstick.
[425] Succeeded McRae Faison.
[426] Succeeded Frank Pierson.
[427] Succeeded Tully Blair.
[428] Succeeded Mildred Southern.
[429] Succeeded Fred Fletcher.
[430] Succeeded O. A. Fetch.
[431] Succeeded Nancy Stamey.
[432] Succeeded Hugh Hines.
[433] Succeeded Lucy Morgan.
[434] Succeeded I. E. Ready.
[435] Succeeded Ray Smith.

Name of Appointee	Address	Date Appointed	Date of Expiration
Martha Jo Chambers	Winston-Salem	1-10-64	7-1-65
G. Paul Carr	Hillsboro	1-10-64	7-1-65
Ronald England	Morganton	1-10-64	7-1-65
William C. Fields	Fayetteville	1-10-64	7-1-65
Janice Hardison	Greenville	1-10-64	7-1-65
Oka T. Hester	Greensboro	1-10-64	7-1-65
Mrs. Arthur C. Jenkins	Fayetteville	1-10-64	7-1-65
Evelyn Peeler	Raleigh	1-10-64	7-1-65
Robert Reed	Efland	1-10-64	7-1-65
Sam Rees	Siler City	1-10-64	7-1-65
LeRoy Sossamon	Bryson City	1-10-64	7-1-65
Mrs. Davetta Steed	Raleigh	1-10-64	7-1-65
William E. Smith	Raleigh	1-10-64	7-1-65
Earle Wallace, *Chairman*	Chapel Hill	1-10-64	7-1-65

COMMISSION ON REORGANIZATION OF STATE GOVERNMENT [436]

Name of Appointee	Address	Date Appointed	Date of Expiration
Allen Barbee[437]	Spring Hope	9-8-61	Report to the governor by December 1, 1962
David Britt †	Fairmont	9-8-61	Report to the governor by December 1, 1962
Robert Calder[438]	Wilmington	9-8-61	Report to the governor by December 1, 1962
Hollis Owens[439]	Rutherfordton	9-8-61	Report to the governor by December 1, 1962
Dwight Quinn, *Chairman* †	Kannapolis	9-8-61	Report to the governor by December 1, 1962
Hector McGeachy[440]	Fayetteville	9-8-61	Report to the governor by December 1, 1962
Stewart Warren[441]	Clinton	9-8-61	Report to the governor by December 1, 1962
Fred H. Weaver †	Chapel Hill	9-8-61	Report to the governor by December 1, 1962
Boyce Whitmire[442]	Hendersonville	9-8-61	Report to the governor by December 1, 1962
Mrs. Max Miller	Greensboro	9-8-61	Report to the governor by December 1, 1962

RESEARCH TRIANGLE REGIONAL PLANNING COMMISSION [443]

Name of Appointee	Address	Date Appointed	Date of Expiration
Arthur W. Clark *[444]	Durham	5-3-62-63	7-1-63-67
Oscar R. Ewing *[445]	Chapel Hill	10-11-62-63	7-1-63-67
Rex Powell[446]	Fuquay-Varina	8-28-63	7-1-67

STAFF OFFICERS OF NORTH CAROLINA RESERVE MILITIA [447]

Name of Appointee	Address	Date Appointed	Date of Expiration
Leslie C. Blankinship	Maxton	8-14-63	At will of the governor

Harry D. Cook	Maxton	8-14-63	At will of the governor
Joseph Stone	Maxton	8-14-63	At will of the governor
Jesse B. Mercer	Maxton	8-14-63	At will of the governor
Ernest M. Blankenship	Maxton	8-14-63	At will of the governor
Thomas C. Maynor	Maxton	8-14-63	At will of the governor
Calvert H. Humbert	Maxton	8-14-63	At will of the governor
Clyde Parrish	Maxton	8-14-63	At will of the governor
Alvin S. Rose	Maxton	8-14-63	At will of the governor
Lacy Taylor	Maxton	8-14-63	At will of the governor
Joseph Creech	Maxton	8-14-63	At will of the governor
Edward B. Dodd	Maxton	8-14-63	At will of the governor
Fred H. Ferguson	Maxton	8-14-63	At will of the governor
Thomas Whiteley	Maxton	8-14-63	At will of the governor
Raymond H. Stokes	Maxton	8-14-63	At will of the governor
Jack Holly	Maxton	8-14-63	At will of the governor
Jimmy Howell	Maxton	8-14-63	At will of the governor
Lloyd C. McCaskill	Maxton	10-31-63	At will of the governor
Lloyd D. Hunter	Maxton	10-31-63	At will of the governor

COMMISSIONER OF REVENUE [448]

William A. Johnson[449]	Lillington	1-1-61	1-1-65
L. Sneed High[450]	Fayetteville	4-23-64	1-1-65

---

[436] The successor to a commission authorized for the same purpose by the 1959 General Assembly, the group is composed of nine members appointed by the governor to study and make recommendations to him on or before December 1, 1962. S. L., 1961, Res. 48.

[437] Succeeded George R. Uzzell.

[438] Succeeded Frank W. Snepp.

[439] Succeeded H. P. Taylor, Jr.

[440] Succeeded Claude Currie.

[441] Succeeded David J. Rose.

[442] Succeeded H. Cloyd Philpott, resigned.

[443] The commission is composed of fifteen members, three of whom are appointed by the governor for four-year terms. One member each must be a resident of the three counties of Durham, Orange, and Wake, and must have an interest in the development of the three-county area. S. L., 1959, c. 642.

[444] Succeeded E. K. Powe, resigned.

[445] Succeeded George L. Simpson, resigned.

[446] Succeeded Hubert C. Sears.

[447] The 1963 General Assembly provided for a complete revision of the commissions of these officers. The governor appoints and commissions as many officers as necessary, provided that specified qualifications, as outlined in the law, are met. G. S. 127-23; S. L., 1963, c. 1095.

[448] The commissioner is appointed by the governor for a four-year term. G. S. 147-87.

[449] Succeeded James S. Currie.

[450] Succeeded William A. Johnson, resigned to become Superior Court judge.

Name of Appointee	Address	Date Appointed	Date of Expiration
NORTH CAROLINA RURAL ELECTRIFICATION AUTHORITY [451]			
Gwyn B. Price, *Chairman* †	Raleigh	6-12-61	6-5-65
Cutlar Lee Ballance †	St. Pauls	9-8-61	6-5-65
Glenn Palmer †	Clyde	9-8-61	6-5-65
Milton V. Scott [452]	Pinetops	9-8-61	6-5-65
S. H. Hobbs, Jr. †	Chapel Hill	8-26-63	6-5-67
Sam J. Burrow, Jr. [453]	Asheboro	10-14-64	6-5-67
NORTH CAROLINA RURAL REHABILITATION CORPORATION BOARD OF DIRECTORS [454]			
Ira O. Schaub, *Chairman* †	Raleigh	1-31-61	11-19-63
Fred E. Harris †*	Bailey	4-9-62-64	11-19-64-67
George R. Ross **[455]	Jackson Springs	4-9-62-64	11-19-64-67
James Spence[456]	Fayetteville	12-19-62	11-19-65
James C. Wallace[457]	Chapel Hill	12-19-62	11-19-65
J. P. Brady[458]	Franklin	3-26-64	11-19-66
THE SALT MARSH MOSQUITO ADVISORY COMMISSION [459]			
W. H. Edens	Scotts Hill	9-26-63	At pleasure of the governor
Charles J. McCotter	Bayboro	9-26-63	At pleasure of the governor
Hugh Ragsdale	Richlands	9-26-63	At pleasure of the governor
R. D. Sawyer, Jr.	Manteo	9-26-63	At pleasure of the governor
NORTH CAROLINA SEASHORE COMMISSION [460]			
James T. Buffaloe	Rocky Mount	11-12-63	8-31-67
George Cherry	Pactolus	11-12-63	8-31-67
Frederick L. Cox	Grifton	11-12-63	8-31-67
William M. Cochrane	Washington, D. C.	11-12-63	8-31-67
Ashley B. Futrell	Washington	11-12-63	8-31-67
Monroe Gaskill	Cedar Island	11-12-63	8-31-67
Thomas B. Hord, Jr.	Lawndale	11-12-63	8-31-67
Eugene Price	Goldsboro	11-12-63	8-31-67
Earl N. Phillips	High Point	11-12-63	**8-31-67**

Name	Location		
Alida Willis	Morehead City	8-31-67	11-12-63
Pascal M. Camak	Wilmington	8-31-65	11-12-63
N. E. Day	Jacksonville	8-31-65	11-12-63
Braxton Bragg Dawson	Washington	8-31-65	11-12-63
Thomas W. Ellis, Jr.	Henderson	8-31-65	11-12-63
C. D. Ferrell	Elizabeth City	8-31-65	11-12-63
Harvey C. Hines	Kinston	8-31-65	11-12-63
Sebastian C. Sommer	Laurinburg	8-31-65	11-12-63
Joe G. Swindell	Lake Landing	8-31-65	11-12-63
Mrs. Estelle Burrus Tillett	Manteo	8-31-65	11-12-63
Fred H. Weaver	Chapel Hill	8-31-65	11-12-63
Angus McKellar[461]	Jackson	8-31-67	1-23-64
Jim F. Mullen[462]	Hatteras	8-31-67	1-23-64
Carroll H. Gillam[463]	Windsor	8-31-67	9-18-64
Woodrow Price, *Chairman*	Raleigh	At pleasure of the governor	11-12-63

NORTH CAROLINA BOARD OF SCIENCE AND TECHNOLOGY [464]

J. H. Black	Shelby	6-30-67	8-15-63

[451] The group is composed of six members appointed by the governor for four-year terms. G. S. 117-1.

[452] Succeeded W. Avery Thompson.

[453] Succeeded Mrs. Fred Davis.

[454] The board is made up of nine members, five of whom are appointed by the governor for three-year terms, and four of whom are ex officio members representing various rural organizations across the state. G. S. 137-31.3; S. L., 1953, c. 724, s. 3.

[455] Succeeded W. P. Morris.

[456] Succeeded J. J. Hamlin, Jr.

[457] Succeeded Dudley Bagley.

[458] Succeeded I. O. Schaub.

[459] Of the six members who make up this commission, four are appointed by the governor and two are ex officio. G. S. 143-346; S. L., 1955, c. 1197; S. L., 1957, c. 831.

[460] As created by the 1963 General Assembly, the commission consists of twenty members and a chairman appointed by the governor, and ex officio members as follows: the chairman of the Board of Water Resources, the property control officer of the Department of Administration, the director of the North Carolina Recreation Commission, a member of the Wildlife Resources Commission, a member of the Highway Commission, the chairman of the State Parks Committee of the Board of Conservation and Development, and the director of North Carolina Civil Defense. Initial terms for appointive members are for two and four years with subsequent appointments for four years. The chairman serves at the pleasure of the governor. G. S. 143-384, 143-385, 143-387; S. L., 1963, c. 989.

[461] Succeeded James T. Buffaloe, deceased.

[462] Succeeded George Cherry, deceased.

[463] Succeeded Ashley B. Futrell, resigned.

[464] As set up by the 1963 General Assembly, the board shall consist of fifteen members and the governor, who serves as ex officio chairman. The appointive members shall be chosen as follows: two from the University of North Carolina at Chapel Hill; two from North Carolina State College at Raleigh; two from Duke University; one from the membership of the Governor's Scientific Advisory Committee; one from the membership of the State Advisory Committee on Atomic Energy; three members from the General Assembly; three members from industry within the state; and one appointed upon nomination by the executive committee of the Board of the Research Triangle Institute. After initial terms of two and four years expire, reappointments are for four years. G. S. 143-379; S. L., 1963, c. 1006, s. 2.

Name of Appointee	Address	Date Appointed	Date of Expiration
George Herbert	Durham	8-15-63	6-30-67
George E. Nicholson	Chapel Hill	8-15-63	6-30-67
Everett Palamatier	Chapel Hill	8-15-63	6-30-65
Sheldon P. Smith	Charlotte	8-15-63	6-30-67
William S. Yeager	Winston-Salem	8-15-63	6-30-67
Paul M. Gross	Durham	8-15-63	6-30-65
Marcus E. Hobbs	Durham	8-15-63	6-30-65
Harry C. Kelly	Raleigh	8-15-63	6-30-65
William Little	Chapel Hill	8-15-63	6-30-65
A. C. Menius, Jr.	Raleigh	8-15-63	6-30-65
R. W. Truitt	Raleigh	8-15-63	6-30-65
Bruce B. Allen[465]	Charlotte	10-7-64	6-30-67

ADVISORY COMMITTEE OF THE SOUTHEASTERN INTERSTATE FOREST FIRE PROTECTION COMPACT [466]

Carlton J. Blades †	Charlotte	1-29-62	Term indefinite
Bruce B. Cameron[467]	Wilmington	1-29-62	Term indefinite
Boyce A. Whitmire[468]	Hendersonville	1-29-62	Term indefinite
Lacy H. Thornburg[469]	Sylva	1-29-62	Term indefinite

STANDARDIZATION COMMITTEE [470]

Hugh Cannon, Chairman[471]	Raleigh	12-4-61	At pleasure of the governor
Ralph H. Scott[472]	Haw River	9-13-61	At pleasure of the governor
J. Shelton Wicker	Sanford	9-13-61	At pleasure of the governor
David M. Britt[473]	Fairmont	4-15-64	At pleasure of the governor

COMMISSION TO STUDY THE IMPACT
OF STATE SOVEREIGNTY UPON FINANCING OF
LOCAL GOVERNMENTAL SERVICES AND FUNCTIONS [474]

Paul L. Bernhardt, Chairman	Salisbury	9-21-61	Report to the governor by December 1, 1962
Joseph F. Ferrell	Elizabeth City	9-21-61	Report to the governor by December 1, 1962
Mrs. Adelaide Walters	Chapel Hill	9-21-61	Report to the governor by December 1, 1962

STATE STREAM SANITATION COMMITTEE [475]

Grady Stevens[476]	Shiloh	7-20-61	7-11-65

H. Grady Farthing †	Boone	7-20-61	7-11-65
William L. Corbin[477]	Dunn	7-20-61	7-11-65
J. Nelson Gibson, Jr. *[478]	Gibson	7-18-62-63	7-11-63-69
P. Greer Johnson †	Asheville	8-19-63	7-11-69
J. Vivian Whitfield †	Burgaw	8-19-63	7-11-69

BOARD OF TRUSTEES OF THE
NORTH CAROLINA SYMPHONY SOCIETY, INCORPORATED [479]

Mrs. Ed Bond [480]	Edenton	11-8-61	3-10-65
J. Spencer Love †	Greensboro	11-8-61	3-10-65
Mrs. J. Spencer Love[481]	Greensboro	5-9-62	3-10-65
Holland McSwain †	Murphy	9-11-63	3-10-67
Mrs. Louis V. Sutton †	Raleigh	9-11-63	3-10-67

[465] Succeeded J. H. Black, resigned.
[466] The compact consists of one member and an alternate from the state Senate, one member and an alternate from the House of Representatives, and two other representatives, one of whom shall be associated with forestry or forests products industries. All are appointed by the governor for indefinite terms, but presumably from one General Assembly to the next. G. S. 113-60.11, 113-60.14; S. L., 1955, c. 803, s. 4.
[467] Succeeded W. Charles Cohoon.
[468] Succeeded Ernest W. Ross.
[469] Succeeded C. R. Crawford.
[470] The committee consists of seven members appointed by the governor to serve at his pleasure. G. S. 143-60.
[471] Succeeded David S. Coltrane, retired.
[472] Succeeded William Copeland.
[473] Succeeded J. Shelton Wicker.
[474] As established by the 1961 General Assembly, the commission is composed of nine members, three of whom shall be appointed by the governor, three by the president of the Senate from the Senate membership, and three by the speaker of the House from the House membership. Members shall serve until a report is made to the governor for transmission to the General Assembly. S. L., 1961, Res. 68.
[475] This permanent committee within the State Board of Health consists of nine members, of whom seven are appointed by the governor for six-year terms, and of whom two serve ex officio (chief engineer of the State Board of Health and chief engineer of the Water Resources and Engineering Division of the Department of Conservation and Development). G. S. 143-213; S. L., 1957, c. 992.
[476] Succeeded J. N. Vann, resigned.
[477] Succeeded Scott B. Berkley.
[478] Succeeded T. B. Upchurch, Jr., resigned.
[479] The board consists of not less than sixteen members, of whom four are named by the governor for four-year terms, ten are chosen by the North Carolina Symphony Society, and two serve ex officio as follows: the governor and the superintendent of public instruction. G. S. 140-6; S. L., 1943, c. 755; S. L., 1947, c. 1049.
[480] Succeeded Mrs. H. E. Latham.
[481] Succeeded J. Spencer Love, deceased.

Name of Appointee	Address	Date Appointed	Date of Expiration
BOARD OF TRUSTEES OF THE TEACHERS' AND STATE EMPLOYEES' RETIREMENT SYSTEM [482]			
Robert E. Williams[483]	Raleigh	6-12-61	4-5-65
George B. Cherry *[484]	Raleigh	2-14-62-63	4-5-63-67
Withers Davis †	Fayetteville	7-31-63	4-5-67
E. L. Phillips[485]	Durham	7-31-63	4-5-67
L. M. Massey[486]	Zebulon	5-15-64	4-5-68
Royal W. Sands †	Reidsville	5-15-64	4-5-68
NORTH CAROLINA TEXTBOOK COMMISSION [487]			
Mrs. Nina DeBruhl Clark [488]	Asheville	10-31-62	4-1-65
Joseph Q. Holliday[489]	Raleigh	10-31-62	4-1-65
Mrs. Helen Rhyne Marvin[490]	Gastonia	10-31-62	4-1-65
Mrs. Catherine D. Penny[491]	Durham	10-31-62	4-1-65
Clyde Pressley[492]	Spray	10-31-62	4-1-65
Reba Proctor[493]	Rocky Mount	10-31-62	4-1-65
Elizabeth Putnam[494]	Boone	10-31-62	4-1-65
Mrs. Sarah Hamilton Richbourg †	Lumberton	10-31-62	4-1-65
Mary B. Thompson[495]	Charlotte	10-31-62	4-1-65
Philip J. Weaver, *Chairman*[496]	Greensboro	10-31-62	4-1-65
Mrs. LaLuce Williams[497]	Fayetteville	10-31-62	4-1-65
Mrs. Dorothy Y. Zimmerman †	Yanceyville	10-31-62	4-1-65
THE TRAFFIC CODE COMMISSION [498]			
David Clark	Lincolnton	11-11-63	To report to the governor by September 1, 1964
Claude M. Hamrick	Winston-Salem	11-11-63	To report to the governor by September 1, 1964
J. Russell Kirby, *Chairman*	Wilson	11-11-63	To report to the governor by September 1, 1964
B. T. Jones	Forest City	11-11-63	To report to the governor by September 1, 1964
Hector MacLean	Lumberton	11-11-63	To report to the governor by September 1, 1964
William R. Pope	Mt. Mourne	11-11-63	To report to the governor by September 1, 1964
Jack Palmer, Jr.	Shelby	11-11-63	To report to the governor by September 1, 1964
R. D. McMillan, Jr.	Red Springs	11-11-63	To report to the governor by September 1, 1964
George R. Uzzell	Salisbury	11-11-63	To report to the governor by September 1, 1964

TRYON PALACE COMMISSION [496]

Robert L. Stallings, Jr.	New Bern	12-22-61	Term Indefinite
Mrs. James M. Tyler[500]	Kinston	8-13-62	Term Indefinite
Robert L. Stallings, Jr.[501]	New Bern	12-1-64	Term Indefinite

THE NORTH CAROLINA TURNPIKE AUTHORITY [502]

George R. Goodwin	Raleigh	8-9-63	7-1-66
Vernon G. James	Elizabeth City	8-9-63	7-1-66
T. Baxter Williams, Jr.*	Currituck	8-9-63-64	7-1-64-68

[482] The board is composed of eight members, six of whom are appointed by the governor with the consent of the Senate for four-year terms, and two of whom are ex officio as follows: the superintendent of public instruction and the state treasurer. One appointee of the governor must be a member of the teaching profession, one must be an employee of the State Highway and Public Works Commission, and one a state employee. The remaining members must not be teachers or state employees. G. S. 135-6; S. L., 1947, c. 259.

[483] Succeeded Clyde W. Gordon; Williams' term ended with his resignation on October 22, 1964.

[484] Succeeded F. Kent Burns, resigned.

[485] Succeeded Annie H. Swindell.

[486] Succeeded H. L. Stephenson.

[487] The commission consists of twelve members appointed jointly by the governor and the superintendent of public instruction to serve four-year terms. Seven of the members must be outstanding teachers or principals in the elementary grades; five members must be outstanding teachers or principals in the high school grades; one member may be a county or city superintendent. G. S. 115-208; S. L., 1945, c. 707; S. L., 1955, c. 1372, s. 3 of art. 24.

[488] Succeeded Catherine Whitener, resigned.

[489] Succeeded Jack Horner, resigned.

[490] Succeeded Marie Haigwood, resigned.

[491] Succeeded Claire Freeman.

[492] Succeeded Lloyd Y. Thayer.

[493] Succeeded Helen D. Wolff.

[494] Succeeded Carrie P. Abbott.

[495] Succeeded Cornelia McLauchlin.

[496] Succeeded A. B. Gibson.

[497] Succeeded Margaret E. McGimsey.

[498] By an act of the 1963 General Assembly this commission was established, consisting of eleven persons appointed by the governor from the membership of the 1963 General Assembly. Members shall file a report with the governor not later than September 1, 1964, and shall present recommendations to the 1965 General Assembly. S. L., 1963, c. 1183.

[499] The commission, acting under the general authority of the Department of Archives and History, consists of twenty-five members appointed by the governor, and six ex officio members as follows: the governor, the attorney general, the director of the Department of Conservation and Development, the director of the Department of Archives and History, the mayor of New Bern, and the chairman of the Craven County Board of County Commissioners. The law does not specify the terms of the appointees. G. S. 121-19; S. L., 1945, c. 791.

[500] Succeeded Robert L. Stallings, Jr., resigned to become director of Conservation and Development.

[501] Succeeded Mrs. Edwin C. Gregory, deceased.

[502] Established by an act of the 1963 General Assembly, the authority is empowered to construct, maintain, and operate toll roads across the state. It consists of four members, including the chairman of the State Highway Commission, ex officio member, and three members appointed by the governor for initial terms of one, two, and three years. Subsequent appointments are for four-year terms. S. L., 1963, c. 757, s. 3.

Name of Appointee	Address	Date Appointed	Date of Expiration
	U.S.S. NORTH CAROLINA BATTLESHIP COMMISSION [503]		
Hugh Morton, *Chairman* *	Wilmington	4-21-61-63	4-4-63-65
Victor S. Bryant *	Durham	4-29-61-63	4-4-63-65
Orville Campbell	Chapel Hill	4-29-61	4-4-63
James S. Craig, Jr.[504]	Wilmington	4-29-61	4-4-63
Percy Ferebee *	Andrews	4-29-61-63	4-4-63-65
John H. Fox *	Wilmington	4-29-61-63	4-4-63-65
G. Andrew Jones, Jr. *[505]	Raleigh	4-29-61-63	4-4-63-65
Thomas W. Morse	Raleigh	4-29-61	4-4-63
Edwin L. Rankin, Jr.*	Raleigh	4-29-61-63	4-4-63-65
William G. Womble, Jr. *	Raleigh	4-29-61-63	4-4-63-65
Jack S. Younts	Southern Pines	4-29-61	4-4-63
William W. Willson *[506]	Wilmington	10-11-61-63	4-4-63-65
J. D. Fitz*	Morganton	12-8-61-63	4-4-63-65
T. Ed Pickard, Jr.	Charlotte	12-8-61-63	4-4-63-65
Marvin Robbins*	Rocky Mount	12-8-61-63	4-4-63-65
E. C. Thompson*	Warsaw	12-8-61-63	4-4-63-65
Kenneth R. Williams	Winston-Salem	9-13-63	4-4-65
Charles H. Craven, Jr.	Raleigh	3-9-64	4-4-65
	NORTH CAROLINA UTILITIES COMMISSION [507]		
Clarence Hugh Noah †	High Point	8-24-61	7-1-67
Samuel Otis Worthington †	Greenville	8-24-61	7-1-67
Robert Brookes Peters, Jr.[508]	Raleigh	8-24-61	7-1-65
Harry T. Westcott, *Chairman* †	Raleigh	7-19-63	7-1-71
	NORTH CAROLINA VETERANS COMMISSION [509]		
Wesley E. Cullipher *[510]	Elizabeth City	1-23-61-63	5-16-63-68
John L. Kallam †	Kinston	9-20-61	5-16-66
John R. Dickerson[511]	Monroe	6-19-62	5-16-67
William Z. Wood[512]	Winston-Salem	4-23-64	5-16-65
William E. Bass[513]	Hickory	6-10-64	5-16-69

THE GEORGE WASHINGTON STATUE COMMISSION [514]

W. Lunsford Crew	Roanoke Rapids	3-20-64	6-20-67
Mrs. Albert G. Edwards	Raleigh	3-20-64	6-20-67
R. O. Everett	Durham	3-20-64	6-20-67
Edwin M. Gill	Raleigh	3-20-64	6-20-67
Louise Hall	Durham	3-20-64	6-20-67
Mrs. Ernest Ives	Southern Pines	3-20-64	6-20-67
John R. Jordan, Jr.	Raleigh	3-20-64	6-20-67
John Kellenberger	Greensboro	3-20-64	6-20-67
Hector MacLean, *Chairman*	Lumberton	3-20-64	6-20-67
Annie S. Ramsey	Raleigh	3-20-64	6-20-67
C. Paul Roberts	Durham	3-20-64	6-20-67
Mrs. John L. Sanders	Chapel Hill	3-20-64	6-20-67
Joseph Sloane	Chapel Hill	3-20-64	6-20-67
Ben F. Williams	Raleigh	3-20-64	6-20-67

BOARD OF WATER RESOURCES [515]

Paul Dexter Davis †	Durham	9-21-61	7-1-67
Wayne Mabry [516]	Albemarle	9-21-61	7-1-67

[503] The commission consists of not more than fifteen members, including as ex officio member at least one person from the board or staff of the Department of Conservation and Development. Members serve on the commission for two years. By an act of the 1963 General Assembly, the commission, originally destined to terminate in 1963, was continued for another biennium. *G. S.* 143-363; *S. L., 1963, c. 52.*

[504] Deceased.

[505] Resigned to become Budget Director, 7-1-63.

[506] Succeeded Thomas W. Morse, resigned.

[507] As amended by the 1963 General Assembly, the terms of the five commissioners appointed by the governor shall be increased from six to eight years. Initial appointments to fill the terms expiring in 1963 and 1965 shall be for eight years, and those to fill the terms expiring in 1967 shall be for two years. Thereafter all appointments are for eight years. The governor designates one of the members as chairman. *G. S. 62-10; S. L., 1963, c. 1165, s. 1.*

[508] Succeeded Richard G. Long, resigned.

[509] The commission consists of five members appointed by the governor for five-year terms. All must be veterans and must represent both major political parties. *G. S. 165-5; S. L., 1945, c. 723.*

[510] Succeeded Claude T. Bowers.

[511] Succeeded Irwin Monk.

[512] Succeeded J. Oscar Thomas, deceased.

[513] Succeeded Chris C. Fordham, Jr.

[514] As established by an act of the 1963 General Assembly, the commission consists of eighteen members, fifteen of whom are appointed by the governor for terms of four years each. The superintendent of the Department of Public Instruction, the director of Conservation and Development, and the director of the Department of Archives and History serve as ex officio members. *S. L., 1963, c. 1082, s. 1.*

[515] The board is made up of seven members appointed by the governor for six-year terms. The director is appointed by the board with the approval of the governor. *G. S. 143-353; S. L., 1959, c. 779, s. 1.*

[516] Succeeded Ben R. Lewis.

Name of Appointee	Address	Date Appointed	Date of Expiration
S. Vernon Stevens, Jr. †	Broadway	9-21-61	7-1-67
Glenn M. Tucker†	Carolina Beach	8-6-63	7-1-69
C. H. Pruden, Jr.	Windsor	8-6-63	7-1-69
Director of Department of Water Resources			
Walter E. Fuller[517]	Raleigh	12-10-63	

North Carolina Wildlife Resources Commission [518]

Name of Appointee	Address	Date Appointed	Date of Expiration
O. L. Woodhouse †*	Grandy	7-27-61-63	6-30-63-69
Robert M. Carr †	Wallace	7-27-61	6-30-65
G. E. Beal †	Red Oak	7-27-61	6-30-67
J. A. Bridger †	Bladenboro	7-27-61	6-30-63
Dickson Phillips[519]	Chapel Hill	7-27-61	6-30-65
Thurman Briggs †	Lexington	7-27-61	6-30-67
R. Floyd Crouse †	Sparta	7-27-61	6-30-63
Chester S. Davis *[520]	Winston-Salem	3-7-62-63	6-30-63-69
Lee L. Powers[521]	Lake Lure	7-27-61	6-30-65
Oscar Ledford[522]	Franklin	7-27-61	6-30-67
Jay Waggoner[523]	Graham	7-24-63	6-30-65
Phil Ellis *	Raleigh	7-27-61-63	6-30-63-67
Walter Lambeth	Charlotte	7-27-61	6-30-65
Tom U. Cameron	Raeford	8-14-63	6-30-69
J. Hewes Parrish	Winston-Salem	1-6-64	6-30-69
Hugh G. Chatham II [524]	Elkin	12-31-64	6-30-69

Wreck Commissioners [525]

Name of Appointee	Address	Date Appointed	Date of Expiration
Alpheus W. Drinkwater †[526]	Manteo	3-15-62	2-21-64
Fairley Fulcher	Sneads Ferry	10-3-63	10-2-65
B. B. Hurst	Hubert	10-3-63	10-2-65

INSTITUTIONS

Agricultural and Technical College of North Carolina Board of Trustees [527]

Name of Appointee	Address	Date Appointed	Date of Expiration
George Sockwell †	Gibsonville	7-27-61	6-30-69
Henry A. Scott †	Haw River	7-27-61	6-30-69
Elbert Edwin Waddell †	Albemarle	7-27-61	6-30-69

Name	Location		
Frontis W. Johnston[528]	Davidson	7-27-61	6-30-67
John S. Stewart[529]	Durham	7-27-61	6-30-67
David W. Morehead[530]	Greensboro	9-20-62	6-30-69
Andrew Best[531]	Greenville	9-23-63	6-30-71
James A. Graham[532]	**Raleigh**	**9-23-63**	**6-30-71**
Otis E. Tillman[533]	High Point	9-23-63	6-30-71

TECHNICAL INSTITUTE OF ALAMANCE BOARD OF TRUSTEES [534]

Name	Location		
Bernie Bean	Mebane	2-27-64	6-30-69
Mrs. B. Tate Horton	Burlington	2-27-64	6-30-67
Stephen B. Thomas	Burlington	2-27-64	6-30-65
D. J. Walker	Burlington	2-27-64	6-30-71

THE ALBEMARLE COMMUNITY COLLEGE BOARD OF TRUSTEES [535]

Name	Location		
William F. Ainsley	Hertford	9-10-63	6-30-69
C. Alden Baker	Elizabeth City	9-10-63	6-30-67

[517] Succeeded Harry E. Brown, retired.

[518] The 1961 General Assembly increased the membership of this commission from nine to eleven persons to be appointed by the governor for six-year terms. Members must be informed on wildlife conservation and restoration problems, and shall be appointed from geographical districts designated in the General Statutes. Vacancies are filled by appointment of the governor for the duration of unexpired terms. G. S. 143-241; S. L., 1961, c. 737, s. 1; S. L., 1947, c. 263, s. 6.

[519] Succeeded S. I. Stewart, resigned.

[520] Succeeded R. Floyd Crouse, resigned; Davis resigned on November 16, 1963.

[521] Succeeded T. N. Massie.

[522] Succeeded James A. Connelly.

[523] Succeeded Dickson Phillips, resigned.

[524] Succeeded J. Hewes Parrish, resigned.

[525] Whenever necessary, the governor appoints wreck commissioners for the various districts in the state's coastal counties to serve for two-year terms. Each commissioner is to live in the district for which he is appointed. G. S. 82-2.

[526] Deceased, September 24, 1962.

[527] The board is composed of twelve members appointed by the governor or for terms of eight years each, the terms to be staggered so that three vacancies occur every two years. The appointments are subject to confirmation by the General Assembly. G. S. 116-46 (1); S. L., 1957, c. 1142.

[528] Succeeded James A. Graham.

[529] Succeeded A. H. Brett.

[530] Succeeded Henry A. Scott, deceased.

[531] Succeeded Robert P. Holding.

[532] Succeeded Joseph M. Hunt, Jr.

[533] Succeeded Murray Davis, deceased.

[534] As organized by the 1963 General Assembly, each community college and technical institute shall be governed by a board of trustees consisting of twelve members. Four of this number are appointed by the governor, four are elected by the city or county board of education located in the administrative area of the institution, and four are elected by the county board of commissioners of the county in which the institution is located. All members must be residents of the administrative area of the institution or contiguous counties. Initial appointments are for two-, four-, six-, and eight-year terms; thereafter all appointments are for eight years. G. S. 115A-7, 115A-8; S. L., 1963, c. 448, s. 23.

[535] See footnote 534.

Name of Appointee	Address	Date Appointed	Date of Expiration
M. Keith Fearing, Jr.	Manteo	9-10-63	6-30-65
Vernon G. James	Elizabeth City	9-10-63	6-30-71

APPALACHIAN STATE TEACHERS COLLEGE BOARD OF TRUSTEES [536]

Name of Appointee	Address	Date Appointed	Date of Expiration
Claude Armfield [537]	Lenoir	8-11-61	6-30-69
William R. Rankin [538]	Lincolnton	8-11-61	6-30-69
Wayne Shoaf [539]	Lexington	8-11-61	6-30-69
John Frank †	Mt. Airy	9-25-63	6-30-71
E. G. Lackey †	Winston-Salem	9-25-63	6-30-71
John H. Vickers [540]	Charlotte	9-25-63	6-30-71
Lester P. Martin, Jr. [541]	Mocksville	9-25-63	6-30-67

THE NORTH CAROLINA SCHOOL OF THE ARTS BOARD OF TRUSTEES [542]

Name of Appointee	Address	Date Appointed	Date of Expiration
James McClure Clarke	Asheville	5-15-64	6-30-70
Wallace Carroll	Winston-Salem	5-15-64	6-30-70
E. N. Richards	Raleigh	5-15-64	6-30-70
Hugh Cannon	Raleigh	5-15-64	6-30-70
Mrs. James Boyd	Southern Pines	5-15-64	6-30-68
Mrs. Martha Muilenburg	Charlotte	5-15-64	6-30-68
Sam Ragan	Raleigh	5-15-64	6-30-68
James Semans	Durham	5-15-64	6-30-68
Smith Bagley	Winston-Salem	5-15-64	6-30-66
R. Philip Hanes, Jr.	Winston-Salem	5-15-64	6-30-66
Mrs. Wilbur Jolly	Louisburg	5-15-64	6-30-66
Mrs. Everette Miller	Raleigh	5-15-64	6-30-66

ADVISORY BOARD OF THE SCHOOL FOR THE PERFORMING ARTS [543]

Name of Appointee	Address	Date Appointed	Date of Expiration
Richard Adler	Upper Saddle River, New Jersey	3-26-64	6-30-69
Sidney Blackmer	Salisbury	3-26-64	6-30-71
Agnes de Mille	New York City	3-26-64	6-30-69
Vittorio Giannini	New York City	3-26-64	6-30-67
Paul Green	Chapel Hill	3-26-64	6-30-71
Jose Limon	New York City	3-26-64	6-30-71
Peter Mennin	New York City	3-26-64	6-30-71

Jan Peerce	New York City	3-26-64	6-30-67
James Christian Pfohl	Charlotte	3-26-64	6-30-67
Julius Rudel	New York City	3-26-64	6-30-69
Jose Ferrer	Beverly Hills, California	6-24-64	6-30-67
Eugenie Ouroussow	New York City	6-23-64	6-30-69

ASHEVILLE-BILTMORE COLLEGE BOARD OF TRUSTEES[544]

Mrs. Virginia Dameron	Asheville	8-22-63	6-30-71
John Reynolds	Asheville	8-22-63	6-30-71
Manly E. Wright	Asheville	8-22-63	6-30-71
Bruce Elmore	Asheville	8-22-63	6-30-69
Dula Hawkins	Marion	8-22-63	6-30-69
J. Aaron Prevost	Waynesville	8-22-63	6-30-69
J. Gerald Cowan	Asheville	8-22-63	6-30-67
William M. Lehmkuhl	Canton	8-22-63	6-30-67
Claude Ramsey, Jr.	Asheville	8-22-63	6-30-67
Edwin Duncan, Jr.	North Wilkesboro	8-22-63	6-30-65
Louis Lipinsky, Sr.	Asheville	8-22-63	6-30-65
Solon Smart	Cliffside	8-22-63	6-30-65

ASHEVILLE-BUNCOMBE TECHNICAL INSTITUTE BOARD OF TRUSTEES[545]

John H. Giezentanner	Asheville	12-10-63	6-30-71
Paul W. Markwood	Asheville	12-10-63	6-30-69
Ernest A. Mills	Asheville	12-10-63	6-30-67
William Dillard	Sylva	12-10-63	6-30-65

[536] See footnote 527.
[537] Succeeded C. Watson Brame.
[538] Succeeded L. A. Dysart.
[539] Succeeded Mrs. Harry B. Caldwell.
[540] Succeeded Kidd Brewer.
[541] Succeeded B. C. Brock, resigned.
[542] As created by the 1963 General Assembly, this board consists of thirteen members, twelve of whom are appointed by the governor, and one of whom is the conductor of the North Carolina Symphony who serves ex officio. Initial appointments are as follows: Four, for six-year terms; four, for four-year terms; four, for two-year terms; reappointments are for six years. G. S. 116-65; S. L., 1963, c. 1116.
[543] The board consis's of at least ten members who shall have achieved national or international distinction as performers, playwrights, or composers. Original appointments are made by the governor for eight, six-, and four-year terms; reappointments shall be for eight years. S. L. 1963, c. 1116, s. 1.
[544] See footnote 527; see also, G. S. 116-45.2.
[545] See footnote 534.

Ben B. Brooks	Hickory	3-9-64	6-30-69
Ira E. Bell	Hickory	3-9-64	6-30-67
C. Ray Morrow	Claremont	3-9-64	6-30-65

CENTRAL PIEDMONT COMMUNITY COLLEGE BOARD OF TRUSTEES[557]

Mrs. Frank A. McClenegham	Charlotte	8-29-63	6-30-65
John R. Milliken	Monroe	8-29-63	6-30-67
Gerald Alton Rudisill	Badin	8-29-63	6-30-69
Mrs. James Boyce Garland	Gastonia	8-29-63	6-30-71

BOARD OF TRUSTEES OF THE NORTH CAROLINA HOSPITAL FOR CEREBRAL PALSY[558]

Thomas Henson[559]	Kinston	7-22-61	7-10-67
Mrs. R. M. Middleton[560]	Lexington	7-22-61	7-10-67
Grizzelle M. Norfleet †	Winston-Salem	7-22-61	7-10-67
J. Leslie Atkins, Jr.[561]	Durham	8-6-63	7-10-69
Harold Meyer[562]	Chapel Hill	8-6-63	7-10-69
J. Fleming Wily, Jr. †	Durham	8-6-63	7-10-69

CHARLOTTE COLLEGE BOARD OF TRUSTEES[563]

| J. M. Atkins | Charlotte | 7-10-63 | 6-30-65 |
| Thomas M. Belk | Charlotte | 7-10-63 | 6-30-65 |

---

[546] In 1963 the name of the institution was changed from the State School for the Blind and the Deaf in Raleigh to the Governor Morehead School. The board consists of eleven members appointed by the governor and confirmed by the Senate for four-year terms. G. S. 116-106; S. L. 1963, Res. 65.
[547] Succeeded Mrs. Homer Wright.
[548] Succeeded James Webb.
[549] Succeeded S. Linton Smith.
[550] Succeeded Mrs. Julian B. Hutaff.
[551] Succeeded Claude Teague.
[552] Succeeded Mrs. Eva Nickols, who did not accept appointment.
[553] See footnote 534.
[554] See footnote 534.
[555] See footnote 534.
[556] See footnote 534.
[557] See footnote 534.
[558] The board composed of nine members appointed by the governor for six-year terms. G. S. 131-127, 131-128.
[559] Succeeded James M. White.
[560] Succeeded Forrest Waller.
[561] Succeeded Mrs. B. V. Hedrick.
[562] Succeeded Roy L. Lindahl.
[563] See footnote 527; see also, G. S. 116-45.2.

Name of Appointee	Address	Date Appointed	Date of Expiration
Jesse Caldwell	Gastonia	7-10-63	6-30-65
James H. Clark	Wadesboro	7-19-63	6-30-67
John L. Fraley	Cherryville	7-10-63	6-30-67
C. Frank Griffin	Monroe	7-10-63	6-30-67
C. A. McKnight	Charlotte	7-10-63	6-30-69
Addison H. Reese	Charlotte	7-10-63	6-30-69
Oliver R. Rowe	Charlotte	7-10-63	6-30-69
Sheldon P. Smith	Charlotte	7-10-63	6-30-71
Mrs. A. W. Thomas, Jr.	Concord	7-10-63	6-30-71
C. H. Wentz	Salisbury	7-10-63	6-30-71
J. E. Burnside[564]	Charlotte	12-10-63	6-30-65
ADVISORY COUNCIL TO CHERRY HOSPITAL AND O'BERRY SCHOOL[565]			
Andrew Best	Greenville	10-18-61	6-30-63
H. V. Brown	Goldsboro	10-18-61	6-30-63
William Gavin	Goldsboro	10-18-61	6-30-63
Mrs. W. L. T. Miller	Greensboro	10-18-61	6-30-63
H. S. Robinson	Chapel Hill	10-18-61	6-30-63
L. H. Robinson	Greensboro	10-18-61	6-30-63
O. L. Sherrill	Raleigh	10-18-61	6-30-63
THE COLORED ORPHANAGE OF NORTH CAROLINA BOARD OF DIRECTORS[566]			
M. S. Currin †	Oxford	7-27-61	5-9-65
Roy L. Noblin †	Oxford	7-27-61	5-9-65
Ben K. Lassiter †	Oxford	7-27-61	5-9-65
John S. Watkins, Jr.[567]	Oxford	7-27-61	5-9-65
W. T. Yancey †	Oxford	7-27-61	5-9-65
COLUMBUS COUNTY COMMUNITY COLLEGE BOARD OF TRUSTEES[568]			
H. P. Bell, Jr.	Currie	2-10-64	6-30-71
James C. Green	Clarkton	2-10-64	6-30-69
P. A. McRae[569]	Proctorville	2-10-64	6-30-65
Mrs. M. H. Rourk	Shallotte	2-10-64	6-30-67
MOSES H. CONE MEMORIAL HOSPITAL BOARD OF TRUSTEES[570]			
Roger A. McDuffie †	Greensboro	5-3-61	5-12-65
L. P. McLendon †	Greensboro	5-3-61	5-12-65
James R. Townsend †	Greensboro	5-3-61	5-12-65

CONFEDERATE WOMAN'S HOME BOARD OF DIRECTORS[571]

Mrs. E. R. MacKethan †*	Fayetteville	6-12-61-63	6-30-63-65
Mrs. W. S. Alexander *[572]	Fairmont	7-22-61-63	6-30-63-65
John R. Jenkins, Jr. †	Aulander	10-25-61	6-30-63
James I. Musgrave *[573]	Pikeville	10-25-61-63	6-30-63-65
Mrs. Arthur F. Pope *[574]	Dunn	10-25-61-63	6-30-63-65
Mrs. Henry L. Stevens, Jr. †*	Warsaw	10-25-61-63	6-30-63-65
Charles G. Rose, Jr. †*	Fayetteville	10-25-61-63	6-30-63-65
Mrs. John D. Boyd[575]	Fayetteville	9-25-63	6-30-65

NORTH CAROLINA BOARD OF DIRECTORS OF SCHOOLS FOR THE DEAF[576]

Ed Beddingfield[577]	Stantonsburg	10-20-61	10-20-65
Arthur Bell Harris	Fairfield	10-20-61	10-20-65
Howard Moose †	Newton	10-20-61	10-20-65
W. S. McCord †	Charlotte	10-20-61	10-20-65
J. G. Northcott †	Black Mountain	10-20-61	10-20-65
Mrs. Pearl O'Donnell	Asheville	7-22-61	10-20-65
O. H. Pons †	Valdese	10-20-61	10-20-65
Samuel McD. Tate †	Morganton	10-20-61	10-20-65
J. M. Vestal	Raleigh	10-20-61	10-20-65
Lawrence O. Weaver	Greensboro	10-20-61	10-20-65
Roy B. Williams	Elm City	10-20-61	10-20-65

564 Succeeded J. M. Atkins, deceased.
565 The council, consisting of seven members appointed by the governor for two-year terms, was made void by action of the 1963 General Assembly. In that year the legislature created the Medical Advisory Council to the State Board of Mental Health which took over the powers and responsibilities of the former commission. S. L., 1961, c. 766; S. L., 1963, c. 668.
566 The board consists of thirteen members, eight of whom are appointed by the General Assembly and five of whom are white persons from Granville County, appointed by the governor for four-year terms. G. S. 116-139.
567 Succeeded N. W. Weldon, resigned.
568 See footnote 534.
569 Deceased in March, 1965.
570 Fifteen members make up this board, three of whom are appointed by the governor for four-year terms. Private Laws of the State of North Carolina . . . 1913, c. 400, hereinafter cited as Private Laws.
571 The board is composed of seven members appointed by the governor for two-year terms. The state treasurer is treasurer of the board. G. S. 112-2.
572 Succeeded J. H. Ross.
573 Succeeded J. Henry Hill, Jr.
574 Succeeded Henry C. Doby.
575 Succeeded John R. Jenkins, Jr., resigned.
576 As organized by the 1961 General Assembly the North Carolina School for the Deaf at Morganton and the Eastern North Carolina School for the Deaf shall be under the control of this board. The governor appoints eleven members to serve for four years. S. L., 1961, c. 968, s. 1.
577 Succeeded Harry L. Wilson, deceased.

Gibson Prather	Fayetteville	9-30-63	6-30-69
Herbert W. Vick	Fayetteville	9-30-63	6-30-65
Mrs. Beth Finch	Fayetteville	9-30-63	6-30-67

FORSYTH COUNTY TECHNICAL INSTITUTE BOARD OF TRUSTEES[600]

Claude M. Hamrick	Winston-Salem	2-25-64	6-30-71
Charles C. Lassiter	Winston-Salem	2-25-64	6-30-69
Claude Frederick	Winston-Salem	2-25-64	6-30-67
Marvin J. Mulhern	Winston-Salem	2-25-64	6-30-65

LENOIR COUNTY TECHNICAL INSTITUTE BOARD OF TRUSTEES[601]

C. Brantley Aycock	Kinston	11-20-64	6-30-71
Robert H. Gilbert	Kinston	11-20-64	6-30-69
Mrs. Paul L. Fletcher	Kinston	11-20-64	6-30-67
William E. Brewer	Pink Hill	11-20-64	6-30-65

NORTH CAROLINA COLLEGE AT DURHAM BOARD OF TRUSTEES[602]

J. M. Hubbard †	Durham	10-18-61	6-30-69

578 See footnote 527.
579 Succeeded Frederick Willetts, Sr.
580 Succeeded Mrs. William B. Umstead.
581 Succeeded Charles H. Larkins, Sr.
582 Succeeded Carl Goerch.
583 Succeeded Elizabeth S. Bennett.
584 Succeeded Baxter Ridenhour.
585 Succeeded Herbert Waldrop.
586 Succeeded Harry L. Dalton, resigned.
587 See footnote 527.
588 Succeeded J. H. Moore.
589 Succeeded O. Ray Symonds.
590 Succeeded Roger R. Jackson, Jr., resigned.
591 Succeeded A. J. Jones, resigned.
592 Succeeded W. Lunsford Long, deceased.
593 Succeeded James C. Sawyer, Sr.
594 See footnote 527.
595 Succeeded Walter Baker, resigned.
596 Succeeded Ed. L. White.
597 Succeeded W. E. Horner, resigned.
598 Succeeded S. R. Rosemond, deceased.
599 See footnote 534.
600 See footnote 534.
601 See footnote 534.
602 See footnote 527.

RICHMOND COUNTY TECHNICAL INSTITUTE BOARD OF TRUSTEES[620]

A. R. Cowan, Jr.	Hamlet	6-23-64	6-30-65
Horace Clenon Coleman	Cordova	6-23-64	6-30-67
Hugh A. Lee	Rockingham	6-23-64	6-30-69
A. L. Cockman	Rockingham	6-23-64	6-30-71
Lindsey G. DeWitt[621]	Ellerbee	10-23-64	6-30-67

ROCKINGHAM COMMUNITY COLLEGE BOARD OF TRUSTEES[622]

Charles W. Campbell	Reidsville	12-16-63	6-30-71
Julius J. Gwyn	Reidsville	12-16-63	6-30-69
Earl W. Vaughn	Draper	12-16-63	6-30-67
Welsford Bishopric	Spray	12-16-63	6-30-65

ROWAN TECHNICAL INSTITUTE BOARD OF TRUSTEES[623]

Mrs. Arnold H. Snider, Jr.	Salisbury	7-28-64	6-30-65
Ozell K. Beatty	Salisbury	7-28-64	6-30-67
Alan F. Scott	Salisbury	7-28-64	6-30-69
Angus J. Currie	China Grove	7-28-64	6-30-71

[603] Succeeded J. W. Black.
[604] Succeeded Hanes Lassiter, resigned.
[605] Succeeded Edwin L. Jones, resigned.
[606] Succeeded John G. Clark, resigned.
[607] The board consists of nine members appointed by the governor for six-year terms. G. S. 131-1.
[608] Succeeded Helen Kaiser.
[609] Succeeded B. C. Trotter, Jr.
[610] Succeeded W. L. Balthis.
[611] The board is composed of nine members, of whom three are appointed by the governor for four-year terms. The Grand Master of Masons of North Carolina serves ex officio, and five members are elected by the Masonic Grand Lodge of North Carolina. Private Laws, 1923, c. 119; S. L., 1953, c. 60.
[612] Succeeded J. E. Rooker, Jr.
[613] Succeeded Thomas L. Simmons, deceased.
[614] See footnote 527.
[615] Succeeded Carl L. Maynor, deceased.
[616] Succeeded Albert E. Hammonds, deceased.
[617] Succeeded Steve Hammonds, Jr.
[618] Succeeded Zeb Lowry, resigned.
[619] See footnote 534.
[620] See footnote 534.
[621] Succeeded Horace Clenon Coleman, resigned.
[622] See footnote 534.
[623] See footnote 534.

Name of Appointee	Address	Date Appointed	Date of Expiration
RUTHERFORD COUNTY COMMUNITY COLLEGE BOARD OF TRUSTEES[624]			
Hollis M. Owens, Jr.	Rutherfordton	11-5-64	6-30-71
Spencer D. Gamble	Bostic	11-5-64	6-30-69
H. Paul Bridges	Cliffside	11-5-64	6-30-67
Lee L. Powers	Lake Lure	11-5-64	6-30-65
BOARD OF TRUSTEES OF THE NORTH CAROLINA SANATORIUMS FOR THE TREATMENT OF TUBERCULOSIS[625]			
Paul S. Cragan †	Sanford	8-21-61	4-29-67
Mrs. Sadie L. McCain †	Wilson	8-21-61	4-29-67
W. G. Suiter †	Weldon	8-21-61	4-29-67
Hardy Talton †	Pikeville	8-21-61	4-29-67
Mrs. Reid S. Monroe[626]	Salisbury	12-19-62	4-29-67
H. Emmett Powell *[627]	Clinton	12-6-62-63	4-29-63-69
O. Arthur Kirkman, Chairman †	High Point	7-17-63	4-29-69
John Lawrence McNeill †	Raeford	7-17-63	4-29-69
Mrs. Roy Parker, Sr. †	Ahoskie	7-17-63	4-29-69
A. E. Gibson, Sr.[628]	Wilmington	2-6-64	4-29-65
Mrs. Cecil L. Sanford[629]	Laurinburg	8-19-64	4-29-69
SANDHILLS COMMUNITY COLLEGE BOARD OF TRUSTEES[630]			
H. Clifton Blue	Aberdeen	11-27-63	6-30-71
Paul Dickson	Raeford	11-27-63	6-30-69
Charles Highsmith	Troy	11-27-63	6-30-67
Thomas B. Hunter	Rockingham	11-27-63	6-30-65
SURRY COUNTY COMMUNITY COLLEGE BOARD OF TRUSTEES[631]			
Robert A. Yarborough	Elkin	4-21-64	6-30-71
Robert E. Merritt	Mt. Airy	4-21-64	6-30-69
W. I. Monday	Mt. Airy	4-21-64	6-30-67
Glenn M. Robertson	Mt. Airy	4-21-64	6-30-65
NORTH CAROLINA VOCATIONAL TEXTILE SCHOOL BOARD OF TRUSTEES[632]			
J. C. Cowan, Jr. †	Greensboro	8-11-61	7-1-65
William B. Shuford †	Hickory	8-11-61	7-1-65

Name	Place	Appointed	Term ends
Council Claudius Dawson †	Cramerton	8-26-63	7-1-67
Carl F. Mauney †	Kings Mountain	8-26-63	7-1-67
Sherwood Hedgepeth [633]	Greensboro	9-15-64	7-1-68
J. Harold Lineberger †	Belmont	9-15-64	7-1-68

WAYNE TECHNICAL INSTITUTE BOARD OF TRUSTEES [634]

Name	Place	Appointed	Term ends
Nancy W. Chase	Eureka	4-10-64	6-30-71
Hal H. Tanner	Goldsboro	4-10-64	6-30-69
Ralph E. Jinnette	Brogden	4-10-64	6-30-67
Earl Whitted, Jr.	Goldsboro	4-10-64	6-30-65

WESTERN CAROLINA COLLEGE BOARD OF TRUSTEES [635]

Name	Place	Appointed	Term ends
Charles O. van Gorder *[636]	Andrews	2-11-61-61	6-30-61-69
Jonathan Woody[637]	Waynesville	10-16-61	6-30-69
Phillip Woollcot †	Asheville	10-16-61	6-30-69
Morgan Cooper[638]	Forest City	10-16-63	6-30-69
Mrs. Dan K. Moore †	Canton	10-16-63	6-30-71
Modeal Walsh[639]	Robbinsville	10-16-63	6-30-71
Boyce Whitmire[640]	Hendersonville	10-16-63	6-30-71

WILKES COUNTY COMMUNITY COLLEGE BOARD OF TRUSTEES [641]

Name	Place	Appointed	Term ends
Robert M. Gambill	Wilkesboro	12-31-64	6-30-71

[624] See footnote 534.
[625] The board consists of twelve members appointed by the governor and confirmed by the Senate for terms of six years. The state health director is an ex officio member. G. S. 131-62, 131-63, 131-64.
[626] Succeeded W. G. Suiter, deceased.
[627] Succeeded P. K. Gravely.
[628] Succeeded Carl C. Council, deceased.
[629] Succeeded H. Emmett Powell, deceased.
[630] See footnote 534.
[631] See footnote 534.
[632] The board is composed of seven members, six of whom are appointed by the governor for four-year terms. The director of vocational education serves ex officio. G. S. 115-255.1: S. L., 1945, c. 806.
[633] Succeeded Harry Carter.
[634] See footnote 534.
[635] See footnote 527.
[636] Succeeded H. A. Helder, deceased.
[637] Succeeded Charles F. Gold.
[638] Succeeded Phillip Woollcot, resigned.
[639] Succeeded W. H. McDonald.
[640] Succeeded James J. Harris.
[641] See footnote 534.

Fred W. Butner, Jr.[650]	Winston-Salem	5-14-62	4-8-67
Shannon Meriwether †	Tryon	7-5-63	4-8-68
Charles H. Wheatley[651]	Charlotte	3-25-64	4-8-69

STATE BOARD OF BARBER EXAMINERS [652]

Claude T. Land †	Rocky Mount	7-10-61	7-1-67
Lloyd O. Crowe[653]	Morehead City	8-1-63	7-1-69

NORTH CAROLINA STATE BOARD OF CERTIFIED PUBLIC ACCOUNTANT EXAMINERS [654]

Theodore N. Grice *[655]	Raleigh	7-26-61-64	6-30-64-67
Richard M. Hunter *[656]	Charlotte	7-26-61-64	6-30-64-67
Richard K. Worsley †	Greenville	5-30-62	6-30-65
Irvin R. Squires[657]	Greensboro	6-29-62	6-30-65
William A. Terrill[658]	Chapel Hill	7-13-62	6-30-65
J. Neveland Brand, Jr.[659]	Wilmington	8-30-63	6-30-65

STATE BOARD OF CHIROPRACTIC EXAMINERS [660]

Ramey F. Kemp *[661]	Mocksville	7-10-61-64	5-5-64-67

[642] See footnote 527; see also, G. S. 116-452.
[643] See footnote 534.
[644] See footnote 527.
[645] Succeeded H. D. Townsend.
[646] Succeeded Bert Bennett, resigned.
[647] Succeeded L. D. Long.
[648] This board is composed of five members appointed by the governor for staggered five-year terms; all must have been engaged in the practice of architecture for at least ten years. G. S. 83-2, 83-10.
[649] Succeeded James W. Griffith, resigned.
[650] Succeeded S. Porter Graves.
[651] Succeeded John E. Ramsay.
[652] The board consists of three members to be appointed by the governor for six-year terms. Each member must be an experienced barber, having practiced barbering in North Carolina for at least five years. G. S. 86-6.
[653] Succeeded Guy Adams.
[654] The board consists of four members appointed by the governor for a term of three years and until their successors are appointed G. S. 93-12.
[655] Succeeded Harry R. Borthwick.
[656] Succeeded John B. Dickinson, Jr.
[657] Succeeded Richard K. Worsley, who did not accept reappointment.
[658] Succeeded Martin L. Black, Jr.
[659] Succeeded William A. Terrill, resigned.
[660] The board consists of three members appointed by the governor for three-year terms. Members must be practicing chiropractors and residents of the state. No more than two members shall be graduates of the same school or college of chiropractic. G. S. 90-140, 90-141.
[661] Succeeded S. S. Stephenson.

Name of Appointee	Address	Date Appointed	Date of Expiration
W. Dillon Chambers †	Asheville	8-3-62	5-5-65
Erle Downing[662]	Fayetteville	8-26-63	5-5-66
STATE LICENSING BOARD FOR GENERAL CONTRACTORS [663]			
Raymond A. Bryan †	Goldsboro	3-14-61	12-31-65
E. P. Bond, Jr. *[664]	Lumberton	6-15-62-64	12-31-64-69
E. G. Singletary †	Greensboro	6-15-62	12-31-66
N. K. Dickerson, Jr. †	Monroe	1-11-63	12-31-67
Jesse P. Phifer †	Rockingham	2-21-64	12-31-68
STATE BOARD OF COSMETIC ART EXAMINERS [665]			
Mrs. Charles B. Noe †	Beaufort	6-11-62	7-1-65
Velma H. Reibel [666]	Charlotte	6-11-62	7-1-65
Joseph E. Snotherly[667]	Raleigh	6-11-62	7-1-65
STATE BOARD OF DENTAL EXAMINERS [668]			
Ralph B. Barden[669]	Wilmington	2-27-62	7-31-64
J. H. Guion †	Charlotte	2-27-62	7-31-64
Wade H. Breeland	Belmont	8-1-62	7-31-65
S. W. Shaffer †	Greensboro	8-1-62	7-31-65
S. L. Bobbitt †	Raleigh	8-1-63	7-31-66
G. Shuford Abernethy †	Hickory	8-1-63	7-31-66
BOARD OF EXAMINERS OF ELECTRICAL CONTRACTORS [670]			
Hector Ray *[671]	Fayetteville	2-6-61-62	4-15-62-65
C. H. Gudger *†	Asheville	9-20-61-64	4-15-64-67
W. P. Seagraves[672]	Raleigh	7-5-63	4-15-66
Thomas L. Watson, Jr.[673]	Wilson	12-31-64	4-15-65
STATE BOARD OF REGISTRATION FOR ENGINEERS AND LAND SURVEYORS [674]			
John Dargan Watson †	Greensboro	10-20-61	12-31-66
Arvin Page †	Winston-Salem	10-20-61	12-31-65
Meriwether Lewis *[675]	Kinston	10-20-61-62	12-31-62-67

Robert B. Rice †	Raleigh	2-6-64	12-31-68
George S. Rawlins †	Charlotte	12-31-64	12-31-69

GASOLINE AND OIL INSPECTION BOARD [676]

William Archie Cobb [677]	Ruffin	12-9-61	At pleasure of the governor
Walter Clark Jones, Jr. [678]	New Bern	12-9-61	At pleasure of the governor
Evander Worth McDaniel †	Elkin	12-9-61	At pleasure of the governor

BOARD OF NURSE REGISTRATION AND NURSING EDUCATION [679]

Robert N. Creadick * [680]	Durham	9-20-61-65	1-1-65-69
Dorothy Dixon [681]	Wilmington	9-20-61	1-1-65
Mrs. Martha M. Adams [682]	Winston-Salem	4-10-62	1-1-66
Mrs. Priscilla D. Ballance †	Rocky Mount	4-10-62	1-1-66

[662] Succeeded C. H. Peters.
[663] The Board is composed of five members appointed by the governor for five-year terms. At least one member must be in the business of highway construction, one in the business of public utilities, and one in the business of construction of buildings. G. S. 87-2, 87-4.
[664] Succeeded R. D. Beam, deceased.
[665] The Board consists of three members appointed by the governor for three-year terms. Each member must be an experienced cosmetologist who has practiced at least five years, and who is not connected with any cosmetic school, college, or academy. G. S. 88-13.
[666] Succeeded James A. Henderson.
[667] Succeeded Eleanor Register Wallace.
[668] The board originally consisted of six members of the North Carolina Dental Society, elected by the society and commissioned by the governor for three-year terms of office. By action of the 1961 General Assembly, the members are to be chosen by the dentists of the state, thus making the gubernatorial appointments thereafter void. G. S. 90-22; S. L., 1961, c. 213.
[669] Succeeded Horace K. Thompson.
[670] The board consists of three members appointed by the governor for three-year terms, and ex officio members as follows: the state electrical engineer, who is also the chairman, and the secretary of the Association of Electrical Contractors of North Carolina. G. S. 87-39.
[671] Succeeded Elwood C. Peele, deceased.
[672] Succeeded Robert J. Pearsall.
[673] Succeeded Hector Ray, resigned.
[674] The board is composed of five members appointed by the governor for five-year terms, the terms so staggered that one expires each year. Four of the members must be registered engineers and one a registered land surveyor, and all must have been engaged in the practice or teaching of his profession for at least ten years. G. S. 89-4; S. L., 1957, c. 1060.
[675] Succeeded Grady S. Harrell, deceased.
[676] The board is composed of five members, of whom three are appointed by the governor and two serve ex officio: the commissioner of agriculture, the director of the Gas and Oil Inspection Division. G. S. 119-26.
[677] Succeeded Garland E. Bobbitt.
[678] Succeeded G. Allen Ives.
[679] The board consists of twelve members appointed by the governor for four-year terms. Five members are to be registered nurses, two are to be physicians, two are to be representatives of hospitals operating nursing schools, and three are to be practical nurses who shall be licensed practical nurses and may be members of the North Carolina Licensed Practical Nurses Association. G. S. 90-158.1; 90-171.1.
[680] Succeeded Louten R. Hedgpeth.
[681] Succeeded Joyce Warren.
[682] Succeeded Dorothy Woods.

Name of Appointee	Address	Date Appointed	Date of Expiration
Mrs. Mae Adams Beard †	Goldsboro	4-10-62	1-1-66
Mrs. Lura K. Davis †	Waynesville	4-10-62	1-1-66
Mrs. Edna E. Koontz[683]	Greensboro	4-10-62	1-1-66
C. F. Irons[684]	Greenville	1-3-63	1-1-67
James M. DeVane[685]	Lumberton	8-8-63	1-1-67
Mrs. W. D. James, Sr. †	Hamlet	8-8-63	1-1-67
J. Grayson Brothers †	Morganton	1-22-64	1-1-68
Mrs. Eloise R. Lewis †	Chapel Hill	1-22-64	1-1-68
Eugene Smith[686]	Charlotte	1-4-65	1-1-69

NORTH CAROLINA STATE BOARD OF OPTICIANS [687]

H. L. Ridgeway, Jr. †	Raleigh	8-11-61	7-1-66
W. B. Fluharty, Jr. †	Asheville	10-3-62	7-1-67
Vinson A. Smith[688]	Winston-Salem	7-5-63	7-1-68
Richard C. Hamilton[689]	Durham	11-20-64	7-1-69

STATE BOARD OF EXAMINERS IN OPTOMETRY [690]

C. Ray Lawrence †	Boone	8-3-61	5-1-66
James S. Bailey †	Charlotte	5-1-62	5-1-67
Lindsay N. Fincannon[691]	Elkin	6-12-63	5-1-68
John D. Robinson[692]	Wallace	5-20-64	5-1-69

STATE BOARD OF OSTEOPATHIC EXAMINATION AND REGISTRATION [693]

R. R. Sermon[694]	Raleigh	10-23-61	5-1-66
Richard C. Baker †	Rockingham	4-24-62	5-1-67
Joseph Huff †	Burlington	7-5-63	5-1-68
Guy Funk †	Winston-Salem	5-1-64	5-1-69

STATE BOARD OF PHARMACY [695]

Harold Vann Day[696]	Spruce Pine	5-22-61	4-28-66
Frank Wilson Dayvault †	Lenoir	5-30-62	4-28-67
David Dortch Claytor[697]	Greensboro	6-5-63	4-28-68
Clarence E. Page, Jr.[698]	Henderson	4-28-64	4-28-69

STATE EXAMINING COMMITTEE OF PHYSICAL THERAPISTS [699]

Robert L. Gossett [700]	Charlotte	8-3-61	1-1-64
Olive Wortman †*	Salisbury	8-3-61-64	1-1-64-67
Eleanor Flanagan* [701]	Durham	4-9-62-65	1-1-65-68
Dan A. Martin [702]	Chapel Hill	9-23-63	1-1-66
Mary Clyde Singleton [703]	Durham	9-23-63	1-1-66
Mrs. Dorothea Wray [704]	Gastonia	2-27-64	1-1-67

STATE BOARD OF EXAMINERS OF PLUMBING AND HEATING CONTRACTORS [705]

J. H. Rogers [706]	Asheville	9-20-61	4-25-68
Finley Lee †	Kinston	6-12-62	4-25-69

[683] Succeeded John K. Lockhart.

[684] Succeeded John Gilmer Mebane.

[685] Succeeded Bessie Perry Burgess.

[686] Succeeded Dorothy Dixon.

[687] The board consists of five members appointed by the governor from a list of names submitted by the North Carolina Opticians Association. Terms of office are for five years. Members shall have been in practice for at least five years. G. S. 90-238; S. L., 1951, c. 1089.

[688] Succeeded John W. Southerland.

[689] Succeeded Everett H. Stamper.

[690] The board is composed of five members elected by the North Carolina State Optometric Society and commissioned by the governor for five-year terms. Members must have engaged in the practice of optometry for five years. Vacancies are filled by the governor for unexpired terms. G. S. 90-116.

[691] Succeeded Kenneth W. Ramsey.

[692] Succeeded John D. Costabile.

[693] The board is composed of five members appointed by the governor for terms of five years each. The membership is selected from a number of not less than five practitioners of osteopathy recommended by the State Osteopathic Society. The governor fills vacancies for unexpired terms in the same manner and may request an increase in the number recommended by the society. G. S. 90-130.

[694] Succeeded S. D. Foster; Sermon died on October 13, 1964.

[695] The board consists of five members, elected by the North Carolina Pharmaceutical Association and commissioned by the governor for five-year terms. G. S. 90-55.

[696] Succeeded William Moss Salley, Jr.

[697] Succeeded Roger A. McDuffie.

[698] Succeeded Norfleet Owen McDowell, Jr.

[699] The committee is composed of five members, including at least one doctor and four physical therapists, appointed by the governor from a list submitted to him by the North Carolina Physical Therapy Association, Inc. Members are appointed for three-year terms. The governor appoints persons to fill unexpired terms and no member is allowed to serve more than two successive three-year terms. G. S. 90-257.

[700] Succeeded Edith Vail, resigned.

[701] Succeeded Anne Parrish.

[702] Succeeded G. Erick Bell, Jr.

[703] Succeeded Rachel L. Nunley.

[704] Succeeded Robert L. Gossett.

[705] The board is composed of seven members, each appointed by the governor for a seven-year term with the term of one member expiring each year. G. S. 87-16.

[706] Succeeded W. H. Sullivan, Jr.

Name of Appointee	Address	Date Appointed	Date of Expiration
J. Frank Sealy[707]	Raleigh	6-11-63	4-25-67
H. G. Baity †	Chapel Hill	7-5-63	4-25-70
J. M. Jarrett †	Raleigh	6-18-64	4-25-71

Committee on Postmortem Medicolegal Examinations [708]

Name of Appointee	Address	Date Appointed	Date of Expiration
Holt McPherson †	High Point	12-16-64	11-29-67

North Carolina Real Estate Licensing Board [709]

Name of Appointee	Address	Date Appointed	Date of Expiration
Kenneth Royster Smith †*	Raleigh	8-14-61-64	7-31-64-67
D. Russell Foster, Jr.†	Kinston	6-26-62	7-31-65
J. Henry Cromartie[710]	Charlotte	6-26-62	7-31-65
James Bartlett Hall †	Belmont	12-9-63	7-31-66
John K. Gallaher[711]	Winston-Salem	12-9-63	7-31-66
Henry C. Doby, Jr.[712]	Albemarle	8-4-64	7-31-65

State Board of Refrigeration Examiners [713]

Name of Appointee	Address	Date Appointed	Date of Expiration
E. T. Chanlett †	Chapel Hill	10-3-61	1-1-68
Karl Hanson †	Raleigh	5-15-62	1-1-69
Wade V. Carter[714]	Charlotte	8-16-63	1-1-67
Billy B. Smith[715]	Lumberton	4-15-64	1-1-70
Walter H. Jones †	Raleigh	11-24-64	1-1-71

State Board of Sanitarian Examiners [716]

Name of Appointee	Address	Date Appointed	Date of Expiration
Robert W. Brown †	Asheville	9-20-61	12-15-65
James N. Fulp †	Statesville	6-18-62	12-15-65
Fred G. Pegg †	Winston-Salem	12-5-62	12-15-66
Marley M. Melvin †	Raleigh	12-9-64	12-15-67
Bob C. Sandford [717]	Rockingham	12-9-64	12-15-67
Joe L. Costin[718]	Kenansville	12-9-64	12-15-66
Hamilton Wright Stevens, Jr.[719]	Asheville	12-9-64	12-15-66

Structural Pest Control Commission [720]

Name of Appointee	Address	Date Appointed	Date of Expiration
H. E. Fry[721]	Raleigh	8-11-61	7-1-64
Clyde F. Smith, *Chairman* †*	Raleigh	8-11-61-65	7-1-64-67

Name	Place		
J. A. Harris †	Raleigh	9-20-62	7-1-65
W. C. McClellan [722]	Raleigh	8-19-63	7-1-66
John L. Reitzel †	Raleigh	8-19-63	7-1-66
David Dodd, Jr. [723]	Monroe	6-12-64	7-1-67

STATE BOARD OF WATER WELL CONTRACTOR EXAMINERS [724]

Name	Place		
R. O. Heater *	Cary	2-12-62-62	12-31-62-65
Boyce T. Green *	Canton	2-12-62-62	12-31-62-65
J. M. Jarrett *	Raleigh	2-12-62-64	12-31-64-67
John R. Lowry, *Chairman*[725]	Laurinburg	2-12-62	12-31-64
Manley S. Martin	Warrenton	2-12-62	12-31-65
G. Allie Moore, Jr.	Wilmington	2-12-62	12-31-65
Harry M. Peek	Raleigh	2-12-62	12-31-65
William E. Godwin, Jr.[726]	Fayetteville	2-10-64	12-31-64

NORTH CAROLINA VETERINARY MEDICAL BOARD [727]

Name	Place		
J. C. Bateman †	Greenville	2-21-62	7-1-66

707 Succeeded L. L. Vaughan, deceased.
708 This committee is organized within the State Board of Health, consists of seven members, six of whom are ex officio and one of whom is appointed by the governor for a four-year term. G. S. 130-192; S. L., 1955, c. 972, s. 1.
709 The board consists of five members appointed by the governor for three-year terms. Not more than two of the members may be licensed real estate brokers or salesmen. S. L., 1957, c. 744; G. S. 93A-3.
710 Succeeded Henry V. Koonts.
711 Succeeded Peter W. Hairston.
712 Succeeded J. Henry Cromartie, resigned.
713 The board consists of seven members, serving staggered terms, appointed by the governor. G. S. 87-52; S. L., 1955, c. 912.
714 Succeeded P. B. Mayo, resigned.
715 Succeeded George Brickle.
716 The board is composed of nine members, six of whom are appointed by the governor and three of whom serve ex officio. Initial appointments were for one, two, three, and four-year terms. Reappointments are for four-year terms. Each member must be a registered sanitarian. G. S. 90A-2; S. L., 1959, c. 1271, s. 2.
717 Succeeded E. R. Spruill.
718 Succeeded Walter C. Lackey.
719 Succeeded Fred G. Gregg, resigned.
720 The commission consists of five members, each appointed by the governor for a three-year term. G. S. 106-65.23; S. L., 1955, c. 1017.
721 Succeeded T. M. Gunn.
722 Succeeded David A. Goforth.
723 Succeeded H. E. Fry.
724 As authorized by the 1961 General Assembly, the board consists of seven members appointed by the governor for initial terms of one, two, and three-year periods. Subsequent appointments are made for three years. G. S. 87-70; S. L., 1961, c. 997, s. 6.
725 Deceased.
726 Resigned.
727 As restated by the 1961 General Assembly, the board is composed of five members, appointed by the governor annually when and as the terms of office of the present members expire. Members, who serve for five-year terms, shall be legal residents of the state and licensed to practice veterinary medicine in the state for not less than five years prior to their appointments. G. S. 90-180; S. L., 1961, c. 353, s. 3.

Name of Appointee	Address	Date Appointed	Date of Expiration
James I. Cornwell †	Asheville	8-15-62	7-1-67
Fred B. Coates †	Reidsville	10-2-64	7-1-68
C. C. McLean728	Southern Pines	7-7-64	7-1-69

STATE OWNED RAILROADS

ATLANTIC AND NORTH CAROLINA RAILROAD [729]

DIRECTORS

Name of Appointee	Address	Date Appointed	Date of Expiration
George A. Moore, Jr. †*	Raleigh	8-7-61-62-63-64	8-7-62-63-64-65
Hugh G. Swan †*	New Bern	8-7-61-62-63	8-7-62-63-64
R. E. Hamlin, Jr.	Kinston	8-7-61	8-7-62
J. E. Ragan, Jr. †*	Oriental	8-7-61-62-63	8-1-62-63-64
Troy Page *	Clayton	8-7-61-62-63	8-7-62-63-64
John S. Butler	St. Pauls	8-7-61	8-7-62
Moses Howard *	Newport	8-7-61-62-63	8-7-62-63-64
W. B. Chalk	Morehead City	8-7-61	8-7-62
W. G. Crawford *	Goldsboro	8-10-62-63-64	8-9-63-64-65
Judson H. Blount *	Greenville	8-10-62-63-64	8-9-63-64-65
Mitchell Allen *	Jacksonville	8-10-62-63	8-9-63-64
A. T. Leary, Jr.	Morehead City	7-30-64	8-7-65
Herbert G. Stiles	Jacksonville	7-30-64	8-7-65
Leon Mann, Jr.	Newport	7-30-64	8-7-65
R. R. Rivenbark	New Bern	7-30-64	8-7-65
E. L. Scott	Kinston	7-30-64	8-7-65

OFFICERS

Name of Appointee	Address	Date Appointed	Date of Expiration
George A. Moore, Jr., President †*	Raleigh	8-7-61-62-63-64	8-7-62-63-64-65
G. Paul LaRoque, Secretary-Treasurer †*	Kinston	8-7-61-62-63-64	8-7-62-63-64-65
Robert Satterfield, Attorney730	Hillsboro	8-7-61-62-63-64	8-7-62-63-64-65

EXECUTIVE COMMITTEE

Name of Appointee	Address	Date Appointed	Date of Expiration
Troy Page *	Clayton	8-7-61-62-63	8-7-62-63-64
Moses Howard *	Newport	8-7-61-62-63	8-7-62-63-64

Name	Location		
R. R. Rivenbark	New Bern	7-30-64	8-7-65
W. G. Crawford	Goldsboro	7-30-64	8-7-65
FINANCE COMMITTEE			
J. R. Carroll*	Jacksonville	8-7-61-62	8-7-62-63
John Gainey*	Morehead City	8-7-61-62-63-64	8-7-62-63-64-65
A. D. Ward*	New Bern	8-7-61-62-63-64	8-7-62-63-64-65
INSPECTOR			
Albert R. Bell †*	New Bern	8-7-61-62-63-64	8-7-62-63-64-65
PROXY			
John A. Williams, Jr.*	Raleigh	8-7-61-62-63-64	8-7-62-63-64-65
NORTH CAROLINA RAILROAD[731]			
DIRECTORS			
John M. Morehead †*	New York City	7-13-61-62-63-64	7-13-62-63-64-65
Trent Ragland, Jr.†	Raleigh	7-13-61	7-13-62
N. K. Dickerson, Jr.†	Monroe	7-13-61	7-13-62
Dan Nicholas*	Salisbury	7-13-61-62-63-64	7-13-62-63-64-65
Smith Richardson, Sr. †	New York City	7-13-61	7-13-62
W. H. Morrow	Albemarle	7-13-61	7-13-62
R. L. Pittman	Fayetteville	7-13-61	7-13-62
Jim Abernethy	Lincolnton	7-13-61	7-13-62
Dexter E. Howard*	Greensboro	7-12-62-63-64	7-12-63-64-65
Richard L. Carnes*	Hamlet	7-12-62-63	7-12-63-64
John M. Belk*	**Charlotte**	7-12-62-63-64	7-12-63-64-65
E. Bruce Peabody, Sr.*	**Raleigh**	7-12-62-63-64	7-12-63-64-65
Walter Rucker	Greensboro	7-12-63	7-12-63
James G. Babb, Jr.*	Charlotte	7-12-62-63-64	7-12-63-64-65

728 Succeeded C. B. Randall.
729 The board of directors is composed of twelve members, eight of whom the governor appoints annually. The governor also nominates the officers and the inspector and appoints the finance committee and the proxy. P. L., 1852, c. 136; P. L., 1858-1859, Resolution, p. 99; P. L., 1891 c. 483; P. L., 1925, c. 157. The Southern Railway, Incorporated, has lease to properties now.
730 Succeeded Malcolm B. Seawell.
731 The board of directors consists of twelve members, eight of whom are appointed by the governor with the advice and consent of the Council of State. The governor also appoints the proxy. See the bylaws of the North Carolina Railroad Company, and charter and amendments thereto. G. S. 147-12(7); P. L., 1854-1855, c. 32; P. L., 1873-1874, c. 33, 54, P. L., 1891, c. 392; P. L., 1925, c. 157.

Name of Appointee	Address	Date Appointed	Date of Expiration
William Z. Wood	Winston-Salem	7-1-63	7-12-63
J. Floyd Henderson	Charlotte	7-9-64	7-9-65
F. C. Franklin	Fayetteville	7-9-64	7-9-65
OFFICERS			
John M. Morehead, *President* †*	New York City	7-13-61-62-63-64	7-13-62-63-64-65
Woodrow Teague, *Secretary-Treasurer* *[732]	Raleigh	7-13-61-62-63-64	7-13-62-63-64-65
Harley B. Gaston, *Attorney* †	Belmont	7-13-61	7-13-62
M. H. Russ, *Expert* *[733]	Rocky Mount	7-12-62-63	7-12-63-64
David E. Henderson, *Attorney* *	Charlotte	7-12-62-63-64	7-12-63-64-65
W. E. Broughton, *Expert*	Rocky Mount	7-9-64	7-9-65
FINANCE COMMITTEE			
Irvin R. Squires †*	Greensboro	7-13-61-62-63-64	7-13-62-63-64-65
Paul Clark	Candor	7-13-61-62-63	7-13-62-63-64
J. V. Morgan	High Point	7-13-61-62-63-64	7-13-62-63-64-65
Henry B. Smith	Monroe	7-9-64	7-9-65
PROXY			
Edwin M. Gill †*	Raleigh	7-13-61-62-63-64	7-13-62-63-64-65

MISCELLANEOUS APPOINTMENTS IN LOCAL GOVERNMENT

TOWN OF ATLANTIC BEACH [734]			
A. B. Cooper, *Mayor* †	Morehead City	4-26-61	5-1-65
R. A. Barefoot †	Atlantic Beach	4-26-61	5-1-65
W. L. Derrickson [735]	Morehead City	4-26-61	5-1-65
Mack G. Smith[736]	Greenville	4-26-61	5-1-65
Charles S. Walters[737]	Atlantic Beach	4-26-61	5-1-65
COMMISSIONERS OF THE TOWN OF BOILING SPRING LAKES [738]			
Harold Greene, *Mayor*	Boiling Spring Lakes	4-7-61	5-31-63
Carl E. Kleimo	Boiling Spring Lakes	4-7-61	5-31-63

Name	Town		
Henry B. Smytte	Boiling Spring Lakes	4-7-61	5-31-63
Grange S. Cuthbert III	Boiling Spring Lakes	4-7-61	5-31-63
Douglass M. Bradham	Boiling Spring Lakes	4-7-61	5-31-63
Earl L. Elwood [739]	Southport	6-1-63	5-31-67
Anson Lewis[740]	Southport	6-1-63	5-31-67
James W. Hufham[741]	Southport	6-1-63	5-31-67
Homer S. King[742]	Southport	6-1-63	5-31-65
Charles A. Tate[743]	Southport	6-1-63	5-31-65

TOWN OF LONG BEACH [744]

Name	Town		
Ed W. Morgan[745]	Long Beach	5-19-61	6-1-65
Wiley W. Snow[746]	Long Beach	5-19-61	6-1-65
Johnie W. Vereen[747]	Long Beach	5-19-61	6-1-65
A. Turner Hight[748]	Long Beach	5-26-61	6-1-65
E. F. Middleton †	Long Beach	5-14-63	6-1-67
E. M. Underwood, Jr.[749]	Long Beach	5-14-63	6-1-67
Woodrow W. Vennel[750]	Long Beach	5-14-63	6-1-67

[732] Succeeded Edwin S. Pou.
[733] Succeeded Charles Heath.
[734] A mayor and four aldermen are appointed every four years by the governor upon the recommendations of the majority of property owners of the town. *Public Local Laws . . . 1937*, c. 433, s. 6, hereinafter cited as *P. L. L.*
[735] Succeeded M. E. Bizzell.
[736] Succeeded A. F. Fleming.
[737] Succeeded M. G. Coyle.
[738] The governing body consists of five commissioners appointed by the governor upon recommendation by the county and town officials. Initial terms are as follows: three for four-year terms and two for two-year terms. Reappointments are made for four years. From their number the commissioners elect their own mayor. *S. L., 1961*, c. 182, s. 4.
[739] Succeeded Harold Greene.
[740] Succeeded Carl E. Kleimo.
[741] Succeeded Henry B. Smytte.
[742] Succeeded Grange S. Cuthbert III.
[743] Succeeded Douglass M. Bradham.
[744] Six commissioners are appointed by the governor for four-year terms. The commissioners elect the mayor from among their number for a two-year term. *S. L., 1955*, c. 1067.
[745] Succeeded **J. A. Woltz.**
[746] Succeeded **A. T. Hight.**
[747] Succeeded **E. M. Underwood, Jr.**
[748] Succeeded **Johnie W. Vereen,** resigned.
[749] Succeeded **A. H. Cromer.**
[750] Succeeded **W. L. Simmons.**

Name of Appointee	Address	Date Appointed	Date of Expiration
COMMISSIONERS OF THE TOWN OF OCEAN ISLE BEACH [751]			
John Roberts	Ocean Isle Beach	5-19-61	6-1-65
Mrs. Mirium Horne	Ocean Isle Beach	5-19-61	6-1-65
Homer L. Johnston	Ocean Isle Beach	5-19-61	6-1-65
Watt Huntley *	Ocean Isle Beach	5-19-61-63	6-1-63-67
John Edwards[752]	Ocean Isle Beach	5-19-61	6-1-63
N. E. Meggs[753]	Ocean Isle Beach	5-19-61	6-1-63
J. C. Fortson[754]	Ocean Isle Beach	5-14-63	6-1-67
Virginia Ervin[755]	Ocean Isle Beach	5-14-63	6-1-67
TOWN OF SUNSET BEACH [756]			
Edward K. Proctor	Shallotte	7-9-63	5-31-67
Edward M. Gore	Shallotte	7-9-63	5-31-67
M. C. Gore	Shallotte	7-9-63	5-31-67
Nivan Milligan	Shallotte	7-9-63	5-31-65
Ben McDonald	Shallotte	7-9-63	5-31-65
L. H. Parramore	Shallotte	7-9-63	5-31-65
TOWN OF SURF CITY [757]			
R. T. Batts, Mayor †	Surf City	6-16-61	6-30-63
M. J. Blizzard[758]	Surf City	6-16-61	6-30-63
Paul A. L. Black[759]	Surf City	6-16-61	6-30-63
TOWN OF WHITE LAKE [760]			
J. J. Womble, Mayor † *	White Lake	6-16-61-63	7-2-63-65
Gordon W. Love †	Garland	6-16-61	7-2-63
William M. Corbett, Jr. †	White Lake	6-16-61	7-2-63
Hiram A. Melvin †	White Lake	6-16-61	7-2-63
Issiah H. Herring[761]	White Lake	6-16-61	7-2-63
Lucy R. Duncan[762]	White Lake	7-18-63	7-6-65
W. K. Evans, Jr.[763]	White Lake	7-18-63	7-6-65
Livious D. Herring[764]	White Lake	7-18-63	7-6-65
Paul G. Strickland[765]	White Lake	7-18-63	7-6-65
William M. Corbett, Jr.[766]	White Lake	4-14-64	7-6-65

TOWN OF WRIGHTSVILLE BEACH [707]

Lawrence C. Rose †	Wrightsville Beach	6-14-63	7-4-67
Jere D. Freeman, Jr. [708]	Wrightsville Beach	6-16-61	7-6-65
Richard F. Meier †	Wrightsville Beach	6-16-61	7-6-65
Kenneth M. Sprunt [709]	Wrightsville Beach	6-16-61	7-6-65
Robert N. Taylor [770]	Wrightsville Beach	10-11-61	7-6-65
Robert M. Williams †	Wrightsville Beach	6-14-63	7-4-67

TOWN OF YAUPON BEACH COMMISSIONERS [771]

G. V. Barbee, Jr.	Yaupon Beach	6-16-61	6-1-65
Clarence E. Murphy †	Yaupon Beach	6-16-61	6-1-65
E. L. Champion	Yaupon Beach	6-16-61	6-1-65
W. R. Price [772]	Yaupon Beach	6-18-63	6-1-67

[751] The governor appoints the six persons receiving the highest number of votes in the municipal election. Initial appointments were for two-year terms. At the end of this period the three persons receiving the highest number of votes would be appointed for four years and the other three for two years. Thereafter all appointments are for four-year terms. S. L., 1959, c. 887.
[752] Succeeded Odell Williamson.
[753] Succeeded W. T. Wimbish.
[754] Succeeded John Edwards.
[755] Succeeded N. E. Meggs.
[756] The governor appoints as six commissioners the persons receiving the highest number of votes in the municipal elections. Initial appointments are for two- and four-year terms; thereafter commissioners serve for four years. From their number the commissioners select a mayor. S. L., 1963, c. 93, ss. 3, 4.
[757] From persons recommended to him as having had the highest number of votes in the general election, the governor appoints biennially a mayor and two other commissioners. S. L., 1949, c. 512, s. 12. (No election was held in 1963; therefore, the same persons continued to serve.)
[758] Succeeded A. H. Ward.
[759] Succeeded M. J. Blizzard, who moved into the position of commissioner of finance.
[760] The five persons receiving the highest number of votes in the biennial election are appointed by the governor as the governing body of White Lake. The law provides that the person with the highest number of votes be appointed mayor and the other four be appointed commissioners. Any vacancies are filled by appointment of the governor upon the recommendation of the remaining commissioners. S. L., 1963, c. 339, s. 2.
[761] Succeeded Rodney Marshburn.
[762] Succeeded Gordon W. Love.
[763] Succeeded William M. Corbett, Jr.
[764] Succeeded Hiram A. Melvin.
[765] Succeeded Issiah H. Herring.
[766] Succeeded Paul G. Strickland, resigned.
[767] Upon recommendation of municipal officials the governor appoints five aldermen for four-year terms. The aldermen choose one of their number as mayor. S. L., 1951, c. 637; S. L., 1955, c. 772.
[768] Succeeded E. F. Peschau.
[769] Succeeded J. C. Thompson.
[770] Succeeded Jere D. Freeman, Jr., resigned.
[771] The commissioners are elected by the qualified voters and appointed by the governor. Initial appointments were for two- and four-year terms; reappointments are for four years. S. L., 1957, c. 899.
[772] Succeeded C. E. Bellamy.

Name of Appointee	Address	Date Appointed	Date of Expiration
Andrew S. Burgess[773]	Yaupon Beach	6-18-63	6-1-67
L. D. King, Jr.[774]	Yaupon Beach	6-18-63	6-1-67
DAVIDSON COUNTY COURT [775]			
Charles E. Williams, Jr., *Judge* †	Lexington	11-30-62	First Monday of December, 1964
Hubert E. Olive, Jr., *Solicitor* *[776]	Lexington	11-30-62-64	First Monday of December, 1964-1966
Jack E. Klass, *Judge* *[777]	Lexington	9-1-64-64	First Monday of December, 1964-1966
DURHAM COUNTY CIVIL COURT [778]			
Oscar G. Banker, *Judge* †	Durham	7-11-61	8-5-63
MUNICIPAL RECORDER'S COURT OF THE TOWN OF SILER CITY[779]			
J. Speight Wrenn, *Judge* †	Siler City	12-22-61	1-1-66
T. F. Baldwin, *Solicitor* †	Siler City	12-22-61	1-1-66
W. C. Webb, *Judge*[780]	Siler City	2-10-64	1-1-66
THOMASVILLE RECORDER'S COURT [781]			
L. Roy Hughes, *Judge* †*	Thomasville	4-1-61-63	4-1-63-65
William B. Mills, *Solicitor* *[782]	Thomasville	4-1-61-63	4-1-63-65
TAX COLLECTOR, TRANSYLVANIA COUNTY[783]			
Lawrence R. Hipp[784]	Brevard	2-10-61	12-7-64
WILKES COUNTY COURT[785]			
E. James Moore, *Judge*	North Wilkesboro	1-20-64	10-6-65

NON-STATUTORY BOARDS AND COMMISSIONS [786]

GOVERNOR'S COORDINATING COMMITTEE ON AGING[787]

Name of Appointee	Address	Date Appointed	Date of Expiration
Mrs. Ellen Winston †	Raleigh	1-25-61	Term indefinite
J. W. R. Norton †	Raleigh	1-25-61	Term indefinite
Ralph Andrews †	Raleigh	1-25-61	Term indefinite
Margaret Blee †	Chapel Hill	1-25-61	Term indefinite

Name	Place	Date	Term
E. N. Brower†	Hope Mills	1-25-61	Term indefinite
Ewald W. Busse†	Durham	1-25-61	Term indefinite
Frank Crane†	Raleigh	1-25-61	Term indefinite
Catherine Dennis†	Raleigh	1-25-61	Term indefinite
Eugene A. Hargrove†	Raleigh	1-25-61	Term indefinite
Mrs. Elizabeth A. Hughey†	Raleigh	1-25-61	Term indefinite
Wingate M. Johnson†	Winston-Salem	1-25-61	Term indefinite
Henry E. Kendall†	Raleigh	1-25-61	Term indefinite
Harold D. Meyer†	Chapel Hill	1-25-61	Term indefinite
David S. Weaver†	Raleigh	1-25-61	Term indefinite
Nathan H. Yelton, *Chairman*†	Raleigh	1-25-61	Term indefinite
R. Eugene Brown[788]	Raleigh	1-3-63	Term indefinite
Edgar T. Beddingfield[789]	Statonsburg	6-16-64	Term indefinite

[773] Succeeded Robert C. Sellers.

[774] Succeeded E. G. Sinclair.

[775] The judge and the solicitor are appointed by the governor to hold office for two years or until their successors are appointed. P. L. L., 1933, c. 82.

[776] Succeeded Thomas H. Suddarth, Jr.

[777] Succeeded Charles E. Williams, Jr., resigned.

[778] By an act of the 1963 General Assembly the term of the judge of Durham County Civil Court was increased from two years to four years. Under the new provision the governor no longer has authority to appoint the judge, as this duty is now delegated to the county commissioners of Durham County. G. S. 7-383.1; S. L., 1963, c. 485.

[779] The judge and the solicitor are appointed by the governor for terms of four years each. S. L., 1953, c. 607.

[780] Succeeded J. Speight Wrenn, deceased.

[781] The judge and solicitor are appointed by the governor for two-year terms each upon the recommendation of the city of Thomasville. P. L. 1933, c. 245.

[782] Succeeded E. W. Hooper.

[783] Officials of the county make recommendations to the governor who appoints one person for a four-year term. P. L. L., 1925, c. 8, as amended by P. L. L., 1933, c. 30.

[784] Succeeded Margaret Whitmire Guilkey.

[785] The governor appoints a qualified judge from Wilkes County to serve a two-year term; any vacancy shall be filled by the governor. G. S. 7-405, 7-406, 7-407.

[786] These commissions, while not authorized by law, are included here because of their significant relationship to the Sanford administration and/or because of their influence on later legislation. The groups selected are by no means inclusive but are perhaps the most important of such unofficial boards which gave the state an unprecedented amount of creative leadership. Unlike the statutory appointments, the number of members and their tenure are not clearly defined in these groups, and thus are not indicated as thoroughly in these data.

[787] The committee "was established in November, 1956, for the purpose of studying the needs of the state's elder citizens, evaluating existing programs designed to meet those needs, and recommending new programs and activities to meet those needs as they arise." The group consists of fifteen members appointed by the governor for indefinite terms. News release of Governor Terry Sanford, January 25, 1961.

[788] Succeeded Ellen Winston as Acting Commissioner of Public Welfare.

[789] Succeeded Wingate M. Johnson, deceased.

Name of Appointee	Address	Date Appointed	Date of Expiration
THE NORTH CAROLINA STATE ARTS COUNCIL[700]			
Mrs. J. Spencer Bell	Matthews	9-10-64	9-1-66
Allen Bone	Durham	9-10-64	9-1-66
Henry Bowers	Raleigh	9-10-64	9-1-66
Vittorio Giannini	Winston-Salem	9-10-64	9-1-66
Russell Graves	Chapel Hill	9-10-64	9-1-66
William C. Fields	Fayetteville	9-10-64	9-1-66
Paul Green	Chapel Hill	9-10-64	9-1-66
R. Philip Hanes, Jr., *President*	Winston-Salem	9-10-64	9-1-66
Robert Lee Humber, *Chairman*	Greenville	9-10-64	9-1-66
Herman Middleton	Greensboro	9-10-64	9-1-66
Ralph McCallister	Rougemont	9-10-64	9-1-66
Mrs. Benjamin Swalin	Chapel Hill	9-10-64	9-1-66
Francis Speight	Greenville	9-10-64	9-1-66
Henry Hall Wilson	Washington, D. C.	9-10-64	9-1-66
Sam T. Ragan	Raleigh	9-10-64	9-1-66
GOVERNOR'S COMMISSION ON EDUCATIONAL TELEVISION[701]			
Hubert Philpott, *Chairman*	Lexington	6-1-62	5-31-64
Harold Essex	Winston-Salem	6-1-62	5-31-64
R. Floyd Crouse	Sparta	6-1-62	5-31-64
E. Hervey Evans	Laurinburg	6-1-62	5-31-64
Horace Stacy, Jr.	Lumberton	6-1-62	5-31-64
Charles F. Carroll	Raleigh	6-1-62	5-31-64
Fred H. Weaver	Chapel Hill	6-1-62	5-31-64
Louis Lipinsky	Asheville	6-1-62	5-31-64
L. Y. Ballentine	Raleigh	6-1-62	5-31-64
Lois Edinger	Chapel Hill	6-1-62	5-31-64
W. H. Wagoner	Wilmington	6-1-62	5-31-64
Howard Holderness	Greensboro	6-1-62	5-31-64
Claude Currie	Durham	6-1-62	5-31-64
H. P. Taylor, Jr.	Wadesboro	6-1-62	5-31-64
Junie Peel	Williamston	6-1-62	5-31-64

J. Carlyle Rutledge	Kannapolis	6-1-62	5-31-64
Harold Coffey	Lenoir	6-1-62	5-31-64
L. W. Allen	Charlotte	6-1-62	5-31-64
L. S. Weaver	Fayetteville	6-1-62	5-31-64
Allen H. Gwyn, Jr.	Reidsville	6-1-62	5-31-64
Wesley Wallace	Chapel Hill	6-1-62	5-31-64
W. C. Harris, Jr.	Raleigh	6-1-62	5-31-64
Budd E. Smith	Wingate	6-1-62	5-31-64
Charles Phillips	Greensboro	6-21-62	5-31-64
Bill Hill	Murfreesboro	6-21-62	5-31-64
James T. Taylor	Durham	6-21-62	5-31-64
D. Grier Martin	Davidson	6-21-62	5-31-64
Hartwell Campbell	Greenville	12-4-62	5-31-64

GOVERNOR'S COMMISSION ON EDUCATION BEYOND THE HIGH SCHOOL[792]

			Report to the governor by
Clifton Blue	Aberdeen	9-29-61	9-1-62
Irving Carlyle, *Chairman*	Winston-Salem	9-29-61	9-1-62
F. Stuart Chapin	Asheville	9-29-61	9-1-62
Bonnie E. Cone	Charlotte	9-29-61	9-1-62
William C. Friday	Chapel Hill	9-29-61	9-1-62
Alfonso Elder	Durham	9-29-61	9-1-62
Deryl Hart	Durham	9-29-61	9-1-62
Mrs. Samuel Hair	Charlotte	9-29-61	9-1-62
W. Dallas Herring	Rose Hill	9-29-61	9-1-62
Leo W. Jenkins	Greenville	9-29-61	9-1-62

[790] Established by executive order in December, 1964, the council has as its purpose the advancement of the arts in North Carolina and the representation of this state in implementing the National Arts and Cultural Development Act of 1964. The twenty-member council appointed by the governor is instructed to report recommendations to the governor before July 1, 1966; it is due to expire not later than September 1, 1966. See Executive Order of Governor Terry Sanford, December 3, 1964, in this volume.

[791] Established by executive order, the commission is charged with the responsibility of advising the governor as to the most efficient, fruitful, and expeditious way in which the benefits of educational television can be provided to all the people of North Carolina (with special attention to federal grants to be used for this purpose). An indefinite number of members appointed by the governor serve terms of two years each. Executive Order of Governor Terry Sanford, May 15, 1962, in this volume.

[792] Established in September, 1961, the commission had a two-fold purpose: to identify and define the state's needs in higher education, and other education beyond or in lieu of the high school, and to recommend the most efficient plans and methods of meeting those needs. The Higher Education Act enacted by the 1963 General Assembly was largely a result of the study of the commission. See statement by Governor Terry Sanford, September 15, 1961, in this volume.

Name of Appointee	Address	Date Appointed	Date of Expiration
John R. Jordan	Raleigh	9-29-61	9-1-62
Colvin Leonard	Greensboro	9-29-61	9-1-62
Alex McMahon	Chapel Hill	9-29-61	9-1-62
L. P. McLendon	Greensboro	9-29-61	9-1-62
H. A. Mattox	Murphy	9-29-61	9-1-62
Thomas J. Pearsall	Rocky Mount	9-29-61	9-1-62
Mrs. L. Richardson Preyer	Greensboro	9-29-61	9-1-62
Samuel Proctor	Greensboro	9-29-61	9-1-62
Mrs. Harry B. Stein	Fayetteville	9-29-61	9-1-62
James Stikeleather	Asheville	9-29-61	9-1-62
Shelton Wicker	Sanford	9-29-61	9-1-62
Thomas Woodard	Wilson	9-29-61	9-1-62
Thomas White	Kinston	9-29-61	final report

North Carolina Film Board[783]

Name of Appointee	Address	Date Appointed	Date of Expiration
James Beveridge, *Director*	Canada	9-18-62	
Benjamin V. Mast, *Assistant Director*	Sugar Grove		
John Ehle, *Special Assistant*	Chapel Hill		
Lewis Dowdy	Greensboro	1-28-63	Term indefinite
Harmon Duncan	Durham	1-28-63	Term indefinite
James A. Gray, Jr.	Winston-Salem	1-28-63	Term indefinite
Paul Green	Chapel Hill	1-28-63	Term indefinite
Horace Hamilton	Raleigh	1-28-63	Term indefinite
Mrs. Guy Johnson	Chapel Hill	1-28-63	Term indefinite
P. R. Latta	Raleigh	1-28-63	Term indefinite
David R. Middleton	Greenville	1-28-63	Term indefinite
Sam Ragan	Raleigh	1-28-63	Term indefinite
W. D. Weatherford	Black Mountain	1-28-63	Term indefinite
Lawrence O. Weaver	Greensboro	2-12-63	Term indefinite
ADVISORY COMMITTEE			
Borden Mace	Beaufort	9-13-62	Term indefinite
George C. Stoney	Winston-Salem	9-13-62	Term indefinite
John Grierson	Scotland	9-13-62	Term indefinite

NORTH CAROLINA GOOD NEIGHBOR COUNCIL.[794]

Name	City	Date	Term
Clark S. Brown	Winston-Salem	6-26-63	Term indefinite
G. K. Butterfield	Wilson	6-26-63	Term indefinite
David S. Coltrane, *Chairman*	Raleigh	6-26-63	Term indefinite
Harry O. Gore	Southport	6-26-63	Term indefinite
J. Marse Grant	Raleigh	6-26-63	Term indefinite
Thompson Greenwood	Raleigh	6-26-63	Term indefinite
Reginald A. Hawkins	Charlotte	6-26-63	Term indefinite
J. W. Jeffries	Mebane	6-26-63	Term indefinite
Bruce F. Jones	Edenton	6-26-63	Term indefinite
John Larkins	Raleigh	6-26-63	Term indefinite
Edward Loewenstein	Greensboro	6-26-63	Term indefinite
Roy D. McLaurin	Laurinburg	6-26-63	Term indefinite
J. A. Nelson	Charlotte	6-26-63	Term indefinite
Ernest W. Ross	Albemarle	6-26-63	Term indefinite
J. S. Stewart	Durham	6-26-63	Term indefinite
J. P. Strother	Kinston	6-26-63	Term indefinite
James T. Taylor	Durham	6-26-63	Term indefinite
John H. Wheeler	Durham	6-26-63	Term indefinite
John W. Winters	Raleigh	6-26-63	Term indefinite
Edward R. Zane	Greensboro	6-26-63	Term indefinite
John E. Jervis	Asheville	8-21-63	Term indefinite
Marshall A. Rauch	Gastonia	8-21-63	Term indefinite
Jefferson Davis Batts[795]	Rocky Mount	9-24-63	Term indefinite
Robert Brown	High Point	11-19-63	Term indefinite
Geneva Jones Bowe	Murfreesboro	11-19-63	Term indefinite
Mrs. Katharine H. Marsh	High Point	5-8-64	Term indefinite
Mrs. Virginia Dameron	Asheville	8-21-64	Term indefinite
Mrs. Geneva B. Hamilton	Goldsboro	8-21-64	Term indefinite
J. W. Pate, Jr.	Fayetteville	8-21-64	Term indefinite
Mrs. Martha McKay	Chapel Hill	12-16-64	Term indefinite

[794] The organization, set up on a grant from the Richardson Foundation of Greensboro and New York and administered by the Department of Conservation and Development, is responsible for overseeing the production of documentary films on behalf of North Carolina and the distribution of these films within and outside the state. Statement of Governor Sanford, February 6, 1963. The twenty-eight member council has as its two-fold objective to encourage employment of qualified people without regard to race, and to urge youth to become better trained and qualified for employment. See statement of Governor Terry Sanford, January 18, 1963, in this volume.

[795] Resigned February 8, 1965.

Name of Appointee	Address	Date Appointed	Date of Expiration
BOARD OF DIRECTORS OF THE LEARNING INSTITUTE OF NORTH CAROLINA[796]			
Harold Howe III, *Executive Director*	Scarsdale, New York		
Ralph McCallister, *Operations Director*	Chapel Hill		
Terry Sanford, *President*	Fayetteville		
Douglas M. Knight	Durham		
Charles F. Carroll	Raleigh		
William C. Friday	Chapel Hill		
W. Dallas Herring	Rose Hill		
William C. Archie	Raleigh		
Donald B. Anderson	Chapel Hill		
Everett Hopkins	Durham		
Guy B. Phillips	Chapel Hill		
Harold L. Trigg	Salisbury		
Mrs. Harry Horton	Pittsboro		
Dan K. Moore	Canton		
GOVERNOR'S COMMISSION TO STUDY THE NEEDS OF THE MENTALLY RETARDED IN NORTH CAROLINA[797]			
Mrs. Charles Babcock	Winston-Salem	1-11-62	Report to the governor 9-30-62
Roland C. Braswell	Goldsboro	1-11-62	Report to the governor 9-30-62
Malcolm Brown	Shelby	1-11-62	Report to the governor 9-30-62
Rose Butler Brown	Durham	1-11-62	Report to the governor 9-30-62
Sam J. Burrow, Jr.	Asheboro	1-11-62	Report to the governor 9-30-62
Mrs. Susan Bash Cobb	Fayetteville	1-11-62	Report to the governor 9-30-62
Courtland H. Davis	Winston-Salem	1-11-62	Report to the governor 9-30-62
Thomas A. Fraser	Raleigh	1-11-62	Report to the governor 9-30-62
W. P. Herbert, Jr.	Charlotte	1-11-62	Report to the governor 9-30-62
Glenn M. Pickard	Burlington	1-11-62	Report to the governor 9-30-62
Mrs. Ruth Stoner	Lexington	1-11-62	Report to the governor 9-30-62
Thelma Thurston	Chapel Hill	1-11-62	Report to the governor 9-30-62
Charles Waddell, *Chairman*	Asheville	1-11-62	Report to the governor 9-30-62
Mrs. Dorothy Wilson	Leaksville	1-11-62	Report to the governor 9-30-62
John K. Wilson	Greensboro	1-11-62	Report to the governor 9-30-62

Harrie R. Chamberlin	Chapel Hill	4-18-62	Report to the governor 9-30-62
C. Douglas Carter	Winston-Salem	4-18-62	Report to the governor 9-30-62
Felix S. Barker	Raleigh	2-28-62	Report to the governor 9-30-62
Joe K. Byrd	Morganton	5-3-62	Report to the governor 9-30-62

BOARD OF DIRECTORS OF THE NORTH CAROLINA FUND[798]

Terry Sanford, *Chairman*	Fayetteville
C. A. McKnight, *President*	Charlotte
John H. Wheeler, *Treasurer*	Durham
George Esser, *Executive Director*	Durham
Hargrove Bowles, Jr.	Greensboro
J. Gerald Cowan	Asheville
Samuel Duncan	Salisbury
Hollis Edens	Winston-Salem
Mrs. H. Frank Forsyth	Winston-Salem
James A. Gray	Winston-Salem
W. Dallas Herring	Rose Hill
Wallace Murchison	Wilmington
Mrs. B. C. Parker	Albemarle
Thomas J. Pearsall	Rocky Mount
John Ehle	Chapel Hill
Mrs. Dan K. Moore	Canton

---

[796] The initial directors of the corporation shall include the following six persons who shall serve on the board as long as they serve in their respective positions: the president of Duke University, the president of the University of North Carolina, the chairman of the State Board of Education, the State Superintendent of Public Instruction, the Director of the State Board of Higher Education, and the chairman of the Board of Higher Education, the North Carolina Fund. Additional directors shall be chosen as follows: two by the Board of Education, and one each by the Board of Higher Education, the University of North Carolina, Duke University, and the North Carolina Fund. *Articles of Incorporation of the Learning Institute of North Carolina, A Non-Profit Corporation.* For explanation of the organization and purposes of LINC, see the statement of Governor Terry Sanford, February 2, 1964, in this volume.

[797] The purpose of the commission is to study the over-all needs of the existing program for the mentally retarded and to explore ways and means of meeting the unmet needs in the state. Fifteen members are appointed by the governor to serve on the commission. News releases of Governor Terry Sanford, January 11, 1962, and February 28, 1962.

[798] The North Carolina Fund was established on July 18, 1963, as a creative effort to improve education and the general welfare in the state by means of generous financial grants. The board, consisting of an indefinite number of persons chosen by initial board members, shall serve until the 1964 meeting, at which time the number of directors and their tenure shall be determined. *By-Laws of the North Carolina Fund,* Article I. For further explanation of the purpose and organization of this corporation see statement of Governor Terry Sanford, July 18, 1963, in this volume.

THE NORTH CAROLINA OUTER BANKS SEASHORE PARK COMMISSION[799]

Name of Appointee	Address	Date Appointed	Date of Expiration
Alden Baker	Elizabeth City	8-1-62	7-31-64
Thomas H. Broughton	Charlotte	8-1-62	7-31-64
Pascal M. Camak	Wilmington	8-1-62	7-31-64
George Cherry	Pactolus	8-1-62	7-31-64
William M. Cochrane	Washington, D. C.	8-1-62	7-31-64
Frederic L. Cox	Grifton	8-1-62	7-31-64
Thomas W. Ellis, Jr.	Henderson	8-1-62	7-31-64
Joseph F. Ferrell	Elizabeth City	8-1-62	7-31-64
Ashley B. Futrell	Washington	8-1-62	7-31-64
Harvey C. Hines	Kinston	8-1-62	7-31-64
Monroe Gaskill	Cedar Island	8-1-62	7-31-64
Thomas B. Hord, Jr.	Lawndale	8-1-62	7-31-64
Mrs. Victor Meekins[800]	Manteo	8-1-62	7-31-64
Lester N. Moore	Harkers Island	8-1-62	7-31-64
H. D. Newbern, Jr.	Powells Point	8-1-62	7-31-64
Julian Oneto	Nags Head	8-1-62	7-31-64
Earl H. Phillips	High Point	8-1-62	7-31-64
Woodrow Price, *Chairman*	Raleigh	8-1-62	7-31-64
Tony Seamon	Morehead City	8-1-62	7-31-64
Mrs. A. O. Smith	Elizabeth City	8-1-62	7-31-64
Harvey Smith	Beaufort	8-1-62	7-31-64
George M. Stephens, Jr.	Raleigh	8-1-62	7-31-64
John Harold Swindell	Swan Quarter	8-1-62	7-31-64
Joe G. Swindell	Lake Landing	8-1-62	7-31-64
Charles P. Wales	Chapel Hill	8-1-62	7-31-64
Roy E. Wilder, Jr.	Morehead City	8-1-62	7-31-64
Alida Willis	Washington	8-1-62	7-31-64
Braxton B. Dawson	Goldsboro	9-5-62	7-31-64
Eugene Price	Laurinburg	8-31-62	7-31-64
Sebastian C. Sommer	Manteo	8-31-62	7-31-64
Mrs. Estelle Tillett		9-19-62	7-31-64

THE PIEDMONT CRESCENT 2000 COMMISSION EXECUTIVE COMMITTEE[801]

Name	Location	Date	Term
Gordon Goodson	Lincolnton	6-30-64	Term indefinite
Wense Grabarek	Durham	6-30-64	Term indefinite
Graeme M. Keith	Greensboro	6-30-64	Term indefinite
W. E. Thompson	Chapel Hill	6-30-64	Term indefinite
Wayne Shoaf, *Chairman*	Lexington	6-30-64	Term indefinite
W. Harold Trentman	Raleigh	9-25-64	Term indefinite
C. Clifford Cameron	Raleigh	9-25-64	Term indefinite
Mrs. Adelaide Walters	Chapel Hill	9-25-64	Term indefinite
W. W. Lambeth	Swepsonville	9-25-64	Term indefinite
Carl O. Jeffress	Greensboro	9-25-64	Term indefinite
Gordon Hanes	Winston-Salem	9-25-64	Term indefinite
S. H. Mitchell	Winston-Salem	9-25-64	Term indefinite
J. E. Lambeth	Thomasville	9-25-64	Term indefinite
C. L. Lineback	Salisbury	9-25-64	Term indefinite
George A. Scott	Statesville	9-25-64	Term indefinite
W. Frank McCray	Kannapolis	9-25-64	Term indefinite
J. B. Holmes	Badin	9-25-64	Term indefinite
E. A. Resch	Siler City	9-25-64	Term indefinite
William B. McGuire	Charlotte	9-25-64	Term indefinite
Joseph G. Claud	Charlotte	9-25-64	Term indefinite
Grier Beam	Cherryville	9-25-64	Term indefinite
J. Hyatt Hammond	Asheboro	9-25-64	Term indefinite
William D. Benton	Monroe	9-25-64	Term indefinite
George W. Martin	Mocksville	9-25-64	Term indefinite
Joseph M. Bryan	Greensboro	12-26-64	Term indefinite
C. A. Cannon	Kannapolis	12-26-64	Term indefinite
S. T. Castleman	Winston-Salem	12-26-64	Term indefinite
Thomas A. Fraser	Raleigh	12-26-64	Term indefinite

[799] As set forth in an executive order, the duties of the commission are "to examine the North Carolina outer banks, to plan and assist in the preservation of the shore line and the establishment of public parks in that area." See Executive Order of August 3, 1962, in this volume. An indefinite number of members serve terms of two years, with six others serving by virtue of the offices they occupy.

[800] Did not accept appointment.

[801] The commission "seeks to involve leaders of the twenty piedmont crescent counties in studying the problems of the region as it grows and in establishing a program to make it the most beautiful, workable, and prosperous metropolis in the nation as it grows over the next forty years." It is so named because it involves between 1,000 and 2,000 people, and its objectives are working toward the year 2000. News release of Governor Sanford, June 30, 1964.

Name of Appointee	Address	Date Appointed	Date of Expiration
Asa T. Spaulding	Durham	12-26-64	Term indefinite
Jimmy Wallace	Chapel Hill	1-6-65	Term indefinite

THE GOVERNOR'S COMMISSION ON THE STATUS OF WOMEN[802]

Name of Appointee	Address	Date Appointed	Date of Expiration
Mrs. C. W. Beasley	Colerain	11-20-63	Report to the governor by 1-1-65
William H. Cartwright	Durham	11-20-63	Report to the governor by 1-1-65
Bonnie E. Cone	Charlotte	11-20-63	Report to the governor by 1-1-65
Mrs. William T. Crisp	Raleigh	11-20-63	Report to the governor by 1-1-65
E. MacArthur Currie	Charlotte	11-20-63	Report to the governor by 1-1-65
Rachel D. Davis	Kinston	11-20-63	Report to the governor by 1-1-65
Mrs. Ruth M. Easterling	Charlotte	11-20-63	Report to the governor by 1-1-65
Oscar R. Ewing	Chapel Hill	11-20-63	Report to the governor by 1-1-65
Mrs. Sarah W. Herbin	Raleigh	11-20-63	Report to the governor by 1-1-65
Mrs. Guion G. Johnson	Chapel Hill	11-20-63	Report to the governor by 1-1-65
Mrs. Juanita M. Kreps	Durham	11-20-63	Report to the governor by 1-1-65
James E. Lambeth, Jr.	Thomasville	11-20-63	Report to the governor by 1-1-65
Arthur Larson	Durham	11-20-63	Report to the governor by 1-1-65
Mrs. C. Odell Matthews	Winston-Salem	11-20-63	Report to the governor by 1-1-65
Mrs. Anne Scott, Chairman	Durham	11-20-63	Report to the governor by 1-1-65
Mrs. Gladys A. Tillett	Charlotte	11-20-63	Report to the governor by 1-1-65
Mrs. Ellen Black Winston	Washington, D. C.	11-20-63	Report to the governor by 1-1-65
Mrs. Annie B. Kennedy	Winston-Salem	2-4-64	Report to the governor by 1-1-65

STAY IN SCHOOL COMMITTEE[803]

Name of Appointee	Address	Date Appointed	Date of Expiration
Jack Wood, Chairman	Charlotte	9-12-61	Term indefinite
T. Earl Yarborough	Charlotte	9-12-61	Term indefinite
Louis Berini	Durham	9-12-61	Term indefinite
Charles F. Carroll	Raleigh	9-12-61	Term indefinite
Robert Bunnelle	Asheville	9-12-61	Term indefinite
Brodie S. Griffith	Charlotte	9-12-61	Term indefinite
Eugene Poston	Boiling Springs	9-12-61	Term indefinite
Lacy Thornburg	Sylva	9-12-61	Term indefinite
Robert Calder	Wilmington	9-12-61	Term indefinite

Name	City	Date	Term
Keith Fearing	Manteo	9-12-61	Term indefinite
Samuel Proctor	Greensboro	9-12-61	Term indefinite
Earle Edwards	Raleigh	9-12-61	Term indefinite
Avery Hightower	Wadesboro	9-12-61	Term indefinite
Archie Laney	Monroe	9-12-61	Term indefinite
B. D. Quinn	Swan Quarter	9-12-61	Term indefinite
Charlie Justice	Asheville	9-12-61	Term indefinite
John Foster	Greensboro	9-12-61	Term indefinite
Mrs. Virginia H. Grier	Raleigh	9-12-61	Term indefinite
Walton Kitchin	Clinton	9-12-61	Term indefinite
Lawson Withers	Goldsboro	9-12-61	Term indefinite
Leon Brogden	Wilmington	9-12-61	Term indefinite
Jack Boone	Greenville	9-12-61	Term indefinite
Syd Dunn	Greenville	9-12-61	Term indefinite
Ed Lilly	Kinston	9-12-61	Term indefinite
Henry Weitz	Durham	9-12-61	Term indefinite
Mrs. Louise Godwin	Greensboro	9-12-61	Term indefinite
Lloyd Y. Thayer	High Point	9-12-61	Term indefinite
T. R. Collins	Smithfield	9-12-61	Term indefinite
C. J. Barber	Oxford	9-12-61	Term indefinite
J. Harold Lineberger	Gastonia	9-12-61	Term indefinite
Daniel E. Moore	Durham	9-12-61	Term indefinite
William L. Beerman	Greensboro	9-12-61	Term indefinite
Howard M. Fitts[804]	Durham	2-28-64	Term indefinite

NORTH CAROLINA TRAFFIC SAFETY COUNCIL[805]

Name	City	Date	Term
J. C. Cowan	Greensboro	2-6-61	Term indefinite
Herbert Dowd	Charlotte	2-6-61	Term indefinite
John F. Fraley	Cherryville	2-6-61	Term indefinite

---

[802] The commission, established by executive order on October 11, 1963, consists of twenty members appointed by the governor. Members are charged "to review the progress, consider the potential, and make recommendations as needed for constructive action" on many problems of women's roles in the state. See Executive Order of Governor Terry Sanford, October 11, 1963, in this volume.

[803] The establishment of this committee in co-operation with the Optimist Clubs of the state is another step in the program to reduce sharply the number of students who drop out of school before the completion of high school. News releases of Governor Terry Sanford, July 13, 1961, September 12, 1961.

[804] Succeeded Daniel E. Moore, deceased.

[805] The council, a privately-supported organization with a full-time staff, is responsible for promoting and co-ordinating traffic safety activities throughout the state. The board consists of eleven persons appointed for an indefinite term. News release of Governor Sanford, February 6, 1961.

Name of Appointee	Address	Date Appointed	Date of Expiration
Alex Galloway, *Chairman*	Winston-Salem	2-6-61	Term indefinite
Robert Holding	Smithfield	2-6-61	Term indefinite
Willis Kirkpatrick	Canton	2-6-61	Term indefinite
William B. McGuire	Charlotte	2-6-61	Term indefinite
O. F. Stafford	Greensboro	2-6-61	Term indefinite
J. M. Wasson	Charlotte	2-6-61	Term indefinite
John Watlington	Winston-Salem	2-6-61	Term indefinite
Lewis E. Woodberry	Wilmington	2-6-61	Term indefinite
Eleanor Benson	Greensboro	4-24-63	Term indefinite
Mrs. Graham Lawrence	Charlotte	4-24-63	Term indefinite

E